P9-CLB-213

CURRICULUM PLANNING
A Contemporary Approach

EIGHTH EDITION

FORREST W. PARKAY
Washington State University

ERIC J. ANCTIL
Washington State University

GLEN HASS
Late, University of Florida

PEARSON

Boston   New York   San Francisco
Mexico City   Montreal   Toronto   London   Madrid   Munich   Paris
Hong Kong   Singapore   Tokyo   Cape Town   Sydney

Series Editor: Traci Mueller
Series Editorial Assistant: James P. Neal, III
Marketing Manager: Krista Groshong
Editorial Production Service: Omegatype Typography, Inc.
Composition and Manufacturing Buyer: Andrew Turso
Electronic Composition: Omegatype Typography, Inc.
Cover Administrator: Kristina Mose-Libon

For related titles and support materials, visit our online catalog at
www.ablongman.com.

Copyright © 2006, 2000, 1993, 1987, 1983, 1980, 1977, 1974
Pearson Education, Inc.

All rights reserved. No part of the material protected by this copyright
notice may be reproduced or utilized in any form or by any means,
electronic or mechanical, including photocopying, recording, or by any
information storage and retrieval system, without written permission
from the copyright owner.

To obtain permission(s) to use materials from this work, please submit a
written request to Allyn and Bacon, Permissions Department, 75 Arlington
Street, Boston, MA 02116 or fax your request to 617-848-7320.

Between the time website information is gathered and then published, it
is not unusual for some sites to have closed. Also, the transcription of
URLs can result in typographical errors. The publisher would appreciate
notification where these occur so that they may be corrected in subsequent
editions.

Library of Congress Cataloging-in-Publication Data

Curriculum planning : a contemporary approach / [edited by] Forrest W. Parkay, Eric J.
    Anctil, Glen Hass. — 8th ed.
        p.   cm.
    Includes bibliographical references and index.
    ISBN 0-205-44960-3
        1. Curriculum planning—United States.   2. Child development—United States.   3.
Learning.   4. Educational psychology.   I.   Parkay, Forrest W.   II. Anctil, Eric J. III.
Hass, Glen.

LB2806.15.C868   2006
375′.001—dc22   2005047443

Printed in the United States of America

10 9 8 7 6 5 4   10 09 08

Credits appear on pp. 524–527, which constitute an extension of the copyright page.

Contents

Preface

The eighth edition of *Curriculum Planning: A Contemporary Approach* presents the knowledge, skills, and understandings needed by curriculum developers and teachers at all levels of education, from early childhood through adulthood. This edition of *Curriculum Planning* has been completely revised and updated; 37 of the 71 articles in the book are new, with most published during the last three years. The book includes a broad spectrum of articles—from historical perspectives on curriculum planning, to contemporary analyses of trends and issues, to first-person accounts of curriculum planning and implementation.

Several features are designed to meet the needs of students with wide-ranging interests, learning styles, and backgrounds. Each chapter includes a "Teachers' Voices—Putting Theory Into Practice" section that presents a teacher-authored article. In addition, each chapter in Part III includes a "Case Study in Curriculum Implementation" section that presents a practitioner-authored article that illustrates the complexities of providing leadership for curriculum planning and implementation at the institutional or system-wide level.

To facilitate instruction and to help students study effectively, *Curriculum Planning* includes the following: focus questions at the beginning of each chapter; abstracts and reflection questions for each article; end-of-chapter critical thinking questions, application activities, field experiences, and Internet activities.

Part I, "Bases for Curriculum Planning," examines the following: goals and values and the three bases of the curriculum (social forces, human development, and learning and learning styles). Part II, "Developing and Implementing the Curriculum," includes two new chapters: Chapter 5, "Approaches to Curriculum Development," examines curriculum designs that can be used to develop (or write) curricula. Chapter 6, "Curriculum and Instruction," focuses on the interrelationships between curriculum and instruction. Part III, "The Curriculum in Action," emphasizes the application of curriculum planning skills for educational programs for children; early, middle, and late adolescents; and adult learners. At each level, current trends, innovations, and issues are examined from both theoretical and practical viewpoints.

The key role of educational philosophy in curriculum planning is highlighted in the first chapter. Seminal articles by key figures representing each of the four philosophical orientations that had a major influence on curriculum planning during the twentieth century are presented. These sharply contrasting statements bring contemporary trends and issues into clearer focus, and they highlight how each position will continue to be relevant for curriculum planning in the future.

Throughout the book, the interrelationships among past, present, and future perspectives on curriculum planning are stressed. Several articles in this edition address the importance of future planning. Topics covered include curriculum planning for the future, education and the Information Age, and technology and the Internet. Other topics that receive increased coverage in this edition are media literacy, inclusion, No Child Left Behind, multicultural education, diversity, curriculum standards, assessment of learning, multiple intelligences, learning styles, commercialism in the schools, and critical perspectives on curriculum planning.

Curriculum Planning is designed for upper-level and graduate students in curriculum and instruction, educational leadership, teacher education, foundations of education, and higher education programs. The key principles and concepts discussed throughout the book apply to educational programs at all levels and, for each chapter, special attention has been paid to identifying commonalities between curriculum planning at the K–12 and higher education levels.

Acknowledgment is given to the many authors who have contributed to this book. Their willingness to republish their ideas reflects their dedication to the continuous improvement of curriculum as a field of study. We also wish to thank the following reviewers who provided concise, helpful suggestions for this edition: Adel T. Al-Bataineh, Illinois State University; Claudette Ligons, Texas Southern University; and Allen H. Seed, University of Memphis. For steadfast support and encouragement while preparing this edition of *Curriculum Planning* and expert advice during all phases of manuscript preparation, we would like to thank Traci Mueller, acquisitions editor at Allyn and Bacon, and Janice Hackenberg, former editorial assistant. In addition, special thanks to Hillary Boman-Dunham, Washington State University, for her behind-the-scenes assistance with all the preproduction details.

Forrest W. Parkay gives a sincere thanks to students in his Basic Principles of Curriculum Design classes at Washington State University. Their insightful comments and suggestions have enriched this edition of the book. In addition, he thanks Wu Mei for her friendship, spiritual support, and encouragement during the revision process—ni shi diyige, ye shi zuihou yige, wode yiqie. Lastly, he wishes to acknowledge his considerable debt to Glen Hass who authored the first edition of *Curriculum Planning* and over the years developed a solid conceptual framework for examining the complexities of curriculum planning. He was an impressive curriculum scholar, an inspirational mentor, a valued colleague, and a good friend—it is to his memory that this and future editions of *Curriculum Planning* is dedicated.

Eric J. Anctil would like to thank his partner, Tina, for her patience during the revision process and Jack, his son, for helping to keep his priorities in order.

F.W.P.
E.J.A.

BASES for CURRICULUM PLANNING

CHAPTER 1

Goals and Values

FOCUS QUESTIONS

1. What is meant by the term *curriculum?*
2. What are the differences between curriculum and instruction?
3. What are the bases for curriculum planning?
4. What criteria can be used to plan, develop, and implement curricula?
5. What are five broad, general goals for the curriculum?
6. How do values influence curriculum planning?

The eighth edition of *Curriculum Planning: A Contemporary Approach* contains the knowledge and resources you will need to plan and implement a curriculum. Whether you are a teacher, principal, supervisor, or curriculum coordinator in a K–12 setting; instructor or academic administrator in higher education; or director of an educational program in business or other nonschool setting, you will make many curriculum-related decisions that will influence student learning. To provide all learners—those with diverse cultural backgrounds, needs, abilities, learning styles, and prior educational experiences—with curricular experiences that are meaningful and growth promoting is not easy; however, this book is designed to guide you through the complex processes of curriculum planning.

While this book raises many questions about curriculum planning, its purpose is not to settle these questions, but to help you understand the processes involved in curriculum planning. The book also suggests ways to improve curriculum planning. For example, if higher standards is currently the public's dominant demand for education (see Kim Marshall's "A Principal Looks Back: Standards Matter" in Chapter 5), then educators must raise questions like the following: What is excellence in education? For what purpose is it sought? How can it be achieved? How can it be measured? Which is more important—the pursuit or the achievement of excellence?

If excellence is a major curriculum goal, its attainment will depend primarily on decisions made by curriculum planners and teachers. A goal of *Curriculum Planning: A Contemporary Approach,* then, is to enable you to be professionally accountable when you make those decisions. Accountability requires that your decisions be informed by an understanding of curriculum goals and values, the bases of the curriculum, and curriculum criteria. In addition, professional accountability requires the ability to apply the knowledge, methods, and skills developed by curriculum theorists, researchers, and practitioners. By studying the processes of curriculum planning as perceived by the contributing authors of this book, you will continue to develop your own professional competencies.

To become competent in curriculum planning, you must understand how society, stages of human development, and theories of learning and learning styles influence the curriculum. In addition, you must understand the importance of achieving a balance among these three elements as you plan and implement the curriculum. At the beginning of this complex process, however, you should be able to answer the following question: What is meant by the term *curriculum?*

DEFINITIONS OF *CURRICULUM*

Educational practitioners, theorists, and researchers have used the term *curriculum* in various ways, with no definition universally accepted. Among the definitions currently used are the following:

1. A course of study; derived from the Latin *currere,* meaning to run a course
2. Course content; the information or knowledge that students are to learn
3. Planned learning experiences
4. Intended learning outcomes; the *results* of instruction as distinguished from the *means* (activities, materials, etc.) of instruction
5. All the experiences that students have while at school or in a nonschool educational program (Parkay & Stanford, 2004, p. 343)

Naturally, no one of these five is the "right" definition. Instead, how we define curriculum reflects our purposes and the educational setting within which we work.

Differences between Curriculum and Instruction

When the term *curriculum* is used to refer to planned learning experiences, it is clear that curriculum and instruction are interdependent, not separate and mutually exclusive. Experiences that are planned for learners, of course, include teachers' planning for instruction and the methods they actually use to teach the material. Thus, curriculum and instruction are part of the same process, a process that consists of planning experiences that lead to students' learning and growth.

While there is some warrant for saying that curriculum refers to the *what* of education and instruction the *how*, each has implications for the other. Chapter 6 is devoted to examining two key points regarding curriculum and instruction: (1) the terms *curriculum* and *curriculum planning* also refer to the *instruction* and *planning for instruction* which are essential elements of effective educational programs, and (2) effective teachers are those who engage in the full spectrum of curriculum and instruction—from planning the *what* of the curriculum to planning the *how* of instruction.

A Comprehensive Definition of *Curriculum*

None of the preceding views of curriculum are adequate in terms of the needs and trends that will characterize our lives in the future. Though mindful of the previous statement that there is no "right" definition of curriculum, we have found the following definition useful: *The curriculum is all of the educative experiences learners have in an educational program, the purpose of which is to achieve broad goals and related specific objectives that have been developed within a framework of theory and research, past and present professional practice, and the changing needs of society.*

In this definition, the term *educational program* has major significance. It means that the curriculum is a planned program developed by teachers and other professionals. In addition, the term means that the planned experiences may occur not only in a school, but in a community agency, a business, or any other setting that has an educational program. This definition of *curriculum* also incorporates the following points:

1. The curriculum is preplanned. *Curriculum planning* involves gathering, sorting, synthesizing, and selecting relevant information from many sources. This information is then used to design experiences that enable learners to attain the goals of the curriculum.
2. The planned objectives of a curriculum are developed in light of theories and research on social forces, human development, and learning and learning styles.
3. Many decisions must be made while planning a curriculum, and these decisions should be made in light of specific, carefully thought out criteria.
4. Planning for instruction is a major part of curriculum planning, since instruction often has a greater influence on learners than the preplanned curriculum, which may be partially, even totally, ignored by the teacher. This is as it should be, since the teacher usually has the greatest knowledge of learners and their needs. Nevertheless, when planning for instruction, the teacher, like the curriculum planner, should be guided by theories and research on social forces, human development, and learning and learning styles.
5. The curriculum that each learner comes to know is the result of experiences had while participating in learning opportunities provided by the teacher. Thus, each student plays an important role in determining the *experienced curriculum*.

BASES OF THE CURRICULUM

The three bases of curriculum planning provide a framework for the organization of much of this book. These bases—*social forces, theories of human development, and the nature of learning and learning styles*—are a major source of guidance for decision making in curriculum planning and planning for instruction. The next three chapters in Part I are devoted to the study of these curriculum bases.

Social Forces

All civilized societies establish schools and programs of education to induct children and youth into the culture and to transmit the society's culture and way of life. K–12 schools, higher education, and educational programs in nonschool settings operate in the midst of an ever-changing array of social forces and trends. Thus, one of the major areas to be considered in curriculum planning must be social forces that include, but are not limited to, the following: (1) social goals, (2) conceptions of culture, (3) the tension between cultural uniformity and diversity, (4) social pressures, (5) social change, and (6) futures planning.

Theories of Human Development

K–12 schools and institutions of higher education emerged in the United States before we knew much about human development and individual differences. However, knowledge of human development and related theories and research expanded significantly during the twentieth century, so that today a vast body of knowledge is available to guide the work of curriculum planners. We understand, for example, that children are not small adults and that human beings are qualitatively different at the various age levels for which we must target curriculum planning and instruction. Therefore, knowledge of human development is an essential basis of the curriculum because it enables curriculum planners to provide for age-related and individual differences among learners.

The Nature of Learning and Learning Styles

Knowledge about how human beings learn also increased significantly during the twentieth century. The complexities of learning and individual differences among learners led to the development of several theories of learning that have been tested and refined through carefully controlled research studies. Today's curriculum planners are guided by many of these theories, some of which describe different kinds of learning. Other theories describe the "learning styles" that individuals prefer to use when they process information and seek meaning. Since there are many differences among learners, various learning theories can guide curriculum planners as they address questions such as: How does each learner process information? How does he or she seek meaning? Answers to these questions can guide curriculum planners as they develop alternative paths for learning that allow for differences in cognitive style.

Emphasizing Curriculum Bases

What degree of emphasis should be placed on each of the three curriculum bases—social forces, human development, and learning and learning styles—when planning the curriculum? While not easily answered, curriculum planners and teachers should consider this question deliberately and thoughtfully. Therefore, Part I of this book is largely devoted to consideration of this question.

At different intervals during the past, some curriculum planners placed major emphasis on one of the three bases to the exclusion of the others. Often, the emphasis preferred by a curriculum planner reflected that person's philosophical orientation to education or significant historical developments. Prior to the twentieth century, knowledge in the subject matter disciplines and level of schooling provided the primary foci for curriculum planning. After 1900, however, theories and research in the new fields of child development, psychology, anthropology, sociology, and learning gave rise to an emphasis on each of these areas as the basis for curriculum planning and instruction. For contemporary curriculum planning, however, a multidimensional approach must be used, and all three of the bases considered in the quest to improve curriculum and instruction.

CURRICULUM CRITERIA

In addition to the three essential bases of the curriculum, other criteria can guide curriculum planners. A *criterion* is a standard on which a decision or judgment can be based; it is a basis for discriminating among elements in a complex field of endeavor. Curriculum criteria, then, are guidelines or standards for addressing the central question in the field of curriculum: What knowledge is of most worth? What to exclude from the curriculum is as difficult to determine as what to include.

The articles in Chapter 1 present varying perspectives on the criteria to be followed in answering this central question. In "Perspectives on Four Curriculum Traditions," for example, William H. Schubert suggests that four positions characterize the approach curriculum planners use to answer this question: intellectual traditionalist, social behaviorist, experientialist, and critical reconstructionist. And, in "A Morally Defensible Mission for Schools in the 21st Century," Nel Noddings explains why "themes of care," rather than the traditional disciplines, should be the criteria around which the curriculum is organized.

The goals or purposes of a curriculum are among the most significant criteria for guiding the curriculum planning process. Other frequently suggested curriculum criteria are diversity among learners, continuity, balance, flexibility, cooperative planning, international comparisons of achievement, standards developed by professional organizations, student–teacher planning, values to be taught, systematic planning, self-understanding, relevance to learners, and problem solving. The importance of these criteria can be derived from the three essential bases of the curriculum. For instance, an understanding of social forces, human development, and learning and learning styles will enhance your ability to develop curricula that allow for diversity among learners.

Similarly, an understanding of all three curriculum bases will help you develop a balanced curriculum. An understanding of social forces will help you provide for relevance and the teaching of values. Knowledge about human development will enable you to provide for continuity in learning and for the development of self-understanding. Lastly, knowledge of learning and learning styles will enable you to plan curricula with learning outcomes that learners find useful and transferable from one situation to another.

The many criteria to guide curriculum-related decision making should suggest the need to develop your own criteria to guide your planning. The ability to articulate how the three curriculum bases and additional curriculum criteria influence your curriculum planning activities should be one of your goals as you study *Curriculum Planning: A Contemporary Approach*.

CURRICULUM GOALS

While most people would agree that one goal of a curriculum should be to prepare students for the future, there is often little consensus about what knowledge and skills will be required in the future. Debate over this matter is not new, however; for example, Aristotle expressed the dilemma this way: "The existing practice [of curriculum development] is perplexing; no one knows on what principle we should proceed— should the useful in life, or should virtue, or should the higher knowledge, be the aim of our training; all three opinions have been entertained" (1941, p. 1306).

Curriculum goals provide general guidelines for determining the learning experiences to be included in the curriculum. Unfortunately, schools commonly lack a comprehensive, consistent set of goals on which to base curriculum decisions, and teachers often fail to use these goals to guide their planning for instruction. According to Deborah Meier's "So What Does It Take to Build a School for Democracy?" in this chapter, goals for curriculum planning should reflect "a steadfast vision of what civic life can be."

Without a set of clearly defined goals in view, teachers and curriculum planners cannot make sound professional judgments. They cannot use their knowledge of the three curriculum bases to choose content, materials, or methods to facilitate students' learning. To choose among curriculum alternatives or instructional strategies, educators must know the goals they seek and the curriculum bases on which they will make their choices. Otherwise, their choices will be little more than random, uninformed by today's knowledge of social forces, human development, and learning and learning styles.

Learners should also be clearly aware of the goals sought by their teachers. In fact, the teacher's instructional strategies should "invite" students to share in clarifying and, if appropriate, modifying the goals. As Glen Hass states in the article, "Who Should Plan the Curriculum?" in Chapter 5, the student is the "major untapped resource in curriculum planning." While the goals the teacher uses to guide his or her planning and those sought by learners need not be identical, they should overlap. The teacher's and learners' goals for a learning experience must be compatible or they are not likely to be achieved. If students are to participate in curriculum planning, teachers must "trust . . . students' innate ability to make good decisions for themselves," as Linda Inlay points out in this chapter's *Teachers' Voices* section ("Values: The Implicit Curriculum").

Broad, general goals are needed to determine the related specific objectives of the curriculum. Once developed, these goals and objectives can be used to identify relevant courses, activities, and other educational experiences. While there is seldom total agreement about what the goals of a curriculum should be, it is useful to think of five broad, general curriculum goals: *citizenship, equal educational opportunity, vocation, self-realization,* and *critical thinking.* In addition, curriculum goals can be clustered into two broad areas, each of which should always be considered in curriculum planning: goals that relate to *society and its values,* and goals that relate to the *individual learner and his or her needs, interests, and abilities.*

VALUES IN CURRICULUM PLANNING

Values enter into every curriculum decision. From planning the curriculum to delivering it in the classroom, there is rarely a moment when teachers are not confronted with situations in which values influence the choices they make. It is their answers (often covert) to questions such as "What is the good person?" "What is the good society?" "What is the good life?" that determine action. While teachers may not consciously pose these philosophical questions, all their curriculum thinking and work are value-based.

Four philosophical positions have had a major influence on curriculum planners and teachers since the early twentieth century—*perennialism, essentialism, progressivism,* and *reconstructionism.* The struggle for influence among these philosophical positions remains visible today. Because of the significance of values in formulating curriculum goals and developing learning experiences, and in deciding how to evaluate learning, a statement of each philosophical position by an influential historical leader in curriculum planning is included in this chapter. Robert F. Hutchins ("The Organization and Subject-Matter of General Education") represents the perennialists, William C. Bagley ("The Case for Essentialism in Education") the essentialists, William Heard Kilpatrick ("The Case for Progressivism in Education") the progressivists, and Theodore Brameld ("A Cross-Cutting Approach to the Curriculum: The Moving Wheel") the reconstructionists.

That these four positions can lead to heated debate among curriculum planners even today testifies to the continuing relevance of each position. Thus, today's curriculum planners might be well advised to pay more attention to areas of agreement among the positions and less to areas of controversy. Toward this end, John Dewey ("Traditional vs. Progressive Education" in this chapter) cautions curriculum planners against using "either-or" positions to guide their work. His *concept of experience,* for example, includes all the bases of the curriculum—the learner (human development and learning and learning styles), and the society (social forces).

CRITERION QUESTIONS—GOALS AND VALUES

As previously stated, curriculum criteria are guidelines or standards for curriculum decision making. Stating criteria in the form of *criterion questions* is a good way to bring the criteria into clear focus, and we shall use this method in Chapters 1 through 6 of this book. The criterion questions for this chapter on goals and values are as follows:

1. Are the goals of the curriculum clearly stated?
2. To the degree that students' developmental levels will allow, have teachers and students engaged in collaborative planning to define the goals and determine how they will be attained?
3. Do some of the planned goals relate to the society or the community within which the curriculum will be implemented?
4. Do some of the planned goals relate to individual learners and their needs, purposes, interests, and abilities?
5. Are the planned goals used as criteria for selecting and developing learning activities and instructional materials?
6. Are the planned goals used as criteria for assessing students' learning and for further planning of learning subgoals and activities?

The criterion questions bring into clear focus (1) the key role teachers play in curriculum planning and (2) the fact that curriculum planning requires interactions with the learners and consideration of the society and community within which the curriculum will be implemented. If all or most of these criterion questions can be answered affirmatively, the goal-setting phase of curriculum planning has been adequate.

REFERENCES

Aristotle. *Politics* (Book VIII). In Richard McKoen (Ed.), *The basic works of Aristotle*. New York: Random House, 1941.

Parkay, F. W., & Stanford, B. *Becoming a teacher* (6th ed.). Boston: Allyn and Bacon, 2004.

So What Does It Take to Build a School for Democracy?

DEBORAH MEIER

ABSTRACT: The goal of the public schools should be to prepare all students to participate equally in a democratic way of life. Meier presents five propositions that can guide schools in carrying out this function and then details how several exemplary schools have gone about putting the propositions into practice.

In the 20 years since *A Nation at Risk* called for a major overhaul of our public schools, we have heard endless talk about standards, accountability, and "toughness." But we have avoided an honest discussion of means and ends. Having that discussion would—for all concerned—force into the open some questions that we would apparently rather not face. But the price for our silence is high.

The most serious silence has to do with ends: What do we want schools to accomplish that is of sufficient public (not just personal) value to justify all the hullabaloo, not to mention expense? The second silence concerns the role of social class: Do we really want the same outcomes for everyone? And the third concerns cost: What price are we willing to pay? I'll revisit each of these below.

First, about the ends of schooling. I reject the idea that the purpose of schooling is to improve the economic opportunities of individuals or groups. And I also reject the idea that it's to improve our competitive position world-wide, above all in economic terms. This was the claim that got everyone exercised in 1983. It has been the organizing principle of the last 20 years of school reform. It was based on false and misleading data then, and subsequent economic history has proved it was nonsense. Our current worldwide preeminence assuredly doesn't rest on our high test scores. But the fiction has persisted. It has distracted us from what should be our agenda and led us to the even more absurd and malicious No Child Left Behind Act of 2001.

The real crisis we face is not a threat to America's economic or military dominance but the ebbing strength of our democratic and egalitarian culture. We have lost sight of the traditional public function of schools: to pass on the skills, aptitudes, and habits needed for a democratic way of life. These skills, aptitudes, and habits are hard to come by; they are not natural to the species. In fact, the ideal of civic virtue is as counterintuitive as is much of modern science. They are as hard to teach as relativity, and teaching them in ways that will make them second nature is even harder. It's no wonder that flourishing democracies are fragile phenomena.

Moreover, if the democratic promise is to thrive, these democratic virtues and skills need to be as firmly part of the repertoire of the poor as of the rich, of people of color as of white people, and of women as of men. The inequities of race, gender, and class that persist in our nation will surely grow worse unless civic equity is nourished by a publicly funded system of schooling with exactly that as its prime target. What does this focus on the pursuit of healthy democracy mean for the life of a school?

FIVE PROPOSITIONS ABOUT DEMOCRATIC SCHOOLS

1. *Schools need focus.* But for every focus, there is a tradeoff. Over the long haul, education for democracy is unlikely to hurt one's test scores and can begin to narrow some of the gaps between rich and poor. But the reverse—a single-minded focus on raising test scores—will not close or even narrow the gaps between rich and poor or black and white. And it will inevitably widen the gaps between rich and poor when it comes to civic participation. A steadfast vision of what civic life can be needs to pervade schooling and must not be sacrificed to other purposes.

The current focus on testing calls for a curriculum that is an inch deep and a mile wide, a curriculum that aims at rote learning, and a pedagogy that focuses on coverage and right answers. Its virtues are simplicity, alignment, measurability. But it is an approach peculiarly sensitive to out-of-school variables and peculiarly insensitive to what it takes to be a powerful citizen. In contrast, teaching a limited number of essential ideas in greater depth, in order to explore the ways in which truth is discovered and uncovered, places all comers on a more even footing and develops the habits of mind needed to tackle contemporary novelties. This is where all the attention needs to be, but getting it right will be hard. Getting to the wrong place faster, however, is not a virtue.

2. *One size does not fit all.* Even if we all agreed that the purpose of public schooling was to prepare young people for democratic life, the schools would look very different from those we have invented in the past century and very different from one another. That's what happens when ordinary folks are involved in deciding things for themselves. And that is why we cannot guarantee that two sets of jurors will always make the same, much less the right, decision.

E. D. Hirsch, Jr., and I agree on the need for rigorous subject matter, not just skills. But we reach different conclusions from this common starting point. The MET Schools, founded by Dennis Littky, teach students through real-life experiences under the guidance of mentors, and they eschew all traditional academic coursework. The school Ted Sizer founded around the same time is built on a deeply serious approach to academic subject matter and course-work. Ann Cook and Herb Mack's Urban Academy is built

around controversial arguments in critical academic and civic domains. On my terms, they are all successful, but the rod used to measure their success cannot be a simple-minded one.

3. *A democratic school culture would have lots of human interaction.* A school that trains people for citizenship in a democracy needs a faculty made up of individuals who can model what it means to value one another's ideas, to be open to new views, and to be comfortable defending their ideas in public—not just in disputes with students but also with colleagues. That would be as true for Hirsch's, Littky's, Cook's, and Sizer's models as for mine. Everyone would see controversy among adults as a golden opportunity to educate, not as a distraction.

Just as young people need models who show what it means to be a historian, mathematician, musician, or soccer player, so too do they need models of adults who engage in the arts of democratic life. Students need to see an adult community that actively and zestfully participates in the oral and written exchange of ideas and the forms of decision making that democracy promotes. By inviting young people into their circle, the adults act much like a religious community or tribe, offering the young ways to gradually assume more and more of the privileges and responsibilities of full membership. It works, of course, only if the young *want* to become such adults.

4. *Forms of governance would differ, too.* Should we include all the members of the school community in decision making? For which decisions? What is the role of students? Of custodians? Complicated tradeoffs are required in each instance, but adults and children learn about democracy in the process. Just as the details of democratic life differ in each of our 50 states, not to mention in a host of countries we call democracies, so would the schools in which adults teach democracy vary. There would be gnashing of teeth if schools "unwisely" decided that creationism should be taught alongside evolution or that early training in mathematical algorithms is worth a loss in understanding or that a love of books is more valuable than training in phonics.

But sometimes such differences would be resolved by experience, not debate, and, in any case, as in society at large, these disputes are not reasons for anyone to despair of democracy. Checks and balances of many sorts are as necessary for schools as for the larger society; in both arenas, they serve to mediate when the majority has overstepped its bounds. Addressing how to hear and respond to sharply held differences is part of the curriculum of such schools. It leads to ways of thinking about the larger world. Pacing such discussions so that they do not overwhelm the school's life and mission takes care, just as in the larger political sphere. Democracy, as Winston Churchill noted, is a thoroughly flawed form of government, except in comparison with all of the others.

5. *Reform consistent with democracy takes time.* The habits of democracy do not develop naturally, any more than mathematical competence does. One learns best by immersion and apprenticeship. Sometimes these habits may be taught by direct teaching and sometimes holistically, by example. Even the fiercest supporter of the direct teaching of reading or math acknowledges that it will not go far if along the way students don't also experience the world of reading or mathematics and aren't immersed in a culture of literacy and numeracy. In a society in which most young people, not to mention adults, have had very little experience with how democracy might work, students will require time to internalize these habits.

It should be clear that schools that set out to train the young to become adults in a democratic society have a tough job ahead; not one of the five propositions above is typical of the schools we have today. Embarking on this journey means taking risky steps—some forward and some backward. These are not paper-and-pencil changes. Ornery little boys and girls need to learn the multiplication tables and U.S. history and modern physics, as well as handwriting, spelling, and how best to use the computer. Ornery adults teach not only all of these things but also how to live together in such a way that new truths are allowed to emerge. They have to juggle when to allow argument and when not to allow it, and they must decide what rules are beyond debate. In addition, all of these things must take place while they help children tie their shoes, make friends, and handle enemies. And the adults in schools must make sure that families and communities are on board. (We forget this last item at our peril.)

RETHINKING ASSESSMENT

Once we've decided to build a democratic school culture, how do we know we're on the right track? Letting children vote on classroom decisions in kindergarten will not necessarily get them to respect the ballot box when they are 18. Nor is representative government the only form of democracy suitable to schools.

Imagine what a school would look like if it had to document its success in terms of its students' participation in decision making and their ability to accept responsibility for their work and the work of others. Imagine if this extended beyond graduation. Suppose a school's success rating were based not on how many students go to college but on how many of them vote. Where would that form of accountability lead us?

Far more serious than the test-score gap—and more remediable—is the gap between the voting patterns of the rich and the poor or the similar gap between whites and blacks. On these counts, the U.S. looks worse than it does in math or literacy. Similarly, we might look at the gap between how many rich as opposed to poor youths or black as opposed to white youths are in jail and for how long—a gap that places the U.S. once again in a class by itself. We might hold ourselves accountable, as a society and as individual schools, for reducing that gap. Or we might assume responsibility for reducing the health gap between rich and poor. Shouldn't a school system devoted to democracy—and committed to equity—judge itself as much by whether the work it does reduces or increases these gaps?

The old Central Park East Secondary School (CPESS) in East Harlem, which I helped start in 1985, had a statistically significant impact on many of the variables in the preceding paragraph. (We knew because we made sure to keep track of these things after our students graduated.) But the school had very little impact on its students' SAT scores, a fact that did not, incidentally, prevent them from going to college.

It was with these kinds of assessments in mind that Central Park East Elementary School was organized in 1974; CPESS, in 1985; and the Mission Hill School in Boston, in 1997. And a great many other schools committed to these same propositions during these same 25 years. All of us in such schools looked for indicators that would help us see how the school had affected its students—and each held itself accountable to responding to such information. In a way, these schools were among the first in public education to put the accountability question on the front burner—although our definition of accountability was rather different from that of George Bush.

IT STILL IS NEWS: THE SECOND SILENCE

We never claimed we could overcome all the odds facing our students. We took for granted that school was but one input, a place where kids spent 180 out of 365 days a year at most, for six out of roughly 16 waking hours each day. Children come to school not at birth but at age 4 or 5. Precisely this limitation makes it critical that we focus on the right stuff—the stuff that lasts when our backs are turned, when the kids are on their own.

It is not merely that students' home lives differ, though they surely do. If schools were prepared to accept these differences as potential assets, not deficits to overcome, these differences might not even matter. But some of the differences bring with them the clearly undesirable side effects of poverty and oppression. Some of our students live in settings where asthma is rampant; they suffer more absenteeism than their more fa-

vored peers. Some have neither the money nor the time, quite apart from the knowledge, to eat nutritiously, to get sufficient exercise, to have access to medical care, to remain in the same stable setting for long, or to have a place to live that is large enough to give family members sufficient space and privacy for intellectual work.

It would be ludicrous to think that such factors don't produce in-school as well as lifelong differentials—not to mention the subtler advantages of being a child whose parents can hire tutors, give expert homework assistance, send you to a luxurious summer camp, and have friends in places of power and influence to get you a leg up at critical moments.

As Billie Holiday reminded us half a century ago:

Them that's got shall get
Them that's not shall lose
So the Bible says,
and it still is news.

This is the second great silence: our pretense that the gaps in the quality of life outside of school are matters of, at most, inconvenience or matters of poor parenting skills.

The Central Park East schools, along with so many others that took on this project in the past 25 years, argued that all children can learn what they need in order to enter into the conversation about their own and society's future as equal partners—or as nearly equal as schooling can get them. However, reaching this point requires care in picking the right goals and an alliance with families that relies on their strengths rather than on their inadequacies.

As we struggled with the five propositions I spelled out above, nearly all of us arrived at the same five corollary conclusions.

1. *Be clear about purpose.* We all decided that our schools could better serve families and children if we were clear about what we were and weren't trying to do: our vision or mission (as we call it nowadays), our methods of assessing both individual students and the school, and finally our specific plan of action. (Ideally, families should also have an opportunity to sample what a school looks, sounds, and "tastes" like—not just read what it claims to be.)

If a school decided, as we did, on multiple-age homerooms, it should relate this choice to its larger purpose. It should do likewise with the organization of the day, the placement of its faculty, and so on. What the school will not be doing— the tradeoffs it has chosen—should be as clear as what it will do. We all got into trouble when we tried to meet too many different goals, and we learned to be more and more explicit about the connection between our mission and what we agreed to be accountable for.

We needed, we all agreed, to explain clearly how we decided when students were ready to graduate. While the goals and criteria for competence were universally applicable for students of a particular school, the ways students met them varied. Today, at Mission Hill, Landmark, and many other schools that modeled themselves on CPESS, a panel of reviewers—faculty members, family members, students, and external community people or professionals—makes the final judgment, subject to a largely pro-forma vote by the faculty. These panels in each major field review a portfolio of work prepared by the student in that field, listen to a major presentation of one piece of that work the student is particularly proud of, ask questions, probe for strengths and weaknesses, and then retire to make a collective judgment. Several on-demand tasks add to the package. At such schools, a substantial number of students are required to redo at least some portions of their work, and on rarer occasions they are required to spend considerably more time at the school before they can move on.

But this is just one of many different approaches to external review of student competence. All depend on a mixture of expert opinion—some close and some distant—in making judgments about a student's readiness to move on. Some rely more than we did on conventional grades and exams or use other forms of

public exhibitions to supplement such grades. But these up-front decisions about what counts help define the meaning of a school's mission statement.

2. *Choice is powerful*. We discovered that schools could better serve democratic ends if they were intentional communities for teachers, students, and families. Once we decided that no school should be generic, that decision had repercussions for the placement of faculty and students. We recognized that whole systems of choice naturally followed and that these had to meet essential democratic principles of fairness and equity. Schools had to weigh the merits of requiring students to take the initiative to apply and of being able to "exile" those who violate a school's norms against the knowledge we have of the unintended consequences of such forms of choice.

We opted for more inclusion and didn't even have an application system, since we operated within a large system of controlled choice that featured a public lottery. But some of our sister schools, especially the high schools, introduced admissions processes that sought to include evidence of a desire to attend a particular school and an interest in engaging in the special tasks the school demanded. Some argued that this was a form of "creaming," while others argued that it was treating students and their intentions with respect. Clearly, such choice is easier to offer in districts with many different buildings (small schools of choice can share a single building, of course) and harder to organize in one-school towns—and maybe less appropriate in such settings. But choice is an inevitable aspect of acknowledging that there is more than one legitimate way to think about democratic imperatives.

3. *Size matters*. There's a good reason why the rich favor small schools over big ones. Relationships between students and between students and adults are at the heart of the education of the well-to-do. Today, the idea that smaller is better has become a truism, almost a fad in the public sector. But to make it work will take more than the proclamation that "this is now a small school." As a mechanism for decentralizing essentially centralized authority, creating a small school is at best a gimmick and at worst a deception. It's probably most important for the power it offers teachers to know one another and one another's work well and to find ways to provide schoolwide coherence in both subject matter and pedagogy, to build upon one another's strengths.

But if the faculty members of a school have no important decisions to make together, then making a school smaller may be time and effort wasted. A smaller school makes the relationships with students—and, probably equally important, with their families—feasible, but only if the will to focus on those relationships exists. Over time, smallness can become the basis for looking each other in the eye and learning how and when to trust each other to make important decisions. Even small schools, we discovered, often need to create subcommunities—sometimes called critical friends groups—in which even more risky learning can take place. Some schools invented common faculty work spaces to replace private classrooms and offices, ensuring greater cross-fertilization of ideas and concerns. Urban Academy, for example, has one huge room in which all adults work, storing their materials in cubbies.

Smallness makes some things possible. But it's also possible, we found out quickly, to run a small school as mindlessly as a big one. Smallness is necessary, but not sufficient. It's the relationships that matter.

4. *Be clear about who's in charge.* Democracy requires acknowledging power and agreeing on its delegation and distribution. Schools also need to work out power structures. At Mission Hill, the co-principals are responsible to a school-based board of governors, which approves the budget and the annual staffing and curricular plan. The board consists of equal numbers of parent and staff representatives, along with an equal number of community members chosen by the parents and staff members, plus two senior students. The dividing line between this board's powers and the responsibilities of the faculty council, the co-principals, and the parent council are always unclear at the edges and occasionally contentious, as are the powers of the executive and legislative branches in our state and local governments. Ultimately, the board, with consent from the city's superintendent, holds the power to evaluate and renew the principals' tenure, to resolve disputes between members of the community, and to review the work plan and operations of the school. With the help of the teacher union, the school sets forth clearly the terms of staff employment and responsibilities, as well as the mechanisms for resolving disputes when they depart from the labor/management contract.

Other schools have very different forms of governance, and some have no formal plan at all. How much power to put into the hands of the principal as opposed to the faculty or the faculty as opposed to a representative board varies from school to school. As public schools within a larger system of schooling, we were constrained by the larger contractual rules and arrangements of the city and state we worked within and the union we worked with. In a way, these ventures at self-governance, which lie at the heart of democratic life, are in cities like New York and Boston quixotic, operating in many cases on the sheer will and belief of the staff and families and against the actual machinery of government in which they are embedded. In both Boston and New York, the teacher union was a willing ally and supporter and helped pave the way for systemwide acceptance. There's a continual balancing that needs to take place between the various parts of the community. And sometimes the best-laid plans—as in the larger world—will come to naught as bad decisions are made, weak leaders prevail, and schools revert to the status quo. Even CPESS experienced such reversals.

5. *Openness makes us stronger.* We learned that in all of its work a school must be open and transparent, the evidence of its strengths and weaknesses accessible to both its immediate community and the larger public. Above all, its standards for awarding diplomas must be accessible

and open to public criticism. Even in our early, vulnerable, half-outlaw state, we paid a price for having to keep too many secrets. Folks may differ in their interpretation of the data, but shared and common data are needed.

At Mission Hill, we built a formal alternative system of assessment in reading, writing, and math to ensure that we were not stuck with only test results and our "reassurances." Wherever possible we looked for direct versus indirect evidence—e.g., biannual tape recordings of students as readers, from kindergarten on. In most of the new schools, students were followed when they graduated, to document the impact of the school on its former students. This proved to be powerful information when, for example, New York State sought to clamp down on the small schools with a history of performance-based graduation. Various forms of public external review—now organized formally by the system in Boston every four years and organized formally by ourselves in New York—attest to and provide critiques of the work of these kinds of schools, as well as help to ward off external attack.

As these five principles suggest, the work of building these little oases of trust between people with very different styles, personalities, histories, beliefs, and racial and ethnic identifications and ties is a never-ending project. Even as schools claim to stand for some particular set of views about curriculum and pedagogy, they will attract people with their own, sometimes differing, interpretations of what it all means. Such schools are always works in progress. That in itself is a lesson in democracy.

ARE WE HAVING FUN YET?

In fact, the fun part is that every difficulty such schools face can be a lesson in and for democracy. The fight for leisure inside the school is related to the fight for leisure outside. The idea that teachers should take responsibility for their collective, not just individual, work carries over to other workplaces and communities. When colleagues

take on additional tasks for the school as a whole—attend parent council meetings, go to union meetings, do research on shared curriculum topics, review their peers' work, or take on schoolwide assessment tasks—it is our shared responsibility to give them the extra time they need. But it's also a reminder that the same thing happens in our towns and cities. The importance of face-to-face encounters between people with differing views and the related capacity to imagine a viewpoint different from one's own are intellectual habits of mind central to our academic work, our school governance, and the governance of the larger society.

At every point in our work, we must connect the dots between our practice and democracy. Why are scientists wary about how easy it is to see results that you want to see? Don't ordinary citizens need to develop similar habits of caution? Why must high-stakes assessment be the work not of one single person but of a group? And are there lessons here for decision making outside of schools? Why do all high-stakes decisions need to be made openly and include a process of appeal? We must make the connection between how a historian weighs historical evidence and how we as citizens weigh daily evidence. We should compare how cautiously a scholar in any field uses analogies with the way we toss around historical or personal analogies in political discourse.

We need to remind ourselves that the villains we denounce in our daily lives are versions of literary characters we have grown to understand and even sympathize with in the novels we have devoured. Could such empathy help inform our respect for often despised minorities? If great literature is to inform our lives, we need to take the time to trace such connections. We need to translate the zeros that differentiate millions from billions into real-life comparisons, as a step toward demystifying school budgets and national budgets.

Such a view of schooling leads us to ask questions about why all jobs, not just all schools, don't have built-in requirements for civic leisure—to attend school meetings, town meetings, and legislative hearings, not to mention to use the library, meet with colleagues, and join study groups. These are tasks of civic life that we view as luxuries, which no one but the individual who "wants" to do them should be concerned with. What would civic life be like if we educated our children to honor such activity as central to the good life?

And because civic life overlaps with just plain human decency and neighborliness, schools like Mission Hill provide the extra time folks need on occasion: when a family member is sick, when a marriage is breaking up, or even when a water main bursts! The school naturally bends and twists to make it possible for its members to take care of their personal business without ignoring the impact on the school's work or its students. We do this for its own sake, but also because such practices should be part of our democratic norms in society. They should be assumed in all workplaces.

Just as democracy is at its most fragile at times of war or civil strife, so will schools that operate against the grain have an even harder time maintaining normal democratic practices in what too often appears to be a war with "the system." Under such circumstances, these schools are easy prey for takeovers, cutting corners, foolish internecine battles, secret budgets, and closed-mindedness (school systems' own forms of ultra-patriotism and fear of treason). The less embattled and the less at risk such schools are, the less they will need to turn to superhuman heroes to be their leaders.

Above all, given the paucity of experience that most of us have had with truly democratic institutions, we will simply often do democracy badly. We may not know how to distinguish a personal battle from an intellectual difference of opinion, or we may see logical argument as a form of bul-

lying and fall back on "it's my opinion and I've got a right to it" arguments out of fear and self doubt. Real democracy will not come without hurt feelings and breaches of civility—and without some losses. It will often confuse parents and students. Sometimes people will pull back and yearn for a benign dictator. In the face of a hostile system, many will fold. Others will keep their problems to themselves, for fear of the enemy.

But with patience we can learn from the experiences of our sister schools and of small local school communities; with patience more of us will come forward to tell our difficult stories; over time, perhaps, the larger system we live within will develop ways to be supportive of rather than hostile to such communities. We may someday learn to build systems to accommodate and cherish these ornery and complex entities. We will have much to learn from the many small schools in America that are struggling to find the balance they need to initiate themselves and their students into the values of democracy, as well as instill the social and intellectual habits that help democracy survive and occasionally thrive. Some lessons will come from ways to organize and teach the formal curriculum, while others will emerge from the culture of everyday life and decision making in the school.

None of this will take us far until a larger number of our fellow citizens begin to see these goals as important and worth some uncomfortable tradeoffs. It turns out one can have varsity football and small serious schools of choice, but one still has to decide which comes first—which is the add-on and which is the essential. In other words: What price are we willing to pay for putting democracy at the head of the line? Whatever answer to that question we come up with, the price of not asking it at all—the cost of the third and final silence—is immeasurably higher.

Deborah Meier is the MacArthur Award-winning founder of Central Park East School in East Harlem and of Mission Hill School in Boston. Her most recent book is *In Schools We Trust* (Beacon Press, 2002).

QUESTIONS FOR REFLECTION

1. Meier suggests that the young must *want* to become "adults who engage in the arts of democratic life." To what extent do you believe today's youth want to become such adults?
2. According to Meier, one measure of school effectiveness might be how many students vote, rather than how many students go to college. How feasible is Meier's approach to assessing school effectiveness?
3. Do you agree with Meier's assertion that "not one of the five propositions [about democratic schools] is typical of the schools we have today"?

A Morally Defensible Mission for Schools in the 21st Century

NEL NODDINGS

ABSTRACT: Arguing that the traditional school curriculum is intellectually and morally inadequate for the twenty-first century, Noddings asserts that the goal of education should be the development of students' capacity to find purpose and meaning through their involvement in "centers of care." Thus, education should be organized around "themes of care" rather than the traditional disciplines.

Social changes in the years since World War II have been enormous. We have seen changes in work patterns, in residential stability, in styles of housing, in sexual habits, in dress, in manners, in language, in music, in entertainment, and—perhaps most important of all—in family arrangements. While schools have responded, albeit sluggishly, to technological changes with various additions to the curriculum and narrowly prescribed methods of instruction, they have largely ignored massive social changes. When they *have* responded, they have done so in piecemeal fashion, addressing isolated bits of the problem. Thus, recognizing that some children come to school hungry, schools provide meals for poor children. Alarmed by the increase in teenage pregnancies and sexually transmitted diseases, schools provide sex education. Many more examples could be offered, but no one of these nor any collection of them adequately meets the educational needs of today's students.

What do we want for our children? What do they need from education, and what does our society need? The popular response today is that students need more academic training, that the country needs more people with greater mathematical and scientific competence, that a more adequate academic preparation will save people from poverty, crime, and other evils of current society. Most of these claims are either false or, at best, only partly true. For example, we do *not* need more physicists and mathematicians; many people already highly trained in these fields are unable to find work. The vast majority of adults do *not* use algebra in their work, and forcing all students to study it is a simplistic response to the real issues of equity and mathematical literacy. Just as clearly, more education will not save people from poverty unless a sufficient number of unfortunate people either reject that education or are squeezed out of it. Poverty is a *social* problem. No person who does honest, useful work—regardless of his or her educational attainments—should live in poverty. A society that allows this to happen is not an educational failure; it is a moral failure.

Our society does not need to make its children first in the world in mathematics and science. It needs to care for its children—to reduce violence, to respect honest work of every kind, to reward excellence at every level, to ensure a place for every child and emerging adult in the economic and social world, to produce people who can care competently for their own families and contribute effectively to their communities. In direct opposition to the current emphasis on academic standards, a national curriculum, and national assessment, I have argued that our main educational aim should be to encourage the growth of competent, caring, loving, and lovable people.[1]

At the present time, it is obvious that our main educational purpose is not the moral one of producing caring people but a relentless—and, as it turns out, hapless—drive for academic adequacy. I am certainly not going to argue for academic *in*adequacy, but I will try to persuade readers that a reordering of priorities is essential. All children must learn to care for other human beings, and all must find an ultimate concern in some center of care: care for self, for intimate others, for associates and acquaintances, for distant others, for animals, for plants and the physical environment, for objects and instruments, and for ideas. Within each of these centers, we can find many themes on which to build courses, topical seminars, projects, reading lists, and dialogue.

Today the curriculum is organized almost entirely around the last center, ideas, but it is so poorly put together that important ideas are often swamped by facts and skills. Even those students who might find a genuine center of care in some arena of ideas—say mathematics or literature—are sorely disappointed. In trying to teach everyone what we once taught only a few, we have wound up teaching everyone inadequately. Further, we have not bothered to ask whether the traditional education so highly treasured was ever the best education for anyone.

I have argued that liberal education (defined as a set of traditional disciplines) is an outmoded and dangerous model of education for today's young. The popular slogan today is "All children can learn!" To insist, however, that all children should get the same dose of academic English, social studies, science, and mathematics invites an important question unaddressed by the sloganeers: Why should children learn what we insist they "can" learn? Is this the material people really need to live intelligently, morally, and happily? Or are arguments for traditional liberal education badly mistaken? Worse, are they perhaps mere political maneuverings?

My argument against liberal education is not a complaint against literature, history, physical science, mathematics, or any other subject. It is an argument, first, against an ideology of control that forces all students to study a particular, narrowly prescribed curriculum devoid of content they might truly care about. Second, it is an argument in favor of greater respect for a wonderful range of human capacities now largely ignored in schools. Third, it is an argument against the persistent undervaluing of skills, attitudes, and capacities traditionally associated with women. . . .

What do we want for our children? Most of us hope that our children will find someone to love, find useful work they enjoy or at least do not hate, establish a family, and maintain bonds with friends and relatives. These hopes are part of our interest in shaping an acceptable child.[2] What kind of mates, parents, friends, and neighbors will our children be?

I would hope that all our children—both girls and boys—would be prepared to do the work of attentive love. This work must be done in every family situation, whether the family is conventionally or unconventionally, constituted. Both men and women, if they choose to be parents, should participate in the joys and responsibilities of direct parenting, of acting as psychological parents. Too often, women have complained about bearing this responsibility almost entirely. When men volunteer to help with child care or with housework, the very language suggests that the tasks are women's responsibilities. Men "help" in tasks they do not perceive as their own. That has to change.

In education today, there is great concern about women's participation in mathematics and science. Some researchers even refer to something called the "problem of women and mathematics." Women's lack of success or low rate of participation in fields long dominated by men is seen as a problem to be treated by educational means. But researchers do not seem to see a problem in men's low rate of participation in nursing, elementary school teaching, or full-time parenting. Our society values activities traditionally associated with men above those traditionally associated with women.[3]

The new education I envision puts a very high valuation on the traditional occupations of women. Care for children, the aged, and the ill must be shared by all capable adults, not just women, and everyone should understand that these activities bring special rewards as well as burdens. Work with children can be especially rewarding and provides an opportunity to enjoy childhood vicariously. For example, I have often wondered why high school students are not more often invited to revisit the literature of childhood in their high school English classes. A careful study of fairy tales, augmented by essays on their psychology, might be more exciting and more generally useful than, for example, the study of *Hamlet*. When we consider the natural interest we have in ourselves—past, present, and future— it is clear that literature that allows us to look forward and backward is wonderful. Further, the study of fairy tales would provide opportunities for lessons in geography, history, art, and music.

Our children should learn something about life cycles and stages. When I was in high school, my Latin class read Cicero's essay "On Old Age." With all his talk of wisdom—of milk, honey, wine, and cheese; of meditating in the afternoon breeze—I was convinced that old age had its own romance. Looking at the present condition of many elderly people, I see more than enough horror to balance whatever romance there may

be. But studies of early childhood, adulthood, and old age (with or without Latin) seem central to education for real life. Further, active association with people of all ages should be encouraged. Again, one can see connections with standard subjects—statistical studies in math; the history and sociology of welfare, medical care, and family life; geographical and cultural differences. We see, also, that the need for such studies has increased as a result of the social changes discussed earlier. Home life does not provide the experience in these areas that it once did.

Relations with intimate others are the beginning and one of the significant ends of moral life. If we regard our relations with intimate others as central in moral life, then we must provide all our children with practice in caring. Children can work together formally and informally on a host of school projects, and, as they get older, they can help younger children, contribute to the care of buildings and grounds, and eventually—under careful supervision—do volunteer work in the community. Looking at Howard Gardner's multiple intelligences, we see that children can contribute useful service in a wide variety of ways; some have artistic talents, some interpersonal gifts, some athletic or kinesthetic abilities, some spiritual gifts.[4]

A moral policy, a defensible mission, for education recognizes a multiplicity of human capacities and interests. Instead of preparing everyone for college in the name of democracy and equality, schools should instill in students a respect for all forms of honest work done well.[5] Preparation for the world of work, for parenting, and for civic responsibility is essential for all students. All of us must work, but few of us do the sort of work implied by preparation in algebra and geometry. Almost all of us enter into intimate relationships, but schools largely ignore the centrality of such interests in our lives. And although most of us become parents, evidence suggests that we are not very good at parenting—and again the schools largely ignore this huge human task.

When I suggest that a morally defensible mission for education necessarily focuses on matters of human caring, people sometimes agree but fear the loss of an intellectual mission for the schools. There are at least two powerful responses to this fear. First, anyone who supposes that the current drive for uniformity in standards, curriculum, and assessment represents an intellectual agenda needs to reflect on the matter. Indeed, many thoughtful educators insist that such moves are truly anti-intellectual, discouraging critical thinking, creativity, and novelty. Second, and more important from the perspective adopted here, a curriculum centered on themes of care can be as richly intellectual as we and our students want to make it. Those of us advocating genuine reform—indeed, transformation—will surely be accused of anti-intellectualism, just as John Dewey was in the middle of this century. But the accusation is false, and we should have the courage to face it down.

Examples of themes that are especially important to young people are love and friendship. Both can be studied in intellectual depth, but the crucial emphasis should be on the relevance of the subjects to self-understanding and growth. Friends are especially important to teenagers, and they need guidance in making and maintaining friendships.

Aristotle wrote eloquently on friendship, and he assessed it as central in moral life. In the *Nicomachean Ethics,* Aristotle wrote that the main criterion of friendship is that a friend wishes a friend well for his or her own sake. When we befriend others, we want good things for them not because those things may enhance our welfare but because they are good for our friends. Aristotle organized friendships into various categories: those motivated by common business or political purposes, those maintained by common recreational interests, and those created by mutual admiration of the other's virtue. The last was, for Aristotle, the highest form of friendship and, of course, the one most likely to endure.

How do friendships occur? What draws people together? Here students should have opportunities to see how far Aristotle's description will carry them. They should hear about Damon and Pythias, of course. But they should also examine some incongruous friendships: Huck and Jim in Mark Twain's *Adventures of Huckleberry Finn;* Miss Celie and Shug in Alice Walker's *Color Purple;* Lenny and George in John Steinbeck's *Of Mice and Men;* Jane and Maudie in Doris Lessing's *Diaries of Jane Somers.* What do each of these characters give to the friendship? Can friendship be part of a personal quest for fulfillment? When does a personal objective go too far and negate Aristotle's basic criterion?

Another issue to be considered is, When should moral principles outweigh the demands of friendship? The question is often cast this way, even though many of us find the wording misleading. What the questioner wants us to consider is whether we should protect friends who have done something morally wrong. A few years ago, there was a terrifying local example of this problem when a teenage boy killed a girl and bragged about it to his friends. His friends, in what they interpreted as an act of loyalty, did not even report the murder.

From the perspective of caring, there is no inherent conflict between moral requirements and friendship, because, as Aristotle teaches us, we have a primary obligation to promote our friends' moral growth. But lots of concrete conflicts can arise when we have to consider exactly what to do. Instead of juggling principles as we might when we say, "Friendship is more important than a little theft" or "Murder is more important than friendship," we begin by asking ourselves whether our friends have committed caring acts. If they have not, something has to be done. In the case of something as horrible as murder, the act must be reported. But true friends would also go beyond initial judgment and action to ask how they might follow through with appropriate help for the murderer. When we adopt caring as an ethical approach, our moral work has just begun where other approaches end. Caring requires staying-with, or what Ruddick has called "holding." We do not let our friends fall if we can help it, and if they do, we hold on and pull them back up.

Gender differences in friendship patterns should also be discussed. It may be harder for males to reject relationships in which they are pushed to do socially unacceptable acts, because those acts are often used as tests of manhood. Females, by contrast, find it more difficult to separate themselves from abusive relationships. In both cases, young people have to learn not only to take appropriate responsibility for the moral growth of others but also to insist that others accept responsibility for their own behavior. It is often a fine line, and—since there are no formulas to assist us—we remain vulnerable in all our moral relations.

A transformation of the sort envisioned here requires organizational and structural changes to support the changes in curriculum and instruction. It requires a move away from the ideology of control, from the mistaken notion that iron-handed accountability will ensure the outcomes we identify as desirable. It won't just happen. We should have learned by now that both children and adults can accomplish wonderful things in an atmosphere of love and trust and that they will (if they are healthy) resist—sometimes to their own detriment—in environments of coercion.

Because I would like to present for discussion my basic recommendations for both structural and curricular changes, I will risk setting them forth here in a skeletal form. Of course, I cannot describe and defend the recommendations adequately in so brief a space, but here is a summary.

The traditional organization of schooling is intellectually and morally inadequate for contemporary society. We live in an age troubled by social problems that force us to reconsider what we do in schools. Too many of us think that we can improve education by merely designing a better curriculum, finding and implementing a better form of instruction, or instituting a better form of classroom management. These things won't work.

We need to give up the notion of *a single* ideal of the educated person and replace it with a multiplicity of models designed to accommodate the multiple capacities and interests of students. We

need to recognize multiple identities. For example, an 11th-grader may be a black, a woman, a teenager, a Smith, an American, a New Yorker, a Methodist, a person who loves math, and so on. As she exercises these identities, she may use different languages, adopt different postures, and relate differently to those around her. But whoever she is at a given moment, whatever she is engaged in, she needs—as we all do—to be cared for. Her need for care may require formal respect, informal interaction, expert advice, just a flicker of recognition, or sustained affection. To give the care she needs requires a set of capacities in each of us to which schools give too little attention.

I have argued that education should be organized around themes of care rather than around the traditional disciplines. All students should be engaged in a general education that guides them in caring for self, intimate others, global others, plants, animals, the environment, objects and instruments, and ideas. Moral life so defined should be frankly embraced as the main goal of education. Such an aim does not work against intellectual development or academic achievement. Rather, it supplies a firm foundation for both.

How can we begin? Here is what I think we must do:

1. *Be clear and unapologetic about our goal.* The main aim of education should be to produce competent, caring, loving, and lovable people.

2. *Take care of affiliative needs.* We must keep students and teachers together (by mutual consent) for several years, and we must keep students together when possible. We should also strive to keep students in the same building for considerable periods of time and help students to think of the school as theirs. Finally, we must legitimize time spent in building relations of care and trust.

3. *Relax the impulse to control.* We need to give teachers and students more responsibility to exercise judgment. At the same time we must get rid of competitive grading and reduce the amount of testing that we do. Those well-designed tests that remain should be used to assess whether people can competently handle the tasks they want to undertake. We also need to encourage teachers to explore material with students. We don't have to know everything to teach well.

In short, we need to define expertise more broadly and instrumentally. For example, a biology teacher should be able to teach whatever mathematics is involved in biology, while a social studies teacher should be able to teach whatever mathematics is required in that subject. We must encourage self-evaluation and teach students how to do it competently, and we must also involve students in governing their own classrooms and schools. Making such changes means that we accept the challenge to care by teaching well the things that students want to learn.

4. *Get rid of program hierarchies.* This will take time, but we must begin now to provide excellent programs for *all* our children. Programs for the noncollege-bound should be just as rich, desirable, and rigorous as those for the college-bound.

We must abandon uniform requirements for college entrance. What a student wants to do or to study should guide what is required by way of preparation. Here we should not worry greatly about students who "change their minds." Right now we are afraid that, if students prepare for something particular, they may change their minds and all that preparation will be wasted. Thus we busily prepare them uniformly for nothing. We forget that, when people have a goal in mind, they learn well and that, even if they change their minds, they may have acquired the skills and habits of mind they will need for further learning. The one essential point is that we give all students what all students need—genuine opportunities to explore the questions central to human life.

5. *Give at least part of every day to themes of care.* We should discuss existential questions—including spiritual matters—freely. Moreover, we need to help students learn to treat each other ethically by giving them practice in caring. We must help students understand how groups and individuals create rivals and enemies and help them learn how to "be on both sides." We should encourage a way of caring for animals, plants, and the environment that is consistent with caring for humans, and we should also encourage caring for the human-made world. Students need to feel at home in technical, natural, and cultural worlds, and educators must cultivate wonder and appreciation for the human-made world.

6. *Teach students that caring in every domain implies competence.* When we care, we accept the responsibility to work continuously on our competence so that the recipient of our care—person, animal, object, or idea—is enhanced. There is nothing mushy about caring. It is the strong, resilient backbone of human life.

NOTES

1. Nel Noddings, *The Challenge to Care in Schools* (New York: Teachers College Press, 1992).
2. Sara Ruddick, "Maternal Thinking," *Feminist Studies,* vol. 6, 1980, pp. 342–67.
3. For an extended and powerful argument on this issue, see Jane Roland Martin, *Reclaiming a Conversation* (New Haven, Conn.: Yale University Press, 1985).
4. Howard Gardner, *Frames of Mind* (New York: Basic Books, 1983).
5. John Gardner, *Excellence: Can We Be Equal and Excellent Too?* (New York: Harper, 1961).

Nel Noddings is the Lee Jacks Professor of Child Education at Stanford University.

QUESTIONS FOR REFLECTION

1.   Do you agree with Noddings's assertion that the "drive for academic adequacy" characterizes contemporary education? What evidence can you cite to support your position?

2. At the level with which you are most familiar (elementary, middle, secondary, or higher education), what would be the key elements of a curriculum based on Noddings's concept of "themes of care"?

3. Noddings suggests that traditional liberal education may perhaps be "mere political maneuverings." Do you agree or disagree with her position? Why or why not?

4. How can curricula based on "themes of care" be as "richly intellectual" as students and teachers wish them to be?

Perspectives on Four Curriculum Traditions
WILLIAM H. SCHUBERT

ABSTRACT: *The history of curriculum planning reveals that various theoretical orientations to curriculum have been proposed. By having hypothetical "speakers" address the central curriculum question, "What is worth knowing?" Schubert suggests that there are four theoretical orientations to curriculum thought—intellectual traditionalist, social behaviorist, experientialist, and critical reconstructionist.*

Since the advent of graded textbooks by the mid-1800s, teachers and school administrators have relied on them to such an extent that when many educators and most noneducators hear the term *curriculum*, they think of textbooks. Pioneers in the curriculum field, however (e.g., John Dewey, Franklin Bobbitt, W. W. Charters, Hollis Caswell, Ralph Tyler), argued in the first half of the twentieth century for a much more complex and variegated conceptualization of curriculum. Although these scholars, the array of others who accompanied them, and their more recent descendants have disagreed on many educational issues, they all agreed that curriculum is a great deal more than the textbook.

The most perceptive curriculum scholars throughout history have realized that *curriculum*, at its root, deals with the central question of what is worth knowing; therefore, it deals with what is worth experiencing, doing, and being. Etymologically, *curriculum* is derived from classic meanings associated with the course of a chariot race. Metaphorically, *race course* can be interpreted to mean *journey* or journey of learning, growing, and becoming. As recent interpretation suggests, the verb form of *curriculum* (the noun) is *currere,* and it can be used to focus attention on the act of running the race or experiencing the journey of becoming who we become in life. Thus, the study of curriculum, taken seriously, invokes questions of the good life for individuals and matters of justice in pursuing life together for societies of human beings.

In several of my surveys of curriculum history, I have identified four recurrent positions on curriculum thought, which I have labeled as *intellectual traditionalist, social behaviorist, experientialist,* and *critical reconstructionist.* Although most curriculum scholars, leaders, and teachers are blends of one or more of these orientations, the pure form of each offers its own unique brand of educational possibility that moves far beyond the curriculum as mere textbook. Instead of writing discursively here *about* each, I will ask each *to speak,* as I have done in several publications and as a pedagogical device that I frequently employ through role-playing in courses or in presentations to groups of teachers, administrators, policy makers, and others interested in education. I have asked the *speakers* to share briefly their basic convictions about the major curriculum question(s) noted above and to augment their responses by explaining how curriculum should be restructured beyond the all-too-pervasive reliance on textbooks.

FOUR CURRICULUM TRADITIONS

Intellectual Traditionalist Speaker

[Appearing somewhat formal, self-assured, and willing to deliver the inspirational lecture or to engage in analytic, Socratic dialogue and debate]

The best answers to the basic curriculum question (What is worth knowing?) are found in the great works and in the organized disciplines of knowledge. The great works are the best expressions of human insight, understanding, and wisdom, and the disciplines are the best organizations of knowledge as created by experts in each field. Most certainly, I am an advocate of what is often called "a liberal education" for all. But why? My rationale for advocating study of the great works (in all fields, e.g., arts, sciences, humanities, social sciences) is that they, more than any other source, stimulate human beings to probe deeply into what Mortimer Adler and Robert M. Hutchins have referred to as the *great ideas,* and more recently what Allan Bloom, E. D. Hirsch, Diane Ravitch, Chester Finn, William Bennett, and others have advocated as necessary and neglected knowledge. Adler, for instance, writes of six great ideas: truth, beauty, goodness, liberty, equality, and justice. These ideas transcend matters of culture, race, gender, class, age, ethnicity, location, health or ableness, national origin, and any other aspects of individual and social life that too many consider reasons for gaining separate or individualized treatment.

This focus on individual differences neglects what all human beings have in common—in fact, it omits what makes them essentially human, namely, the great ideas. Every human who has ever lived is concerned about these matters in his or her own life and in the social context of that life. The best expressions of insight into the great ideas is found, not in the intellectual pabulum of textbooks, but in the best expressions that human beings have produced, namely the great works of literature, art, music, philosophy, social and psychological theory, mathematics, history, and the natural sciences.

Whenever possible, the primary sources should be read; however, due to barriers of language, cultural frame of reference, and ability, I admit that secondary sources need to be used. These are adequately found in good translations and in the summaries of essential knowledge available in the disciplines of knowledge.

SOCIAL BEHAVIORIST SPEAKER

[Less formal attire, not quite a lab coat—but in that spirit, oozing with the desire to discover and invent, analytically and scientifically, what works for the needs of today's world; a little rough around the edges]

Basically, I am a grubby empiricist *[with a gleam of eye that shows great respect for scientific investigation, with the "grubby" merely being a way of asking listeners to put more stock in results than in appearances].* I don't ask for too much, only that one have evidence for one's advocacy. The Intellectual Traditionalist seems to think that just because a content area has stood the test of time, so to speak, it is valuable for what students need today.

Textbooks of today carry little more than redigested relics of past textbooks, and the same unquestioned curriculum is passed from generation to generation. These textbooks rarely even get to the level of "great ideas" that the Intellectual Traditionalist promotes. Even those ideas, however, need to be looked at for their relevance to today's students. Taking a cue from one of the greatest Intellectual Traditionalists of all (though I disagree with much that he promotes), I recall that Socrates warned that the unexamined life is not worth living. I want to add that the unexamined curriculum is not worth offering.

To that end I want to tell you a little story from a curriculum classic called *The Saber-Tooth Curriculum,* written by Harold Benjamin in 1939. (By the way, intellectual traditionalists were so powerful in education at the time that Benjamin had to write under a pseudonym, J. Abner Peddiwell.) Being an advocate of economy of time (an earlier version of "time on task"), I am pleased to tell you that the book is short and to the point, even if it is literary and one of the only funny curriculum books in existence!

The story line has a young man who just graduated from college, planning to be a teacher, on a celebratory vacation seated at the longest bar in the world in Tijuana. He sees his old professor from an introduction to education course, strikes up a conversation, and learns that the professor has been on sabbatical studying the educational system of prehistoric peoples.

The conversations are about what he learned. He learned, for example, that prehistoric education classes bore such titles as "Fish Grabbing with the Bare Hands" and "Saber-tooth Tiger Chasing with Fire." The practical value of these courses for prehistoric life is obvious. However, as time went on and as the climate became intensely colder (glaciers arrived), the streams froze up and the saber-tooth tigers migrated to warmer parts of the world. Nevertheless, even then, there were Intellectual Traditionalist educators who argued that the *great ideas* embedded in fish grabbing and tiger chasing would build the mind and must be preserved for all generations. The absurdity of this hardly needs to be noted . . . (or does it, given contemporary intellectual traditionalists?).

With this in mind, I want to say that I am a *behaviorist* in the sense that we need to identify the kinds of behaviors that help students become successful in today's world (as well as the behaviors of teachers that lead to achievement of the desired behaviors in students). I am *social* in the sense that I think that such behaviors should not be taken mindlessly from traditional curriculum values and practices, but rather from systematic investigation of what it takes to be successful in society today.

EXPERIENTIALIST SPEAKER

[Very casual, trying to "tune in" to the audience, obviously desirous of engaging them in an interpersonal fashion, rather than by lecture or by precept]

Sometimes we think of curriculum as a configuration of experiences that leads to the acquisition of skills, bodies of knowledge, and values or beliefs. I am not altogether happy with this three-part separation, and see skill, knowledge, and value as part of a seamless fabric; nevertheless, each of these categories has a heuristic value for my present purposes.

I want you to think of a skill you have that helps you frequently. I want you to think of a body of knowledge that you are glad you have. Similarly, I want you to think of a value or belief that guides your life and helps you deal with difficult circumstances.

Take some time to ponder. *[pause]* Then ask yourself how and where you acquired the skill, or body of knowledge, or guiding value. Tell someone else stories about getting to the place that you now are regarding this skill, knowledge, or value. Try to understand the conditions under which you gained these capacities. If these are powerful learnings, then understanding more about the conditions under which they occurred (in your own life and the lives of others with whom you exchange) will help you to understand powerful learning for your students. Are the conditions of powerful learning in your life, and in the lives of others you know, present in the lives of your students in your school?

What I am trying to convey here is a natural way of learning and teaching, one that we all experience outside of formal learning contexts. Learning, teaching, and curriculum of formal learning contexts, however, are often contrived. My position is that we learn best when learning springs from our genuine interests and concerns.

John Dewey argued this in his many writings. He referred to a progressive curriculum organization centered not in authority outside of the learner, but derived from each learner's experience. He referred to this organization as movement from *the psychological* to *the logical*. By *psychological* he meant concerns and interests of learners and by *logical* he meant the disciplines or funds of knowledge accumulated by the human race. He said that we need to move back and forth on a continuum between the psychological and the logical as we learn and grow.

In other words, Dewey's view is that the usual way of teaching (whether textbook-based, or even as either the Intellectual Traditionalist or the Social Behaviorist recommends) is the antithesis of the natural way of teaching. It is artificial and contrived, and needs to be turned on its head. The *logical* organization of the disciplines of knowledge is fine for encyclopedias and computer banks, but it is not pedagogically sound. The *logical,* however, has the power to inform and illuminate the *psychological*. The reverse is also true.

CRITICAL RECONSTRUCTIONIST SPEAKER

[Starkly serious, upset with injustice and the complicity of the status quo about it; suspicious of conspiracies—intentional and unintentional—restless about the lack of time to right wrongs before injustice reigns supreme]

Although I do agree, in principle, with my Experientialist colleague, I think he is a bit too hopeful—maybe even naive. I am convinced that schools are "sorting machines" for society, as Joel Spring has put it so well. Thus, students are accorded different opportunities to grow and learn, depending on different dimensions of their lives or contexts. I guess that the Social Behaviorist would refer to them as "variables." In any case these dimensions include socioeconomic class, gender, race, ethnicity, health, ableness, appearance, place of living or location, marital status, religion or beliefs, age, nationality, and more.

Much has been written about most of these aspects of life and their impact on providing differential treatment of students, giving them a great disparity of kinds and qualities of educational experiences. For instance, students of a particular race, or ethnicity, or social class background, or status of health, ableness/disableness, and so on may not be given equal access to certain kinds of textbooks, instructional materials, and teaching-learning environments. The variables are often covert sources of tracking students, and it is well-known that students in different tracks are taught in different and unequal ways with materials of unequal quality.

All of this is part of a process that the critical theory literature refers to as *hegemony. Hegemony* is the process whereby a society or culture reproduces patterns of inequity. Each institution of a society, school being a prominent one, passes along the hierarchies of the society at large. Students of a given race or social class or gender, for instance, are given messages in schools similar to what they receive from the society at large or from other institutions within the society.

CONCLUSION

The speakers portrayed here represent four quite different curriculum positions. They might be considered akin to archetypes of curriculum that re-emerge in different incarnations and under different labels in each generation all around our globe. Intellectual Traditionalists call for realization of the power of the classics and the great ideas embedded in them (and the accompanying disciplines of knowledge) to overcome the problems of any day. Social Behaviorists, in contrast, call for a new look at what knowledges, skills, and values lead to success in each generation. Experientialists and Critical Reconstructionists decry what they consider to be the authoritarianism of Social Behaviorists and Intellectual Traditionalists, and call for greater grassroots participation. This means that students themselves and the concerns, interests, and injustices they feel deeply must be the starting point for meaningful and worthwhile learning.

What does this all mean? Must the reader (any educator or policymaker, teacher, parent, or student) choose one side or another? In the heat of an earlier battle in the progressive era, John

Dewey argued that choosing either progressive or traditional education as superficially practiced was not the main point. In *Experience and Education,* one of Dewey's last books on education, he said prophetically, in the preface, "It is the business of an intelligent theory of education to ascertain the causes for the conflicts that exist and then, instead of taking one side or the other, to indicate a plan of operations proceeding from a level deeper and more inclusive than is represented by the practices and ideas of the contending parties." Dewey's admonition makes it necessary not to become a card-carrying Experientialist, Critical Reconstructionist, Social Behaviorist, or Intellectual Traditionalist, but instead to remember and develop relevant aspects of all of these positions as possibilities for each educational situation encountered.

The fundamental question is not merely whether to have textbooks, but to ask continuously what should be done and why it should be done—with or without textbooks. Each of the curriculum positions offers an avenue to curriculum that transcends most textbooks available, enabling teachers to meet student needs, concerns, and interests more fully. This, however, does not mean that textbooks and other more interactive instructional materials are irrelevant. In fact, rather than rejecting textbooks and related instructional materials, it would be better to ask how instructional media (teacher made, commercially prepared, or student generated) can be created to deeply capture the essence of the Social Behaviorist, Intellectual Traditionalist, Critical Reconstructionist, and Experientialist, alike. Surely, these positions do contradict one another at many points, and practices that bespeak mindless contradiction should be avoided at all costs. However, it is also possible to see each position as complementary to one another, speaking at once to different needs in any complex educational context.

Thus, the great curriculum development task before us is to draw upon all curriculum traditions for the insights and understandings that best fit situations at hand. This means that no text or policy or written curriculum is the final answer. Good answers lie in continuously asking what knowledge and experiences are most worthwhile now, and now, and now . . . throughout the whole panoply of situations that lie ahead. Moreover, such asking must be done by all who are affected by the consequences of that asking, including students who have the greatest vested interest, yet are too often left out of the process of considering matters of purpose that affect them so dearly.

William H. Schubert is Professor of Education and Coordinator of Graduate Curriculum Studies at the University of Illinois at Chicago.

QUESTIONS FOR REFLECTION

1. Is the intellectual traditionalist orientation elitist? How might Schubert's intellectual traditionalist speaker respond to this criticism?
2. The social behaviorist speaker states that "we need to identify the kinds of behaviors that help students become successful in today's world." How would this person determine what will make students "successful"? How would this contrast with the approach used by the other three speakers?
3. If, as the experientialist speaker suggests, the curriculum should be based on students' "genuine interests and concerns," will students acquire the knowledge and skills they will need to function effectively in our society?
4. At this point in your study of curriculum planning, which curriculum orientation is most compatible with your views? Least compatible?

A Cross-Cutting Approach to the Curriculum: The Moving Wheel

THEODORE BRAMELD (1904–1987)

ABSTRACT: Often acknowledged as the founder of reconstructionism, Brameld believed that schools should become the primary agent for planning and directing social change, or "reconstructing" society. Here, he describes a "cross-cutting," integrated approach to the curriculum—an approach that would replace "conventional" subject-matter structures and subdivisions of knowledge. According to the "cross-cutting" approach, the curriculum would be shaped around the critical problems and issues that currently beset humankind. Brameld also explains how the structure of the curriculum can be likened to a wheel, an idea he originally introduced in Patterns of Educational Philosophy *(1950).*

A number of presuppositions must underlie a cross-cutting approach to the curriculum. Let me merely sketch several of these presuppositions.

1. The prime responsibility of the curriculum on any level, but most focally on the lagging senior high school and undergraduate college levels, is the confrontation of young people with the array of severe, indeed ominous, disturbances that now beset the "naked ape" himself.

2. These disturbances are by no means of exclusive concern to the "social studies." Rather, they pervade every aspect of human life across the planet—whether we are thinking either of the political, economic, esthetic, moral, and religious, or of the so-called "objective" sciences and skills of, say, chemistry, botany, and mathematics. Nothing that man has begun to understand or to utilize can any longer be considered as separable from the crucial roles that he now plays, and the extraordinary obligations that these roles entail.

3. The interpenetrating, interfusing, and evolving character of nature, including human nature, compels us to recognize the universality of the critical period through which we are passing. And education, in turn, is compelled to create new models of the curriculum that express and dramatize this universality.

4. By the same token, the new curriculum models and applications of them in experimental practice repudiate and supersede the entire conventional structure of subjects and subdivisions of knowledge that, for much too long a time,

have reflected a grossly outworn, atomistic model of both the universe and man.

5. The legitimate place that special subjects and skills occupy in transformed conceptions of the curriculum undergoes its own metamorphosis. The part no more remains merely a part than does the heart or the hand when it becomes dissevered from the total human body.

6. To follow the same metaphor another step, the human species requires abundant opportunity to reach inward, outward, and upward toward increasing fulfillment of its ever-developing powers both individually and cooperatively. To the degree that men are denied this opportunity, life becomes a failure for them. When education is not completely geared to this same purpose, it too becomes a failure.

7. The necessarily comprehensive presuppositions that we have made above apply, as norms, to any period of culture and history. But they apply with peculiar urgency to our own period. Fearful warnings, often heard, that the birth of the twenty-first century may never be attended by any historian, because no historian will have survived on our planet thirty years hence, are not warnings that any serious-minded citizen, much less any serious-minded educator, can conscientiously ignore. Unless, of course, he chooses to scoff at such an absurdity.

I am aware that each of these bald statements could be refined and supplemented almost endlessly. Nevertheless, for purposes of discussion, I intend to point directly toward one prospective design for a secondary school curriculum constructed upon the bases that they provide. This is not at all to claim that only one defensible curriculum is possible. It is to claim, however, that models at least comparable to this model should be pulled off the drawing boards and put to the test.

What are the interrelated problems and issues that illustrate the educational agenda inherent in our several presuppositions? I shall state them, again baldly, and without pretense of either order of priority or novelty. They do, however, serve as catalysts for the model to follow.

1. Can the ordinary human being conceivably hope to approach anywhere near optimal fulfillment of his own capacities in the face of accelerating technologized and depersonalized forces?

2. Can the ordinary human being develop a sense of inner personal tranquility and harmony amidst the alienating, divisive, disillusioning experiences by which he is constantly bombarded?

3. Does one (that is, you or I) hold substantial expectations of maintaining any deep sense of relationship with others (that is, with one's mate or family, with one's friends or associates) either amidst chronic instabilities or under the aegis of the folk belief of modern Western culture that self-interest (however "enlightened") still remains the only "realistic" justification for one's daily conduct?

4. Can neighborhoods and other relatively homogeneous communities learn to work together in attacking their own difficulties, in acting concertedly to remove them, and in achieving even a modicum of well-planned, cooperatively organized programs of constructive change?

5. Can racial, ethnic, and other disadvantaged minorities learn to act similarly both among themselves and with other groups of different backgrounds?

6. It is actually plausible to expect that human conflicts—for example between the sexes, the generations, and socioeconomic classes—can be ameliorated by more humane, viable patterns of living and working?

7. Can religious institutions, with all their rigidities of custom and tradition, still find ways to emulate the same general processes suggested above?

8. Can we reasonably aspire to the expectation that nations will find powerful means to conquer and control the ever-advancing threat of human annihilation?

9. Can the fine arts become a vastly wider, richer experience of unique as well as communal creativity for people across the globe, to be shared freely and openly among diverse cultures?

10. Can communication, in every form (such as travel) and through every medium (such as television), occur without restriction or intimidation not only within but between nations?

11. Can the sciences become equally available to all men, devoted to their welfare and advancement (for example, through the sciences of human health or of the control and growth of natural riches), without depletion and decay?

12. Can economic and accompanying political establishments be rebuilt so that people in every part of the earth have access to and become the exclusive directors of (through their chosen representative) physical and human resources?

13. Can a converging awareness and unity of mankind as one species—a species with unique, life-affirming, life-controlling powers—be achieved, and will this awareness and unity prove translatable into workable guidelines for political, scientific, esthetic, religious direction and renewal?

14. Can education, finally, direct its attention and energy not only toward the past or toward the present of man's experience, but even more persistently and painstakingly toward man's future as well?

That this agenda is far from all-inclusive is surely obvious. Each question could proliferate into dozens of others; indeed, students themselves, stimulated by mankind-oriented teachers, could and should raise innumerable others. All of these questions, moreover, invite explorations into learning not only by means of books and laboratories; above all, they invite firsthand involvement in the experiences of people in nearby or more distant communities who frequently share the same kinds of questions and seek the same kinds of answers.

To approach the problem somewhat more directly, what does all this mean for the organization and operation of the cross-cutting curriculum? It is possible again to summarize only a number of potentialities. According to this normative model:

1. A minimum of one-half of the entire time devoted to the curriculum is spent outside the classroom—in the laboratory of direct participation with people and institutions, and always with the close support of teacher-consultants equipped to deal with whatever situations or issues have been selected for analysis and prognosis.

2. The circumference of this kind of participation is as wide as the earth, extending all the way from the family and neighborhood outward to the region, nation, and eventually to distant nations. Learning therefore occurs *directly* through intra- and international travel (let us not be deluded by financial bugaboos; more than adequate funds are available if we insist upon them enough), and *vicariously* through films, the fine arts, and contact with experts such as anthropologists. There are countless other resources.

3. "Team teaching," so often applied adventitiously these days, is supplanted by flexible partnerships of interdisciplinary study, research, and field involvement.

4. The structure of the curriculum may be symbolized (I have developed this proposal at length elsewhere) in the form of a moving "wheel." The "rim" is the unifying theme of mankind—its predicaments and its aspirations. The "hub" is the central question of any given period of learning (perhaps extending over one week, perhaps a semester), while the "spokes" are the supporting areas of concentrated attention that bear most directly upon each respective question. The "spokes" may thus be termed "courses" in art, science, foreign language, or any

other pertinent subject or skills. But these are not to be construed as *mere* courses. At all times they are as supportive of the "hub" as it is of them.

5. To the extent that a particular student discovers whatever special interests and talents he may possess, the individual is given every opportunity to develop fields of concentration in his own "spoke." Never is he encouraged to do so, however, for the sake of completing a "major" or passing "college entrance examinations," or other dubious appendages of conventional school systems.

The normative target of this theme is, I contend, far more "practicable" than are most of those advocated in the name of "practicality." This is so because a cross-cutting curriculum of the kind I urge meets the ever more insistent demands of young people for audacious, unconventional, but directly meaningful experiences in both learning and action.

If it is to succeed, students themselves should, of course, share throughout in the planning and implementation of each year's program. Jointly with their teachers, they should decide what issues are most significant to concentrate upon in a selected period. They should help to pre-plan each successive year. They should take heavy responsibilities for all field involvements both in arranging and in following them through. They should support the deviant student who may not always be interested in "problems" at all, but rather in his own "thing" (music, for example). They should engage in the dialogic process of learning that demonstrates (as Martin Buber has so brilliantly urged) how it is possible to face the profound dilemmas of human existence through the mutualities of shared emotion, reflection, and aggressive action.

I suggest, in short, that the time is long overdue when theories of the integrative curriculum should be revived and reconstructed. The trend among influential curriculum experts who have managed during the post-progressive-education period to reverse those theories should itself now be reversed.

Theodore Brameld was Professor of Education, Boston University.

QUESTIONS FOR REFLECTION

1. What is the current "status" of the reconstructionist orientation to the curriculum? How widespread is this approach to curriculum planning at the elementary, middle, secondary, and higher education levels?
2. What are the strengths and weaknesses of a reconstructionist curriculum?
3. Brameld presents a list of fourteen "interrelated problems and issues" that confronted humankind three decades ago. Which of these problems and issues are still significant today, and should additional ones be added?
4. To what extent do you believe that schools should take an activist position regarding social problems?

The Organization and Subject-Matter of General Education

ROBERT M. HUTCHINS (1899–1977)

ABSTRACT: *As president of the University of Chicago, Hutchins developed an undergraduate curriculum based on the Great Books. A well-known advocate for using perennialist philosophy to guide curriculum planning, he championed the need to preserve the intellectual traditions of Western culture. This article reflects the key elements of perennialist educational philosophy: education should (1) promote humankind's continuing search for truth, which is universal and timeless; (2) focus on ideas and the cultivation of human rationality and the intellect; and (3) stimulate students to think thoughtfully and critically about significant ideas.*

I assume that we are all agreed on the purpose of general education and that we want to confine our discussion to its organization and subject-matter. I believe that general education should be given as soon as possible, that is, as soon as the student has the tools and the maturity it requires. I think that the program I favor can be experienced with profit by juniors in high school. I therefore propose beginning general education at about the beginning of the junior year in high school. Since I abhor the credit system and wish to mark intellectual progress by examinations taken when the student is ready to take them, I shall have no difficulty in admitting younger students to the program if they are ready for it and excluding juniors if they are not.

The course of study that I shall propose is rigorous and prolonged. I think, however, that the ordinary student can complete it in four years. By the ingenious device I have already suggested I shall be able to graduate some students earlier and some later, depending on the ability and industry that they display.

General education should, then, absorb the attention of students between the ages of fifteen or sixteen and nineteen or twenty. This is the case in every country of the world but this. It is the case in some eight or nine places in the United States.

If general education is to be given between the beginning of the junior year in high school and the end of the sophomore year in college and if a bachelor's degree is to signify the completion of it, the next question is what is the subject-matter that we should expect the student to master in this period to qualify for this degree.

I do not hold that general education should be limited to the classics of Greece and Rome. I do not believe that it is possible or desirable to insist that all students who should have a general education must study Greek and Latin. I do hold that tradition is important in education; that its primary purpose, indeed, is to help the student understand the intellectual tradition in which he lives. I do not see how he can reach this understanding unless he understands the great books of the western world, beginning with Homer and coming down to our own day. If anybody can suggest a better method of accomplishing the purpose, I shall gladly embrace him and it.

Nor do I hold that the spirit, the philosophy, the technology, or the theology of the Middle Ages is important in general education. I have no desire to return to this period any more than I wish to revert to antiquity. Some books written in the Middle Ages seem to me of some consequence to mankind. Most Ph.D.'s have never heard of them. I should like to have all students read some of them. Moreover, medieval scholars did have one insight; they saw that in order to read books you had to know how to do it. They developed the techniques of grammar, rhetoric, and logic as methods of reading, understanding and talking about things intelligently and intelligibly. I think it can not be denied that our students in the highest reaches of the university are woefully deficient in all these abilities today. They cannot read, write, speak, or think. Most of the great books of the western world were written for laymen. Many of them were written for very young laymen. Nothing reveals so clearly the indolence and inertia into which we have fallen as the steady decline in the number of these books read in our schools and colleges and the steady elimination of instruction in the disciplines

through which they may be understood. And all this has gone on in the sacred name of liberalizing the curriculum.

The curriculum I favor is not too difficult even for ordinary American students. It is difficult for the professors, but not for the students. And the younger the students are the better they like the books, because they are not old enough to know that the books are too hard for them to read.

Those who think that this is a barren, arid program, remote from real life and devoid of contemporary interest, have either never read the books or do not know how to teach. Or perhaps they have merely forgotten their youth. These books contain what the race regards as the permanent, abiding contributions its intellect and imagination have made. They deal with fundamental questions. It is a mistake to suppose that young people are interested only in football, the dramatic association, and the student newspaper. I think it could be proved that these activities have grown to their present overwhelming importance in proportion as the curriculum has been denatured. Students resort to the extracurriculum because the curriculum is stupid. Young people are interested in fundamental questions. They are interested in great minds and great works of art. They are, of course, interested in the bearing of these works on the problems of the world today. It is, therefore, impossible to keep out of the discussion, even if the teacher were so fossilized as to want to, the consideration of current events. But these events then take on meaning; the points of difference and the points of similarity between then and now can be presented. Think what a mine of references to what is now going on in the world is Plato's "Republic" or Mill's "Essay on Liberty." If I had to prescribe an exclusive diet for young Americans, I should rather have them read books like these than gain their political, economic, and social orientation by listening to the best radio commentators or absorbing the *New York Times.* Fortunately, we do not have to make the choice; they can read the books and listen to the commentators and absorb the *New York Times,* too. I repeat: these important agencies of instruction—the radio and the newspaper—and all other experiences of life, as a matter of fact—take on intelligibility as the student comes to understand the tradition in which he lives. Though we have made great advances in technology, so that the steam turbine of last year may not be of much value in understanding the steam turbine of 1938, we must remember that the fundamental questions today are the same with which the Greeks were concerned; and the reason is that human nature has not changed. The answers that the Greeks gave are still the answers with which we must begin if we hope to give the right answer today.

Do not suppose that in thus including the ancients in my course of study I am excluding the moderns. I do not need to make a case for the moderns. I do apparently need to remind you that the ancients may have some value, too.

Do not suppose, either, that because I have used as examples the great books in literature, philosophy and the social sciences, I am ignoring natural science. The great works in natural science and the great experiments must be a part and an important part of general education.

Another problem that has disturbed those who have discussed this issue is what books I am going to select to cram down the throats of the young. The answer is that if any reasonably intelligent person will conscientiously try to list the one hundred most important books that have ever been written I will accept his list. I feel safe in doing this because (a) the books would all be worth reading, and (b) his list would be almost the same as mine. There is, in fact, startling unanimity about what the good books are. The real question is whether they have any place in education. The suggestion that nobody knows what books to select is put forward as an alibi by those who have never read any that would be on anybody's list.

Only one criticism of this program has been made which has seemed to me on the level. That is that students who can not learn through books will not be able to learn through the course of study that I propose. This, of course, is true. It is what might be called a self-evident proposition. I suggest, however, that we employ this curriculum for students who can be taught to read and that we continue our efforts to discover methods of teaching the rest of the youthful population how to do it. The undisputed fact that some students can not read any books should not prevent us from giving those who can read some the chance to read the best there are.

I could go on here indefinitely discussing the details of this program and the details of the attacks that have been made upon it. But these would be details. The real question is which side are you on? If you believe that the aim of general education is to teach students to make money; if you believe that the educational system should mirror the chaos of the world; if you think that we have nothing to learn from the past; if you think that the way to prepare students for life is to put them through little fake experiences inside or outside the classroom; if you think that education is information; if you believe that the whims of children should determine what they should study—then I am afraid we can never agree. If, however, you believe that education should train students to think so that they may act intelligently when they face new situations; if you regard it as important for them to understand the tradition in which they live; if you feel that the present educational program leaves something to be desired because of its "progressivism," utilitarianism, and diffusion; if you want to open up to the youth of America the treasures of the thought, imagination, and accomplishment of the past—then we can agree, for I shall gladly accept any course of study that will take us even a little way along this road.

Robert M. Hutchins was both President of the University of Chicago and Head of the Center for the Study of Democratic Institutions.

QUESTIONS FOR REFLECTION

1. What is the current "status" of the perennialist orientation to the curriculum? In other words, how widespread is this approach to curriculum planning at the elementary, middle, secondary, and higher education levels?
2. What are the strengths and weaknesses of a perennialist curriculum?
3. Hutchins states that he "wish[es] to mark intellectual progress by examinations." What additional strategies can educators use to assess students' "intellectual progress"?
4. What does Hutchins mean when he says "The curriculum I favor is not too difficult even for ordinary American students. It is difficult for the professors [and teachers], but not for the students."?

The Case for Essentialism in Education

WILLIAM C. BAGLEY (1874–1946)

ABSTRACT: *Founder of the Essentialistic Education Society and author of* Education and Emergent Man *(1934), Bagley was critical of progressive education, which he believed damaged the intellectual and moral standards of students. This article reflects the essentialist belief that our culture has a core of common knowledge that should be transmitted to students in a systematic, disciplined manner. Though similar to perennialism, essentialism stresses the "essential" knowledge and skills that productive citizens should have, rather than a set of external truths.*

What kind of education do we want for our children? Essentialism and Progressivism are terms currently used to represent two schools of educational theory that have been in conflict over a long period of time—centuries in fact. The conflict may be indicated by pairing such opposites as: effort vs. interest; discipline vs. freedom; race experience vs. individual experience; teacher-initiative vs. learner-initiative; logical organization vs. psychological organization; subjects vs. activities; remote goals vs. immediate goals; and the like.

Thus baldly stated, these pairings of assumed opposites are misleading, for every member of every pair represents a legitimate—indeed a needed—factor in the educative process. The two schools of educational theory differ primarily in the relative emphasis given to each term as compared with its mate, for what both schools attempt is an integration of the dualisms which are brought so sharply into focus when the opposites are set off against one another.

The fundamental dualism suggested by these terms has persisted over the centuries. It appeared in the seventeenth century in a school of educational theory the adherents of which styled themselves the "Progressives." It was explicit in reforms proposed by Rousseau, Pestalozzi, Froebel, and Herbart. It was reflected in the work of Bronson Alcott, Horace Mann, and later of E. A. Sheldon and Francis W. Parker; while the present outstanding leader, John Dewey, first came into prominence during the 1890s in an effort to resolve the dualism in his classic essay, now called "Interest and Effort in Education."

PROBLEMS OF AMERICAN EDUCATION

The upward expansion of mass education, first to the secondary and now to the college level, has been an outcome not alone of a pervasive faith in education, but also of economic factors. Power-driven machinery, while reducing occupations on routine levels, opened new opportunities in work for which general and technical training was essential. That young people should seek extended education has been inevitable. In opening high schools and colleges to ever-increasing numbers, it was just as inevitable that scholastic standards should be reduced. Theories that emphasized freedom, immediate needs, personal interest, and which in so doing tended to discredit their opposites—effort, discipline, remote goals—naturally made a powerful appeal. Let us consider, in a few examples, these differences in emphasis.

1. *Effort against Interest*—Progressives have given the primary emphasis to interest, and have maintained that interest in solving a problem or in realizing a purpose generates effort. The Essentialists would recognize clearly enough the motivating force of interest, but would maintain that many interests, and practically all the higher and more nearly permanent interests grow out of efforts to learn that are not at the outset interesting or appealing in themselves. If higher interests can grow out of initial interests that are intrinsically pleasing and attractive, well and good; but if this is not the case, the Essentialists provide a solution for the problem (at least, with some learners) by their recognition of discipline and duty—two concepts which the Progressives are disposed to reject unless discipline is self-discipline and duty self-recognized duty.

2. *Teacher against Learner Initiative*—Progressive theory tends to regard teacher-initiative as at best a necessary evil. The Essentialist holds

that adult responsibility for the guidance and direction of the immature is inherent in human nature—that it is, indeed, the real meaning of the prolonged period of necessary dependence upon the part of the human offspring for adult care and support. It is the biological condition of human progress, as John Fiske so clearly pointed out in his essay, "The Meaning of Infancy." The Essentialists would have the teachers responsible for a systematic program of studies and activities to develop the recognized essentials. Informal learning through experiences initiated by the learners is important, and abundant opportunities for such experiences should be provided; but informal learning should be regarded as supplementary rather than central.

3. *Race against Individual Experience*—It is this plastic period of necessary dependence that has furnished the opportunities for inducting each generation into its heritage of culture. The cultures of primitive people are relatively simple and can be transmitted by imitation or by coming-of-age ceremonies. More highly organized systems of education, however, become necessary with the development of more complicated cultures. The need of a firmer control of the young came with this development. Primitive peoples pamper and indulge their offspring. They do not sense a responsibility to provide for their own future, much less for the future of their children. This responsibility, with its correlative duty of discipline, is distinctly a product of civilization. The Progressives imply that the "child-freedom" they advocate is new, whereas in a real sense it is a return to the conditions of primitive social life.

4. *Subjects against Activities*—The Essentialists have always emphasized the prime significance of race-experience and especially of organized experience or culture—in common parlance, *subject-matter*. They have recognized, of course, the importance of individual or personal experience as an indispensable basis for interpreting organized race-experience, but the former is a means to an end rather than an educational end in itself. The Progressives, on the other hand, have tended to set the "living present" against what they often call the "dead past." There has been an element of value in this position of the Progressives, as in many other of their teachings. Throughout the centuries they have been protestants against formalism, and especially against the verbalism into which book-ish instruction is so likely to degenerate. Present day Essentialists clearly recognize these dangers.

5. *Logical against Psychological Organization*—The Essentialists recognize, too, that the organization of experience in the form of sub-jects involves the use of large-scale concepts and meanings, and that a certain proportion of the members of each generation are unable to mas-ter these abstract concepts. For immature learn-ers and for those who never grow up mentally, a relatively simple educational program limited in the earliest years of childhood to the most simple and concrete problems must suffice. This the Es-sentialists (who do not quarrel with facts) readily admit. The tendency throughout the long his-tory of Progressivism, however, has been to dis-credit formal, organized, and abstract learnings *in toto*, thus in effect throwing the baby out with the bath, and in effect discouraging even compe-tent learners from attempting studies that are "exact and exacting."

WHAT ABOUT FAILURE?

The Essentialists recognize that failure in school is unpleasant and that repetition of a grade is costly and often not effective. On the other hand, lack of a stimulus that will keep the learner to his task is a serious injustice to him and to the demo-cratic group which has a stake in his education. Too severe a stigma has undoubtedly been placed upon school failure by implying that it is sympto-matic of permanent weakness. By no means is this always the case. No less a genius than Pasteur did so poorly in his efforts to enter the Higher Nor-mal School of Paris that he had to go home for further preparation. One of the outstanding sci-entists of the present century had a hard time in

meeting the requirements of the secondary school, failing in elementary work of the field in which he later became world-famous.

WHAT ARE THE ESSENTIALS?

There can be little question as to the essentials. It is no accident that the arts of recording, comput-ing, and measuring have been among the first con-cerns of organized education. Every civilized society has been founded upon these arts, and when they have been lost, civilization has invari-ably collapsed. Nor is it accidental that a knowl-edge of the world that lies beyond one's immediate experience has been among the recog-nized essentials of universal education, and that at least a speaking acquaintance with man's past and especially with the story of one's country was early provided for in the program of the universal school. Investigation, invention, and creative art have added to our heritage. Health instruction is a basic phase of the work of the lower schools. The elements of natural science have their place. Nei-ther the fine arts nor the industrial arts should be neglected.

ESSENTIALISTS ON DEMOCRACY

The Essentialists are sure that if our democratic society is to meet the conflict with totalitarian states, there must be a discipline that will give strength to the democratic purpose and ideal. If the theory of democracy finds no place for disci-pline, then before long the theory will have only historical significance. The Essentialists stand for a literate electorate. That such an electorate is in-dispensable to its survival is demonstrated by the fate that overtook every unschooled democracy founded as a result of the war that was "to make the world safe for democracy." And literacy means the development and expansion of ideas; it means the basis for the collective thought and judgment which are the essence of democratic in-stitutions. These needs are so fundamental that it would be folly to leave them to the whim or caprice of either learner or teacher.

SUMMARY OF THE CASE FOR ESSENTIALISM

To summarize briefly the principal tenets of the present-day Essentialists:

1. Gripping and enduring interests frequently, and in respect of the higher interests almost always, grow out of initial learning efforts that are not intrinsically appealing or attractive. Man is the only animal that can sustain effort in the face of immediate desire. To deny to the young the benefits that may be theirs by the exercise of this unique human prerogative would be a gross injustice.

2. The control, direction, and guidance of the immature by the mature is inherent in the prolonged period of infancy or necessary dependence peculiar to the human species.

3. While the capacity for self-discipline should be the goal, imposed discipline is a necessary means to this end. Among individuals, as among nations, true freedom is always a conquest, never a gift.

4. The freedom of the immature learner to choose what he shall learn is not at all to be compared with his later freedom from want, fraud, fear, superstition, error, and oppression—and the price of this latter freedom is the effortful and systematic mastery of what has been winnowed and refined through the long struggle of mankind upward from the savage—and a mastery that, for most learners, must be under guidance of competent and sympathetic but firm and exacting teachers.

5. Essentialism provides a strong theory of education; its competing school offers a weak theory. If there has been a question in the past as to the kind of educational theory that the few remaining democracies of the world need, there can be no question today.

William C. Bagley was Professor of Education, Teachers College, Columbia University.

QUESTIONS FOR REFLECTION

1. What is the current "status" of the essentialist orientation to the curriculum? How widespread is this approach to curriculum planning at the elementary, middle, secondary, and higher education levels?
2. What are the strengths and weaknesses of an essentialist curriculum?
3. How might Bagley respond to critics who charge that a tradition-bound essentialist curriculum indoctrinates students and makes it more difficult to bring about desired changes in society?
4. Bagley states that "There can be little question as to the essentials. It is no accident that the arts of recording, computing, and measuring have been among the first concerns of organized education." Do you agree with his view? What "basics" might be overlooked in an essentialist curriculum?

The Case for Progressivism in Education

WILLIAM HEARD KILPATRICK (1871–1965)

ABSTRACT: *Often called "the father of progressive education," Kilpatrick believed that the curriculum should be based on "actual living." In this article, Kilpatrick sets forth the key tenets of a progressive curriculum: (1) the curriculum, which begins with children's natural interests, gradually prepares them to assume more socially responsible roles; (2) learning is most effective if it addresses students' purposes and concerns; (3) students learn to become worthy members of society by actively participating in socially useful work; (4) the curriculum should teach students to think intelligently and independently; (5) the curriculum should be planned jointly by teachers and students; and (6) students learn best what they practice and live.*

The title of this article is the editor's. The writer himself questions whether labels as applied to a living and growing outlook may not do more harm than good. Still, for certain purposes, a name is desirable. In what follows the writer tries to state his own position in a way to seem fair and true to that growing number who approve the same general outlook.

1. The center and nub of what is here advocated is that we start with the child as a growing and developing person and help him live and grow best; live now as a child, live richly, live well; and thus living, to increase his effective participation in surrounding social life so as to grow steadily into an ever more adequate member of the social whole.

Among the signs that this desirable living and consequent growth are being achieved, two seem especially significant. One is child happiness—for best work is interested work, and to be zestfully interested and reasonably successful is to be happy. The other, less obvious, but highly desirable is that what is done now shall of itself continually sprout more of life, deeper insights bringing new suggestions with new desires to pursue them.

2. The second main point has to do with learning and how this best goes on so as most surely to come back helpfully into life. For the test of learning is whether it so builds mind and character as to enhance life.

Two types of learning must here be opposed, differing so much in degree as to amount to a difference in kind. In one the learner faces a situation of his own, such that he himself feels inwardly called upon to face it; his own interests are inherently at stake. And his response thereto is also his own; it comes out of his own mind and heart, out of his own very self. He may, to be sure, have had help from teacher or book, but the response when it comes is his.

With the other kind of learning, the situation is set by the school in examination or recitation demands. This accordingly seems to the typical learner as more or less artificial and arbitrary; it does not arise out of his own felt needs. Except for the school demands there would be no situation to him. His response to this hardly felt situation is itself hardly felt, coming mainly out of words and ideas furnished by the textbook or, with older students, by the professor's lectures.

This second, the formal school kind of learning, we all know. Most of us were brought up on it. Except for those more capable in abstract ideas, the learning thus got tends to be wordy and shallow. It does little for mind or heart, and possibly even less for character, for it hardly gets into life.

The first kind has great possibilities. We may call it life's kind. It furnishes the foundation for the type of school herein advocated. Since what is learned is the pupil's own response to a situation felt to be his own, it is at once both heartfelt and mind-created. It is learned as it is lived; in fact, it is learned because it is lived. And the more one's heart is in what he does, the more important (short of too painful solicitude) it is to him, the more impelling will be the situation he faces; and the stronger accordingly will be his response and in consequence the stronger the learning. Such learning comes from deeper down in the soul and carries with it a wider range of connection both in its backward and in its forward look.

If we take the verb "to live" in a full enough sense, we may then say that, by definition, *learning has taken place when any part or phase of experience, once it has been lived, stays on with one to affect pertinently his further experience.* And we assert that *we learn what we live and in the degree that we live it.*

A further word about the school use of this life-kind of learning may help. Suppose a class is studying Whittier's "Barefoot Boy." I as teacher cannot hand over appreciation to John, nor tell it to him, nor can I compel him to get it. He must in his own mind and heart see something in the poem that calls out in him approval and appreciation. He must first respond that way before he can learn appreciation. Learning here is, in fact, the felt appreciation so staying with John as to get into his mind and character and thence come out appropriately into his subsequent life.

It is the same way with any genuinely moral response attitude. I cannot compel it. John must first feel that way in his own heart and accept it as his way of responding. Such an acceptance on John's part fixes what is thus learned in his character there to stay till the right occasion shall bring it forth again in his life. As it is accepted, so is it learned.

It is the same with ideas. These can be learned only as they are first lived. I cannot simply give John an idea, no matter how skillful I am with words. He may read and I may talk, but he has to respond *out of his own mind* with the appropriate idea as his own personal insight. He has to *see it* himself; something has to *click* inside him; the idea has to come from within, with a certain degree of personal creative insight, as his response to the problematic situation. Otherwise he hasn't it even though he may fool himself and us by using the appropriate words. I as teacher may help John to see better than otherwise he would, and his fellow pupils and I may help him make up his own mind and heart more surely to the good,

but he learns only and exactly his own response as he himself accepts this as his way of behaving.

We may sum all this up in the following words: *I learn my responses, only my responses, and all my responses, each as I accept it to act on. I learn each response in the degree that I feel it or count it important, and also in the degree that it interrelates itself with what I already know. All that I thus learn I build at once into character.*

The foregoing discussion makes plain once more how the presence of interest or purpose constitutes a favorable condition for learning. Interest and felt purpose mean that the learner faces a situation in which he is concerned. The purpose as aim guides his thought and effort. Because of his interest and concern he gets more whole-heartedly into action; he puts forth more effort; what he learns has accordingly more importance to him and probably more meaningful connections. From both counts it is better learned.

3. Each learner should grow up to be a worthy member of the social whole. Thus to grow up means to enter more fully and responsibly into the society of which one is a member and in so doing to acquire ever more adequately the culture in terms of which the group lives.

The school exists primarily to foster both these aspects of growing up. The older type school, holding itself relatively secluded within its own four walls, shut its pupils off from significant contact with actual surrounding life and instead had them learn words about life and about the actual culture. The newer school aims explicitly to have its pupils engage actively in life, especially in socially useful work within the community, thus learning to manage life by participation in life, and acquiring the culture in life's varied settings where alone the culture is actually at work.

4. The world in which we live is changing at so rapid a rate that past-founded knowledge no longer suffices. Intelligent thinking and not mere habit must henceforth rule. Youth must learn better to think for themselves. They must understand the why of our institutions, of our system of legal rights, of moral right and wrong—because only then can they use these essential things adequately or change them intelligently. The newer school thus adds to its learning by living the further fact of pervasive change and undertakes to upbuild its pupils to the kind of thoughtful character and citizenship necessary for adequate living in such a changing social world. The older school cared little either for living or for change. Stressing book study and formal information and minimizing present-day problems, it failed to build the mind or character needed in modern life.

5. The curriculum, where pupil and teacher meet, is of necessity the vital focus of all educational theory.

The older curriculum was made in advance and given to the teacher who in turn assigned it as lessons to the pupils. It was a bookish content divided into separate subjects, in result remote from life. The pupils in their turn "learned" the lessons thus assigned and gave them back to the teacher in recitation or examination, the test being (in the main) whether what was given back was the same as what had been given out. Even the few who "succeeded" on this basis tended to get at best a pedantic learning. The many suffered, being denied the favorable opportunity for living sketched above. The lowest third suffered worst; such a curriculum clearly did not fit them, as becomes now more obvious with each advance of school leaving age.

The newer curriculum here advocated is first of all actual living—all the living of the child for which the school accepts responsibility. As we saw earlier, the child learns what he actually lives and this he builds at once into character. The quality of this living becomes then of supreme importance. The school, as we say, exists precisely to foster good living in the children, the kind of living fit to be built into character. The teacher's work is to help develop and steer this desirable living. This kind of curriculum, being real child living, cannot be made in advance and handed down either to teachers or to pupils. Living at the external command of another ceases by that much to be living for the person himself and so fails to meet desirable learning conditions.

The curriculum here sought is, then, built jointly by pupils and teacher, the teacher remaining in charge, but the pupils doing as much as

they can. For these learn by their thinking and their decisions. The teacher helps at each stage to steer the process so as to get as rich living and, in the long run, as all-round living as possible. The richness of living sought includes specifically as much of meaning as the children can, with help from teacher and books, put into their living, meanings as distinctions made, knowledge used, considerations for others sensed, responsibilities accepted. The all-roundedness refers to all sides and aspects of life, immediately practical, social-moral, vocational, esthetic, intellectual. To base a curriculum on a scheme of set subjects is for most children to feed them on husks; the plan here advocated is devised to bring life to our youth and bring it more abundantly.

6. Are we losing anything in this new type school?

a. Do the children learn? Yes. Read the scientific studies (Wrightstone's, for example, and Aikin's report on the Thirty Schools) and see that the evidence is overwhelming. The "tool subjects" are learned at least as well, while the others depending on initiative and creative thinking are learned better. Honesty is much better built.

b. Does the new plan mean pupils will not use books? Exactly no; they do now show far more actual use of books. Textbooks as such will decrease perhaps to nothing, but the use of other books will appreciably increase, as experience already well shows.

c. Will children be "spoiled" by such a regime? Exactly no. For character building, this kind of school far surpasses the old sit-quietly-at-your-desk type of school. Modern psychology is well agreed that one cannot learn what one does not practice or live. The school here advocated offers abundant opportunity to associate on living terms with others and to consider them as persons. The schoolroom of the older school, in the degree that it succeeded with its rules, allowed no communication or other association except through the teacher. Accordingly, except for a kind of negative morality, it gave next to no chance to practice regard for others. The discipline of the school here advocated is positive and inclusive, consciously provided by the school, steered by the teacher, and lived by the pupils. Prejudiced journalists have caricatured the liberty as license; intelligent observation of any reasonably well run school shows exactly the contrary. This discipline is emphatically the constructive kind.

William Heard Kilpatrick was Professor of Education, Teachers College, Columbia University.

QUESTIONS FOR REFLECTION

1. What is the current "status" of the progressive orientation to the curriculum? How widespread is this approach to curriculum planning at the elementary, middle, secondary, and higher education levels?
2. What are the strengths and weaknesses of a progressive curriculum?
3. What does Kilpatrick mean when he says, *"we learn what we live and in the degree that we live it"*? What learning experiences from your own life support Kilpatrick's view?
4. What is Kilpatrick's view of *discipline* as reflected in the following: "The discipline of the school here advocated is positive and inclusive, consciously provided by the school, steered by the teacher, and lived by the pupils"? How does this view differ from that usually associated with the term *discipline*?

Traditional vs. Progressive Education

JOHN DEWEY (1859–1952)

ABSTRACT: The most influential thinker of his time, John Dewey had a profound influence on educational theory and practice, philosophy, psychology, law, and political science. He was an eloquent spokesperson for progressive education; however, his ideas were adopted and often distorted by other educators. He protested these distortions in Experience and Education *(1938), the book from which this article was taken. In what follows, he expresses concern about how some progressive schools of the day were focusing on the learner while giving little or no attention to organized subject matter and the need for adults to provide guidance to learners.*

Mankind likes to think in terms of extreme opposites. It is given to formulating its beliefs in terms of *Either-Ors,* between which it recognizes no intermediate possibilities. When forced to recognize that the extremes cannot be acted upon, it is still inclined to hold that they are all right in theory but that when it comes to practical matters circumstances compel us to compromise. Educational philosophy is no exception. The history of educational theory is marked by opposition between the idea that education is development from within and that it is formation from without; that it is based upon natural endowments and that education is a process of overcoming natural inclination and substituting in its place habits acquired under external pressure.

At present, the opposition, so far as practical affairs of the school are concerned, tends to take the form of contrast between traditional and progressive education. If the underlying ideas of the former are formulated broadly, without the qualifications required for accurate statement, they are found to be about as follows: The subject-matter of education consists of bodies of information and of skills that have been worked out in the past; therefore, the chief business of the school is to transmit them to the new generation. In the past, there have also been developed standards and rules of conduct; moral training consists in forming habits of action in conformity with these rules and standards. Finally, the general pattern of school organization (by which I mean the relations of pupils to one another and to the teachers) constitutes the school a kind of institution sharply marked off from other social institutions. Call up in imagination the ordinary schoolroom, its time-schedules, schemes of classification, of examination and promotion, of rules of order, and I think you will grasp what is meant by "pattern of organization." If then you contrast this scene with what goes on in the family for example, you will appreciate what is meant by the school being a kind of institution sharply marked off from any other form of social organization.

The three characteristics just mentioned fix the aims and methods of instruction and discipline. The main purpose or objective is to prepare the young for future responsibilities and for success in life, by means of acquisition of the organized bodies of information and prepared forms of skill which comprehend the material of instruction. Since the subject-matter as well as standards of proper conduct are handed down from the past, the attitude of pupils must, upon the whole, be one of docility, receptivity, and obedience. Books, especially textbooks, are the chief representatives of the lore and wisdom of the past, while teachers are the organs through which pupils are brought into effective connection with the material. Teachers are the agents through which knowledge and skills are communicated and rules of conduct enforced.

I have not made this brief summary for the purpose of criticizing the underlying philosophy. The rise of what is called new education and progressive schools is of itself a product of discontent with traditional education. In effect it is a criticism of the latter. When the implied criticism is made explicit it reads somewhat as follows: The traditional scheme is, in essence, one of imposition from above and from outside. It imposes adult standards, subject-matter, and methods upon those who are only growing slowly toward maturity. The gap is so great that the required subject-matter, the methods of learning and of behaving are foreign to the existing capacities of the young. They are beyond the reach of the experience the young learners already possess. Consequently, they must be imposed; even though good teachers will use devices of art to cover up the imposition so as to relieve it of obviously brutal features.

But the gulf between the mature or adult products and the experience and abilities of the young is so wide that the very situation forbids much active participation by pupils in the development of what is taught. Theirs is to do—and learn, as it was the part of the six hundred to do and die. Learning here means acquisition of what already is incorporated in books and in the heads of the elders. Moreover, that which is taught is thought of as essentially static. It is taught as a finished product, with little regard either to the ways in which it was originally built up or to changes that will surely occur in the future. It is to a large extent the cultural product of societies that assumed the future would be much like the past, and yet it is used as educational food in a society where change is the rule, not the exception.

If one attempts to formulate the philosophy of education implicit in the practices of the newer education, we may, I think, discover certain common principles amid the variety of progressive schools now existing. To imposition from above is opposed expression and cultivation of individuality; to external discipline is opposed free activity; to learning from texts and teachers, learning through experience; to acquisition of isolated skills and techniques by drill, is opposed acquisition of them as means of attaining ends which make direct vital appeal; to preparation for a more or less remote future is opposed making the most of the opportunities of present life; to static aims and materials is opposed acquaintance with a changing world.

Now, all principles by themselves are abstract. They become concrete only in the consequences which result from their application. Just because the principles set forth are so fundamental and far-reaching, everything depends upon the interpretation given them as they are put into practice in the school and the home. It is at this point that the reference made earlier to *Either-Or* philosophies becomes peculiarly pertinent. The general philosophy of the new education may be sound, and yet the difference in abstract principles will not decide the way in which the moral and intellectual preference involved shall be worked out in practice. There is always the danger in a new movement that in rejecting the aims and methods of that which it would supplant, it may develop its principles negatively rather than positively and constructively. Then it takes its clue in practice from that which is rejected instead of from the constructive development of its own philosophy.

I take it that the fundamental unity of the newer philosophy is found in the idea that there is an intimate and necessary relation between the processes of actual experience and education. If this be true, then a positive and constructive development of its own basic idea depends upon having a correct idea of experience. Take, for example, the question of organized subject-matter—which will be discussed in detail later. The problem for progressive education is: What is the place and meaning of subject-matter and of organization *within* experience? How does subject-matter function? Is there anything inherent in experience which tends towards progressive organization of its contents? What results follow when the materials of experience are not progressively organized? A philosophy which proceeds on the basis of rejection, of sheer opposition, will neglect these questions. It will tend to suppose that because the old education was based on ready-made organization, therefore it suffices to reject the principle of organization *in toto,* instead of striving to discover what it means and how it is to be attained on the basis of experience. We might go through all the points of difference between the new and the old education and reach similar conclusions. When external control is rejected, the problem becomes that of finding the factors of control that are inherent within experience. When external authority is rejected, it does not follow that all authority should be rejected, but rather that there is need to

search for a more effective source of authority. Because the older education imposed the knowledge, methods, and the rules of conduct of the mature person upon the young, it does not follow, except upon the basis of the extreme *Either-Or* philosophy, that the knowledge and skill of the mature person has no directive value for the experience of the immature. On the contrary, basing education upon personal experience may mean more multiplied and more intimate contacts between the mature and the immature than ever existed in the traditional school, and consequently more, rather than less, guidance by others. The problem, then, is how these contacts can be established without violating the principle of learning through personal experience. The solution of this problem requires a well thought-out philosophy of the social factors that operate in the constitution of individual experience.

What is indicated in the foregoing remarks is that the general principles of the new education do not of themselves solve any of the problems of the actual or practical conduct and management of progressive schools. Rather, they set new problems which have to be worked out on the basis of a new philosophy of experience. The problems are not even recognized, to say nothing of being solved, when it is assumed that it suffices to reject the ideas and practices of the old education and then go to the opposite extreme. Yet I am sure that you will appreciate what is meant when I say that many of the newer schools tend to make little or nothing of organized subject-matter of study; to proceed as if any form of direction and guidance by adults were an invasion of individual freedom, and as if the idea that education should be concerned with the present and future meant that acquaintance with the past has little or no role to play in education. Without pressing these defects to the point of exaggeration, they at least illustrate what is meant by a theory and practice of education which proceeds negatively or by reaction against what has been current in education rather than by a positive and constructive development of purposes, methods, and subject-matter on the foundation of a theory of experience and its educational potentialities.

John Dewey was, at various times during his career, Professor of Philosophy, Columbia University; head of the Department of Philosophy and director of the School of Education at the University of Chicago; and Professor of Philosophy at the University of Michigan.

QUESTIONS FOR REFLECTION

1. Using Dewey's concept of *Either-Or* thinking, can you identify other current examples of such thinking in education?
2. A key tenet of progressive education is that there is a close, vital relationship between actual experience and education. What is the nature of this relationship?
3. What does Dewey mean in the following: "When external control is rejected, the problem becomes that of finding the factors of control that are inherent within experience"? In regard to the curricular area with which you are most familiar, what are some examples of how "control" might reside within the experiences students have while they are learning?

TEACHERS' VOICES— *Putting Theory Into Practice*

Values: The Implicit Curriculum

LINDA INLAY

ABSTRACT: The "implicit curriculum" of a school teaches values; however, there is often a gap between the values a school espouses and the values students experience. The author describes the development of a charter middle school culture that teaches character through the explicit curriculum of reading, writing, and arithmetic and through an implicit curriculum of values.

Whether teachers intend to or not, they teach values. Teachers' behaviors are, in fact, moral practices that are deeply embedded in the day-to-day functioning of the classroom (Jackson, Boostrom, & Hansen, 1993). Likewise, a school's culture communicates values through the ways in which faculty, parents, and students treat one another and through school policies on such issues as discipline and decision making.

In his eight-year study of more than 1,000 classrooms, Goodlad found a "great hypocrisy" (1984, p. 241) in the differences between what schools espouse as values and what students ex-

perience. This disparity produces cynical students who don't take seriously what schools say about character (Postman & Weingartner, 1969).

At River School, a charter middle school of approximately 160 students, we work hard to develop an entire school culture that teaches character through the explicit curriculum of reading, writing, and arithmetic and through an implicit curriculum of values—what Adlerian psychologist Raymond Corsini called the implicit four *R*s: responsibility, respect, resourcefulness, and responsiveness (Adler, 1927/1992; Ignas & Corsini, 1979). My introduction to this schoolwide approach to character education began 30 years ago when school director and Catholic nun Sr. Joan Madden, who was collaborating with Corsini in implementing what they called Individual Education, hired me as a teacher. She told me, "You are not teaching subjects. You are teaching who you are."

At River School, we rarely talk about character—nor do we have posters or pencils that trumpet values—because we know that the most effective character education is to model the values that we want to see in our students. We attempt to align every part of our school—from assessment to awards, from decision making to discipline—to encourage and foster students' character development. Our mission is to help students cultivate a strong sense of self through demonstrations of personal and social responsibility.

FOSTERING PERSONAL RESPONSIBILITY

We have barely spent a month in our school's new location when the fire alarm goes off. We have not yet established our safety protocols, and two of our students have pulled the fire alarm while horsing around, a typical middle school antic. Before I even get back to my office, the two students who pulled the alarm have voluntarily acknowledged the mistake that they made. They decide to "clean up their mistake" by apologizing to the affected people on campus, from the caretakers in the toddler program to the senior citizens in the Alzheimer's Center. One student voluntarily talks with the fire chief about her error. The mistake becomes an important lesson, as all mistakes should be.

These students are willing to be accountable for their actions. We view negative behavior as a sign of neediness, and we respond with positive contact, not just discipline of the behavior. Humans resist the diminution of spirit that comes with typical messages implying that they are "bad" or "wrong." These students have instead heard a call to responsibility:

You made a mistake. To be human means making mistakes and learning from them.

What do you think you should do to clean up this mistake?

Teachers focus on creating an atmosphere in which it is emotionally safe to make mistakes. We acknowledge when we have made a mistake and work hard not to get angry at students' mistakes. Within this emotionally safe terrain, we hold students accountable for their actions, allowing them to experience appropriate and natural consequences. Parents know, for example, that they are not responsible for bringing their children's forgotten homework to school.

The view of responsibility is the essential notion of our systems approach to character and relates to our underlying assumption about human beings. Humans are self-determining creatures; we have free will to make choices. Because of our ability to think, discern, and reflect, we want to make our own choices.

If humans have free will and the capacity to choose, then experiencing the consequences of "good" or "poor" choices is how humans learn to make choices. At the River School, we organize our school's curriculum and culture to provide many age-appropriate choices so that students learn, through trial and error, what works and what doesn't work for growing as independent learners and human beings.

The middle school years are about testing limits and shedding the old skin of the elementary school years, and we expect our students to cross boundaries as a way to learn about choice, consequences, freedom, and responsibility. Students say that they notice that our discipline system is different because we treat them like adults, even when they don't act like adults. We trust in our students' innate ability to make good decisions for themselves—with practice over time.

We define responsibility as an attitude that reflects a willingness to see oneself as cause, instead of victim. Students who see themselves as active rather than passive don't blame others. They see the mistake or the situation as the result of the choices that they have made. If the situation is out of their control, they see their responses to the situation as their own choice to be positive or to be negative.

This approach lessens extrinsic control, nurtures our students' intrinsic motivation to learn, and increases their self-confidence to meet and overcome challenges.

FOSTERING SOCIAL RESPONSIBILITY

Self-determination is one side of human need; a sense of community and belonging is the other. Our vision of students developing fully as individuals cannot occur without the community being a safe place that accepts the different qualities of each individual. Particularly in middle school, we see students struggling to meet these two needs. They desperately want to belong, so they assume the external trappings and mannerisms of their peer group. At the same time, they try to break away from traditions and develop their individual identities.

To grow as individuals, students must believe that the school community accepts individual differences. One test of a school's effectiveness in teaching social responsibility is how well students treat those who are socially inept on the playground. Most of the time, our students respect one another. When they do not, the school community has opportunities to learn about making our school safe for everyone.

Last year, for example, students were picking on a classmate who we suspected had a mild form of autism. With the student's consent, we devoted several team meetings to helping the school community understand why he sometimes stared at others or made odd noises. As a result of these conversations, students began to include him at lunch tables, lessened the teasing considerably, and defended him when teasing occasionally occurred. Such open conversations help each student become aware of how he or she makes a difference to every other student in school.

How do we teach *responsiveness,* this value of being responsible for one another? We begin with the recognition that we need to fulfill our students' needs for significance ("I matter") and for belonging (being part of a community) by structuring the school's culture so that we listen to students, take their concerns seriously, and depend on them.

We organize students into homeroom advisories in which the homeroom teacher is their advocate. The homeroom groups further divide into smaller "listening groups" that meet every other week with their teachers to share concerns and acknowledge successes. These meetings provide one of the ways in which we allow students to participate in solving problems in the school.

In one case, for example, someone was trashing the boys' bathroom. Student advisories discussed the problem, and one homeroom class volunteered to monitor the bathrooms throughout the day. Instead of the unspoken code of silence often practiced by middle schoolers, students reported the boy involved because they trusted that he would be treated with respect in the discipline process. In another case, students disliked some features of the dress code that had been developed by the student council and teachers. Students presented a proposal for changes at a staff meeting and did such an outstanding job of responding to the purposes of the dress code that the changes were approved.

We also take time to listen to students' ideas and questions as we develop the school's curriculum, modeling responsiveness by taking their concerns seriously. We follow the approach of the National Middle School Association (2002) to curriculum integration by asking students to develop their own questions for dealing with particular standards. The student question "What do you wish you could say but don't have the courage to say?" was the impetus for a unit last year that studied the First Amendment; various positions on evolution; and Galileo, Gandhi, Susan B. Anthony, and other figures who dared to take an unpopular stand.

If a student has problems with a teacher, he or she can call on a facilitator to mediate a conference. The purpose of a facilitating conference with a teacher is not to question his or her authority or to find out who is wrong and who is right. The goal of the conference is common understanding; the teacher works to understand the student's point of view and the student works to understand the teacher's point of view. Earlier this year, for example, a student felt picked on by his teacher and asked for a conference. Following the protocol of the facilitating conference, the teacher began with an "invitation" and asked, "What do you want to say to me?" After the student spoke, the teacher rephrased what the student said, and after the teacher spoke, the student rephrased what the teacher said. Through this active listening format, each came to a better understanding of the reasons for the other's behavior, and their relationship and classroom interactions improved.

We use this same conference format with students, faculty, and parents. Facilitators for conflicts are usually the advisors or the principal, with new teachers learning these communication skills primarily through observation and special training during faculty meetings. In some situations, students facilitate their own conflicts in listening groups, or they ask teachers to allow them time to do so. Last year, for example, two students began harassing each other on Halloween, when one laughed at the other's costume. When their conflict came to a head four months later, a facilitating conference helped them come to a resolution. They apologized to each other without being asked to and were friendly for the rest of the year.

Once understanding occurs, both sides can reach a solution together. Conflicts in the community become opportunities to learn how to deal with differences, to learn how to listen and solve problems. In this way, we empower our students to voice their beliefs and opinions more effectively. Whether expressing their beliefs and

opinions about personal relationships, the dress code, or the First Amendment, students have to think through the logic and rationale of their position. This active engagement results in improved critical thinking skills, and the students develop a sense of responsibility for their community and their learning.

Students also learn that the community depends on them as they perform community chores, offer community service, and plan school meetings and events. When the school's environment meets students' needs for significance and belonging, students are more likely to cooperate with others and look toward the common good.

Throughout our school, the implicit message is clear: We deeply respect our students, not just because they are our students, but because all human beings have the right to be respected in these ways. The seminal ideas of our program are not new. We have simply translated them into practical, day-to-day applications embedded in the school setting so that the entire school's culture becomes our implicit curriculum. Everything that we do and say teaches character.

REFERENCES

Adler, A. (1927/1992). (Trans. C. Brett.) *Understanding human nature.* Oxford, UK: One World Publications.

Goodlad, J. (1984). *A place called school.* New York: McGraw-Hill.

Ignas, E., & Corsini, R. J. (1979). *Alternative educational systems.* Itasca, IL: F. E. Peacock Publisher.

Jackson, P., Boostrom, R., & Hansen, D. (1993). *The moral life of schools.* San Francisco: Jossey-Bass.

National Middle School Association. (2002). NMSA position statement on curriculum integration [Online]. Available: www.nmsa.org/cnews/positionpapers/integrativecurriculum.htm

Postman, N., & Weingartner, C. (1969). *Teaching as a subversive activity.* New York: Delacourt Press.

Linda Inlay is Director of the River School in Napa, California.

QUESTIONS FOR REFLECTION

1. With reference to the grade level and subject area with which you are most familiar, what examples can you cite to support Inlay's assertion that "whether teachers intend to or not, they teach values"?

2. Inlay suggests that "we need to fulfill our students' needs for significance ('I matter') and for belonging (being part of a community)." To what extent do you agree (or disagree) with Inlay's position?

3. According to Inlay, the culture at River School has become part of the school's "implicit curriculum." Reflect on the schools you have attended and describe the implicit curricula you have experienced.

LEARNING ACTIVITIES

Critical Thinking

1. Imagine that Dewey was alive today, teaching in the subject area and at the level with which you are most familiar. Describe the curricular experiences students would have in his classes. Develop similar hypothetical scenarios for the other influential historical curriculum theorists whose work appears in this chapter: Robert M. Hutchins, William C. Bagley, William Heard Kilpatrick, and Theodore Brameld.

2. Think back to the teachers you had during your K–12 and undergraduate years in school. Which ones would you classify as being predominantly perennialist? Essentialist? Progressive? Reconstructionist?

3. How do you imagine teachers at the elementary, middle/junior, senior high, and higher education levels differ in regard to their preferred philosophical orientation to curriculum?

4. Of the four philosophical orientations to curriculum covered in this chapter, which one do you prefer? Least prefer? If you look ahead ten years, do you anticipate any shift in your preference?

5. Study the goals of a curriculum plan of your choice and try to determine whether they are "subject-centered," "society-centered," or "learner-centered." Which do you think they should be? Which of the four philosophical orientations covered in this chapter is closest to each of these three approaches to curriculum goals? Share your findings with other students in your class.

6. There were many important statements about the goals of education during the 1900s, each of which has influenced the processes of curriculum planning. One of the best-known statements of broad goals is known as the "Seven Cardinal Principles of Education," issued in 1918 by the Commission on Reorganization of Secondary Education. The seven goals in *Cardinal Principles of Secondary Education* included the following: health, command of fundamental processes

(reading, writing, and computation), worthy home membership, vocation, citizenship, worthy use of leisure time, and ethical character. More recently, the U.S. Department of Education, under the Clinton Administration, developed Goals 2000, which called for the attainment of goals in the following eight areas: school readiness; school completion; student achievement and citizenship; mathematics and science; adult literacy and lifelong learning; safe, disciplined, and alcohol- and drug-free schools; teacher education and professional development; and parental participation. How have the goals changed? In what respects have they remained the same?

Application Activities

1. What specific steps will you take throughout the remainder of your professional career to ensure that your philosophical orientation to curriculum remains dynamic, growing, and open to new perspectives rather than becoming static and limited?
2. Conduct a survey of current journals in education and try to locate articles that reflect the four philosophical orientations to curriculum that are covered in this chapter: perennialism, essentialism, progressivism, and reconstructionism.
3. Help your instructor set up a group activity wherein four to six students role-play teachers who are meeting for the purpose of determining broad, general goals for a curriculum. (The students should focus on a level and subject with which they are most familiar.) The rest of the class should observe and take notes on the curricular orientations expressed by the role-players. After the role-play (about 15–20 minutes), the entire class should discuss the curriculum planning process it has just observed.
4. For a one-month period, keep a tally of all the comments that are made in the mass media regarding what is (or should be) taught in schools, colleges, and universities. Compare your list with those of other students and identify the philosophical orientations to curriculum that are reflected in the comments.

Field Experiences

1. Visit a school and interview the principal or other member of the administrative team about the broad goals of the school's curriculum. Which of the following educational philosophies are reflected in his or her comments: perennialism, essentialism, progressivism, and reconstructionism? Conduct a similar interview at the higher education level by interviewing one of the following: the director of a university undergraduate honors program, director of general education, dean of instruction, academic dean, or department chair.
2. Observe the classes of two different teachers at the level with which you are most familiar. Which *one* of the four philosophical orientations to curriculum most characterizes each teacher?

3. Ask your instructor to arrange for a curriculum coordinator from the local school district to visit your class. In addition to finding out about this individual's work, ask him or her to describe the curriculum planning process in the district. On another occasion, ask your instructor to arrange for a similar visit by an individual with responsibility for planning curricula at the higher education level—the director of a university undergraduate honors program, director of general education, dean of instruction, academic dean, or department chair, for example.

Internet Activities

The Internet Activities for each chapter of *Curriculum Planning: A Contemporary Approach* are designed to help you use the Internet to further your study of curriculum planning. Use key words related to curriculum planning and your favorite search engine to gather the latest information and resources.

1. Visit the following three sites on the Internet and begin a search for materials of interest on philosophical orientations to curriculum: the home page of the American Philosophical Association (APA) "WWW Philosophy Sites" maintained by the University of Waterloo, and "Philosophy in Cyberspace."
2. Visit the Center for Dewey Studies maintained by Southern Illinois University at Carbondale and compile a list of online publications, associations, and reference materials related to the influence of Dewey's work on education.
3. Subscribe to the John Dewey Discussion Group ("open to anyone with an interest in any facet of Dewey's philosophy") on the Internet. Then participate in discussions, seminars, and other online activities of interest.
4. Numerous organizations influence the development of curriculum goals in the United States. Visit the WWW sites of two or more of the following organizations and compare the curriculum goals reflected in their position statements and political activities with regard to education.

   Alternative Public Schools Inc. (APS)
   American Federation of Teachers (AFT)
   National Education Association (NEA)
   Chicago Teachers Union (or other municipal teachers' organization)
   National Congress of Parents and Teachers (PTA)
   Parents as Teachers (PAT)
   Texas State Teachers Association (or other state teachers' organization)

C H A P T E R 2

Social Forces:
Present and Future

FOCUS QUESTIONS

1. What are ten contemporary social forces that influence the curriculum?
2. What are three developmental tasks that effective curricula help learners accomplish?
3. What are three levels of social forces, and how do they influence the curriculum?
4. Which concepts from the social sciences can help curriculum planners understand the social forces that influence the curriculum?
5. What is the role of futures planning in developing a curriculum that prepares students for an unknown future?

Although education plays an important role in shaping the world of tomorrow, it is also shaped by current and future economic, political, social, demographic, and technological forces. Since education reflects the goals and values of a society, schools must harmonize with the lives and ideas of people in a particular time and place. Curriculum planners, therefore, must understand how schools and school systems mirror the surrounding societal milieu.

Since social environments are dynamic rather than static, descriptions of a society must be modified continually. A critical dimension of curriculum planning and instruction, then, is the continuous reconsideration of present social forces and future trends. Though no one can foretell the future, it has a profound effect on curriculum planning. As Alvin Toffler (1970, p. 363) stated in *Future Shock,* a book that captured the nation's attention more than three decades ago, "All education springs from some image of the future. If the image of the future held by a society is grossly inaccurate, its educational system will betray its youth." Thus, current social forces and future trends should be examined regularly and an attempt made to understand their significance for curricula from kindergarten through higher education.

Today, we are faced with an array of challenges and opportunities unimagined at the start of the previous century. Though we don't know what the future holds, we do know that there will be a vital link between education and the quality of that future. Now, more than ever, we are aware of the role education can play in shaping a desired future—virtually every country in the world realizes that education is essential to the individual and collective wellbeing of its citizens in the future.

CURRICULUM AND THE FUTURE

For curriculum planners, the key question becomes "How do I incorporate an unknown future into the curriculum?" Lined up behind this question, like so many airplanes on a runway, are major trends and issues that will have a profound influence on education at all levels in the future: increasing ethnic and cultural diversity; the environment; changing values and morality; the family; the microelectronics revolution; the changing world of work; equal rights; crime and violence; lack of purpose and meaning; and global interdependence. Each of these trends and issues has profound implications for the processes of curriculum planning.

1. *Increasing Ethnic and Cultural Diversity.* The percentage of ethnic minorities in the United States has been growing steadily since the end of World War II. According to the Census Bureau, 28.4 million foreign-born people lived in the United States in 2000, and there is a net increase of one international migrant every thirty seconds.

New immigration and births to immigrants now account for more than three-fourths of U.S. population growth (Center for Immigration Studies, 2004). Twenty percent of U.S. senators are grandchildren of immigrants, a claim than can be made by no other nation in the world about its leading legislative body (Wirt and Kirst, 1997). In addition, the Census Bureau estimates that

- By 2010, African Americans and Hispanics will equal the number of whites
- By 2025, half of U.S. youth will be white and half "minority"
- By 2050, no one group will be a majority among adults

Increasing diversity in the United States is reflected, of course, in the nation's schools, colleges, and universities. In 2000, 39 percent of public school students were considered to belong to a minority group, an increase of 17 percent from 1972. This increase was largely due to the growth in the proportion of Hispanic students. In 2000, Hispanic students accounted for 17 percent of the public school enrollment, up by 11 percent from 1972. African Americans were 17 percent of the public school enrollment in 2000, up by 2 percent from 1972. The percentage of students from other racial and ethnic minority groups also increased, from 1 percent in 1972 to 5 percent in 2000 (National Center for Education Statistics, 2002).

At one time it was believed that the United States was a "melting pot" in which ethnic cultures would meld into one; however, ethnic and cultural diversity has remained very much a part of our society. A "salad bowl" analogy captures more accurately the cultural pluralism of our society—the distinguishing characteristics of cultures are to be preserved rather than blended into a single culture. The United States has always derived strength from the diversity of its people, and curriculum planners see cultural diversity as an asset to be preserved and valued.

2. *The Environment.* People have become increasingly proficient in their efforts to control and use nature to increase their safety, comfort, and convenience. Scientific and technological advances and the increased industrialization of the United States led many to believe that people could indeed control and use nature as they pleased. We now realize that is not the case. Sophisticated computer simulations and ecological experts warn us that we must become careful stewards of the planet. Some people believe that we have already passed the point of no return—that we have so polluted our air and water and plundered our natural resources that it is only a matter of time before we perish, regardless of what corrective measures we now take. The number of species that have become extinct or been placed on the endangered species list during our lifetimes indicates that the worldwide ecosystem is in peril. Clearly, problems such as overpopulation, pollution, depletion of the ozone layer, and the grim possibility of other environmental disasters should be addressed by curricula at all levels.

3. *Changing Values and Morality.* For some time, we have been losing faith in many of our institutions, including government, schools, religion, and the professions. The dizzying pace of events around the globe pushes aside values almost as rapidly as styles come and go in the fashion world. For example, in a short period of time we have undergone a shift in values ranging from frugality to conspicuous consumption to ecologically oriented frugality to renewed conspicuous consumption. There is much unrest in today's middle-aged generation because of its inability to pass its values on to the young. Our fluctuating moral standards contribute to adult and child drug abuse, teen alcoholism, and the divorce rate. Our private lives are played out in a world where much of the landscape seems threatening and constantly changing.

There is an increasing belief on the part of many educators that curricula should include experiences in the process of valuing and values clarification. One approach to teaching values and moral reasoning is known as *character education*. The need for character education is reflected in the *2004 Report Card: The Ethics of American Youth,* based on a national survey of nearly 25,000 high school students conducted by the Josephson Institute of Ethics, a nonprofit, nonsectarian corporation. The survey revealed that nearly two-thirds (62 percent) cheated on exams and more than one in four (27 percent) stole from a store within the past 12 months. Additionally, 40 percent admitted they "sometimes lie to save money."

Some educators, who support their positions with extensive research, assert that the processes of moral judgment can and should be taught at all school levels to help students develop so that they live according to principles of equity, justice, caring, and empathy (see, for example, Lawrence Kohlberg's "The Cognitive-Developmental Approach to Moral Education" in Chapter 3). Many parents and teachers oppose the inclusion of values and morals as part of the curriculum. They believe this is an area of instruction that should be reserved for the home and church or synagogue. At the very least, our various social institutions—the schools, the media, the government, organized religion, the family—must redefine and clarify their responsibilities for instruction in values and morality.

4. *Family.* The family has traditionally been one of the most important institutions in American society. In many cases today, however, the family no longer functions as a closely knit unit. There is great mobility among a large segment of the population—the family is not tied closely to the community, and family members are spread out over a wide geographical area. More and more children are raised without benefit of their natural father's or mother's presence. The roles of father and mother have undergone change.

The stress placed on families in a complex society is extensive and not easily handled. For some families, such stress can be overwhelming. The structure of families who are experiencing the effects of financial problems, substance abuse, or violence, for example, can easily begin to crumble. Children in these families are more likely to experience health and emotional problems as well as difficulties at school.

With the high rise in divorce and women's entry into the workforce, family constellations have changed dramatically. No longer is a working father, a mother who stays at home, and two or three children the only kind of family in the United States. The number of single-parent families, stepparent families, blended families, and extended families has increased dramatically during the last decade. Three million children are now being raised by their grandparents, and an equal number are raised by same-sex parents (Hodgkinson, 2002). Twenty-eight percent of families with children were headed by a single parent in 2000. Of these children, 20 percent lived with only their mothers, about 4 percent lived with only their fathers, and four percent with neither parent (Federal Interagency Forum on Child and Family Statistics, 2003).

5. *Microelectronics Revolution.* Learners in the future will need to attain extensive skills in computer-based technologies; they will use computers to communicate worldwide and to generate creative solutions to complex problems. To equip students to access vast stores of information available on the Internet, on CD-ROMs, and in countless data banks, schools, colleges, and universities will need to become more technologically rich and teachers more technologically sophisticated. No longer able to resist the "irresistible force" of Information Age technology (Mehlinger, 1996), they will need to understand that computers are not merely tools—their expanding capabilities and interactivity now provide students with structured learning environments with complex, comprehensive capabilities to access and manipulate information.

Clearly, the Internet, the World Wide Web, and related telecommunications technologies have transformed the world in which we live. This includes the times and places where work is done; the range of products and services available; and how, when, and where we learn. Computers, interactive multimedia, and communication devices that employ the awesome power of tiny silicon microchips are having a profound effect on curriculum and instruction at all levels. Within the context of expanding telecommunications technologies, Erica Scharrer stresses the importance of media literacy curricula in schools, after-school programs, and programs for adults run by community-based organizations (see "Making a Case for Media Literacy in the Curriculum" in this chapter). Similarly, Kevin Maness suggests that teachers should "protect" children from a "bombardment of media exposure" by providing them with critical media literacy skills (see "Teaching Media-Savvy Students about the Popular Media" in this chapter).

6. *Changing World of Work.* The microelectronics revolution is radically changing work and the workplace. Clearly, we are in the midst of a revolution that will leave virtually no form of work unchanged.

A key aim that should guide curriculum planners from the preschool to the graduate school and beyond is to develop educational experiences that create within students the ability, and the desire, to continue self-directed learning over a lifetime. In a rapidly changing job market, career changes will be the norm, and the ability to continue learning throughout one's career a necessity.

7. *Equal Rights.* Women and minority groups in America have become more vocal and more active in demanding equal rights. African Americans, Latino and Hispanic Americans, Asian Americans and Pacific Islanders, and Native Americans and Alaskan natives often do not agree among themselves about how to proceed, but they share in a common cause of fighting back against years of inequality, inferior status, marginalization, and often inhumane treatment. In addition, those who know poverty, regardless of ethnicity or race, also struggle for a better life. Lastly, some members of the historically dominant Anglo-European American culture believe that their rights are now being violated in favor of other groups.

Though much has been accomplished to provide equal educational opportunity to all students, regardless of social class, abilities or disabilities, gender, sexual orientation, ethnicity, or race, much remains to be done. According to Frederick M. Hess and Chester E. Finn, Jr. (see "Inflating the Life Rafts of NCLB: Making Public School Choice and Supplemental Services Work for Students in Troubled Schools" in this chapter) a key purpose of No Child Left Behind legislation is to ensure equal educational opportunity: "No Child Left Behind commits the nation to finally ensuring that all of its children are given an opportunity to pursue the American dream." On the other hand, Lisa Guisbond and Monty Neill believe that NCLB is aggravating, not solving, the problem of educational inequities (see "Failing Our Children: No Child Left Behind Undermines Quality and Equity in Education" in this chapter).

In spite of legislation such as NCLB, the curricular and instructional experiences provided to students are not always appropriate. Many students who have no disabilities now end up in special education classes because of a lack of adequate education options designed to meet the needs of children and youth with diverse learning styles. With the continuing emphasis on higher standards, there is the risk that many low-achieving students will be inappropriately labeled as having a disability. In "The 'Three A's' of Creating an Inclusive Curriculum and Classroom" in this chapter, Tina M. Anctil provides guidelines for teachers to follow as they meet the needs of students with differing abilities.

In spite of a general consensus that schools should promote social change and equal opportunity, some individuals believe that educational practices reproduce the existing social order by providing qualitatively different curricular and instructional experiences to children from different socioeconomic classes. In effect, schools help to maintain the existing stratification in society and the differences between the "haves" and the "have nots." As Joel Spring (1999, pp. 290–291) asserts: "the affluent members of U.S. society can protect the educational advantages and, consequently, economic advantages, of their children by living in affluent school districts or by using private schools. [T]heir children will attend the elite institutions of higher education, and their privileged educational backgrounds will make it easy for them to follow in the footsteps of their parents' financial success." Similarly, in "Remembering Capital: On the Connections between French Fries and Education" in this chapter, Michael W. Apple maintains that a conservative power bloc in the United States "has integrated education into a wider set of ideological commitments [and] one of its major achievements has been to shift the blame for unemployment and underemployment, for the loss of economic competitiveness, and for the supposed breakdown of 'traditional' values and standards in the family, education, and paid and unpaid workplaces *from* the economic, cultural, and social policies and effects of dominant groups *to* the school and other public agencies."

8. *Crime and Violence.* Ours is a violent, crime-ridden world, as terrorism, street crime, family violence, gang violence, hate crimes, and organized crime attest. Repeated investigations into crime and dishonesty at the highest levels of government, welfare and tax fraud, corruption in business, television and movie violence, and drug abuse have contributed to an alarming erosion of concern for the rights and property of others.

The impact of crime on education is staggering; more than $600 million is spent annually on school vandalism, a figure the National Parent-Teacher Association pointed out exceeds the amount spent on textbooks for our nation's schools. The National Association of School Security Directors gives the following estimates of school-based crimes committed each year:

(handwritten margin note: often gender bullying)

- 12,000 armed robberies
- 270,000 burglaries
- 204,000 aggravated assaults
- 9,000 rapes

The rate of victimization in U.S. schools has decreased since 1992, according to *Indicators of School Crime and Safety, 2003,* jointly published by the Bureau of Justice Statistics and the National Center for Education Statistics. However, students aged 12–18 were victims of about 764,000 violent crimes and 1.2 million crimes of theft at school in 2001 (Bureau of Justice Statistics and the National Center for Education Statistics, 2003). Seventy-one percent of public schools experienced one or more violent incidents, while 36 percent reported one or more such incidents to the police.

In addition, the U.S. Department of Justice estimates that there are more than 30,500 gangs and approximately 816,000 gang members (Moore and Terrett, 1999). According to *Indicators of School Crime and Safety, 2003,* 22 percent of students in public schools reported that there were street gangs in their schools, compared with 5 percent in private schools. Urban students were more likely to report street gangs at their schools (29 percent) than were suburban and rural students (18 percent and 13 percent, respectively).

Since 1996, the nation's concern about school crime and safety heightened as a result of a string of school shootings. Among the communities that had to cope with such tragic incidents were Moses Lake, Washington (1996); Pearl, Mississippi (1997); West Paducah, Kentucky (1997); Jonesboro, Arkansas (1998); Springfield, Oregon (1998); Littleton, Colorado (1999); Conyers, Georgia (1999); and Santee and El

Cajon, California (2001). Since the recurring question after each instance of horrific school violence was "Why?" there was a renewed effort to understand the origins of youth violence.

9. *Lack of Purpose and Meaning.* The inability of many individuals to develop and pursue goals they consider worthwhile has led to a lack of purpose and meaning in their lives. Fragmented communities, changes in family structure, the seeming immorality of many leaders, injustice, income disparities, the dizzying pace of technological changes, sharp fluctuations in the global economy, our loss of faith in science and the "experts"—all make it difficult to establish a sense of purpose and meaning. An alarming number of people feel disconnected from the larger society, their families, and themselves.

An increasing number of children and youth live in situations characterized by extreme stress, family violence, grinding poverty, crime, and lack of adult guidance. Searching for purpose and meaning in their lives, they may escape into music, video games, movies, sex, cruising shopping malls, or hanging out with friends on the street. The vulnerability of today's adolescents was vividly portrayed in *Great Transitions: Preparing Adolescents for a New Century,* a report by the Carnegie Council on Adolescent Development: "Altogether, nearly half of American adolescents are at high or moderate risk of seriously damaging their life chances. The damage may be near-term and vivid, or it may be delayed, like a time bomb set in youth" (Carnegie Council on Adolescent Development, 1995). The list of alarming concerns among children and youth is sobering: academic failure, retention, and dropping out; accidents; anorexia; violent behavior; criminal activity; cultism; depression; drug abuse; suicide; teenage pregnancy; and sexually transmitted diseases.

10. *Global Interdependence.* The relationships among the nations of the world can have a significant impact on curriculum development at all levels. It is crucial that education help us understand our interconnectedness with all countries and all people and become more sensitive to our own and other's motives and needs. Our future well-being depends on being able to participate intelligently and empathetically in the global community. Curricula of the future must emphasize global interdependence, respect for the views and values of others, and an orientation toward international cooperation for resolving global threats to security, health, the environment, and human rights.

Our fate is inextricably bound up with that of the rest of the world. For example, the horrific events of September 11, 2001, were felt around the world. Thus, an important aim of the curriculum at all levels is to cultivate an understanding of the social, psychological, and historical settings that cause others to think and act as they do.

Social Forces and the Individual

The close relationship between the social environment and the development of curricula is evident if we consider three developmental tasks that citizens in a democratic society must accomplish. First, each person must select an occupation. With the exception of the family, the work environment is the setting for most individuals' day-to-day experiences. Second, a democratic society requires citizens who are prepared to deal with the current issues of government. Finally, each person faces the challenge of achieving self-fulfillment and self-development. Thus, from the learner's standpoint, an appropriate school program—from preschool through the graduate level—must enhance his or her ability to accomplish developmental tasks in three areas: *vocation, citizenship,* and *self-fulfillment.* In every society the nature of these developmental tasks is different. In industrialized societies such as ours, for example, rapid change is the norm; thus pathways for accomplishing life's developmental tasks are continually changing.

Since social forces are constantly changing, educational programs should change with them. Moreover, few social forces exist independent of each other. They are interrelated, and each individual in the society experiences the influence of most, if not all, of them at the same time. This point is illustrated by the following hypothetical situation.

> Liza is an African American who lives in the ghetto of a large city. She is fourteen years old, the oldest of a family of nine children. Her father left the family five years ago because he could not find employment and knew that his children could receive more financial support from the government if he left home. Liza's mother works during the evening, so Liza is expected to care for the apartment and children when she gets home from school. The apartment has only two rooms and is infested with rats. It has poor plumbing and toilet facilities, and the heating system works only occasionally. The children get only one real meal a day and have no money to spend at school. Their clothing is old and worn.
>
> Kevin is a white boy who lives in a middle-class suburb. He is fourteen years old, and has a seventeen-year-old sister. His father is a lawyer who works downtown and commutes daily, often arriving home very late in the evening. Kevin's mother attends many social functions and has a serious drinking problem. His parents often have loud arguments and are openly talking about divorce. Kevin's sister uses cocaine. She often spends the weekend with her boyfriend. Kevin is well fed, lives in an attractive home with a good-sized yard, and is given a generous allowance.
>
> Roy is a white boy who lives near a factory on the outer fringe of the city. He is fourteen years old, and he has one older brother and one older sister. His father is employed at the nearby factory as a blue collar worker. Roy lives in a small but comfortable house. His family does not have many luxuries, but their needs are well satisfied. His parents are deeply religious and take Roy to church with them twice on Sunday and again on Wednesday evening. His father is a veteran and proudly displays several medals. He also belongs to the local VFW. Roy's parents spend much time with their children. He often hears them talk about how radicals and the minority groups are taking over the country.

All three of these young people attend the same school and most of the same classes. Roy walks three blocks to school, but both Liza and Kevin ride the bus. Consider these questions and try to formulate some answers to them in your own mind.

1. How are all three of these young people alike?
2. How are they different?
3. What social forces have played a significant part in their lives?
4. How can the school curriculum plan for meeting the needs of these students, considering the social setting from which they come?
5. How would you, as the teacher of these three students, deal with the similarities and differences they bring from diverse social backgrounds?

It is obvious that each person is unique in the way that social forces have affected his or her life, and the school curriculum is challenged to deal with that individuality. But the curriculum is also asked to meet the needs of the total society. This problem can be seen as you consider the following questions:

1. How actively involved should the school become in dealing with social forces? (Should the faculty lead the students in picket lines?)
2. What percentage of the curriculum should be devoted to learning about social issues?
3. How should the school respond to parents who feel that the curriculum is either overemphasizing or underemphasizing particular social issues?

Levels of Social Forces

Curriculum planners should consider three levels of social forces that influence the curriculum (see Figure 2.1). First, there is the *national and international level* where concerns such as the preceding ten trends and issues should be identified and utilized in planning.

There is also the level of social forces found in the *local community,* including family structure; class structure; the ethnic, racial, and religious backgrounds of students; and the values of the community in which the curriculum will be implemented. Social forces at the community level significantly affect learners and decidedly influence their perceptions regarding the appropriateness of the curriculum they experience.

Finally, there is the *culture* of the educational setting within which the curriculum is implemented—the social forces that determine the quality of life at the school.

FIGURE 2.1
Levels of Social Forces that Influence the Curriculum

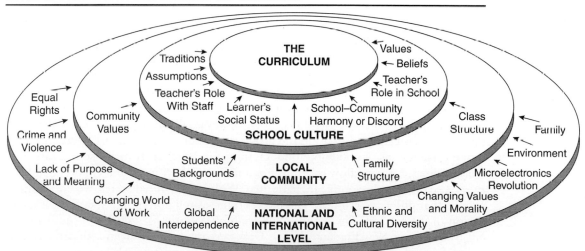

The many social forces at this level include the individual learner's social status, the teacher's role in the school, the teacher's role in relation to other professional staff, and the degree of harmony or discord that characterizes school–community relationships. On one level, schools, colleges, and universities are much alike; on another, they are very unique. Each has a distinctive culture—a set of guiding beliefs, assumptions, values, and traditions that distinguish it from other educational settings at the same level. Some may be characterized as communal places where there is a shared sense of purpose and a commitment to providing students with meaningful, carefully thought out curricular experiences. Others lack a unified sense of purpose or direction, and they drift, rudderless, from year to year. Still others may be characterized by internal discord, conflict, and devisiveness. Regardless of how they become manifest in a school's culture, social forces at this level are of major significance in curriculum planning and instruction.

Concepts from the Social Sciences

Several concepts from sociology, anthropology, and social psychology are very useful in defining and describing the social forces to be considered in curriculum planning. Among these concepts are *humanity, culture, enculturation* or *socialization, subculture,* and *cultural pluralism.* This list of relevant concepts could be extended greatly, but these are among the most salient when considering the influence of social forces on contemporary curriculum planning.

The concept of *humanity* can be a significant organizing element in curriculum planning, and it is one that is particularly needed as the nations of the world become more interdependent and together address problems of pollution, energy and food shortages, and terrorism. In addition to trying to understand the social forces that affect society in the United States or Canada, curriculum planners should consider forces that affect humanity as a whole. The issues and information to be considered and the curricular approaches developed should go well beyond national borders. These "cultural universals" would be a major guiding focus in curriculum planning. For example, an increased global perspective on the arts could enlarge students' understanding in many areas of the curriculum.

The concept of culture has been defined in many ways. Simply put, *culture* is the way of life common to a group of people; it represents their way of looking at the world. It also consists of the values, attitudes, and beliefs that influence their behavior. There are hundreds of different cultures, and no one can hope to learn about all of them. In spite of their specific differences, however, all cultures are alike in that they serve important functions within the group. For example, a group's culture may prescribe certain ways of obtaining food, clothing, and shelter. It may also indicate how work is divided up and how relationships among men, women, and children, and between the old and the young, are patterned. Within the United States, we find cultural groups that differ according to language, ethnicity, religion, politics, economics, and region of the country. The regional culture of the South, for example, is quite different from that of New England. North Dakotans are different from Californians, and so on. Socioeconomic factors, such as income and occupation, also contribute to the culture of communities. Recall, for instance, the hypothetical scenario earlier in this chapter—Liza, Kevin, and Roy had very different cultural backgrounds.

From birth to death, each person is immersed in a culture or cultures. Early in life, each person learns the patterns of behavior supported by the culture into which he or she was born. Learning this first culture is called *enculturation* or *socialization*. As our society becomes more complex and places ever-increasing demands and stresses on parents, various agencies assume more responsibility for enculturating and socializing children and youth.

A *subculture* is a division of a cultural group consisting of persons who have certain characteristics in common while they share some of the major characteristics of the larger culture. For example, our society consists of varied subcultures, and many children from these subcultures come to school with life experiences that differ significantly from those of children the schools and teachers are used to encountering. Therefore, curriculum planners and teachers should understand the differences and similarities among the subcultures in a community, as well as those within the national culture.

An additional critical point is that the individual learner should have positive feelings about his or her culture. This is possible only if curriculum planners and teachers understand that the behaviors, attitudes, and beliefs that children from nonmainstream cultures bring to school are just *different,* not wrong—a point Shirley Brice Heath (1996) brings out in *Ways with Words,* an insightful analysis of how children from two subcultures, "Roadville" and "Trackton," come to school possessing "ways with words" that are incongruent with the "school's ways":

> Roadville and Trackton residents have a variety of literate traditions, and in each community these are interwoven in different ways with oral uses of language, ways of negotiating meaning, deciding on action, and achieving status. . . . Roadville parents believe it their task to praise and practice reading with their young children; Trackton adults believe the young have to learn to be and do, and if reading is necessary for this learning, that will come. . . . In Trackton, the written word is for negotiation and manipulation—both serious and playful. Changing and changeable, words are the tools performers use to create images of themselves and the world they see. For Roadville, the written word limits alternatives of expression; in Trackton, it opens alternatives. Neither community's ways with the written word prepares it for the school's ways (Heath, 1996, pp. 234–235).

Cultural pluralism refers to a comingling of a variety of ethnic and generational lifestyles, each grounded in a complexity of values, linguistic variations, skin hues, and perhaps even cognitive world views. The term *pluralism* implies that, theoretically at least, no one culture takes precedence over any other. Cultural pluralism means that each person, regardless of self- or group-identification, is entitled to the respect, dignity, freedom, and citizen rights promised by law and tradition.

Cultural pluralism requires that curriculum planners and teachers develop learning experiences and environments in which each group's contribution to the richness of the entire society is genuinely validated and reflected to the extent possible in the curriculum. Schools that facilitate understanding of cultural pluralism radiate a tone of inclusiveness in policies, practices, and programs. So significant are the implications of cultural pluralism for contemporary curriculum planning that the concept is discussed in several articles throughout this book. (In "Multicultural Education and Curriculum Transformations" in this chapter, James A. Banks explains how the cultural assumptions, frames of reference, and perspectives of mainstream scholars have resulted in the construction of academic knowledge that legitimizes institutional inequality.)

Futures Planning

What curricula will best prepare learners to meet the challenges of the future? Of course, no one has *the* answer to this question. Nevertheless, it is important for curriculum planners to think carefully about the future. *Futures planning* is the process of conceptualizing the future as a set of possibilities and then taking steps to create the future we want. As Alvin Toffler (1970, p. 460) pointed out in *Future Shock,* we must choose wisely from among several courses of action: "Every society faces not merely a succession of *probable* futures, but an array of *possible* futures, and a conflict over *preferable* futures. The management of change is the effort to convert certain possibles into probables, in pursuit of agreed-on preferables. Determining the probable calls for a science of futurism. Delineating the possible calls for an art of futurism. Defining the preferable calls for a politics of futurism."

Futures planners project current social forces into the future with the hope of identifying and developing ways to meet the challenges associated with those forces. Unlike past futurists, today's futures planners seldom predict a single future; to use Toffler's term, they develop a set of *possible* futures.

In using the processes of futures planning, curriculum planners and teachers work with students, parents, and other members of the community in identifying and discussing present trends, and forecasting and projecting the effects of one trend compared to another. Alternative scenarios are developed based on efforts to "change" the future, either by taking action or by doing nothing.

For example, the Internet, the World Wide Web, and related telecommunications technologies illustrate how planning for the future in light of present social forces influences the curriculum. For more than thirty years, there have been continued improvements in microelectronics. Computers have moved from the laboratories, universities, and big companies into the mainstream of everyday life. They are at the grocery checkout counter, the neighborhood service station, and in our homes. Each day, millions of people around the world spend countless hours in cyberspace where they visit chat rooms, make business transactions, participate in distance learning programs, and receive instantaneous reports on newsworthy events. In light of the continued dazzling pace of developments in microelectronics, what are the implications for today's curriculum planners? Clearly, a critical form of literacy for the future is the ability to use computers for learning and solving problems.

The rapid pace of change demands that the curriculum prepare children, youth, and adults for the present as well as the future. Learning to look ahead—to see local, national, and global forces and trends in terms of alternative futures and consequences—must be part of the curriculum. Today, the curriculum should help learners participate in the development of the future through their involvement in meaningful, authentic learning experiences in the present.

CRITERION QUESTIONS—SOCIAL FORCES

What criterion questions may be derived from the social forces discussed in this chapter? Providing for individual differences among learners, the teaching of values, the development of self-understanding, and the development of problem-solving skills are four important curriculum planning criteria that illustrate how social forces influence the curriculum.

First, individual differences among learners are related to family and home background, subculture, and community background. The descriptions of Liza, Kevin, and Roy earlier in this chapter illustrate how social forces provide a key to understanding individual differences which should be provided for in the curriculum. In light of individual differences among learners, then, the criterion questions for curriculum planners and teachers are as follows:

1. What social or cultural factors contribute to individual differences among learners?
2. How can the curriculum provide for these differences?

Second, all curricula are implemented within a social climate that teaches values that may or may not be clearly stated, or about which curriculum planners and teachers may be unaware. This "hidden curriculum," as it is commonly termed, also refers to the attitudes and knowledge the culture of a school unintentionally teaches students. The discussion of cultural pluralism earlier in this chapter illustrates the relationship between social forces and the teaching of values. Thus, the criterion questions in regard to teaching values are as follows:

3. What values *are* we teaching?
4. What values do we *wish* to teach?

Third, self-understanding as a curriculum criterion is related to cultural pluralism and to various social forces such as changing values and changes in family life. Effective educational programs help students—regardless of cultural background, family situation, or challenging life circumstances—to understand themselves more fully. Thus, a salient criterion question in regard to facilitating self-understanding is:

5. How can the school program assist learners in achieving their goals of self-understanding and self-realization?

Finally, problem solving as a curriculum criterion asks whether the curriculum and the teaching of that curriculum help learners to clarify problems and develop appropriate problem-solving strategies. Three criterion questions to gauge the effectiveness of a curriculum at promoting problem-solving skills are as follows:

6. Has the curriculum been planned and organized to assist learners in identifying and clarifying personal and social problems?
7. Does the curriculum help learners acquire the problem-solving skills they will need now and in the future?
8. Does the curriculum include the development of skills in futures planning?

REFERENCES

Annie E. Casey Foundation. *Kids Count Data Book 1998.* Baltimore, MD: The Annie E. Casey Foundation, 1998.

Bureau of Justice Statistics and National Center for Education Statistics. *Indicators of School Crime and Safety, 2003.* Washington, DC: Authors, 2003.

Carnegie Council on Adolescent Development. *Great Transitions: Preparing Adolescents for a New Century.* New York: Carnegie Corporation of New York, 1995.

Center for Immigration Studies. 2004. (Retrieved from: http://www.cis.org/topics/currentnumbers .html).

Heath, Shirley Brice. *Ways with Words: Language, Life and Work in Communities and Classrooms.* Cambridge: Cambridge University Press, 1996.

Henry, Eric, et al. *To Be a Teacher: Voices from the Classroom.* Thousand Oaks, CA: Corwin Press, Inc., 1995.

Lickona, Thomas. "The Return of Character Education." *Educational Leadership* 51, no. 3 (November 1993): 6–11.

Mehlinger, Howard D. "School Reform in the Information Age." *Phi Delta Kappan* 77, no. 6 (February 1996): 400–407.

Moore, J. P., & Terrett, C. P. *Highlights of the 1997 national youth gang survey. Fact sheet.* Washington, DC: U.S. Department of Justice, Office of Justice Programs, Office of Juvenile Justice and Delinquency Prevention, 1999.

National Center for Education Statistics. *Projection of Education Statistics to 2006,* 25th Ed. Washington, DC: National Center for Education Statistics, 1996.

National Center for Education Statistics. *The condition of education 2002.* Washington, DC: U.S. Department of Education: Author, 2002a.

Spring, Joel. *American Education,* 8th Ed. New York: McGraw-Hill, Inc., 1999.

Toffler, Alvin. *Future Shock.* New York: Random House, 1970.

U.S. Department of Justice. *Sourcebook of Criminal Justice Statistics, 1998.* Washington, DC: U.S. Department of Justice, 1998.

U.S. Department of Justice. *1995 National Youth Gang Survey.* Washington, DC: U.S. Department of Justice, 1995.

Wirt, F. M., & Kirst, M. W. *The political dynamics of American education.* Berkeley: McCutchan, 1997.

Inflating the Life Rafts of NCLB: Making Public School Choice and Supplemental Services Work for Students in Troubled Schools

FREDERICK M. HESS
CHESTER E. FINN, JR.

ABSTRACT: The No Child Left Behind Act's remedies for students whose schools have been identified as needing improvement may not be working as intended. In this article, the authors analyze the choice-related provisions of the law and offer suggestions for making midcourse corrections to help the law achieve its intended outcomes.

To no one's surprise, the No Child Left Behind (NCLB) Act has become a political football. Amidst the heated rhetoric and impassioned claims, it can be easy to forget that NCLB is no one thing but rather an awkward compendium of many disparate pieces. While public officials are pressed to render absolute judgments—that NCLB is a wondrous advance or a malign mistake—observers and educators must recognize that anything as unwieldy and complex as this law will inevitably yield mixed results.

Sorting through those mixed results requires sifting through the law's many elements and learning how each of them works. In this piece, we turn our attention to the first remedies prescribed by NCLB for children in schools identified as needing improvement: the supplemental educational services and public school choice provisions, both of which constitute the choice-based element of the NCLB design. These provisions are a limited, but crucial, component of NCLB. They are the life rafts that Congress is throwing to children in our most troubled schools, and they are also hammers intended to pound districts into taking the hard steps that are so essential to improving those schools.

Less than three years after passage, it's premature to gauge NCLB's "success"—whether it has helped or hindered student achievement. But it's not too early to ask whether various provisions are being conscientiously and constructively implemented or appear likely to work as intended. If yes, then those provisions of NCLB should be given time to work while being closely watched and objectively evaluated. If no, then federal policy makers should consider making midcourse corrections in these elements of the law. Such steps, taken at an early stage when states and districts are still formulating policies, could prove far easier than efforts at a later date to alter ingrained practices and entrenched assumptions.

Nothing is gained by avoiding the question of how the law is working or innocently assuming that well-intentioned efforts will suffice. As veteran policy analyst Michael Kirst has noted, it took more than a decade and multiple legislative and administrative adjustments before the Title I program in the original 1965 Elementary and Secondary Education Act (ESEA) really functioned as intended.[1] That's the norm for ambitious new federal programs: they rarely work smoothly at the outset. Instead, they bring a raft of unforeseen problems, unintended consequences, unwanted loopholes, and unworkable features.

In fact, NCLB is vastly more ambitious than the original ESEA. The original Title I program sought to spread additional money to established institutions and interests. ESEA's mechanisms were purely fiscal, and the main implementation challenges were how to get the new money to its intended recipients and ensure that it was spent in permissible ways. Though that entailed complex calculations and intricate procedures, in reality the original Title I program nestled reasonably well into existing arrangements. By contrast, NCLB's goals, mechanisms, and remedies do not fit neatly into the status quo. One may fairly say they ask states and school districts to engage in unfamiliar, even unnatural, acts.

At NCLB's heart is the insistence that public schools annually test all students in grades 3 through 8 in reading and math and that every state measure whether its public schools are making "adequate yearly progress" (AYP) toward universal pupil proficiency in those two core subjects. Schools must show steady improvement in every grade and for multiple demographic groups. If they do not, various sanctions and interventions are supposed to follow in a scripted sequence.

Among those interventions are the twin NCLB provisions designed to offer better education options to students stuck in faltering schools and also intended, via competitive pressures, to create incentives for those schools to improve. If a Title I school fails to make its AYP target for two consecutive years, its students are supposed to be offered "public school choice." The local district is to provide each student with a choice of alternative public (including charter) schools that are making adequate yearly progress. If a student's school fails to make AYP for three consecutive years, the district is supposed to provide that child with the opportunity to enroll in "supplemental educational services"—which in practice typically amount to about 30 hours of free after school tutoring. Various providers, including private vendors, can deliver the tutoring, which is to be paid for with a portion of the school's Title I dollars.

It is important to recognize that NCLB's choice provisions were not designed primarily to enhance school options or to foster choice per se. Rather they were, first, to give students in failing schools access to other places and service providers whereby they could learn reading and math and meet NCLB standards and, second, to give failing schools an incentive to improve by threatening to reduce their enrollments and budgets.

Because it's early in the implementation cycle, it is difficult for evaluators to assess the performance of these measures in any conclusive fashion, in truth, there is immense variability across communities in how parents and districts are making use of the remedies.[2] The appropriate question to ask today about the choice provisions (and, indeed, about all provisions of NCLB) is whether, as presently constituted, they have a reasonable chance of succeeding given time and practice or whether they assume things that are extremely unlikely to happen. If the latter is the case, then the provisions need rethinking and reshaping, not just patience, practice, and minor adjusting.

LESSONS LEARNED

Thus far, we think six key lessons have emerged regarding the workings of the NCLB choice provisions.[3]

First, NCLB's choice provisions currently rely on local school systems to engage in what, for most, are unfamiliar and unnatural actions that clash with what they perceive to be their own interests. Districts, and to some extent states, are instructed to tackle tasks that many of them cannot do, will not do, or won't be able to do with the energy and finesse required by the new responsibilities and unfamiliar tasks. This reality makes it likely that NCLB's choice provisions will fare poorly except in circumstances where they happen to mesh with preexisting policy preferences and practices.

One dilemma is that effective schools that find room to attract students from troubled schools are likely to suffer in terms of academic results, while schools that shed these pupils may either benefit or worsen under NCLB-style accountability. This depends on which students change schools. If relatively high-performing students leave a low-performing school, its results may deteriorate, even as those same youngsters tug downward on test scores in the high-performing schools that they enter. Where, in this picture, is the incentive for either the sending or receiving school to facilitate choice?

Second, the NCLB supplemental service and public choice provisions are playing out very differently, with the former unexpectedly proving to be somewhat more acceptable to school districts. Many policy skeptics, ourselves included, assumed when the law was passed that districts would be more comfortable with public school choice, which at least keeps all the federal money inside the public education system. That, we supposed, was why Congress treated the supplemental services provision as the more draconian intervention, to kick in only after three years of school failure, including a year of public school choice. In reality, it appears that districts are more troubled by the challenges of choice than by the supplemental services mandate.[4] Perhaps this is because districts are themselves purveyors of services while also serving as referees and gatekeepers for other providers.

Still, we are struck that supplemental services (viewed by some proponents as "mini-vouchers") are widely regarded by districts as minimally disruptive. Students using them remain in their accustomed schools, which means that identifying eligible pupils and service providers relatively late in the school year is not an insuperable problem. With the choice option, on the other hand, districts must find space in schools that are making adequate yearly progress. Because districts don't want to disrupt bus routes and are often restricted by laws, policies, or court orders governing student assignment and ethnic balance, they frequently regard the public choice mandate as a huge bother.

Moreover, some principals and district officials seem to view providing supplemental services as a

potentially useful tool that can help boost student performance, improve school outcomes, and increase the prospects for making AYP. By contrast, they see choice as a mechanism for shifting children from one school to another, not solving any problems at the sending school and perhaps creating new ones at the receiving school.

Third, statutory constraints built into NCLB's public choice provision create such limited options—namely, other public schools within district boundaries—that, in many communities, they'll prevent most children from availing themselves of better educational opportunities. The Citizens' Commission on Civil Rights reports that just 5.6% of eligible students requested transfers to higher-performing schools in 2003–04 and that fewer than one-third of those (just 1.7% of eligible students) ultimately transferred.[5]

Student movement is constrained both by the paucity of existing options and by the lack of incentives to create new ones. Since districts must offer pupils the opportunity to transfer only into schools that are making their AYP targets, youngsters in the most troubled school districts can find few real options. Because students coming from poorly performing schools are unlikely to boost a receiving school's performance, principals at AYP-compliant schools have no incentives to accommodate more children. Most good charter schools already boast waiting lists, and high-performing, often suburban, school districts have shown no inclination to accept students from poor schools in adjacent communities. Rural communities may have but a single school and may also lack the population density to attract private providers of supplemental services. The result: there is not enough space in high-performing schools to provide attractive alternatives for more than a handful of students.

Meanwhile, NCLB contains few incentives for states or districts to create more high-performing schools. Nothing in the law suggests that state or district leaders will benefit by taking such steps, nor does the law identify sanctions for failing to do so. Instead, the status quo remains intact, with all its preexisting obstacles and logjams.

For instance, in the past two years, charter schools have come under increased political opposition and scrutiny, with more states moving to limit their growth and expansion, curb their funding, and burden them with added regulations. NCLB does nothing to encourage districts or states to create more room in effective public schools, while the law's accountability mechanisms can actually backfire on AYP-compliant schools that make room for more than a handful of students from failing schools. Some of the perverse consequences of NCLB's choice and accountability policies may even deter a school district that was considering its own choice programs. Consider: students who move may aggravate the AYP prospects of both the sending and receiving school.

NCLB's fiscal considerations may also serve to dissuade districts from enthusiastically promoting the law's choice options. The more that students avail themselves of NCLB's options, the more that districts will have to devote their mandatory 20% Title I budget "set-aside" to these activities rather than to extant programs—and the more likely that even 20% won't be sufficient to pay for the demand.

Fourth, the NCLB choice mechanisms, besides yielding few viable options for children, are unlikely to be "felt" by schools or districts in ways that prompt them to improve. Hence, they are unlikely to cause schools to alter their practices in the achievement-enhancing and customer-satisfying ways that the law's framers envisioned. It's unrealistic to imagine that a school is going to turn itself inside out because it's losing 10 or 20 kids to intradistrict choice or because 75 students sign up for tutoring through a nondistrict provider. After all, few tangible consequences flow to individual schools. Moreover, some of those consequences—like less-crowded facilities—are more attractive than repugnant. And many troubled schools are in states or districts where sundry forms of school choice, including interdistrict choice, magnet schooling, and charter schools, have long been the norm. In communities like Milwaukee, Philadelphia, Houston, Dayton,

Miami, Los Angeles, San Diego, Boston, or Washington, D.C., schools have operated for a number of years within a framework of burgeoning choice programs. If a number of district schools are failing to make AYP after years of discipline exerted by this "competition," one must wonder why NCLB's marginal changes would dramatically alter the picture.

Fifth, state school chiefs have been unenthusiastic about using the NCLB choice provisions as levers to drive school improvement. For the most part, state education and political leaders seem to regard themselves as bystanders when it comes to NCLB's choice provisions. They have left these provisions to local districts, and they appear to believe that the burden for ensuring that districts are behaving responsibly falls squarely on the U.S. Department of Education. Although the federal agency has been blessed with uncommonly creative and committed leadership in its Office of Innovation and Improvement (the unit charged with implementing NCLB's choice programs), states have not done their parts.

States have been unhurried about identifying failing schools; ensuring that eligible students receive timely, accurate information and appropriate choices; demanding that districts find desirable placements for students who wish to exit from failing schools; or pressing districts to fulfill the spirit of the law.[6] States do not even gather good data on how many students are being served by NCLB's public school choice and supplementary services provisions or how well their districts are complying with these features of the law. And they're doing little to reward and encourage districts to develop more options for children. Yet decades of federal education law make clear that Washington's proper relationship is with states and that the states are supposed to work with districts to ensure that federal programs are successfully implemented.

Finally, the clash between the rules dictated by NCLB and preexisting accountability systems in states like California and Florida is yielding immense confusion. This problem goes beyond the choice programs, to be sure, but it has a palpable effect on them. Neither parents nor educators entirely understand which schools and children are eligible for what or the actual meaning of dual school ratings under the state and federal systems. The confusion deepens in states (e.g., Michigan) where the penalties associated with failing to make AYP have led to an easing of academic standards or a softening of accountability systems.

NCLB's calendar is also unrealistic. Educationally, it makes sense to conduct student assessments near the end of a school year, so as to measure what pupils learned that year. Yet states that test in late spring are experiencing huge difficulty identifying failing schools before Labor Day, which causes havoc for the choice option and difficulty for the supplemental services option. While it's surely possible to score and report test results faster, it may also be that a one-year lag time needs to be built into the imposition of sanctions on schools.

THE PROBLEM WITH SELF-POLICING

An inherent difficulty in the design of NCLB's remedy provisions is their reliance on state and district educators to police themselves. In places blessed with gifted leadership and the courage to take tough steps, such federal stimuli can provide a useful spur to ongoing reform efforts. However, these aren't typically the states and districts that the law sought to target.

Districts unenthusiastic about the NCLB remedies can and do drag their feet in myriad ways: sending parents indecipherable letters, making a "needs improvement" label on a school sound like a badge of honor, providing unclear direction (and plenty of red tape) to parents regarding their options, moving reluctantly to contract with supplemental service providers, making little effort to find new space for public choice transfers, and erecting logistical roadblocks to outside providers of tutoring services. Meanwhile, many states are not identifying in a timely fashion the schools that are eligible, not providing effective guidance on fulfilling the mandates of the law, or not supporting the creation of new options.

It's hard to believe, therefore, that NCLB's choice provisions are on track to make a big difference in many troubled districts. Yet one ought not be too critical of the implementers. They are behaving in normal and predictable ways, and a free society gives them much lee-way to continue doing precisely that. Organizations simply do not do things that they perceive as inimical to their own self-interest unless they are forced to—and the choice provisions of NCLB contain little by way of compulsion, coercion, or punishment (or, for that matter, inducement or reward). In that sense, NCLB is a law defined more by its aspiration than by its muscle.

Further, superintendents have raised two concerns that strike us as legitimate. First, no matter what Washington may say about not allowing space constraints to impede school choice, the fact is that buildings can accommodate only so many students. Moreover, it's a stark reality that in many districts with schools from which NCLB gives students the right to exit, there just aren't many high-performing schools with empty seats.

Second, with regard to supplemental services, a district may legitimately ask whether a provider's education program is reasonably aligned with the district's (or state's) course of study. Considering that the district schools attended by these students are still obliged to demonstrate AYP on state tests, if the provider of supplemental services is teaching something different, it may do neither district nor students much good.

RECOMMENDATIONS

What to do? Though experience will likely yield some improvement in the current functioning of NCLB-mandated public choice and supplemental services programs, we don't expect that time alone will bring significant gains. This situation is not due to any grand conspiracy of resistance or to ill intentions on the part of the law's authors.

It's simply a consequence of the awkward compromises that shaped the statute's convoluted provisions. In short, if NCLB's authors are serious about using choice to give children access to more effective educational opportunities, they will need to modify this part of the law. We make no attempt here to spell out a detailed blueprint for revising it. Instead, we suggest 10 principles for lawmakers, addressing three major areas of concern: providing an effective system of choices; making choice work in concert with NCLB-style accountability; and ensuring that parents, educators, and public officials have the information they need to make sensible decisions.

Structuring the choice system. First, the same amount of attention needs to be paid to the supply of potential alternatives (i.e., effective schools and viable service providers) as to the demand-related rules by which students gain access to them. The supply of adequate schools into which eligible students can transfer needs to be expanded, whether by increasing district options, widening the availability of charter schooling, or putting greater emphasis on nondistrict options, such as interdistrict transfers and cyber schools. In particular, it will be imperative to offer incentives and support to entrepreneurs—within or beyond existing district borders—who wish to provide new classrooms and tutoring programs. Rural areas will need to rely more heavily on inventive options such as virtual schools, distance learning, schools-within-schools, and other learning modes that can mitigate the constraints imposed by geography.

Today, NCLB offers no incentives or recognition for procuring space or otherwise being proactive. This must change. For instance, schools that attract low-performing students might be given a per-pupil state "bonus." Or extra federal or state funds might be set aside to fund expansion of AYP-qualifying schools that are willing to grow.

Second, when a state or district is eager to use choice as a vehicle for school reform and can convincingly demonstrate this inclination by pointing to its own policies and programs, it should be given the flexibility to blend NCLB's provisions into its own. Some states and districts—such as Colorado, Florida, and San Diego—have made school choice a central tenet of their improvement efforts for years. Rather than being asked to alter these arrangements in deference to NCLB, these locales should be treated as beta sites and allowed to demonstrate new and effective approaches.

States have the ability to pursue such waivers from the U.S. Department of Education, and state superintendents should not be shy about doing so. Federal officials say that "EdFlex" states already have the authority to grant districts such waivers. A useful tack would be for the U.S. Department of Education to encourage states to promote an "earn your freedom" approach, whereby districts that meet certain benchmarks in terms of choice provision or utilization are exempted from some regulations. Districts might, for example, install district wide choice systems that favor students in troubled schools, cultivate a portfolio of charter schools, focus on interdistrict mobility, or develop a number of other creative approaches.

Third, school districts need to function either as providers of supplemental services or as regulators of other providers, not both. It's never a good idea to allow the fox to guard the hen house—however noble the fox's intentions. In districts that wish to provide services themselves, the state ought to be responsible for identifying another entity to screen, negotiate with, and oversee all local providers, including the school system. The likely result, which could be encouraged by federal seed funding, would be the emergence of organizations that could fill this referee-and-broker role. Some of these service coordinators might eventually operate in dozens or hundreds of districts, permitting them to build expertise in managing and evaluating providers, negotiating contracts with them, and ensuring that they deliver the promised services.

Harmonizing the accountability apparatus. Fourth, it may make sense to reverse the order in which supplemental services and public school choice must be provided. While many people supposed that districts would resist service provision more than school choice, in fact they seem more comfortable with the tutoring provision than with adopting public school choice. Moreover, it would seem to make sense to help children improve their performance within a school prior to offering them the chance to leave that school. We see a case for changing NCLB so that students would become eligible for supplemental services if their school misses AYP two years in a row and for public school choice if it misses it for the third consecutive year.

Fifth, the manner in which AYP is currently calculated works to punish principals who would otherwise embrace the public choice mandate. Schools that succeed in attracting a lot of transfer students will, by definition, receive an influx of pupils from low-performing schools. This is likely to pull down the performance of the receiving school, perhaps causing it to miss its AYP target. In other words, the law discourages rational principals from wanting to attract many students from weak schools via NCLB-mandated public choice.

It would make sense to amend the evaluation system so that schools are not penalized for enrolling these students. Perhaps all students in the school could be tested but AYP calculation would be based only on the performance of pupils who have been in attendance for at least two years. Or new arrivals could be judged on academic improvement, ensuring that students are adequately served by their receiving school without penalizing the school for having attracted low-performing students. In fact, this illustrates why it would be desirable to modify NCLB's AYP calculations more generally so as to attend to the rate at which students are gaining as well as their absolute level of performance.

Sixth, the failure of the law to distinguish between truly horrendous schools and those that barely miss AYP in one or two of the dozens of scrutinized student categories creates too many "failing" schools and too few "successful" schools. And this makes adequately performing schools nervous about small fluctuations in performance at particular grade levels or among specific pupil groups, resulting in little effort to make new seats available for transferring students. Refining the law so that the choice options are mandated only for pupils in schools that are clearly inadequate would help districts focus resources, ensure that fewer students seek transfers and that more schools can receive them, and reduce the management problems. Admittedly, this suggestion conflicts with the goals of some of NCLB's architects whose purpose for including choice provisions in the law was primarily to advance the school choice cause.

Seventh, states should revamp their testing and reporting cycles to identify targeted schools at least three months prior to the opening of the following school year. This would allow districts to prepare their choice and supplemental services programs and at the same time would help families to make intelligent decisions. No doubt this will mean reworking testing systems (and perhaps information technology systems) so that student performance can be analyzed and reported in a more timely fashion. Such revision should not entail moving assessments up into January or February, but rather retooling operations and investing in information technology so as to dramatically shorten the turnaround time for reporting.

Alternatively, NCLB might be amended so that the sanctions would lag a year behind the test results: a school's performance in 2003–04 would thus determine its students' choice options in 2005–06. A third approach is to hinge a school's status on a three-year aggregate or average performance, thus smoothing the year-to-year fluctuations that can be triggered by a wide array of phenomena, some of them purely statistical.

Informing parents and policy makers. Eighth, most parents of students in schools that fail to make AYP are unaware of the true status of their children's school. Survey data make this devastatingly clear.[7] This widespread public ignorance is due to confusion about accountability systems, the fact that parents have other matters on their minds, and the unenthusiastic efforts by many districts to inform parents of the status of their children's school.

States should take steps to prod districts to notify parents of their options early, often, and in plain, user-friendly terms. For example, the state could provide all districts with the opening paragraphs of letters to be used to notify parents, thus ensuring that the language of such letters is clear and to the point. However, it would still be a mistake to assume that troubled districts will aggressively encourage parents to transfer or to utilize nondistrict tutoring services. Hence we must look to states to provide clear models, ensure that districts take the requisite steps, and monitor the implementation of these sometimes-painful provisions.

Under NCLB, there is room for state education leaders to take a much more active role. For years, Title I has authorized state officials to withhold or reallocate funding from a district that does not comply with the law. Because the provision has been used so infrequently, its full potential remains unknown. It may, however, be possible for the state to redirect some of the federal money to provide information directly to parents in communities that are failing to adequately notify families of their options. While further federal guidance on this front would help, imaginative state officials have opportunities to redefine the permissible.

Ninth, there is an acute need for better federal data on how choice options are being utilized and how they are working. Today, nobody is responsible for compiling information on the number of students who are receiving supplemental services or on which providers are serving how many students. Nor is there any systematic data on how many districts are notifying families of their alternatives in a timely fashion, how many public school choices are being offered to eligible students, or how many students are exercising choice. Such information is essential. This strikes us as a worthy assignment for the National Center for Education Statistics.

Finally, if families are to make informed choices, it is imperative that they actually be provided with both information and options, whether or not the district wishes to cooperate. When a district wants no part of NCLB's mandated choice options, families must have a viable bypass mechanism whereby choice can be exercised notwithstanding district recalcitrance or incapacity. In such places, states should identify a private organization to ensure that families are adequately served. One possible model is the longstanding arrangement in several states (Missouri, for example) whereby a private organization provides Title I services to private school students who cannot be served directly by the state department or by a local district.

A FINAL WORD

No Child Left Behind commits the nation to finally ensuring that all of its children are given an opportunity to pursue the American dream. In an effort to make the law more than a noble aspiration, lawmakers sought to impose sanctions on schools, districts, and states that fail to meet their obligations and to provide recourse for students trapped in ineffective schools. This was a laudable and courageous effort that policy makers and public officials at every level are now struggling, for the most part in good faith, to put into practice.

Yet good intentions are never enough. The Elementary and Secondary Education Act of 1965 was landmark legislation in its day, yet in the four decades since its passage we have seen little evidence that it has made a significant difference in the schooling of disadvantaged youngsters or in the performance of schools in poor communities. For NCLB to do better, it will not be enough to offer rousing speeches and calls to action. It is also necessary to reflect soberly on how the law is working.

The supplemental services and public school choice provisions are but a limited part of NCLB, yet they have a crucial role to play. Making these provisions work as intended will not ensure that NCLB succeeds across the board, but it will be a promising and important step.

Congress was wise to craft NCLB in a manner that sought to harness the power of choice, enterprise, and market forces. Parents can be an energetic source of education reform, and competition can be a powerful spur to educational improvement. But as we have seen in a variety of locales, choice-based school reform is no simple thing. Now Congress and the White House face a choice of their own: whether to learn the emerging lessons quickly and capitalize on them at an early stage or to close their eyes and insist that things will somehow work out. To us that seems like an easier decision than choosing between two schools.

NOTES

1. Michael Kirst, "To Glimpse NCLB's Future, Look to the Past," *Education Gadfly,* January 2004, available at www.edexcellence.net/foundation/gadfly/issue.cfm?id=129#1610.
2. Cynthia G. Brown, *Choosing Better Schools: A Report on Student Transfers Under the No Child Left Behind Act* (Washington, D.C.: Citizens' Commission on Civil Rights, 2004); and Michael Casserly, "Choice and Supplemental Services in America's Great City Schools," in Frederick M. Hess and Chester E. Finn, Jr., eds., *Leaving No Child Behind?: Options for Kids in Failing Schools* (New York: Palgrave Macmillan, 2004), pp. 191–211.
3. Hess and Finn, op. cit.
4. Casserly, op. cit.
5. Brown, op. cit.
6. Robert Maranto and April Gresham Maranto, "Options for Low-Income Students: Evidence from the States," in Hess and Finn, pp. 63–88.
7. William Howell, "Fumbling for an Exit Key: Parents, Choice, and the Future of NCLB," in Hess and Finn, pp. 161–90.

Frederick M. Hess, a former high school social studies teacher, is director of education policy studies at the American Enterprise Institute, Washington, D.C. *Chester E. Finn* is president of the Thomas B. Fordham Foundation, Washington, D.C. Hess and Finn are co-editors of *Leaving No Child Behind? Options for Kids in Failing Schools* (Palgrave Macmillan, 2004), from which this article is adapted.

QUESTIONS FOR REFLECTION

1. Based on this article, are the authors supporters of the No Child Left Behind Act (NCLB), or are they critics? What evidence within the text can you point to to support your conclusion?
2. What do the authors suggest are the key "midcourse corrections" that need to be made to make the NCLB legislation better able to achieve its intended outcomes? Do you think their suggestions are reasonable?
3. What are the main reasons for the authors' criticism of the choice-related provisions of NCLB? What are your thoughts regarding these provisions? How do you feel about "choice" in public education?

Failing Our Children: No Child Left Behind Undermines Quality and Equity in Education

LISA GUISBOND
MONTY NEILL

ABSTRACT: The No Child Left Behind Act (NCLB) describes a "worthy goal" for the United States according to the authors. However, NCLB is aggravating, not solving, the problems that cause many children to be left behind. Guisbond and Neill propose a new approach to accountability as the basis for a comprehensive revamp of NCLB.

The No Child Left Behind Act (NCLB), the title of the federal Elementary and Secondary Education Act, describes a worthy goal for our nation. Tragically, the reality is that NCLB is aggravating, not solving, the problems that cause many children to be left behind. For the federal government to truly contribute to enhancing the duality of education for low-income and minority group students, NCLB must be overhauled.

FairTest, our nonprofit organization that strives to end misuses of standardized testing and promote fair evaluation of both teachers and students, has tracked the first two years of NCLB's implementation and identified fundamental errors in its conception, design, and execution. Rather than accept NCLB's dangerous prescriptions for public education, we propose a new approach to accountability as the basis for a comprehensive revamp of NCLB (Neill and Guisbond 2004).

Many false assumptions undergird NCLB. The most serious of the suppositions are the following:

1. *Boosting standardized test scores should be the primary goal of schools.* This assumption leads to one-size-fits-all teaching that focuses primarily on test preparation and undermines efforts to give all children a high-quality education. This exclusive focus on test scores ignores the widespread desire for schools that address a broad range of academic and social goals, as reported in public opinion polls. One recent public opinion survey found Americans believe the most important thing schools should do is prepare responsi-

ble citizens. The next most important role for public schools was to help students become economically self-sufficient (Rose and Gallup 2000). Another recent survey found that people's key concerns about schools were mostly social issues not addressed by standards, tests, or accountability (Goodwin 2003).

2. *Because poor teaching is the primary cause of unsatisfactory student performance, schools can best be improved by threats and sanctions.* Such threats encourage teachers to focus narrowly on boosting test scores. However, these punitive actions fail to address underlying problems such as family poverty and inadequate school funding, which are major reasons that many students start off behind and never catch up.

A new accountability system must start from accurate assumptions, including a richer vision of schooling that will lead away from NCLB's test-and-punish methodology. This new approach assumes that educators want to do their jobs but need assistance to do better. We believe that rather than threatening educators with sanctions based on test results, our more effective approach focuses on gathering multiple forms of evidence about many aspects of schooling and using them to support school improvements. Because schools need to build the capacity to ensure that all children receive a high-quality education, all levels of government, therefore, must fulfill their responsibilities to provide adequate and equitable resources. FairTest's proposal also gives parents and the community central roles in the accountability process rather than excluding them through incomprehensible statistical procedures and bureaucratically mandated reports currently required by NCLB.

SET UP TO FAIL

At NCLB's destructive core is a link between standardized testing and heavy sanctions through the rigid and unrealistic "adequate yearly progress" (AYP) formula. The problem is that NCLB's AYP provision is not grounded in any proven theory of school improvement. As Harvard Graduate School of Education Professor Richard Elmore explains: "The AYP requirement, a completely arbitrary mathematical function grounded in no defensible knowledge or theory of school improvement, could, and probably will, result in penalizing and closing schools that are actually experts in school improvement" (Elmore 2003, 6–10).

Moreover, many other expert analysts also have concluded that the AYP mechanism, the heart of the NCLB accountability provisions, guarantees failure for a substantial majority of the nation's schools. For example, the National Conference of State Legislatures estimated that, according to these standards, some 70 percent of schools nationwide will fail (Prah 2002). More recently, a study conducted for the Connecticut Education Association projected that more than nine out of ten Connecticut elementary and middle schools will fail to meet AYP targets within ten years (Moscovitch 2004).

The reason for the high failure rate is that the pace of progress envisioned in the law—that all students will reach the proficient level within fourteen years of its passage—is implausible. Part of the problem lies in the word "proficiency," which Education Secretary Rod Paige defines as solid, grade-level achievement. In fact, the term comes from the National Assessment of Educational Progress (NAEP), where it has been widely criticized for being an unrealistic and inaccurate standard, as well as a political construct engineered to depict a national academic crisis (Bracey 2003). Only about three in ten American students now score at the proficient level on NAEP reading and math tests (NCES 2004). Thus, within a little more than a decade, all students are expected to do as well as only a third now do—a goal far more stringent than simply "grade level."

Based on trends on NAEP tests over the past decade, prominent measurement expert Robert Linn calculated that it would take 166 years for all twelfth graders to attain proficiency, as defined by NCLB, in both reading and math (Linn 2003; Linn, Baker, and Herman 2002). In addition, due to requirements that all demographic groups make AYP, several studies have concluded that schools with more integrated student bodies are far more likely to fail than schools that lack diversity (Kane and Staiger 2002; Novak and Fuller 2003). Adding to the confusion, states' definitions of proficiency vary wildly, making it difficult to make meaningful state-to-state comparisons (Kingsbury et al. 2003).

The AYP provisions further reflect the flawed reasoning behind NCLB by assuming that schools already have adequate resources to get all students to a proficient level, if they would only use those resources better. The implication is that administrators and teachers are not working hard enough, not working well, or both. Thus, with willpower and effort, schools and districts can bootstrap their way to unprecedented results. This reasoning ignores real factors that impede improvements in teaching and learning, such as large class sizes, inadequate books, and outmoded technology, as well as nonschool factors like poverty and high student mobility.

THE LIMITS OF TEST SCORES

For NCLB proponents, the law's near-total reliance on test scores to determine the progress of students, teachers, and schools reflects a desire for objective assessments of educational outcomes. For example, President Bush has said, "Without yearly testing, we don't know who is falling behind and who needs help. Without yearly testing, too often we don't find failure until it is too late to fix" (Bush 2001). But standardized test scores offer nothing more than snapshots, often fuzzy ones, of student achievement at a single moment in time. When used to make important decisions about students and schools, they can be misleading and damaging. Moreover, good teachers already know which students are falling behind.

The national obsession with using standardized test scores to drive school improvement and reform is not new. Education researchers have examined this trend only to come up with results that cast serious doubts about the efficacy of test-based reform. Among the findings:

- Test scores do not necessarily indicate real progress when they rise or deterioration when they fall. Annual fluctuations should not be used to reward or sanction schools, teachers or school officials (Haney 2002).
- Many of the tests used to judge our students, teachers, and schools are norm-referenced, meaning they are specifically designed to ensure a certain proportion of "failures" (Haney 2002).
- Errors in question design, scoring and reporting have always been a part of standardized testing and are likely to increase substantially with the increase in testing mandated by NCLB (Rhoades and Madaus 2003).

NCLB's rigid AYP mechanism and the sanctions it triggers exacerbate standardized exams' weaknesses, such as their cultural biases, their failure to measure higher-order thinking, and the problem of measurement error. Exams with such narrow scopes and strong sanctions promote intensive teaching to the test, which undermines efforts to improve educational quality (von Zastrow 2004).

As one seventh-grade Kentucky student explained, "The test is taking away the real meaning of school. Instead of learning new things and getting tools for life, the mission of the schools is becoming to do well on the test" (Mathison 2003).

Even before NCLB became law, there was ample evidence that many of its assumptions and the model on which it was based had fundamental flaws:

- Little evidence supports the idea that the model of standards, testing, and rewards and punishments for achievement is the cure for public schooling's ailments. On the contrary, several studies show a decline in achievement in states with high-stakes testing programs relative to those with low-stakes testing (Stecher, Hamilton, and Gonzalez 2003; Amrein and Berliner 2002).
- Surveys of educators confirm that the model promotes teaching to the test and narrowed curricula, particularly in schools that serve low-income and minority students (Pedulla et al. 2003; Clarke et al. 2002).
- Independent analysts have found that tests often fail to measure the objectives deemed most important by educators who determine academic standards. Thus, students taught to such tests will not be exposed to high-quality curricula, and the public will not be informed about student achievement relative to those standards (Rothman et al. 2002).
- The instructional quality suffers under such a model because it is often assumed that all students who fail need the same type of remediation. On the contrary, researchers have found that students fail for a variety of reasons and need different instructional approaches to get on track (Riddle Buly and Valencia 2002; Moon, Callahan, and Tomlinson 2003; Hinde 2003; Mabry et al. 2003).
- Research refutes the assumption that low-achieving students are motivated to work harder and learn more in a high-stakes context. On the contrary, low-achieving students are most likely to become discouraged and give up in that environment (Harlen and Deakin-Crick 2002; Ryan and La Guardia 1999).
- There is evidence of falling graduation rates in high-stakes states, as well as evidence that schools retain additional students in hopes of reaping higher test scores in key grades.

Decades of research support the contention that retained students are more likely to drop out of school (Haney 2003).

Within its more than one thousand pages, NCLB does include some potentially helpful provisions. However, the law's flaws overwhelm them and end up damaging educational quality and equity. For example:

- NCLB calls for multiple measures that assess higher-order thinking and are diagnostically useful. However, these provisions are neither enforced nor embedded in most state practices.
- The law mandates school (or district) improvement plans. In practical terms, however, improvement means boosting test scores. Disruptive sanctions based on unrealistic rates of AYP deny schools the opportunity to see if their own improvement efforts work.

Another potentially useful component of NCLB is the call for high-quality teachers for all students. Unfortunately, the law's requirements fall short of the attractive label: A teacher may be deemed "highly qualified" if she or he has a bachelor's degree and passes a paper-and-pencil standardized exam. This minimal definition can in no way ensure that all children have good teachers.

There is no persuasive evidence demonstrating a strong relationship between passing a standardized test and being competent in the classroom. A National Academy of Sciences report, *Testing teaching candidates: The role of licensure tests in improving teacher quality,* offers the most comprehensive study of this issue. It found that raising cut-off scores on the exams may reduce racial diversity in the teaching profession without improving quality (Mitchell et al. 2001). Furthermore, the study concludes that the tests cannot "predict who will become effective teachers" (FairTest 2001).

NCLB, however, allows groups such as the American Board for Certification of Teacher Excellence (ABCTE) to promote quick and inadequate fixes. For example, the group offers a standardized test as a solution to the serious problem low-income areas have attracting strong teachers to their schools (Jacobson 2004). ABCTE is a project of the conservative, pro-NCLB Education Leaders Council, cofounded by Department of Education Deputy Secretary Eugene Hickok. ABCTE has received roughly $40 million in federal support for this scheme, although two of the three members of the department's own review panel rejected it.

A strong definition of "highly qualified" ensures that teachers work successfully with a variety of students to attain a range of important outcomes, not just test scores. And although NCLB does contain some good ideas for improving the teaching force, such as mentoring and ongoing professional development, they must be separated from the drive to narrow schooling to test preparation. These favorable elements easily could become key parts of a revamped accountability and school improvement system that would replace NCLB.

NCLB also harms rather than helps schools in need in other ways. Sanctions intended to force school improvement eventually divert funds away from efforts to help all children succeed toward helping a few parents obtain transfers and tutoring for their children. The law's ultimate sanctions—privatizing school management, firing staff, state takeovers, and similar measures—have no proven record of success.

As many educators have pointed out, the federal government has failed to adequately fund the law (National Conference of State Legislatures 2004). Just as schools are hit with the demands of the current law, most states' education budgets are shrinking. Worse, neither federal nor state governments address either the dearth of resources required to bring all children to educational proficiency or the deepening poverty that continues to hinder some children's learning.

A MOVEMENT FOR AUTHENTIC ACCOUNTABILITY

These problems have catalyzed a growing movement seeking to overhaul NCLB. State officials, parents, teachers, and students are mobilizing against the law. Unfortunately, some efforts, such as proposals to modify the AYP formula or spend more money without changing the law, seek only to minimize the damage caused by NCLB and would further perpetuate educational inequality. Others address only peripheral issues rather than the law's faulty premises and assumptions.

Effective opposition to NCLB must embrace genuine accountability, stronger equity, and concrete steps toward school improvement. FairTest has been working with educators, civil rights organizations, parent groups, and researchers across the nation to devise new models of accountability. Based on a set of draft principles, core elements of a better accountability system include:

1. *Getting federal, state, and local governments to work together to provide a fair opportunity for all children to learn a rich curriculum.* Current governments have failed to meet this fundamental accountability requirement because they have not ensured adequate, equitable funding and have overemphasized test scores.

2. *Using multiple forms of evidence to assess student learning.* If we want to know how well students are doing, we need to look at a range of real student work. If we want students to learn more or better, we have to provide teachers and students with useful feedback based on high-quality classroom assessments that reflect the various ways children really learn.

3. *Focusing on helping teachers and schools ensure educational success for all students.* Reaching that goal requires schools to be safe, healthy, supportive, and challenging environments. This means providing schools with data that can help improve academic and social aspects of education and making certain that the schools are equipped to use the data.

4. *Localizing the primary accountability mechanisms.* These mechanisms must involve educators, parents, students, and the local community. Open, participatory processes, including local school councils, annual reports, and meetings to review school progress, are necessary.

5. *Focusing the primary responsibility of state governments to provide tools and support for schools and teachers while maintaining equity and civil rights.* Intervention should take place only when localities have been given adequate resources and support but still fail to improve performance or when uncorrected civil rights violations occur.

In the short term, NCLB's rigid AYP provisions and draconian penalties should be amended. States should no longer have to annually test all students in grades 3–8 in reading and math, and the amount of required testing should be reduced. Additional measures of school performance and student learning should be included in progress evaluations. Congress also should appropriate the full amount authorized under NCLB.

FairTest's report, *Failing our children,* uses work in Nebraska and the Massachusetts Coalition for Authentic Reform in Education's community-based assessment systems as models in the construction of a different approach to accountability.

More fundamentally, policymakers must seriously consider both the damage that NCLB has wrought and the problem of inadequate educational funding around the nation. They should begin by listening to the voices of educators, parents, and community people asking for high-quality education, not test preparation, for children.

Stripped of its bureaucratic language, NCLB is a fundamentally punitive law that uses flawed standardized tests to label many schools as failures and then punishes them with harmful sanctions. NCLB must be transformed into a law that supports lasting educational improvement and makes good on the promise, in the words of the Children's Defense Fund, to "leave no child behind."

NOTE

FairTest's report on NCLB, *Failing our children: How "No Child Left Behind" undermines quality and equity in education and an accountability model that supports school improvement,* is available at www.fairtest.org/Failing_Our_Children_Report.html.

REFERENCES

Amrein, A., and D. Berliner. 2002. An analysis of some unintended and negative consequences of high-stakes testing. Tempe, AZ: Education Policy Studies Laboratory, Arizona State Univ. http://www.asu.edu/educ/epsl/EPRU/documents/EPSL-0211–125-EPRU.pdf (accessed June 18, 2004).

Bracey, G. 2003. NCLB—A plan for the destruction of public education: Just say no! *NoChildLeft.com* 1, no. 2 (February). http://www.nochildleft.com/2003/feb03no.html (accessed June 29, 2004).

Bush, G. W. 2001. Press conference with President Bush and Education Secretary Rod Paige to introduce the President's education program. http://www.whitehouse.gov/news/releases/2001/01/20010123-2.html (accessed June 18, 2004).

Clarke, M., A. Shore, K. Rhoades, L. Abrams, J. Miao, and J. Lie. 2002. *Perceived effects of state-mandated testing programs on teaching and learning: Findings from interviews with educators in low-, medium-, and high-stakes states.* Boston: National Board on Educational Testing and Public Policy, Boston College. http://www.bc.edu/research/nbetpp (accessed June 18, 2004).

Elmore, R. F. 2003. A plea for strong practice. *Education Leadership* 61 (3): 6–10.

FairTest. 2001. Reports blast teacher tests. *Examiner.* http://www.fairtest.org/examarts/Winter%2000-01/Reports%20Blast%20Teacher%20Tests.html (accessed April 29, 2004).

Goodwin, B. 2003. *Digging deeper: Where does the public stand on standards-based education?* Aurora, CO: Mid-continent Research for Education and Learning.

Haney, W. 2002. Lake Woebeguaranteed: Misuse of test scores in Massachusetts, Part 1. *Education Policy Analysis Archives* 10 (24), http://epaa.asu.edu/epaa/v10n24/ (accessed June 14, 2004).

——. 2003. Attrition of students from New York schools. Invited testimony at public hearing, "Regents Learning Standards and High School Graduation Requirements," before the New York Senate Standing Committee on Education, New York. http://www.timeoutfromtesting.org/testimonies/923_Testimony_Haney.pdf (accessed June 16, 2004).

Harlen, W., and R. Deakin Crick. 2002. A systematic review of the impact of summative assessment and tests on students' motivation for learning. Evidence for Policy and Practice Information and Coordinating Centre (EPPI-Centre), Univ. of London.

Hinde, E. R. 2003. The tyranny of the test. *Current Issues in Education* 6, no. 10 (May 27), http://cie.asu.edu/volume6/number10/ (accessed June 16, 2004).

Jacobson, L. 2004. Education Dept. ignored reviewers in issuing grant for teachers' test. *Education Week* 23 (27): 10. http://www.edweek.org/ew/ewstory.cfm?slug=27Amboard.h23&keywords=education%20leaders%20council (accessed June 21, 2004).

Kane, T. J., and D. O. Staiger. 2002. Volatility in school test scores: Implications for test-based accountability systems. Brookings Papers on Education Policy. Washington, DC: Brookings Institution.

Kingsbury G. G., A. Olson, J. Cronin, C. Hauser, and R. Houser. 2003, *The state of standards.* Portland, OR: Northwest Evaluation Association. http://www.young-roehr.com/nwea/ (accessed June 14, 2004).

Linn, R. L. 2003. *Accountability: Responsibility and reasonable expectations.* Los Angeles: National Center for Research on Evaluation, Standards, and Student Testing, Univ. of California.

Linn, R. I., E. L. Baker, and J. L. Herman. 2002. Minimum group size for measuring adequate yearly progress. *The CRESST Line* 1 (Fall): 4–5. Los Angeles: National Center for Research on Evaluation, Standards, and Student Testing, Univ. of California. http://www.cse.ucla.edu/products/newsletters/CL2002fall.pdf.

Mabry, L., J. Poole, L. Redmond, and A. Schultz. 2003. Local impact of state testing in Southwest Washington. *Education Policy Analysis Archives* 11, no. 21 (July 18), http://epaa.asu.edu/epaa/v11n22 (accessed June 16, 2004).

Mathison, S. 2003. The accumulation of disadvantage: The role of educational testing in the school career of minority children. *Workplace* 5, no. 2, http://www.louisville.edu/journal/workplace/issue5p2/mathison.html (accessed April 26, 2004).

Mitchell, K. J., D. Z. Robinson, B. S. Plake, and K. T. Knowles, eds. 2001. *Testing teacher candidates: The role of licensure tests in improving teacher quality.* Committee on Assessment and Teacher Quality, Board on Testing and Assessment, National Research Council, Washington, DC: National Academy Press.

Moon, T. R., C. M. Callahan, and C. A. Tomlinson. 2003. Effects of state testing programs on elementary schools with high concentrations of student poverty: Good news or bad news? *Current Issues in Education* 6, no. 8 (April 28), http://cie.asu.edu/volume6/number8/index.html (accessed July 15, 2004).

Moscovitch, E. 2004. Projecting AYP in Connecticut Schools. Prepared for the Connecticut Education Association. Gloucester, MA: Cape Ann Economics.

National Center for Education Statistics. 2004. *The nation's report card.* Washington, DC: National Center for Education Statistics, Institute of Education Sciences, U.S. Department of Education. http://nces.ed.gov/nationsreportcard/ (accessed June 14, 2004).

National Conference of State Legislatures. 2004. *Mandate Monitor* 1, no. 1 (March 31). http://www.ncsl.org/programs/press/2004/pr040310.htm (accessed June 18, 2004).

Neill, M., and Guisbond, L. 2004. *Failing our children: How "No Child Left Behind" undermines quality and equity in education and an accountability model that supports school improvement.* Cambridge, MA: FairTest. http://www.fairtest.org/Failing_Our_Children_Report.html (accessed June 14, 2004).

Novak, J. R., and B. Fuller. 2003. Penalizing diverse schools? Similar test scores but different students bring federal sanctions. Policy Analysis for California Education (PACE), policy brief 03-4. http://pace.berkeley.edu/pace_publications.html (accessed June 18, 2004).

Pedulla, J., L. Abrams, G. Madaus, M. Russell, M. Ramos, and J. Miao. 2003. *Perceived effects of state-mandated testing programs on teaching and learning: Findings from a national survey of teachers.* Boston: National Board on Educational Testing and Public Policy, Boston College. http://www.bc.edu/research/nbetpp/reports.html (accessed June 18, 2004).

Prah, P. M. 2002. New rules may guarantee "F's" for many schools. *Stateline.org,* December 9. http://stateline.org/stateline/?pa=story&sa=showStoryInfo&id=275753.

Rhoades, K., and C. Madaus. 2003. Errors in standardized tests: A systemic problem. National Board on Educational Testing and Public Policy, Boston College. http://www.bc.edu/nbetpp (accessed June 14, 2004).

Riddle Buly, M., and S. W. Valencia. 2002. Below the bar: Profiles of students who fail state reading assessments. *Educational Evaluation and Policy Analysis* 24 (3): 219–39. http://depts.washington.edu/ctpmail/PDFs/Reading-MRBSV-04-2003.pdf (accessed June 14, 2004).

Rose, L. C., and A. M. Gallup. 2000. The 32nd annual Phi Delta Kappan Gallup poll of the public's attitudes toward the public schools. *Phi Delta Kappan* 82 (1): 41–58.

Rothman, R., J. B. Slattery, J. L. Vranek, and L. B. Resnick. 2002. *Benchmarking and alignment of standards and testing.* Los Angeles: National Center for Research on Evaluation, Standards, and Student Testing. http://www.cse.ucla.edu/CRESST/Reports/TR566.pdf, Univ. of California.

Ryan, R. M., and J. G. La Guardia, 1999. Achievement motivation within a pressured society: Intrinsic and extrinsic motivations to learn and the politics of school reform. In *Advances in motivation and achievement,* ed. T. Urdan, 45–85. Greenwich, CT: JAI Press.

Stecher, B., L. Hamilton, and G. Gonzalez. 2003. *Working smarter to leave no child behind: Practical insights for school leaders.* Santa Monica, CA: RAND Corp.

von Zastrow, C. 2004. *Academic atrophy: The condition of the liberal arts in America's public schools.* Washington, DC: Council for Basic Education. http://www.c-b-e.org/PDF/cbe_principal_Report.pdf.

Lisa Guisbond is a researcher and advocate for the National Center for Fair and Open Testing (FairTest), where *Monty Neill,* Ed.D., is the executive director.

QUESTIONS FOR REFLECTION

1. Guisbond and Neill are highly critical of the No Child Left Behind (NCLB) Act. What are their major complaints and is their criticism justified?
2. According to the authors, in what way is NCLB *aggravating* the problems that cause many children to be left behind?
3. What do the authors propose as a new approach to accountability as the basis for a comprehensive overall of the NCLB Act? Is their proposal feasible? What would it take to win support from education policy makers to see their ideas carried forward? Who would be most likely to oppose them?

The "Three A's" of Creating an Inclusive Curriculum and Classroom

TINA M. ANCTIL

ABSTRACT: Tina Anctil provides an overview of inclusive teaching practices for regular education teachers. The legal basis for inclusion, disability prevalence, and curricular and assessment strategies for teaching students with disabilities are also discussed. Anctil provides information all teachers need to know as they confront students of differing abilities in today's classroom.

Since the landmark passage of P.L. 94-142, the Education of All Handicapped Children Act (1975), which guaranteed all children with disabilities a free, appropriate public education (FAPE), children with disabilities have been attending public schools. Prior to this legislation, children with disabilities were largely uneducated, residing in institutions or with family members. Today, the inclusion of students with disabilities in the "regular" education classroom has been coined a revolution. This recent excerpt from *The New York Times Magazine* captures the experience of one classroom.

Thomas, one of two motor impaired, nonverbal children, was in a custom built wheelchair, his blue eyes wide, his gentle face animated, watching from on high as the others drew and chattered and explored. [The parents] noticed that while the class list, posted by the cubbies, had barely a dozen names, a small army of teachers—including an occupational therapist, a speech therapist, an augmentative communication expert and several other aids—had greeted them at the door. Even those who were arriving as kindergarten parents for the first time could sense that this class was different. 'Inclusion', said Suzanne Blake, the head teacher (Belkin, 2001).

While this example may not be typical of students with disabilities in today's classrooms—as most students with more significant physical disabilities are still not fully included in the regular classroom—95% of students with disabilities are served in regular school buildings (U.S. Department of Education, 2002). In the 2001–2002 school year, over 5 million school aged children, or 9% of the U.S. resident population, had been identified as requiring special education services due to specific disabilities. The most common disabilities represented in

U.S. schools are specific learning disabilities, speech or language impairments, mental retardation, and emotional disturbance. Of those students, white students made up 62.3% of the students served; 19.8% were African American; 14.5% were Hispanic; 1.9% were Asian/Pacific Islander; and 1.5% were American Indian/ Alaska Native (U.S. Department of Education, 2002). There continues to be overrepresentation of disabilities in some racial/ethnic groups according to specific disability categories, as well as under representation of certain disabilities in some racial/ethnic groups, when compared with the special education student population as a whole (U.S. Department of Education, 2002). Table 1 provides more details about the special education population according to disability type and race/ethnicity.

The Phi Delta Kappa Center for Evaluation, Development and Research (Rogers, 1993) provided a summary of the various terms used to describe the inclusion of students with disabilities in regular classrooms as these terms are often used incorrectly and interchangeably in practice:

- *Mainstreaming* generally refers to selectively placing a student with a disability into one or more regular education classrooms. There is often the assumption that mainstreamed students will need to "keep up" with the other students through the same instructional strategies (Rogers, 1993).
- *Inclusion* is a more global term referring to a commitment to educate each child in the same classroom or school as his or her peers. The assumption is that the necessary "supports will be brought to the child (rather than moving the child to the services) and requires only that the child will benefit from being in the class (rather than keeping up with the other students)" (Rogers, 1993, p. 2).

TABLE 1
Percentage of Students Ages 6 through 21 Served Under IDEA During 2000–2001

Disability	American Indian/ Alaska Native	Asian/ Pacific Islander	Black (non-Hispanic)	Hispanic	White (non-Hispanic)	All Students Served
Specific learning disabilities	56.3	43.2	45.2	60.3	48.9	50.0
Speech or language impairments	17.1	25.2	15.1	17.3	20.8	18.9
Mental retardation	8.5	10.1	18.9	8.6	9.3	10.6
Emotional disturbance	7.5	5.3	10.7	4.5	8.0	8.2
Multiple disabilities	2.5	2.3	1.9	1.8	1.8	2.1
Hearing impairments	1.1	2.9	1.0	1.5	1.2	1.2
Orthopedic impairments	.08	2.0	0.9	1.4	1.1	1.3
Other health impairments	4.1	3.9	3.7	2.8	5.9	5.1
Visual impairments	0.4	0.8	0.4	0.5	0.5	0.4
Autism	0.6	3.4	1.2	0.9	1.4	1.4
Deaf-blindness	0.0	0.0	0.0	0.0	0.0	0.0
Traumatic brain injury	0.3	0.3	0.2	0.2	0.3	0.3
Developmental delay	0.7	0.6	0.7	0.2	0.6	0.5
All disabilities	100.00	100.00	100.00	100.00	100.00	100.00

Note: Does not include New York State

Source: U.S. Department of Education, Office of Special Education Programs, Data Analysis System, (DANS)

- *Full inclusion* indicates that a school has the instructional capacity available to "accommodate all students in the schools and classrooms they would normally attend if not disabled" (Rogers, 1993, p. 2). Many proponents of full inclusion view the role of the special education teacher to be that of a trainer and technical assistance provider to the regular education teachers.

LEGAL BASIS FOR INCLUSION

Today, P.L. 94-142 has been amended five times and has evolved into the Individualized Disability Education Act (IDEA), with the most recent amendments passed in 2004. The amendments of 1997 were particularly significant in creating a renewed focus requiring children with disabilities be guaranteed the "least restrictive environment" for learning while also addressing the importance of a thorough evaluation for services (including diagnosis by qualified professionals), individualized education programs for each student, student and parent participation in decision making, and the procedural safeguards to insure that the regulations and the rights of students with disabilities are being followed (Individuals with Disabilities Act Amendments of 1997). The recent passage of the 2004 amendments address discipline, paperwork, overrepresentation of minorities in certain special education categories, hiring highly qualified teachers, litigation, and other issues.

Also important to curricular planning is Section 504 of the Rehabilitation Act, originally passed in 1973, as the first civil rights law that prohibited discrimination on the basis of disability. Specifically, this law required that all federally funded entities (e.g., schools, libraries, universities, local and state government agencies) provide physical as well as programmatic accommodations for people with disabilities of all ages. Many students with health impairments, such as juvenile diabetes, that do not interfere with classroom learning receive 504 accommodations instead of IDEA related services. For example, if a seventh

grade student with diabetes needs regular breaks throughout the day to administer and monitor his insulin, the school will establish a 504 plan, rather than an individualized education plan (IEP) in order to assure that this student has the necessary accommodations to do so.

The latest flagship regular education law, No Child Left Behind (NCLB), was authorized in 2002, replacing the Elementary and Secondary Education Act (ESEA) and bringing broad changes to U.S. educational systems. Although not a special education law in particular, NCLB does have significant impact on students with disabilities, especially in the terms of assessment. Building on IDEA, NCLB requires schools to measure how well students with disabilities have learned reading and mathematics curriculum. The law includes provisions for students with the most significant cognitive disabilities, allowing for designed alternate assessments when appropriate. Since the majority of students with disabilities are required to meet the academic achievement goals of their schools, they must also have access to the general education curriculum. Shrag (2003) contends that, "Clearly, students with disabilities cannot demonstrate knowledge about content that they have not been taught. Our current challenge is to ensure this access to these students" (p. 10). Furthermore, Shrag warns that with the emphasis on high stakes testing and academic achievement success, some schools may be tempted to place more students in more restrictive environments, which only distances them from the general curriculum and their peers (2003).

Other indirect effects of NCLB for students with disabilities may be that schools will be less welcoming of students with special learning needs because they may threaten the schools' assessment results. Finally, because NCLB includes this assessment mandate of students with disabilities—*without* adequate funding to implement the mandate—it may be very difficult for schools to "provide the appropriate remediation or special education services that many students with disabilities may need if they are going to reach the levels of proficiency on statewide assessments that NCLB requires" (Shrag, 2003, p. 10).

In summary, classroom teachers need to understand that these laws mandate the education of students with disabilities with the expectation that both regular education and special education teachers provide instruction for students with disabilities. Understanding how one's teaching practices fit into the national legal mandates provides a framework for implementing best practices in the classroom, including designing educational tasks and providing assessment accommodations.

THE THREE A'S OF CREATING AN INCLUSIVE CURRICULUM AND CURRICULUM

To many teachers, meeting the educational needs of students with disabilities can be both overwhelming and frightening. Fortunately, the regular education teacher is not alone in this endeavor. Special education teachers, school counselors, school psychologists, nurses, speech pathologists, occupational therapists, educational assistants, and educational administrators all play a unique role in supporting the regular education teacher to educate students with disabilities. However, it is absolutely necessary for the regular education teacher to be proactive and knowledgeable regarding inclusion.

How can a regular education teacher ensure he or she is practicing effective instructional techniques that meet the educational needs of all students in the classroom? Practicing the three A's of creating an inclusive curriculum (aware, active, and achieve) is an excellent place to begin.

Consider the three A's of creating an inclusive curriculum to be like a garden, with each component necessary for growth. In gardens some plants are hardier than others—many need special attention, accommodations, and pruning before they can flourish. Teachers tend to the needs of the classroom and the students in the same way a gardener tends to the individual plants in the garden.

AWARE   Think of awareness as the soil of the garden. Effective gardeners understand the unique needs of each plant and make certain the soil is formulated to maximize the success of all plants in the garden.

An aware teacher can articulate the individual needs to various students in the classroom. The aware teacher not only knows which students are on IEPs and/or 504 plans, but also knows the content of the plans.

ACTIVE   Effective gardeners must tend to the plants in the garden on a regular basis—some plants require daily watering, others are drought resistant, and still others require regular pruning. If the soil nutrients are perfectly balanced but the plants are not maintained properly, many will not survive or thrive.

Similarly, successful inclusionary practices require the teacher to be constantly active and engaged in the students' learning. Beyond knowing what the students need, the curriculum should be designed and frequently modified with these diverse learning styles in mind. The teacher must reach out to the students rather than expect the student to reach out to him or her. Students with disabilities may have become academically disengaged by other teachers who have not met their needs and may need to be "nurtured" back to learning. Many *active* teachers attend and participate in IEP meetings, with the goal of learning more about students' strengths and weaknesses to better accommodate their learning and curricular needs.

ACHIEVE   Now that the garden is filled with rich soil, and a variety of plants with unique needs that are carefully tended to, the gardener expects the plants to grow, thrive, and bloom. However, despite these perfect conditions for growth, not all plants may mature: perhaps environmental conditions have become challenging, such as extreme weather or an insect infestation; or maybe some other *unseen* threat to plant health and vitality. Does the gardener give up on the deteriorating plant or stay the course and continue to try and address the plant's needs?

In the same manner, a successful inclusive teacher provides all students with a rich, engaging curriculum, and expects all students will succeed. However, when a student does not achieve adequately, effective inclusionary practices require the teacher to assess why. Why was the student not able to achieve the learning objectives with the current curriculum and what must be addressed, adapted, or changed for the student to succeed? Many times environmental factors impede a student's ability to learn. For example, a student with a behavioral disorder whose parents are divorcing may require intervention from the school counselor, rather than a modification of the curriculum. Regardless, the teacher must assess the reasons for academic failure and be prepared to address them.

AUTHENTIC PEDAGOGY AND INCLUSION

Beyond practicing the *Three A's of Inclusion,* NCLB emphasizes the importance of implementing research-based practices for schools to meet state educational standards. Braden, Schroeder, and Buckley (2001) note the importance of high quality inclusionary practices across the curriculum:

> A commitment to educational equity demands inclusion. Students cannot learn what they have not been taught; educators must include students with disabilities in opportunities to learn, and they must provide the supports those students need to gain access to general education (Braden, Schroeder, & Buckley, 2001).

Authentic pedagogy is an outstanding example of a research based practice that has emerged from the education reform movement, and has been shown to increase the learning of students with disabilities educated in inclusive classrooms (King, Schroeder, & Chawszczewski, 2001; Newman, Marks, & Garmoran, 1996).

Authenticity is defined as the extent to which a lesson, assessment task, or sample of student performance represents construction of new knowledge, through the use of disciplined inquiry, which has some value or meaning beyond success in school (Newmann, Secada, & Wehlage, 1995). According to Newman et al. (1995) the three primary components of authentic intellectual work include *higher order thinking, depth of knowledge and understanding, and connectedness to the real world.*

Higher order thinking requires that students manipulate information and ideas in ways that transfer their meaning and their implications, rather than rote memorization, for example. Depth of knowledge and student understanding in authentic schools and classrooms requires that students successfully produce new knowledge by discovering relationships, solving problems, constructing explanations, and drawing conclusions. The final key component of authentic education—connectedness to the real world—implies that there is a connection to the larger social context within which students live. For example, a science experiment that relates to the environment or a history assignment that relates an historical event to a current event.

When curriculum is designed with authentic tasks that include the above components, all students achieve; however, students with disabilities achieve at a higher rate. According to a study by King, Schroeder, and Chawszczewski (2001) there is a significant relationship between authentic tasks and student learning. In other words, when teachers assigned authentic tasks, students produced authentic work. Furthermore, in their study, "sixty-two percent of the students with disabilities produced work that was the same, or higher, in authenticity than that produced by their nondisabled peers" (p. 12).

Finally, learning how to design authentic tasks requires practice and skill; however, once mastered can transform a teacher's pedagogical practice.

For more information and examples of highly authentic tasks, see the Research Institute on Secondary Education Reform at the University of Wisconsin-Madison: http://www.wcer.wisc.edu/riser.

ASSESSMENT ACCOMMODATIONS AND STUDENTS WITH DISABILITIES

Another issue essential for inclusionary practice is that of assessment accommodations for students with disabilities. Assessment accommodations is a hotly contested topic within education, especially as it pertains to large scale standardized tests such as the SAT or state-wide high stakes tests. For the purposes of this article, only classroom assessment will be addressed.

The classroom teacher must always address each assessment accommodation separately as each student and each assessment task vary. What is a necessary accommodation for one student with a learning disability may not be necessary for another. The I.E.P. and any supporting medical or psychological documentation are important foundational data to consider when making assessment decisions. For example, does the psychological evaluation indicate that the student requires a distraction free environment for test taking?

It is also important to distinguish assessment accommodations from assessment modifications and instructional supports. Accommodations do not change the assessment content but may change the assessment process components, such as setting, time, administration, or response format. Conversely, the nature of the assessment is changed with assessment modifications which alter assessment content. Meanwhile, instructional supports help students gain access to the general education curriculum (Braden et al., 2001).

With those distinctions in mind, Braden, Schroeder, and Buckley have suggested an assessment accommodations framework, along with principles for implementation of accommoda-

tions for students with disabilities (2001). This framework will allow teachers to make more informed assessment accommodation decisions. Referring to Table 2, the guiding framework includes the following provisions: students should not receive accommodations unless they are needed; accommodations decisions presume target and access skills are clearly identified; accommodations should address access, not target, or skills; target skill complexity should be modified when access is insufficient to allow for reasonable assessment of skills; and assessments should retain authenticity, even if they are modified to a simpler skill level.

The principles further assist the teacher with assessment accommodation decision making. Teachers should encourage risk taking by allowing the student to try the task without accommodations. The option for later accommodations without penalty should always be offered. Teachers should know what knowledge and skills the assessment intends to measure and what skills are required to respond to the assignment. An accommodation should allow access to the task, but not if it changes the skill targeted by the assessment. An accommodation may be appropriate in one circumstance but not another. Some skill levels are so different from the level targeted, even with successful access, the task is of no educational value. In these cases, teachers should consider modifying the assessment to assess a less complex level of targeted skills. Lastly, the teacher should not substitute an assessment with limited authenticity (e.g., labeling the parts of a rocket diagram rather than producing an experiment) (Braden et al., 2001).

For teachers to practice effective inclusive education, teachers must have an awareness of who the students with disabilities are in the classroom, as well as the unique educational needs of each of those students. Having a solid appreciation of the legal mandates of education for students with disabilities provides a framework for understanding the teacher's role in providing an education to this population.

TABLE 2
Assessment Accommodations Framework: Principles for Implementation

Accommodations Framework	Implementation
Students should not receive accommodations unless they are needed.	Encourage risk taking by allowing the student to try to task without accommodations. Offer the option for later accommodations without penalty.
Accommodations decisions presume target and access skills are clearly identified.	Know what knowledge and skills the assessment intends to measure and what skills are required to respond to the assignment.
Accommodations should address access, not target, skills.	An accommodation should allow access to the task, but not if it changes the skill targeted by the assessment. An accommodation may be appropriate in one circumstance but not another.
Target skill complexity should be modified when access is insufficient to allow for reasonable assessment of skills.	Some skills levels are so far below the level targeted, even with successful access, the task is of no educational value. One should always seek to eliminate barriers posed by access skills. However, with some target skills, the task demands are so different from the test taker's current skill that the assessment is meaningless.
Assessments should retain authenticity, even if they are modified to a simpler skill level.	The teacher should not substitute an assessment with limited authenticity (e.g., labeling the parts of a rocket diagram rather than producing an experiment).

Source: Braden et al., 2001, p. 8

REFERENCES

Belkin, L. (2001, September 4, 2004). The lessons from classroom 506. *The New York Times Magazine*, 40–49.

Braden, J., Schroeder, J., & Buckley, J. (2001). *Secondary school reform, inclusion, and authentic assessment.* Madison, Wisconsin: Research Institute on Secondary Education Reform: Author.

Individuals with Disabilities Act Amendments of 1997.

King, M. B., Schroeder, J., & Chawszczewski. (2001). *Authentic assessment and student performance in inclusive schools.* Madison, WI: Research Institute on Secondary Education Reform: Author.

Newman, F. M., Marks, H. M., & Garmoran, A. (1996). Authentic pedagogy and student performance. *American Journal of Education, 104,* 208–312.

Newmann, F. M., Secada, W. G., & Wehlage, G. G. (1995). *A guide to authentic instruction and assessment: Vision, standards and scoring.* Madison, WI: University of Wisconsin-Madison, Wisconsin Center for Education Research.

Rogers, J. (1993). *The inclusion revolution.* Bloomington, IN: Phi Delta Kappa Center for Evaluation, Development, and Research: Author.

Shrag, J. A. (2003). No Child Left Behind and its implications for students with disabilities. *The Special Edge, 16*(2), 1–12.

U.S. Department of Education. (2002). *Twenty-fourth annual report to Congress on the implementation of the Individuals with Disabilities Education Act.* Washington, DC.

Tina M. Anctil is an assistant professor in the Department of Educational Leadership and Counseling Psychology at Washington State University.

QUESTIONS FOR REFLECTION

1. Did this article challenge any stereotypes you may have about people with disabilities? Did the statistical data on the number and type of students with disabilities in the classroom surprise you?
2. The author explained how some disabilities are "over-diagnosed" for some ethnicities. How might this happen and what might be done to prevent this practice? How does this over-diagnosis harm children?
3. When thinking about applying the three A's of inclusive curriculum to your own teaching, which "A" is most challenging for you to consider doing? Why? What might you need to do to successfully integrate all three A's in your teaching?

Multicultural Education and Curriculum Transformation

JAMES A. BANKS

ABSTRACT: In this article, James A. Banks describes five dimensions of multicultural education, focusing on the knowledge construction process. This dimension is emphasized to show how the cultural assumptions, frames of reference, and perspectives of mainstream scholars and researchers influence the ways in which they construct academic knowledge to legitimize institutionalized inequality. The process by which transformative scholars create oppositional knowledge and liberatory curricula that challenge the status quo and sanction action and reform is also described. This process is endorsed as a means of helping students become effective citizens in a pluralistic, democratic society.

The racial crisis in America, the large number of immigrants that are entering the nation each year, the widening gap between the rich and the poor, and the changing characteristics of the nation's student population make it imperative that schools be reformed in ways that will help students and teachers to re-envision, rethink, and reconceptualize America. Fundamental changes in our educational system are essential so that we can, in the words of Rodney King, "all get along." The nation's student population is changing dramatically. By 2020, nearly half (about 48%) of the nation's students will be students of color. Today, about 31% of the youth in the United States under 18 are of color and about one out of every five students is living below the official poverty level (U.S. Bureau of the Census, 1993).

Multicultural education, a school reform movement that arose out of the civil rights movement of the 1960s and 1970s, if implemented in thoughtful, creative, and effective ways, has the potential to transform schools and other educational institutions in ways that will enable them to prepare students to live and function effectively in the coming century (Banks & Banks, 1995a). I will describe the major goals and dimensions of multicultural education, discuss knowledge construction and curriculum transformation, and describe how transformative academic knowledge can be used to re-invent and re-imagine the curriculum in the nation's schools, colleges, and universities.

MULTICULTURAL EDUCATION AND SCHOOL REFORM

There is a great deal of confusion about multicultural education in both the popular mind and among teachers and other educational practitioners. Much of this confusion is created by critics of multicultural education such as Schlesinger (1991), D'Souza (1995), and Sacks and Theil (1995). The critics create confusion by stating and repeating claims about multiculturalism and diversity that are documented with isolated incidents, anecdotes, and examples of poorly conceptualized and implemented educational practices. The research and theory that have been developed by the leading theorists in multicultural education are rarely cited by the field's critics (Sleeter, 1995).

The critics of multicultural education often direct their criticism toward what they call multiculturalism. This term is rarely used by theorists and researchers in multicultural education. Consequently, it is important to distinguish what the critics call multiculturalism from what multicultural education theorists call multicultural education. Multiculturalism is a term often used by the critics of diversity to describe a set of educational practices they oppose. They use this term to describe educational practices they consider antithetical to the Western canon, to the democratic tradition, and to a universalized and free society.

Multiculturalism and multicultural education have different meanings. I have conceptualized multicultural education in a way that consists of three major components: an idea or concept, an educational reform movement, and a process (Banks, 1993a). As an idea or concept, multicultural education maintains that all students should have equal opportunities to learn regardless of the racial, ethnic, social-class, or gender group to which they belong. Additionally, multicultural education describes ways in which some students are denied equal educational opportunities because of their racial, ethnic, social-class, or gender characteristics (Lee & Slaughter-Defoe, 1995; Nieto, 1995). Multicultural education is an educational reform movement that tries to reform schools in ways that will give all students an equal opportunity to learn. It describes teaching strategies that empower all students and give them voice.

Multicultural education is a continuing process. One of its major goals is to create within schools and society the democratic ideals that Myrdal (1944) called "American Creed" values—values such as justice, equality, and freedom. These ideals are stated in the nation's founding documents—in the Declaration of Independence, the Constitution, and the Bill of Rights. They can never be totally achieved, but citizens within a democratic society must constantly work toward attaining them. Yet, when we approach the realization of these ideals for particular groups, other groups become victimized by racism, sexism, and discrimination. Consequently, within a democratic, pluralistic society, multicultural education is a continuing process that never ends.

THE DIMENSIONS OF MULTICULTURAL EDUCATION

To effectively conceptualize and implement multicultural education curricula, programs, and practices, it is necessary not only to define the concept in general terms but to describe it programmatically. To facilitate this process, I have developed a typology called the dimensions of multicultural education (Banks, 1993b, 1995a). This dimensions typology can help practitioners identify and formulate reforms that implement multicultural education in thoughtful, creative, and effective ways. It is also designed to help theorists and researchers delineate the scope of the field and identify related research and theories.

The dimensions typology is an ideal-type construct in the Weberian sense. The dimensions are highly interrelated, and the boundaries between and within them overlap. However, they are conceptually distinct.

A description of the conceptual scope of each dimension facilitates conceptual clarity and the development of sound educational practices. As Gay (1995) has pointed out, there is a wide gap between theory, research, and practice in multicultural education. The practices within schools that violate sound principles in multicultural education theory and research are cannon fodder for the field's critics, who often cite questionable practices that masquerade as multicultural education to support the validity of their claims. Although there is a significant gap between theory and practice within all fields in education, the consequences of such a gap are especially serious within new fields that are marginal and trying to obtain legitimacy within schools, colleges, and universities. Thus, the dimensions of multicultural education can serve as benchmark criteria for conceptualizing, developing, and assessing theory, research, and practice.

In my research, I have identified five dimensions of multicultural education (Banks, 1995a). They are: (a) content integration, (b) the knowledge construction process, (c) prejudice reduction, (d) an equity pedagogy; and an (e) empowering school culture and social structure. I will briefly describe each of these dimensions.

Content integration describes the ways in which teachers use examples and content from a variety of cultures and groups to illustrate key concepts, principles, generalizations, and theories in their subject area or discipline. The knowledge construction process consists of the methods, activities, and questions used by teachers to help students understand, investigate, and determine how implicit cultural assumptions, frames of reference, perspectives, and biases within a discipline influence the ways in which knowledge is constructed. When the knowledge construction process is implemented, teachers help students to understand how knowledge is created and how it is influenced by the racial, ethnic, and social-class positions of individuals and groups (Code, 1991; Collins, 1990).

The prejudice reduction dimension of multicultural education relates to the characteristics of students' racial attitudes and strategies that teachers can use to help them develop more democratic values and attitudes. Since the late 1930s, researchers have been studying racial awareness, racial identification, and racial preference in young children (Clark & Clark, 1939; Cross, 1991; Spencer, 1982). This research is too vast and complex to summarize here; however, studies indicate, for example, that both children of color and White children develop a "White bias" by the time they enter kindergarten (Phinney & Rotheram, 1987; Spencer, 1982). This research suggests that teachers in all subject areas need to take action to help students develop more democratic racial attitudes and values. It also suggests that interventions work best when children are young. As children grow older, it becomes increasingly difficult to modify their racial attitudes and beliefs (Banks, 1995b).

An equity pedagogy exists when teachers modify their teaching in ways that will facilitate the academic achievement of students from diverse racial, ethnic, cultural, and gender groups (Banks & Banks, 1995b). A number of researchers such as Au (1980), Boykin (1982), Delpit (1995), Kleinfeld (1975), Ladson–Billings (1995), and Shade and New (1993) have described culturally sensitive (sometimes called culturally congruent) teaching strategies whose purpose is to enhance the academic achievement of students from diverse cultural and ethnic groups and the characteristics of effective teachers of these students. This research indicates that the academic achievement of students of color and low-income students can be increased when teaching strategies and activities build upon the cultural and linguistic strengths of students, and when teachers have cultural competency in the cultures of their students. Kleinfeld, for example, found that teachers who were "warm demanders" were the most effective teachers of Indian and Eskimo youths. Other researchers maintain that teachers also need to have high academic expectations for these students, to explicitly teach them the rules of power governing classroom interactions, and to create equal-status situations in the classroom (Cohen & Lotan, 1995).

An empowering school culture and social structure conceptualizes the school as a complex social system, whereas the other dimensions deal with particular aspects of a school or educational setting. This dimension conceptualizes the school as a social system that is larger than any of its constituent parts such as the curriculum, teaching materials, and teacher attitudes and perceptions. The systemic view of schools requires that in order to effectively reform schools, the entire system must be restructured, not just some of its parts. Although reform may begin with any one of the parts of a system (such as with the curriculum or with staff development), the other parts of the system (such as textbooks and the assessment program) must also be restructured in order to effectively implement school reform related to diversity.

A systemic view of educational reform is especially important when reform is related to issues as complex and emotionally laden as race, class, and gender. Educational practitioners—because of the intractable challenges they face, their scarce resources, and the perceived limited time they have to solve problems due to the high expectations of an impatient public—often want quick fixes to complex educational problems. The search for quick solutions to problems related to race and ethnicity partially explains some of the practices, often called multicultural education, that violate theory and research. These include marginalizing content about ethnic groups by limiting them to specific days and holidays such as Black History month and Cinco de Mayo. A systemic view of educational reform is essential for the implementation of thoughtful, creative, and meaningful educational reform.

KNOWLEDGE CONSTRUCTION AND CURRICULUM TRANSFORMATION

I will focus on only one of the dimensions of multicultural education: knowledge construction. In my latest book, *Multicultural Education, Transformative Knowledge, and Action* (1996), I describe a typology of knowledge that consists of five types: (a) personal/cultural, (b) popular, (c) mainstream academic, (d) transformative academic, and (e) school knowledge. I will discuss only two of these knowledge types: mainstream academic and transformative academic.

Mainstream Academic Knowledge

Mainstream academic knowledge consists of the concepts, paradigms, theories, and explanations that constitute traditional and established knowledge in the behavioral and social sciences. An important tenet within mainstream academic knowledge is that there is a set of objective truths that can be verified through rigorous and objective research procedures that are uninfluenced by human interests, values, and perspectives. Most of the knowledge that constitutes the established canon in the nation's schools, colleges, and universities is mainstream academic knowledge.

The traditional conceptualization of the settlement of the West is a powerful example of the way in which mainstream academic knowledge has shaped the paradigms, canons, and perspectives that become institutionalized within the college, university, and school curriculum. In an influential paper presented at a meeting of the American Historical Association in 1893, Frederick Jackson Turner (1894/1989) argued that the frontier, which he regarded as a sparsely populated wilderness and as lacking in civilization, was the main source of American democracy and freedom. Although Turner's thesis is now being criticized by revisionist historians, his paper established a conception of the West that has been highly influential in American scholarship, popular culture, and school books. His ideas, however, are closely related to other European conceptions of the Americas, of "the other" (Todorov, 1982), and of the native peoples who lived in the land that the European conceptualized as "the West." Turner's paradigm, and the interpretations that derive from it, largely ignore the large number of indigenous peoples who were living in the Americas when the Europeans arrived (Thornton [1995] estimates seven million). It also fails to acknowledge the rich cultures and civilizations that existed in the Americas, and the fact that the freedom the Europeans found in the West meant destruction and genocide for the various groups of Native Americans. By the beginning of the 20th century, most American Indian groups had been defeated by U.S. military force (Hyatt & Nettleford, 1995). Their collective will, however, was not broken, as evidenced by the renewed quest for Indian rights that emerged during the civil rights movement of the 1960s and 1970s.

Today, the West paradigm in American history and culture is powerful, cogent, and deeply entrenched in the curriculum of the nation's institutions of learning. As such, it often prevents students at all levels of education from gaining a sophisticated, complex, and compassionate understanding of American history, society, and culture. The West paradigm must therefore be seriously examined and deconstructed in order for students to acquire such an understanding. Students must be taught, for example, that the concept of the West is a Eurocentric idea, and they must be helped to understand how different groups in American society conceptualized and viewed the West differently.

For example, the Mexicans who became a part of the United States after the Treaty of Guadalupe Hidalgo in 1848 did not view or conceptualize the Southwest as the West. Rather, they viewed the territory that Mexico lost to the United States after the war as Mexico's "North." The Indian groups living in the western territories did not view their homelands as the West but as the center of the universe. To the various immigrants to the U.S. from Asia such as those from Japan and China, the land to which they immigrated was "the East" or the "land of the Golden Mountain." By helping students view Eurocentric concepts such as the West, "the Discovery of America," and "the New World" from different perspectives and points of view, we can increase their ability to conceptualize, to determine the implicit perspectives embedded in curriculum materials, and to become more thoughtful and reflective citizens.

Transformative Academic Knowledge

Teachers can help students acquire new perspectives on the development of American history and society by reforming the curriculum with the use of paradigms, perspectives, and points of view from transformative academic knowledge. Transformative academic knowledge consists of the concepts, paradigms, themes, and explanations that challenge mainstream academic knowledge and that expand the historical and literary canon (Banks, 1996). It thus challenges some of the key assumptions that mainstream scholars make about the nature of knowledge as well as some of their major paradigms, findings, theories, and interpretations. While mainstream academic scholars claim that their findings and interpretations are universalistic and unrelated to human interests, transformative scholars view knowledge as related to the cultural experiences of individuals and groups (Collins, 1990). Transformative scholars also believe that a major goal of knowledge is to improve society (Clark, 1965).

TRANSFORMATIVE SCHOLARSHIP AND THE QUEST FOR DEMOCRACY

Within the last two decades, there has been a rich proliferation of transformative scholarship developed by scholars on the margins of society (Banks & Banks, 1995a). This scholarship challenges many of the paradigms, concepts, and interpretations that are institutionalized within the nation's schools, colleges, and universities. Much, but not all, of this scholarship has been developed by scholars of color and feminist scholars. For example, in his book, *Margins and Mainstreams: Asians in American History and Culture,* Gary Okhiro (1994) argues that groups on the margins of society have played significant roles in maintaining democratic values in American society by challenging practices that violated democracy and human rights. Okhiro notes that America's minorities were among the first to challenge institutionalized racist practices such as slavery, the forced removal of American Indians from native lands, segregation, and the internment of Japanese Americans during World War II. By so doing, they helped to keep democracy alive in the United States.

As I point out in my most recent book, transformative scholars and transformative scholarship have long histories in the United States (Banks, 1996). Transformative scholars and their work have helped to maintain democracy in the academic community by challenging racist scholarship and ideologies that provided the ideological and scholarly justification for institutionalized racist practices and policies. This lecture honors Charles H. Thompson, a transformative scholar and educator who was founding editor of the *Journal of Negro Education.* The *Journal* was established to provide a forum for transformative scholars and researchers to publish their findings and interpretations related to the education of Black people throughout the world. Much of their research challenged mainstream research and contributed to the education and liberation of African Americans.

In his editorial comment in the first issue of the *Journal,* entitled "Why a Journal of Negro Education?" Thompson (1932) advocated Black self-determination. He believed that the *Journal* would provide African Americans with a vehicle for assuming a greater role in their own education. As Thompson stated:

. . . leadership in the investigation of the education of Negroes should be assumed to a greater ex-

tent by Negro educators . . . [yet there is] no ready and empathetic outlet for the publication of the results of [the Negro's] investigations. . . . Thus, it is believed that the launching of this project will stimulate Negroes to take a greater part in the solutions of the problems that arise in connection with their own education. (p. 2)

Black self-determination is as important today as when Thompson penned these words. The first issue of the *Journal of Negro Education* was published in April 1932. The *Journal* has continued its transformative tradition for 63 years. Other transformative journals founded by African American scholars include the *Journal of Negro History,* founded by Carter G. Woodson in 1916, and *Phylon,* founded by W. E. B. DuBois at Atlanta University in 1940. Prior to the founding of these journals, transformative scholars had few outlets for the publication of their works. The mainstream academic community and its journal editors had little interest in research and work on communities of color prior to the 1960s, especially work that presented positive descriptions of minority communities and that was oppositional to mainstream racist scholarship. When we examine the history of scholarship in the United States, it is striking how both racist scholarship and transformative scholarship have been consistent through time. Near the turn of the century, research and theories that described innate distinctions among racial groups was institutionalized within American social science (Tucker, 1994). A group of transformative scholars including thinkers as DuBois, Kelly Miller, and Franz Boas seriously challenged these conceptions (Banks, 1996).

The relationship between transformative and mainstream social science is interactive; each influences the other. Over time, transformative knowledge influences mainstream knowledge, and elements of transformative knowledge become incorporated into mainstream knowledge. For example, the conceptions about race that were constructed by transformative scholars near the turn of the century became the accepted concepts and theories in mainstream social science during the 1940s and 1950s. Nevertheless, a group of scholars continued to invent research and construct ideas about the inferiority of particular racial groups.

The history of research about race in America indicates that theories about the racial inferiority of certain groups—and challenges to them from transformative scholars—never disappear (Tucker, 1994). What varies is the extent to which theories of racial inferiority and other theories that support inequality attain public legitimacy and respectability. Since the beginning of the 20th century, every decade has witnessed the development of such theories. The extent to which these theories, and the individuals who purported them, experienced public respectability, awards, and recognitions has varied considerably. The amount of recognition that transformative scholars who challenged these theories have received from the public and academic communities has also varied considerably through time.

Prior to the civil rights movement of the 1960s and 1970s, the White mainstream academic community ignored most of the scholarship created by African American scholars. Most African American scholars had to take jobs in historically Black colleges. Most of these colleges were teaching institutions that had few resources with which to support and encourage research. Professors at these institutions had demanding teaching loads. Nevertheless, important research was done by African American and by a few White transformative scholars prior to the 1960s. Yet, because this research was largely ignored by the mainstream academic community, it had little influence on the knowledge about racial and ethnic groups that became institutionalized within the popular culture and the mainstream academic community. Consequently, it had little influence on the curriculum and the textbooks used in most of the nation's schools, colleges, and universities.

Although it was largely ignored by the mainstream community, a rich body of transformative scholarship was created in the years from the turn of the century to the 1950s. Much of this re-

search was incorporated into popular textbooks that were used in Black schools and colleges. For example, Carter G. Woodson's *The Negro in Our History,* first published in 1930, was published in a 10th edition in 1962. John Hope Franklin's *From Slavery to Freedom,* first published in 1947, is still a popular history textbook in its seventh edition. Scholarly works published during this period included *The Philadelphia Negro* by W. E. B. DuBois (1899/1975), *American Negro Slave Revolts* by Herbert Aptheker (1943), *The Negro in the Civil War* by Benjamin Quarles (1953), *The Free Negro in North Carolina, 1790–1860,* by John Hope Franklin (1943), and Woodson's *The Education of the Negro Prior to 1861* (1919/1968).

THE NEED FOR A TRANSFORMATIVE, LIBERATORY CURRICULUM

Prior to the 1960s, African American scholars and their White colleagues who did research on the African American community remained primarily at the margins of the mainstream academic community. Most of the paradigms and explanations related to racial and ethnic groups that became institutionalized within the mainstream academic community were created by scholars outside these groups. Most of the paradigms, concepts, and theories created by mainstream scholars reinforced the status quo and provided intellectual justifications for institutionalized stereotypes and misconceptions about groups of color. An important example of this kind of scholarship is *American Negro Slavery* by Ulrich B. Phillips, published in 1918. Phillips described slaves as happy, inferior, and as benefiting from Western civilization. His interpretation of slavery became the institutionalized one within American colleges and universities, and he became one of the nation's most respected historians.

Phillips's view of slavery was not seriously challenged within the mainstream scholarly community until historians such as Stanley M. Elkins (1959), Kenneth M. Stampp (1956), John

Blassingame (1972), and Eugene D. Genovese (1972) published new interpretations of slavery during the 1950s, 1960s, and 1970s. Transformative scholarship that presented other interpretations of slavery had been published as early as 1943, when Aptheker published *American Negro Slave Revolts*. However, this work was largely ignored and marginalized by the mainstream community partly because it was inconsistent with established views of slaves and slavery.

More recent research on the cognitive and intellectual abilities of African Americans indicates the extent to which antiegalitarian research is still influential in the mainstream academic community. In 1969, for example, the prestigious *Harvard Educational Review* devoted 123 pages of its first issue that year to Arthur Jensen's article on the differential intellectual abilities of Whites and African Americans. Papers by transformative scholars who embraced paradigms different from Jensen's were not published in this influential issue, although comments on the article by other scholars were published in the next issue of the *Review* (Kagan et al., 1969). Even though Jensen's article occupied most of the pages in an issue of a well-known scholarly journal, he experienced much public scorn and rejection when he appeared in public lectures and forums on university campuses.

Published nearly a quarter century after Jensen's article, *The Bell Curve* by Herrnstein and Murray (1994) received an enthusiastic and warm reception in both the academic and public communities. It was widely discussed in the public media and remained on the *New York Times* bestseller list for many weeks. Although it evoked much discussion and controversy (Jacoby & Glauberman, 1995), it attained a high degree of legitimacy within both the academic and public communities.

The publication of *The Bell Curve,* its warm and enthusiastic public reception, and the social and political context out of which it emerged provide an excellent case study for discussion and analysis by students who are studying knowledge construction. They can examine the arguments made by the authors, their major assumptions, and find out how these arguments and assumptions relate to the social and political context. Students can discuss these questions: Why, at this time in our history, was *The Bell Curve* written and published? Why was it so widely disseminated and well-received by the educated public? Who benefits from the arguments in *The Bell Curve?* Who loses? Why do arguments and theories about the genetic inferiority of African Americans keep re-emerging? How do such arguments relate to the social and political climate?

Stephen Jay Gould (1994) responded to the last question in a *New Yorker* article by noting the following:

> *The Bell Curve,* with its claim and supposed documentation that race and class differences are largely caused by genetic factors and are therefore essentially immutable, contains no new arguments and presents no compelling data to support its anachronistic social Darwinism, so I can only conclude that its success in winning attention must reflect the depressing temper of our time—a historical moment of unprecedented ungenerosity, when a mood for slashing social programs can be powerfully abetted by an argument that beneficiaries cannot be helped, owing to inborn cognitive limits expressed as low IQ scores. (p. 139)

The publication and public reception of *The Bell Curve* is a cogent example of the extent to which much institutionalized knowledge within our society still supports inequality, dominant group hegemony, and the disempowerment of marginalized groups. *The Bell Curve,* its reception, and its legitimacy also underscore the need to educate students to become critical consumers of knowledge, to become knowledge producers themselves, and to be able to take thoughtful and decisive action that will help to create and maintain a democratic and just society. Works such as *The Bell Curve,* and the public response to them, remind us that democracies are fragile and that the threats to them are serious. Fortunately, the work of transformative scholars indicates that the quest for human freedom is irrepressible.

REFERENCES

Aptheker, H. (1943). *American Negro slave revolts.* New York: International Publishers.

Au, K. H. (1980). Participation structures in a reading lesson with Hawaiian children. *Anthropology and Education Quarterly, 11*(2), 91–115.

Banks, J. A. (1993a). Multicultural education: Characteristics and goals. In J. A. Banks & C. A. M. Banks (Eds.), *Multicultural education: Issues and perspectives* (2nd ed.) (pp. 3–28). Boston: Allyn & Bacon.

Banks, J. A. (1993b). *Multiethnic education: Theory and practice* (3rd ed.). Boston: Allyn & Bacon.

Banks, J. A. (1995a). Multicultural education: Historical development, dimensions, and practice. In J. A. Banks & C. A. M. Banks (Eds.), *Handbook of research on multicultural education* (pp. 3–24). New York: Macmillan.

Banks, J. A. (1995b). Multicultural education: Its effects on students' racial and gender role attitudes. In J. A. Banks & C. A. M. Banks (Eds.), *Handbook of research on multicultural education* (pp. 617–627). New York: Macmillan.

Banks, J. A. (Ed.). (1996). *Multicultural education, transformative knowledge, and action.* New York: Teachers College Press.

Banks, J. A., & Banks, C. A. M. (Eds.). (1995a). *Handbook of research on multicultural education.* New York: Macmillan.

Banks, J. A., & Banks, C. A. M. (1995b). Equity pedagogy: An essential component of multicultural education. *Theory into Practice, 34*(3), 152–168.

Blassingame, J. W. (1972). *The slave community: Plantation life in the antebellum south.* New York: Oxford University Press.

Boykin, A. W. (1982). Task variability and the performance of Black and White school children: Vervistic explorations. *Journal of Black Studies, 12,* 469–485.

Clark, K. B. (1965). *Dark ghetto: Dilemmas of social power.* New York: Harper & Row.

Clark, K. B., & Clark, M. P. (1939). The development of consciousness of self and the emergence of racial identification in Negro preschool children. *Journal of Social Psychology, 10,* 591–599.

Code, L. (1991). *What can she know? Feminist theory and the construction of knowledge.* Ithaca, NY: Cornell University Press.

Cohen, E. G., & Lotan, R. A. (1995). Producing equal-status interactions in the heterogeneous classroom. *American Educational Research Journal, 32*(1), 99–120.

Collins, P. H. (1990). *Black feminist thought: Feminist theory and the construction of knowledge.* New York: Routledge.

Cross, W. E., Jr. (1991). *Shades of Black: Diversity in African American identity.* Philadelphia: Temple University Press.

Delpit, L. (1995). *Other people's children: Cultural conflict in the classroom.* New York: The New Press.

D'Souza, D. (1995). *The end of racism: Principles for a multicultural society.* New York: The Free Press.

DuBois, W. E. B. (1940). Apology. *Phylon, 7*(1), 3–5.

DuBois, W. E. B. (1975). *The Philadelphia Negro: A social study.* Millwood, NY: Kraus–Thomson Organization Limited. (Original work published in 1899)

Elkins, S. M. (1959). *Slavery: A problem in American institutional and intellectual life.* Chicago: The University of Chicago Press.

Franklin, J. H. (1943). *The free Negro in North Carolina, 1790–1860.* New York: Russell & Russell.

Franklin, J. H. (1947). *From slavery to freedom: A history of Negro Americans.* New York: Knopf.

Gay, G. (1995). Curriculum theory and multicultural education. In J. A. Banks & C. A. M. Banks (Eds.), *Handbook of research on multicultural education* (pp. 25–43). New York: Macmillan.

Genovese, E. D. (1972). *Roll, Jordan, roll: The world the slaves made.* New York: Pantheon.

Gould, S. J. (1994, November 28). Curveball. *The New Yorker, 70*(38), 139–149.

Herrnstein, R. J., & Murray, C. (1994). *The bell curve: Intelligence and class structure in American life.* New York: The Free Press.

Hyatt, V. L., & Nettleford, R. (Eds.). (1995). *Race, discourse, and the origin of the Americas: A new world view.* Washington, DC: Smithsonian Institution Press.

Jacoby, R., & Glauberman, N. (Eds.). (1995). *The Bell Curve debate: History, documents, opinions.* New York: Times Books/Random House.

Jensen, A. R. (1969). How much can we boost IQ and scholastic achievement? *Harvard Educational Review, 39*(1), 1–123.

Kagan, J. S., Hunt, J. M., Crow, J. F., Bereiter, C., Elkin, D., & Cronbach, L. (1969). Discussion: How much can we boost IQ and scholastic achievement? *Harvard Educational Review, 39*(2), 274–347.

Kleinfeld, J. (1975). Effective teachers of Eskimo and Indian students. *School Review, 83,* 301–344.

Ladson–Billings, G. (1995). Toward a theory of culturally relevant pedagogy. *American Educational Research Journal, 32*(3), 465–491.

Lee, C., & Slaughter–Defoe, D. T. (1995). Historical and socio-cultural influences on African American education. In J. A. Banks & C. A. M. Banks (Eds.), *Handbook of research on multicultural education* (pp. 348–371). New York: Macmillan.

Nieto, S. (1995). A history of the education of Puerto Rican students in U.S. mainland schools: "Losers," "outsiders," or "leaders"? In J. A. Banks & C. A. M. Banks (Eds.), *Handbook of research on multicultural education* (pp. 388–411). New York: Macmillan.

Myrdal, D. (with R. Sterner & A. Rose). (1944). *An American dilemma: The Negro problem in modern democracy*. New York: Harper.

Okhiro, G. (1994). *Margins and mainstreams: Asians in American history and culture*. Seattle, WA: University of Washington Press.

Phillips, U. B. (1918). *American Negro slavery*. New York: Appleton.

Phinney, J. S., & Rotheram, M. J. (Eds.). (1987). *Children's ethnic socialization: Pluralism and development*. Beverly Hills, CA: Sage Publications.

Quarles, B. (1953). *The Negro in the Civil War*. Boston: Little, Brown.

Sacks, D. O., & Theil, P. A. (1995). *The diversity myth: "Multiculturalism" and the politics of intolerance at Stanford*. Oakland, CA: The Independent Institute.

Schlesinger, A., Jr. (1991). *The disuniting of America: Reflections on a multicultural society*. Knoxville, TN: Whittle Direct Books.

Shade, B. A., & New, C. A. (1993). Cultural influences on learning: Teaching implications. In J. A. Banks & C. A. M. Banks (Eds.), *Multicultural education: Issues and perspectives* (2nd ed.) (pp. 317–331). Boston: Allyn & Bacon.

Sleeter, C. A. (1995). An analysis of the critiques of multicultural education. In J. A. Banks & C. A. M. Banks (Eds.), *Handbook of research on multicultural education* (pp. 81–94). New York: Macmillan.

Spencer, M. B. (1982). Personal and group identity of Black children: An alternative synthesis. *Genetic Psychology Monographs, 106,* 59–84.

Stampp, K. M. (1956). *The peculiar institution: Slavery in the ante-bellum south*. New York: Vintage.

Thompson, C. H. (1932). Editorial comment: Why a journal of Negro education? *Journal of Negro Education, 1*(1), 1–4.

Thornton, R. (1995). North American Indians and the demography of contact. In V. L. Hyatt & R. Nettleford (Eds.), *Race, discourse, and the origin of the Americas: A new world view* (pp. 213–230). Washington, DC: Smithsonian Institution Press.

Todorov, T. (1982). *The conquest of America: The question of the other*. New York: HarperCollins.

Tucker, W. H. (1994). *The science and politics of racial research*. Urbana, IL: University of Illinois Press.

Turner, F. J. (1989). The significance of the frontier in American history. In C. A. Milner, II (Ed.), *Major problems in the history of the American West* (pp. 2–21). Lexington, MA: Heath. (Original work published in 1894)

U.S. Bureau of the Census. (1993). *We, the American children*. Washington, DC: U.S. Government Printing Office.

Woodson, C. G. (1930). *The Negro in our history*. Washington, DC: The Associated Publishers.

Woodson, C. G. (1968). *The education of the Negro prior to 1861*. New York: Arno Press. (Original work published in 1919)

James A. Banks is Russell R. Stark University Professor and Director of the Center for Multicultural Education at the University of Washington, Seattle.

QUESTIONS FOR REFLECTION

1. What are the five dimensions of multicultural education that Banks writes about? Which one resonates with you most? Why?

2. Banks focuses on the knowledge construction process to illustrate how mainstream scholars and researchers influence the ways in which they construct academic knowledge to legitimize institutionalized inequality. What is it about the knowledge construction process that allows this institutionalized inequality to occur? What could be done to change this practice? Can it be changed?

3.   In your own educational experience, what kinds of multicultural experiences helped you frame how you see the pluralistic, democratic society we live in? Is there any one event that had a bigger impact on you than the others? If so, what was it and what made it so significant for you?

Making a Case for Media Literacy in the Curriculum: Outcomes and Assessment

ERICA SCHARRER

ABSTRACT: In an effort to bring key media literacy issues to the curriculum table, the author lays some groundwork for the identification and potential assessment of outcomes associated with media literacy—a crucial step in the argument for the widespread adoption of media literacy curricula in schools, after-school programs, and programs for adults run by community-based organizations.

There is surprisingly little discussion of the goals or "outcomes" ideally associated with participation in a media-literacy program. However, the literature on media literacy is growing. How should we expect people who have participated in a media-literacy program to be different from people who have not? What outcomes can be anticipated? In this article I attempt to lay some groundwork for the identification and potential assessment of outcomes associated with media literacy—a crucial step in the argument for the widespread adoption of media-literacy curricula in schools, after-school programs, and programs for adults run by community-based organizations.

The results of participation in media-literacy curricula are not often explicitly defined and measured, but there is a generalized notion about what these outcomes are. Media literacy often incorporates the goal of "discriminating responsiveness" or the fostering of critical analysis in its participants (Brown, 1998). Media literacy involves "asking questions about what you watch, see and read" (Hobbs, 2001, p. 5), thus encouraging the outcome of ongoing critical inquiry. Indeed, among the most commonly stated goals of media literacy is the development of "critical

viewers" (Singer & Singer, 1998). Elizabeth Thoman (1999), director of the Center for Media Literacy, defined critical viewing as "learning to analyze and question what is on the screen, how it is constructed and what may have been left out" (p. 133). Another crucial component of media literacy, as discussed by Silverblatt (1995), is awareness of the multitude of messages received daily from the media and the effects they can have on attitudes and behavior. Thus, media literacy can help foster critical thinking and discussion of media-related issues, including how media messages are created, marketed, and distributed as well as their potential influence (or how they are received).

GUIDELINES FOR MEDIA LITERACY

In order to move toward increased adoption and acceptance of media literacy in the K–12 curriculum and elsewhere, however, it is necessary to move beyond implicit assumptions about the benefits such efforts can achieve and toward their explicit definition and measurement. Christ and Potter (1998) pointed out that there are no national standards in the United States regarding media-literacy assessment and whether outcomes generated from it should consist of knowledge, skills, behaviors, attitudes, or values. Christ and Potter called the guidelines being advanced by the Speech Communication Association (now known as the National Communication Association) "the closest attempt at a 'certified' national standard" (p. 11). These guidelines suggested individuals should be able to "demonstrate the effects of the various types of electronic audio and visual media" and "identify and use skills necessary for competent participation in communication across various types of audio and visual media" (Speech Communication Association in Christ & Potter, 1998, pp. 11–12). The former suggestion is a cognitive, critical thinking type of outcome, whereas the latter is a behavioral outcome that entails learning the technical skills (e.g., for computers, video, and audio equipment) and creative expression needed to produce one's own media messages. Beyond these somewhat general standards, however, there is little else that serves as an official guide for media-literacy practice.

Little research exists that has defined and tested these or other anticipated outcomes from a social science research perspective (Hobbs & Frost, 2001; Singer & Singer, 1998). Though there are noteworthy exceptions (e.g., Dorr, Graves, & Phelps, 1980; Hobbs & Frost, 2001; Quin & McMahon,1993; Singer, Zuckerman, & Singer, 1980), research evidence supporting the effectiveness of media-literacy curricula is generally rare. More effort is needed to discover (a) whether critical thinking has increased and whether critical viewing has been encouraged, (b) whether students are asking questions about the media, and (c) what other outcomes are appropriate in determining the effects of participation in media literacy.

MEDIA-LITERACY PERSPECTIVES

There are two philosophical perspectives on media literacy, and any discussion of potential outcomes is conceived differently based on alignment with one or the other. One perspective, a cultural studies approach, places great emphasis on students' own, often pleasurable, experiences with media. Members of this camp might take issue with the facilitator of a media-literacy program who has a predetermined set of "learning outcomes" on the grounds of paternalism and protectionism (Buckingham, 1998; Collins, 1992; Halloran & Jones, 1992, Hart, 1997; Masterman, 1985). In other words, those taking this philosophical perspective might object to the views the instructor imposes upon the students, especially if delivered in a top-down approach.

Masterman (1985) reported on curriculum statements published by the British Film Institute. Instead of identifying skills or competencies individuals should acquire, these statements outlined areas that can be explored in media literacy, including media agencies, categories, technologies, languages, audiences, and representations (Bazalgette, 1989; Bowker, 1991). Thus, the outcomes emphasized in this school of thought pertain to the ways in which media literacy is conceived and the topics addressed as well as to the analysis and discussion that ensues.

The other philosophical perspective, called impact mediation (Anderson, 1983), inoculation (Kubey, 1998), or interventionism, often focuses on negative issues pertaining to the media (e.g., violence, sex-role stereotyping, or manipulation in advertising) and interprets media literacy as a strategy to help protect young people from harmful effects (Hobbs, 1998). The outcome this perspective appears to advance is for the media to have less of an influence on individuals who participate in a media-literacy program. A program on television violence, for example, would be viewed as most effective if it led to children responding less aggressively to or being less desensitized by violent programs. Doolittle (1975) and Huesmann and colleagues (Huesmann, Eron, Klein, Brice, & Fischer, 1983) took this approach in their studies of intervention programs (early media-literacy curricula) that emphasized the fictional nature of production techniques used to create violent television scenes. Their results show that intervention programs had only modest success in reducing children's subsequent aggressive responses to television violence. If interventionist media literacy doesn't make people less susceptible to negative media effects, can it accomplish different outcomes that are potentially important and useful?

CAN MEDIA LITERACY HELP?

Why might media literacy be unsuccessful in helping individuals resist media's effects? Perhaps holding such a goal for media literacy is an unfair and inappropriate test. The media-literacy curriculum may be insufficient to change such a complex phenomenon as an individual's unique and various responses to media messages. Just as exposure to media is but one (important but not individually operating) factor shaping our ideas, views, and actions, participation in a media-literacy curriculum is only one factor to weigh against a multitude of others in determining a person's susceptibility to media effects at any given point in time. It may be a grave oversimplification to expect that participation in a potentially short and topically limited curriculum will make an immediate, profound difference in how we respond to the media we encounter every day.

Indeed, the theoretical link between increased awareness about, or sensitivity to, media-related issues via media literacy (e.g., violence, gender stereotypes) and the influence of media exposure is not as obvious as it may seem on the surface. Does a critical view of the media lead to diminished media influence? It's possible that such a connection may not always occur. We may criticize a movie for being too violent or graphic but still be interested in an exciting action sequence or suspenseful plot. We may be well aware that media characters have body sizes that bear little resemblance to that of the general public, but we may still have a lapse in self-esteem as we watch them. We may know that the news media doesn't allot much airtime to third-party political candi-

dates, but we still get the impression from news viewing that such candidates don't stand a chance of election. In short, I argue that critical thinking cannot always lead neatly to resistance to the media's effects.

Furthermore, if media criticism *can* make us resistant to media effects, it may not occur immediately after our first ventures into media literacy, and it may not endure powerfully enough beyond the confines of the media-literacy setting. Even if participation in media-literacy curricula were successful in inspiring resistance to the effects of the media, how long would that resistant state last? Would one media-literacy unit in the curriculum create a permanent resistant view? If not, would resistance still occur one week after participation? One month? One year? It's possible that any resistance achieved would decay over time.

Resistance to media effects may also be viewed as an inappropriate outcome because it may not be retained due to the onslaught of potentially competing information from the media themselves. Effects of participation in a media-literacy curriculum in which critical thinking is encouraged are inevitably limited in duration due to the competing media messages that bombard us every day. Young people in the United States watch an average of three-and-a-half hours of television per day (Comstock & Scharrer, 1999) and spend an average of six-and-a-half hours per day with all media, including computers, video games, radio, and CD players (Roberts, Foehr, Rideout, & Brodie, 1999). On the day or days in which media literacy is included in the curriculum, presumably students will be exposed to a massive number of messages from the media as well. To expect that participation in some part of a media-literacy curriculum would lower the potential influence of these ubiquitous media seems like a tall order.

Finally, research on media effects suggests that differences among audience members (e.g., personality traits as well as variable emotional states) and external factors in one's environment (e.g., influence of family and friends) help to determine whether, and to what degree, individuals are affected by media. Similarly, differences in individual personality in a media-literacy setting would also have to be taken into account to determine the effects of a media-literacy program. Just as the media are not presumed to affect all audience members in a universal way, participation in media literacy should also not be presumed to operate similarly for all those involved. The differences that individuals bring to the experience (e.g., prior critical media discussions with parents or others) and situational differences (e.g., how the curriculum was administered or the students' current mood) should also be taken into account in determining and measuring outcomes.

POSITIVE OUTCOMES

Is media literacy ineffective or uninstructive if the outcome of resistance to media effects only occurs for some participants some of the time, under some circumstances, and probably only in the long term after sustained participation in multiple media-literacy lessons and curricula? I believe that, even if it might not decrease negative media influences, media literacy can contribute to important outcomes having to do with thoughts, opinions, and attitudes. It is possible that these outcomes, when accumulated and considered in the long term through sustained and prolonged engagement in media literacy, can perhaps mitigate the negative behavioral effects of media. Thus, as knowledge, awareness, attitudes, and opinions take shape and become stronger, more fleshed out, and more reinforced over time, they may shape future behaviors. Perhaps then we can expect repeated media-literacy efforts to contribute to a diminished likelihood of negative effects from the media. But in the short term, and in response to participation in as few as only one media-literacy unit in the curriculum, outcomes in the realm of cognition and affect are more feasible and likely to occur, and they are immensely important in their own right.

Indeed, such outcomes should not be underestimated. If participation in media-literacy curricula allows individuals to learn something new or something more about media messages, practices, processes, institutions, or influence, then that shows important cognitive development. These outcomes entail increased knowledge of key concepts or terms used in the study of media and increased awareness of central issues. Some examples might include knowledge of strategies used in advertising to encourage favorable responses; awareness of the ways that violence is shown in the media that make it look cool; or attention to roles that women, people of color, and other "minorities" are given in the media. Similarly, if such participation contributes to a student's approval of some media messages, practices, processes, institutions, or influence and the disapproval of others, this, too, is a laudable accomplishment of media literacy.

Overall, if a student develops the ability to "deconstruct"—break down the components of and closely analyze—media messages, practices, processes, institutions, or influence, then media literacy has been effective and that student is becoming a "critical thinker" about the media. Outcomes such as these are better measures of the effectiveness of media-literacy curricula (from a cultural studies or from an interventionist point of view) than expecting to find increased resistance to media effects. The process of questioning key media-related issues—Who owns the media? What kinds of themes are present in media content? How are media produced? What role do the media play in our lives? What influences can media have on our thoughts, feelings, and behaviors?—and the thoughts and beliefs that result are significant achievements. Not only, I believe, is it critical to identify the outcomes to be gained from media literacy, but it is also crucial to assess whether those outcomes have been achieved. A number of techniques can measure student learning. They include having students write essays; answer open or closed questions; critique a television show, a song's lyrics, or a commercial; and create their own media content (e.g., constructing a miniature billboard, writing a newspaper opinion piece, scripting a scene from a sitcom). Such measures document the effectiveness of media-literacy and are a necessary step in making the case for a central role for media literacy in the K–12 curriculum.

REFERENCES

Anderson, J. A. (1983). Television literacy and the critical viewer. In J. Bryant & D. R. Anderson (Eds.), *Children's understanding of television: Research on children's attention and comprehension* (pp. 297–330). New York: Academic Press.

Bazalgette, C. (Ed.). (1989). *Primary media education: A curriculum statement.* London: British Film Institute.

Bowker, J. (Ed.). (1991). *Secondary media education: A curriculum statement.* London: British Film Institute.

Brown, J. A. (1998). Media literacy perspectives. *Journal of Communication, 48*(1), 44–57.

Buckingham, D. (1998). Media education in the UK: Moving beyond protectionism. *Journal of Communication, 48*(1), 33–43.

Christ, W. G., & Potter, W. J. (1998). Media literacy, media education, and the academy. *Journal of Communication, 48*(1), 5–15.

Collins, R. (1992). Media studies: Alternative or oppositional practice? In M. Alvarado & O. Boyd-Barrett (Eds.), *Media education: An introduction* (pp. 57–62). London: British Film Institute.

Comstock, G., & Scharrer, E. (1999). *Television: What's on, who's watching, and what it means.* San Diego, CA: Academic Press.

Doolittle, J. C. (1975). *Immunizing children against the possible antisocial effects of viewing television: A curricular intervention.* Unpublished doctoral dissertation, University of Wisconsin, Madison.

Dorr, A., Graves, S., & Phelps, E. (1980). Television literacy for young children. *Journal of Communication, 30*(3), 71–83.

Halloran, J. D., & Jones, M. (1992). The inoculation approach. In M. Alvarado & O. Boyd-Barrett (Eds.), *Media education: An introduction* (pp. 10–13). London: British Film Institute.

Hart, A. (1997). Textual pleasures and moral dilemmas: Teaching media literacy in England. In R. Kubey (Ed.), *Media literacy in the information age* (pp. 199–211). New Brunswick, NJ: Transaction.

Hobbs, R. (1998). The seven great debates in the media literacy movement. *Journal of Communication, 48*(1), 16–32.

Hobbs, R. (2001, Spring). The great debates circa 2001: The promise and the potential of media literacy. *Community Media Review,* pp. 25–27.

Hobbs, R., & Frost, R. (2001, May). *Measuring the acquisition of media literacy skills: An empirical investigation.* Paper presented at the annual meeting of the International Communication Association, Washington, DC.

Huesmann, L. R., Eron, L. D., Klein, R., Brice, P., & Fischer, P. (1983). Mitigating the imitation of aggressive behavior by changing children's attitudes about media violence. *Journal of Personality and Social Psychology, 44,* 899–910.

Kubey, R. (1998). Obstacles to the development of media education in the United States. *Journal of Communication, 48*(1), 58–69.

Masterman, L. (1985). *Teaching the media.* London: Routledge.

Quin, R., & McMahon, B. (1993). Monitoring standards in media studies: Problems and strategies. *Australian Journal of Education, 37*(2), 182–197.

Roberts, D. F., Foehr, U. G., Rideout, V. J., & Brodie, M. (1999, November). *Kids and media at the new millennium.* Menlo Park, CA: Kaiser Family Foundation Report.

Silverblatt, A. (1995). *Media literacy: Keys to interpreting media messages.* Westport, CT: Praeger.

Singer, D. G., & Singer, J. L. (1998). Developing critical viewing skills and media literacy in children. *The Annals of the American Academy of Political and Social Science, 557,* 164–180.

Singer, D. G., Zuckerman, D. M., & Singer, J. L. (1980). Helping elementary school children learn about TV. *Journal of Communication, 30*(3), 84–93.

Thoman, E. (1999). Media literacy education can address the problem of media violence. In B. Leone (Ed.), *Media violence: Opposing viewpoints* (pp. 131–136). San Diego, CA: Greenhaven Press.

Erica Scharrer is an assistant professor in the Department of Communications at the University of Massachusetts, Amherst.

QUESTIONS FOR REFLECTION

1. What is media literacy and why is it important to the curriculum today? What features distinguish a media literate person from someone who is media illiterate?
2. What are some of the potential assessments of outcomes that Scharrer sees as critical to the widespread adoption of media literacy in the curriculum?
3. With all of the media images that we see on a daily basis, why do you think media literacy has been slow to catch on as a main curriculum topic? What needs to change within education to make media literacy a basic requirement of classroom learning?

Remembering Capital: On the Connections between French Fries and Education

MICHAEL W. APPLE

ABSTRACT: Education in the United States is experiencing the effects of a "tense alliance" between neoconservatism and neoliberalism. Neoconservative educational policies and proposals are evidenced by choice plans, the standards movement, increasing attacks on the school curriculum for its failure to promote conservative values, and pressure to make the needs of business and industry the primary goals of education. Neoliberalism, which claims that a democratic society should be founded on a free market perspective, is seen as complementing efforts to implement a neoconservative educational agenda. Thus, schooling should be seen as fundamentally connected to patterns of domination and exploitation in the larger society.

Everyone stared at the department chair in amazement. Jaws simply dropped. Soon the room was filled with a nearly chaotic mixture of sounds of anger and disbelief. It wasn't the first time she had informed us about what was "coming down from on high." Similar things had occurred before. After all, this was just another brick that was being removed. Yet, to each and every one of us in that room it was clear from that moment on that for all of our struggles to protect education from being totally integrated into the rightist project of economic competitiveness and rationalization, we were losing.

It was hard to bring order to the meeting. But, slowly, we got our emotions under control long enough to hear what the State Department of Public Instruction and the Legislature had determined was best for all of the students in Wisconsin—from kindergarten to the university. Starting the next year, all undergraduate students who wished to become teachers would have to take a course on Education for Employment, in essence a course on the "benefits of the free enterprise system." At the same time, all school curricula at the elementary and secondary levels—from five year olds on up—would have to integrate within their teaching a coherent program of education for employment as well. After all, you can't start too young, can you? Education was simply the supplier of "human capital" for the private sector, after all.

I begin with this story because I think it is often better to start in our guts so to speak, to start with our experiences as teachers and students in this time of conservatism. I begin here as well because, even though the administration in Washington may attempt to rein in some of the excesses of the rightist social agenda—in largely ineffectual ways—the terms of debate and the existing economic and social conditions have been transformed remarkably in a conservative direction (Apple 1993). We should not be romantic about what will happen at our schools and universities, especially given the fiscal crisis of the state and the acceptance of major aspects of the conservative social and economic agenda within both political parties. The story I told a moment ago can serve as a metaphor for what is happening to so much of educational life at universities and elsewhere.

Let me situate this story within the larger transformations in education and the wider society that the conservative alliance has attempted. Because of space limitations in an article of this size, my discussion here will by necessity be brief. A much more detailed analysis can be found in my newest book, *Cultural Politics and Education* (Apple 1996).

BETWEEN NEO-CONSERVATISM AND NEO-LIBERALISM

Conservatism by its very name announces one interpretation of its agenda. It conserves. Other interpretations are possible of course. One could say, something more wryly, that conservatism believes that nothing should be done for the first time (Honderich 1990, 1). Yet in many ways, in the current situation this is deceptive. For with the Right now in ascendancy in many nations, we are witnessing a much more activist project. Conservative politics now are very much the politics of alteration—not always, but clearly the idea of "Do nothing for the first time" is not a sufficient explanation of what is going on either in education or elsewhere (Honderich 1990, 4).

Conservatism has in fact meant different things at different times and places. At times, it will involve defensive actions; at other times, it will involve taking initiative against the status quo (Honderich 1990, 15). Today, we are witnessing both.

Because of this, it is important that I set out the larger social context in which the current politics of official knowledge operates. There has been a breakdown in the accord that guided a good deal of educational policy since World War II. Powerful groups within government and the economy, and within "authoritarian populist" social movements, have been able to redefine—often in very retrogressive ways—the terms of debate in education, social welfare, and other areas of the common good. What education is for is being transformed (Apple 1993). No longer is education seen as part of a social alliance which combined many "minority" groups, women, teachers, community activists, progressive legislators and government officials, and others who acted together to propose (limited) social democratic policies for schools (e.g., expanding educational opportunities, limited attempts at equalizing outcomes, developing special programs in bilingual and multicultural education, and so on).[1] A new alliance has been formed, one that has increasing power in educational and social policy. This power bloc combines business with the New Right and with neo-conservative intellectuals. Its interests are less in increasing the life chances of women, people of color, or labor. (These groups are obviously not mutually exclusive.) Rather it aims at providing the educational conditions believed necessary both for increasing international competitiveness, profit, and discipline and for returning us to a romanticized past of the "ideal" home, family, and school (Apple 1993). There is no need to control the White House for this agenda to continue to have a major effect.

The power of this alliance can be seen in a number of educational policies and proposals. These include: 1) programs for "choice" such as voucher plans and tax credits to make schools like the thoroughly idealized free-market economy; 2) the movement at national and state levels throughout the country to "raise standards" and mandate both teacher and student "competencies" and basic curricular goals and knowledge increasingly now through the implementation of statewide and national testing; 3) the increasingly effective attacks on the school curriculum for its anti-family and anti-free enterprise "bias," its secular humanism, its lack of patriotism, and its supposed neglect of the knowledge and values of the "western tradition" and of "real knowledge"; and 4) the growing pressure to make the perceived needs of business and industry into the primary goals of education at all levels (Apple 1988; Apple 1993; Apple 1996). The effects of all this—the culture wars, the immensity of the fiscal crisis in education, the attacks on "political correctness," and so on—are being painfully felt in the university as well.

In essence, the new alliance in favor of the conservative restoration has integrated education into a wider set of ideological commitments. The objectives in education are the same as those which serve as a guide to its economic and social welfare goals. These include the expansion of the "free market," the drastic reduction of government responsibility for social needs (though the Clinton Administration will mediate this in not very extensive—and not very expensive—ways), the reinforcement of intensely competitive structures of mobility, the lowering of people's expectations for economic security, and the popularization of what is clearly a form of Social Darwinist thinking (Bastian, Fruchter, Gittell, Greer, & Haskins 1986).

As I have argued at length elsewhere, the political right in the United States has been very successful in mobilizing support *against* the educational system and its employees, often exporting the crisis in the economy onto the schools. Thus, one of its major achievements has been to shift the blame for unemployment and underemployment, for the loss of economic competitiveness, and for the supposed breakdown of "traditional" values and standards in the family, education, and paid and unpaid workplaces *from* the economic, cultural, and social policies and effects of dominant groups *to* the school and other public agencies. "Public" now is the center of all evil; "private" is the center of all that is good (Apple 1995).

In essence, then, four trends have characterized the conservative restoration both in the United States and Britain—privatization, centralization, vocationalization, and differentiation (Green 1991, 27). These are actually largely the results of differences within the most powerful wings of this tense alliance—neo-liberalism and neo-conservatism.

Neo-liberalism has a vision of the weak state. A society that lets the "invisible hand" of the free market guide *all* aspects of its forms of social interaction is seen as both efficient and democratic. On the other hand, neo-conservatism is guided by a vision of the strong state in certain areas, especially over the politics of the body and gender and race relations, over standards, values, and conduct, and over what knowledge should be passed on to future generations (Hunter 1988).[2] While these are no more than ideal types, those two positions do not easily sit side by side in the conservative coalition.

Thus the rightist movement is contradictory. Is there not something paradoxical about linking all of the feelings of loss and nostalgia to the unpredictability of the market, "in replacing loss by sheer flux"? (Johnson 1991, 40).

At the elementary and secondary school level, the contradictions between neo-conservative and neo liberal elements in the rightist coalition are "solved" through a policy of what Roger Dale has called *conservative modernization* (Dale quoted in Edwards, Gewirtz, & Whitty in press, 22). Such a policy is engaged in:

> simultaneously "freeing" individuals for economic purposes while controlling them for social purposes; indeed, in so far as economic "freedom" increases inequalities, it is likely to increase the need for social control. A "small, strong state" limits the range of its activities by transferring to the market, which it defends and legitimizes, as much welfare [and other activities] as possible. In education, the new reliance on competition and choice is not all pervasive; instead, "what is intended is a dual system, polarized between . . . market schools and minimum schools." (Dale quoted in Edwards, Gewirtz, & Whitty in press, 22)

That is, there will be a relatively less regulated and increasingly privatized sector for the children of the better off. For the rest—and the economic status and racial composition in, say, our urban areas of the people who attend these minimum schools will be thoroughly predictable—the schools will be tightly controlled and policed and will continue to be underfunded and unlinked to decent paid employment.

One of the major effects of the combination of marketization and strong state is "to remove educational policies from public debate." That is, the choice is left up to individual parents and "the hidden hand of unintended consequences does the rest." In the process, the very idea of education being part of a *public* political sphere in which its means and ends are publicly debated atrophies (Education Group II 1991, 268).

There are major differences between democratic attempts at enhancing people's rights over the policies and practices of schooling and the neo-liberal emphasis on marketization and privatization. The goal of the former is to *extend politics,* to "revivify democratic practice by devising ways of enhancing public discussion, debate, and negotiation." It is inherently based on a vision of democracy that sees it as an educative practice. The latter, on the other hand, seeks to *contain politics.* It wants to *reduce all politics to economics,* to an ethic of "choice" and "consumption" (Johnson 1991, 68). The world, in essence, becomes a vast supermarket (Apple 1993).

Enlarging the private sector so that buying and selling—in a word competition—is the dominant ethic of society involves a set of closely related propositions. It assumes that more individuals are motivated to work harder under these conditions. After all, we "already know" that public servants are inefficient and slothful while private enterprises are efficient and energetic. It assumes that self-interest and competitiveness are the engines of creativity. More knowledge, more experimentation, is created and used to alter what we have now. In the process, less waste is created. Supply and demand stay in a kind of equilibrium. A more efficient machine is thus created, one

which minimizes administrative costs and ultimately distributes resources more widely (Honderich 1990, 104).

This is of course not meant simply to privilege the few. However, it is the equivalent of saying that everyone has the right to climb the north face of the Eiger or scale Mount Everest without exception, providing of course that you are very good at mountain climbing and have the institutional and financial resources to do it (Honderich 1990, 99–100).

Thus, in a conservative society, access to a society's private resources (and, remember, the attempt is to make nearly *all* of society's resources private) is largely dependent on one's ability to pay. And this is dependent on one's being a person of an *entrepreneurial or efficiently acquisitive class type.* On the other hand, society's public resources (that rapidly decreasing segment) are dependent on need (Honderich 1990, 89). In a conservative society, the former is to be maximized, the latter is to be minimized.

However, most forms of conservatism do not merely depend in a large portion of their arguments and policies on a particular view of human nature—a view of human nature as primarily self-interested. They have gone further, they have set out to degrade that human nature, to force all people to conform to what at first could only be pretended to be true. Unfortunately, in no small measure they have succeeded. Perhaps blinded by their own absolutist and reductive vision of what it means to be human, many of our political "leaders" do not seem to be capable of recognizing what they have done. They have set out, aggressively, to drag down the character of a people (Honderich 1991, 81), while at the same time attacking the poor and the disenfranchised for their supposed lack of values and character.

But I digress here and some of my anger begins to show. You will forgive me I trust; but if we cannot allow ourselves to be angry about the lives of our children, what can we be angry about?

Unfortunately, major elements of this restructuring are hardly on the agenda of discussions of some of the groups within the critical and "progressive" communities within education itself, especially by *some* (not all) of those people who have turned uncritically to postmodernism.

LOSING MEMORY

What I shall say here is still rather tentative, but it responds to some of my intuitions that a good deal of the storm and fury over the politics of one form of textual analysis over another or even over whether we should see the world as a text, as discursively constructed, for example, is at least partly beside the point and that "we" may be losing some of the most important insights generated by, say, the neo-marxist tradition in education and elsewhere.

In what I say here, I hope I do not sound like an unreconstructed Stalinist (after all I've spent all too much of my life writing and speaking about the reductive tendencies within the marxist traditions). I simply want us to remember the utterly essential—not essentialist—understandings of the relationships (admittedly very complex) between education and some of the relations of power we need to consider but seem to have forgotten a bit too readily.

The growth of the multiple positions associated with postmodernism and poststructuralism is indicative of the transformation of our discourse and understandings of the relationship between culture and power. The rejection of the comforting illusion that there can (and must) be one grand narrative under which all relations of domination can be subsumed, the focus on the "micro-level" as a site of the political, the illumination of the utter complexity of the power-knowledge nexus, the extension of our political concerns well beyond the "holy trinity" of class, gender, and race, the idea of the decentered subject where identity is both non-fixed and a site of political struggle, the focus on the politics and practices of consumption, not only production—all of this has been important, though not totally unproblematic to say the least (Clarke 1991; Best & Kellner 1991).

With the growth of postmodern and poststructural literature in critical educational and cultural studies, however, we have tended to move too quickly away from traditions that continue to be filled with vitality and provide essential insights into the nature of the curriculum and pedagogy that dominate schools at all levels. Thus, for example, the mere fact that class does not explain all can be used as an excuse to deny its power. This would be a serious error. Class is of course an analytic construct as well as a set of relations that have an existence outside of our minds. Thus, what we mean by it and how it is mobilized as a category needs to be continually deconstructed and rethought. Thus, we must be very careful when and how it is used, with due recognition of the multiple ways in which people are formed. Even given this, however, it would be wrong to assume that, since many people do not identify with or act on what we might expect from theories that link, say, identity and ideology with one's class position, this means that class has gone away (Apple 1992).

The same must be said about the economy. Capitalism may be being transformed, but it still exists as a massive structuring force. Many people may not think and act in ways predicted by class essentializing theories, but this does *not* mean the racial, sexual, and class divisions of paid and unpaid labor have disappeared; nor does it mean that relations of production (both economic *and* cultural, since how we think about these two may be different) can be ignored if we do it in non-essentializing ways (Apple 1992).

I say all this because of very real dangers that now exist in critical educational studies. One is our loss of collective memory. While there is currently great and necessary vitality at the "level" of theory, a considerable portion of critical research has often been faddish. It moves from theory to theory rapidly, often seemingly assuming that the harder something is to understand or the more it rests on European cultural theory (preferably French) the better it is. The rapidity of its movement and its partial capture by an upwardly mobile function of the new middle class within the academy—so intent on mobilizing its cultural resources within the status hierarchies of the university that it has often lost any but the most rhetorical connections with the multiple struggles against domination and subordination at the university and elsewhere—has as one of its effects the denial of gains that have been made in other traditions or restating them in new garb (Apple 1992). Or it may actually move backwards, as in the reappropriation of, say, Foucault into just another (but somewhat more elegant) theorist of social control, a discredited and a-historical concept that denies the power of social movements and historical agents. In our rush toward post-structuralism, we may have forgotten how very powerful the structural dynamics are in which we participate. In the process, we seem to be losing our capacity to be angry.

One of the major issues here is the tendency of all too many critical and oppositional educators to become overly theoretical. Sometimes, in this process, we fail to see things that are actually not that hard to understand. I want to tell a story here that I hope makes my arguments clear. It is a story that perhaps will be all too familiar to those of you who have opposed the North American Free Trade Agreement (NAFTA).

EATING FRENCH FRIES

The sun glared off of the hood of the small car as we made our way along the two lane road. The heat and humidity made me wonder if I'd have any liquid left in my body at the end of the trip and led me to appreciate Wisconsin winters a bit more than one might expect. The idea of winter seemed more than a little remote in this Asian country for which I have a good deal of fondness. But the topic at hand was not the weather; rather, it was the struggles of educators and social activists to build an education that was considerably more democratic than what was in place in that country now. This was a dangerous topic. Discussing it in philosophical and formalistically academic terms was tolerated. Openly calling for it

and situating it within a serious analysis of the economic, political, and military power structures that now exerted control over so much of this nation's daily life was another matter.

As we traveled along that rural road in the midst of one of the best conversations I had engaged in about the possibilities of educational transformations and the realities of the oppressive conditions so many people were facing in that land, my gaze somehow was drawn to the side of the road. In one of those nearly accidental happenings that clarify and crystallize what reality is *really* like, my gaze fell upon a seemingly inconsequential object. At regular intervals, there were small signs planted in the dirt a few yards from where the road met the fields. The sign was more than a little familiar. It bore the insignia of one of the most famous fast food restaurants in the United States. We drove for miles past seemingly deserted fields along a flat hot plain, passing sign after sign, each a replica of the previous one, each less than a foot high. These were not billboards. Such things hardly existed in this poor rural region. Rather, they looked exactly—exactly—like the small signs one finds next to farms in the American mid-west that signify the kinds of seed corn that each farmer had planted in her or his fields. This was a good guess it turned out.

I asked the driver—a close friend and former student of mine who had returned to this country to work for the social and educational reforms that were so necessary—what turned out to be a naive but ultimately crucial question in my own education. "Why are those signs for ***** there? Is there a ***** restaurant nearby?" My friend looked at me in amazement. "Michael, don't you know what these signs signify? There's no western restaurant within fifty miles of where we are. These signs represent exactly what is wrong with education in this nation. Listen to this." And I listened.

The story is one that has left an indelible mark on me, for it condenses in one powerful set of historical experiences the connections between our struggles as educators and activists in so many countries and the ways differential power works in ordinary life. I cannot match the tensions and passions in my friend's voice as this story was told; nor can I convey exactly the almost eerie feelings one gets when looking at that vast, sometimes beautiful, sometimes scarred, and increasingly depopulated plain. Yet the story is crucial to hear. Listen to this.

The government of the nation has decided that the importation of foreign capital is critical to its own survival. Bringing in American, German, British, Japanese, and other investors and factories will ostensibly create jobs, will create capital for investment, and will enable the nation to speed into the 21st century. (This is of course elite group talk, but let us assume that all of this is indeed truly believed by dominant groups.) One of the ways the military dominated government has planned to do this is to focus part of its recruitment efforts on agri-business. In pursuit of this aim, it has offered vast tracts of land to international agri-business concerns at very low cost. Of particular importance to the plain we are driving through is the fact that much of this land has been given over to a large American fast food restaurant corporation for the growing of potatoes for the restaurant's french fries, one of the trademarks of its extensive success throughout the world.

The corporation was eager to jump at the opportunity to shift a good deal of its potato production from the U.S. to Asia. Since many of the farm workers in the United States were now unionized and were (correctly) asking for a livable wage, and since the government of that Asian nation officially frowned on unions of any kind, the cost of growing potatoes would be lower. Further, the land on that plain was perfect for the use of newly developed technology to plant and harvest the crop with considerably fewer workers. Machines would replace living human beings. Finally, the government was much less concerned about environmental regulations. All in all, this was a fine bargain for capital.

Of course, *people* lived on some of this land and farmed it for their own food and to sell what might be left over after their own—relatively minimal—needs were met. This deterred neither

agri-business nor the government. After all, people could be moved to make way for "progress." And after all, the villagers along that plain did not actually have deeds to the land. (They had lived there for perhaps hundreds of years, well before the invention of banks, and mortgages, and deeds—no paper, no ownership). It would not be too hard to move the people off of the plain to other areas to "free" it for intensive potato production and to "create jobs" by taking away the livelihood of thousands upon thousands of small scale farmers in the region.

I listened with rapt attention as the rest of the story unfolded and as we passed by the fields with their miniature corporate signs and the abandoned villages. The people whose land had been taken for so little moved, of course. As in so many other similar places throughout what dominant groups call the Third World, they trekked to the city. They took their meager possessions and moved into the ever expanding slums within and surrounding the one place that held out some hope of finding enough paid work (if *everyone*—including children—labored) so that they could survive.

The government and major segments of the business elite officially discouraged this, sometimes by hiring thugs to burn the shanty towns, other times by keeping conditions so horrible that no one would "want" to live there. But still the dispossessed came, by the tens of thousands. Poor people are not irrational, after all. The loss of arable land had to be compensated for somehow and if it took cramming into places that were deadly at times, well what were the other choices? There *were* factories being built in and around the cities which paid incredibly low wages—sometimes less than enough money to buy sufficient food to replace the calories expended by workers in the production process—but at least there might be paid work if one was lucky.

So the giant machines harvested the potatoes and the people poured into the cities and international capital was happy. It's not a nice story, but what does it have to do with *education*? My friend continued my education.

The military dominated government had given all of these large international businesses twenty years of tax breaks to sweeten the conditions for their coming to that country. Thus, there was now very little money to supply the health care facilities, housing, running water, electricity, sewage disposal, and schools for the thousands upon thousands of people who had sought their future in or had literally been driven into the city. The mechanism for not building these necessities was quite clever. Take the lack of any formal educational institutions as a case in point. In order for the government to build schools it had to be shown that there was a "legitimate" need for such expenditure. Statistics had to be produced in a form that was *officially* accepted. This could only be done through the official determination of numbers of registered births. Yet, the very process of official registration made it impossible for thousands of children to be recognized as actually existing.

In order to register for school, a parent had to register the birth of the child at the local hospital or government office—none of which existed in these slum areas. And even if you could somehow find such an office, the government officially discouraged people who had originally come from outside the region of the city from moving there. It often refused to recognize the legitimacy of the move as a way of keeping displaced farmers from coming into the urban areas and thereby increasing the population. Births from people who had no "legitimate" right to be there did not count as births at all. It is a brilliant strategy in which the state creates categories of legitimacy that define social problems in quite interesting ways. (See, e.g., Curtis 1992 and Fraser 1989.) Foucault would have been proud, I am certain.

Thus, there are no schools, no teachers, no hospitals, no infrastructure. The root causes of this situation rest not in the immediate situation. They can only be illuminated if we focus on the chain of capital formation internationally and nationally, on the contradictory needs of the state, on the class relations and the relations between country and city that organize and disorganize that country.

My friend and I had been driving for quite a while now. I had forgotten about the heat. The ending sentence of the story pulled no punches. It was said slowly and quietly, said in a way that made it even more compelling. "Michael, these fields are the reason there's no schools in my city. There's no schools because so many folks like cheap french fries."

I tell this story about the story told to me for a number of reasons. First, it is simply one of the most powerful ways I know of reminding myself and all of us of the utter importance of seeing schooling relationally, of seeing it as connected—fundamentally—to the relations of domination and exploitation of the larger society. Second, and equally as importantly, I tell this story to make a crucial theoretical and political point. Relations of power are indeed complex and we do need to take very seriously the postmodern focus on the local and on the multiplicity of the forms of struggle that need to be engaged in. It is important as well to recognize the changes that are occurring in many societies and to see the complexity of the "power/knowledge" nexus. Yet in our attempts to avoid the dangers that accompanied some aspects of previous "grand narratives," let us *not* act as if capitalism has somehow disappeared. Let us not act as if class relations don't count. Let us not act as if all of the things we learned about how the world might be understood politically have been somehow overthrown because our theories are now more complex.

The denial of basic human rights, the destruction of the environment, the deadly conditions under which people (barely) survive, the lack of a meaningful future for the thousands of children I noted in my story—all of this is not only or even primarily a "text" to be deciphered in our academic volumes as we pursue our postmodern themes. It is a reality that millions of people experience in their very bodies everyday. Educational work that is not connected deeply to a powerful understanding of these realities (and this understanding cannot evacuate a serious analysis of political economy and class relations without losing much of its power) is in danger of losing its soul. The lives of our children demand no less.

NOTES

1. I put the word "minority" in inverted commas here to remind us that the vast majority of the world's population is composed of persons of color. It would be wholly salutary for our ideas about culture and education to remember this fact.
2. Neo-liberalism doesn't ignore the idea of a strong state, but it wants to limit it to specific areas (e.g., defense of markets).

REFERENCES

Apple, Michael W. *Teachers and Texts: A Political Economy of Class and Gender Relations in Education*. New York: Routledge, 1988.

Apple, Michael W. "Education, Culture and Class Power." *Educational Theory* 42 (Spring 1992): 127–145.

Apple, Michael W. *Official Knowledge: Democratic Education in a Conservative Age*. New York: Routledge, 1993.

Apple, Michael W. *Education and Power*, second edition. New York: Routledge, 1995.

Apple, Michael W. *Cultural Politics and Education*. New York: Teachers College Press, 1996.

Bastian, Ann, Fruchter, Norm, Gittell, Marilyn, Greer, Colin, & Haskins, Kenneth. *Choosing Equality*. Philadelphia: Temple University Press, 1986.

Best, Steven, & Kellner, Douglas. *Postmodern Theory*. London: Macmillan, 1991.

Clarke, John. *New Times and Old Enemies*. London: HarperCollins, 1991.

Curtis, Bruce. *True Government By Choice Men?* Toronto: University of Toronto Press, 1992.

Education Group II, eds. *Education Limited*. London: Unwin Hyman, 1991.

Edwards, Tony, Gewirtz, Sharon, & Whitty, Geoff. "Whose Choice of Schools." *Sociological Perspectives on Contemporary Educational Reforms*. Edited by Madeleine Arnot and Len Barton. London: Triangle Books, in press.

Fraser, Nancy. *Unruly Practices*. Minneapolis: University of Minnesota Press, 1989.

Green, Andy. "The Peculiarities of English Education." *Education Limited*. Edited by Education Group II. London: Unwin Hyman, 1991.

Honderich, Ted. *Conservatism*. Boulder, CO: Westview Press, 1990.

Hunter, Allen. *Children in the Service of Conservatism*. Madison, WI: University of Wisconsin Law School, Institute for Legal Studies, 1988.

Johnson, Richard. "A New Road to Serfdom." *Education Limited*. Edited by Education Group II. London: Unwin Hyman, 1991.

Michael W. Apple is Professor of Curriculum and Instruction and Educational Policy Studies at the University of Wisconsin-Madison.

QUESTIONS FOR REFLECTION

1.   What evidence can you cite to illustrate the influence of conservatism on curricula at the K–12 through higher education levels?
2.   Do you agree with Apple's assertion that " 'Public' now is the center of all evil; 'private' is the center of all that is good"?
3.   How might issues of domination and exploitation be incorporated into the curriculum with which you are most familiar?

TEACHERS' VOICES— Putting Theory Into Practice

Teaching Media-Savvy Students about the Popular Media

KEVIN MANESS

ABSTRACT: *It seems natural that teachers should wish to protect children from what seems to be a bombardment of media exposure by providing them with critical media literacy skills. Kevin Maness offers a framework for media education that helps students enhance their understanding of the media and use their knowledge to influence individual and community action.*

When I began teaching about the media in my high school English classes, it was with the best sense of crusading zeal. I wanted to save students from all manner of societal ills, foremost among them the scourge of consumerism. I think my experience is common—many media teachers are initially moved by alarm about what the media are doing to our children. One teacher in the January 1998 *English Journal,* an issue dedicated to media literacy, begins her article by reciting a litany of disturbing statistics: 162 million TV sets viewed by American families seven hours a day; 260,000 billboards; 23,076 magazines and newspapers; and "between 350,000 and 640,000 TV commercials" seen by students by the time they graduate from high school (Curry-Tash 43). It seems natural that teachers should wish to protect children from what seems to be a bombardment of media exposure by providing them with critical media literacy skills.

COMMON ASSUMPTIONS

The problem with educating children *against,* rather than *about,* the media is the assumption that students are passive audiences of the media, lacking the critical, analytical skills necessary to

resist media manipulation. Although holding this assumption is now unfashionable, evidence of its existence persists in the ways that some teachers talk about media literacy education. I often see an implicit distinction made between the "bad" viewing *habits* of young people and the "good" critical-viewing *skills* held by adults. When media teachers assume that students are passive, disengaged viewers, they risk designing media curricula that fail to acknowledge students' fluency in the languages of the mass media. Students' media savvy, gained through years of informal media literacy training before they reach high school, poses a dilemma for English teachers designing media literacy programs.

My own sense—based on years of teaching media in a high school English classroom and, now, on substantial research about media education—is that media literacy education cannot be effective until teachers find out what students already understand about the popular media (see Fisherkeller, "Learning from"; Shor, esp. chs. 1–2). When media education is not based on students' prior experience, it often deteriorates into "teaching" students media literacy skills that they already possess or into futile attempts to impose new, "good" media habits on students who have no interest in relinquishing their old, "bad" habits. Understanding students' media literacy is the important and often-overlooked first step in making them more media literate.

CHALLENGING OUR PRECONCEPTIONS: HOW MEDIA LITERATE ARE OUR STUDENTS?

Young people do, in fact, bring considerable expertise to their use of mass media products. In the last twenty-five years or so, the research on children's media experience has drawn from a new set of perspectives in psychology, sociology, semiotics, and cultural studies (Buckingham 106–11). Instead of focusing on the ways that mass media use and manipulate audiences, contemporary audience research emphasizes the many ways young people use the media, as well as the sophisticated (if often implicit) media skills and media knowledge that they employ in their everyday media experiences.

Media Uses

Jeanne R. Steele and Jane D. Brown observe that adolescents, like adults, use media for a variety of purposes: to enhance their mood, to sort through cultural norms and values, to make statements about their identity, to emulate desired behaviors (e.g., imitating role models), and to fantasize about a possible (alternative) self (565–69). The writers describe a circular process in which teenagers draw from their lived experience to *select* particular media products; *interact* with those media in an interpretive and evaluative process; and then *apply* aspects of the media product to their lives, appropriating them as part of their lived experience, which then serves to motivate new selections of media and continue the process (556).

David Buckingham and Julian Sefton-Green insist that the media are not all-powerful conditioning forces in the lives of young people; rather, media provide "symbolic resources" that young audiences use "to define and to resist the various social identities that are available to them." While that freedom is limited by numerous factors, it is difficult to know or guess, without asking, how students experience and use the media (30).

Junior high school girls were the subjects of a study by Margaret Finders, who states that students' use of media serves powerful social functions involving belonging, membership, status, and power (*Just Girls* 32). Of particular interest is her inquiry into the use of teen magazines by a group of girls who used the magazines to mark their womanhood and distinguish themselves from other girls ("Queens" 74). The magazines served important purposes within the group as well—the girls read the magazines together, negotiating for consensus on which models and celebrities were cool, pretty, or otherwise desirable. In addition to creating and maintaining intragroup norms, these group readings served as rehearsals where the girls could practice adolescent roles with the magazines as scripts; the magazines, therefore, provided a stable set of roles at a time when the girls' identities were particularly shifting and fluid (78–79). Clearly, these young women were engaged in a markedly critical, evaluative activity.

At the heart of JoEllen Fisherkeller's work with young people in New York City is the question of how they use television. A young male student who had recently moved to New York City found assurance in televised basketball, not only for the pleasure of watching, but also explicitly to learn techniques and styles that would allow him to enter into schoolyard basketball games; moreover, watching the games gave him something he could talk about with the other boys, whom he wanted to befriend. This young man used television for individual identity development and coping as well as to foster his entry into the social interactions of his school and neighborhood environment ("It's Just Like" 158).

There are two important insights that may be gained from this partial account of the purposes for which young people use the media. First, adolescents' uses of media are as wide-ranging and complex as adults' uses of media. Second, young people use media to achieve goals that are intimately connected with their identity and their social interaction. These media uses are neither good nor bad, healthy nor unhealthy. These uses are significant in the lives of young people, necessitating considerable awareness and sensitivity on the part of the critical media teacher. Fisherkeller asks an important question: How often are we expecting—implicitly or explicitly—students to reject the very media stories that provide them with a sense of who they are and of how to achieve empowerment and mainstream acceptance? Surely media representations of power, success, beauty, and belonging demand critical scrutiny, but teachers must remain mindful of what is at stake for their students ("Learning about" 207).

Media Skills

To accomplish their purposes, young people must use a substantial array of critical media skills. Although these skills may be used unconsciously, they are effective and often sophisticated.

Young people may be quite critical of the media they use. Fisherkeller reminds us that we should not let students' enjoyment of the media suggest that they are not also critical of media products. She points out that young viewers evaluate television as a storytelling medium (focusing on narrative quality and plausibility), as "an organizer of stories" (focusing on narrative structure and patterns), and as "an industry" ("Writers" 596).

Before beginning critical media study in class, therefore, teachers should take stock of the critical media skills their students already have, so that they can encourage students to use them more consciously, more effectively, and in new ways for different purposes.

Media Knowledge

Youth also possess considerable media knowledge that they can apply to their media experiences. Fisherkeller compares students' everyday

media knowledge to the information objectives that generally characterize media education curricula, finding that the children in her study already understood a great deal about media agencies, categories, technologies, languages, and representations, but that they were not as knowledgeable about media audiences ("Learning from" 158–61). This does not suggest that all students enter the classroom with knowledge about these aspects, but the fact that they already have some command of the information generally taught in media education classes reinforces the need for a careful assessment of what students actually know about media.

A MODEL FOR MEDIA TEACHING: LISTEN, ACTIVATE, EXTEND

I offer a framework that can help media educators conceptualize their media teaching and design instruction more effectively. The model I propose is based predominantly on the work of Buckingham and Sefton-Green (who draw from the theories of Lev Vygotsky) and Fisherkeller.

For Buckingham and Sefton-Green, a Vygotskian approach to media education consists of teachers helping students make their existing knowledge explicit and more deliberately organized. This more systematic and generalized knowledge can then be used to help students move beyond their original, self-taught knowledge (148). The purpose of media education is not primarily to teach new knowledge—although this does happen—but to "encourage students to make explicit, to reformulate and to question the knowledge which they already possess" (163–64). Reflection is the vital element—students must be given the opportunity and encouragement not just to make meaning out of media texts or to produce their own but to reflect on and understand the processes of "reading" and "writing" media texts (148).

Fisherkeller agrees. She introduces what, for me, becomes a three-stage model for media education when she lists three major insights that can be drawn from her audience research:

It shows how researchers and educators can: (a) recognize the integrity of young people's "informal" media knowledge and experience, (b) categorize their current understandings according to media educational objectives, and (c) make meaningful connections with their actual cultural experiences. ("Learning from" 164)

In formulating my proposed model for media education, I distill the essence of the research of Fisherkeller and Buckingham and Sefton-Green into three stages. The stages are not steps to be followed sequentially; they will often occur simultaneously and repeatedly in the course of a class period, unit, semester, or school year. However, by presenting three distinct stages, I hope that this model can serve as a framework for planning media instruction. The three stages are Listen, Activate, and Extend.

Listen

The first stage in any media education practice should be listening to students to determine their prior understanding and their needs for further understanding. I know that I often placed my own intentions, assumptions, and agendas first, failing to hear the voices of my students. Consequently, although students in my media education classes were generally engaged and motivated, I am not confident that instruction was truly based on the students' needs and experiences.

Listening for students' prior understanding leads directly to the second stage—Activate—while listening for students' needs helps to inform the third stage—Extend.

Activate

Teachers must help students to make their media expertise explicit and to see it as socially and academically valuable. Although students possess a great deal of media skill and knowledge, they are often unaware of it as skill and knowledge, and they are sometimes unaware of how it might benefit them in school or in life beyond the classroom.

Deconstructing advertisements, producing spoof ads, analyzing film, comparing television news to print journalism, analyzing pop music lyrics, and even comparing popular texts to canonical literary ones make use of critical media skills and knowledge that students generally possess when they walk into the classroom. Ending the unit with an oral presentation, a video, or an essay can limit media education to activating students' spontaneous concepts without really encouraging students to understand them, question them, or to change their media behavior as needed.

Students must do more. Encouraging students to reflect on their media writing and reading process—both during and after the process is complete—helps them to develop the metalinguistic and metacognitive skills that Máire Messenger Davies describes as crucial to students' media understanding (Davies 16–17).

Extend

When media teachers listen to their students, we may discover not only areas of media expertise but also needs. Students may need specific kinds of media skills and knowledge, or they may need to understand relationships between themselves, the media, and society. For instance, the girls in Finders' study may need specific instruction to enable them to perceive the difference between advertisements and the editorial content of magazines, as well as an understanding of the constraints on media industries that create an increasingly thin line between editorial content and advertising.

Fisherkeller, believing strongly that one of the imperatives of school is to help students achieve power and success in society, stresses the importance of linking students' media experience to their goals and dreams, their "sense of possibility and purpose" ("Learning from" 163). Extensions of students' media understanding may lead into "political" regions, which may trouble some teachers. But Curry-Tash reminds us that ignoring the social and political implications of media "is itself a political act" (48). If the goal of media education is to enable students to become critically autonomous, then it is vital that we help them extend their media skills and knowledge beyond self-contained textual deconstruction exercises and classroom oral reports to the larger society beyond the classroom walls.

SUGGESTIONS FOR THE MEDIA EDUCATION CLASSROOM

Many of the media education activities that I have read about, in *English Journal* and in other teacher resources both in print and online, can be easily adapted to include all three stages of the model I suggest here. Media literacy activities could be enhanced by (1) determining students' prior media expertise and their educational needs, (2) incorporating more teacher-assisted reflection on the process of media writing and reading, (3) treating the "final product" as a further opportunity for reflective discussion rather than the end of a teaching unit, and (4) extending the "final product" into the world outside the classroom where it can influence the actions of students and other community members.

When I taught high school, I emphasized learning about the media industries themselves since industry constraints (economics, politics, and so forth) have such a significant influence on media experience. This can be difficult because it involves a considerable amount of information that can seem dry and overwhelming. In addition to traditional textbook readings and photocopied articles, I also found videos helpful in teaching about industry dynamics. PBS–Frontline's *The Merchants of Cool* and the Media Education Foundation's *Advertising and the End of the World* stimulated discussion of the advertising industry and, specifically, marketing to young audiences. I learned that it is very important to present these films as texts to be interpreted and questioned rather than as straightforward, authorita-

tive information about other media products. I showed approximately ten minutes of the video at a time, while students watched and reflected in journals; then we discussed the viewpoints represented and the issues raised. This allowed students to draw from their media experience to raise questions and make comparisons and judgments, while also urging them to consider information and opinions that were new to them.

Suggestions from Fisherkeller

My teaching could have benefited from additional recommendations based on current research, but when I was teaching, I did not really know where to look. This year, as a student myself, I have found a lot of value in the work of Fisherkeller, who provides numerous suggestions for media educators. The ideas that follow reflect her influence on my thinking.

Media education can and should address students' hopes for the future. Teachers can listen to students discuss the careers they want to pursue (and why) and explore media models of "success," evaluate their strengths and weaknesses, and look for alternative models. This can help students refine their aims and seek creative ways of accomplishing them, while at the same time scrutinizing media representations and asking critical questions about them ("Learning from" 163; "Learning about" 208).

Teachers can encourage comparisons between mainstream media and alternative media, asking critical questions to account for the similarities and differences. Students can experiment with producing media texts that both emulate conventional media and explore alternatives ("Writers" 603).

Media educators should be wary of overemphasizing deconstructive exercises at the expense of production because media education that relies more on direct structural analysis and criticism often seems to encourage students to reject commercial media products that, as I discuss above, are sometimes very dear to them.

A strength of production-oriented media activities is that they can support community action. Students can make short documentary features about their neighborhoods and screen the films for an audience that includes members of the community. Such a project allows students to "correct" the omissions of the popular media and to tell their stories using their own voices. Students simultaneously learn about the intricacies of media production and draw attention to their daily realities.

Educators can encourage students to compare "adult-sanctioned" media with the students' favorites. How are the symbolic worlds different, especially in terms of identity and social power ("Learning about" 206)? This can help students develop important metacognitive understanding of how value judgments are made regarding media and can lead to inquiry about where the values come from.

THE NEED FOR EDUCATION

If students are so media savvy, why bother to teach them about media at all? There are many important reasons for engaging in critical media education in our classrooms.

Although it may be true that the media are serving students by providing symbolic resources for identity formation, it is also true that those resources are terribly constrained by the commercial nature of media industries. Even the most critical adolescent will find only a limited range of identity resources from which to choose (Steele and Brown 553). Communications researcher Paul Willis cites the need for a greater "range of usable symbolic resources available" for the identity work of youth, and he suggests that media critics—and I think the suggestion applies to media educators as well—focus on what is missing or disappearing from programming, rather than simply on what is there (37).

At the same time, many researchers are careful to demarcate the limits on young people's media savvy. Finders, in particular, is alarmed by some of the blind spots in the media literacy of the girls she studied. She finds that the young girls in her research lacked critical distance from the magazines they enjoyed ("Queens" 81). Many of the girls believed that the articles and advice columns in teen magazines were authored by the teen models pictured (75), and one girl she interviewed saw the ads as informational pieces providing her with facts and advice about products she might purchase (82–83). There is considerable need for instruction about popular media, despite students' significant media uses, skills, and knowledge.

Chances are that listening, activating, and extending are already part of most teachers' media education curricula. My hope is that this model can help media teachers incorporate these three vital elements more consciously. Doing so would have increased my effectiveness.

I started teaching about the popular media because there is a freshness and currency about today's popular media that energized my teaching and because study of the media appealed to the students. I think that there is great activist potential in studying the media—it is my hope that by encouraging students to become more independent, critical agents, they will question the relationship between the media, their identities, their dreams for future success, and the society in which they live. Media teachers who can master the art of listening to students' experiences and needs, activating their prior knowledge, and extending that knowledge to new territory are enabling and empowering students to become active, informed, thoughtful, and intentional participants in all aspects of American society.

WORKS CITED

Advertising and the End of the World. Written, edited, and produced by Sut Jhally. Media Education Foundation, 1997.

Buckingham, David. *After the Death of Childhood: Growing Up in the Age of Electronic Media*. Cambridge: Polity, 2000.

Buckingham, David, and Julian Sefton-Green. *Cultural Studies Goes to School: Reading and Teaching Popular Media*. London: Taylor, 1994.

Curry-Tash, Marnie W. "The Politics of Teleliteracy and Adbusting in the Classroom." *English Journal* 87.1 (1998): 43–48.

Davies, Máire Messenger. *Fake, Fact, and Fantasy: Children's Interpretations of Television Reality*. Mahwah: Erlbaum, 1997.

Finders, Margaret J. *Just Girls: Hidden Literacies and Life in Junior High*. New York: Teachers College, 1997.

———. "Queens and Teen Zines: Early Adolescent Females Reading Their Way toward Adulthood." *Anthropology and Education Quarterly* 27.1 (1996): 71–89.

Fisherkeller, JoEllen. "It's Just Like Teaching People 'Do the Right Things' ": Using TV to Become a Good and Powerful Man. *Say It Loud! African-American Audiences, Media, and Identity*. Ed. Robin R. Means Coleman. New York: Routledge, 2002. 147–85.

———. "Learning about Power and Success: Young Urban Adolescents Interpret TV Culture." *The Communication Review* 3.3 (1999): 187–212.

———. "Learning from Young Adolescent Television Viewers." *The New Jersey Journal of Communication* 6.2 (1998): 149–69.

———. " 'The Writers Are Getting Kind of Desperate': Young Adolescents, Television, and Literacy." *Journal of Adolescent and Adult Literacy* 43.7 (2000): 596–606.

The Merchants of Cool. Dir. Barak Goodman. PBS–Frontline, 2001.

Shor, Ira. *Empowering Education: Critical Teaching for Social Change*. Chicago: U of Chicago P, 1992.

Steele, Jeanne R., and Jane D. Brown. "Adolescent Room Culture: Studying Media in the Context of Everyday Life." *Journal of Youth and Adolescence* 24.5 (1995): 551–76.

Willis, Paul. *Common Culture: Symbolic Work at Play in the Everyday Cultures of the Young*. Boulder: Westview, 1990.

Kevin Maness is a Ph.D. student in media ecology at New York University. Before going back to school as a student, he taught English at Penncrest High School in Media, Pennsylvania.

QUESTIONS FOR REFLECTION

1. Why does Maness believe students today are media-savvy in a way that no generation has been before? What makes the students of today so media-savvy and why could this be a problem? What are they *lacking* in their savvy approach to media?

2. Maness claims that media literacy cannot be effective until teachers find out what students already understand about the popular media. Why does he make this claim? What do teachers risk doing when they don't survey the experiences their students have with media?

3. What is the "listen, activate, extend" model for media teaching that Maness proposes? Do you think it is a model that most, if not all, teachers can teach? What would be some barriers for getting teachers to adopt such a model? How might you use the model within your own classroom?

LEARNING ACTIVITIES

Critical Thinking

1.   Have your personal beliefs and attitudes about social forces changed as a result of reading this chapter? If so, how?
2.   With respect to a school, college, or university with which you are familiar, describe the social forces that *are* reflected in the curriculum and compare these with the social forces that *should be* reflected in the curriculum. To what extent is there a lack of fit between the two sets of social forces?
3.   Some people have suggested that emphasizing our nation's multicultural heritage exalts racial and ethnic pride at the expense of social cohesion. How might a curriculum that emphasizes multicultural diversity also *contribute* to social cohesion?
4.   To what extent do you believe that schools in the United States reproduce the existing class and social structure   that curricula tend not to prepare students from the lower socioeconomic classes for upward social mobility?

Application Activities

1.   Review the section on futures planning in this chapter and then identify several objectives and some appropriate learning activities for a futures-oriented curriculum at the level of education with which you are most familiar.
2.   Herbert A. Thelen has developed a model for teaching called *group investigation*. The model combines the democratic process and the processes of problem solving. (You can read about this model of teaching in Bruce Joyce and Marsha Weil's *Models of Teaching,* seventh edition [Allyn and Bacon, 2004, pp. 214–227]). Describe how you might use this approach to address a social force that influences the curriculum with which you are most familiar.
3.   Examine several recent curriculum guides to determine what, if any, provisions have been made to consider changing social forces in the curriculum (e.g., changes in values, work, the environment, family). In light of the material presented in this chapter, what changes or additions would you suggest in these curriculum guides?
4.   In this chapter's discussion of concepts from the social sciences, it was pointed out that "the concept of *humanity* can be a significant organizing element in curriculum planning." To gain further understanding of how this concept might be applied to curriculum planning, look at the 503 photographs from 68 countries that Edward Steichen presents in *The Family of Man* (New York: Museum of Modern Art, 2002). What does one learn about humanity by viewing these photographs, often referred to as the "greatest photographic exhibition of all time"? How might this learning be applied to curriculum planning?

Field Experiences

1. Visit a local school and then develop a case study of that school's culture. (If your primary interest is at the higher education level, modify this field experience activity as appropriate). Organize your case in terms of the following: (1) *Environment:* Describe the school facility in regard to material and human resources. Describe the climate of the school. To what extent is the surrounding social milieu reflected in the school's curriculum? (2) *Formal practices:* What grades are included at the school? What are the goals of the curriculum? (3) *Traditions:* What events, activities, and rituals are important to students, teachers, administrators, and parents? How do community members describe the school?
2. Visit a local school and gather information on activities, programs, and services the school has developed to meet the needs of students placed at risk by social problems and their families.

Internet Activities

1. Visit the Equity Online home page funded by the Women's Educational Equity Act and compile a list of gender-fair curriculum materials related to the level and subject area with which you are most familiar.
2. Go to the "Futures-Related Links and World-Wide Resources" home page and gather resources you could use to incorporate a futures-oriented perspective into your curriculum planning activities.
3. Explore the U.S. government's Children, Youth and Families Education and Research Network (CYFERNet) and gather information and resources related to several of the social forces discussed in this chapter.
4. Conduct an online keyword search for sources of information on one or more of the ten social forces discussed in this chapter. Share your findings with others in your class.

CHAPTER 3

Human Development

FOCUS QUESTIONS

1. How do learners differ in their stages of development?
2. What are five aspects of human development that should guide curriculum planners?
3. What is the "problem of the match," and how does it influence curriculum planning?
4. What are the salient characteristics of learners' cognitive, psychosocial, and moral development?

Human development throughout the life span is a significant basis of the curriculum. For decades, the study of child and adolescent development has been regarded as an important part of the knowledge base for K–12 education. Now, with the increasing significance of lifelong learning, curriculum planners must also focus attention on human development during adulthood.

The generally accepted stages of human development include infancy, childhood, early adolescence, middle adolescence, late adolescence, and adulthood. The elementary school years correspond roughly to the stage known as childhood. Early, middle, and late adolescence correspond roughly to the middle school, high school, and community college levels of education. And the various stages of adulthood are of considerable importance to curriculum planners at the higher education level.

Knowledge of human development enables curriculum planners to design curricula that are shaped, in part, by the nature and needs of individual learners. Articles that focus on various aspects of human development are included in this chapter. For example, in "Organize Schools around Child Development," James P. Comer discusses how to design school programs around students' developmental needs in several areas; and David A. Hamburg's "Toward a Strategy for Healthy Adolescent Development" examines the biological, physical, behavioral, and social transformations that characterize adolescence. These and other articles in this chapter illustrate the need for curriculum planning to be guided by the five aspects of human development presented in Figure 3.1: the biological basis of individual differences, physical maturation, intellectual development and achievement, emotional growth and development, and cultural and social development.

The concept of stages of human development is a useful tool for understanding the needs of learners at various levels of education, but it cannot define the development of any one learner at a particular age. Each learner is innately unique, and this inborn individuality indicates the importance of providing many alternatives in educational programs. Nevertheless, humans as learners have much in common. In the first article in this chapter, for example, Ashley Montagu ("My Idea of Education") emphasizes the educability of each human being from the perspective of anthropology. Montagu points out that the human person is capable of learning anything, under the appropriate environmental conditions. He states that we need to "grow up into children" and not into adults—that is, we need to preserve some of the traits that children so conspicuously exhibit.

Maturation and change in human development occur over the entire life span, providing one of the bases for curriculum planning at all age levels, including higher and adult education. Maturation follows different courses of development for different individuals. One of the guidelines for curriculum planning derived from the study

FIGURE 3.1
Five Aspects of Human Development to Guide Curriculum Planning and Planning for Instruction

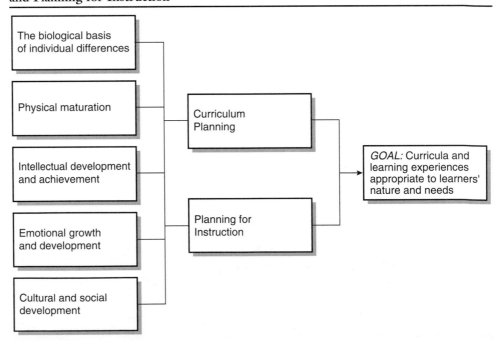

of human development, then, is the *problem of the match*. In other words, there must be a match between the learner's developmental stage and the explicit curriculum. There should also be a match between the learner's developmental stage and the informal, "hidden" curriculum. For example, the informal curriculum often forces students to develop their identity within a school climate that communicates rejection and intolerance. In addition, some students must work through their developmental challenges in over-crowded, under-funded schools situated in impoverished communities and neighborhoods. As first-year teacher Molly Ness points out in this chapter's *Teachers' Voices* section, "A First-Year Teacher Tells It All," "My students have been handed immeasurable challenges, and have tackled them with the courage, grace, and strength that some adults fail to demonstrate."

Research on brain growth periodization has significance for curriculum planning and the problem of the match at various age levels. This research suggests that there are five periods of growth spurt, which alternate with intervals of growth lag, in the development of the human brain from birth to about the age of seventeen. Herman Epstein (1978, 1990), a biologist, reports that growth spurts occur at 3–10 months, 2–4 years, 6–8 years, 10–12 or 13 years, and 14–16 or 17 years. He suggests that "intensive intellectual input should be situated at the spurt ages" (Epstein, 1978, p. 362) and that too much input during the plateau periods may reduce the learner's ability to absorb information at a later, more appropriate age. The challenge for curriculum planners, then, is to make the timing and content of learning experiences fit these known patterns of brain growth.

THEORIES OF HUMAN DEVELOPMENT

Several theorists' and researchers' theories in the area of human development have had a significant influence on curriculum planning. They include Jean Piaget's theory of cognitive development, Erik Erikson's developmental outline for stages of "growth toward a mature personality," and Lawrence Kohlberg's cognitive-developmental view of moral development. These three human development theorists maintain that the developmental stages they describe have a fixed order, and that each person passes through these stages in this order. Sufficient resolution of the challenges and developmental tasks associated with each stage is necessary for the individual to proceed with vigor and confidence to the next stage, and there is a "teachable moment" or opportune time for this development to occur.

Piaget's Model of Cognitive Development

Piaget's theory maintains that children learn through interacting with their environments, much as scientists do, and that a child's thinking progresses through a sequence of four cognitive stages. (In "Waldorf Schools: Education for the Head, Hands, and Heart" in this chapter, Christopher Bamford and Eric Utne describe an educational program that incorporates Piaget's theory.) At the sensorimotor intelligence stage (birth to 2 years), behavior is largely sensory and motor, and, while cognitive development is occurring, the child does not yet "think" conceptually. At the preoperational thought stage (2–7 years), the development of language occurs, and the child can think of objects and people beyond the immediate environment. At the concrete operations stage (7–11 years), the child explores and masters basic concepts of objects, number, time, space, and causality and can use logical thought to solve problems. Finally, at the formal operations stage (11–15 years), the child can make predictions, think hypothetically, and think abstractly about language.

Erikson's Model of Psychosocial Development

"Erik Erikson's Developmental Stages: A Healthy Personality for Every Child" in this chapter presents Erikson's views on the emotional growth and development of human beings. His model is based on eight stages of growth—from infancy to old age. Each stage is characterized by a psychosocial crisis for the individual's emotional and social growth. These crises are expressed in polar terms; for example, in infancy, the psychosocial crisis is trust versus mistrust. The infant must come to trust the world sufficiently in order to move on to the next stage, autonomy versus shame and doubt. Shortly before his death in 1994, Erikson postulated a ninth stage in the human life cycle, *gerotranscendence,* during which humans must confront—and, if possible, transcend—the reality of their deteriorating bodies and faculties. In the final chapter of an extended version of Erikson's *The Life Cycle Completed,* first published in 1982, his wife and lifelong colleague, Joan M. Erikson, describes the challenges of moving into gerotranscendence:

> Old age in one's eighties and nineties brings with it new demands, reevaluations, and daily difficulties. . . . Even the best cared-for bodies begin to weaken and do not function as they once did. In spite of every effort to maintain strength and control, the body continues to lose its autonomy. Despair, which haunts the eighth stage, is a close companion in the ninth, because it is almost impossible to know what emergencies and losses of physical ability are imminent. As independence and control are challenged, self-esteem and confidence weaken. Hope and trust, which once provided firm support, are no longer the sturdy props of former days. To face down despair with faith and appropriate humility is perhaps the wisest course. (Erikson, 1997, pp. 105–106)

Kohlberg's and Gilligan's Models for Moral Development

Among the many perspectives on the moral development of human beings, Kohlberg's cognitive-developmental approach to moral education, based on Piaget's stages of cognitive development and John Dewey's levels of moral development, has had perhaps the greatest influence on curriculum planning. However, one might ask: Should moral education be an aspect of human development that is considered by curriculum planners and teachers? Perhaps the question is moot, since education is not value-free—it is a moral enterprise whether we wish it to be or not. Students' curricular experiences, including countless hours observing their teachers as moral models, have a profound influence on how they think and behave regarding moral issues.

In "The Cognitive-Developmental Approach to Moral Education" in this chapter, Kohlberg states that moral principals are ultimately "principles of justice," and that at each stage of moral development the concept of justice is reorganized. However, Carol Gilligan, at one point a colleague of Kohlberg's, believes that his research depends too heavily on studies of men and that women's moral judgments are more likely to reflect care and concern for others. In "Woman's Place in Man's Life Cycle" in this chapter, Gilligan examines these two perspectives and suggests that the female perspective on morality is based on the understanding of responsibility and relationships, while the male perspective is based on rights and rules.

CRITERION QUESTIONS—HUMAN DEVELOPMENT

Although stages of human development can be identified, no two individuals of the same age are alike in physical, emotional, intellectual, or social development. Knowing how development occurs in each of these areas helps curriculum planners and teachers identify two important curriculum criteria that should be reflected in the curriculum: individual differences and continuity in learning (i.e., the curriculum and teaching begin "where the learner is").

The following are among the criterion questions that can be derived from the theories of human development discussed in this chapter.

1. Does the curriculum reflect the inborn individuality and innate uniqueness of each learner?
2. Does the curriculum provide for developmental differences among the learners being taught?
3. Does the curriculum provide for continuity of learning?
4. Have the significance of developmental tasks, stages of growth toward a mature personality, and the development of morality been considered when planning the curriculum?
5. Does the curriculum attempt to provide for earlier tasks inadequately achieved, and for their maintenance when successfully achieved?
6. Does the curriculum reflect social and cultural changes that have occurred in recent years at each stage of human development?

REFERENCES

Epstein, Herman T. "Stages in Human Mental Growth." *Journal of Educational Psychology* 82, no. 4 (December 1990): 876–880.

———. "Growth Spurts During Brain Development: Implications for Educational Policy and Practice." In Jeanne S. Chall and Allan F. Mirsky, eds., *Education and the Brain, The 77th Yearbook of the National Society for the Study of Education, Part II.* Chicago: University of Chicago Press, 1978.

Erikson, Erik H. *The Life Cycle Completed: Extended Version with New Chapters on the Ninth Stage of Development by Joan M. Erikson.* New York: W. W. Norton & Company, 1997.

My Idea of Education

ASHLEY MONTAGU (1905–1999)

ABSTRACT: One of the world's preeminent anthropologists asserts that educability and the need for love distinguishes human beings from other creatures. The implications of children's individual rates of development for schools and teachers are discussed.

As an anthropologist who has been studying the six-million-year course of human evolution for nearly sixty years, I have become convinced that the characteristic that distinguishes humans from all other creatures is educability and that the most important of all basic human psychological needs is the need for love. Both of these findings have profound implications for schools and teachers.

The human is capable of learning anything, under the appropriate environmental conditions.

The human brain is an organ for the assimilation of diverse kinds of experiences and for turning accidents into opportunities. It is the most flexible, the most malleable, and the most educable of all the brains in the world.

It is capable of making the most of the improbable. Some people use their brains to arrive at truth and conclusions that others might conceive as utterly impossible. For example, at the very time the flying machine was invented, leading experts of the world said it was a physical impossibility.

We must recognize the educability of the human brain, particularly in dealing with children, who are the most educable of all human beings.

One thing most of us don't understand is the nature of the child and his or her extraordinary educability. Furthermore, we don't understand that we need to grow up into children and not adults. By this I mean we should preserve some of the traits that the child so conspicuously exhibits.

What are these traits? Besides educability, they are the need to love, sensitivity, the need to think soundly, the need to learn, the need to work, the need to organize, curiosity and wonder, open-mindedness, experimental-mindedness, imagina-

tion, creativity, playfulness, sense of humor, joyfulness, laughter, optimism, honesty, trust, compassionate intelligence, and the desire to grow and develop in all these traits.

Frequently, we feel we ought to limit this desire to grow to certain stages that we arbitrarily designate as infancy, childhood, and adolescence or to this one stage or another. Then we treat children of the same chronological age as if they were developmentally of the same age, too.

This is a damaging idea, and it has done an enormous amount of harm to children. Every child has his or her own developmental rate. To treat children, even children the same age, as if they were all equal is to commit a biological and social absurdity. The equal treatment of unequals is the most unequal way of dealing with human beings ever devised. We're all very different, and because we're all very different, we require individual attention. We should not be treated as if we were an agglutinated mass affixed to one another on the basis of our particular age level.

Even though many teachers recognize the great differences among children, they are not in a position to do anything about them because of the way school systems are organized and the inadequacy of those who are presiding at their top levels. These top level officials are usually unequipped to understand what the child is, what the teacher's needs are, and what education is all about.

What education is all about is being human, in other words, developing those traits that are uniquely human for the benefit of the individual, the family, the community, the society, and the world. Eventually what teachers do in the classroom is going to determine what the world is going to be like; for it is there that children learn all about being human if they have not learned it in the home.

Unfortunately, the probabilities are that children have not learned this in the home, because most parents are not equipped to do the job of parenting. Why? Simply because they have lived in a society that has not recognized the nature of the child, the nature of the human being, and the nature of what the child ought to be.

We now know what human beings ought to be because we understand for the first time in the history of our species that the most important of all human basic psychological needs is the need for love. It stands at the center of all human needs just as our sun stands at the center of our solar system with the planets orbiting around it. So the basic needs, the need for oxygen, food, liquid, rest, for activity, and so on, these revolve around the need for love—the sun of the human being.

It is this need for love that nature designates the mother to satisfy and that we have interfered with for a very long time by having mothers give birth to babies in hospitals, by taking babies away from their mothers in hospitals, by bottlefeeding babies, and by committing many other frightful offenses against babies at the very beginnings of their lives. These are offenses not only against the baby but against the mother and the family. The family should be involved in the ceremony and the celebration of welcoming a new member into the family. It is the family's job to turn this educable creature into the kind of human being that he or she is striving to be from the moment of birth.

Now that's quite a statement for a scientist to make. How do I know what this baby is striving to be? Well, I have discussed this with hundreds of babies. I've observed them, and I've talked with them. So have a good many other people. What they and I have observed is that the baby wants more than anything else to learn to love. Not only to be loved, but to love, because if the baby fails in this, then he or she fails to grow up as a warm, loving human being.

It's as simple as that. Nothing very complicated, but it's taken a long time for us to understand this.

The child who has not been loved is biochemically, physiologically, and psychologically very different from the one who has been loved. The former even grows differently from the latter. What we now know is that the human being is born to live as if to live and love were one.

This is not, of course, new. This is a validation of the Sermon on the Mount. I who am not a Christian and who am not a member of any religious affiliation say this.

The only religion I believe in is goodness and love. This is what we should be teaching in our schools. The greatest gift a teacher has to give a student is his or her love.

A teacher can recognize that the biggest behavior problems in the classroom are the ones who have been failed in their need for love and that what their need is is not to be sent to the principal but to be loved by the teacher. They will try the teacher again and again because they have been failed so many times and they don't trust anyone.

Every time the teacher offers them love, they may not improve their behavior, but if the teacher persists, then the teacher will win the children over. I speak from experience as an old teacher. I know very well how this works, because I've frequently done it myself.

I know this is very difficult in many cases—and it's extremely difficult in certain parts of America where teachers face behavior problems of the worst kind and where violence and vandalism are increasing at an accelerating rate in the schools. Even in those places, however, I think each teacher can make a difference by doing what he or she ought to do: behaving as a warm, loving human being.

How do we become warm, loving human beings? We act *as if* we were warm, loving human beings. If we act as if we were, someday we may find we've become what we've been trying to be, because what we are is not what we say but what we do.

I have been discussing love, but I have not defined it yet for the simple reason that a definition isn't meaningful at the beginning of an inquiry. It can be so only at the end of one.

Love is the ability to communicate by demonstrative acts to others our profound involvement in their welfare. We communicate our deep interest in them because we are aware that to be born human is to be born in danger, and therefore we will never commit the supreme treason against others of not helping them when they are most in need of us. We will minister to their needs and give them all the supports, all the stimulation, all the succor that they need or want.

That's love, and that's what we should be teaching in the schools, and everything else should be secondary to that. Reading, writing, and arithmetic, yes—but not of primary importance, of secondary importance in the development of a warm, loving human being.

This is my idea of education. If we put this idea into action, we stand a chance of solving most of the problems that bedevil the world at the present time, for teachers are the unacknowledged legislators of the world.

Ashley Montagu was an anthropologist. Among the books he authored are *Growing Young* (1981), *The Human Connection* (1979), *Touching* (2nd Ed., 1978), *Life Before Birth* (2nd Ed., 1978), *The Direction of Human Development* (2nd Ed., 1970), *On Being Human* (2nd Ed., 1966), and *Growing Young* (2nd Ed., 1988).

QUESTIONS FOR REFLECTION

1. What does Montagu mean when he states that "we don't understand that we need to grow up into children and not adults"? Do you agree?
2. To what extent do you agree or disagree with Montagu's statement that "the equal treatment of unequals is the most unequal way of dealing with human beings ever devised"? What implications does his position have for curriculum and teaching?
3. What evidence can you cite to support Montagu's claim that our society "has not recognized the nature of the child, the nature of the human being, and the nature of what the child ought to be"?
4. Do you agree with Montagu when he states that reading, writing, and arithmetic are "of secondary importance in the development of a warm, loving human being"? What would be the key elements of a school curriculum organized around this belief?

Toward a Strategy for Healthy Adolescent Development

DAVID A. HAMBURG

ABSTRACT: Adolescence is a critical transition period for young people. Contemporary society confronts adolescents with formidable stresses and risks that, for some youth, impair physical and mental health, erode motivation for success in school and workplace, and damage their relationships with others. With support from families, schools, health care professionals, and the community, however, adolescents can grow up to assume the responsibilities of democratic citizenship. For example, schools can promote healthy development by emphasizing a life sciences curriculum, life skills training, and social support.

Adolescence is one of the most complex transitions in the lifespan—a time of metamorphosis from childhood to adulthood. Its beginning is associated with biological, physical, behavioral, and social transformations that roughly correspond with the move from elementary school to middle or junior high school. The events of this crucially formative phase can shape an individual's entire lifespan.

Many adolescents manage to negotiate their way through this critical transition. With caring families, good schools, preventive health care, and supportive community institutions, they grow up healthy and vigorous, reasonably well educated, committed to families and friends, and prepared for the workplace and the responsibilities of democratic citizenship. For many others, however, the obstacles in their path can impair their physical and emotional health, erode their motivation and ability to succeed in school and the workplace, and damage their human relationships.

Adolescents from the ages of 10 to 15 are being confronted with pressures to use legal and illegal drugs and weapons and to engage in premature, unprotected sexual behavior. Many are depressed, and one-third report that they have contemplated suicide. Others lack the competence to handle interpersonal conflict without resorting to violence. By age 17, about one-quarter of all adolescents have engaged in behaviors that are harmful to themselves and others, such as getting pregnant, using drugs, taking part in antisocial activity, and failing in school. Altogether, nearly half of American adolescents are at high or moderate risk of seriously damaging their life chances.

The technological and social changes of recent decades have provided many young people with remarkable material benefits and opportunities but have also brought formidable stresses and risks into the adolescent experience. These changes are most striking in relation to their effect on family configurations: high divorce rates, both parents working full time outside the home, and the growth of single-parent families. Indeed, about half of all young Americans will spend part or all of their childhood and adolescence living with only one parent. These problems are exacerbated by the erosion of neighborhood networks and other traditional social support systems. Children now spend less time in the company of adults than a few decades ago; more of their time is spent either watching television or on the street, generally with peers in age-segregated, largely unsupervised environments.

Such conditions are common among families of all economic strata, social backgrounds, and geographic areas. But these conditions are especially prevalent in neighborhoods of concentrated poverty, where young adolescents so often lack two crucial prerequisites for their healthy growth and development: a close relationship with at least one dependable adult and the perception that meaningful opportunities exist in the adult life course.

What are fundamental requirements for healthy adolescent development? Adolescents must 1) find a valued place in a constructive group; 2) learn how to form close, durable human relationships; 3) feel a sense of worth as individuals; 4) achieve a reliable basis for making informed choices; 5) know how to use the support systems available to them; 6) express constructive curiosity and exploratory behavior; 7) believe in a promising future with real opportunities; 8) find ways of being useful to others; 9) learn to live respectfully with others in circumstances of democratic pluralism; and 10) cultivate the inquiring and problem-solving skills that serve lifelong learning and adaptability.

Early adolescence—the phase during which young people are just beginning to engage in very risky behaviors but before damaging patterns have become firmly established—offers an excellent opportunity for intervention to prevent later casualties and promote successful adult lives. Over a 10-year span in which several major reports were published, the Carnegie Council on Adolescent Development recommended ways in which pivotal institutions can adapt to contemporary circumstances so as to meet the requirements for healthy adolescent development. These institutions are the family, schools, health care systems, community organizations, and the media.

Many current interventions on behalf of young adolescents are targeted to one problem behavior, such as drug abuse or teenage pregnancy. While targeted approaches are useful, they often do not take adequate account of two important findings from research: 1) serious problem behaviors tend to cluster in the same individual and reinforce one another, and 2) such behaviors often have common antecedents in childhood experience.

Therefore, generic approaches that address the fundamental requirements in a comprehensive way—a youth development strategy—are attractive. The pivotal, frontline institutions that have a daily impact on adolescent experience have a special opportunity and obligation to foster healthy lifestyles in childhood and adolescence, while taking into consideration the underlying factors that promote either positive or negative outcomes. For better and worse, these institutions have powerful effects on adolescent development.

DISEASE PREVENTION IN ADOLESCENCE

Over the past few decades, the burden of adolescent illness has shifted from traditional causes of disease toward the "new morbidities" associated with health-damaging behaviors such as depression, suicide, substance use (alcohol, tobacco, and drugs), sexually transmitted diseases—including HIV and AIDS—and gun-related homicides.

Early adolescence is characterized by exploratory behavior in which the individual seeks adult-like roles and status. This is developmentally appropriate and socially adaptive, even though it involves some high-risk behavior. Yet such behavior can readily become dangerous and inflict damage, such as sexually transmitted diseases, death or trauma from violence, and disabling accidents related to alcohol. In addition, long-term consequences include cancer and cardiovascular disease, which are made more likely by high-calorie, high-fat dietary patterns, inadequate exercise, and heavy smoking. Destructive behaviors may constrict life options. For example, a teenage mother who drops out of junior or senior high school diminishes her prospects for lifetime employment and increases the risk of living in poverty, with the associated risks to her own health and the health of her child.

Early adolescence is a time of opportunity for the formation of healthy practices that have both short-term and long-term effects. Research of recent years has shown how the frontline institutions can provide accurate and personally meaningful information about health risks as well as foster the skills and motivation to avoid these risks and adopt healthy practices.

The health-related perceptions of adolescents can be helpful in motivating them to adopt healthy behavior. Their health concerns vary according to their gender, ethnicity, and socioeconomic status. Still, most are preoccupied with how they look, how they feel about themselves, their relationships to their peers, and educational pressures. Many adolescents are similarly concerned about substance abuse, sexuality, nutrition, and exercise. They tend wishfully to minimize the potentially damaging effects of high-risk behavior, in effect saying, "It can't happen to me." Such views are relevant to the design of social supports to adolescents, including clinical contacts. If health services are not user-friendly, they are not likely to be used by the individuals who need them most. By responding in meaningful ways to the interests, concerns, and perceptions of adolescents, health professionals can be helpful in ways that may have enduring value.

EDUCATION FOR HEALTH IN EARLY ADOLESCENCE

There is an inextricable link between education and health. Adolescents in poor health have difficulty learning (e.g., substance abuse destroys attention to instruction). Conversely, young people fully engaged in learning tend to form health-promoting habits. Many adolescents arrive at middle school with inadequate skills to cope with their great transition to adulthood. Much of what they need goes beyond the traditional curriculum offered by the public school system.

Middle schools can play a crucial role in fostering health among young adolescents through the curriculum, school policy, and clear examples of health-promoting behavior. A substantial approach to education for health includes 1) teaching adequate nutrition in the classroom and offering a corresponding diet in the cafeteria; 2) smoke-free buildings and programs to help students and staff avoid tobacco; 3) education on the effects of alcohol and illicit drugs on the brain and other organs; 4) opportunities for exercise not just for students in varsity competition but for all in the school community; and 5) emphasis on safety and the prevention of violence, including violence inherently associated with drug dealing and the carrying of weapons.

In 1989, the Carnegie Council on Adolescent Development published an interdisciplinary analysis of middle-grade education entitled *Turning Points*. This task force recommended reforms that were aimed at creating health-promoting, developmentally appropriate middle schools. For example, by organizing smaller units out of large schools, these new units can function on a human scale and provide sustained individual attention to students in a supportive group setting. A mutual aid ethic can be fostered among teachers and students, e.g., through interdisciplinary team teaching, cooperative learning, and academically supervised community service. These units can stimulate thinking skills, especially through a substantial life sciences curriculum, and can offer life skills training, especially in decision making, constructive interpersonal relations, nonviolent problem solving, and the ability to take advantage of opportunities. Since three approaches (life skills curriculum, life skills training, and social supports) offer sufficient potential for healthy development, some further words are in order.

Life sciences curriculum. The life sciences tap into the natural curiosity that surges in early adolescence. Students are intensely interested in the changes taking place in their own bodies. The life sciences clarify growth and development and specifically address adolescent development. The study of human biology includes the scientific study of behavior and illuminates ways in which high-risk behavior, especially in adolescence, bears on health throughout the lifespan.

Life skills training. The vital knowledge obtained from the life sciences curriculum is crucial but needs augmentation to be effective in shaping behavior. Such information becomes more useful when combined with training in interpersonal and decision-making skills. These skills can be useful in a variety of ways, such as helping students to

1) resist pressure from peers or from the media to engage in high-risk behaviors, 2) increase their self-control, 3) acquire ways to reduce stress without engaging in dangerous activity, 4) learn how to make friends and overcome isolation, and 5) learn how to avoid violence. Research shows that such skills can be effectively taught by using systematic instruction and practice through role playing.

Social supports. Research evidence shows that social supports that involve dependable relationships and shared values can provide leverage in the promotion of adolescent health. Schools, community organizations, and health care providers can supplement the family by arranging constructive social support programs.

Taken together, the life sciences curriculum, life skills training, and social supports constitute effective facilitators of healthy adolescent development.

Categorical or targeted approaches are complementary to the generic comprehensive approach of educating youth for lifelong health. Four issues are selected for brief illustration here: responsible sexuality, preparation for parenthood, prevention of youth violence, and prevention of drug abuse. Clearly, other problems also deserve attention and none more so than mental health, particularly depression.

RESPONSIBLE SEXUALITY

Early adolescence is not a time to become seriously engaged in sexual activity, yet adolescents are sorely tempted to do so. They get conflicting messages about desirable body image and appropriate sexual behavior, especially from the media and from peers. They badly need to understand sexuality, including the dynamics of intimate relationships, when to become sexually active, the biological process of conception, and the risks of contracting sexually transmitted diseases, including HIV infection.

Young adolescents get their information about sexuality primarily from peers but also from fam-

ily, school, television, and movies. Peer information is often inaccurate; for example, the assumption is widespread that "everybody does it." This assumption applies to a variety of risky behaviors such as smoking and alcohol use. Families and schools are in a better position to provide accurate information and health-protective choices. Adolescents who rate communication with their parents as poor are likely to initiate sex, smoking, and drinking earlier than peers who rate communication with their parents as good. However, parents need help in becoming well informed about reproductive health and in overcoming embarrassment about discussing sex with their children.

Adolescents need information about human sexuality and reproduction before they become sexually active. Organized efforts to meet these needs should begin not later than early adolescence in middle schools and in community organizations. Information about preventing the transmission of the AIDS virus is now a crucial although controversial part of health education for young adolescents. Adolescents typically do not know that the incubation period for AIDS can be a decade and that mothers can transmit the virus to their offspring. Interventions should identify the emotionally charged situations that adolescents are likely to encounter and provide life skills training on how to manage or avoid those situations of high risk. Schools, families, and the media, through health-promoting knowledge and skills, can contribute to this effort.

Even so, good information and skills may not be enough; motivation for constructive choices is crucial. Determining how to bring this about remains a formidable task. A recent Institute of Medicine study concluded that fewer than 25 programs to reduce unintended pregnancy have been carefully evaluated; of these programs, about half were found to be effective in the short term. This is one of the many indications that research in this field has not been given adequate priority.

The vast majority of adolescent pregnancies are unintended. Education for health must make it clear that to be sufficiently mature to raise a family, an individual not only must be knowledgeable about reproductive information, birth control, and the prevention of unwanted pregnancies but also must be aware that raising a family brings responsibilities as well as joys and that it takes a lot of learning and coping to become a reliable, competent parent.

PREPARATION FOR PARENTHOOD

Preparing adolescents for the time when they form families of their own is a neglected aspect of healthy development. All too many adolescents become pregnant only to find later that they are poorly prepared for the challenge of raising a child. The fulfillment of each child's potential requires a profound parental investment of time, energy, caregiving, resources, persistence, and resilience in coping with adversity.

The 1994 Carnegie report, *Starting Points: Meeting the Needs of Our Youngest Children,* emphasized the importance of preparing adolescents for responsible parenthood. When people make an informed, thoughtful commitment to have children, they are more likely to be good parents, and their children are more likely to develop in healthy ways. By the same token, when young parents are unprepared for the opportunities and responsibilities of parenthood, the risks to their children are formidable.

Therefore, *Starting Points* recommended a substantial expansion of efforts to educate young people about parenthood. Families are the first source of such education, but schools, places of worship, and community organizations can also be useful. Performing community service in child care centers can provide a valuable learning experience for adolescents about what is required to raise young children. Age-appropriate education about parenthood should begin in late elementary school but no later than early adolescence. It can be a part of either a life sciences curriculum or health education. In either case, it must be substantial and meaningful to adolescents.

PREVENTION OF YOUTH VIOLENCE

Nearly one million adolescents between the ages of 12 and 19 are victims of violent crimes each year. This problem has been accelerating, yet evidence is emerging on ways to prevent adolescent violence. To be effective, prevention requires a comprehensive approach that addresses both individual and social factors. Optimally, this would build on generic approaches that meet essential requirements for healthy adolescent development through developmentally appropriate schools, supportive families, and youth-oriented community organizations. In addition, specific interventions that target youth violence can enhance adolescents' ability to deal with conflict in nonviolent ways. Policy changes, such as implementing stronger measures to restrict the availability of guns, are urgently needed, especially in light of the growing propensity of juveniles to use guns, even semiautomatic weapons.

One promising strategy for preventing youth violence is the teaching of conflict resolution skills as part of health education in elementary and middle schools. Research indicates that conflict resolution programs can reduce violence; best results are achieved if these skills are embedded in long-term, comprehensive programs that address the multiple risk factors that lead to empty, shattered lives, which offer little recourse except violence. Serious, in-depth conflict resolution training over extended periods is increasingly important in a culture that is saturated with media and street violence. Supervised practice of conflict-resolution skills is important. Assertiveness, taught as a social skill, helps young people learn how to resist unwanted pressures and intimidation, resolve conflicts nonviolently, and make sound decisions about the use of weapons.

High-risk youth in impoverished communities urgently need social support networks and life skills training. Both can be provided in schools and school-related health centers as well as in community organizations, including church-related youth activities and sports programs. These programs work best by building enduring relationships with adults as well as with constructive peers. Such an approach offers alternatives to violent groups by providing a sense of belonging, a source of enjoyable activity, a perception of opportunity, a basis for mentoring, and a chance to prepare for social roles that earn respect.

PREVENTION OF DRUG ABUSE

Drugs are cheaper and more plentiful today than they were a decade ago. The United States has the highest addiction rates in its history, and the judicial system is clogged with drug-related cases. Adolescents consider alcohol and other drugs less harmful today than they did a few years ago. For many, the use of drugs, even the sale of drugs, constitutes an attractive path to what they perceive as adult status. Society has been searching desperately for answers. Meanwhile, serious research efforts oriented to prevention have gone through several "generations" of insight, and some promising evidence is at hand.

Community-wide preventive interventions in a few places have substantially diminished the use of "gateway" substances (tobacco, alcohol, and marijuana) in early adolescence, concomitantly enhancing personal and social competence. These efforts have used rigorous research designs on a long-term basis. Several preventive programs for young adolescents have been shown to reduce drug use. The learning of life skills has been effective in the prevention of cigarette smoking and alcohol and marijuana use if applied with sufficient intensity and duration. The systematic, explicit teaching of these skills can contribute to personal competence and provide constructive alternatives to health-damaging behavior.

When booster sessions are provided in high school, the preventive effects of early interventions are sustained through the senior year. The prevention of cigarette smoking is very important, both because of its "gateway" function and the many pathologies throughout the lifespan

that flow from this addiction in early adolescence. The well-designed, community-wide interventions are encouraging in this respect. Their success suggests that social norms on cigarette use can be changed by systematic, intensive, and long-term efforts. A striking example is the recent decline in smoking reported by African American adolescents.

Beyond the targeted approach to substance abuse, parents, teachers, and health professionals should understand that adolescent immersion in high-risk behavior is exacerbated by developmental problems such as low self-esteem, poor performance in school, depression, or inability to make deliberate, informed decisions. Using drugs may be a way of feeling mature, courageous, sophisticated, or otherwise grown-up. Disadvantaged youth need to be shown how individuals from comparable backgrounds have done well in the mainstream economy—in contrast to the putatively successful drug dealers who are involved in crime and violence. The fostering of family-augmenting functions by community organizations and health-social services can provide accurate, pertinent information and supportive human relationships that facilitate healthy development even in circumstances of adversity.

STRENGTHENING HEALTH SERVICES FOR ADOLESCENTS

A comprehensive study of adolescent health, conducted by the U.S. Office of Technology Assessment in 1991, pointed to serious barriers to establishing developmentally appropriate health services for adolescents. Current services are particularly lacking in disease prevention and health-promotion services. Recent studies and innovations show what can be done, but there is a long way to go.

One in seven American adolescents has no health insurance coverage; many more have very little. Within the Medicaid population, only one-third of eligible adolescents are currently covered because of funding constraints. Health insurance, even when provided by employers for working families, often excludes their adolescent children.

As managed care spreads rapidly throughout the United States, it is essential to include explicit provisions for coverage of adolescents. This will be especially important to monitor as states increasingly enroll their Medicaid population in managed care plans. Managed care organizations can contract with school-based health centers that serve adolescents. Some community health and school-based adolescent health centers have shown how various barriers can be overcome so that adolescents can get adequate care during these years that are crucially formative for healthy lifestyles.

At present, there is a shortage of experienced and well-trained health providers who can sensitively treat the health problems of adolescents. The conjunction of psychiatry with pediatrics and internal medicine is important in this context.

One promising approach to filling the service gap for adolescents is manifested in school-related health facilities, either at or near the school, and functionally integrated with respect to curriculum and accessibility. Such facilities have demonstrated their ability to deal with acute medical problems, including mental health. They have strong potential for disease prevention and health promotion.

Since students often request help with feelings of depression, loneliness, and anxiety, these centers must provide mental health services. Treatment of depression can represent an important opportunity to prevent further problems, for example, self-medication that leads to substance abuse and addiction.

CONCLUSIONS

The early adolescent years have become the starting point for an upsurge of health-compromising behaviors that have lifelong consequences. Yet early adolescence presents a neglected and overlooked opportunity for health promotion. The interest of adolescents in their own developing bodies can be a potent force for building healthy lifestyles of enduring significance. The best chance to fulfill this promise lies in enhancing understanding of adolescent development among health care professionals, schools, community organizations, families, and media.

A crucial ingredient is the guiding and motivating influence of caring adults. Information and skills are necessary but not sufficient to shape the behavior of adolescents unless they are motivated to put them to use in the service of their own health. This requires the protection and support of families and health professionals who are trained to work effectively with adolescents as distinctive individuals. Health policy makers must find ways to improve adolescents' access to health care through dependable primary care providers and school-linked preventive services, including services for mental health.

A comprehensive health-promotion strategy would optimally involve a community-wide commitment from the full range of institutions with which adolescents are involved. Such a commitment to adolescents is potentially a powerful means of shaping young lives in healthy, constructive patterns of lifelong learning and adaptation. This approach is highly congruent with Mel Sabshin's career-long vision of research, education, and care for healthy development and social responsibility.

David A. Hamburg is President Emeritus of the Carnegie Corporation of New York and former Chair of Psychiatry at Stanford University School of Medicine. In 1996, he received the Presidential Medal of Freedom, the nation's highest civilian honor, and in 1998, he received the Public Welfare Medal from the National Academy of Sciences.

QUESTIONS FOR REFLECTION

1. Reflect on your experiences as an adolescent. In what ways did your school experiences help you to cope with the stresses associated with this transition period?
2. What concerns might some teachers, parents, and community members raise about Hamburg's call for schools to emphasize a life sciences curriculum, life skills training, and social support? How might Hamburg respond to these concerns?
3. What evidence indicates that some adolescents in your local community may not be on the path toward healthy adult development?

The Cognitive-Developmental Approach to Moral Education

LAWRENCE KOHLBERG (1927–1987)

ABSTRACT: Building on Dewey's and Piaget's ideas about moral development, Kohlberg suggests that the reasoning processes people use to differentiate between right and wrong progress through three levels of development. At the preconventional level, people decide what is right on the basis of personal needs and rules developed by others; at the conventional level, moral decisions reflect a desire for others' approval and a willingness to conform to expectations of family, community, and country; and at the postconventional level, decisions are based on rational, personal choices that can be separated from conventional values.

In this article, I present an overview of the cognitive-developmental approach to moral education and its research foundations, compare it with other approaches, and report the experimental work my colleagues and I are doing to apply the approach.

I. MORAL STAGES

The cognitive-developmental approach was fully stated for the first time by John Dewey. The approach is called *cognitive* because it recognizes that moral education, like intellectual education, has its basis in stimulating the *active thinking* of the child about moral issues and decisions. It is

called developmental because it sees the aims of moral education as movement through moral stages. According to Dewey:

> The aim of education is growth or *development*, both intellectual and moral. Ethical and psychological principles can aid the school in the *greatest of all the constructions—the building of a free and powerful character*. Only knowledge of the *order and connection of the stages in psychological development can insure this*. Education is the work of *supplying the conditions* which will enable the psychological functions to mature in the freest and fullest manner.[1]

Dewey postulated three levels of moral development: (1) the *pre-moral* or *preconventional* level "of behavior motivated by biological and social impulses with results for morals," (2) the *conventional* level of behavior "in which the individual accepts with little critical reflection the standards of his group," and (3) the *autonomous* level of behavior in which "conduct is guided by the individual thinking and judging for himself whether a purpose is good, and does not accept the standard of his group without reflection."[2]

Dewey's thinking about moral stages was theoretical. Building upon his prior studies of cognitive stages, Jean Piaget made the first effort to define stages of moral reasoning in children through actual interviews and through observations of children (in games with rules).[3] Using this interview material, Piaget defined the premoral, the conventional, and the autonomous levels as follows: (1) the *premoral stage*, where there was no sense of obligation to rules; (2) the *heteronomous stage,* where the right was literal obedience to rules and an equation of obligation with submission to power and punishment (roughly ages four to eight); and (3) the *autonomous stage*, where the purpose and consequences of following rules are considered and obligation is based on reciprocity and exchange (roughly ages eight to twelve).[4]

In 1955 I started to redefine and validate (through longitudinal and cross-cultural study) the Dewey-Piaget levels and stages. The resulting stages are presented in Table 1.

We claim to have validated the stages defined in Table 1. The notion that stages can be *validated* by longitudinal study implies that stages have definite empirical characteristics.[5] The concept of stages (as used by Piaget and myself) implies the following characteristics:

1. Stages are "structured wholes," or organized systems of thought. Individuals are *consistent* in level of moral judgment.
2. Stages form an *invariant sequence.* Under all conditions except extreme trauma, movement is always forward, never backward. Individuals never skip stages; movement is always to the next stage up.
3. Stages are "hierarchical integrations." Thinking at a higher stage includes or comprehends

within it lower-stage thinking. There is a tendency to function at or prefer the highest stage available.

Each of these characteristics has been demonstrated for moral stages. Stages are defined by responses to a set of verbal moral dilemmas classified according to an elaborate scoring scheme. Validating studies include:

1. A twenty-year study of fifty Chicago-area boys, middle- and working-class. Initially interviewed at ages ten to sixteen, they have been reinterviewed at three-year intervals thereafter.
2. A small, six-year longitudinal study of a Turkish village and city boys of the same age.
3. A variety of other cross-sectional studies in Canada, Britain, Israel, Taiwan, Yucatan, Honduras, and India.

With regard to the structured whole or consistency criterion, we have found that more than 50 percent of an individual's thinking is always at one stage, with the remainder at the next adjacent stage (which he is leaving or which he is moving into).

With regard to invariant sequence, our longitudinal results have been presented in the *American Journal of Orthopsychiatry* (see note 12), and indicate that on every retest individuals were either at the same stage as three years earlier or had moved up. This was true in Turkey as well as in the United States.

With regard to the hierarchical integration criterion, it has been demonstrated that adolescents exposed to written statements at each of the six stages comprehend or correctly put in their own words all statements at or below their own stage but fail to comprehend any statements more than one stage above their own.[6] Some individuals comprehend the next stage above their own; some do not. Adolescents prefer (or rank as best) the highest stage they can comprehend.

To understand moral stages, it is important to clarify their relations to stage of logic or intelligence, on the one hand, and to moral behavior on

TABLE 3.1
Definition of Moral Stages

I. Preconventional level

   At this level, the child is responsive to cultural rules and labels of good and bad, right or wrong, but interprets these labels either in terms of the physical or the hedonistic consequences of action (punishment, reward, exchange of favors) or in terms of the physical power of those who enunciate the rules and labels. The level is divided into the following two stages:

   Stage 1: *The punishment-and-obedience orientation.* The physical consequences of action determine its goodness or badness, regardless of the human meaning or value of these consequences. Avoidance of punishment and unquestioning deference to power are valued in their own right, not in terms of respect for an underlying moral order supported by punishment and authority (the latter being Stage 4).

   Stage 2: *The instrumental-relativist orientation.* Right action consists of that which instrumentally satisfies one's own needs and occasionally the needs of others. Human relations are viewed in terms like those of the marketplace. Elements of fairness, of reciprocity, and of equal sharing are present, but they are always interpreted in a physical, pragmatic way. Reciprocity is a matter of "You scratch my back and I'll scratch yours," not of loyalty, gratitude, or justice.

II. Conventional level

   At this level, maintaining the expectations of the individual's family, group, or nation is perceived as valuable in its own right, regardless of immediate and obvious consequences. The attitude is not only one of *conformity* to personal expectations and social order, but of loyalty to it, of actively *maintaining,* supporting, and justifying the order, and of identifying with the persons or group involved in it. At this level, there are the following two stages:

   Stage 3: *The interpersonal concordance or "good boy-nice girl" orientation.* Good behavior is that which pleases or helps others and is approved by them. There is much conformity to stereotypical images of what is majority or "natural" behavior. Behavior is frequently judged by intention—"he means well" becomes important for the first time. One earns approval by being "nice."

   Stage 4: *The "law and order" orientation.* There is orientation toward authority, fixed rules, and the maintenance of the social order. Right behavior consists of doing one's duty, showing respect for authority, and maintaining the given social order for its own sake.

III. Postconventional, autonomous, or principled level

   At this level, there is a clear effort to define moral values and principles that have validity and application apart from the authority of the groups or persons holding these principles and apart from the individual's own identification with these groups. This level also has two stages:

   Stage 5: *The social-contract, legalistic orientation,* generally with utilitarian overtones. Right action tends to be defined in terms of general individual rights and standards which have been critically examined and agreed upon by the whole society. There is a clear awareness of the relativism of personal values and opinions and a corresponding emphasis upon procedural rules for reaching consensus. Aside from what is constitutionally and democratically agreed upon, the right is a matter of personal "values"; and "opinion." The result is an emphasis upon the "legal point of view," but with an emphasis upon the possibility of changing law in terms of rational considerations of social utility (rather than freezing it in terms of Stage 4 "law and order"). Outside the legal realm, free agreement and contract is the binding element of obligation. This is the "official" morality of the American government and constitution.

   Stage 6: *The universal-ethical-principle orientation.* Right is defined by the decision of conscience in accord with self-chosen *ethical principles* appealing to logical comprehensiveness, universality, and consistency. These principles are abstract and ethical (the Golden Rule, the categorical imperative); they are not concrete moral rules like the Ten Commandments. At heart, these are universal principles of *justice,* of the *reciprocity* and *equality* of human *rights,* and of respect for the dignity of human beings as *individual persons* ("From Is to Ought," pp. 164, 165).

From *Journal of Philosophy* 70, no. 18 (October 25, 1973): 631–632. Reprinted by permission.

the other. Maturity of moral judgment is not highly correlated with IQ or verbal intelligence (correlations are only in the 30s, accounting for 10 percent of the variance). Cognitive development, in the stage sense, however, is more important for moral development than such correlations suggest. Piaget has found that after the child learns to speak there are three major stages of reasoning: the intuitive, the concrete operational, and the formal operational. At around age seven, the child enters the stage of concrete logical thought: He can make logical inferences, classify, and handle quantitative relations about concrete things. In adolescence individuals usually enter the stage of formal operations. At this stage they can reason abstractly, i.e., consider all possibilities, form hypotheses, deduce implications from hypotheses, and test them against reality.[7]

Since moral reasoning clearly is reasoning, advanced moral reasoning depends upon advanced logical reasoning; a person's logical stage puts a certain ceiling on the moral stage he can attain. A person whose logical stage is only concrete operational is limited to the preconventional moral stages (Stages 1 and 2). A person whose logical stage is only partially formal operational is limited to the conventional moral stages (Stages 3 and 4). While logical development is necessary for moral development and sets limits to it, most individuals are higher in logical stage than they are in moral stage. As an example, over 50 percent of late adolescents and adults are capable of full formal reasoning, but only 10 percent of these adults (all formal operational) display principled (Stages 5 and 6) moral reasoning.

The moral stages are *structures of moral judgment* or *moral reasoning*. *Structures* of moral judgment must be distinguished from the *content* of moral judgment. As an example, we cite responses to a dilemma used in our various studies to identify moral stage. The dilemma raises the issue of stealing a drug to save a dying woman. The inventor of the drug is selling it for ten times what it costs him to make it. The woman's husband cannot raise the money, and the seller re-

fuses to lower the price or wait for payment. What should the husband do?

The choice endorsed by a subject (steal, don't steal) is called the *content* of his moral judgment in the situation. His reasoning about the choice defines the structure of his moral judgment. This reasoning centers on the following ten universal moral values or issues of concern to persons in these moral dilemmas:

1. Punishment
2. Property
3. Roles and concerns of affection
4. Roles and concerns of authority
5. Law
6. Life
7. Liberty
8. Distributive justice
9. Truth
10. Sex

A moral choice involves choosing between two (or more) of these values as they *conflict* in concrete situations of choice.

The stage or structure of a person's moral judgment defines: (1) *what* he finds valuable in each of these moral issues (life, law), i.e., how he defines the value, and (2) *why* he finds it valuable, i.e., the reasons he gives for valuing it. As an example, at Stage 1 life is valued in terms of the power or possessions of the person involved; at Stage 2, for its usefulness in satisfying the needs of the individual in question or others; at Stage 3, in terms of the individual's relations with others and their valuation of him; at Stage 4, in terms of social or religious law. Only at Stages 5 and 6 is each life seen as inherently worthwhile, aside from other considerations.

Moral Judgment vs. Moral Action

Having clarified the nature of stages of moral *judgment*, we must consider the relation of moral judgment to moral *action*. If logical reasoning is a necessary but not sufficient condition for mature moral judgment, mature moral judgment is a necessary but not sufficient condition for mature moral action. One cannot follow moral principles if one does not understand (or believe in) moral principles. However, one can reason in terms of principles and not live up to these principles. As an example, Richard Krebs and I found that only 15 percent of students showing some principled thinking cheated as compared to 55 percent of conventional subjects and 70 percent of preconventional subjects.[8] Nevertheless, 15 percent of the principled subjects did cheat, suggesting that factors additional to moral judgment are necessary for principled moral reasoning to be translated into "moral action." Partly, these factors include the situation and its pressures. Partly, what happens depends upon the individual's motives and emotions. Partly, what the individual does depends upon a general sense of will, purpose, or "ego strength." As an example of the role of will or ego strength in moral behavior, we may cite the study by Krebs: Slightly more than half of his conventional subjects cheated. These subjects were also divided by a measure of attention/will. Only 26 percent of the "strong-willed" conventional subjects cheated; however, 74 percent of the "weak-willed" subjects cheated.

If maturity of moral reasoning is only one factor in moral behavior, why does the cognitive-developmental approach to moral education focus so heavily upon moral reasoning? For the following reasons:

1. Moral judgment, while only one factor in moral behavior, is the single most important or influential factor yet discovered in moral behavior.
2. While other factors influence moral behavior, moral judgment is the only distinctively *moral* factor in moral behavior. To illustrate, we noted that the Krebs study indicated that "strong-willed" conventional stage subjects resisted cheating more than "weak-willed" subjects. For those at a preconventional level

of moral reasoning, however, "will" had an opposite effect. "Strong-willed" Stages 1 and 2 subjects cheated more, not less, than "weak-willed" subjects, i.e., they had the "courage of their (amoral) convictions" that it was worthwhile to cheat. "Will," then, is an important factor in moral behavior, but it is not distinctively moral; it becomes moral only when informed by mature moral judgment.
3. Moral judgment change is long-range or irreversible; a higher stage is never lost. Moral behavior as such is largely situational and reversible or "losable" in new situations.

II. AIMS OF MORAL AND CIVIC EDUCATION

Moral psychology describes what moral development is, as studied empirically. Moral education must also consider moral philosophy, which strives to tell us what moral development ideally *ought to be*. Psychology finds an invariant sequence of moral stages; moral philosophy must be invoked to answer whether a later stage is a better stage. The "stage" of senescence and death follows the "stage" of adulthood, but that does not mean that senescence and death are better. Our claim that the latest or principled stages of moral reasoning are morally better stages, then, must rest on considerations of moral philosophy.

The tradition of moral philosophy to which we appeal is the liberal or rational tradition, in particular the "formalistic" or "deontological" tradition running from Immanuel Kant to John Rawls.[9] Central to this tradition is the claim that an adequate morality is *principled*, i.e., that it makes judgments in terms of *universal* principles applicable to all mankind. *Principles* are to be distinguished from *rules*. Conventional morality is grounded on rules, primarily "thou shalt nots" such as are represented by the Ten Commandments, prescriptions of kinds of actions. Principles are, rather, universal guides to making a moral decision. An example is Kant's "categorical imperative," formulated in two ways. The first is the maxim of respect for human personality "Act always toward the other as an end, not as a means." The second is the maxim of universalization, "Choose only as you would be willing to have everyone choose in your situation." Principles like that of Kant's state the formal conditions of a moral choice or action. In the dilemma in which a woman is dying because a druggist refuses to release his drug for less than the stated price, the druggist is not acting morally, though he is not violating the ordinary moral rules (he is not actually stealing or murdering). But he is violating principles: He is treating the woman simply as a means to his ends of profit, and he is not choosing as he would wish anyone to choose (if the druggist were in the dying woman's place, he would not want a druggist to choose as he is choosing). Under most circumstances, choice in terms of conventional moral rules and choice in terms of principles coincide. Ordinarily, principles dictate not stealing (avoiding stealing is implied by acting in terms of a regard for others as ends and in terms of what one would want everyone to do). In a situation where stealing is the only means to save a life, however, principles contradict the ordinary rules and would dictate stealing. Unlike rules which are supported by social authority, principles are freely chosen by the individual because of their intrinsic moral validity.[10]

The conception that a moral choice is a choice made in terms of moral principles is related to the claim of liberal moral philosophy that moral principles are ultimately principles of justice. In essence, moral conflicts are conflicts between the claims of persons, and principles for resolving these claims are principles of justice, "for giving each his due." Central to justice are the demands of *liberty, equality,* and *reciprocity.* At every moral stage, there is a concern for justice. The most damning statement a school child can make about a teacher is that "he's not fair." At each higher stage, however, the conception of justice is reorganized. At Stage 1, justice is punishing the bad in terms of "an eye for an eye and a tooth for a tooth." At Stage 2, it is exchanging favors and goods in an equal manner. At Stages 3 and 4, it is

treating people as they desire in terms of the conventional rules. At Stage 5, it is recognized that all rules and laws flow from justice, from a social contract between the governors and the governed designed to protect the equal rights of all. At Stage 6, personally chosen moral principles are also principles of justice, the principles any member of a society would choose for that society if he did not know what his position was to be in the society and in which he might be the least advantaged.[11] Principles chosen from this point of view are, first, the maximum liberty compatible with the like liberty of others and, second, no inequalities of goods and respect which are not to the benefit of all, including the least advantaged.

As an example of stage progression in the orientation to justice, we may take judgments about capital punishment.[12] Capital punishment is only firmly rejected at the two principled stages, when the notion of justice as vengeance or retribution is abandoned. At the sixth stage, capital punishment is not condoned even if it may have some useful deterrent effect in promoting law and order. This is because it is not a punishment we would choose for a society if we assumed we had as much chance of being born into the position of a criminal or murderer as being born into the position of a law abider.

Why are decisions based on universal principles of justice better decisions? Because they are decisions on which all moral men could agree. When decisions are based on conventional moral rules, men will disagree, since they adhere to conflicting systems of rules dependent on culture and social position. Throughout history men have killed one another in the name of conflicting moral rules and values, most recently in Vietnam and the Middle East. Truly moral or just resolutions of conflicts require principles which are, or can be, universalizable.

Alternative Approaches

We have given a philosophic rationale for stage advance as the aim of moral education. Given this rationale, the developmental approach to moral education can avoid the problems inherent in the other two major approaches to moral education. The first alternative approach is that of indoctrinative moral education, the preaching and imposition of the rules and values of the teacher and his culture on the child. In America, when this indoctrinative approach has been developed in a systematic manner, it has usually been termed "character education."

Moral values, in the character education approach, are preached or taught in terms of what may be called the "bag of virtues." In the classic studies of character by Hugh Hartshorne and Mark May, the virtues chosen were honesty, services and self-control.[13] It is easy to get superficial consensus on such a bag of virtues—until one examines in detail the list of virtues involved and the details of their definition. Is the Hartshorne and May bag more adequate than the Boy Scout bag (a Scout should be honest, loyal, reverent, clean, brave, etc.)? When one turns to the details of defining each virtue, one finds equal uncertainty or difficulty in reaching consensus. Does honesty mean one should not steal to save a life? Does it mean that a student should not help another student with his homework?

Character education and other forms of indoctrinative moral education have aimed at teaching universal values (it is assumed that honesty or service is a desirable trait for all men in all societies), but the detailed definitions used are relative; they are defined by the opinions of the teacher and the conventional culture and rest on the authority of the teacher for their justification. In this sense character education is close to the unreflective valuings by teachers which constitute the hidden curriculum of the school.[14] Because of the current unpopularity of indoctrinative approaches to moral education, a family of approaches called "values clarification" has become appealing to teachers. Values clarification takes the first step implied by a rational approach to moral education: the eliciting of the child's own judgment or opinion about issues or situations in which values conflict, rather than imposing the

teacher's opinion on him. Values clarification, however, does not attempt to go further than eliciting awareness of values; it is assumed that becoming more self-aware about one's values is an end in itself. Fundamentally, the definition of the end of values education as self-awareness derives from a belief in ethical relativity held by many value-clarifiers. As stated by Peter Engel, "One must contrast value clarification and value inculcation. Value clarification implies the principle that in the consideration of values there is no single correct answer." Within these premises of "no correct answer," children are to discuss moral dilemmas in such a way as to reveal different values and discuss their value differences with each other. The teacher is to stress that "our values are different," not that one value is more adequate than others. If this program is systematically followed, students will themselves become relativists, believing there is no "right" moral answer. For instance, a student caught cheating might argue that he did nothing wrong, since his own hierarchy of values, which may be different from that of the teacher, made it right for him to cheat.

Like values clarification, the cognitive-developmental approach to moral education stresses open or Socratic peer discussion of value dilemmas. Such discussion, however, has an aim: stimulation of movement to the next stage of moral reasoning. Like values clarification, the developmental approach opposes indoctrination. Stimulation of movement to the next stage of reasoning is not indoctrinative, for the following reasons:

1. Change is in the way of reasoning rather than in the particular beliefs involved.
2. Students in a class are at different stages; the aim is to aid movement of each to the next stage, not convergence on a common pattern.
3. The teacher's own opinion is neither stressed nor invoked as authoritative. It enters in only as one of many opinions, hopefully one of those at a next higher stage.
4. The notion that some judgments are more adequate than others is communicated. Funda-

mentally, however, this means that the student is encouraged to articulate a position which seems most adequate to him and to judge the adequacy of the reasoning of others.

In addition to having more definite aims than values clarification, the moral development approach restricts value education to that which is moral or, more specifically, to justice. This is for two reasons. First, it is not clear that the whole realm of personal, political, and religious values is a realm which is nonrelative, i.e., in which there are universals and a direction of development. Second, it is not clear that the public school has a right or mandate to develop values in general.[15] In our view, value education in the public schools should be restricted to that which the school has the right and mandate to develop: an awareness of justice, or of the rights of others in our Constitutional system. While the Bill of Rights prohibits the teaching of religious beliefs, or of specific value systems, it does not prohibit the teaching of the awareness of rights and principles of justice fundamental to the Constitution itself.

When moral education is recognized as centered in justice and differentiated from value education or affective education, it becomes apparent that moral and civic education are much the same thing. This equation, taken for granted by the classic philosophers of education from Plato and Aristotle to Dewey, is basic to our claim that a concern for moral education is central to the educational objectives of social studies.

The term *civic education* is used to refer to social studies as more than the study of the facts and concepts of social science, history, and civics. It is education for the analytic understanding, value principles, and motivation necessary for a citizen in a democracy if democracy is to be an effective process. It is political education. Civic or political education means the stimulation of development of more advanced patterns of reasoning about political and social decisions and their implementation directly derivative of broader patterns of moral reasoning. Our studies show that reasoning and decision making about political decisions are directly derivative of broader patterns of moral reasoning and decision making. We have interviewed high school and college students about concrete political situations involving laws to govern open housing, civil disobedience for peace in Vietnam, free press rights to publish what might disturb national order, and distribution of income through taxation. We find that reasoning on these political decisions can be classified according to moral stage and that an individual's stage on political dilemmas is at the same level as on nonpolitical moral dilemmas (euthanasia, violating authority to maintain trust in a family, stealing a drug to save one's dying wife). Turning from reasoning to action, similar findings are obtained. In 1963 a study was made of those who sat in at the University of California, Berkeley, administration building and those who did not in the Free Speech Movement crisis. Of those at Stage 6, 80 percent sat in, believing that principles of free speech were being compromised, and that all efforts to compromise and negotiate with the administration had failed. In contrast, only 15 percent of the conventional (Stage 3 or Stage 4) subjects sat in. (Stage 5 subjects were in between.)[16]

From a psychological side, then, political development is part of moral development. The same is true from the philosophic side. In the *Republic,* Plato sees political education as part of a broader education for moral justice and finds a rationale for such education in terms of universal philosophic principles rather than the demands of a particular society. More recently, Dewey claims the same.

In historical perspective, America was the first nation whose government was publicly founded on postconventional principles of justice, rather than upon the authority central to conventional moral reasoning. At the time of our founding, postconventional or principled moral and political reasoning was the possession of the minority, as it still is. Today, as in the time of our founding, the majority of our adults are at the conventional level, particularly the "law and order" (fourth) moral stage. (Every few years the Gallup Poll circulates the Bill of Rights unidentified, and every year it is turned down.) The Founding Fathers intuitively understood this without benefit of our elaborate social science research; they constructed a document designing a government which would maintain principles of justice and the rights of man even though principled men were not the men in power. The machinery included checks and balances, the independent judiciary, and freedom of the press. Most recently, this machinery found its use at Watergate. The tragedy of Richard Nixon, as Harry Truman said long ago, was that he never understood the Constitution (a Stage 5 document), but the Constitution understood Richard Nixon.[17]

Watergate, then, is not some sign of moral decay of the nation, but rather of the fact that understanding and action in support of justice principles are still the possession of a minority of our society. Insofar as there is moral decay, it represents the weakening of conventional morality in the face of social and value conflict today. This can lead the less fortunate adolescent to fixation at the preconventional level, the more fortunate to movement to principles. We find a larger proportion of youths at the principled level today than was the case in their fathers' day, but also a larger proportion at the preconventional level.

Given this state, moral and civic education in the schools becomes a more urgent task. In the high school today, one often hears both preconventional adolescents and those beginning to move beyond convention sounding the same note of disaffection for the school. While our political institutions are in principle Stage 5 (i.e., vehicles for maintaining universal rights through the democratic process), our schools have traditionally been Stage 4 institutions of convention and authority. Today more than ever, democratic schools systematically engaged in civic education are required.

Our approach to moral and civic education relates the study of law and government to the actual creation of a democratic school in which moral dilemmas are discussed and resolved in a manner which will stimulate moral development.

Planned Moral Education

For many years, moral development was held by psychologists to be primarily a result of family upbringing and family conditions. In particular, conditions of affection and authority in the home were believed to be critical, some balance of warmth and firmness being optimal for moral development. This view arises if morality is conceived as an internalization of the arbitrary rules of parents and culture, since such acceptance must be based on affection and respect for parents as authorities rather than on the rational nature of the rules involved.

Studies of family correlates of moral stage development do not support this internalization view of the conditions for moral development. Instead, they suggest that the conditions for moral development in homes and schools are similar and that the conditions are consistent with cognitive-developmental theory. In the cognitive-developmental view, morality is a natural product of a universal human tendency toward empathy or role taking, toward putting oneself in the shoes of other conscious beings. It is also a product of a universal human concern for justice, for reciprocity or equality in the relation of one person to another. As an example, when my son was four, he became a morally principled vegetarian and refused to eat meat, resisting all parental persuasion to increase his protein intake. His reason was, "It's bad to kill animals." His moral commitment to vegetarianism was not taught or acquired from parental authority; it was the result of the universal tendency of the young self to project its consciousness and values into other living things, other selves. My son's vegetarianism also involved a sense of justice, revealed when I read him a book about Eskimos in which a seal hunting expedition was described. His response was to say, "Daddy, there is one kind of meat I would eat—Eskimo meat. It's all right to eat Eskimos because they eat animals." This natural sense of justice or reciprocity was Stage 1—an eye for an eye, a tooth for a tooth. My son's sense of the value of life was also Stage 1 and involved no differentiation between human personality and physical life. His morality, though Stage 1, was, however, natural and internal. Moral development past Stage 1, then, is not an internalization but the reconstruction of role taking and conceptions of justice toward greater adequacy. These reconstructions occur in order to achieve a better match between the child's own moral structures and the structures of the social and moral situations he confronts. We divide these conditions of match into two kinds: those dealing with moral discussions and communication and those dealing with the total moral environment or atmosphere in which the child lives.

In terms of moral discussion, the important conditions appear to be:

1. Exposure to the next higher stage of reasoning
2. Exposure to situations posing problems and contradictions for the child's current moral structure, leading to dissatisfaction with his current level
3. An atmosphere of interchange and dialogue combining the first two conditions, in which conflicting moral views are compared in an open manner.

Studies of families in India and America suggest that morally advanced children have parents at higher stages. Parents expose children to the next higher stage, raising moral issues and engaging in open dialogue or interchange about such issues.[18]

Drawing on this notion of the discussion conditions stimulating advance, Moshe Blatt conducted classroom discussions of conflict-laden hypothetical moral dilemmas with four classes of junior high and high school students for a semester.[19] In each of these classes, students were to be found at three stages. Since the children were not all responding at the same stage, the arguments they used with each other were at different levels. In the course of these discussions among the students, the teacher first supported and clarified those arguments that were one stage above the lowest stage among the children; for example,

the teacher supported Stage 3 rather than Stage 2. When it seemed that these arguments were understood by the students, the teacher then challenged that stage, using new situations, and clarified the arguments one stage above the previous one: Stage 4 rather than Stage 3. At the end of the semester, all the students were retested; they showed significant upward change when compared to the controls, and they maintained the change one year later. In the experimental classrooms, from one-fourth to one-half of the students moved up a stage, while there was essentially no change during the course of the experiment in the control group.

Given the Blatt studies showing that moral discussion could raise moral stage, we undertook the next step: to see if teachers could conduct moral discussions in the course of teaching high school social studies with the same results. This step we took in cooperation with Edwin Fenton, who introduced moral dilemmas in his ninth- and eleventh-grade social studies texts. Twenty-four teachers in the Boston and Pittsburgh areas were given some instruction in conducting moral discussions around the dilemmas in the text. About half of the teachers stimulated significant developmental change in their classrooms—upward stage movement of one-quarter to one-half a stage. In control classes using the text but no moral dilemma discussions, the same teachers failed to stimulate any moral change in the students. Moral discussion, then, can be a usable and effective part of the curriculum at any grade level. Working with filmstrip dilemmas produced in cooperation with Guidance Association, second-grade teachers conducted moral discussions yielding a similar amount of moral stage movement.

Moral discussion and curriculum, however, constitute only one portion of the conditions stimulating moral growth. When we turn to analyzing the broader life environment, we turn to a consideration of the *moral atmosphere* of the home, the school, and the broader society. The first basic dimension of social atmosphere is the role-taking opportunities it provides, the extent to which it encourages the child to take the point of view of others. Role taking is related to the amount of social interaction and social communication in which the child engages, as well as to his sense of efficacy in influencing attitudes of others. The second dimension of social atmosphere, more strictly moral, is the level of justice of the environment or institution. The justice structure of an institution refers to the perceived rules or principles for distributing rewards, punishments, responsibilities, and privileges among institutional members. This structure may exist or be perceived at any of our moral stages. As an example, a study of a traditional prison revealed that inmates perceived it as Stage 1, regardless of their own level.[20] Obedience to arbitrary command by power figures and punishment for disobedience were seen as the governing justice norms of the prison. A behavior-modification prison using point rewards for conformity was perceived as a Stage 2 system of instrumental exchange. Inmates at Stage 3 or 4 perceived this institution as more fair than the traditional prison, but not as fair in their own terms.

These and other studies suggest that a higher level of institutional justice is a condition for individual development of a higher sense of justice. Working on these premises, Joseph Hickey, Peter Scharf, and I worked with guards and inmates in a women's prison to create a more just community.[21] A social contract was set up in which guards and inmates each had a vote of one and in which rules were made and conflicts resolved through discussions of fairness and a democratic vote in a community meeting. The program has been operating four years and has stimulated moral stage advance in inmates, though it is still too early to draw conclusions as to its overall long-range effectiveness for rehabilitation.

One year ago, Fenton, Ralph Mosher, and I received a grant from the Danforth Foundation (with additional support from the Kennedy Foundation) to make moral education a living matter in two high schools in the Boston area (Cambridge and Brookline) and two in Pittsburgh. The plan had two components. The first was training counselors and social studies and English teachers in conducting moral discussions and making moral discussion an integral part of the curriculum. The second was establishing a just community school within a public high school.

We have stated the theory of the just community high school, postulating that discussing real-life moral situations and actions as issues of fairness and as matters for democratic decision would stimulate advance in both moral reasoning and moral action. A participatory democracy provides more extensive opportunities for role taking and a higher level of perceived institutional justice than does any other social arrangement. Most alternative schools strive to establish a democratic governance, but none we have observed has achieved a vital or viable participatory democracy. Our theory suggested reasons why we might succeed where others failed. First, we felt that democracy had to be a central commitment of a school, rather than a humanitarian frill. Democracy as moral education provides that commitment. Second, democracy in alternative schools often fails because it bores the students. Students prefer to let teachers make decisions about staff, courses, and schedules, rather than to attend lengthy, complicated meetings. Our theory said that the issues a democracy should focus on are issues of morality and fairness. Real issues concerning drugs, stealing, disruptions, and grading are never boring if handled as issues of fairness. Third, our theory told us that if large democratic community meetings were preceded by small-group moral discussion, higher-stage thinking by students would win out in later decisions, avoiding the disasters of mob rule.[22]

Currently, we can report that the school based on our theory makes democracy work or function where other schools have failed. It is too early to make any claims for its effectiveness in causing moral development, however.

Our Cambridge just community school within the public high school was started after a small summer planning session of volunteer teachers, students, and parents. At the time the school opened in the fall, only a commitment to democracy and a skeleton program of English and social studies had been decided on. The school started with six teachers from the regular school and sixty students, twenty from academic professional homes and twenty from working-class homes. The other twenty were dropouts and trouble-makers or petty delinquents in terms of previous record. The usual mistakes and usual chaos of a beginning alternative school ensued. Within a few weeks, however, a successful democratic community process had been established. Rules were made around pressing issues: disturbances, drugs, hooking. A student discipline committee or jury was formed. The resulting rules and enforcement have been relatively effective and reasonable. We do not see reasonable rules as ends in themselves, however, but as vehicles for moral discussion and an emerging sense of community. This sense of community and a resulting morale are perhaps the most immediate signs of success. This sense of community seems to lead to behavior change of a positive sort. An example is a fifteen-year-old student who started as one of the greatest combinations of humor, aggression, light-fingeredness, and hyperactivity I have ever known. From being the principal disturber of all community meetings, he has become an excellent community meeting participant and occasional chairman. He is still more ready to enforce rules for others than to observe them himself, yet his commitment to the school has led to a steady decrease in exotic behavior. In addition, he has become more involved in classes and projects and has begun to listen and ask questions in order to pursue a line of interest.

We attribute such behavior change not only to peer pressure and moral discussion but to the sense of community which has emerged from the democratic process in which angry conflicts are resolved through fairness and community decision. This sense of community is reflected in statements of the students to us that there are no cliques—that the blacks and the whites, the professors' sons and the project students, are friends. These statements are supported by observation. Such a sense of community is needed where stu-

dents in a given classroom range in reading level from fifth-grade to college.

Fenton, Mosher, the Cambridge and Brookline teachers, and I are now planning a four-year curriculum in English and social studies centering on moral discussion, on role taking and communication, and on relating the government, laws, and justice system of the school to that of the American society and other world societies. This will integrate an intellectual curriculum for a higher level of understanding of society with the experiential components of school democracy and moral decision.

There is very little new in this—or in anything else we are doing. Dewey wanted democratic experimental schools for moral and intellectual development seventy years ago. Perhaps Dewey's time has come.

NOTES

1. John Dewey, "What Psychology Can do for the Teacher," in Reginald Archambault, ed., *John Dewey on Education: Selected Writings* (New York: Random House, 1964).
2. These levels correspond roughly to our three major levels: the preconventional, the conventional, and the principled. Similar levels were propounded by William McDougall, Leonard Hobhouse, and James Mark Baldwin.
3. Jean Piaget, *The Moral Judgment of the Child,* 2nd ed. (Glencoe, Ill.: Free Press, 1948).
4. Piaget's stages correspond to our first three stages: Stage 0 (premoral), Stage 1 (heteronomous), and Stage 2 (instrumental reciprocity).
5. Lawrence Kohlberg, "Moral Stages and Moralization: The Cognitive-Developmental Approach," in Thomas Lickona, ed., *Man, Morality, and Society* (New York: Holt, Rinehart and Winston, in press).
6. James Rest, Elliott Turiel, and Lawrence Kohlberg, "Relations Between Level of Moral Judgment and Preference and Comprehension of the Moral Judgment of Others," *Journal of Personality,* vol. 37, 1969, pp. 225–52, and James Rest, "Comprehension, Preference, and Spontaneous Usage in Moral Judgment," in Lawrence

Kohlberg, ed., *Recent Research in Moral Development* (New York: Holt, Rinehart and Winston, in preparation).

7. Many adolescents and adults only partially attain the stage of formal operations. They do consider all the actual relations of one thing to another at the same time, but they do not consider all possibilities and form abstract hypotheses. A few do not advance this far, remaining "concrete operational."

8. Richard Krebs and Lawrence Kohlberg, "Moral Judgment and Ego Controls as Determinants of Resistance to Cheating," in Lawrence Kohlberg, ed., *Recent Research.*

9. John Rawls, *A Theory of Justice* (Cambridge, Mass.: Harvard University Press, 1971).

10. Not all freely chosen values or rules are principles, however. Hitler chose the "rule," "exterminate the enemies of the Aryan race," but such a rule is not a universalizable principle.

11. Rawls, *A Theory of Justice.*

12. Lawrence Kohlberg and Donald Elfenbein, "Development of Moral Reasoning and Attitudes Toward Capital Punishment," *American Journal of Orthopsychiatry,* Summer, 1975.

13. Hugh Hartshorne and Mark May, *Studies in the Nature of Character: Studies in Deceit,* vol. 1; *Studies in Service and Self-Control,* vol. 2; *Studies in Organization of Character,* vol. 3 (New York: Macmillan, 1928–30).

14. As an example of the "hidden curriculum," we may cite a second-grade classroom. My son came home from this classroom one day saying he did not want to be "one of the bad boys." Asked "Who are the bad boys?" he replied, "The ones who don't put their books back and get yelled at."

15. Restriction of deliberate value education to the moral may be clarified by our example of the second-grade teacher who made tidying up of books a matter of moral indoctrination. Tidiness is a value, but it is not a moral value. Cheating is a moral issue, intrinsically one of fairness. It involves issues of violation of trust and taking advantage. Failing to tidy the room may under certain conditions be an issue of fairness, when it puts an undue burden on others. If it is handled by the teacher as a matter of cooperation among the group in this sense, it is a legitimate focus of deliberate moral education. If it is not, it simply represents the arbitrary imposition of the teacher's values on the child.

16. The differential action of the principled subjects was determined by two things. First, they were more likely to judge it right to violate authority by sitting in. But second, they were also in general more consistent in engaging in political action according to their judgment. Ninety percent of all Stage 6 subjects thought it right to sit in, and all 90 percent lived up to this belief. Among the Stage 4 subjects, 45 percent thought it right to sit in, but only 33 percent lived up to this belief by acting.

17. No public or private word or deed of Nixon ever rose above Stage 4, the "law and order" stage. His last comments in the White House were of wonderment that the Republican Congress could turn on him after so many Stage 2 exchanges of favors in getting them elected.

18. Bindu Parilch, "A Cross-Cultural Study of Parent-child Moral Judgment," unpublished doctoral dissertation, Harvard University, 1975.

19. Moshe Blatt and Lawrence Kohlberg, "Effects of Classroom Discussions upon Children's Level of Moral Judgment," in Lawrence Kohlberg, ed., *Recent Research.*

20. Lawrence Kohlberg, Peter Scharf, and Joseph Hickey, "The Justice Structure of the Prison: A Theory and an Intervention," *The Prison Journal,* Autumn-Winter, 1972.

21. Lawrence Kohlberg, Kelsey Kauffman, Peter Scharf, and Joseph Hickey, *The Just Community Approach to Corrections: A Manual, Part I* (Cambridge, Mass.: Education Research Foundation, 1973).

22. An example of the need for small-group discussion comes from an alternative school community meeting called because a pair of the students had stolen the school's video-recorder. The resulting majority decision was that the school should buy back the recorder from the culprits through a fence. The teachers could not accept this decision and returned to a more authoritative approach. I believe if the moral reasoning of students urging this solution had been confronted by students at a higher stage, a different decision would have emerged.

Lawrence Kohlberg was Professor of Education and Psychology and Director, Center for Moral Education, Graduate School of Education, Harvard University.

QUESTIONS FOR REFLECTION

1.   Are there universal moral values that educators, parents, and community members—regardless of philosophical, political, or religious beliefs—would include in the school curriculum? What are these values?
2.   What does Kohlberg mean when he makes a distinction between the *structures* of moral judgment and the *content* of moral judgment? Give an example of a moral dilemma to illustrate this point.
3.   What is the relationship between moral *judgment* and moral *action?* What factors determine whether an individual's moral judgment will be translated into moral action?

Woman's Place in Man's Life Cycle

CAROL GILLIGAN

ABSTRACT: Arguing that Kohlberg's model of moral reasoning is based on a male perspective and addresses the rights of the individual, Gilligan suggests that moral reasoning from a female perspective stresses the individual's responsibility to other people. Life-cycle theories, she concludes, should encompass the experiences of both sexes.

. . . Relationships, and particularly issues of dependency, are experienced differently by women and men. For boys and men, separation and individuation are critically tied to gender identity since separation from the mother is essential for the development of masculinity. For girls and women, issues of femininity or feminine identity do not depend on the achievement of separation from the mother or on the progress of individuation. Since masculinity is defined through separation while femininity is defined through attachment, male gender identity is threatened by intimacy while female gender identity is threatened by separation. Thus males tend to have difficulty with relationships, while females tend to have problems with individuation. The quality of embeddedness in social interaction and personal relationships that characterizes women's lives in contrast to men's, however, becomes not only a descriptive difference but also a developmental liability when the milestones of childhood and adolescent development in the psychological literature are markers of increasing separation. Women's failure to separate then becomes by definition a failure to develop.

When one begins with the study of women and derives developmental constructs from their lives, the outline of a moral conception different from that described by Freud, Piaget, or Kohlberg begins to emerge and informs a different description of development. In this conception, the moral problem arises from conflicting responsibilities rather than from competing rights and requires for its resolution a mode of thinking that is contextual and narrative rather than formal and abstract. This conception of morality as concerned with the activity of care centers moral development around the understanding of responsibility and relationships, just as the conception of morality as fairness ties moral development to the understanding of rights and rules.

This different construction of the moral problem by women may be seen as the critical reason for their failure to develop within the constraints of Kohlberg's system. Regarding all constructions of responsibility as evidence of a conventional moral understanding, Kohlberg defines the highest stages of moral development as deriving from a reflective understanding of human rights. That the morality of rights differs from the morality of responsibility in its emphasis on separation rather than connection, in its consideration of the individual rather than the relationship as primary, is illustrated by two responses to interview questions about the nature of morality. The first comes from a twenty-five-year-old man, one of the participants in Kohlberg's study:

> [*What does the word morality mean to you?*] Nobody in the world knows the answer. I think it is recognizing the right of the individual, the rights of other individuals, not interfering with those rights. Act as fairly as you would have them treat you. I think it is basically to preserve the human being's right to existence. I think that is the most important. Secondly, the human being's right to do as he pleases, again without interfering with somebody else's rights.
>
> [*How have your views on morality changed since the last interview?*] I think I am more aware of an individual's rights now. I used to be looking at it strictly from my point of view, just for me. Now I think I am more aware of what the individual has a right to.

Kohlberg (1973) cites this man's response as illustrative of the principled conception of human rights that exemplifies his fifth and sixth stages. Commenting on the response, Kohlberg says: "Moving to a perspective outside of that of his society, he identifies morality with justice (fairness, rights, the Golden Rule), with recognition of the rights of others as these are defined naturally or intrinsically. The human being's right to do as he pleases without interfering with somebody else's rights is a formula defining rights prior to social legislation" (pp. 29–30).

The second response comes from a woman who participated in the rights and responsibilities study. She also was twenty-five and, at the time, a third-year law student:

> [*Is there really some correct solution to moral problems, or is everybody's opinion equally right?*] No, I don't think everybody's opinion is equally right. I think that in some situations there may be opinions that are equally valid, and one could conscientiously adopt one of several courses of action. But there are other situations in which I think there are right and wrong answers, that sort of inhere in the nature of existence, of all individuals here who need to live with each other to live. We need to depend on each other, and hopefully it is not only a physical need but a need of fulfillment in ourselves, that a person's life is enriched by cooperating with other people and striving to live in harmony with everybody else, and to that end, there are right and wrong, there are things which promote that end and that move away from it, and in that way it is possible to choose in certain cases among different courses of action that obviously promote or harm that goal.
>
> [*Is there a time in the past when you would have thought about these things differently?*] Oh, yeah, I think that I went through a time when I thought that things were pretty relative, that I can't tell you what to do and you can't tell me what to do, because you've got your conscience and I've got mine.
>
> [*When was that?*] When I was in high school. I guess that it just sort of dawned on me that my own ideas changed, and because my own judgment changed, I felt I couldn't judge another person's judgment. But now I think even when it is only the person himself who is going to be affected I say it is wrong to the extent it doesn't cohere with what I know about human nature and what I know about you, and just from what I think is true about the operation of the universe, I could say I think you are making a mistake.
>
> [*What led you to change, do you think?*] Just seeing more of life, just recognizing that there are an awful lot of things that are common among people. There are certain things that you come to learn promote a better life and better relationships and more personal fulfillment than other things that in general tend to do the opposite, and the things that promote these things, you would call morally right.

This response also represents a personal reconstruction of morality following a period of questioning and doubt, but the reconstruction of moral understanding is based not on the primacy and universality of individual rights, but rather on what she describes as a "very strong sense of being responsible to the world." Within this construction, the moral dilemma changes from how to exercise one's rights without interfering with the rights of others to how "to lead a moral life which includes obligations to myself and my family and people in general." The problem then becomes one of limiting responsibilities without abandoning moral concern. When asked to describe herself, this woman says that she values "having other people that I am tied to, and also having people that I am responsible to. I have a very strong sense of being responsible to the world, that I can't just live for my enjoyment, but just the fact of being in the world gives me an obligation to do what I can to make the world a better place to live in, no matter how small a scale that may be on." Thus while Kohlberg's subject worries about people interfering with each other's rights, this woman worries about "the possibility of omission, of your not helping others when you could help them."

The issue that this woman raises is addressed by Jane Loevinger's fifth "autonomous" stage of ego development, where autonomy, placed in a context of relationships, is defined as modulating an excessive sense of responsibility through the recognition that other people have responsibility for their own destiny. The autonomous stage in Loevinger's account (1970) witnesses a relinquishing of moral dichotomies and their replacement with "a feeling for the complexity and multifaceted character of real people and real situations" (p. 6). Whereas the rights conception of morality that informs Kohlberg's principled level (stages five and six) is geared to arriving at an objectively fair or just resolution to moral dilemmas upon which all rational persons could agree, the responsibility conception focuses instead on the limitations of any particular resolution and describes the conflicts that remain.

Thus it becomes clear why a morality of rights and noninterference may appear frightening to women in its potential justification of indifference and unconcern. At the same time, it becomes clear why, from a male perspective, a morality of responsibility appears inconclusive and diffuse, given its insistent contextual relativism. Women's moral judgments thus elucidate the pattern observed in the description of the developmental differences between the sexes, but they also provide an alternative conception of maturity by which these differences can be assessed and their implications traced. The psychology of women that has consistently been described as distinctive in its greater orientation toward relationships and interdependence implies a more contextual mode of judgment and a different moral understanding. Given the differences in women's conceptions of self and morality, women bring to the life cycle a different point of view and order human experience in terms of different priorities.

The myth of Demeter and Persephone, which McClelland (1975) cites as exemplifying the feminine attitude toward power, was associated with the Eleusinian Mysteries celebrated in ancient Greece for over two thousand years. As told in the Homeric *Hymn to Demeter,* the story of Persephone indicates the strengths of interdependence, building up resources and giving, that McClelland found in his research on power motivation to characterize the mature feminine style. Although, McClelland says, "it is fashionable to conclude that no one knows what went on in the Mysteries, it is known that they were probably the most important religious ceremonies, even partly on the historical record, which were organized by and for women, especially at the onset before men by means of the cult of Dionysos began to take them over." Thus McClelland regards the myth as "a special presentation of feminine psychology" (p. 96). It is, as well, a life-cycle story par excellence.

Persephone, the daughter of Demeter, while playing in a meadow with her girlfriends, sees a beautiful narcissus which she runs to pick. As she does so, the earth opens and she is snatched away by Hades, who takes her to his underworld kingdom. Demeter, goddess of the earth, so mourns the loss of her daughter that she refuses to allow anything to grow. The crops that sustain life on earth shrivel up, killing men and animals alike, until Zeus takes pity on man's suffering and persuades his brother to return Persephone to her mother. But before she leaves, Persephone eats some pomegranate seeds, which ensures that she will spend part of every year with Hades in the underworld.

The elusive mystery of women's development lies in its recognition of the continuing importance of attachment in the human life cycle. Woman's place in man's life cycle is to protect this recognition while the developmental litany intones the celebration of separation, autonomy, individuation, and natural rights. The myth of Persephone speaks directly to the distortion in this view by reminding us that narcissism leads to death, that the fertility of the earth is in some mysterious way tied to the continuation of the mother-daughter relationship, and that the life

cycle itself arises from an alternation between the world of women and that of men. Only when life-cycle theorists divide their attention and begin to live with women as they have lived with men will their vision encompass the experience of both sexes and their theories become correspondingly more fertile.

REFERENCES

Kohlberg, L. (1973). "Continuities and Discontinuities in Childhood and Adult Moral Development Revisited." In *Collected Papers on Moral Development and Moral Education*. Moral Education Research Foundation, Harvard University.

Lovinger, J., and Wessler, R. (1970). *Measuring Ego Development*. San Francisco: Jossey-Bass.

McClelland, D. C. (1975). *Power: The Inner Experience*. New York: Irvington.

Carol Gilligan is Professor at New York Univesity and Professor in the Human Development and Psychology Program at the Graduate School of Education, Harvard University.

QUESTIONS FOR REFLECTION

1. What does the word *morality* mean to you? With whose view of morality is your answer most congruent—Kohlberg's or Gilligan's?
2. Do you agree with Gilligan's statement that "masculinity is defined through separation while femininity is defined through attachment, [and] male gender identity is threatened by intimacy while female gender identity is threatened by separation"? According to Gilligan, how are these gender differences reflected in moral reasoning?
3. What are the implications for the curriculum of Gilligan's view of male and female moral reasoning?

Organize Schools around Child Development

JAMES P. COMER

ABSTRACT: Drawing from the principles of child development, Comer describes an approach to school reform (now called the School Development Program) that provides children with the support and role models they need. Through a team approach involving a Governance and Management Team (now called the School Planning and Management Team), a Mental Health Team (now called the Student and Staff Support Team), and the Parents Program (now called the Parent Team), schools are restructured to meet students' developmental needs in the social-interactive, psycho-emotional, moral, linguistic, and intellectual-cognitive areas.

When you don't have a map—or some other way of setting direction—trying to go from New York to Los Angeles by way of Paris is not unreasonable. Americans have been pursuing school improvement in this way—without a conceptual map, without an organizing, direction-giving theme. That's why everything from establishing standards to restructuring to school choice appears to be a reasonable way to improve schools to one group or another.

There is an obvious point of focus for any organizing theme—students—how they grow and learn and, in turn, how policies must be established and resources deployed to promote development and learning. There is abundant evidence that young people learn at an adequate to optimal level when they are able to meet their developmental needs—with support for growth in social-interactive, psycho-emotional, moral, linguistic, and intellectual-cognitive areas. But neither our traditional educational approaches nor our school reform efforts of the past decade has focused adequately on child development.

Many teachers know very little about child development and even less about how to promote it. Until very recently, the pre- and in-service education of teachers largely ignored development; even now, the subject is not taught in a way that prepares teachers to support the development of students in school. Most schools are not organized and managed in a way that facilitates child development. Only recently and grudgingly has it been acknowledged that parents can play a direct role in schooling; and even now, the emphasis is on increasing their power to promote accountability rather than on enabling them to collaborate with the school staff in promoting the development of their children. Most curricula are not informed by an understanding of child development, and education policy often is not made by people with expertise in child development.

Based on our Yale Child Study Center-New Haven School System intervention, I believe school-reform efforts should focus on and be guided by child development principles. The program started in 1968, when a four-person Yale Child Study Center team went into two elementary schools in New Haven that were at the bottom in achievement, attendance, and behavior of the 33 elementary schools in the city. The students were nearly without exception Black, and almost all were from poor families.

In the beginning, our staff had no way to understand the problems of our students that often were manifested in fighting, disrespectful attitudes towards teachers, an inability to concentrate and take in information when it was important to do so, an inability to be spontaneous and curious when it was important, and to get along well with other students. Staff members often viewed the students as bad or not smart, not interested, and not motivated. Their response—consistent with our cultural norms—was to attempt to punish and control them, and to have low academic expectations for them. And even when staff members wanted to be supportive or better respond to the needs of students, the hierarchical and authoritarian organization and management of the school would not permit it. Teachers were expected to teach and control the children, or refer them to the principal or professional support staff when there was a problem.

In working with the schools, we eventually came to understand the difficult interactions in school to be a result of underdevelopment of children from families under economic and social stress, the punitive and controlling response of teachers that made matters worse, and an organization and management that did not allow the staff to respond in a supportive way. In a chaotic environment, children cannot adequately imitate, identify with, and internalize the attitudes and values of adult caretakers in the way needed to gain the confidence and personal discipline necessary for academic learning.

Our solution was to create a Governance and Management Team representative of all the adult stakeholders in the school—parents, teachers, administrators, and non-professional support staff. The Governance Team enabled parents and staff together to identify problems and opportunities, and to develop strategies and direction for the school, thus gradually decreasing the apathy and chaos, alienation and anger, hopelessness and despair. It was school-based management. But because we were more interested in creating a sense of community in the school, we didn't call it that. Order, control, and accountability eventually increased, largely due to the work of an effective Governance and Management Team—but even more because the team helped to create a school climate that supported student development and a growth in school effectiveness rather than through a use of rules, regulations, and power.

Our focus on creating a good climate for children led to the creation of a Mental Health Team and a Parents Program. In traditional schools, social workers, psychologists, special education teachers, and other support staff work individually in a way that leads to fragmentation and duplication—expensive and ineffective. By working as a team, our support staff coordinated their efforts, but more importantly, they were able to share systematically their knowledge of child development and relationship skills with other staff and parents. This enabled all the school staff—not just the support staff—to begin to support

development rather than simply punish children. The parent program enabled the parents to work with the school staff to create a good social climate in the school.

As we assessed what was going on in our program, we realized that we were giving low-income children the social skills that many middle-class children gained simply by growing up in families engaged in activities utilizing skills that prepared them to meet the expectations of school. We reasoned that our improved social climate in school could accomplish the same thing if we made the effort more systematic. Out of this developed a program called "A Social Skills Curriculum for Inner-City Children."

By 1984, the two project schools we were working with were among the top five in attendance, achievement, and behavior (one of the initial schools was replaced with another with a similar profile in the course of the study). Using the same principles, we are now involved with more than 165 schools in 17 school districts across the country; many are showing improvement, and in several instances there have been dramatic gains—40 to 60 percentile points—measured on nationally standardized achievement tests.

We have seen a large number of school-reform initiatives in this country that have been minimally successful, failed, or are destined to fail because they do not adequately address the developmental issues that should be central to any reform. Many educators have in mind a vaguely industrial model for teaching and learning: students as raw material, staff as assembly-line workers functioning more or less independently of each other. Our work—and that of many others—shows that this system of schooling prevents many capable staff, parents, and students from functioning adequately.

The decision we must now make about how to improve education is similar to the one manufacturers were faced with after World War II. American manufacturers chose to stick with the principles advanced by Frederick Taylor tied to mechanistic, assembly-line mass production. Japanese manufacturers were guided by the principles of William Demming, which were people-centered and recognized the interrelatedness of areas of work and the need for continuous quality control, and to change, adapt, and find appropriate ways to do a job rather than be locked into a rigid system. A half-century later, American manufacturing is on the ropes and Japanese manufacturing is thriving. If American education is to thrive, it must be guided by a people-centered—in this case, child-development—approach.

James P. Comer is the Maurice Falk Professor of Child Psychiatry at the Yale University Child Study Center, Associate Dean of the Yale University School of Medicine, and Director of the School Development Program.

QUESTIONS FOR REFLECTION

1.   Comer states that "most curricula are not informed by an understanding of child development." What do you think might account for the fact that this important basis of the curriculum is often overlooked?
2.   What objections might some teachers, parents, and community members raise about Comer's approach to school reform? As an educational leader, how would you respond to these objections?
3.   What evidence can you cite to support Comer's contention that "many educators have in mind a vaguely industrial model for teaching and learning"? How is this model reflected in school curricula?

Waldorf Schools: Education for the Head, Hands, and Heart

CHRISTOPHER BAMFORD
ERIC UTNE

ABSTRACT: The authors provide a worldwide vision of how the innovative alternative Waldorf School System has come about, which is part of the vision for a better human condition created by the social vision of Rudolf Steiner. Steiner's vision of a better human future has been played out in many different fields of human endeavor, education being one of them.

Beginning at the end of the 19th century, a relatively unknown Austrian philosopher and teacher began to sow the seeds of what he hoped would blossom into a new culture. The seeds were his ideas, which he sowed through extensive writings, lectures, and countless private consultations. The seeds germinated and took root in the hearts and minds of his students, among whom were individuals who would later become some of the best known and most influential figures of the 20th century. Since the teacher's death in 1925, a quiet but steadily growing movement, unknown and unseen by most people, has been spreading over the world, bringing practical solutions to the problems of our global, technological civilization. The seeds are now coming to flower in the form of thousands of projects infused with human values. The teacher, called by some "the best kept secret of the 20th century," was Rudolf Steiner.

Steiner, a truly "Renaissance man," developed a way of thinking that he applied to different aspects of what it means to be human. Over a period of 40 years, he formulated and taught a path of inner development or spiritual research he called "anthroposophy." From what he learned, he gave practical indications for nearly every field of human endeavor. Art, architecture, drama, science, medicine, economics, religion, care of the dying, social organization—there is almost no field he did not touch.

Today, wherever there is a human need you'll find groups of people working out of Steiner's ideas. There are an estimated ten thousand initiatives worldwide—the movement is a hotbed of entrepreneurial activity, social and political activism, artistic expression, scientific research, and community building. In this report we limit our investigation to a tiny, representative sampling of these initiatives, primarily from North America.

Waldorf education is probably the most widespread and mature of Steiner's many plantings. There are more than 150 Waldorf schools in North America and over 900 worldwide, double the number just a decade ago, making it possibly the fastest growing educational movement in the world. Steiner's interest in education was lifelong. As a young man, he earned a living as a tutor, starting at 14 helping fellow students. Then, from the age of 23 to 29, he lived in Vienna with the family of Ladislaus and Pauline Specht, undertaking the education of their four sons, one of whom, Otto, was hydrocephalic. At the age of 10, Otto could hardly read or write. His parents were uncertain whether he could be educated at all. Steiner took responsibility for him. Believing that, despite appearances, the boy had great intellectual capacities, Steiner saw his task as slowly waking the boy up and bringing him into his body. To do this, he knew he first had to gain the child's love. On this basis, he was able to awaken his dormant faculties. He was so successful that Otto went on to become a doctor.

For Steiner, Otto was a learning experience. As he says in his *Autobiography:* "The educational methods I had to adopt gave me insight into the way that the human soul and spirit are connected with the body. It became my training in physiology and psychology. I came to realize that education and teaching must become an art, and must be based upon true knowledge of the human being."

As with everything Steiner did, his curriculum for Waldorf education began with a question. In 1919, in the chaos following the First World War, Emil Molt, director of the Waldorf Astoria Cigarette Company, asked Steiner to help with the creation of a school for his workers. Four months later, the first Independent Waldorf School opened in Stuttgart, Germany. From that spontaneous beginning arose the now worldwide Waldorf School Movement.

WALDORF EDUCATION: IT'S ALL IN THE CURRICULUM

Whenever he visited a Waldorf school, Rudolf Steiner's first question to the students was always, "Do you love your teacher?" Similarly, he would ask the teachers, "Do you love your students?" The class teacher accompanies the children from first grade through eighth grade, i.e., from childhood into the beginning of adolescence. Children and teacher grow together. Making and doing, creating beauty, and working with one's hands—knitting, crocheting, painting, drawing, and woodworking—are an integral part of the educational and developmental process. Besides teaching manual dexterity and training eye-hand coordination, the work with color, form, and different materials develops an aesthetic sense, which permeates all other activities. Coordinated physical movement, learning through the body, accompanies all stages of development. The practice of Eurythmy—Steiner's art of movement, which makes speech and music visible through action and gesture—allows the child to develop a sense of harmony and balance. Rhythm is an important component of all these activities. Rhythm (order or pattern in time) permeates the entire school day, as well as the school year, which unfolds around celebrating festivals drawn from different religions and cultures.

The curriculum is based upon an understanding of the developing child. From birth through ages six or seven, children absorb the world through their senses and respond primarily through imitation. As they enter the primary school years, they are centered more in feeling and imagination. Then, as they continue their journey into the middle school, rational, abstract thinking begins to emerge. The curriculum respects this developmental process and gives it substance. Based on the idea that "ontogeny recapitulates phylogeny," that a developing child goes through the phases of human cultural evolution, children at different ages study what is appropriate to their development. Thus they learn reading by first "becoming" the letters, through physical gesture. In their "main lesson" books that are their textbooks, crayoned pictures of mountains and trees metamorphose into the letters M and T, and form drawings of circles and polygons become numbers.

Movement, music, and language (including foreign languages) begin in first grade. They hear fables and stories of the holy ones of different cultures. They learn to knit and crochet and play the recorder. Leaving the "paradise" of the first two grades, they encounter the sacred teachings of their culture. For example, in North America, the stories of the Old Testament are taught. In Japan, ancient Shinto stories are told. Farming, gardening, house building, measurement, and grammar now enter the curriculum. They memorize poems and begin to play stringed instruments. With the fourth grade comes mythology, embroidery, zoology, geography, and geometric drawing. Mathematics and languages become more complex; art becomes more representational. In the fifth grade, history enters; they recite poems, begin botany, learn to knit with four needles, and start woodworking. And thus it continues, each grade providing more wonders.

Rather than pursuing several subjects at a time, the Waldorf curriculum unfolds in main lesson blocks of three or four weeks. The students create their own texts, or "main lesson books" for each subject. This enables students to live deeply into the subject. In this age of distraction, Waldorf children learn to be able to concentrate and focus.

With high school, the mood changes in harmony with the tremendous developmental changes occurring at this time. Students no longer have a class teacher, but specialists in different fields who teach the various blocks and encourage dialog and discussion. Exact observation and reflection are prized. The aim is to engage students in the present and build on the confidence and ability to think for oneself that developed in the lower grades.

AN EXAMPLE: THE GREEN MEADOW WALDORF SCHOOL

The Green Meadow Waldorf School in Spring Valley, New York, founded in 1950, is one of the oldest Waldorf schools in North America. As you approach the wooded suburban enclave you realize that this is a different kind of school. The several buildings are clustered around a courtyard, forming a little campus, which in turn is surrounded by mature oaks and white ash. Gardens, large climbing logs and stones, and sculpture abound. Each building has its own character and form, yet the entire assemblage works as a whole. The colors are warm and natural, not bright. There's no graffiti. The roofs are shingled and gently sloped. Many of the walls are set at softer, more oblique angles. Even many of the windows have their rectangular shapes softened with another edge, making them five- or six-sided instead of just four-sided.

There is something peaceful in the air. The impression intensifies as you enter. Warmth pervades the space. Your senses begin to dance. Beauty, color, and natural flowing forms surround you. Children's paintings adorn the walls. Muffled sounds filter through the classroom walls and doors as you walk down a corridor. You can hear musical instruments, singing, children reciting a poem, the calm voice of a class teacher. And the smells! Bread baking in the kindergarten, fragrant plants and nontoxic paints.

When you enter a classroom, the impression is confirmed—this is what a school ought to be. The children are happy, they are learning, they seem to love their teachers and each other.

The Green Meadow School is home to a veritable United Nations of religious diversity. Of the 388 students (K–12) in Green Meadow, more than 60 are of Jewish descent, approximately 25 are the children of members of the nearby Jerrahi Islamic Mosque, and the rest come from Protestant, Catholic, Buddhist, agnostic, atheistic, and who-knows-what other religious traditions. Waldorf schools are sometimes assumed to be Eurocentric because of their European origins, yet the curriculum turns out to have universal appeal, adapting well in cultures as diverse as the *favelas* (slums) of Sao Paolo, Brazil, the black settlements of South Africa, rural Egypt and urban Israel, Eastern Europe, India, Southeast Asia, Australia, Japan, and the Pine Ridge Lakota Indian reservation in South Dakota.

From our own observations, Waldorf students seem to share certain common characteristics. They are often independent and self-confident self-starters. They have genuine optimism for the future. They also tend to be highly ethical and are compassionately intelligent. They keep their sense of wonder about learning and the interdisciplinary sense that everything is connected. They seem to have a very healthy measure of what author Daniel Goleman calls "emotional intelligence," a much more reliable predictor of "success" in life, by any definition, than IQ or SAT scores. Generally speaking, they are both artistic and practical. They seem to know intuitively how to do many things.

Waldorf grad Paul Asaro, an architect, says: "I still draw upon the problem-solving skills that were nurtured . . . during my adolescent years." Other graduates stress independent thinking, imagination, and the relationships they developed and enjoyed with faculty and fellow students. "That's what's so wonderful about Waldorf education," says actress Julianna Margulies. "You're exposed to all these different ideas, but you're never given one view of it. You're encouraged to think as an individual."

Rachel Blackmer, a veterinarian, writes: "Waldorf education is learning in its purest form. It is learning to think, to feel, and to act appropriately and with conscience." Mosemare Boyd, president and CEO, American Women Presidents, adds: "At Waldorf, we were taught to see things from the perspective of others. We saw that doing things together . . . was always more fun. . . . We learned to love learning."

EARLY CHILDHOOD INITIATIVES

The Waldorf approach to education is not limited to school-age kids. Recent students have pointed repeatedly to the critical importance of the nurturing children receive in early childhood, when infants and children are especially at risk. The combination of the breakdown of the family, the need for two working parents, and the growing number of single-parent families has left caregivers, whether at home or in daycare, uncertain how to care for children. Activities that were once natural and instinctive, like what to eat and how to bring up a baby, must now be learned consciously.

"Children," says Cynthia Aldinger, "are like sponges. They drink in everything and everyone around them." It is not only a question of the physical surroundings. What we say and do around a child, even how we think, is critical. A grassroots organization growing out of the Waldorf Early Childhood Association, Life Ways is devoted to the deinstitutionalization of child care. Founded in 1998, Life Ways provides courses and training in parenting and child care and is expanding to establish child care homes, centers, and parenting programs throughout North America.

A related effort is Sophia's Hearth in Keene, New Hampshire. Taking its name from the ancient goddess of wisdom, Sophia's Hearth works with "the art of becoming a family." As founder Susan Weber puts it, "Our work supports families in creating an atmosphere of loving warmth, joy, and respect for their infants and young children, while at the same time nurturing each parent."

The Caldwell Early Life Center at Rudolf Steiner College acts as a center for these and similar initiatives. Only two years old, but with a prestigious advisory board including naturalist Jane Goodall, well-known authors and researchers Jane Healy and Joseph Chilton Pearce, and education and child advocate Sally Bickford, it is halfway through raising the $2.5 million needed to complete a building to house its activities. These will cover the full range of early childhood needs, from working to reduce stress and isolation for families in ethnically and economically diverse neighborhoods to the creation of a demonstration daycare component.

Christopher Bamford is the editor in chief of SteinerBooks and its imprint, Lindisfarne Books. *Eric Utne* founded *Utne Magazine* in 1984. Bamford and Utne co-wrote *An Emerging Culture: Rudolf Steiner's Continuing Impact in the World* (Utne Reader, © 2003).

QUESTIONS FOR REFLECTION

1. What is Rudolf Steiner's vision of a better human future and how might a more "mainstream" curriculum benefit from the characteristics at the center of his philosophy?

2. Is spirituality key to successful education? How might the core tenets of spirituality be covered in the classroom in a manner that would allow for religious difference and tolerance?

3. What is at the center of the Waldorf curriculum? How is it structured and what are its main learning goals? How is it different than the education you received and would you have preferred this method? Why or why not? What are limitations in the Waldorf curriculum?

TEACHERS' VOICES—
Putting Theory Into Practice

A First-Year Teacher Tells It All
MOLLY NESS

ABSTRACT: Molly Ness reflects on the lessons she has learned as a first year teacher placed in an overcrowded, under-funded Oakland, CA school by Americorps' Teach For America program. She relates her realization that the difficult challenge of teaching these children was easier than being in the children's own situations, living in poverty and urban chaos.

Upon graduating from college, I joined Teach For America and committed the next two years of my life to teaching in one of the nation's most under-resourced school districts.

Part of the Americorps service program, Teach For America has a clear mission: to give every child—regardless of race, ethnicity, background, or religion—the opportunity to attain an excellent education. Founded 10 years ago, Teach For America places more than 800 college graduates every year in the nation's 12 most impoverished school districts: in urban areas—such as Baltimore, Los Angeles, the Bay Area, and New York—and in rural areas, such as the Mississippi Delta and the Rio Grande Valley.

Corps members fill vacancies in districts that suffer from teacher shortages, most often taking the most challenging placements in the most difficult schools. In an intensive five-week training program before taking up placements, corps members focus on theories of education, holding children to high expectations, practical ways of becoming an effective teacher, and leveling the playing field for students in an effort to provide them with the educational opportunities that children from better backgrounds have.

Corps members are hired directly by the school district, and many complete state credentialing programs during their two years of service. Upon the completion of their two-year commitment, over 60% of corps members continue teaching, while others change paths towards graduate school and the private sector.

I became a first-year teacher of sixth-graders at Roosevelt Middle School, in East Oakland, California. Roosevelt is an extremely overcrowded school, with an annual teacher retention rate of 60%. The student body is 50% Asian, 25% Latino, and 25% African-American. Located in a rough area notorious for drug use, gangs are an ever-present force.

My students are nonnative English speakers. They speak 10 languages, including Arabic, Cambodian, Spanish, Vietnamese, and Chinese. Many of my students are recent immigrants, and I am expected to teach them conversational and written English, as well as the state-mandated social studies curriculum.

HARSHER REALITY

Although I had been told before I began my Teach For America commitment that I was about to experience a harsher reality than anything I had previously known, I nonetheless believed that teaching was a 9-to-3 job, that I could leave my work at school and keep my personal and professional lives totally separate from one another.

I thought I could bring my students into my classroom, shut the door, and leave the problems of the inner-city community at the doorstep. I believed that I could instill the love of learning in my students, and somehow forget all the turmoil they faced in their lives outside school.

I vowed that the passion and enthusiasm I felt for the children who were my students and for teaching would never diminish. I would never allow myself to suffer emotionally, as many first-year teachers do. I would stay positive and avoid the disillusionment that so many teachers feel.

I would go into my classroom every day, with the same energy and passion which I had started with in September. It wouldn't matter if it was a gloomy Thursday afternoon in late October, or if I had been battling the flu for the previous two weeks.

I would never become a "worksheet teacher." Rather than slide grammar worksheets under the noses of my students, I would have them build the Pyramids out of sugar cubes. I set high expectations not only for my students, but for myself as well.

ENDLESS CHALLENGE

In one swift move, I had graduated from college, packed my belongings, and driven cross-country to start life anew in an entirely unfamiliar environment without the comforts of family, friends, and home. It was an exciting adventure at first—relocating, getting my first real job, and having the responsibilities of adult life. It was a whirlwind of adventure, embarking on a new chapter in my life.

But by early November, the excitement had worn off, and the reality had begun to sink in. I was in a new city, far away from my home, from my roots to my past. Maintaining a positive learning environment in an otherwise depressing place was an endless challenge—the constant planning, the discipline, the paperwork, the headaches of the district bureaucracy.

I felt under-appreciated by my school administration, and abused by my students. I would come home from school, sit on my couch, and think, "I can't go back tomorrow." I felt drained. And gradually, I felt as though I was letting my students down, as though nothing I was doing in my classroom would ever be enough to make life fair for them.

I was becoming the worksheet teacher that I swore I would never be. I felt as though I had lost myself in this process of trying to serve my students. And so I started asking the really hard questions, about myself, about my life, and about my commitment.

Often I feel that Teach For America is too eager to dismiss the frustrations that we teachers inevitably feel about our lives and our jobs. It sometimes seems as if I am just supposed to grin and bear it through two years, until finally I can reflect upon what has happened to me, and say, "That was an impossibly difficult experience, but I am a richer person because of it."

Given the passion and dedication of most corps members, it seems taboo to question your commitment to Teach For America and to your students, but in fact, I question my commitment nearly every day. I have a vivid memory of calling a friend in Los Angeles, also a 1999 corps member placed in Compton, to ask "Will you quit with me?"

At first, I thought that doubting my commitment made me a bad person, and that some omniscient Teach for America presence was frowning down upon me. But in fact, maybe all this questioning of my commitment is actually a positive force that makes me push to achieve more in my classroom.

When I went home for the winter break, I wasn't sure exactly what to tell my friends and family about my Teach For America experience thus far. Should I focus on the good or on the bad of teaching?

Should I tell them how I teach 97 students who speak little to no English? Should I tell them how there are never enough markers, or enough

scissors, or even enough textbooks to go around? Should I tell them about my 12-year-old student who is now serving time in juvenile hall for armed robbery? Or maybe I should tell them about my 13-year-old student who cannot spell "dog" because he is a victim of social promotion? I slowly realized that any platitudes I would provide would be trite, and simply untrue.

I could barely make sense of the sort of tension of opposites I felt in my life. Did I want to quit and get out, or did I want to devote all of my life and energy to the Teach for America vision? How should I characterize the way I felt—cynicism or optimism? Should I tell about the bad experiences, or dismiss them in light of the positive ones?

I began to reflect on my initial impressions of teaching. I remembered feeling overwhelmed upon first entering the classroom. Where did I even begin to teach these children English and social studies? More important, how could I teach them that education would be their way out of poverty and into successful and meaningful futures?

How could I teach them to be upstanding citizens and to practice civility in their everyday lives? How could I teach them conflict resolution, responsibility, and self-respect?

When I told my father about my worries, he told me, "Do your best. You have been handed an unrealistic situation. All that anybody can ask you to do is your best. Don't beat yourself up over what you cannot accomplish."

For a long time, I believed my father's advice—that I did have an unrealistic situation at Roosevelt Middle School. I believed it was unrealistic to think that a first-year teacher would be given such a difficult placement, in such an under-resourced school, with so little support.

TOO REALISTIC

But after a while, I realized that my father was wrong. It *was* realistic—and that was exactly the problem. Far too many of our nation's children go to over-crowded schools like mine that cannot provide adequate materials, instruction, or attention. Too many of our children will receive a sub-par education, seeming to warrant that a cycle of poverty will not soon be broken.

Too many teachers are thrown into their classrooms with meager tangible support. Teachers do not receive enough concrete incentives to make teaching a life-long profession. Our best teachers are often lost before they even start to achieve success in the classroom. It is no secret that teachers are overworked, underpaid, and underappreciated; I am living proof of that.

Upon completing my first year of teaching, I struggled to make sense of the lessons I had learned thus far. I truly believe that I have learned more about the world in a few months of teaching than I did in several semesters of college.

I have learned that children are unbelievably resilient. My students have been handed immea-surable challenges, and have tackled them with the courage, grace, and strength that some adults fail to demonstrate.

I have learned how to make personal sacrifices for the sake of a greater good. I have learned that many people in the world today would rather let school districts like Oakland be forgotten than try to solve their problems headfirst.

I have learned that it is rather easy to be idealistic in thoughts and words, but much harder to keep that idealism in actions and in everyday life. I have realized that not enough people in our society today devote their lives, their energy, and their souls to making this world a little better than they found it.

I have learned the meaning and value of humility. And lastly, I have learned that I am only one person, but my power as a teacher will extend further than I could have ever guessed.

Molly Ness, author of *Lessons to Learn: Voices from the Front Lines of Teach for America,* is currently a doctoral student of literacy education at the University of Virginia. She was a teacher with Teach for America in Oakland, California when she wrote this article.

QUESTIONS FOR REFLECTION

1. What do you think is the most valuable lesson Ness learned in her first year of teaching in Oakland? What might be her biggest regret?
2. Americorps' Teach For America program is known for placing inexperienced, young people in some of the most challenging teaching environments anywhere. Is this a good way to introduce future teachers to the profession? What are some of the potential drawbacks of this kind of practice? Likewise, what might be considered some of the strengths?
3. How might school districts be better structured to serve schools like Roosevelt Middle School without having to place such a burden on the classroom teacher? Is lack of adequate funding the main problem, or are there other societal issues at work?

LEARNING ACTIVITIES

Critical Thinking

1. With respect to a school, college, or university with which you are familiar, describe the curriculum as it relates to human development. To what extent are the theories of human development presented in this chapter reflected in the curriculum?

2. In *All Grown Up and No Place to Go: Teenagers in Crisis* (Addison-Wesley, 1998), David Elkind suggests that adolescents behave according to an "imaginary audience" (the belief that others are preoccupied with one's appearance and behavior) and the "personal fable" (the belief that one is immortal and not subject to the limitations that affect other human beings). How might the school curriculum help students to become more realistic in both of these areas?

3. In *Blackberry Winter: My Earlier Years* (Kodansha, 1995), noted anthropologist Margaret Mead expresses the view that the lack of a close relationship between grandparents and grandchildren in today's society is a serious loss to society and the child. She states that children need to grow up with three generations. Do you agree? Why? Will "adopt a grandparent" programs which many communities have implemented help this developmental need of children?

4. Studies by the Center on Organization and Restructuring of Schools at the University of Wisconsin-Madison have found that students at "successfully restructured" schools are more likely to conform to their school's expectations if they believe the school "cares" about students. Compare this finding with Ashley Montagu's statement in this chapter that the "greatest gift a teacher has to give a student is his or her love." How can teachers convey this attitude toward their students?

5. Piaget's theory of cognitive development has been criticized for having only four discrete stages tied to chronological age and for underestimating the cognitive abilities and competence of young children. To what extent do you agree with these criticisms? (For more information see Gelman, R., and Baillargeon, R. (1983). "A Review of Some Piagetian Concepts." In P. Mussen, ed., *Carmichael's Manual of Child Psychology, Vol. 3: Cognitive Development* (E. Markman and J. Flavel, volume eds.). New York: Wiley, 1983; Woolfolk, A. *Educational Psychology*, 6th Ed. Boston: Allyn and Bacon, 1995, pp. 44–46; and Lourenco, Orlando, and Machado, Armando. "In Defense of Piaget's Theory: A Reply to 10 Common Criticisms." *Psychological Review* 103 (January 1996): 143–164.).

6. What are some developmental challenges that today's children and youth must confront that were unknown or little known to their parents or grandparents?

Application Activities

1. Ask your instructor to invite a counselor from the K–12 or higher education levels to your class. Ask this individual to discuss the most frequent developmental

needs they encounter among students and to suggest ways that the curriculum can address those needs.

2.   The March 2003 issue of *Educational Leadership* is devoted to the theme of creating caring schools. Read the articles in this journal and make a list of learning experiences that, with appropriate modification, could be incorporated into the curriculum with which you are most familiar.

Field Experiences

1.   Visit a classroom at the level with which you are most familiar. What differences do you note among learners that are related to their stages of development? How might these differences affect their learning?
2.   At the level with which you are most familiar, interview a student and, if possible, observe his or her classroom behavior. Then write a brief case study that focuses on common developmental tasks of learners in that age group. As appropriate, make references to the articles on human development included in this chapter.

Internet Activities

1.   Go to the home page for James P. Comer's School Development Program and gather information on the structure and "operational expectations" of the three "teams" that make up the School Development Program.
2.   Visit a few of the following web sites for K–12 students and determine to what extent each site reflects the developmental needs of children and youth:

The Awesome Lists
Berit's Best Sites for Children
Canada's SchoolNet
KidLink
Kid's Web
Newton's Apple
Online Educator
Young Person's Guide to the Internet
Discovery Channel School

CHAPTER 4

Learning and Learning Styles

FOCUS QUESTIONS

1. What are the key principles of behavioral learning theories?
2. What role does socialization play in learning?
3. What are the key principles of cognitive learning theories?
4. What is the constructivist view of learning?
5. How do learning styles influence learning?
6. What are multiple intelligences?

The third basis of the curriculum is the nature of learning and learning styles. An understanding of how human beings learn is obviously of central importance for curriculum planners. Learning theorists and researchers have not arrived at a universally accepted, precise definition of *learning;* however, most agree that learning is a change in an individual's knowledge or behavior that results from experience (Mazur, 1997; Slavin, 2003; Woolfolk, 2005). It is generally acknowledged that there are two families of learning theories—*behavioral* and *cognitive*—and that many subgroups exist within these two families. At the very least, curriculum planners should understand the distinguishing features of each family, because each defines the curriculum differently, and each leads to or supports different instructional strategies. In addition, curricula and teaching practices are usually based on both families of theories to allow for the diverse needs of learners or different types of knowledge to be learned.

BEHAVIORAL LEARNING THEORIES

Behavioral learning theories emphasize observable changes in behavior that result from stimulus-response associations made by the learner. Thinking is part of a stimulus-response (S-R) sequence that begins and ends outside the individual learner, and learning is the product of design rather than accident. Learning is a conditioning process by which a person acquires a new response; and motivation is the urge to act, which results from a stimulus. Behavior is directed by stimuli from the environment, and a person selects one response instead of another because of the particular combination of prior conditioning and physiological drives operating at the moment of action. A person does not have to want to learn something in order to learn it. People can learn anything of which they are capable if they are willing to go through the pattern of activity necessary for conditioning to take place.

A major construct of S-R behavioral learning theories is the *rewarded response*. A response must be rewarded for learning to take place. What counts as a "reward" varies from learner to learner; although the reward must be important to the learner in some way. Rewards are often effective for certain types of learners: slow learners, those less prepared for the learning task, and those in need of step-by-step learning. Some teachers set up a system of rewards in their classrooms based on the concept of the rewarded response.

John B. Watson (1878–1958) and B. F. Skinner (1904–1990) are the two principal originators of behaviorist approaches to learning. Watson asserted that human behavior was the result of specific stimuli that elicited certain responses. Watson's view of learning was based partially on experiments conducted by Russian psychologist Ivan Pavlov (1849–1936), who noticed that a dog he was working with salivated shortly before he was given food. Pavlov discovered that by ringing a bell when food was given and repeating this several times, the sound of the bell alone (a conditioned stimulus) would make the dog salivate (a conditioned response). Watson believed that all learning conformed to the Pavlovian S-R model, which has become known as *classical* or *type S conditioning*.

Expanding on Watson's basic S-R model, Skinner developed a more comprehensive view of conditioning known as *operant* (or *type R*) *conditioning*. His model was based on the premise that satisfying responses are conditioned, unsatisfying ones are not; as he put it: "the things we call pleasant have an energizing or strengthening effect on our behaviour" (Skinner, 1972, p. 74).

Skinner believed that a "scientific" S-R approach to learning could serve humanitarian aims and help to create a better world. He maintained that notions about human free will based on an eighteenth-century political philosophy should not be allowed to interfere with the application of scientific methods to human affairs. In his novel *Walden Two* (1962), Skinner describes how a utopian society could be created through "behavioral engineering." By focusing on external conditions that shape and maintain human behavior, educators could turn their attention from ill-defined inner qualities and faculties to the observable and manipulable.

Social Learning Theories

While social learning theories reflect many of the principles of behavioral learning theories, they place greater emphasis on the influence of external cues on behavior and on how thinking influences action and vice versa. Social learning theories—which are widely endorsed by sociologists, anthropologists, and social psychologists—maintain that human beings have an unlimited capacity to learn. This capacity, however, *is* limited by social expectations and by constraints on behavior patterns that the immediate social environment considers appropriate. According to this view, the learning process is primarily social, and learning occurs through socialization. Socialization occurs in a variety of social settings, including the family, the peer group, the school, and the job, and it continues throughout life. According to Albert Bandura (1977, p. 12), the originator of social learning theory, "virtually all learning phenomena resulting from direct experience occur on a vicarious basis by observing other people's behavior and its consequences for them." Bandura's view of learning is often referred to as *modeling* or *observational learning*.

COGNITIVE LEARNING THEORIES

Cognitive learning theories focus on the mental processes people use as they acquire new knowledge and skills. Unlike behavioral learning theories which focus on observable behavior, cognitive theories focus on the unobservable processing, storage, and retrieval of information from the brain. According to cognitive learning theories, the individual acts, originates, and thinks, and this is the important source of learning; according to behavioral learning theory, however, the individual learns by reacting to external forces.

Cognitive learning theories emphasize personal meaning, generalizations, principles, advance organizers, discovery learning, coding, and superordinate categories. In "Structures in Learning" in Chapter 6, Jerome Bruner, a leading cognitive learning theorist, applies generalizations concerning the following to curriculum planning: structure, organization, discovery learning, the "connectedness" of knowledge, meaningfulness, and the "problems approach."

Cognitive views of learning provide the theoretical basis for current approaches to "authentic" pedagogy and assessment of learning. As M. Bruce King, Jennifer Schroeder, and David Chawszczewski point out in "Authentic Assessment and Student Performance in Inclusive Secondary Schools" in this chapter: "teaching and learning of high intellectual quality and teaching for understanding offer compelling alternatives to more traditional forms of instruction focused on basic skills and content." Moreover, such approaches increase the learning of students with and without disabilities. Similarly, Kathie F. Nunley calls for a "Layered Curriculum" that integrates three keys of learning: choice, accountability, and complex thinking (see "Giving Credit Where Credit Is Due" in this chapter).

Cognitive Science

By adding to our understanding of how people think and learn, research in the field of cognitive science has contributed to the development of cognitive learning theories. Drawing from research in linguistics, psychology, anthropology, and computer science, cognitive scientists study the mental processes learners use as they acquire new knowledge. Often, cognitive scientists develop computer flow charts to illustrate how learners use their short- and long-term memory to manipulate symbols and process information. In "Cognitive Science and Its Implications for Education" in this chapter, Gary D. Kruse discusses how school programs should be changed to reflect recent findings from cognitive research. And, in "Let's Put Brain Science on the Back Burner," John T. Bruer clarifies the difference between cognitive science and neuroscience (the biological science of the brain) and cautions educators against assuming that developments in neuroscience can serve as a guide for developing curricular and instructional practices.

Gestalt-Field Views of Learning

During the first few decades of the twentieth century, several psychologists in Germany—and later in the United States—began to look at how learners organize information into patterns and wholes. *Gestalt* is a German term meaning "configuration" or "pattern," and Gestalt theorists maintain that "wholeness" is primary; one should start with the total aspects of a learning situation and then move to particulars in light of the whole. Thus, obtaining an "overview" is often an important step in learning, for without it we may be, as the popular saying goes, "unable to see the forest for the trees."

Another major element of the Gestalt view of learning is that the whole is always greater than the sum of its parts. Experiencing a moving symphony is more than hearing individual musical notes; watching a movie is more than looking at the thousands of individual still pictures that make up the movie. The nature of the whole determines the meaning of its parts, and individual perceptions determine meaning.

Constructivist Learning Theories

Since the mid-1980s, several educational researchers have attempted to identify how learners *construct* understanding of new material. Constructivist views of learning, therefore, focus on how learners make sense of new information—how they construct meaning based on what they already know. In part, the roots of constructivism can be traced back to Gestalt views of learning in that learners seek to organize new information into meaningful wholes.

According to constructivism, "*students develop new knowledge through a process of active construction.* They do not merely passively receive or copy input from teachers or textbooks. Instead, they actively mediate it by trying to make sense of it and relate it to what they already know (or think they know) about the topic" (Good and Brophy 2003, p. 398). Constructivist-oriented curricula and instructional strategies focus on students' thinking about the material to be learned and, through carefully thought out prompts and questions, enable students to arrive at a deeper understanding of new material. Among the common elements of constructivist approaches to curriculum and teaching, research has identified the following effective practices:

1.   The curriculum is designed to equip students with knowledge, skills, values, and dispositions that they will find useful both inside and outside of school.

2. Instructional goals emphasize developing student expertise within an application context and with emphasis on conceptual understanding of knowledge and self-regulated application of skills.
3. The curriculum balances breadth with depth by addressing limited content but developing this content sufficiently to foster conceptual understanding.
4. The content is organized around a limited set of powerful ideas (basic understandings and principles).
5. The teacher's role is not just to present information but also to scaffold and respond to students' learning efforts.
6. The students' role is not just to absorb or copy input but also to actively make sense and construct meaning.
7. Students' prior knowledge about the topic is elicited and used as a starting place for instruction, which builds on accurate prior knowledge and stimulates conceptual change if necessary (Good and Brophy, 2003, pp. 420–421).

A common element of constructivist approaches to curriculum planning and teaching is known as *scaffolding*—that is, providing learners with greater support during the early phases of learning and then gradually reducing support as their competence and ability to assume responsibility increase. The concept of scaffolding is based on the work of Lev Semenovich Vygotsky (1896–1934), a well-known Russian psychologist. Vygotsky coined the phrase *zone of proximal development* to refer to the point at which the learner needs assistance to continue learning. According to this view, effective instruction neither exceeds the learner's current level of understanding nor underestimates the learner's ability to learn independent of the teacher. The effective teacher varies the amount of help given to learners

> on the basis of their moment-to-moment understanding. If they do not understand an instruction given at one level, then more help is forthcoming. When they do understand, the teacher steps back and gives the child more room for initiative. In this way, the child is never left alone when he [or she] is in difficulty nor is he [or she] "held back" by teaching that is too directive and intrusive. (Wood, 1988, p. 81)

LEARNING STYLES

Much of the recent research on learning focuses on students' learning styles—that is, the approaches to learning that work best for them. Put differently, *learning styles* refers to individual typical ways of processing information and seeking meaning. These differences have also been called *learning modes, learning style preferences,* or *cognitive styles.*

Students' preferred learning styles are determined by a combination of hereditary and environmental factors. Some learners rapidly acquire new knowledge that they encounter; others learn best when they are independent and can shape their own learning. Some learn best in formal academic settings, while others learn best in informal, relaxed settings. Some learners require almost total silence, while others learn well in noisy, busy environments. Some learn intuitively, while others learn best in a step-by-step, linear, concrete fashion.

Learning style is an emerging concept, and there is no single "correct" view of learning styles to guide curriculum planners. In this chapter's *Teachers' Voices* section, Elsa C. Bro chronicles how she used ethnographic research methods to identify the preferred learning style of a high school sophomore with learning difficulties. In addition, cultural differences in learning styles are subtle and difficult to identify. For example, in "Learning Styles from a Multicultural Perspective: The Case for Culturally Engaged Education" in this chapter, Cynthia B. Dillard and Dionne A. Blue point out that no single learning style is preferred by any particular ethnic or cultural group and that learning style diversity within and among cultures is great.

Within the last decade, much research has been conducted on students' preferred learning styles, and scores of conceptual models and accompanying learning-style assessment instruments have been developed. While critics have pointed out flaws in many learning-style schemes and maintain that there is little evidence to support their validity (Snider, 1990, 1992), curriculum planners should be aware of the concept of learning styles and realize that some curricula may be more effective for some students than for others. In addition, though preferences for learning styles can be strong, they can also change as a person matures.

Multiple Intelligences

While many learning theorists believe that intelligence is the general ability to learn—to acquire and use new knowledge—others believe that "the weight of the evidence at the present time is that intelligence is multidimensional, and that the full range of these dimensions is not completely captured by any single general ability" (Sternberg, 1996, p. 11). For example, in response to cognitive theories of learning, which he believed were limited to logical-mathematical or scientific forms of intelligence valued in the West, Howard Gardner proposed in *Frames of Mind: The Theory of Multiple Intelligences* (1983, 1993a, p. 8) that "there is persuasive evidence for the existence of several relatively autonomous human intellectual competencies, [referred to] as 'human intelligences' . . . [The] exact nature and breadth of each has not so far been satisfactorily established, nor has the precise number of intelligences been fixed." Gardner suggested that there were at least seven human intelligences: logical-mathematical, linguistic, musical, spatial, bodily-kinesthetic, intrapersonal, and interpersonal (in the mid-1990s, he identified an eighth intelligence, that of the naturalist).

The concept of multiple intelligences is clearly useful in curriculum planning and teaching. However, in his reflections twelve years after the publication of *Frames of Mind* (Gardner, 1995, p. 206), Gardner asserted that "MI [multiple intelligences] theory is in no way an educational prescription. [E]ducators are in the best position to determine the uses to which MI theory should be put. . . ." And, in "Probing More Deeply into the Theory of Multiple Intelligences" in this chapter, Gardner states that "educators should be cautious about characterizing the intellectual profiles of students."

CRITERION QUESTIONS—LEARNING AND LEARNING STYLES

In light of individual differences among learners, curriculum planners and teachers need many ways to encourage learning. Knowledge and use of theories about learning and learning styles offer important guidelines in providing for individual differences and instructional alternatives. The following are among the criterion questions that can be derived from the theories of learning and learning styles discussed in this chapter.

1. Have both behavioral and cognitive views of learning been considered in planning the curriculum?
2. Has the significance of individual learning styles and how learners construct meaning been considered in planning the curriculum?
3. Does the curriculum include diverse activities for learning?
4. Does the curriculum allow learners to exhibit and develop different forms of intelligence?
5. Is the significance of learning theory concepts such as the following reflected in the curriculum: rewarded response, socialization, modeling, scaffolding, and zones of proximal development?

REFERENCES

Bandura, Albert. *Social Learning Theory.* Englewood Cliffs, NJ: Prentice-Hall, 1977.
Gardner, Howard. *Frames of Mind: The Theory of Multiple Intelligences.* New York: Basic Books, 1983. (A tenth-anniversary edition with a new introduction was published in 1993).
———. "Reflections on Multiple Intelligences: Myths and Messages. *Phi Delta Kappan 77,* no. 3 (November 1995): 200–203, 206–209.
Good, Thomas E., and Brophy, Jere E. *Looking in Classrooms,* 9th Ed. Boston: Allyn and Bacon, 2003.
Mazur, J. *Learning and Behavior,* 4th Ed. Englewood Cliffs, NJ: Prentice-Hall, 1997.
Skinner, B. F. "Utopia through the Control of Human Behavior." In John Martin Rich, ed., *Readings in the Philosophy of Education.* Belmont, CA: Wadsworth, 1972.
Slavin, Robert. *Educational Psychology: Theory and Practice,* 7th Ed. Boston: Allyn and Bacon, 2003.
Snider, Vicki E. "Learning Styles and Learning to Read: A Critique." *Remedial and Special Education (RASE)* 13, no. 1 (January–February, 1992): 6–18.
———. "What We Know about Learning Styles from Research in Special Education. *Educational Leadership* 48, no. 2 (October, 1990): 53.
Sternberg, Robert J. "Myths, Countermyths, and Truths about Intelligence. *Educational Researcher* 25, no. 2 (March 1996): 11–16.
Wood, David. *How Children Think and Learn.* New York: Basil Blackwell, 1988.
Woolfolk, Anita. *Educational Psychology,* 9th ed. Boston: Allyn and Bacon, 2005.

Cognitive Science and Its Implications for Education

GARY D. KRUSE

ABSTRACT: Cognitive science has provided a better understanding of the structure and functions of the human brain—for example, the brain is rarely at rest and constantly searches for meaning. Ten findings from cognitive science that are relevant to the teaching learning process are presented. Schools should incorporate these findings and adopt new views of time, curriculum, learning, and the teacher's role.

A much clearer understanding of the brain's functions and processes has been developed during the last several decades. This growing body of knowledge has far-reaching implications for educational methods and practices. The brain is the result of thousands of years of human evolution. Only recently, largely due to advanced technology, have we begun to unravel the mind's secrets at the molecular, cellular, and functional level.

THE ARCHITECTURE OF THE BRAIN

The basic working units of the brain are 100 billion specialized nerve cells (neurons), each capable of making up to 50,000 connections as meaning is detected. It is this ability to discriminate, register, store, and retrieve meaning that is the essence of all human learning. Neurons communicate or make connections through the use of chemical messengers called neurotransmitters. The process takes the form of electrochemical impulses traveling from one neuron to another by crossing a minute gap called the synapse. This electrochemical "dance" between neurons using chemical messengers is believed to give rise to our power to derive or evoke meaning (Sylwester, 1995).

The earliest structure of the brain, the brain stem, appears to be an extension of our spinal cord. The brain stem contributes to our general alertness and serves as an early warning system to the rest of the brain regarding incoming sensory information. Hence, all learning initially begins at a sensory level of cognitive processing. Mean-

ing and understanding are the result of further cognitive functions within the brain (Ornstein and Thompson, 1984).

Located atop the brain stem lies the limbic system. This system provides the chemicals that influence focus, attention, and concentration. The thalamus, located near the limbic system, is the "gateway valve" for the flow of all information into the brain. The hippocampus, a part of the system, serves as a way station for the temporary storage of information. Short-term memory may reside within this structure.

The largest part of the brain is the cerebrum. It is divided into two hemispheres that are connected by the largest band of neurons found in the brain, the corpus callosum. Its role is to act as a communication "bridge" between hemispheres, which work in concert to make sense out of incoming information. Each hemisphere contributes various forms of thinking to derive meaning.

This lateralization of cognitive processing by hemisphere gives us the ability to think both divergently and convergently. It allows us to approach complexities in life from an intuitive as well as a logical manner. The hemispheres of the cerebrum process information from both a "parts-to-whole" and "whole-to-parts" perspective, allowing us to conceive a holistic as well as a detailed pattern of thought regarding an object, event, or relationship (Ornstein and Thompson, 1984).

Covering the cerebrum is the cortex, which houses two-thirds of all neurons in the brain. It is within this thin layer composed of billions of columns of neurons that genuine learning occurs (Suzuki, 1994).

The cortex is divided into lobes, each lobe carrying out a variety of functions. Researchers have found neurons of similar function grouped together within these lobes. At the rear of the brain lies the visual processing area; within this area are about 100,000 neurons whose purpose is to work to identify facial features such as the height of a hairline or exact distance between the eyes on a facial image (Ackerman, 1994). These "face cells" help us recognize a face as that of a friend or foe, brother or sister.

Temporal lobes contain a number of critical attributes for learning. An area in the left temporal lobe the size of a silver dollar is responsible for receiving all spoken words and forwarding these sounds for further processing to determine semantic meaning. This area discriminates between just 44 "sound bits" that comprise the entire English language. An area of similar size in the right temporal lobe helps process spatial information for meaning. It is also in the temporal lobes that researchers have found evidence of permanent episodic memory (Ornstein and Thompson, 1984; Damasio and Damasio, 1992).

Frontal lobes of the cortex serve as our center for thought. It is here that such purposeful actions as planning or deciding occur. Neurons found throughout the cortex help to complete the construction of understanding. Alphabet letter symbols, for example, strung together in the temporal lobe to create words are forwarded onto associative fields in the parietal lobes to become sentences, paragraphs and, eventually, a story. These associative fields take in previously processed information and aid in developing conceptual understanding (Damasio and Damasio, 1992).

SOME NOTIONS REGARDING HUMAN LEARNING

Human learning is a direct result of the brain's associative properties and memory systems, the origins of which are currently being investigated by scientists. The ability, however, of one neuron to communicate with another places these associative mechanisms at the heart of all human learning. Though complex, we are moving closer toward the realization that a biological basis exists for learning. The implications of this fact for education are awesome (Kandel and Hawkins, 1992).

Researchers describe the brain as an extremely dynamic organ. It appears that it is rarely at rest and constantly searches for meaning. Moreover, the organ grows as meaning is attached and new synaptic connections are laid down. Hemispheres of the cerebrum provide their owner with a number of different perspectives when interpreting information for meaning. Besides helping to decipher the world outside us, the brain also appears to have the capability to go off on its own to evoke new ideas (Suzuki, 1994).

It is obvious this organ of learning is by no means the passive repository for skills and facts it was once thought to be. Current evidence would suggest the following regarding cognitive processing:

1. The brain is our learning organ.
2. The brain constantly searches for meaning.
3. The brain is a dynamic processor of information.
4. We can enhance or inhibit the operation of the brain.
5. Learning is a "sociocognitive act" tying social interaction, cognitive processing, and language together in an interactive manner.
6. Multi-sensory activities that embed skills and facts into natural experiences appear to enhance the brain's search for meaning.
7. A school day in which "connectiveness" exists between concepts taught enhances the brain's search for meaning.
8. The pace of instruction appears to influence the brain's search for meaning.
9. Information delivered within the student's context, tied to his or her prior understanding, and moving from concrete to abstract levels of processing appears to enhance the brain's search for the meaning.
10. To learn (beyond a perceptual level) requires the student to "act on the learning." To act means involvement.

A MOST IMMODEST PROPOSAL

Educational methods and practices have traditionally treated the brain as a passive repository. Knowledge has been transmitted by subject-area specialists inside a self-contained classroom setting. Current practices promote passive learning through a heavy reliance on students listening, reading, and practicing in isolation. The school day is composed of small increments of time (e.g., 50- to 90-minute periods) in which a subject specialist delivers discrete skills and memorizable facts period by period. In assembly-line fashion, students move from subject to subject, rarely encountering a conceptual tie or relationship (Gardner, 1991; Brooks and Brooks, 1993).

Both traditional instruction and student evaluation have become more a measure of the ability to recognize and recall than a genuine understanding of the concepts. Under the current scheme, curricula are viewed vertically (K–12). No consideration is given to what knowledge and concepts are being taught across the day, week, or semester. No ties or connections exist for the student to attach between subject areas.

This arrangement is built on the false notion that human learning is a linear progression within the mind, a notion that cognitive researchers dispute. They point out that knowledge is constructed by the brain through situational and experiential encounters influenced to a large degree by pace, context, connectiveness, prior understanding, and one's ability or freedom to act on the learning. The traditional vertical view of curriculum has resulted in a system of education driven by a textbook and taught at a rapid pace, causing many students difficulty in cognitively processing information (Brooks and Brooks, 1993).

Many characteristics of our schools disagree with the findings of cognitive research. The isolation as well as fragmentation of knowledge neither complements nor enhances the associative powers of the human mind. The current methods of transmitting knowledge may eliminate the "whole to parts" processing ability of the cere-

brum, thereby eliminating the larger picture or understanding for the student. A heavy reliance on the spoken or printed word effectively shuts down other sensory input available to the brain in its search for meaning. At times the message sent to youngsters today is that one's ability to recognize and recall (remember) is of far more value than understanding or applying a concept to life.

Finally, the practice of delivering information out of context, then assuming the student will be able to transfer it to changing life situations, may be totally unrealistic. Information taught out of context is neither meaningful nor relevant to most young people, causing them serious problems in attempting to process it. This common form of instruction could be the major reason we find such inordinate amounts of rote practice occurring in the current school setting.

To move schools toward a greater sensitivity in cognitive processing, we should adopt new views of time, curriculum, learning, and the role of teachers. This will require major shifts on the part of the educational community (Hart, 1983; Kruse and Kruse, 1995).

Our view of time needs to change dramatically. The Carnegie unit equates "seat time" with learning by awarding students credit for successfully completing coursework. For most of the 20th century we have been locked into a view that the school day should be composed of standard increments of time. Common sense, as well as research, should tell us otherwise. Genuine learning occurs at different rates and to different degrees for each student. The best judges of "how fast" or "how much" are the student and the teacher.

The traditional role of teachers must also change. Teachers should be trained and organized into teams composed of various grade levels or content specialties. The need to create a coherent school day in which the student's mind encounters conceptual ties and connections throughout, necessitates dialogue on a daily basis between subject area specialists. Integration can be two teachers doing something together—however, integration can be a much fuller and richer act, involving an entire team of specialists making conceptual connections as they appear in real life. This type of organization requires a complete change from the traditional "department," which is a working unit originally designed to search for truth, not teach youngsters (Kruse, 1994).

Curriculum should be viewed across the school day. Constant dialogue between team members should occur to make the curriculum coherent. Activities designed by the team embedding essential facts and skills into natural experiences will be a major team responsibility. Finally, the future school day should place utmost value on developing student understanding through honoring student questions, allowing students to work cooperatively, and encouraging student interaction in order to initiate a full array of cognitive functions (Kruse and Zulkoski, 1997).

CONCLUSION

Understanding the ability of the mind to attach novel information to already stored understandings has major implications for current instructional practices, setting, and the manner in which we organize teachers. A greater coherency is needed within the school day to tap into the associative powers of the mind. To accomplish this a new view of time, curriculum, learning, and teacher role will be necessary. Greater authenticity toward knowledge and its delivery is essential to provide relevance and meaning.

To achieve this a much higher degree of collegiality by teachers will be called for in the future, implying a completely different product than has been stamped out over the past century by training institutions. Perhaps the most critical factor being suggested by cognitive research is that of the brain's potential to learn. It appears, barring major insults, this organ's potential to learn is limitless if educational practices and methods "complement, not complicate" its search for meaning.

REFERENCES

Ackerman, S. J. "Face Facts, How Does the Circuitry of Our Brain Allow Us To Recognize Faces?" *Brainwork—The Neuroscience Newsletter,* November/December 1994.

Arwood, E. *Pragmatism, Theory and Application.* London: Aspen, 1983.

Brooks, J. G., and Brooks, M. G. *In Search of Understanding. The Case for Constructivist Classrooms.* Alexandria, Va.: ASCD, 1993.

Caine, R. N., and Caine, G. C. *Making Connections: Teaching and the Human Brain.* Menlo Park, Calif.: Addison Wesley Longman, 1994.

Damasio, A. R., and Damasio, H. "Brain and Language." *Scientific American,* September 1992.

Gardner, H. *The Unschooled Mind. How Children Think and How Schools Should Teach.* New York: Basic Books, 1991.

Goldman-Rakic, P. S. "Working Memory and the Mind." *Scientific American,* September 1992.

Hart, L. *Human Brain and Human Learning.* New York: Longman, 1983.

Kandel, E. R., and Hawkins, R. D. "The Biological Basis of Learning and Individuality." *Scientific American,* September 1992.

Kotulak, R. "Unraveling the Mysteries of the Brain." (A series of articles) *Chicago Tribune,* April 1993.

Kruse, C. A., and Kruse, G. D. "The Master Schedule: Improving the Quality of Education." *NASSP Bulletin,* May 1995.

Kruse, G. D. "Thinking, Learning, and Public Schools: Preparing for Life." *NASSP Bulletin,* September 1994.

Kruse, G. D., and Zulkoski, M. "The Northwest Experience: A Lesser Road Traveled." *NASSP Bulletin,* December 1997.

LeDoux, J. "Emotion, Memory, and the Brain." *Scientific American,* 1994.

Ornstein, R., and Thompson, R. F. *The Amazing Brain.* Boston, Mass.: Houghton-Mifflin, 1984.

Suzuki, J. *The Brain.* (A five-part television series) Discovery Channel, 1994.

Sylwester, R. *A Celebration of Neurons: An Educators Guide to the Human Brain.* Alexandria, Va.: ASCD, 1995.

Gary D. Kruse is assistant principal of Northwest High School in Grand Island, Nebraska.

QUESTIONS FOR REFLECTION

1. In what ways might a curriculum "enhance or inhibit" the operation of the human brain?
2. Kruse states that "multi-sensory activities that embed skills and facts into natural experiences appear to enhance the brain's search for meaning." What are the implications of this statement for the curriculum with which you are most familiar?
3. In what ways does a curriculum that is "vertically" arranged conflict with findings from cognitive science?
4. To what extent do you believe K–12 schools and higher education will implement the recommendations contained in Kruse's "immodest proposal"?

Let's Put Brain Science on the Back Burner

JOHN T. BRUER

ABSTRACT: Current knowledge of brain development and neural functioning is not adequate to guide educational practice. Three misconceptions about neuroscience and education are discussed, and educators are urged to use cognitive science, rather than brain science, to develop learning environments that exploit the brain's lifelong plasticity.

There has long been a simmering interest in brain research among educators. Recently, however, that interest has gone from simmer to full boil. In the past 18 months, for example, we have seen special issues of *The American School Board Journal* (February 1997), *Educational Leadership* (March 1997), and *The School Administrator* (January 1998). Now the *NASSP Bulletin* addresses the implications of the new brain research for educators.

These issues contain a variety of articles—articles by advocates of brain-based curricula, articles by educational futurists, articles by cognitive (not brain) scientists. In fact, it is rare to find an article written by a neuroscientist in the educational literature. Of these articles, those citing cognitive research on learning, intelligence, memory, and specific subject matter learning provide the most useful advice to educators.

Educators should be aware that cognitive science—the behavioral science of the mind—is not the same as neuroscience—the biological science of the brain. Most cognitive theories are formulated without regard for how the brain might implement or execute mental processes. Nonetheless these cognitive theories are most useful to educators (Bruer, 1993; McGilly, 1994). When "brain-based" curricula do provide sound advice, they might better be called "mind-based," because they often draw from cognitive rather than brain research. Most other claims found in the emerging brain and education literature are vague, outdated, metaphorical, or based on misconceptions. This article will address some of those misconceptions.

NEUROSCIENCE AND EDUCATION

Despite all the interest and media attention, I do not believe we currently know enough about brain development and neural function to link that understanding, in any meaningful way, to educational practice. Most of the "brain" articles you will read, both in the media and the professional journals, will explicitly state or allude to what I call the "neuroscience and education argument."

The neuroscience and education argument relies on and embellishes three important and reasonably well-established findings from developmental neurobiology. *First,* starting in infancy and continuing into later childhood there is a period of exuberant synapse growth, followed by a period of synaptic "pruning" in the brain. *Second,* there are experience-dependent critical periods in the development of at least some sensory and motor systems. *Third,* in rats, at least, complex or enriched environments cause new synapses to form.

The argument fails to provide guidance to educators because it relies on misconceptions about and overgeneralizations from these three results. I have discussed these misinterpretations elsewhere (Bruer, 1997). Rather than repeat those arguments here, I will concentrate on misconceptions about one of the three findings—misconceptions about the significance of synapse formation and loss during childhood—that have crept into the educational literature.

Most neuroscientists agree that the brain is not mature at birth and that significant development events take place post-natally. One such significant developmental event is a post-natal phase of rapid synapse formation. In the mid-1970s, neuroscientists first observed this by counting synapses in samples of brain tissue taken from the visual cortex of cats and monkeys (Cragg, 1975a; Lund, Booth, and Lund, 1977). Since the mid-1970s, research, mostly on rhesus monkeys, has shown that this developmental phase occurs in all areas of the monkey brain that scientists have examined—visual, motor, somatosensory, and frontal cortex—brain areas fundamental for seeing, moving, feeling, and planning/remembering (Rakic, 1994; Rakic, Bourgeois, and Goldman-Rakic, 1994; Goldman-Rakic, Bourgeois, and Rakic, 1997).

In monkeys, rapid synapse formation begins two months before the monkey is born. At birth

the number of synapses per unit volume (synaptic density) of tissue in the monkey brain is approximately the same as the synaptic density found in adult monkey brains. This process of rapid synapse formation continues for another two to three months after birth, until synaptic density in the monkey brain far exceeds that found in adult brains.

From age three months to three years, the age of sexual maturity for rhesus monkeys, there is a "high plateau" period for synaptic density. At puberty, a period of rapid synapse elimination begins, during which synaptic densities settle at adult levels by age five years. Thus, in the monkey, synaptic densities (as well as the number of synapses) follow an inverted-U pattern—low at birth, high during adolescence, low thereafter.

Although fewer data are available, it appears that during development the human brain follows the same inverted-U pattern. Since 1979, Peter Huttenlocher at the University of Chicago has counted synapses in brain tissue taken from 53 human patients at autopsy. The patients' ages at death ranged from pre-term infants to more than 70 years old. Huttenlocher has counted synapses in three brain areas—the visual area, the auditory area, and the frontal area (Huttenlocher, 1979, 1990; Huttenlocher and de Courten, 1987; Huttenlocher and Dabholkar, 1997).

Synapse Formation in Humans

Unlike in the monkey, where rapid synapse formation appears to occur concurrently in all brains, in the human it appears that rapid synapse formation occurs at different times in different brain areas. (Because we do not have comparable data for monkeys and humans, however, this remains an unresolved, contested issue.)

In the human visual cortex, there is a rapid increase in the number of synaptic connections at around 2 months of age, which reaches a peak at 8–10 months. Then there is a steady decline in synaptic density, until it reaches adult levels at around 10 years of age. In the auditory cortex, there is also a rapid rise in the months following birth, with peak density occurring at age 3 months, followed by a plateau period and stabilization at adult levels at puberty. In the human frontal cortex, peak densities occur at around two years of age and remain at these high levels until 8 years of age, when they slowly decline to adult levels at around age 16 (Huttenlocher, 1990).

In humans, there is also indirect evidence for this developmental pattern. Many of the education articles mention brain scanning technologies, such as Positron Emission Tomography (PET), that allow scientists to measure brain activity in normal, living human subjects. PET uses radioactively labeled substances, like oxygen or glucose, that the brain requires for energy. When these substances are administered to a subject, they go via the bloodstream to brain areas requiring energy and there eventually emit positrons. Detectors pick up these emissions, and data on the paths of the emissions allow scientists to construct images of where in the brain the oxygen or glucose is being consumed.

The PET study most often cited in the education literature is a study of 29 epileptic children. (Because PET scans require the injection of a radioactive substance almost no images are available from healthy children [Chugani, Phelps, and Mazziota, 1987].) This study revealed a rapid rise in glucose uptake in children's brains that started at 1 year, peaked at 3 years, and stayed at this level until age 9 or 10, after which levels of glucose uptake receded to adult levels. If one assumes, as the authors of this study do, that the brain's increased energy demands result from the need to fuel and maintain excess synapses, the study provides indirect evidence of the inverted-U developmental pattern.

IMPLICATIONS FOR CHILDREN

Although neuroscientists have documented the time course of this apparent synaptic waxing and waning, they are less sure about what it means for changes in children's behavior, intelligence, and capacity to learn. Generally, they point to correlations between changes in synaptic density or numbers and observed changes in children's behavior documented by developmental and cognitive psychologists. Typically, they all rely on the same small set of examples (Chugani, Phelps, and Mazziota, 1987; Huttenlocher and de Courten, 1987; Goldman-Rakic, Bourgeois, and Rakic, 1997).

At the time rapid synapse formation begins, at around two months of age, human infants start to lose their innate, infantile reflexes. At age three months, when the process is well underway in the visual cortex, infants can reach for an object while visually fixating on it. At four–five months, infants' visual capacities increase. At eight months, when rapid synapse formation begins in the frontal cortex, infants first show the ability to hold information, like the location of hidden objects, in working memory for a short period of time, say several seconds. The time delay over which they can remember this information improves steadily during the next four months up to more than 10 seconds. These examples are all significant developmental milestones that no doubt depend somehow on brain development. We know these milestones are correlated with changes in synaptic densities and number, but that is all we know.

Educators should note one thing about these examples. They are examples of the emergence or changes in basic sensory, motor, and memory functions. The changes are developmentally significant. These are not abilities and skills children learn in school or pre-school, however. Normal children in almost any environment acquire these capacities at approximately the same age—children in affluent suburbs, children in inner cities, children in rural-pastoral settings throughout the world. It takes severely deprived environments and highly unnatural situations to prevent these skills and abilities from developing, in both children and animals.

No doubt, in some way, the development of these capacities supports future school learning, but currently, we have little idea, certainly no idea based on neuroscientific research, how the emergence of these species-wide capacities relates to later school learning. We do not know much about how these capacities contribute to the acquisition of culturally transmitted knowledge and skills like reading, writing, mathematics, and science.

NEUROSCIENCE AND EDUCATION: MISCONCEPTIONS

This is the neuroscience, most of it more than 20 years old, at the basis of the neuroscience and education argument. Educators interpret these findings to develop what appears to be a commonsense, highly compelling argument. One reason this argument is so beguiling is that it lends itself to a "quantitative" view of brain development, intelligence, and learning. More synapses are better. Saving as many synapses as we can is important. The right experiences at the right times can result in optimal "synaptic conservation" and learning. Beguiling, but misconceived. Here are three of the most common misconceptions.

1. *Enriched early childhood environments cause synapses to multiply rapidly.*

It not unusual to see claims like these: "With proper stimulation brain synapses will form at a rapid pace, reaching adult levels by the age two and far surpassing them in the next several years" (Clinton, 1996, Chapter 4). Or, "Growing evidence indicates that early mental stimulation promotes the growth of synaptic connections between brain cells" (Kotulak, 1996, p. 186).

What little direct evidence we have—all based on studies of monkeys—indicates these claims are inaccurate. Experience, the environment, and sensory stimulation appear to have no impact on the brain's rapid formation of synapses early in life. Evidence comes from both deprivation and stimulation experiments. Rhesus monkeys, whose retinas were removed in utero midway

through gestation, had the same synaptic densities in the visual cortex at each stage of development as age-matched normal, sighted monkeys.

Although the visual cortex in the blind animals was smaller than that of the sighted monkeys, total visual deprivation had no impact on the rate of synapse formation (Rakic, 1994; Rakic, Bourgeois, and Goldman-Rakic, 1994; Goldman-Rakic, Bourgeois, and Rakic, 1997).

In the stimulation experiment, monkeys delivered three weeks pre-term received intensive visual stimulation to see if such stimulation would accelerate synapse formation in the visual cortex. Contrary to the experimenters' expectations, the synaptic densities of the pre-term, highly stimulated monkeys were no different than those of the full-term, normally stimulated control monkeys.

The rate of synapse formation and synaptic density seems to be impervious to quantity of stimulation. The rate of synapse formation appears to be linked to the animal's developmental age, the time since it was conceived, and to be under genetic control. It is not linked to birth age and amount of postnatal experience. Some features of brain development, including the rapid burst of synapse formation in infancy and early childhood, rather than being acutely sensitive to deprivation or increased stimulation, are in fact surprisingly resilient to them. Early experience does not cause synapses to form rapidly. Early enriched environments will not put our children on synaptic fast tracks.

2. *More synapses mean more brainpower.*

One often sees claims that neuroscientific evidence indicates that the more synapses you have, the smarter you are. The assumption is that there is a linear relationship between the number of synapses in the brain and brainpower or intelligence (Kotulak, 1996, p. 20; Education Commission of the States, 1997; National Education Association, 1997, p. 9).

The neuroscientific evidence does not support this claim, either. The evidence shows that synaptic numbers and densities follow an inverted-U pattern—low, high, and low—over the life span.

However, our behavior, cognitive capacities, and intelligence obviously do not follow an inverted-U pattern over our life span.

Synaptic densities at birth and in early adulthood are approximately the same, yet by any measure adults are more intelligent, have more highly flexible behavior, and learn more readily than infants. Furthermore, early adulthood, the period of rapid synaptic loss, follows the high plateau period of synaptic densities from early childhood to puberty. Young adults do not become less intelligent or less able to learn once they start to lose synapses. Furthermore, learning complex subjects continues throughout life, with no apparent, appreciable change in synaptic numbers.

Studies of brain tissue taken from individuals suffering forms of mental retardation also undermine this claim. Some forms of mental retardation seem to be associated with abnormally low synaptic densities and numbers, but other forms seem to be associated with abnormally high synaptic densities and numbers (Cragg, 1975b; Huttenlocher and Dabholkar, 1997). Whatever the relationship is between synapses and brain power, it is not a simple, linear, numerical one: ". . . no one believes that there will be a simple and linear relationship between any given dimension of neural development and functional competence" (Goldman-Rakic, 1986, p. 234; Huttenlocher, 1990). It is not true that more synapses mean more brainpower.

3. *The plateau of high synaptic density and high brain metabolism is the optimal period for learning.*

One sees claims that during the plateau period the brain is super-dense and is "a super-sponge that is most absorbent from birth to around the age of 12" (Kotulak, 1996, p. 4). "It is a time during which the human computer has so much memory capacity that . . . it can store more information than any army of humans could possibly input" (Clinton, 1996, Chapter 4). This is *the* critical period for learning (Carnegie, 1996,

pp. 10–11; Kotulak, 1996; U.S. Department of Education, 1996, p. 22; Shore, 1997).

The idea that periods of high brain growth or activity are optimal periods for learning is an old one. In the 1970s, Herman Epstein argued those periods of high brain growth, as determined by changes in head circumference, might be periods where children are most receptive to learning (1978). To his credit, he put this forward as a hypothesis, not as a fact. There is still not much evidence to support it, but in the brain and education literature, this hypothesis has risen to the status of fact.

The neuroscientific evidence for this claim is extremely weak. The neuroscientists who count synapses in humans and monkeys merely point out that during the plateau period, monkeys and humans develop a variety of skills and behaviors. They develop from infants to adolescents. At adolescence, when rapid synapse loss begins, young primates are essentially like adults in their capacities. They can move, sense, communicate, behave, and procreate like adults.

This is another correlational argument where neuroscientists have observed something about the brain and look to commonsense experience or results from behavioral science in an attempt to explain the possible broader significance of what they have observed. They use what we know about development and behavior to generate hypotheses about the significance of changes observed in the brain. The observed changes in the brain are not being used to explain what we see in child development and classroom behavior. Brain science, at least at the level of studying synapses, is just not that far along yet.

Even, as it appears, that there is this high-plateau period from age 3 to 10, it is still difficult to provide evidence for or against a claim that children learn more during this period than during any other. We have not, and probably have no way, to quantify learning and knowledge. Claims about peak learning periods thus depend more on one's intuitions than on established scientific claims.

When educators say that the first decade of life is a unique time of enormous information acquisition and that the brain is in its most sponge-like phase of learning, they are making an intuitive conjecture, not stating a research result. Needless to say, peoples' intuitions differ. The neuroscientific study that is most often cited to support the claim that age 3–10 is the optimal time for learning is the PET study of brain metabolism. This study showed there was a high plateau period of cerebral metabolism between the ages of 3 and 10. In the educational literature, "high glucose metabolism" becomes "high brain activity," which in turn becomes "high learning potential."

Note, however, that these PET studies did not look at "learning" at all. These studies measured resting brain metabolism—how much energy the brain used when it was doing as little as possible, when the subjects were in a dark room intended to minimize sensory input. We do not know what relationship exists between high resting brain metabolism and learning, any more than we know what relation exists between high synaptic numbers and ability to learn. Any such claims are again conjecture, correlating commonsense behavioral observations with a neuroscientific result in an attempt to understand what the brain is doing.

We can as readily make the opposite conjecture, as one neuroscientist has done. Peter Huttenlocher once speculated that the presence of excess synaptic activity might have negative effects on children's brain function because the large number of unspecified synapses might interfere with efficient information processing in the cortex (Huttenlocher, 1990). This might make it difficult for children to learn.

Although children's brains are metabolically more active than adults, high resting metabolic activity does not necessarily mean high cognitive activity or heightened ability to learn. Childhood is a time of rapid brain growth, as it is a time of rapid physical growth. Growth requires energy. For all we know, and for all that neuroscience can tell us, periods of rapid growth may not be the best time to learn. Little Leaguers should not throw curve balls. It's bad for their growing arms. Maybe they shouldn't learn calculus, either.

WHAT DOES ALL THIS MEAN?

The brain does and should fascinate all of us and we should find advances in neuroscience exciting. As educators, we should also be interested in how basic research might contribute to and improve educational practice. However, we should be wary of claims that neuroscience has much to tell us about educational practice. The neuroscience and education argument attempts to link learning, particularly early childhood learning, with what neuroscience has discovered about neural development and synaptic change.

Neuroscience has discovered a great deal about neurons and synapses, but not nearly enough to guide educational practice in any meaningful way. Currently, it is just too much of a leap from what we know about changes in synapses to what goes on in a classroom. Educators, like all well-informed citizens, should be aware of what basic science can contribute to our self-understanding and professional practice. However, educators should consider carefully what neuroscientists are saying before leaping on the brain and education bandwagon.

Truly new results in neuroscience, rarely mentioned in the brain and education literature, point to the brain's lifelong capacity to reshape itself in response to experience. The challenge for educators is to develop learning environments and practices that can exploit the brain's lifelong plasticity. The challenge is to define the behaviors we want to teach; design learning environments to impart them; and constantly test the educational efficacy of these environments. We will best meet this challenge by careful study of human behavior and behavioral change. How the brain does it will be of less significance. For the present, educators should critically read and evaluate those articles on cognitive science and put brain science on the back burner.

REFERENCES

Bruer, J. T. "Education and the Brain: A Bridge Too Far." *Educational Researcher* 8(1997): 4–16.

———. *Schools for Thought: A Science of Learning in the Classroom*. Cambridge, Mass.: 1993.

Carnegie Corporation of New York. *Years of Promise: A Comprehensive Learning Strategy for America's Children*. New York: Carnegie Corporation, 1996.

Chugani, H. T.; Phelps, M. E.; and Mazziota, J. C. "Positron Emission Tomography Study of Human Brain Function Development." *Annals of Neurology* 22(1987): 487–97.

Clinton, H. *It Takes a Village*. New York: Touchstone, 1996.

Cragg, B. G. "The Density of Synapses and Neurons in Normal, Mentally Defective and Aging Human Brains." *Brain* 98(1975b): 81–90.

———. "The Development of Synapses in the Visual System of the Cat." *Journal of Comparative Neurology* 160(1975a): 147–66.

Education Commission of the States. "1997 Education Agenda/Priorities." September 1997. http://www.ecs.org/ecs/231e.htm.

Epstein, H. T. "Growth Spurts During Brain Development: Implications for Educational Policy and Practice." In *Education and the Brain*, edited by J. S. Chall and A. F. Mirsky, pp. 343–70. Chicago, Ill.: University of Chicago Press, 1978.

Goldman-Rakic, P. S. "Development of Cortical Circuitry and Cognitive Function." *Child Development* 58(1987): 601–22.

———. "Setting the Stage: Neural Development Before Birth." In *The Brain, Cognition, and Education*, edited by S. L. Friedman, K. A. Klivington, and R. W. Peterson. Orlando, Fla.: Academic Press, 1986, pp. 233–58.

Goldman-Rakic, P. S.; Bourgeois, J. P.; and Rakic, P. "Synaptic Substrate of Cognitive Development: Synaptogenesis in the Prefrontal Cortex of the Nonhuman Primate." In *Development of the Prefrontal Cortex: Evolution, Neurobiology, and Behavior*, edited by N. A. Krasnegor, G. R. Lyon, and P. S. Goldman-Rakic, pp. 27–47. Baltimore, Md.: Paul H. Brooks, 1997.

Huttenlocher, P. R. "Morphometric Study of Human Cerebral Cortex Development." *Neuropsychologia* 6(1990): 517–27.

———. "Synaptic Density in Human Frontal Cortex—Developmental Changes of Aging." *Brain Research* 163(1979): 195–205.

Huttenlocher, P. R., and Dabholkar, A. S. "Regional Differences in Synaptogenesis in Human Cerebral Cortex." *The Journal of Comparative Neurology* 387(1997): 167–78.

Huttenlocher, P. R., and de Courten, Ch. "The Development of Synapses in Striate Cortex of Man." *Human Neurobiology* 6(1987): 1–9.

Kotulak, R. *Inside the Brain: Revolutionary Discoveries of How the Mind Works*. Kansas City: Andrews and McNeel, 1996.

Lund, J. S.; Boothe, R. G.; and Lund, R. D. "Development of Neurons in the Visual Cortex (Area 17) of the Monkey (*Macaca Nemestrina*): A Golgi Study From Fetal Day 127 to Postnatal Maturity." *Journal of Comparative Neurology* 176(1977): 149–88.

McGilly, K., ed. *Classroom Lessons: Integrating Cognitive Theory and Classroom Instruction*. Cambridge, Mass.: MIT Press, 1994.

National Education Association. "The Latest on How the Brain Works." *NEA Today*, April 1997.

Rakic, P. "Corticogenesis in Human and Nonhuman Primates." In *The Cognitive Neurosciences*, edited by M. Gazzaniga. Cambridge, Mass.: MIT Press, 1994.

Rakic, P.; Bourgeois, I. P.; and Goldman-Rakic, P. S. "Synaptic Development of the Cerebral Cortex: Implications for Learning, Memory, and Mental Illness." In *Progress in Brain Research*, edited by J. van Pelt, M. A. Corner, H. B. M. Uylings, and F. H. Lopes da Silva. Amsterdam: Elsevier ScienceBV, 1994.

Shore, R. *Rethinking the Brain*. New York: Families and Work Institute, 1997.

U.S. Department of Education. *Building Knowledge for a Nation of Learners: A Framework for Education Research 1997*. Washington, D.C.: U.S. Department of Education, 1996.

John T. Bruer is President, James S. McDonnell Foundation, St. Louis, Missouri.

QUESTIONS FOR REFLECTION

1. Why does Bruer prefer the term *mind-based* curricula than *brain-based* curricula?
2. Bruer discusses several limitations of the "neuroscience and education argument." What might account for the misapplication of neuroscience to the teaching–learning process?
3. In regard to the content area and level with which you are most familiar, what would be the characteristics of a learning environment that exploits the brain's plasticity? In what ways would this environment differ from that which currently exists?

Probing More Deeply into the Theory of Multiple Intelligences

HOWARD GARDNER

ABSTRACT: The originator of multiple intelligences theory discusses several misconceptions educators have about how to apply the theory to the teaching–learning process. The seven intelligences are based on explicit criteria and "come into being" when they interact with specific real-world content. While educators can assess proficiency at using intelligences for different tasks, they cannot assess intelligences per se.

No one has been more surprised than I by the continuing interest among educators in the theory of multiple intelligences ("MI," as it has become known). Almost 15 years after the manuscript of *Frames of Mind* (1983; 1993a) was completed, I continue on a nearly daily basis to hear about schools that are carrying out experiments in implementing MI. And, on occasion, I encounter a series of thoughtful essays such as the set assembled here.

As a result of the almost constant interaction with the "field," I have come to expect certain understandings and misunderstandings of MI. I began to respond to these interpretations, first through correspondence and then through "replies" to reviews and critiques. In 1995, after 10 years of relative silence, I issued a more formal response, in the form of reflections on seven "myths about multiple intelligences" (Gardner, 1995). This article gave me an opportunity to address directly some of the most common misconceptions about the theory and, as best I could, to set the record straight.

Since publishing these reflections, I have begun to think about the theory from a different perspective. Like any new formulation, "MI theory" is prone to be apprehended initially in certain ways. Sometimes the initial apprehensions (and misapprehensions) endure; more commonly, they alter over time in various, often in predictable, ways.

It may surprise readers to know that I have observed this process even in myself; I have held some of the common misconceptions about MI theory, even as I have come over time to understand aspects of the theory more deeply. In these notes, I identify a series of steps that seem to me to reflect increasingly deep readings of the theory.

Judging the book by its title. Anyone who has published a book of non-fiction will recognize symptoms of the most superficial readings of the book (or, more likely, examination of its cover). Such individuals show no evidence of having even cracked the binding. I have read and heard individuals talk about "multiple intelligence" (sic) as if there were a single intelligence, composed of many parts—in direct contradiction to my claim that there exist a number of relatively autonomous human intellectual capacities. Displaying the ability to read the table of contents but not further, many have written about the "six intelligences," though I have never asserted that there were fewer than seven intelligences. The apparent reason for this misstep: in *Frames of Mind* I devote a single chapter to the two personal intelligences, thus suggesting to the skimmer that I consider these two as if they are one. Finally, I cannot enumerate how often I have been said to posit a "spiritual intelligence" though I have never done so, and have in fact explicitly rejected that possibility both orally and in writings (Gardner, 1995; 1999).

"MI-Lite" based on a skim or a cocktail party conversation. Those who have made at least a half-hearted effort to understand what the author had in mind usually recognize that "multiple intelligence" (sic) is plural, that there are at least seven separate intelligences, and that the only newly accepted intelligence is that of the Naturalist. Of equal importance, they appreciate that my theory constitutes a critique of the hegemony of one or two intelligences—usually the linguistic and logical varieties that are (over-) valued in school. And they infer that I am not fond of tests of the standard psychometric variety. Indeed, such readers are often attracted more by what they think I oppose (IQ tests, the SAT, a one-dimensional approach to students) than by the actual claims of the theory.

Still, these individuals prove most susceptible to the misconceptions to which I earlier referred. It is from them that I am likely to hear that:

1. One ought to have seven tests. (Alas, you can't get from MI to psychometrics-as-usual.)
2. An intelligence is the same as a domain, discipline, or craft. (Actually, any domain can use several intelligences, and any intelligence can be drawn upon in numerous domains.)
3. An intelligence is indistinguishable from a "learning style." (In fact "style" turns out to

be a slippery concept, one quite different from an intelligence.)
4. There is an official Gardner or "MI approach" to schools. (There is not such an approach, and I hope there never will be.)

My psychologist colleagues are more likely to succumb to three other myths:

5. MI theory is not based on empirical data. (This nonsensical view could not be held by anyone who has ever spent more than five minutes skimming through the book.)
6. MI theory is incompatible with hereditarian or environmental accounts. (In fact, the theory takes no position on the sources of different intellectual profiles.)
7. Gardner's notion of intelligence is too broad. (Actually, it is the psychometric view that is too narrow, substituting one form of scholasticism for the rich set of capacities that comprise the human mind.)

One further misconception unites many skimmers with those who do not even bother to skim. That is a belief that I favor an un-rigorous curriculum, one that spurns the standard disciplines, hard work, and regular assessment.

Nothing could be further from the truth. I am actually a proponent of teaching the classical disciplines and I attempt to adhere to the highest standards, both for others and for myself. Unlike many readers, I see no incompatibility whatsoever between a belief in MI and pursuit of a rigorous education. Rather, I feel that only if we recognize multiple intelligences can we reach more students, and give those students the opportunity to demonstrate what they have understood.

TOWARD A DEEPER GRASP OF THE THEORY

Those who have studied key writings and have engaged in reflection and dialogue about the theory have come to appreciate a number of important insights. In what follows, I state these insights and suggest their possible educational implications.

The intelligences are based on explicit criteria.
What makes MI theory more than a parade of personal preferences is a set of eight criteria that were laid out explicitly in Chapter 4 of *Frames of Mind*. These range from the existence of populations that feature an unusual amount of a certain intelligence (e.g., prodigies); to localization of an intelligence in particular regions of the brain; to susceptibility to encoding in a symbolic system. Of the many candidate intelligences proposed and reviewed so far (e.g., auditory or visual; humor or cooking; intuitive or moral), only eight have qualified in terms of these criteria. Those who would posit additional intelligences have the obligation to assess candidates on these criteria, and to make available the results of this evaluation (Gardner, 1999).

The intelligences reflect a specific scientific wager. As I envision them, the intelligences have emerged over the millennia as a response to the environments in which humans have lived. They constitute, as it were, a cognitive record of the evolutionary past. If my list of intelligences is close to the mark, it will mean that my colleagues and I have succeeded in figuring out what the brain has evolved to do—to use a current phrase, that we have carved nature at its proper joints.

To be sure, culture has not evolved simply to fit nature, but the kinds of skills that we expect individuals to achieve do reflect the capacities that individuals actually possess. The challenge confronting educators is to figure out how to help individuals employ their distinctive intellectual profiles to help master the tasks and disciplines needed to thrive in the society.

The intelligences respond to specific content in the world.
Scientifically, an intelligence is best thought of as a "biopsychological construct": that is, if we understood much more than we do about the ge-

netic and neural aspects of the human mind, we could delineate the various psychological skills and capacities that humans are capable of exhibiting. Despite the convenient existence of the word, however, it makes little sense to think of intelligences in the abstract. Intelligences only come into being because the world in which we live features various contents—among them, the sounds and syntax of language, the sounds and rhythms of music, the species of nature, the other persons in our environment, and so on.

These facts lead to the most challenging implication of MI theory. If our minds respond to the actual varied contents of the world, then it does not make sense to posit the existence of "all-purpose" faculties. There is, in the last analysis, no *generalized* memory: There is memory for language, memory for music, memory for spatial environments, and so on. Nor, despite current buzzwords, can we speak about critical or creative thinking in an unmodified way. Rather, there is critical thinking using one or more intelligences, and there is creativity in one, or in more than one, domain.

Powerful educational implications lurk here. We must be leery about claiming to enhance general abilities like thinking or problem solving or memory; it is important to examine *which* problem is being solved, *which* kind of information is being memorized. Even more important, the teacher must be wary of claims about transfer. Though transfer of skill is a proper goal for any educator, such transfer cannot be taken for granted—and especially not when such transfer is alleged to occur across intelligences. The cautious educator assumes that particular intelligences can be enhanced, but remains skeptical of the notion that use of one set of intellectual skills will necessarily enhance others.

Despite the seductive terminology, we cannot assess intelligences: We can at most assess proficiency in different tasks.
Given the positing of multiple intelligences, there is an almost inevitable slippage toward the idea

that we could assess an individual's intelligences, or profile of intelligences. And even those who recognize the limits (or inappropriateness) of standard measures are still tempted to create some kind of a battery or milieu that "takes the temperature" of different intelligences. I know: I have more than once succumbed to this temptation myself.

But because intelligences are the kinds of constructs that they are, it is simply not possible to assess an individual intelligence or an individual's intelligences with any degree of reliability. All that one can ever assess in psychology is performance on some kind of task. And so, if an individual does well in learning a melody and in recognizing when that melody has been embedded in harmony, we do not have the right to proclaim her "musically intelligent"; the most that we can infer is that the individual has presumptively exhibited musical intelligence on this single measure.

The greater the number of tasks sampled, the more likely it is that a statement about "strength" or "weakness" in an intelligence will acquire some validity. Even here, however, one must be careful. For just because it *appears* that a task was solved by the use of a particular intelligence, we cannot be certain this is so. A person is free to solve a task in whichever manner he likes. Inferences about mind or brain mechanisms can only be made as a result of carefully designed experiments, ones that most educators (and, truth to tell, most researchers) are in no position to conduct.

For informal purposes, it is certainly acceptable to speculate that a person is relying on certain intelligences rather than others, or that she exhibits a strength in one but not another intelligence. Because actual inference about intelligences is problematic, however, educators should be cautious about characterizing the intellectual profiles of students. While seven or eight labels may be preferable to one (smart or stupid), labeling can still be pernicious, and particularly so when there is little empirical warrant for it.

The road between theory and practice runs in two directions.

Many individuals, practitioners as well as researchers, adopt a jaundiced view of the relation between theory and practice. On this "conduit" view, researchers collect data and then develop theories about a topic (say, the nature of human intelligence); the implications of the theories are reasonably straightforward (e.g., let's train all intelligences equally); and practitioners consume the material and attempt to apply the theory as faithfully as possible (Voilà—behold a multiple intelligences classroom!).

This description is wrong in every respect. Within the research world, the relations among theory, data, and inference are complex and ever-changing. Any theoretical statement or conclusion can lead to an indefinite number of possible practical implications. Only actual testing "in the real world" will indicate which, if any, of the implications holds water. And most important, those who theorize about the human world have as much to learn from practitioners as vice versa.

Continuing the confessional mode of this essay, I freely admit that I once held a version of this mental model. While I was not initially bent on applying my theory in practical settings, I assumed that the theory would be revised in the light of further research and nothing else.

Here the events of the past decade have been most auspicious—and most enlightening. My colleagues and I have learned an enormous amount from the various practical projects that have been inspired by MI theory—those that we designed ourselves (Gardner, 1993b) and equally, those generated by ingenious practitioners such as the writers of these essays (cf., Krechevsky, Hoerr, and Gardner, 1995). Readers of this theme section will profit as they ponder Sue Teele's documentation of shifting intellectual enthusiasms over time; Peter Smagorinsky's and Ellen Weber's efforts to engage the passions and imaginations of secondary school students; the pioneering steps taken by Tom Hoerr and his staff to place the personal intelligences at the center of curriculum and assessment; Shirley Jordan's exhortation to broaden our notion of what youngsters can achieve; Richard Colwell and Lyle Davidson's potent arguments for the cultivation of musical intelligence; and Patricia Bolaños' thoughtful reflections on the "mental models" of a staff that is attempting to break open a multiple intelligences pathway. Reminding us that new approaches to intelligence and education are not restricted to the present author, readers may also be instructed by the writings of Robert Sternberg and Joseph Gauld.

Developmental psychology and cognitive psychology confirm an important lesson: It is not possible to short-circuit the learning process. Even those with more than a nodding acquaintance with "MI theory" need to work out their understandings in their own way and at their own pace. And if my own understanding of the theory continues to change, I can hardly expect anyone else to accept any "reading" as conclusive—even that of the founding theorist. Still, I hope that these reflections may help to frame readers' encounters with MI theory and efforts to draw on these ideas in ways that are helpful to students.

REFERENCES

Gardner, H. *Frames of Mind: The Theory of Multiple Intelligences.* New York: Basic Books, 1983. (A tenth anniversary edition with a new introduction was published in 1993.)

———. *Multiple Intelligences. The Theory in Practice.* New York: Basic Books, 1993b.

———. "Reflections on Multiple Intelligences: Myths and Messages." *Phi Delta Kappan,* November 1995.

———. "Are There Additional Intelligences?" In *Education, Information, and Transformation: Essays on Learning and Thinking,* edited by J. Kane. Englewood Cliffs, NJ.: Prentice-Hall, 1999.

Krechevsky, M.; Hoerr, T.; and Gardner, H. "Complementary Energies: Implementing MI Theory from the Laboratory and the Field." In *Creating New Educational Communities,* 94th Yearbook of the National Society for the Study of Education (Part 1), edited by J. Oakes and K. H. Quartz. Chicago, Ill.: University of Chicago Press, 1995.

Howard Gardner is professor of education and codirector of Project Zero at the Harvard Graduate School of Education and an adjunct professor of neurology at the Boston University School of Medicine.

QUESTIONS FOR REFLECTION

1. Why does Gardner believe "we must be leery about claiming to enhance general abilities like thinking or problem solving or memory"? What are the implications of this statement for curriculum planners?
2. Why should educators be cautious about characterizing the intellectual profiles of students?
3. What does Gardner mean when he states that "The road between theory and practice runs in two directions"? What professional experiences have you had that confirm Gardner's view?

Giving Credit Where Credit Is Due

KATHIE F. NUNLEY

ABSTRACT: Kathie F. Nunley discusses the need for a student-centered education to improve student learning. Students have different learning capabilities, so it is important to develop a variety of instructional strategies fit to students in order to catch their attention—attention is the gateway to learning. Moreover, she introduces the Layered Curriculum that integrates the three keys of learning: choice, accountability, and complex thinking.

The educational system may be slow to change, but education practitioners are not. We have been quick to grab the wealth of brain research we have received over the last decade and have made some significant changes in the way we think about delivering instruction. Teachers are finding that some simple changes in their teaching strategy can have a huge effect on classroom effectiveness.

Research continues to reveal some basic keys to a student's brain and how it learns. First, variety in instructional strategies is one key to a successful classroom. No two brains are alike; from conception to puberty, students' brains weed out nearly 80% of their cells, keeping only the 20% or so that are most useful. And the nerve cells they do keep form pathways of differing strengths based on the frequency of their use (Ratey, 2001; Shepherd, 1998). So the first thing classroom teachers must realize is that every brain—and every student—is unique. Therefore, even the very best instructional strategy will not be best for everyone.

Second, attention is a very primitive function in the brain, but it is the gateway to learning. As James (1890/1955) noted more than 100 years ago, "Millions of items of the outward order are present to my senses which never properly enter into my experience. Why? Because they have no interest for me. My experience is what I agree to attend to. Only those items which I notice shape my mind" (p. 402). Consequently, if a teacher doesn't have a student's attention, no learning is taking place. Providing students with assignment choices makes a student-centered classroom. The student must be attending to the task at hand, and the easiest way to get their attention is through the perception of choice and control. Any type of student-centered classroom increases learning because students perceive that they have made their own decision to do an assignment and they take ownership in the work. Although classrooms certainly need structure and routine, they should never be dictatorships. The traditional "my way or no way" type of teaching stigmatizes learning, not only because it limits choice, but also because it limits the students' perception of control.

Everyone wants to feel like they have some control over the decisions that affect them. When people have no control, they often try to take it. The vast majority of classroom management problems are control issues. Nothing reduces classroom management struggles quicker than shifting some of the control, or at least the perception of control, to the students.

With this shift of control comes additional student responsibility. Because students are making their own choices, they now are also responsible for those choices and the consequences of their decisions. Many students initially may balk at this shift toward personal responsibility as they adjust from a traditional teacher-centered classroom, but decisiveness and responsibility must be learned. We simply cannot control all aspects of a student's life from 8 a.m. until 3 p.m. every day for 12 years, and then turn that young person loose in society and expect him or her to make good decisions and assume responsibility for his or her actions. If students are not taught in school, they will be taught in society where the consequences can be much more severe.

LEARNER ACCOUNTABILITY

The cells in a child's brain grow branches from stimulation and continue to grow throughout his or her life, although this cell branching occurs on a much larger scale during childhood and adolescence. It is this branching that results in strong, useful brains and ultimately determines the quality of our lives. We teachers might think of ourselves as gardeners, helping students grow beautifully branched brains. But for that to happen, we must first have students' attention and cooperation. We can accomplish that with choice; control; opportunities to tie new knowledge to previous knowledge; and above all else, by increasing learner accountability.

While visiting a high school classroom in Maryland recently, I stopped by the desk of a student engaged in a vocabulary assignment. He was copying the work of a classmate onto his paper. I asked him what he was doing, and he was forthright in telling me that he was "copying definitions."

Amazed at the blatant copying from another student's paper to his own, I asked, "Aren't you supposed to be doing this on your own so that you will learn these words?"

"Oh, I know all of them. I just need to copy the definitions down on paper," he said.

"Why?" I asked.

"I don't know. That's just what we're supposed to do."

Unfortunately, this scenario is all too common in schools. Students have lost (or have never found) the connection between day to day schoolwork, homework, and learning. Perhaps it is because teachers don't stop often enough and ask themselves, Why? Why am I assigning this? Why are students doing this? Why this number, this paper, this task?

One reason is that there is rarely any accountability at this level. Despite the fact that educational accountability has become a popular topic in the political arena and in the media, few people address the topic of student accountability. How can teachers and schools be held accountable for student learning until students are held accountable for their own? Accountability must be bottom-up, not top-down.

The problem is not necessarily the fault of education practitioners. It has been an integral part of the system for so long that it has become the norm. Education has focused far too long on the process to the extent that we have forgotten the product. We only ask, "Did you do your homework?" rather than, "Did you learn from your homework?" If you did the assignment, credit is awarded, thus implying that the value was in the doing without regard for any learning. We often hear even parents say, "Well, she did it; doesn't that count?"

As many of us know, sometimes "doing" an assignment just means you know who to sit with at lunch, because the reality is that anyone can complete an assignment if he or she has enough friends. What frequently happens is that students do a lot of assignments, which gives them enough points in the grade book to offset low test scores, which leads to a passing grade at the end of the term or school year. And that is part of the reason that some students progress through grade levels and subjects learning very little, if anything.

A decade ago, when Layered Curriculum was in its infancy and still just a student-centered model primarily for high school classrooms, few people understood why I held student accountability in such high regard. Although today we see hundreds of modifications and uses for the model, accountability remains its cornerstone. The model was designed to ensure students' attention, encourage higher-level thinking, and increase student accountability.

When curriculum is layered, assignment choices are used to gain student attention and ownership, as well as allow for the huge variety of brains in the classroom. Grades are aligned with the complexity of the assignment to encourage students to think at higher levels. And all assignments require some type of oral defense to assess learning and award points. Points, and subsequently grades, are given to students on the basis of what they learned, not on what they did.

For example, a vocabulary flash card assignment may be worth 10 points. Simply making the flash cards, however, does not give the student any points. The points come from the oral assessment. Oral assessments are done one-on-one at the student's desk as the teacher moves around the classroom. As the teacher, I choose five flash cards at random, ask the student the words, and award two points for each one he or she can explain correctly. If the student knew four of the five vocabulary words, he or she earned eight points, two out of five would be worth four points, and so on.

In the beginning of the year, oral defense is always met with surprise and sometimes a bit of anger. Students have never been asked to defend day-to-day work. I get such responses as, "Oh, you mean I did all this for nothing?" Students are surprised to discover that if they did not learn anything from the assignment, then it was, in fact, done for nothing.

The purpose of doing an assignment like vocabulary flash cards is not to see who can make flash cards. The purpose is to learn vocabulary. So the points come from the learning, not the doing. As you can see, this is a real shift in thinking on the part of both teacher and student.

What I'm really saying to students is, "Here is what I want you to learn. I don't care how you learn it, just learn it. Let me give you some suggestions and ideas for how other people have learned this. It doesn't matter which method you choose as long as you learn it." This variety of assignment choices in the curriculum provides several options for learning a task or meeting the objective.

As another example, let's look at a typical math homework assignment. We might say to a class, "Work these 40 sample problems for homework." But why 40? Why not 4 or 400? We all know that some students will catch the skill by the 5th problem and some students will still not have mastered it after the 40th sample problem. What is the real purpose to the homework? To work 40 sample problems or to learn the skill?

My favorite example is from a math teacher who assigned such homework as, "Work these 40 practice problems or as many as you need to work to master the skill. But work at least 5." Homework points were awarded in one of two ways. Students could either turn in all 40 practice problems or they could draw a 3×5 index card out of a pile of sample problems and work it correctly. Either way, you got the homework points.

In this classroom, students understood the why of the homework The purpose was clearly defined: "You need to be able to work this type of problem." Running this type of classroom clearly puts the responsibility on the students. The teacher plays the role of facilitator or coach. We say to the student, "You need to learn this. How you do it is up to you. I'll help you in whatever way I can, but the bottom line is you need to learn it, so points and grades will be awarded on what you've learned, not how you got there."

DESIGNING LAYERED CURRICULUM

In the early 1990s, I sought to integrate some of the new research into my high school science classroom. As new information emerged, changes were made and the result was the student-centered model of Layered Curriculum that integrates the three keys: choice, accountability, and increasingly complex thinking.

To write a layered lesson plan, the teacher simply takes the main concepts, tasks, and skills that need to be taught in a lesson and divides them into 3 layers based on the complexity of the task, along the lines of Bloom's Taxonomy. Simple, basic concepts go into the C layer; more complex thinking skills in the B layer; and the most complex, higher level thinking skills go in the A layer. Labeled *C*, *B*, and *A*, the layers correspond to the actual letter grade the student earns. So a grade of C is earned by students who complete a specified number of basic knowledge and rote learning assignments. A grade of B is earned by students who work through the C layer and the B layer that includes more complex activities, such as manipulating the information or applying new skills. A grade of A is earned by students who work through the C layer, B layer, and the A layer, which asks students to think critically and mix research with ethics, values, and opinion.

Each layer provides a menu of assignment choices that represent different learning styles, abilities, and disability accommodations. Students can choose which assignments they'd like to complete. Assignments vary in the number of points they are worth based on their complexity. Students work their way through the increasingly complex layers, and all assignments require an oral defense.

SUCCESSFUL INCLUSION

Shifting the attention from doing to learning has another advantage as well: It allows more students to be successful. During a recent visit to a California high school, I had the opportunity to work with some students in a biology classroom.

Many of the students were being mainstreamed into the regular classroom for the first time.

I stopped to help a young man answer some questions from his textbook. He had been staring at his blank sheet of paper for some time, so I pulled up a chair and we began what turned into a delightful conversation about the material in the text that the class had been reading. The young man seemed to be genuinely interested in the topic. We took each question from the book and discussed it.

After we finished the discussion of the entire section, I was duly impressed. "Why, that's wonderful," I said. "You really know your material! I guess you've finished with this assignment."

"No," the young man replied. "I have to write it all out."

"Why?" I asked.

"I don't know. We just have to."

And with that, he put the pencil down, put his head on the desk, and remained that way until the bell rang. At the end of class, students turned

FIGURE 1

Layered Lesson Plan	
Layers	**Grades**
A Most complex, higher-level thinking skills. Mix research with ethics, values, and opinions.	A
B More complex thinking skills such as manipulation of information or application of new skills.	B
C Completion of a specific number of basic knowledge and rote learning assignments.	C

In a layered lesson plan, simple, basic concepts go into the C layer; more complex thinking skills in the B layer; and the most complex, higher-level thinking skills go in the A layer.

in their class work as they left the room. But this young man had nothing to pass in. He took a zero for the day rather than have to write down his answers. For this student, writing was such an overwhelming task that he would rather not receive credit for his learning than go through, for him, a very painstaking process.

Oral defense frees students from many of the obstacles that hold them back in school. It gives credit where credit is due and often determines where credit is not due. It takes time for teachers to develop efficient oral defense skills, however, especially in large classes. In the beginning, don't try to grade every assignment from every student every day. Work up to that goal. To start, teachers may just want to visit with each student at least once during each unit. Or perhaps the students can put together a portfolio of assignments and choose two or three to discuss with the teacher. Most teachers find the oral defense gets much easier and more efficient with practice.

Shifting the power of control in the classroom from teacher to student not only makes class-rooms more effective, but also puts the fun back in teaching. Most of us don't teach because of the huge paycheck, the delicious school lunch, or the dynamic faculty meetings on Monday afternoon. We teach because we love the relationships we build with our students. When you spend your class time moving around to meet students one-on-one and let them share with you what they have discovered and learned, you revel in the true joy of teaching. It is indeed what calls us back to the classroom year after year.

REFERENCES

James, W. (1890/1950). *Principles of psychology*. Mineola, NY: Dover.

Ratey, J. J. (2001). *A user's guide to the brain: Perception, attention, and the four theaters of the brain.* New York: Pantheon Books.

Shepherd, G. M. (Ed.). (1998). *The synaptic organization of the brain* (4th ed.). New York and Oxford: Oxford University Press.

Kathie F. Nunley, author of *A Student Brain: The Parent/Teacher Manual,* is an educator and researcher residing in Salt Lake City, Utah. She co-founded the Brains.org web site and developed the Layered Curriculum method of teaching.

QUESTIONS FOR REFLECTION

1.   What is the Layered Curriculum that Nunley writes about in her article? What makes this approach to teaching different from other models currently used today? How different are her three keys to learning (choice, accountability, and complex thinking) to what many teachers already teach?

2.   Why does Nunley stress learning accountability in her writing? What curricular benefit is there in placing the learner at the center of what is expected in terms of outcomes? According to Nunley, how have students lost the connection between school work and learning?

3.   Do you agree with Nunley that education has "focused far too long on the process to the extent that we have forgotten the product"? Does today's accountability movement signal a shift to more "product driven" education and outcomes?

Learning Styles from a Multicultural Perspective: The Case for Culturally Engaged Education

CYNTHIA B. DILLARD
DIONNE A. BLUE

ABSTRACT: When developing educational experiences for students from ethnically and culturally diverse backgrounds, teachers should recognize that their personal perspectives influence their curricular decisions. Since no particular learning style is preferred by an ethnic or cultural group, effective teachers use an array of strategies to facilitate students' learning and growth. By using the concept of "culturally engaged education" as a framework for curriculum planning, teachers can create educational experiences that support and develop both their students and themselves.

The idea of multiculturalism is not new to public education. Although there are still a few public schools in the United States with relatively homogeneous ethnic and linguistic populations, it is difficult to ignore the rapidly changing students in our schools. America is truly a multicultural society.

The number of students from diverse cultural and linguistic backgrounds is increasing. According to estimates in *One Third of a Nation,* a report published in 1988 by the American Council on Education and the Education Commission of the States, at least one-third of Americans will be people of color by the year 2000. Many will come from homes where the primary language is not English. The National Clearinghouse for Bilingual Education (1980) reports that the number of people from non-English-speaking homes and communities is expected to increase from about 33 million in 1987, to nearly 40 million by the year 2000. This increase in multicultural and multilingual populations is creating a new ethos for schooling in our nation.

Providing an appropriate education for students from ethnically and culturally diverse backgrounds is not an easy task. Delpit (1995) reminds us that "it is impossible to create a model for the good teacher without taking issues of culture and community context into account" (p. 37). Unfortunately, some have tended to view these students

as inherently deficient—culturally, linguistically, economically, and socially. This deficit perspective has led some teachers to view the education of ethnically diverse students as remedial, rather than developmental or growth-oriented. This view often leads to student alienation. Students may reject the school's culture and codes of power in lieu of patterns that allow for alternative ways of creativity and empowerment, a type of "counter culture" (Delpit, 1995).

Others see ethnically and culturally diverse students as a source of enrichment and embrace diversity as a way to inform their own teaching and enhance all students' learning. They realize the importance of their role in accepting and integrating multicultural perspectives into their teaching.

BEYOND CONTENT: THE ROLE OF TEACHER PERSPECTIVE

Teaching is more than a matter of following a set of strategies. Our choices of subject matter and teaching techniques are grounded in our personal perspectives. Shibutani (1955) defines *perspective* as:

An ordered view of one's world—what is taken for granted about the attributes of various objects, events and human nature. It is an order of things remembered and expected as well as things actually perceived, an organized conception of what is plausible and what is possible; it constitutes the matrix through which one perceives their environment. (p. 564)

Such a perspective guides teachers in making decisions about the curriculum and strategies to be used in the classroom. If we seek to embrace a more culturally diverse perspective related to planning a curriculum, we must also recognize the need to broaden our own perspectives. We must acknowledge, in an explicit manner, the personal perspectives from which we teach and realize, as well as admit to our students, their limited scope (Greene, 1978; Vogeler, 1990). Further, we must acknowledge that in our classrooms there will be a myriad of perspectives held by our students, some of which may be contradictory to the ones we hold. Our own perspective should not become the normative experience by which we judge our students as morally or intellectually correct (Brown, 1988). Instead, our task is one of structuring the curriculum to help our students and ourselves "center" our personal histories and experiences. According to Brown (1988), this is not simply an intellectual process, but rather "about coming to believe in the possibility of a variety of experiences, a variety of ways of understanding the world, a variety of frameworks of operation, without imposing consciously or unconsciously a notion of the norm" (p. 10). What Brown describes has profound implications for curriculum development.

Education, by its very nature, is a social activity. In our classrooms, students observe and experience a wide range of lessons, both intended and unintended. They are involved in relationships of power and authority. They engage in decision making about learning. They see and are involved in a variety of participation structures enacted in classrooms and schools. They are exposed to new and old information and multiple presentations of it. Thus, Harste, Woodward, and Burke (1984) suggest that developing a true multicultural curriculum includes understanding

the key role we must play in participating *with* our students in classrooms.

Hence, curriculum development may be seen as a social, collaborative effort involving teachers, students, parents, and others. Further, an understanding of our students' learning styles fosters an awareness of and appreciation for the multitude of experiences represented in our classrooms and our world. It implies that our interpretation of what is important for our students needs to be open for negotiation with our students. Thus, learning styles in an environment that fosters multicultural understandings focuses on the social nature of education, where everyone and everything is a learning possibility. We turn now to an examination of learning styles within the social and cultural environment of the multicultural classroom.

LEARNING STYLES IN A SOCIOCULTURAL CONTEXT

Many attempts have been made to understand learning styles, from the simply definitional, to elaborate categorizations of elements that make up a particular style. However, it is important to remember that no particular learning style is strictly preferred by an ethnic or cultural group. In fact, the diversity within and among cultures is great and depends on such factors as geography, language, and social class. Furthermore, according to Scarcella (1990), the task, subject matter, and curriculum will influence which style of learning students prefer to use in a given situation. Heath (1986), in her research on the sociocultural contexts of language development suggests further that styles of learning can differ dramatically between the home and community and the schools and classroom. Therefore, as Scarcella (1990) suggests, teachers should use a variety of strategies to facilitate learning for students with various learning styles.

Although there are a number of definitions of learning styles, we will use the broad definition advocated by Hunt (1979) in the early learning styles literature: "Learning style describes a student in terms of those educational conditions under which he/she is most likely to learn. Learning style describes *how* a student learns, not what he/she has learned" (p. 27). Hunt's definition implies the need for teachers to consider not only the place where the student's personal culture meets that of the school, but also the nature of the social context of such a meeting. On the one hand, a student's learning style is distinct and personal, inseparable from the lived experiences of that individual. On the other, one's learning style is followed (or not followed) in relation to the larger social contexts of schools. Thus, the concept of *authenticity* is important in building on the learning styles of students in a multicultural setting. For this discussion, *authenticity* refers to *genuinely inviting students to learn in ways that are appropriate and meaningful to them*. Facilitating such authenticity is an important act of personal affirmation for all of our students. Students from historically marginalized backgrounds and linguistic traditions can see that their personal style of learning is as valid as their teacher's and that of other students. Learning that one's way of knowing is valid and important may have profound meaning for students from groups who have been ignored or pushed to the margins of our classrooms (Dillard, 1994). According to Shor and Freire (1987), such knowledge is truly empowering and important for student success. Further, when we provide spaces in the curriculum for a variety of styles to be enacted, we help students understand different approaches to the processes of learning.

NEGOTIATING THE CURRICULUM: CONSIDERATIONS FOR CURRICULUM PLANNERS

From this discussion, it is clear that learning styles must be considered from both a student's individual and personal culture and the sociocultural environment of the school. With so many necessary elements to consider in the development of multicultural curriculum, where does this leave

the teacher? How, with such variety both within and across ethnic and cultural groups, can we most appropriately develop a curriculum that responds to and respects such diversity?

Slavin (1987) suggests that the age of negotiation is upon us. In contrast to the teacher-centered instruction often found in our nation's schools, a classroom environment in schools that is founded on collaboration and negotiation can help to provide all learners with access to a meaningful education. The goal of such a multicultural education, according to Bennett (1995), is "to maximize the number of stars that can exist simultaneously in the classroom, to formulate a plan that can work with the most diverse group of students" (p. 163). Such an environment will require alternative ways of thinking about learning and teaching, often simultaneously. It will also require that we "re-think" not only how we facilitate learning for ourselves and our students, but also ways to move the discussion of student learning styles in multicultural classrooms beyond stereotypes and into a more useful conversation about multicultural pedagogy and practice. Banks (1995) also outlines elements of multicultural education that would serve to move that conversation forward. His notion of multicultural education, as "content integration; the knowledge construction process; prejudice reduction; an equity pedagogy; and an empowering school culture and social structure" (p. 4) provides a framework educators can use to create pedagogy which is culturally relevant, that engages each student, and values the various learning styles they bring to the classroom. Understanding learning style patterns that seem to characterize various ethnic groups is not enough. Teachers must also consider ways to restructure the curriculum to truly allow students to learn in different ways, grounded in harmony with their cultural backgrounds. This requires broadening our own perspectives to see learning styles as an extension of who our students are as individuals.

Many scholars advocate an integrated approach for curriculum development that is sensitive to the diverse learning styles of students and applicable to the multicultural and linguistically diverse student populations in our schools. They advocate a curriculum that is a cooperative venture between teachers and students, one that embraces learning styles not so much as ethnic-specific characteristics, but as ways in which all students' culture, language, and ways of being in the classroom are valued. For example, Shor (1986) suggests that the following elements be considered in all curriculum plans if they are to be responsive to multiple learning styles:

1. *Problem solving:* Allowing all students to know that their participation and critical contribution is expected, valued, and needed to solve problems of interest to the learning community.
2. *Critical literacy:* Questioning aspects of literacy, including reading, writing, speaking, listening, and thinking; also extends students' knowledge, and assists them in moving beyond memorization.
3. *Situated pedagogy:* Integrating the experiential with the conceptual, both of which should necessarily be grounded in the life experiences of those in the learning–teaching environment of the classroom.
4. *Cross-cultural communication:* Providing opportunities for students to have long-term and authentic experiences with students and peoples of diverse backgrounds and cultures.
5. *Education as a change agent:* Recognizing that schools are intimately influenced and connected with the broader society.
6. *An integrated interdisciplinary approach:* Seeing the content of schools as related and influential, assisting our students in developing their own understandings and perspectives.
7. *Participatory learning:* Modeling democratic ideals by allowing students to be responsive to and responsible for other persons in the learning environment.

Ladson-Billings's (1994) notion of *culturally relevant pedagogy* provides another model for negotiating multicultural learning styles in curriculum development. Operating along a continuum, Ladson-Billings (1992) operationally describes culturally relevant teaching as an approach that

> serves to empower students to the point where they will be able to examine critically educational content and process and ask what its role is in creating a truly democratic and multicultural society. It uses the students' culture to help them create meaning and understand the world. Thus, not only academic success, but social and cultural success are emphasized. (p. 110)

Thus, culturally relevant teachers make pedagogical moves that envision themselves as part of the communities in which they teach and see their role as giving something back to the community. They believe that success is possible for all students and at least part of that success is helping students make connections between themselves and their communities, as well as their national, ethnic, and global identities. There is a connectedness with all students and encouragement for cooperation and collaboration. Finally, culturally relevant teaching recognizes that knowledge is continuously recreated, reconstructed, and shared. However, culturally relevant teachers take a critical view of knowledge as culturally and socially constructed and demonstrate a passion for teaching critical thinking to their students (Ladson-Billings, 1992, 1994).

A related idea is hooks's (1994) concept of *engaged pedagogy. Engaged pedagogy* is an approach to teaching and learning that acknowledges the politics of both, seeks to engage in reciprocal and authentic ways on more intimate terrain in learning communities, and encourages teachers and students to recognize, discuss, and ultimately act through our politics as dynamic and changing sites of transformation towards freedom. In this way, hooks extends Ladson-Billings' definition by seeing teaching and learning as intimate and reciprocal educative processes.

While Ladson-Billings's culturally relevant pedagogy and hooks's engaged pedagogy provide strong bases for attention to learning styles in a multicultural classroom environment, each construct is limited in its ability to describe a deeply influential, more encompassing way in which students and teachers actually experience the impact of learning styles—as *personal, cultural affirmation and interaction between teachers, students, curriculum, and contexts that attend to and support everyone's educational interests, motivations, and needs as individuals.* Thus, we'd like to introduce another construct, one that might be salient for reconceptualizing learning styles in multicultural education in ways more responsive to the diverse student populations in our nation's schools. This construct is *culturally engaged education* (Dillard & Ransom, 1998). Culturally engaged education seeks the integration, interconnectedness, and extension of teaching and learning relationships for the purposes of the overall support and development of both the teacher and the taught. Thus, pedagogy and curriculum take on an expanded meaning here, beyond simply a set of discreet tasks carried out by teachers, to a confluence of involvement in personal, academic, and intellectual lives, creating relationships that inform and support both teachers and students, as well as a broader agenda of transformation and liberation through education, particularly for people of color.

It is important to note that within this construct, even the terms *teacher* and *student* are problematic, given the hierarchical assumptions embedded within them. While one cannot ignore the relative nature of power held by the teacher, we suggest that culturally engaged education assumes that teachers are also transformed through the act of teaching since they must attempt to be fully present with students as they learn. With this perspective as a more encompassing way to reconceptualize teaching, we close with ten guiding principles for culturally engaged education that meets the diverse styles of learning found in today's multicultural classrooms.

1. Culturally engaged education begins with self-inquiry. Understanding one's self as a culturally constructed being is key, and can be fostered through explorations of one's autobiography, life narratives, and stories as a first step toward understanding one's style of learning (and teaching). It is the basis upon which to build coalitions and connections across cultures.

2. Culturally engaged education must foster and include voices from multiple cultural and ethnic groups and from multiple perspectives. Student and teacher self-knowledge are both valid and relevant versions of "truth."

3. Culturally engaged education is inherently reciprocal, built in relationships based on all parties being both teacher and taught, and contingent upon who has the knowledge and experiences to teach at any given moment.

4. Culturally engaged education sees experiential knowledge as necessary and requires long-term direct experiences with diverse peoples, languages/discourses, and contexts, and cultural and social support for diverse ways of knowing (theory) and ways of being (culture).

5. Culturally engaged education requires acknowledgment of "differences" as real and valuable, not deviant and undesirable.

6. Culturally engaged education requires strong efforts to include all voices in the learning community in issues of curricular, political, and cultural development and in real versus solely symbolic or "token" ways. This includes the voices of children.

7. Culturally engaged education acknowledges the systematic nature of racism, discrimination in all forms, other societal ills, and one's own contributions/complicity in these ills, while also engaging in individual and social action to address and remedy these problems.

8. Culturally engaged education requires ongoing efforts to deconstruct myths and privilege and facilitate access to knowledge and opportunity, particularly in K–12 schools.

9. Culturally engaged education attends to the aesthetic, encourages creativity in knowing

and being, and is spiritual, seeking wholeness of individual realities.

10. Culturally engaged education holds humility, passion for education, and caring at the
center of all work, seeking the betterment of
one's self and humanity as its purpose.

REFERENCES

Banks, J. A. (1995). Multicultural education: Historical development, dimensions and practice. In J. A.
Banks & C. A. M. Banks (Eds.), *Handbook of research on multicultural education* (pp. 3–24). New
York: Macmillan Publishing.

Bennett, C. I. (1995). *Comprehensive multicultural
education: Theory and practice* (4th edition).
Boston: Allyn and Bacon.

Brown, E. B. (1988). African-American women's quilt-
ing: A framework for conceptualizing and teaching
African-American women's history. In M. R. Mal-
son, E. Mudimbe-boyi, J. F. O'Barr & M. Wyer
(Eds.), *Black women in America: Social science perspectives*. Chicago: University of Chicago Press.

Commission on Minority Participation in Education
and American Life (1988). *One-third of a nation*.
Washington, DC: American Council on Education
and the Education Commission of the States.

Delpit, L. (1995). *Other people's children: Cultural
conflict in the classroom*. New York: The New Press.

Dillard, C. B., & Ransom, R. M. (1998, February).
*(Re)defining recruitment and retention: A model of
cultural engagement for colleges of education*. Paper
presented at the annual meeting of the American
Association of Colleges for Teacher Education,
New Orleans, LA.

Dillard, C. B. (1994). Beyond supply and demand:
Critical pedagogy, ethnicity, and empowerment in
recruiting teachers of color. In *Journal of teacher
education, 45,* 9–17.

Fine, M. (1989). Silencing and nurturing voice in an
improbable context: Urban adolescents in public
schools. In H. A. Giroux & P. McLaren (Eds.),
Critical pedagogy, the state and cultural struggle.
New York: SUNY Press.

Greene, M. (1978). Teaching: The question of personal reality. In *Teachers College Record, 80,* 23–35.

Harste, J., Woodward, V., & Burke, C. (1984).
Methodological implications. *Language Stories
and Literacy Lessons*. Exeter, NH: Heinemann.

Heath, S. B. (1986). Sociocultural contexts of language development. In *Beyond language: Social
and cultural factors in schooling language minority
students*. Sacramento: California State Department
of Education Bilingual Education Office.

Hunt, D. E. (1979). Learning style and student
needs: Introduction to conceptual level. In *Student
learning styles: Diagnosing and prescribing programs*. Reston, VA: National Association of Secondary School Principals.

hooks, b. (1994). *Teaching to transgress: Education as
the practice of freedom*. New York: Routledge.

Ladson-Billings, G. (1994). *The dreamkeepers: Successful teachers of African American children*. San
Francisco: Jossey-Bass Publishers.

Ladson-Billings, G. (1992). Culturally relevant teaching: The key to making multicultural education
work. In C. Grant (Ed.), *Research and multicultural education: From the margins to the mainstream* (pp. 106–121). London: Falmer Press.

National Clearinghouse for Bilingual Education
(1980). *Non-English Language Background Projec-
tions by Language Groups, 1976–2000*. Rosslyn, VA:
National Clearinghouse for Bilingual Education.

Scarcella, R. (1990). Appealing to a variety of learning
styles. In *Teaching language minority students in
the multicultural classroom*. Englewood Cliffs, NJ:
Prentice-Hall.

Shibutani, T. (1955). Reference group as perspectives.
American Journal of Sociology, LX, 564.

Shor, I., & Freire, P. (1987). *A pedagogy for liberation*.
South Hadley, MA: Bergin and Garvey.

Shor, I. (1986). Equality is excellence: Transforming
teacher education and the learning process. *Harvard Education Review, 56,* 406–426.

Slavin, R. (1987). Cooperative learning and the cooperative school. *Educational Leadership, 45,* 7–13.

Vogeler, I. (1990). Cultural diversity: Ideology of content. *Issues in Teaching and Learning, 3,* 17–20.

Cynthia B. Dillard is Assistant Dean for Diversity and Outreach, College of Education, and Associate
Professor, School of Teaching and Learning, The Ohio State University; and *Dionne A. Blue* is a doctoral candidate and Graduate Associate, School of Teaching and Learning, The Ohio State University.

QUESTIONS FOR REFLECTION

1.   What are the "personal perspectives" that influence your curriculum planning activities?
2.   What is "culturally engaged education"? In regard to the subject matter and level of schooling with which you are most interested, describe two instances when the concept of "culturally engaged education" might be a useful curriculum criterion.
3.   Why do Dillard and Blue suggest that "the terms *teacher* and *student* are problematic, given the hierarchical assumptions embedded within them"?

Authentic Assessment and Student Performance in Inclusive Secondary Schools

M. BRUCE KING

JENNIFER SCHROEDER

DAVID CHAWSZCZEWSKI

ABSTRACT   This article outlines the model of Authentic Intellectual Work and presents initial findings from a study of inclusion and reform in four secondary schools across the United States. Generally, teachers were able to adapt assessments for special education students while maintaining intellectual challenge. Consistent with other research, there was a significant relationship between the authenticity of task demands and the authenticity of the work that students produced. With more authentic and challenging tasks, students with disabilities performed better than both students with and students without disabilities who received less authentic tasks.

In the current context of school reform, teaching and learning of high intellectual quality (e.g., Newmann & Wehlage, 1995) and teaching for understanding (e.g., Cohen, McLaughlin, & Talbert, 1993) offer compelling alternatives to more traditional forms of instruction focused on basic skills and content. In schools that restructure around a vision of authentic pedagogy and student achievement, students learn more and learning occurs more equitably across student groups (Newmann, Marks, & Gamoran, 1996). At the same time, calls for reform in special education focus on the inclusion of students with disabilities in general education classes (e.g., Lipsky & Gartner, 1996).

In this brief, we investigate the intersection of these reform movements. Specifically, we address two questions:

1. In secondary schools with inclusionary practices, to what extent are teacher-designed assessments authentic?
2. How do students with and without disabilities perform on these assessments?

Data comes from high schools that are participating in a 5-year national study conducted by the Research Institute on Secondary Education Reform (RISER) for Youth with Disabilities at the University of Wisconsin–Madison.

AUTHENTIC AND INCLUSIVE REFORM

Most recent education reforms have been generated with limited research on or consideration of the implications of the reforms for students with disabilities. But changes in special education do not evolve in isolation from broader national policy interests and issues. Thus, RISER is focused on schools engaged in reform efforts that include students with disabilities and seeks to identify educational practices that benefit *all* students.

RISER is grounded in the model of authentic intellectual work. Developed as part of a national study of school restructuring (Newmann & Wehlage, 1995), authentic teaching and learning provide the framework for the study of classroom practices that include both students with and students without disabilities. Authentic intellectual work is consistent with the recent emphasis on constructivist teaching, which has been advocated as a productive alternative to traditional instructional approaches in special education. These traditional approaches have been criticized for operating from a deficit model in which learning expectations for students with disabilities are significantly lowered (Trent, Artiles, & Englert, 1998).

---

*AUTHENTIC
INTELLECTUAL WORK*

- *Construction of Knowledge*
- *Disciplined Inquiry*
- *Value Beyond School*

Authentic intellectual work is defined by three general characteristics (Newmann & Wehlage, 1995). The first characteristic is *construction of knowledge*. In the conventional curriculum, students largely identify the knowledge that others have produced (e.g., by recognizing the difference between verbs and nouns, labeling parts of a plant, or matching historical events to their dates). In authentic work, however, students go beyond memorizing and repeating facts, information, definitions, or formulas to produce new knowledge or meaning. This kind of work involves higher order thinking in which students analyze, interpret, or evaluate information in a novel way. The mere reproduction of knowledge does not constitute authentic academic achievement.

A second defining feature of authentic achievement is its reliance on a particular type of cognitive work called *disciplined inquiry*. Disciplined inquiry consists of (a) using a knowledge base, (b) striving for in-depth understanding of relevant knowledge and concepts, and (c) expressing conclusions through elaborated communication. By contrast, much of the traditional pedagogy in schools asks students to show only a superficial awareness of a vast number of topics and requires only brief responses from students (e.g., true–false, multiple-choice, or short answers).

A third characteristic of authentic achievement is that it has *value beyond school*—that is, it has meaning or value apart from documenting or certifying the learner's competence. In authentic work, students make connections between what they are learning and important personal or social issues. Achievements of this sort—whether a performance, exhibition, or written communication—actually influence others and thus have a value that is missing in tasks such as quizzes and standardized tests that only assess an individual student's knowledge or skills.

These three characteristics are the basis for the standards we are using to assess the intellectual quality of teaching and learning in participating schools. (See sidebar for examples of standards for scoring teachers' assignments in writing and math. For all standards and scoring criteria used in this study, see the RISER Web site, www.wcer.wisc.edu/riser.) Teachers' lessons, assignments, and student work can score high on some of these characteristics but lower on others, and one would not expect all activities to score high on all three all of the time. *Practice, memorization, and drill are necessary to build the knowledge and skills needed for more challenging tasks or to prepare for exams required for promotion or advancement. But teachers should provide as much opportunity as possible for all students, including those with disabilities, to engage in and become competent in challenging intellectual work.*

Standards for Teachers' Assignments in Writing

Standard 1: Construction of Knowledge

The assignment asks students to interpret, analyze, synthesize, or evaluate information in writing about a topic, rather than merely to reproduce information.

Standard 2: Disciplined Inquiry Through Elaborated Written Communication

The assignment asks students to draw conclusions or make generalizations or arguments and support them through extended writing.

Standard 3: Value Beyond School Through Connection to Students' Lives

The assignment asks students to connect the topic to experiences, feelings, or situations significant in their lives.

Standards for Teachers' Assignments in Math

Standard 1: Construction of Knowledge

The assignment asks students to organize and interpret information in addressing a mathematical concept, problem, or issue.

Standard 2: Disciplined Inquiry Through Elaborated Written Communication

The assignment asks students to elaborate on their understanding, explanations, or conclusions through extended writing—for example, by explaining a solution path through prose, tables, equations, or diagrams.

Standard 3: Value Beyond School Through Connection to Students' Lives

The assignment asks students to address a concept, problem, or issue that is similar to one they have encountered or are likely to encounter in daily life outside school.

Also central to the SAIL model is the inclusion of special education students in the mainstream of the general education curriculum. Critics point to potentially serious problems with inclusion (see Hanley-Maxwell et al., 1999, for a summary), however, inclusion is prominent in the national reform agenda of special education. Proponents argue that with appropriate accommodations for students' disabilities, both special and regular education students should benefit from inclusive environments. Across the United States, students with a wide range of disabilities are being educated in inclusive settings. In this study of secondary schools that practice inclusion, we explore the degree of authenticity in teacher-designed assessments and the performance of regular and special education students on these assessments.

RESEARCH METHODOLOGY AND ANALYSIS

We present findings from two sets of data collected during the 1999–2000 school year. The first data set (*whole class*) included assessment tasks and the student work on those tasks from 8 teachers in each of two schools. These 16 teachers represented the main academic subject areas of language arts, science, math, and social studies—one teacher in each area from Grades 9–10, and one in each area from Grades 11–12 at each school. The teachers submitted one assessment task that they considered to be an important indicator of what students learned in one of their classes, along with the work the students in that class completed for that task. They also submitted a checklist of accommodations they made, if any, for students with disabilities.

The second data set (*matched pairs*) came from 35 teachers in three of the schools (Schroeder, 2000). The teachers represented the main academic subject areas of language arts, science, math, and social studies (8, 7, 10, and 10 teachers, respectively) across Grades 9–12. These teachers also submitted one assessment task that they considered to be an important indicator of what students learned in one of their classes.

However, this set of data differed from the first in that teachers submitted work completed by just two students in the classroom, one student with a disability and one student without a disability, allowing for comparisons between students with and without disabilities on each task. Teachers also submitted a checklist of accommodations they made, if any, for both regular and special education students.

For both data sets, each task was rated on the extent to which the intellectual work it required met each of three standards corresponding to the general characteristics of authentic achievement—construction of knowledge, in-depth understanding through elaborated written communication, and connection to students' lives. For example, a writing task that scored high on construction of knowledge would meet the following criterion: "The task's dominant expectation is for students to interpret, analyze, synthesize, or evaluate information, rather than merely to reproduce information." To score high on elaborated written communication, a mathematics task would need to ask explicitly for generalization and support in students' responses; that is, the task would require students to show through writing their solution paths and to explain the solution paths with evidence such as models or examples. To score high on the third standard—connection to students' lives—a science task would need to present students with a scientific question, issue, or problem that they would have actually encountered or would be likely to encounter in their daily lives; it would ask students to make connections between the topic and real-world situations.

Student work was also evaluated on three standards consistent with the characteristics of authentic intellectual work, but these standards varied somewhat by subject areas. The standards for student work in math, science, and social studies were analysis, disciplinary concepts, and elaborated written communication. The standards for student work in writing were construction of knowledge, forms and conventions, and elaborated written communication.

For both sets of data, scores assigned to the tasks and student work for each of the three standards of authenticity were added to yield two overall scores, one for authenticity of the task and one for authenticity of work produced by students. The scores for each of the standards and the two overall scores were then compared and statistical analyses run to determine if any differences existed between standards, between academic subjects, or between students with and without disabilities. Correlational analyses were also run on the overall scores to determine if any relationships existed between task authenticity and authenticity of work produced by students with and without disabilities. We report these results below.

FINDINGS (DATA SET 1, WHOLE CLASS)

Overall degree of authenticity of tasks. Across the 16 classes, the mean rating for task authenticity on all submitted tasks was 6.53 (*SD* = 1.33; SD stands for the standard deviation which is a measure of how much scores deviate from the mean.). Task authenticity scores can range from a low of 3 to a high of 10, which means that the mean score across all tasks fell in the middle of the range of possible scores. Despite this fact, the actual range for the scores on the assessment tasks included in this sample was from 3 to 8. Therefore, no task received the highest score possible for task authenticity, whereas one received the lowest score.

Across the 16 teachers in the four subject areas, the first two standards (construction of knowledge and elaborated written communication) received roughly equal emphasis on the tasks. Tasks in social studies, science, and writing scored consistently higher on construction of knowledge and elaborated written communication than did math tasks. Standard 3, connection to students' lives, scored consistently lower with all the tasks but one scoring a 1. This result exemplifies the persisting difficulty of developing assignments that ask students to address real-world problems and to explore the connections between topics or concepts and these problems.

Previous research has shown that student performance in math, social studies, and writing is higher in classes with higher levels of authentic pedagogy (Avery, 1999; Newmann & Associates, 1996; Newmann, Lopez, & Bryk, 1998; Newmann et al., 1996). We now explore whether this relationship holds in our study, both for regular and special education students.

Overall degree of authenticity of student work. For the 16 tasks submitted, the mean overall rating for the authenticity of work produced by students was 7.21 (SD = 2.41). Overall student work authenticity scores can range from a low of 3 to a high of 12, which means that the mean score across all student work fell close to the middle of the range of possible scores. The range of scores for the student work included in this sample was from 4 to 12. Therefore, some student work did receive the highest score possible for work authenticity, but none received the lowest score.

The authenticity ratings given to student work were further compared by student disability status. The scores on work produced by students *without* disabilities were compared to the scores on work produced by students *with* disabilities to determine if there were any significant differences between the work produced by the two groups. Overall, the mean rating of work authenticity for students without disabilities was 7.42 (SD = 2.47) and for students with disabilities was 6.54 (SD = 2.05). This difference was statistically significant, indicating that students with disabilities produced work lower in authenticity than that produced by their nondisabled peers.

Relationship between tasks and student achievement. Finally, we summarize findings on (a) the relationship between task authenticity and student achievement on the tasks and (b) achievement results for students with and without disabilities. The first important finding is that, consistent with previous research, there was a significant relationship between the authenticity of task demands and the authenticity of the work that students pro-

duced. That is, task demands that were rated lower in authenticity were associated with student work that was rated lower in authenticity. Conversely, task demands that were higher in authenticity were associated with student work that was also higher in authenticity. This relationship was the same for tasks and work produced by students with and without disabilities.

Categorizing tasks as below average in task authenticity (< 6.5) or above average in task authenticity (≥ 6.5) provides a further illustration of this relationship. The average authenticity score for student work when task demands were *below average* in authenticity was 6.24 (SD = 2.27). When task authenticity demands were *above average,* however, the average authenticity score for student work was 8.43 (SD = 2.01), a difference of more than two points (see Figure 1).

When task demands and student work were analyzed by student disability status, similar results were found (see Figure 2). On tasks that

FIGURE 1

Mean Ratings for Authenticity of All Student Work When Task Demands Are Categorized as Below or Above Average (First Data Set)

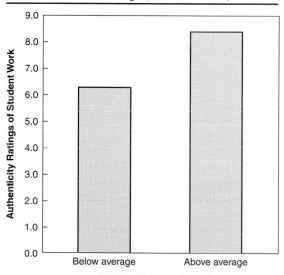

FIGURE 2

Mean Ratings for Authenticity of Student Work for Students with and without Disabilities Relative to Tasks Rated Below or Above Average in Authenticity (First Data Set)

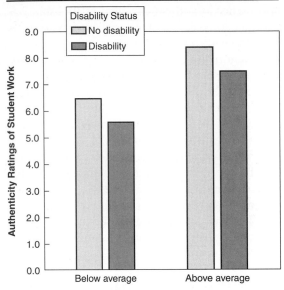

were below average in authenticity, students without disabilities produced work that received an average score of 6.42 (*SD* = 2.39). Students with disabilities produced work that received an average score of 5.63 (*SD* = 1.66) when given the same task demands. This score is slightly lower than that produced by their nondisabled peers, but the difference is not statistically significant.

When students were given task demands that were above average in authenticity, students without disabilities produced work that received an average score of 8.62 (*SD* = 2.00). Students with disabilities produced work that received an average score of 7.72 (*SD* = 1.92) when given the same task demands—again, a slightly lower score than that of their nondisabled peers.

Although students with disabilities did not score, on average, as well as students without disabilities, we note two important trends. First, stu-

dents with disabilities who were given higher scoring (i.e., above-average) tasks performed considerably better (7.72) than students with disabilities who were given below-average tasks (5.63). That is, *special education students in these classes who received tasks with higher intellectual challenge outperformed those who received tasks with less challenge.*

Second, students with disabilities who were given higher scoring (i.e., above-average) tasks performed better (7.72) than students without disabilities who were given below-average tasks (6.42). *Special education students in these classes who received tasks with higher intellectual challenge outperformed their nondisabled peers who received tasks with less challenge.*

FINDINGS (DATA SET 2, MATCHED PAIRS)

The matching of pairs of students in the second set of data allows for much of the same information to be gathered about tasks and student work. However, differences between the two data sets allow for comparisons within pairs of students.

Overall degree of authenticity of tasks. Across the 35 teachers in the second data set, the mean rating for task authenticity on all tasks was 7.30 (*SD* = 2.09). This average fell just above the middle of the range of possible scores (slightly higher than the first data set, which had a mean of 6.53). The actual range for the scores on the assessment tasks included in this data set was from 3 to 10. Therefore, some tasks in this data set, unlike those in the first data set, did receive the highest score possible for task authenticity.

These data yield an additional comparison. Ratings of task authenticity were compared for the tasks given to students with and without disabilities to determine whether the accommodations given to students changed the intellectual demands of the tasks. To benefit from the general education setting and to be able to complete the same tasks as their peers, students with disabilities often require accommodations (McGee, Mutch, & Leyland, 1993). An accommodation that involved eliminating certain parts of a task could lower task authenticity if the parts eliminated were those requiring students to analyze information (construction of knowledge), elaborate on their explanations through extended writing (elaborated written communication), or connect the topic to their lives (connection to students' lives). Accommodations could conceivably increase the authenticity of a task, although none did so in this set of data.

Although the task was generally the same for each pair of students in the second data set, some differences were found in task authenticity. Because of accommodations, students without disabilities received tasks with an overall mean rating of 7.43 (*SD* = 2.12), whereas students with disabilities received tasks with an overall mean rating of 7.17 (*SD* = 2.06). This difference, though small, is statistically significant. Because of the evidence that indicates that task authenticity and the authenticity of student work are related, changes in task demands due to accommodations may be important in determining what students produce. We note, however, that for the vast majority of tasks (85.7%), accommodations made no difference in the degree of intellectual demands.

Overall degree of authenticity of student work. For the 35 tasks submitted, the mean overall rating for the authenticity of work produced by students was 7.47 (*SD* = 2.64). The mean score across all student work fell in the middle of the range of possible scores. The range of scores for the student work included in this sample was from 3 to 12.

The authenticity ratings given to student work in the second data set, as in the first, were compared by student disability status. The mean rating of work authenticity for students without disabilities was 8.03 (*SD* = 2.64), and for students with disabilities it was 6.91 (*SD* = 2.65). This difference was statistically significant, indicating that students with disabilities produced work lower in authenticity than that produced by

their nondisabled peers. However, despite this overall difference, it is interesting to note that whereas 37% of the students with disabilities produced work that was lower in authenticity than that produced by their matched nondisabled peer, *nearly 63% produced work that was the same, or higher, in authenticity than that produced by their matched peer* (see Figure 3).

Relationship between tasks and student achievement. Consistent with previous research and the data provided by the first data set, there was a significant relationship between the authenticity of task demands and the authenticity of the work that students produced. That is, task demands that were rated lower in authenticity were associated with student work that was rated lower in authenticity. Conversely, task demands that were higher in authenticity were associated with student work that was also higher in authenticity.

FIGURE 3
Percentage of Work Produced by Students with Disabilities (SWD) Receiving Authenticity Ratings Lower or Higher Than, or the Same as, the Work Produced by Students without Disabilities (Second Data Set)

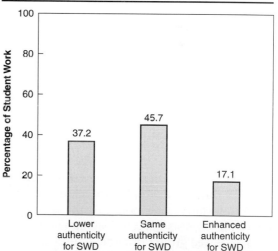

Authenticity Ratings for Work by Students with Disabilities Compared to Work by Students without Disabilities

CONCLUSIONS

Teachers who use more authentic assessments elicit more authentic work from students with and without disabilities. As these data demonstrate, teachers who design and give assessment tasks that call for higher order thinking, requiring analysis or interpretation, in-depth understanding, direct connections to the field under study, and an appeal to an audience beyond the classroom, will enable students to respond in a more sophisticated manner. Students are encouraged to demonstrate their understanding through the construction of knowledge rather than the mere reproduction of facts. Assessments that call for students to respond constructively create opportunities for them to achieve in a manner not captured through a variety of traditional assessment procedures.

These findings suggest that students with disabilities can respond well to more authentic tasks. Although students with disabilities did not score as well on more authentic tasks as their nondisabled peers, *with more challenging tasks, students with disabilities performed better than students with and without disabilities who received less challenging tasks.* Student achievement generally seems to benefit from the use of more authentic forms of assessment, and the achievement of students with disabilities, who are typically unaccounted for at the secondary level, is no exception.

Although accommodations were used extensively in Data Set 2, they altered the authenticity of only 14% of the 35 tasks. This result demonstrates that *teachers are able to adapt assessments for special education students while maintaining the level of intellectual challenge.* Significantly, teachers can sustain high expectations of students in inclusive classrooms. At the same time, the result suggests that challenging tasks can be given to mixed groups of students, including students with disabilities, with relatively minor accommodations.

That said, some explanations are needed for the continuing differences between the scores of disabled and nondisabled students, regardless of the level of a task's authenticity. For one, the assessments included here demanded a certain level of literacy, in both reading and writing, which may make tasks more difficult for certain students because of their disabilities. A broad definition of *elaborated communication* would allow students to show in-depth understanding through a variety of media, not simply through writing as was required for this study. Alternative student products such as demonstrations or exhibitions may provide a solution for this particular problem but are still atypical in schools. A second explanation arises from the pedagogical context in which the assessments are administered. Although not considered in this study, the curriculum and instruction employed before a given assessment may have an impact on disabled students' abilities to respond, given the nature of their disabilities and classroom accommodations. Put simply, the instruction provided to students will affect their ability to access and successfully complete an assessment task.

There is more work to be done with regard to these issues. We are collecting additional assessment data (teacher tasks and student work) from all four high schools participating in the study. We are also visiting the schools to conduct observations of teachers' lessons in the four main subject areas. The lessons are rated according to criteria for authentic instruction. These data will provide further insight into the promise of authentic and inclusive reforms for students with disabilities.

REFERENCES

Avery, P. (1999). Authentic instruction and assessment. *Social Education, 63*(6), 368–373.

Cohen, D. K., McLaughlin, M. W., & Talbert, J. E. (Eds.). (1993). *Teaching for understanding: Challenges for policy and practice.* San Francisco: Jossey-Bass.

Hanley-Maxwell, C., Phelps, L. A., Braden, J., & Warren, V. W. (1999). *Schools of authentic and inclusive learning* (Brief #1). Madison, WI: Research Institute on Secondary Education Reform for Youth with Disabilities.

Lipsky, D. K., & Gartner, A. (1996). Inclusive education and school restructuring. In W. Stainback & S. Stainback (Eds.), *Controversial issues confronting special education* (pp. 3–15). Boston: Allyn & Bacon.

McGee, A. M., Mutch, L. M., & Leyland, A. (1993). Assessing children who cannot be "tested." *Educational Psychology, 13*(1), 43–48.

Newmann, F. M., & Associates. (1996). *Authentic achievement: Restructuring schools for intellectual quality.* San Francisco: Jossey-Bass.

Newmann, F. M., Lopez, G., & Bryk, A. S. (1998). *The quality of intellectual work in Chicago schools.* Chicago: Consortium on Chicago School Research.

Newmann, F. M., Marks, H. M., & Gamoran, A. (1996). Authentic pedagogy and student performance. *American Journal of Education, 104,* 280–312.

Newmann, F. M., & Wehlage, G. G. (1995). *Successful school restructuring: A report to the public and educators.* Madison, WI: University of Wisconsin, Wisconsin Center for Education Research.

Schroeder, J. L. (2000). *Authentic learning and accommodations for students with disabilities and without disabilities in restructuring secondary schools.* Unpublished master's thesis, University of Wisconsin–Madison.

Trent, S. C., Artiles, A. J., & Englert, C. S. (1998). From deficit thinking to social constructivism: A review of theory, research, and practice in special education. *Review of Research in Education, 23,* 277–307.

M. Bruce King is a research scientist with the Wisconsin Center for Education Research at the University of Wisconsin–Madison. *Jennifer Schroeder* is an assistant professor at Texas A&M University-Commerce and works as a school psychology consultant in the public schools. *David Chawszczewski* works as a teacher educator and consultant in Milwaukee, Wisconsin.

QUESTIONS FOR REFLECTION

1. What is authentic assessment and why is it important to education? Likewise, what would you say authentic *pedagogy* is?

2. How would you go about applying the lessons learned from this research to your own classroom? What features or characteristics of the initial findings would guide you as you sought to make this transition?

3. The authors conclude that teachers who use more authentic assessments elicit more authentic work from students, regardless of whether the students have or do not have disabilities. What does this tell you about the nature of the work done in schools? How might you share what you have learned from this research with your colleagues in education?

AUTHORS' NOTE: This chapter is adapted from "Authentic Assessment and Student Performance in Inclusive Schools," Brief #5, Research Institute on Secondary Education Reform for Youth with Disabilities (RISER), December, 2001. See www.wcer.wisc.edu/riser/Brief%205.pdf. The brief was supported by a grant from the U.S. Department of Education, Office of Special Education and Rehabilitative Services, Office of Special Education Programs (#H158J970001) and by the Wisconsin Center for Education Research, School of Education, University of Wisconsin–Madison. Any opinions, findings, or conclusions are those of the authors and do not necessarily reflect the views of the supporting agencies.

TEACHERS' VOICES—
Putting Theory Into Practice

Lifelines: An Ethnographic Study of an IEP Student

ELSA C. BRO

ABSTRACT: *Teaching is a challenging job where river guides and teachers share important characteristics. Here, Elsa C. Bro relates her insightful experiences and realizations as she studies a high school sophomore with learning difficulties.*

Because sometimes I live in a hurricane of words and not one of them can save me.

—Naomi Shihab Nye, "You Know Who You Are"

Several summers ago in raft-guide school, I learned a valuable lesson that can be applied in the classroom: Have a prepared rescue plan for nearly every imaginable scenario. Anticipate. More often than not, however, this nugget of knowledge was passed down to novice guides without the opportunity to practice the skills in low-stakes situations. As a result, my only summer as a raft guide I depended on luck. Guiding by intuition may have been acceptable for pleasure payers but not for students who would be left in my trust in the classroom.

Whether teaching or guiding vacationers down rivers, there is a chance that something could go wrong. Some days are calm; others are turbulent. Before I student taught, while I had the time to observe other teachers in action, my goal was to become a knowledgeable guide who understands the nature and nebulous patterns of learning differences so that I could steer students to success.

In a Literacy and Culture class at Lewis and Clark College, I had an aha moment: If I was going to be able to recognize, anticipate, and prevent the holes that swallow students' ability to participate in a community of learners, I needed data. I became an ethnographer, collecting copious amounts of field notes in a study of one student with literacy challenges. After too many near-death experiences as a river guide, I appreciated having the time to prepare a thoughtful teaching plan for my first year. I intended to use this case study as a reference for how I could modify instruction for future students with diverse learning needs.

Teaching Journal	September 8

This week I learned that being a good observer is not easy, especially when I am grasping for any little drip of free time to get to know the sea of faces that I will be teaching in December. What's easy is accepting an offer to jump into a small group activity to get an insider's look. Solving analogies, for example, is more engaging and fun than lurking on the periphery.

However, my senses are sharper when I am left alone to observe from a distance. From my corner spot next to the student portfolios, I notice Shannon's lackadaisical nature, how his attention remains on sleep's threshold. I note the incessant tap-tap-tapping of Tyrone's feet and muse over his mind's music. The same students read and return text messages. Laticia eats sliced green-apple spears from a plastic bag. Lacrosse team?

Observation time is a privilege, a gift that many teachers aren't granted while navigating new curriculum, diverse learning needs, and growing class sizes. While in this privileged position I'm going to get to know who these students are as individuals. A prediction: cultivating and maintaining this keen awareness will be a challenging task for a first-year teacher.

READING THE LANDSCAPE

As a student intern observing Ms. Lewis's fifth-period sophomore English class, I was drawn into the landscape of ebullient faces, swirling voices, and swift minds. The energy in the room reaffirmed my commitment to teach. For ten weeks, my mission in the classroom was reconnaissance, scouting for potential obstacles that could impede the learning success of any one of thirty fifteen- and sixteen-year-olds. I looked for eddies, the mysterious cross-currents that can suck victims into their roiling vortices, spilling gear and carefully prepared plans for a smooth ride.

On my third day observing at Central High, I joined a heterogeneous group reading scenes 2 and 3 from *Antigone*. The group included two students on individual education plans (IEPs)—Courtney and Carla—and Josh and Patterson, two advanced placement students. Voices sounded out in a chorus of characters' voices from the play. Josh and Patterson claimed their parts with alacrity while Carla read without affect.

"It was not God's procla . . . proclammae. . . ."

"Proclamation," corrected Patterson, one of Central High's all-state racquetball champions.

Carla's soft voice fell off, becoming almost inaudible as she continued, "that final Justice that rules the world below makes no such laws. Your edet, edit. . . ."

"Edict!" Patterson interjected.

"Your edict, King, was strong. But all your strength is weakness itself against the immoooaa-tal. . . ."

As Carla struggled to match sound and symbol, Josh and Courtney kept their eyes on the text. *Just give her time to sound it out,* I wanted to say.

At that instant Patterson sighed, shaking his head in exasperation. "Immortal!"

With her head down now, Carla's giggles hid the fact that she was drowning in embarrassment. "OK," she said at last, straightening up in her desk. She drew in a deep breath and salvaged her last line: "Immortal unrecorded laws of God."

After completing the reading, our group decided to do the summary questions individually. The volume of the other voices in the room made it difficult to concentrate. I reread the first question several times. With my years of reading and learning in various environments, I was surprised at how distracted I was. If I couldn't focus, how could the students?

My mind drifted to Carla. She kept to herself, which made the story of her mind mysterious and intriguing. Her visible lack of the usual teenage-girl behavior—giggling, whispering, and lip-reading conversations with friends while the teacher was instructing—disturbed me. How could I get to know her better without pushing her away? From my adolescence I knew that being singled out from the crowd is a bummer; generally, teens are more receptive to one-on-one talks. With only two minutes until the lunch bell, I decided to address Carla in front of her peers.

"Carla, how are you doing today?" I asked, motioning to her blank sheet of paper. "You didn't answer any questions."

"I'm tired. I didn't go to bed until 2:00 a.m." Her body drooped in her desk.

"Why?"

"Because I got in a fight with my mother and had to go to my brother's."

"What happened?"

"Well, my mom's an alcoholic, and we've never gotten along," she continued. "I used to live with my dad, but I won't go there to live again."

I did not know what to say. What does one say when confronted with the realization that some teens do not have a home to go to? "I'm sorry to hear that. Do you have enough people to talk to about this?"

"Yes," she said definitively. The lunch bell buzzed. All students surged for the hall except Carla, who sauntered slowly to the door, alone.

Teaching Journal   September 14

Imagine reading two whole scenes from a play out loud in front of your classmates and stumbling over words in every sentence. Patterson has made himself the authority on pronunciation, correcting Carla every time she stumbles. I wonder how this reading exercise makes her feel. What is it that makes certain words difficult for Carla to read? Is she getting the help she needs to become a better reader? Need to watch for patterns.

I am surprised at how comfortable she was opening up to me in front of her peers. She was completely unconcerned about disclosing personal info. Now her faded look in class is starting to make sense. It sounds like she has some real challenges to face at home, which could be impeding her progress on schoolwork.

SEEKING RESOURCES

The rotating block schedule went round and round. With school holidays, assemblies, and student absences, I considered myself lucky if I was able to take a half hour of field notes on my case study and squeeze in a twenty-minute conference each week. As my December start date for teaching approached, I had to seek other resources to make sense of Carla's reading difficulty so that I would know how to differentiate instruction for her and other students.

How far would I have to stretch myself as a teacher to reach her? How would I manage to prepare individualized instruction for every student? Would I have to do this alone? While searching for the answers to my questions, I became familiar with another reality of teaching: Taking work home is inevitable. To be a great teacher, one must research.

Readers and Writers with a Difference illuminates some useful clues for identifying troubled readers. Rhodes and Dudley-Marling note, "miscues . . . follow a pattern . . . and give us information about readers' thought processes during reading. . . . When good readers produce miscues they err on the side of meaning. Poor readers tend to err on the side of phonics" (42). The authors suggest that teachers watch for students relying too heavily on one system for reading. In addition, considering whether the miscues vary as a function of the texts themselves or of the students' background experiences aids in preparing developmentally appropriate, challenging lesson plans.

I discovered that Carla's miscues while reading *Antigone* clearly demonstrated a dependence on phonics. Her focus was on making the right sounds, not on decoding the meaning of the text. The abstract language of a Greek tragedy may have been too dense for her, making word recognition spotty at best. Speaking with her ninth-grade English teacher and conducting a reading interview would help to further fill in the blanks.

Teaching Journal   October 1

During a conference with my mentor teacher this morning, we discussed her disappointment that over half of the students did not pass the Certificate of Initial Mastery (CIM) requirements on their narrative essays [Oregon requires that sophomores be assessed on specific reading and writing benchmarks]. Carla is the only student who did not turn in her essay. Even though it was due over a week ago, Ms. Lewis is willing to let Carla turn her essay in whenever she can. Overall, Carla has good attendance, which makes me further question why she is falling behind. I wonder what I can do to help her turn assignments in on time.

CONDUCTING A READING INTERVIEW

The next day I met Carla in first-period Marketing to shadow her for the day. I was curious to see if her behavior and reading patterns were consistent in her other classes. My essential questions were: How do various instructional activities interface with Carla's learning needs? Which processes aid her reading comprehension?

Carla plopped down a cell phone on her desk and began reading a memo from the color guard coach about the upcoming competition. She looked tired.

"Is it hard for you to get up for class this early?" I asked.

"Sometimes, but right now I am sick with a cold, and I can't get better."

"Did you eat breakfast?"

"No, I didn't have time," she replied quietly.

I was drawn to the scene on her desk: a white, plastic binder papered with pictures of horses. "Are you passionate about horses?"

"Yes, I go to my uncle's on the weekends to train horses to be ridden. I used to have my own horse there, too, but not anymore."

I wondered how Carla learned to ride and train horses and if this process carried over into the classroom.

Mr. Resch handed out three photocopied articles while explaining the different ways advertisers categorize target markets. He instructed us to read the articles and write down who the target market was. I watched Carla read while I read.

Carla completed the reading and supporting evidence for the target markets without any noticeable challenges. Her answers were nondescript and in incomplete sentences, although there were no spelling errors. My answers contained more details. Glancing at other students' answers, I found brevity.

Teaching Journal   October 2

Me: I saw that you are finishing your reading at the same time as your classmates. You mentioned before that you have a hard time following along with the story when you have to read it out loud. What helps you to understand the reading in Marketing class?

Carla: I don't know. These articles aren't so hard to read, and it helps that I don't have to listen to anyone else reading aloud.

Me: I see. Is it easier to read quietly or out loud?

Carla: They're both hard. I am a slower reader, and so I need more time. I usually need some-

one to explain to me what is going on in the book. That's why I'm so slow.

Me: What makes it difficult to get your homework done?

Carla: Well, I have color guard practice after school, and when I come home it's hard to do my homework, because my mom blames me for not giving her enough attention. When I'm in my room she bangs on my door, so it's hard to concentrate. Also, I have dyslexia.

Me: Oh. I didn't know. How does this make reading challenging?

Carla: I am a very slow reader and writer. I need more time to understand what's going on, and I feel bored in class.

Me: What do you mean you feel bored?

Carla: Well, it's hard to take notes while listening in class, so a lot of times I feel lost.

Me: Well, if it's OK with you I will talk to Ms. Lewis to see what we can do to adjust our instruction so that it serves you better.

Carla: OK.

Journal Reflection   October 5

On two separate occasions Carla has clued me in on the predicament she faces at home trapped between two difficult choices: homework or Mom. Due to the overwhelming stress and guilt accompanying the mind of a child with an alcoholic parent, Carla is starved for guidance, resources, and support. After school and color guard practice with the band, there is little quiet, uninterrupted time to complete homework. Carla has determined that isolation is the only way; she locks herself in her room to avoid her mother, who is easily angered when not given enough attention.

Concentrating on writing a narrative essay often becomes impossible, as does reading a tenth-grade text like *Antigone* or "Where Have You Gone, Charming Billy?" After rereading the same lines countless times, Carla gives up. For someone like Carla it is imperative that reading time, proofreading, and answers to questions are provided in class, due to the dearth of support at home.

RELYING ON LABELS

In third-period French I, Mr. Rainier moved to the overhead and, before I could take out my notepad, my ears were flooded with French dialogue. His arms flagged the students like a composer. While the rest of the class scribbled down conjugations, Carla just listened. The situation reminded me of Mr. Thelan, my authoritarian, incessantly perspiring high school French teacher. The recollection of relentless drills and the D that I received on the final oral exam made me shudder.

Mr. Rainier squeezed between rows to check that the day's assignment was complete. Carla's worksheet was half blank, and as Mr. Rainier swept by, she expertly hid the incomplete part underneath a messy pile of vocabulary sheets. Saved!

Mr. Rainier whisked around the class with a stack of homework to return. A worksheet fluttered onto Carla's desk; the F in the top margin seemed to leap off the page. She quickly flipped it over.

"Carla, we need to meet sometime to talk about this, OK?" he said, nodding his head.

Carla mirrored Mr. Rainier, nodding her head in compliance.

The French lesson continued, but Carla was not invited to participate. I wondered if teachers purposely did not call on students with IEPs because they were trying to avoid the possibility of humiliating a student. Had Mr. Rainier and Carla agreed on alternative ways to assess her progress? Was there a plan in place that ensured that Carla was able to set and achieve some attainable goals?

"So, what's the story on your French homework?" I asked as subtly as possible on our way to the cafeteria.

"Everything's OK," she responded, "because Mr. Rainier knows I have an IEP."

I did not see it that way.

Teaching Journal   October 26

Apparently, scrambling to copy or cover up incomplete assignments at the last minute is a way of life for students who don't have a quiet place to do homework in the evening. I am curious to learn what other unsanctioned literacies are used to beat a system that doesn't support all students equitably. I understand that Carla definitely has more challenges affecting learning success than the average teenager. Yet, I can't help but wonder if her lack of concern in the classroom is a result of her taking advantage of the flexibility her IEP grants her.

In *Between Worlds,* Freeman and Freeman warn educators about the irreversible damage of labeling students. Students who are labeled "begin to see themselves as limited" (140). Teachers who lower their expectations about students' performance give the perception that students are not capable of being challenged, taking risks, and stretching themselves as learners. Once students learn that they are "different," they often disown and disengage from their academic experience. Consequently, lowered student performance confirms teachers' beliefs, and a "cycle of failure is established" (141).

After observing consistent performance patterns in all of Carla's classes, I came to a troubling conclusion. Instead of asking for help when she was having difficulty reading or writing, Carla relied on her IEP to bump her through her classes. Under the Accommodations and Modifications heading, her IEP required the following: partial credit for work considered late; break down long-term assignments into smaller, more manageable parts; extended time on tests, reading, and writing assignments; may take tests, quizzes, or work on assignments in the resource room as needed; preferential seating away from distractions. Under Assessment Modifications and Accommodations, it states that when taking multiple-choice tests or on-demand performance assessments and work samples, Carla may have extended time if needed. The categories Supplementary Aids and Services and Supports for School Personnel remain blank.

My mentor teacher abhors the burdensome paper trail that depersonalizes teacher-student relationships, yet she is not doing anything to change the system. At the beginning of the school year she is given IEPs, which go into a file. That is it. Throughout my observations of the fifth-period sophomore English class, none of the students with IEPs were called on during whole-class discussions until I asked Ms. Lewis what her rationale was. She admitted that she purposely does not call on students with IEPs for fear of embarrassing them. I think that teachers need to ask themselves if this practice is honoring students or allowing them to slip through the cracks.

Teaching Journal   November 3

I have found no evidence of adaptations or accommodations being exercised to help Carla become an active participant in any of her classes. Since I have been at my internship site, she has never requested, or been offered, extra time on tests or quizzes, nor have teachers broken down larger assignments into chunks for easier understanding. First action to take: create seating chart that places Carla in close proximity to teacher; this would lessen distractions.

IDENTIFYING DIFFICULTIES

Seeing that Carla may never turn in her narrative essay, Ms. Lewis employed me to offer a writing conference. I still did not understand what Carla meant when she told me that she is dyslexic. Her IEP does not state this, as dyslexia falls under the mysterious heading of "learning disabled," offering a vague understanding of how to accommodate students' needs. I was not sure how I could help her. With Carla's permission, I took a copy of her essay, hoping that together we could identify the words and letters that tripped her up in the writing process. What I found was baffling.

Teaching Journal   November 12

At first glance, Carla's handwritten narrative essay is reminiscent of a ball of barbed wire; sentences have been erased and rewritten, scratched out, and redirected with arrows going this way and that. There are significant spelling and sentence structure errors, although she's got a good lead and conclusion. Luckily, she was here on peer edit day; she got some good feedback.

Her areas of trouble included homophones, contractions, mixing up vowels, using a single consonant when there should be double consonants, and switched letters in words (see fig. 1). Based on what I knew about Carla's invented spelling, I could provide one minilesson per week that targeted a repeated spelling error. In addition, I would provide corrections on two troublesome conventions per essay until the mistake was corrected through revision and review.

Whereas my ethnographic study began with observations and a collection of literary artifacts, the lack of resources for "learning disabled" students motivated me to question school counselors and special education caseworkers. Where were they? Who were they, and why wasn't my mentor teacher familiar with them?

I went to the office of Carla's counselor to seek out who could be Carla's "school safety" when home life got rough and oversee Carla's progress to make sure she was not being left behind. In my idealistic mind I assumed that there must be a mentoring program for younger students. After all, Central had just implemented a fully staffed career center for older students.

FIGURE 1
Patterns of Error in Spelling and Usage

Incorrect	Correct
restronts	restaurants
licycle	Lysol
Wecks	weeks
to	too
though	threw/through
deiced	decided
Over	over
druk	drunk
achool	alcohol
grams	germs
brake	break
thought	through
we're	were
but	put
tal	tall
fravorit	favorite

"Unfortunately, Carla does not have priority visitations unless she is a junior, is in crisis, or is high risk," the counselor explained, handing me brochures to two off-campus counseling groups for girls. "There are scholarships for low-income students," she said with a smile.

The groups could give Carla the self-esteem and support that she lacked at home, yet I had the sinking feeling that transportation would present a challenge. For a split second I pondered the possibility of arranging rides for Carla but then realized that I had to draw the line somewhere. Even though I wanted the best for Carla, as a new teacher it was imperative to set up appropriate boundaries from the beginning.

"Since Carla's on an IEP, she does have a caseworker who will know how to better serve her academic needs. If you go to the main office, they can tell you where to find the resource room."

I was beginning to feel resistance. "Is there *anything* I can do to help Carla be more successful in her classes?"

"Does she have a student planner? Here," the counselor said, pointing to a box of orange Central High student handbooks. "Take one for yourself and one for Carla. Usually grades improve when students learn organization and time-management skills."

I left the counseling office feeling waterlogged. I was disappointed by the lack of support for students who may depend on school to give them a sense of accomplishment. If students were not learning at school, what would they do once they were in the real world? Certainly Carla's home life and difficulty reading placed her in the high-risk category, didn't they?

Teaching Journal   November 15

Carla's classroom performance is plummeting. With two incomplete assignments today, she's standing at a 64% in Sophomore English and is failing French. No one is seriously addressing the obtuse patterns of her writing or the frequency that she does not turn in assignments. I fear that if we, the resource guides of this student, do not collaborate to get her back onboard soon, we will be looking at a case of hypothermia.

ACCOMMODATING INDIVIDUAL NEEDS

I was relieved to discover that I would not have to cross these uncharted waters alone. In the resource room, Mr. Blair, Carla's caseworker, told me how IEPs function. Once a student is assessed as being "learning disabled," a caseworker monitors the student's attendance and grades, maintaining a three-week conference schedule unless there is an obvious risk of failure or conflict to address. In between the three-week cycles, Mr. Blair assured me that he is available for writing consultations, proofreading, homework help, and goal setting for high-stakes projects. He also offered to be the "bad guy" if I needed support taking disciplinary action.

Most students on IEPs are encouraged to take at least one special education class, such as an English learning lab where they receive help on assignments. The accommodations on an IEP are designed to lighten class loads while tailoring learning objectives to meet individuals' needs. Special education classes may be appropriate for some students; however, others may benefit from being in mainstream classrooms alongside students with varying abilities. Freeman and Freeman tell us that students doing interactive activities learn more when placed in heterogeneous groups. For example, classes structured around thematic units that take an interdisciplinary approach are apt to be more relevant and inclusive to all students (197).

Unfortunately, it takes assertive parents or a proactive student to receive the support that is needed to overcome reading challenges that sabotage successful learning experiences. In fact, most students do not want to be singled out as "different" and battle it out in regular classes to save face. This seemed to be Carla's case. In Mr. Blair's opinion, she was not keeping in touch with him as she should. In the same way that instruction and assessment are inseparable, Carla's way of navigating and coping with home life spilled over into school life; she prefers to be invisible. After moving from one bad home situation with her father to another with her mother,

Carla has internalized the negative relationships she has had with adults. Adults who are close to her inevitably hurt her. Adults cannot be trusted.

Rescue Kit Strategies   November 21

I am determined to reach her. First, I will make myself accountable for following through with the accommodations outlined on her IEP. I will provide large reading texts and projects in advance to give Carla adequate time. Mr. Blair will also receive copies of high-stakes assignments in order to provide support and assessment. Finally, if Carla feels comfortable I am going to offer to meet her once a week to check in. During our conferences I will offer to read texts or test questions aloud to her, dictate answers to test questions, have writing workshop, or just talk.

Throughout classroom instruction I will strategically frame students' thinking by providing visuals of essential and unit questions. Daily agendas will be posted to anchor the focus of students who have fleeting attention spans; students will know when they will be able to stretch and socialize around learning. I will offer "hurdle help" by chunking information and adjusting individual goals to meet students' varying skill levels. Groups of varying abilities will support learning while cultivating perspective and empathy.

I am as curious about Carla's home life, school literacies, and learning needs today as I was when I started my study. However, I celebrate the leap in understanding I have made around Carla's reading and writing challenges. My experiences as observer and ethnographer have been invaluable to my development as a teacher. I now feel confident that I can prevent unnecessary calamities in the classroom by providing accommodations that make learning enjoyable and accessible, and it is my hope that this ethnographic study will help other new teachers find multiple pathways to knowing their dynamic, unique, and differently abled students.

Even after this ethnographic study, I wonder how we, as teacher-researchers, are truly able to know individual students. I realize, though, that we are not alone out there. By making the time to seek out staff supports and resources within the school, being a first-year teacher does not seem as daunting. I know where to find an ally to work with, someone to toss lifelines with, in hopes that they will be caught and held onto.

WORKS CITED

Freeman, David F., and Yvonne S. Freeman. *Between Worlds: Access to Second Language Acquisition*. 2nd ed. Portsmouth: Heinemann, 2001.

Rhodes, Lynn K., and Curt Dudley-Marling. *Readers and Writers with a Difference: A Holistic Approach to Teaching Learning Disabled and Remedial Students*. Portsmouth: Heinemann, 1988.

Elsa C. Bro, originally from Iowa, teaches English as a second language at an elementary school in the French Alps.

QUESTIONS FOR REFLECTION

1. What does Bro's use of ethnography as a data collection method allow her to learn about her students? How might another form of data collection have yielded different results?

2. Would this article "lose" something if Bro had elected not to include her journal writing and the interview transcripts?

3. What characteristics of Bro's approach to Carla's learning difficulties can you imagine using in your classroom? How could they be applied to all students, not just those with obvious learning challenges?

LEARNING ACTIVITIES

Critical Thinking

1. In light of constructivist views of learning, how can teachers increase their understanding of students' understanding? How should teachers take into account students' social, cultural, linguistic, and academic backgrounds?
2. What is your preferred learning style? Where, when, and how do you learn best?
3. In regard to multiple intelligences theory, in which intelligences are you most proficient? Least proficient? How do these areas of greatest (and least) proficiency affect your learning?
4. What are the risks of using learning styles and/or multiple intelligences theory to design learning activities for students?
5. Herbert A. Thelen has pointed out that "If we get too comfortable, we stop growing. Students can put pressure on us to work within their comfort zone. Let's be kind about that. Kind enough to help them learn to be uncomfortable" (quoted in *Models of Teaching,* 7th edition [Allyn and Bacon, 2004, p. 337]). What are the implications of Thelen's statement for curriculum planners who develop learning activities to "fit" students' learning styles?

Application Activities

1. Examine a recent curriculum guide of interest to you or in your field of study to identify the learning theory (or theories) that is the basis for the suggested learning activities. What additional learning activities, based on other theories of learning, could be added?
2. In *Practical Intelligence for School* (HarperCollins, 1996), Howard Gardner and a team of researchers have proposed another form of intelligence—*practical intelligence,* "the ability to understand one's environment, and to use this knowledge in figuring out how best to achieve one's goals" (p. ix). They believe that practical intelligence consists of five themes that can be taught: *knowing why, knowing self, knowing differences, knowing process,* and *reworking.* In planning curricula at the level with which you are most interested, how useful is the concept of practical intelligence?
3. At the level and in the content area of greatest interest to you, identify several learning activities that address each of the seven multiple intelligences identified by Gardner.

Field Experiences

1. Interview a teacher at your level of greatest interest, K–12 through higher education, for the purpose of clarifying the learning theory (or theories) that guides the teacher. Formulate your interview questions in light of the material in this chapter.

2.   At the level and in the subject area of greatest interest to you, observe a teacher to identify the learning theory (or theories) he or she uses. What differences do you note among the students' responses to their teacher? Is there evidence of different learning styles among the students?

Internet Activities

1.   Conduct an Internet search on one or more of the topics listed below. Gather resources and information relevant to your current, or anticipated, curriculum planning activities.

multiple intelligences	learning styles
learning theories	behavior modification
cognitive science	brain research
constructivism	neuroscience

2.   Go to the site for Harvard Project Zero codirected by Howard Gardner. For almost 40 years Project Zero has studied how children and adults learn. At this site, gather information relevant to your current, or anticipated, curriculum planning activities.

CHAPTER **5**

Approaches to Curriculum Development

FOCUS QUESTIONS

1. How should curriculum theory and research be used during the curriculum development process?
2. What is the nature of curriculum development at the macro- and micro-levels?
3. What are the differences between subject-centered and student-centered curricula?
4. What is the role of standards in the curriculum development process?
5. What are some arguments for and against higher standards for the curriculum?
6. What are some recent trends in curriculum development?
7. What role can students play in curriculum development?

From your reading of Chapters 1–4, you now understand the significance of goals and values and the three bases of curriculum planning—social forces, human development, and learning and learning styles. A major aim of this chapter, then, is to move from *planning* the curriculum to *developing* (or writing) the curriculum.

The title of Franklin Bobbitt's classic work, *How to Make a Curriculum* (1924), might suggest that developing a curriculum is a straightforward process. According to Bobbit, a curriculum should be developed "scientifically" by analyzing the daily activities of adult life and then creating behavioral objectives for those activities.

Bobbitt's approach suggests that one need only apply curriculum theory and research to the processes of curriculum development. However, curriculum theory and research do not set forth, in cookbook fashion, exactly how one should develop a curriculum. Instead, it may be helpful to think of curriculum theory and research as providing "rules of thumb" for developing a curriculum.

Clearly, there is no single right way to develop a curriculum. As John Dewey points out in "The Sources of a Science of Education" in this chapter, "No conclusion of scientific research can be converted into an immediate rule of educational art. For there is no educational practice whatever which is not highly complex; that is to say, which does not contain many other conditions and factors than are included in the scientific finding." The significance of any one research study for educational practice, then, can be determined only as the results of that study are balanced with an understanding of the "conditions and factors" that influence the situation. Connections among research results and surrounding environmental influences should be made until they reciprocally confirm and illuminate one another, or until each gives the other added meaning.

When these connecting principles are understood, the curriculum developer is more likely to make the "best" decisions throughout the curriculum development process. To make such informed decisions, Dewey (1904, p. 10) maintains elsewhere that educators should acquire and develop a fundamental mental process the ultimate aim of which is "the intellectual method and material of good workmanship." According to Dewey, this intellectual method is the criterion against which educational decisions—from curriculum development to selecting instructional strategies—should be made. Dewey also suggests several personal dispositions that characterize those who use the method: intellectual independence (p. 16) and responsibility, initiative, skill in scholarship (p. 21), willingness to be a "thoughtful and alert" student of education (p. 15), and a spirit of inquiry. In addition, Dewey stresses the need to develop the "habit of viewing the entire curriculum as a continuous growth, reflecting the growth of mind itself" (p. 26).

APPROACHES TO CURRICULUM DEVELOPMENT

The articles on goals and values and the three bases of the curriculum in the first four chapters of this book make it evident that many different designs can be followed in planning a curriculum. These designs are not mutually exclusive; they can be used together or separately to address various types of curricular goals, differences among learners, and different types of knowledge.

There is no easy-to-follow set of procedures for developing a curriculum. While there are many "models" for curriculum design, none are intended to provide step-by-step procedures for developing curricula. However, Ralph Tyler's classic text, *Basic*

Principles of Curriculum and Instruction, contained four salient questions, now known as the *Tyler rationale,* that must be considered, in some fashion, at least, when planning a curriculum:

1. What educational purposes should the school seek to attain?
2. What educational experiences can be provided that are likely to attain these purposes?
3. How can these educational experiences be effectively organized?
4. How can we determine whether these purposes are being attained? (Tyler, 1949, p. 1).

The Tyler rationale has been used by many curriculum planners as a set of general guidelines for developing a curriculum; however, others have criticized the rationale as being a linear, means-end model that oversimplifies the complexities of curriculum planning. They believe the Tyler rationale underestimates the complexities of curriculum development. The rationale advocates a straightforward, step-by-step process that, in reality, is difficult to follow in the "real" world of schools. Nevertheless, Tyler's classic work has been used by many school systems to bring some degree of order and focus to the curriculum development process. Thus, as curriculum theorists Francis P. Hunkins and Patricia A. Hammill (1994, p. 7) observe, "Despite all the criticism of Tyler, his thinking is still dominant in schools across the nation."

When first introduced, Tyler's model represented a modern view of curriculum design. Developing the curriculum, according to Tyler, required a mechanical, rational approach that could be followed systematically in any context, with any group of students. Today, however, postmodernist views of the world are leading to curriculum designs that are based on diverse voices, meanings, and points of view. As Hunkins and Hammill (1994, p. 10) point out:

> we are realizing with increasing sophistication that life is organic, not mechanical; the universe is dynamic, not stable; the process of curriculum development is not passive acceptance of steps, but evolves from action within the system in particular contexts; and that goals emerge oftentimes from the very experiences in which people engage.

Similarly, in "Teachers, Public Life, and Curriculum Reform" in this chapter, Henry A. Giroux points out that "the language of curriculum, like other discourses, does not merely reflect a pregiven reality; on the contrary, it selectively offers depictions of the larger world through representations that people struggle over to name what counts as knowledge, what counts as communities of learning, what social relationships matter, and what visions of the future can be represented as legitimate."

The Focus of Curriculum Development

In discussing curriculum development, it is helpful to clarify two dimensions of curriculum development: the target and the time orientation (see Figure 5.1). The target of curriculum development may be at the macro- or the micro-level.

FIGURE 5.1
Two Dimensions of Curriculum Development: The Target and Time Orientation

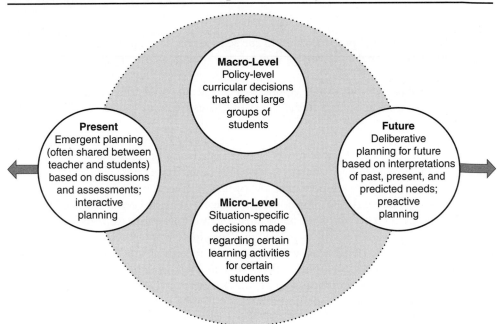

Macro-Level
Policy-level curricular decisions that affect large groups of students

Present
Emergent planning (often shared between teacher and students) based on discussions and assessments; interactive planning

Future
Deliberative planning for future based on interpretations of past, present, and predicted needs; preactive planning

Micro-Level
Situation-specific decisions made regarding certain learning activities for certain students

Source: Forrest W. Parkay and Beverly Stanford, *Becoming a Teacher,* 6th ed. Boston: Allyn and Bacon, 2004, p. 349.

At the macro-level, decisions about the content of the curriculum apply to large groups of students. National goals for education and state-level curriculum standards are examples of macro-level curricular decisions. At the micro-level, curriculum decisions are made that apply to groups of students in a particular school or classroom. To some extent, all teachers are micro-level curriculum developers—that is, they make numerous decisions about the curricular experiences they provide students in their classrooms.

Another dimension of curriculum development is the time orientation—does the curriculum focus on the present or the future? In addition to national goals and state-level curriculum standards, the semester-long or monthly plans or unit plans that teachers make are examples of future-oriented curriculum development. Present-oriented curriculum development usually occurs at the classroom level and is influenced by the unique needs of specific groups of students. The daily or weekly curriculum decisions and lesson plans that teachers make are examples of present-oriented curriculum development.

Student-Centered versus Subject-Centered Curricula

A key concern in curriculum development is whether greater emphasis should be given to the requirements of the subject area or to the needs of the students. It is helpful to imagine where a school curriculum might be placed on the following continuum.

Although no curriculum is entirely subject- or student-centered, curricula vary considerably in the degree to which they emphasize one or the other. The subject-centered curriculum places primary emphasis on the logical order of the discipline students are to study. The teacher of such a curriculum is a subject-matter expert and is primarily concerned with helping students understand the facts, laws, and principles of the discipline. Subject-centered curricula are more typical of high school education.

Some teachers develop curricula that reflect greater concern for students and their needs. Though teachers of the student-centered curriculum also teach content, they emphasize the growth and development of students. This emphasis is generally more typical of elementary school curricula.

THE CURRICULUM DEVELOPMENT PROCESS

The process of developing a curriculum usually begins with an examination of the knowledge, skills, attitudes, and values students should exhibit upon completion of a unit of study. The following are among the factors to consider at this stage of the curriculum development process:

- the desired balance between the *acquisition of content* and *mastery of processes*
- sequencing of content
- students' prior knowledge
- identifying methods for assessing student learning
- short-term versus long-term performance
- quality versus quantity

The Appendix on page 230 presents a "generic" plan for developing a unit of study. At minimum, a plan for a unit of study should include the following six elements:

1. Introduction
2. Objectives
3. Content of Unit
4. Methods and Activities
5. Teaching Materials and/or Resources
6. Assessment of Student Learning

Standards and Curriculum Development

Since the 1990s, curriculum development has focused increasingly on higher, "world-class" standards. Standards-based education (SBE) is based on the belief that *all* students are capable of meeting high standards.

In the past, expectations for students from poor families and students who are members of minority groups were sometimes lower than for other students. Today, SBE is seen as a way of ensuring that excellence and equity become part of our nation's public school system. As President George W. Bush pointed out prior to his election for a second term in 2004: "The educational divide [between African Americans and Hispanic students and white students] is caused by the soft bigotry of low expectations" (Bush 2004, 114). Similarly, in "A Principal Looks Back: Standards Matter" in this chapter, Kim Marshall reflects on 15 years as principal of an inner-city elementary school and notes that "the absence of meaningful external standards before 1998 prevented our strenuous and thoughtful efforts [at school improvement] from having much traction."

In response to the call for higher standards, state departments of education, school districts, and schools undertook numerous curricular reforms and developed more exacting, authentic methods for assessing student learning. Typically, "higher standards" was interpreted by parents, the public, and lawmakers to mean that teachers should expect more of their students. Toward this end, various macro-level mandates were made: detailed statements of the knowledge and skills students were to acquire under the more rigorous standards; higher test scores to receive passing grades or to be promoted to the next level; and more English, science, and mathematics. By 2004, forty-nine states (Iowa is the exception) have adopted state standards for what students should know and be able to do. For example, here are standards in geometry from three states:

Colorado: Students use geometric concepts, properties, and relationships in problem-solving situations and communicate the reasoning used in solving these problems.

North Dakota: Students understand and apply geometric concepts and spatial relationships to represent and solve problems in mathematical and nonmathematical situations.

Wyoming: Students apply geometric concepts, properties, and relationships in problem-solving situations. Students communicate the reasoning used in solving these problems.

Responses to SBE have been mixed. On the one hand, advocates of higher standards agreed with observers such as Diane Ravitch, educational historian and author of *National Standards in American Education: A Citizen's Guide (1995)*, who pointed out that:

- Standards can improve achievement by clearly defining what is to be taught and what kind of performance is expected.
- Standards (national, state, and local) are necessary for equality of opportunity.
- National standards provide a valuable coordinating function.
- Standards and assessments provide consumer protection by supplying accurate information to students and parents.
- Standards and assessments serve as an important signaling device to students, parents, teachers, employers, and colleges (Ravitch, 1996, pp. 134–135).

On the other hand, numerous concerns were expressed by opponents of the effort to develop "world-class" standards for America's educational system. The following are among the arguments these critics raised:

- Higher standards further bias educational opportunities in favor of students from advantaged backgrounds, intensify the class-based structure of American society, and increase the disparities between rich and poor schools.
- Raising standards might eventually lead to the development of a national curriculum, thereby increasing the role of federal government in education.
- The push for higher standards is fueled by conservative political groups that wish to undo educational gains made by historically underrepresented groups.
- Preoccupation with raising standards diverts attention from more meaningful educational reform.
- "World-class" standards are often vague and not linked to valid assessments and scoring rubrics.

Perhaps the most controversial standards to come forth during the 1990s were those developed for U.S. and world history by the National Center for History in the Schools. Immediately after the standards were issued in 1994, conservative groups, including the Council for Basic Education, asserted that the standards covered discrimination experienced by minority groups and women, while they omitted certain historical figures and positive features of the westward expansion and other aspects of American life. Some critics even charged that the standards were so "politically correct" that they reflected an anti-Western bias. In response to such widespread criticism, the Center rewrote the standards, this time with input from the Council for Basic Education, thirty-three national education organizations, and more than 1,000 educators. The revised standards were issued in 1996 with endorsements from many groups that were critical of the previous standards.

Content and Performance Standards

Standards documents prepared by state education agencies, local school districts, and professional associations typically refer to two types of standards—content standards and performance standards. *Content standards,* as the term implies, refer to the agreed-upon content—or knowledge and skills—students should acquire in different academic areas. A common phrase in standards documents is that content standards represent "what students should know and be able to do."

Content standards are often subdivided into benchmarks (frequently called *indicators*). Benchmarks are content standards that are presented as specific statements of what students should understand and be able to do *at specific grade levels or developmental stages.* The following is an example of a benchmark: "at the end of the eighth grade, the student understands basic properties of two- and three-dimensional figures."

In addition, many standards documents refer to *performance standards.* A performance standard specifies "how good is good enough." Performance standards are used to assess the *degree to which* students have attained standards in an academic area.

Performance standards require teacher judgment about the quality of performance or level of proficiency required. Performance standards differ from content standards because performance standards reflect levels of proficiency. A performance standard for evaluating students' written essays, for example, might be as follows: 5 = outstanding, 4 = exemplary, 3 = proficient, 2 = progressing, and 1 = standard not met.

Standards Developed by Professional Associations

In addition to national, state, and local efforts to raise standards, professional associations are playing a key role in SBE by developing standards that reflect the knowledge, skills, and attitudes students should acquire in the subject-matter disciplines. In many cases, professional associations have developed specific, grade-level performance standards. These standards include statements that reflect desired levels of achievement, quality of performance, or level of proficiency. In addition, professional associations have developed classroom activities related to standards.

Educational stakeholders can use standards developed by professional associations in the following ways.

- State departments of education, school districts, and schools can use the standards as a guide for developing curricula and assessments of student learning.
- Teachers can use standards to (1) develop goals and objectives for units and courses, (2) evaluate their teaching, and (3) develop ideas for instructional activities and classroom assessments.
- Parents and community members can use standards to assess the quality of education in their local schools and to monitor the achievement levels of their children.

Aligning Curricula and Textbooks with Standards

An important part of SBE in the United States is "aligning" curricula and textbooks with national and state standards and "curriculum frameworks." Curriculum alignment may take two forms. A curriculum is *horizontally aligned* when teachers within a specific grade level coordinate instruction across disciplines and examine their school's curriculum to ensure that course content and instruction dovetail across and/or within subject areas. A curriculum is *vertically aligned* when subjects are connected across grade levels so that students experience increasingly complex instructional programs as they move through the grades.

Like teachers, textbook publishers and authors have been influenced significantly by the development of academic standards throughout the nation. Since the "bottom line" for publishing companies is making a profit, they pay close attention to the calls of educational policy makers for more rigorous standards in our nation's schools.

Many publishers are revising their textbooks so they are in alignment with state standards and curriculum frameworks, particularly in populous states that make statewide adoptions of textbooks, such as California and Texas. In states such as these, school districts can only purchase textbooks that are on state textbook adoption lists.

Since highly populated states influence publishers more than less populated states, it has been observed that "As California and Texas go [regarding the development of state-approved textbook adoption lists], so goes the rest of the nation."

Curriculum Frameworks

A curriculum framework is a document, usually published by a state education agency, that provides guidelines, recommended instructional and assessment strategies, suggested resources, and models for teachers to use as they develop curricula that are aligned with national and state standards. Curriculum frameworks are usually written by teams of teachers and state agency personnel, and they serve as a bridge between national and state standards and local curriculum and instructional strategies. In Alaska, for example, curriculum frameworks in CD-ROM format and "Frameworks Resource Kits" in specific subjects are given to teachers by the Department of Education & Early Development. The CD-ROM provides state-of-the-art information in different formats, including videoclips of educators explaining standards-based curricula.

Standards and No Child Left Behind (NCLB)

In 2002, President George W. Bush signed the No Child Left Behind (NCLB) legislation. High standards are a key element of NCLB. As President Bush said immediately after his election to a second term in 2004: "We must continue to work on education reform to bring high standards and accountability, not just to elementary schools, but to the high schools as well" (White House News Conference, November 4, 2004).

Rather than emphasize academic goals per se, the NCLB reform bill mandated statewide testing in reading and mathematics each year in grades 3–8, and schools would be held accountable for students' performance on state proficiency tests. Key features of NCLB are:

- States create their own standards for what a child should know and learn for all grades. Standards must be developed in math and reading immediately. Standards must also be developed for science by the 2005–06 school year.
- With standards in place, states must test every student's progress toward those standards by using tests that are aligned with the standards. Beginning in the 2002–03 school year, schools must administer tests in each of three grade spans: grades 3–5, grades 6–9, and grades 10–12 in all schools. Beginning in the 2005–06 school year, tests must be administered every year in grades 3 through 8 in math and reading. Beginning in the 2007–08 school year, science achievement must also be tested.
- Each state, school district, and school will be expected to make Adequate Yearly Progress (AYP) toward meeting state standards. This progress will be measured for all students by sorting test results for students who are economically disadvantaged, from racial or ethnic minority groups, have disabilities, or have limited English proficiency.

- School and district performance will be publicly reported in district and state report cards. Individual school results will be on the district report cards.
- If the district or school continually fails to make Adequate Yearly Progress toward the standards, then they will be held accountable (U.S. Department of Education 2002).

While the NCLBA allows each of the 50 states to select the test it wishes to use, the Gallup Poll of the Public's Attitudes Toward the Public Schools revealed that 68 percent of respondents favor requiring all 50 states to use a nationally standardized test (Rose and Gallup, 2002).

Technology and Curriculum Development

According to the editor of *Technological Horizons in Education (T.H.E.) Journal*, technology should be reflected in the curriculum development process:

> We [must] revisit our state and national core content standards for students and teachers. Can we have science standards with no mention of technology when scientists rely so heavily on technology to do science? Can we have English/Language Arts standards with no mention of technology when most anyone who writes a sentence in his or her job uses word processing, and anyone in the business world doing research goes to the Internet for information? We need to bring our curriculum up to 21st century reality. We need to assess our students' knowledge and skills in a way that is consistent with how that knowledge and those skills are used in the real world. This is the context in which we should be integrating technology throughout all of curriculum and instruction (Fletcher 2004, p. 6).

No Child Left Behind requires that all students will be technologically literate by the end of the eighth grade. The definition of "technologically literate" is left up to the states, and there is no requirement for states to report their progress on this goal. However, NCLB requires states to show how they will ensure that technology is integrated throughout all of their curriculum and instruction by the beginning of 2007.

Students and Curriculum Development

As pointed out in Chapter 1, learners should be clearly aware of the goals being sought by their teachers and the goals embedded in the curriculum they are experiencing. In addition, though, learners formulate their own curricular goals throughout the process of instruction. In fact, as Jane Gilness states in "How to Integrate Character Education into the Curriculum" in this chapter's *Teachers' Voices* section: "I've . . . found that giving students ownership of the curriculum promotes a positive classroom climate and gives them a sense of being a vital part of a community."

While the goals teachers use to guide their planning and those sought by the learners need not be identical, they should overlap. The teacher's and learner's goals for a learning experience must be understood by both the teacher and the learners, and the goals must be compatible or they are not likely to be achieved. An effective way to achieve this congruence is through some form of student–teacher planning. As Glen Hass states in "Who Should Plan the Curriculum?" in this chapter, the student is the "major untapped resource in curriculum planning."

CRITERION QUESTIONS—CURRICULUM DEVELOPMENT

The articles in this chapter present varying perspectives on the processes of curriculum development. Curriculum development should reflect careful consideration of goals and values and all three of the curriculum bases. The following are among the criterion questions that can be derived from the different perspectives on curriculum development presented in this chapter.

1. Does the curriculum reflect an appropriate balance between subject-centeredness and student-centeredness?
2. Does the curriculum reflect a desired balance between acquisition of content and mastery of processes?
3. Are clear, appropriately high standards reflected in the curriculum?
4. Does the curriculum development process consider students' prior knowledge?
5. Does the curriculum include methods for assessing student learning?

REFERENCES

Bobbitt, F. *How to make a curriculum*. Boston: Houghton Mifflin, 1924.

Bush, G. W. The essential work of democracy. *Phi Delta Kappan 86*, no. 2, 114 (2004): 118–121.

Dewey, John. "The Relation of Theory to Practice in Education." In *The Relation of Theory to Practice in Education*, the Third Yearbook of the National Society for the Scientific Study of Education, Part 1. Bloomington, IN: Public School Publishing Co., 1904, pp. 9–30.

Fletcher, G. H. Integrating technology throughout education. *Technological Horizons in Education (T.H.E.) Journal, 32*, no. 3 (2004): 4, 6.

Hunkins, Francis P., & Hammill, Patricia A. "Beyond Tyler and Taba: Reconceptualizing the Curriculum Process." *Peabody Journal of Education 69*, no. 3 (Spring 1994): 4–18.

Ravitch, Diane. "The Case for National Standards and Assessments." *The Clearing House 69*, no. 3 (January/February 1996): 134–135.

———. *National Standards in American Education: A Citizen's Guide*. Washington, DC: The Brookings Institution, 1995.

Rose, L. C., & Gallup, A. M. The 34th annual Phi Delta Kappa/Gallup poll of the public's attitudes toward the public schools. *Phi Delta Kappan, 84*(1), (September, 2002): 41–56.

Tyler, Ralph W. *Basic Principles of Curriculum and Instruction*. Chicago: The University of Chicago Press, 1949.

U.S. Department of Education. Introduction. *No Child Left Behind*. Washington, DC: U.S. Department of Education, 2002. http://www.nclb.gov/next/overview/index.html [Accessed May, 2003].

A P P E N D I X

"Generic" Plan for a Unit of Study

Teacher _____   Grade Level _____   Subject _____

Unit Topic _____   Length of Time _____

1. *Introduction:* What is the nature and scope of the unit? How will the unit benefit students? Briefly, what skills, concepts, issues, and activities will the unit address?

2. *Objectives:* (expected learning outcomes—i.e., what will students be expected to be able to do? Objectives can cover the cognitive, psychomotor, and affective domains).
    a. What do I expect students to be able to do?
    b. What changes in students' behavior do I wish to see?
    c. What should each be able to do to demonstrate that he/she has mastered each objective in the unit?

3. *Content of Unit*
    a. What topics will I cover in my teaching? When will I teach those topics?
    b. Skills, topics, subtopics, concepts, issues, information, etc. covered in unit.
    c. List of activities and time for each (e.g., 1 week, 2 class sessions).

4. *Methods and Activities:*
    a. How am I going to teach the unit?
    b. What methods will I use: large group discussions, cooperative learning groups, discovery learning, mastery learning, etc.?
    c. In what activities will students participate: e.g., preparing oral and/or written reports, working in small committees, going on field trips, playing educational games, listening to guest speakers, etc.?

5. *Teaching Materials and/or Resources:*
    a. What materials and/or resources will you need to teach the unit?
    b. What materials will students need?
    c. What textbooks, software, or reference materials will be used?

6. *Assessment of Student Learning:*
    a. How will I measure and evaluate students' progress or achievement?
    b. How will I know if I have achieved the objectives for the unit?
    c. What assessments will I use to measure students' learning: quizzes, tests, observations of classroom behavior, portfolios, projects, performances, etc.

The Sources of a Science of Education

JOHN DEWEY (1859–1952)

ABSTRACT: Dewey suggests that "science" can be seen as a systematic method of inquiry within an area of professional practice. Thus, educational activities such as curriculum planning, instruction, and the organization and administration of schools may be said to be "scientific" if they are done systematically, with particular attention to a rigorous intellectual technique. However, science should not be seen as providing rules that should be applied to the art of education; instead, science enriches professional judgment and provides a wider range of alternatives that can be applied to educational problems.

EDUCATION AS A SCIENCE

The title may suggest to some minds that it begs a prior question: Is there a science of education? And still more fundamentally, Can there be a science of education? Are the procedures and aims of education such that it is possible to reduce them to anything properly called a science? Similar questions exist in other fields. The issue is not unknown in history; it is raised in medicine and law. As far as education is concerned, I may confess at once that I have put the question in its apparently question-begging form in order to avoid discussion of questions that are important but that are also full of thorns and attended with controversial divisions.

It is enough for our purposes to note that the word "science" has a wide range.

There are those who would restrict the term to mathematics or to disciplines in which exact results can be determined by rigorous methods of demonstration. Such a conception limits even the claims of physics and chemistry to be sciences, for according to it the only scientific portion of these subjects is the strictly mathematical. The position of what are ordinarily termed the biological sciences is even more dubious, while social subjects and psychology would hardly rank as sciences at all, when measured by this definition. Clearly we must take the idea of science with some latitude. We must take it with sufficient looseness to include all the subjects that are usually regarded as sciences. The important thing is to discover those traits in virtue of which various fields are called

scientific. When we raise the question in this way, we are led to put emphasis upon methods of dealing with subject-matter rather than to look for uniform objective traits in subject matter. From this point of view, science signifies, I take it, the existence of systematic methods of inquiry, which, when they are brought to bear on a range of facts, enable us to understand them better and to control them more intelligently, less haphazardly and with less routine.

No one would doubt that our practices in hygiene and medicine are less casual, less results of a mixture of guess work and tradition, than they used to be, nor that this difference has been made by development of methods of investigating and testing. There is an intellectual technique by which discovery and organization of material go on cumulatively, and by means of which one inquirer can repeat the researches of another, confirm or discredit them, and add still more to the capital stock of knowledge. Moreover, the methods when they are used tend to perfect themselves, to suggest new problems, new investigations, which refine old procedures and create new and better ones.

The question as to the sources of a science of education is, then, to be taken in this sense. What are the ways by means of which the function of education in all its branches and phases—selection of material for the curriculum, methods of instruction and discipline, organization and administration of schools—can be conducted with systematic increase of intelligent control and understanding? What are the materials upon which we may—and should—draw in order that educational activities may become in a less degree products of routine, tradition, accident, and transitory accidental influences? From what sources shall we draw so that there shall be steady and cumulative growth of intelligent, communicable insight, and power of direction?

Here is the answer to those who decry pedagogical study on the ground that success in teaching and in moral direction of pupils is often not in any direct ratio to knowledge of educational principles. Here is "A" who is much more successful than "B" in teaching, awakening the enthusiasm of his students for learning, inspiring them morally by personal example and contact, and yet relatively ignorant of educational history, psychology, approved methods, etc., which "B" possesses in abundant measure. The facts are admitted. But what is overlooked by the objector is that the successes of such individuals tend to be born and to die with them: beneficial consequences extend only to those pupils who have personal contact with such gifted teachers. No one can measure the waste and loss that have come from the fact that the contributions of such men and women in the past have been thus confined, and the only way by which we can prevent such waste in the future is by methods which enable us to make an analysis of what the gifted teacher does intuitively, so that something accruing from his work can be communicated to others. Even in the things conventionally recognized as sciences, the insights of unusual persons remain important and there is no levelling down to a uniform procedure. But the existence of science gives common efficacy to the experiences of the genius; it makes it possible for the results of special power to become part of the working equipment of other inquirers, instead of perishing as they arose.

The individual capacities of the Newtons, Boyles, Joules, Darwins, Lyells, Helmholtzes, are not destroyed because of the existence of science; their differences from others and the impossibility of predicting on the basis of past science what discoveries they would make—that is, the impossibility of regulating their activities by antecedent sciences—persist. But science makes it possible for others to benefit systematically by what they achieved.

The existence of scientific method protects us also from a danger that attends the operations of men of unusual power: dangers of slavish imitation, partisanship, and such jealous devotion to them and their work as to get in the way of her progress. Anybody can notice today that the effect of an original and powerful teacher is not all to the good. Those influenced by him often show a one-sided interest; they tend to form schools, and to become impervious to other problems and truths; they incline to swear by the words of their master and to go on repeating his thoughts after him, and often without the spirit and insight that originally made them significant. Observation also shows that these results happen oftenest in those subjects in which scientific method is least developed. Where these methods are of longer standing students adopt methods rather than merely results, and employ them with flexibility rather than in literal reproduction.

This digression seems to be justified not merely because those who object to the idea of a science put personality and its unique gifts in opposition to science, but also because those who recommend science sometimes urge that uniformity of procedure will be its consequence. So it seems worthwhile to dwell on the fact that in the subjects best developed from the scientific point of view, the opposite is the case. Command of scientific methods and systematized subject-matter liberates individuals; it enables them to see new problems, devise new procedures, and, in general, makes for diversification rather than for set uniformity. But at the same time these diversifications have a cumulative effect in an advance shared by all workers in the field.

EDUCATION AS AN ART

This theme is, I think, closely connected with another point which is often urged, namely, that education is an art rather than a science. That, in concrete operation, education is an art, either a mechanical art or a fine art, is unquestionable. If there were an opposition between science and art, I should be compelled to side with those who assert that education is an art. But there is no opposition, although there is a distinction. We must not be misled by words. Engineering is, in actual practice, an art. But it is an art that progressively incorporates more and more of science into itself, more of mathematics, physics, and chemistry. It is the kind of art it is precisely because of a content of scientific subject-matter which guides it as a practical operation. There is room for the original and daring projects of exceptional individuals. But their distinction lies not in the fact that they turn their backs upon science, but in the fact that they make new integrations of scientific material and turn it to new and previously unfamiliar and unforeseen uses. When, in education, the psychologist or observer and experimentalist in any field reduces his findings to a rule which is to be uniformly adopted, then, only, is there a result which is objectionable and destructive of the free play of education as an art.

But this happens not because of scientific method but because of departure from it. It is not the capable engineer who treats scientific findings as imposing upon him a certain course which is to be rigidly adhered to: it is the third- or fourth-rate man who adopts this course. Even more, it is the unskilled day laborer who follows it. For even if the practice adopted is one that follows from science and could not have been discovered or employed except for science, when it is converted into a uniform rule of procedure it becomes an empirical rule-of-thumb procedure—just as a person may use a table of logarithms mechanically without knowing anything about mathematics.

The danger is great in the degree in which the attempt to develop scientific method is recent. Nobody would deny that education is still in a condition of transition from an empirical to a scientific status. In its empirical form the chief factors determining education are tradition, imi-

tative reproduction, response to various external pressures wherein the strongest force wins out, and the gifts, native and acquired, of individual teachers. In this situation there is a strong tendency to identify teaching ability with the use of procedures that yield immediately successful results, success being measured by such things as order in the classroom, correct recitations by pupils in assigned lessons, passing of examinations, promotion of pupils to a higher grade, etc.

For the most part, these are the standards by which a community judges the worth of a teacher. Prospective teachers come to training schools, whether in normal schools or colleges, with such ideas implicit in their minds. They want very largely to find out how to do things with the maximum prospect of success. Put baldly, they want recipes. Now, to such persons science is of value because it puts a stamp of final approval upon this and that specific procedure. It is very easy for science to be regarded as a guarantee that goes with the sale of goods rather than as a light to the eyes and a lamp to the feet. It is prized for its prestige value rather than as an organ of personal illumination and liberation. It is prized because it is thought to give unquestionable authenticity and authority to a specific procedure to be carried out in the school room. So conceived, science is antagonistic to education as an art.

EXPERIENCE AND ABSTRACTION

The history of the more mature sciences shows two characteristics. Their original problems were set by difficulties that offered themselves in the ordinary region of practical affairs. Men obtained fire by rubbing sticks together and noted how things grew warm when they pressed on each other, long before they had any theory of heat. Such everyday experiences in their seeming inconsistency with the phenomena of flame and fire finally led to the conception of heat as a mode of molecular motion. But it led to this conception only when the ordinary phenomena were reflected upon in detachment from the conditions and uses under which they exhibit themselves in practices. There is no science without abstraction, and abstraction means fundamentally that certain occurrences are removed from the dimension of familiar practical experience into that of reflective or theoretical inquiry.

To be able to get away for the time being from entanglement in the urgencies and needs of immediate practical concerns is a condition of the origin of scientific treatment in any field. Preoccupation with attaining some direct end or practical utility, always limits scientific inquiry. For it restricts the field of attention and thought, since we note only those things that are immediately connected with what we want to do or get at the moment. Theory is in the end, as has been well said, the most practical of all things, because this widening of the range of attention beyond nearby purpose and desire eventually results in the creation of wider and farther-reaching purposes and enables us to use a much wider and deeper range of conditions and means than were expressed in the observation of primitive practical purposes. For the time being, however, the formation of theories demands a resolute turning aside from the needs of practical operations previously performed.

This detachment is peculiarly hard to secure in the case of those persons who are concerned with building up the scientific content of educational practices and arts. There is a pressure for immediate results, for demonstration of a quick, short-time span of usefulness in school. There is a tendency to convert the results of statistical inquiries and laboratory experiments into directions and rules for the conduct of school administration and instruction. Results tend to be directly grabbed, as it were, and put into operation by teachers. Then there is the leisure for that slow and gradual independent growth of theories that is a necessary condition of the formation of a true science. This danger is peculiarly imminent in a science of education because its very recentness and novelty arouse skepticism as to its possibility and its value. The human desire to prove that the scientific mode of attack is really

of value brings pressure to convert scientific conclusions into rules and standards of schoolroom practice.

It would perhaps be invidious to select examples too near to current situations. Some illustration, however, is needed to give definiteness to what has been said. I select an instance which is remote in time and crude in itself. An investigator found that girls between the ages of eleven and fourteen mature more rapidly than boys of the same age. From this fact, or presumed fact, he drew the inference that during these years boys and girls should be separated for purposes of instruction. He converted an intellectual finding into an immediate rule of school practice.

That the conversion was rash, few would deny. The reason is obvious. School administration and instruction is a much more complex operation than was the factor contained in the scientific result. The significance of one factor for educational practice can be determined only as it is balanced with many other factors. Taken by itself, this illustration is so crude that to generalize from it might seem to furnish only a caricature. But the principle involved is of universal application. No conclusion of scientific research can be converted into an immediate rule of educational art. For there is no educational practice whatever which is not highly complex; that is to say, which does not contain many other conditions and factors than are included in the scientific finding.

Nevertheless, scientific findings are of practical utility, and the situation is wrongly interpreted when it is used to disparage the value of science in the art of education. What it militates against is the transformation of scientific findings into rules of action. Suppose for the moment that the finding about the different rates of maturing in boys and girls of a certain age is confirmed by continued investigation, and is to be accepted as fact. While it does not translate into a specific rule of fixed procedure, it is of some worth. The teacher who really knows this fact will have his personal attitude changed. He will be on the alert to make certain observations which would otherwise escape him; he will be enabled to interpret some facts which would otherwise be confused and misunderstood. This knowledge and understanding render his practice more intelligent, more flexible, and better adapted to deal effectively with concrete phenomena of practice.

Nor does this tell the whole story. Continued investigation reveals other relevant facts. Each investigation and conclusion is special, but the tendency of an increasing number and variety of specialized results is to create new points of view and a wider field of observation. Various special findings have a cumulative effect; they reinforce and extend one another, and in time lead to the detection of principles that bind together a number of facts that are diverse and even isolated in their *prima facie* occurrence. These connecting principles which link different phenomena together we call laws.

Facts which are so interrelated form a system, a science. The practitioner who knows the system and its laws is evidently in possession of a powerful instrument for observing and interpreting what goes on before him. This intellectual tool affects his attitudes and modes of response in what he does. Because the range of understanding is deepened and widened, he can take into account remote consequences which were originally hidden from view and hence were ignored in his actions. Greater continuity is introduced;

he does not isolate situations and deal with them in separation as he was compelled to do when ignorant of connecting principles. At the same time, his practical dealings become more flexible. Seeing more relations he sees more possibilities, more opportunities. He is emancipated from the need of following tradition and special precedents. His ability to judge being enriched, he has a wider range of alternatives to select from in dealing with individual situations.

WHAT SCIENCE MEANS

If we gather up these conclusions in a summary we reach the following results. In the first place, no genuine science is formed by isolated conclusions, no matter how scientifically correct the technique by which these isolated results are reached, and no matter how exact they are. Science does not emerge until these various findings are linked together to form a relatively coherent system—that is, until they reciprocally confirm and illuminate one another, or until each gives the others added meaning. Now this development requires time, and it requires more time in the degree in which the transition from an empirical condition to a scientific one is recent and hence imperfect.

John Dewey was, at various times during his career, Professor of Philosophy, Columbia University; head of the Department of Philosophy and director of the School of Education at the University of Chicago; and Professor of Philosophy at the University of Michigan.

QUESTIONS FOR REFLECTION

1. What does Dewey mean when he says that the effect of an "original and powerful teacher is not all to the good"? What remedy is available to offset the sometimes unfavorable effects of such teachers, according to Dewey? Have you been taught by this type of teacher? If so, how did those experiences influence your learning?
2. Under what circumstances does Dewey consider science to be "antagonistic" to education as an art?
3. When, according to Dewey, is "theory the most practical of all things"? Do you agree with his argument?

Teachers, Public Life, and Curriculum Reform

HENRY A. GIROUX

ABSTRACT: Discourse related to curriculum and teaching reflects the points of view of those involved and cannot be separated from issues of history, power, and politics. Dominant views of curriculum and teaching claim objectivity, but they fail to link schooling to complex political, economic, and cultural forces; and they see teachers as technicians, bureaucratic agents, and deskilled intellectuals. Thus, a critical theory of curriculum must consider questions of representation, justice, and power. Toward this end, teachers' roles should be restructured so they become critical agents who take risks (or "go for broke") and act as "public intellectuals" who bring issues of equity, community, and social justice to the fore.

REASSERTING THE PRIMACY OF THE POLITICAL IN CURRICULUM THEORY

The connection between curriculum and teaching is structured by a series of issues that are not always present in the language of the current educational reform movement. This is evident, for instance, in the way mainstream educational reformers often ignore the problematic relationship between curriculum as a socially constructed narrative on the one hand, and the interface of teaching and politics on the other. Mainstream curriculum reformers often view curriculum as an objective text that merely has to be imparted to students.[1]

In opposition to this view, I want to argue that the language used by administrators, teachers, students, and others involved in either constructing, implementing, or receiving the classroom curriculum actively produces particular social identities, "imagined communities," specific competencies, and distinctive ways of life. Moreover, the language of curriculum, like other discourses, does not merely reflect a pregiven reality; on the contrary, it selectively offers depictions of the larger world through representations that people struggle over to name what counts as knowledge, what counts as communities of learning, what social relationships matter, and what visions of the future can be represented as legitimate (Aronowitz & Giroux, 1993).

Of course, if curriculum is seen as a terrain of struggle, one that is shot through with ethical considerations, it becomes reasonable to assume that talk about teaching and curriculum should not be removed from considerations of history, power, and politics. After all, the language of curriculum is both historical and contingent. Theories of curriculum have emerged from past struggles and are often heavily weighted in favor of those who have power, authority, and institutional legitimation.

Curriculum is also political in that state governments, locally elected school boards, and powerful business and publishing interests exercise enormous influence over teaching practices and curriculum policies (Apple & Christian-Smith, 1992). Moreover, the culture of the school is often representative of those features of the dominant culture that it affirms, sustains, selects, and legitimates. Thus, the distinction between high and low status academic subjects, the organization of knowledge into disciplines, and the allocation of knowledge and symbolic rewards to different groups indicates how politics work to influence the curriculum.

Within dominant versions of curriculum and teaching, there is little room theoretically to understand the dynamics of power as they work in schools, particularly around the mechanisms of tracking, racial and gender discrimination, testing, and other mechanisms of exclusion (Oaks, 1985). Mainstream educational reformers such as William Bennett, Chester Finn, Jr., and Dianne Ravitch exhibit little understanding of schooling as a site that actively produces different histories, social groups, and student identities under profound conditions of inequality. This is true, in part, because many dominant versions of curriculum and teaching legitimate themselves through unproblematized claims to objectivity and an obsession with empiricist forms of accountability. But, more importantly, many mainstream theorists of curriculum refuse to link schooling to the complex political, economic, and cultural relations that structure it as a borderland of movement and translation rather than a fixed and unitary site.

When inserted into this matrix of power, difference, and social justice, schools cannot be abstracted from the larger society where histories mix, languages and identities intermingle, values clash, and different groups struggle over how they are represented and how they might represent themselves. Questions of representation, justice, and power are central to any critical theory of curriculum. This is especially true in a society in which Afro-Americans, women, and other people of color are vastly underrepresented in both schools and other dominant cultural institutions. Of course, the issue of representation as I am using it here suggests that meaning is always political, actively involved in producing diverse social positions, and inextricably implicated in relations of power.

Educators generally exhibit a deep suspicion of politics, and this is not unwarranted when politics is reduced to a form of dogmatism. And, yet, it is impossible for teachers to become agents in the classroom without a broader understanding of politics and the emancipatory possibilities it provides for thinking about and shaping their own practices. Recognizing the politics of one's location as an educator should not imply that one's pedagogical practice is inflexible, fixed, or intolerant. To insist that teachers recognize the political nature of their own work can be understood as part of a broader critical effort to make them self-reflective of the interests and assumptions that shape their classroom practices. Roger Simon (1992) captures this sentiment by arguing that by inserting the political back into the discourse of teaching educators can "initiate rather than close off the problem of responsibility" (p. 16) for those classroom practices generated by their claim to knowledge and authority.

In what follows, I want to offer an alternative language for defining the purpose and meaning of teacher work. While I have talked about teachers as intellectuals in another context, I want to extend this analysis by analyzing what the implications are for redefining teachers as public intellectuals.[2] In part, I want to explore this position by drawing upon my own training as a teacher and some of the problems I had to face when actually working in the public schools. I will conclude by highlighting some of the defining principles that might structure the content and context of what it means for teachers to assume the role of a public intellectual.

TRADITION AND THE PEDAGOGY OF RISK

Let me begin by saying that we are living through a very dangerous time. . . . We are in a revolutionary situation, no matter how unpopular that word has become in this country. The society in which we live is desperately menaced, not by [the cold war] but from within. So any citizen of this country who figures himself as responsible—and particularly those of you who deal with the minds and hearts of young people—must be prepared to "go for broke." Or to put it another way, you must understand that in the attempt to correct so many generations of bad faith and cruelty, when it is operating not only in the classroom but in society, you will meet the most fantastic, the most brutal, and the most determined resistance. There is no point in pretending that this won't happen. . . . [And yet] the obligation of anyone who thinks of him or herself as responsible is to examine society and try to change it and to fight it—at no matter what risk. This is the only hope society has. This is the only way societies change. (Baldwin, 1988, p. 3)

I read the words of the famed African-American novelist James Baldwin less as a prescription for cynicism and powerlessness than I do as an expression of hope. Baldwin's words are moving because he confers a sense of moral and political responsibility upon teachers by presupposing that they are critical agents who can move between theory and practice in order to take risks, refine their visions, and make a difference for both their students and the world in which they live. In order to take up Baldwin's challenge for teachers to "go for broke," to act in the classroom and the world with courage and dignity, it is important for educators to recognize that the current challenge facing public schools is one of the most serious that any generation of existing and prospective teachers has ever had to face. Politically, the U.S. has lived through 12 years of reforms in which teachers have been invited to deskill themselves, to become technicians, or, in more ideological terms, to accept their role as "clerks of the empire." We live at a time when state legislators and federal officials are increasingly calling for the testing of teachers and the implementation of standardized curriculum; at the same time, legislators and government officials are ignoring the most important people in the reform effort, the teachers. Within this grim scenario, the voices of teachers have been largely absent from the debate about education. It gets worse.

Economically, the working conditions of teachers, especially those in the urban districts with a low tax base, have badly deteriorated. The story is a familiar one: overcrowded classrooms, inadequate resources, low salaries, and a rise in teacher-directed violence. In part, this is due to the increased financial cutbacks to the public sector by the Federal Government, the tax revolt of the 1970s by the middle-class that put a ceiling on the ability of cities and states to raise revenue for public services, and the refusal by wide segments of the society to believe that public schooling is essential to the health of a democratic society. Compounding these problems is a dominant vision of schooling defined largely through the logic of corporate values and the imperatives

of the marketplace. Schools are being treated as if their only purpose were to train future workers, and teachers are being viewed as corporate footsoldiers whose role is to provide students with the skills necessary for the business world. In short, part of the crisis of teaching is the result of a vision of schooling that subordinates issues of equity, community, and social justice to pragmatic considerations that enshrine the marketplace and accountability schemes that standardize the social relations of schooling. The political and ideological climate does not look favorable for teachers at the moment. But it does offer prospective and existing teachers the challenge to engage in dialogue and debate regarding important issues such as the nature and purpose of teacher preparation, the meaning of educational leadership, and the dominant forms of classroom teaching.

I think that if existing and future teachers are willing to "go for broke," to use Baldwin's term, they will need to re-imagine teaching as part of a project of critique and possibility. But there is more at stake here than simply a change in who controls the conditions under which teachers work. This is important, but what is also needed is a new language, a new way of naming, ordering, and representing how power works in schools. It is precisely through a more critical language that teachers might be able to recognize the power of their own agency in order to raise and act upon such questions as: What range of purposes should schools serve? What knowledge is of most worth? What does it mean for teachers and students to know something? In what direction should teachers and students desire? What notions of authority should structure teaching and learning? These questions are important because they force educators to engage in a process of self-critique while simultaneously highlighting the central role that teachers might play in any viable attempt to reform the public schools.

My own journey into teaching was largely shaped by undergraduate education training and my first year of student teaching. While the content and context of these experiences shaped my initial understanding of myself as a teacher, they did not prepare me for the specific tasks and problems of what it meant to address the many problems I had to confront in my first job. In what follows, I want to speak from my own experiences in order to illuminate the shortcomings of the educational theories that both shaped my perceptions of teaching and the classroom practices I was expected to implement.

LEARNING TO BE A TECHNICIAN

During the time that I studied to be a teacher, for the most part I learned how to master classroom methods, read Bloom's taxonomy, and became adept at administering tests, but I was never asked to question how testing might be used as a sorting device to track and marginalize certain groups. Like many prospective teachers of my generation, I was taught how to master a body of knowledge defined within separate academic disciplines, but I never learned to question what the hierarchical organization of knowledge meant and how it conferred authority and power. For example, I was never taught to raise questions about what knowledge was worth knowing and why, why schools legitimated some forms of knowledge and ignored others, why English was more important than art, and why it was considered unworthy to take a course in which one worked with one's hands. I never engaged in a classroom discussion about whose interests were served through the teaching and legitimation of particular forms of school knowledge, or how knowledge served to silence and disempower particular social groups. Moreover, I was not given the opportunity to reflect upon the authoritarian principles that actually structure classroom life and how these could be understood by analyzing social, political, and economic conditions outside of schools. If a student slept in the morning at his or her desk, I was taught to approach the issue as a problem of discipline and management. I was not alerted to recognize the social conditions that may have caused such behavior. That is, to the possibility that the student may

have a drug-related problem, be hungry, sick, or simply exhausted because of conditions in his or her home life. I learned quickly to separate out the problems of society from the problems of schooling and hence became illiterate in understanding the complexity of the relationship between schools and the larger social order.

My initial teaching assignment was in a school in which the teacher turnover rate exceeded 85% each year. The first day I walked into that school I was met by some students hanging out in the lobby. They greeted me with stares born of territorial rights and suspicion and one of them jokingly asked me: "Hey man, you're new, what's your name?" I remember thinking they had violated some sort of rule regarding teacher student relationships by addressing me that way. Questions of identity, culture, and racism had not been factored into my understanding of teaching and schooling at the time. I had no idea that the questions that would be raised for me that year had less to do with the sterile language of methods I had learned as an undergraduate than they did with becoming culturally and politically literate about the context-specific histories and experiences that informed where my students came from and how they viewed themselves and others. I had no idea of how important it was to create a meaningful and safe classroom for them so that I could connect my teaching to their own languages, cultures, and lived experiences. I soon found out that giving students some sense of power and ownership over their own educational experience has more to do with developing a language that was risk taking and self-critical for me and meaningful, practical, and transformative for them. During that first year, I also learned something about the ways in which many school administrators are educated.

LEADERSHIP WITHOUT VISION

During that first year, I rented movies from the American Friends Service Committee, ignored the officially designated curriculum textbooks, and eventually put my own books and magazine articles on reserve in the school library for my students to read. Hoping to give my students some control over the conditions for producing knowledge, I encouraged them to produce their own texts through the use of school video equipment, cameras, and daily journals. Within a very short time, I came into conflict with the school principal. He was a mix between General Patton and the Encino Man. At six foot three, weighing in at 250 pounds, his presence seemed a bit overwhelming and intimidating. The first time he called me into his office, I learned something about how he was educated. He told me that in his mind students should be quiet in classrooms, teachers should stick to giving lectures and writing on the board, and that I was never to ask a student a question that he or she could not answer. He further suggested that rather than developing my own materials in class I should use the curricula packages made available through the good wishes of local businesses and companies. While clearly being a reflection, if not a parody, of the worst kind of teacher training, he adamantly believed strict management controls, rigid systems of accountability, and lock step discipline were at the heart of educational leadership. Hence, I found myself in a secular version of hell. This was a school in which teaching became reduced to the sterile logic of flow charts. Moreover, it was a school in which power was wielded largely by white, male administrators further reinforcing the isolation and despair of most of the teachers. I engaged in forms of guerrilla warfare with this administration, but in order to survive I had to enlist the help of a few other teachers and some members of the community. At the end of the school year, I was encouraged not to come back. Fortunately, I had another teaching job back east and ended up in a much better school.

In retrospect, the dominant view of educational leadership has had a resurgence during the Reagan and Bush eras. Its overall effect has been to limit teachers' control over the development and planning of curriculum, to reinforce the bureaucratic organization of the school, and to re-

move teachers from the process of judging and implementing classroom instruction. This is evident in the growing call for national testing, national curriculum standards, and the concerted attack on developing multicultural curricula. The ideology that guides this model and its view of pedagogy is that the behavior of teachers needs to be controlled and made consistent and predictable across different schools and student populations. The effect is not only to remove teachers from the process of deliberation and reflection, but also to routinize the nature of learning and classroom pedagogy. In this approach, it is assumed that all students can learn from the same standardized materials, instructional techniques, and modes of evaluation. The notion that students come from different histories, experiences, and cultures is strategically ignored within this approach. The notion that pedagogy should be attentive to specific contexts is ignored.

TEACHERS AS PUBLIC INTELLECTUALS

I want to challenge these views by arguing that one way to rethink and restructure the nature of teacher work is to view teachers as public intellectuals. The unease expressed about the identity and role of teachers as public intellectuals has a long tradition in the United States and has become the focus of a number of recent debates. On one level, there are conservatives who argue that teachers who address public issues from the perspective of a committed position are simply part of what they call the political correctness movement. In this case, there is a deep suspicion of any attempt to open up the possibility for educators to address pressing social issues and to connect them to their teaching. Moreover, within the broad parameters of this view schools are seen as apolitical institutions whose primary purpose is to both prepare students for the work place and to reproduce the alleged common values that define the "American" way of life.[3] At the same time, many liberals have argued that while teachers should address public issues they should do so from the perspective of a particular teaching methodology. This is evident in Gerald Graff's (1992) call for educators to teach the conflicts. In this view, the struggle over representations replaces how a politics of meaning might help students identify, engage, and transform relations of power that generate the material conditions of racism, sexism, poverty, and other oppressive conditions. Moreover, some radical feminists have argued that the call for teachers to be public intellectuals promotes leadership models that are largely patriarchal and overly rational in the forms of authority they secure. While there may be an element of truth in all of these positions, they all display enormous theoretical shortcomings. Conservatives often refuse to problematize their own version of what is legitimate intellectual knowledge and how it works to secure particular forms of authority by simply labeling as politically correct individuals, groups, or views that challenge the basic tenets of the status quo. Liberals, on the other hand, inhabit a terrain that wavers between rejecting a principled standpoint from which to teach and staunchly arguing for a pedagogy that is academically rigorous and fair. Caught between a discourse of fairness and the appeal to provocative teaching methods, liberals have no language for clarifying the moral visions that structure their views of the relationship between knowledge and authority and the practices it promotes. Moreover, they increasingly have come to believe that teaching from a particular standpoint is tantamount to imposing an ideological position upon students. This has led in some cases to a form of McCarthyism in which critical educators are summarily dismissed as being guilty of ideological indoctrination. While the feminist critique is the most interesting, it underplays the possibility for using authority in ways which allow teachers to be more self-critical while simultaneously providing the conditions for students to recognize the possibility for democratic agency in both themselves and others. Operating out of a language of binarisms, some feminist education critics essentialize the positions of their opponents and in doing so

present a dehistoricized and reductionistic view of critical pedagogy. Most importantly, all of these positions share in the failure to address the possibility for teachers to become a force for democratization both within and outside of schools.

As public intellectuals, teachers must bring to bear in their classrooms and other pedagogical sites the courage, analytical tools, moral vision, time, and dedication that is necessary to return schools to their primary task: being places of critical education in the service of creating a public sphere of citizens who are able to exercise power over their own lives and especially over the conditions of knowledge acquisition. Central to any such reform effort is the recognition that democracy is not a set of formal rules of participation, but the lived experience of empowerment for the vast majority. Moreover, the call for schools as democratic public spheres should not be limited to the call for equal access to schools, equal opportunity, or other arguments defined in terms of the principles of equality. Equality is a crucial aspect of democratizing schools, but teachers should not limit their demands to the call for equality. Instead, the rallying cry of teachers should be organized around the practice of empowerment for the vast majority of students in this country who need to be educated in the spirit of a critical democracy.[4]

This suggests another dimension in defining the role of public intellectuals. Such intellectuals must combine their role as educators and citizens. This implies they must connect the practice of classroom teaching to the operation of power in the larger society. At the same time, they must be attentive to those broader social forces that influence the workings of schooling and pedagogy. What is at issue here is a commitment on the part of teachers as public intellectuals to extend the principles of social justice to all spheres of economic, political, and cultural life. Within this discourse, the experiences that constitute the production of knowledge, identities, and social values in the schools are inextricably linked to the quality of moral and political life of the wider society. Hence, the reform of schooling must be seen as a part of a wider revitalization of public life.

This should not suggest that as public intellectuals, teachers represent a vanguardist group dedicated to simply reproducing another master narrative. In fact, as public intellectuals it is important for them to link their role as critical agents to their ability to be critical of their own politics while constantly engaging in dialogue with other educators, community people, various cultural workers, and students. As public intellectuals, teachers need to be aware of the limits of their own positions, make their pedagogies context specific, challenge the current organization of knowledge into fixed disciplines, and work in solidarity with others to gain some control over the conditions of their work. At the very least, this suggests that teachers will have to struggle on many different fronts in order to transform the conditions of work and learning that go on in schools. This means not only working with community people, teachers, students, and parents to open up progressive spaces within classrooms, but also forming alliances with other cultural workers in order to debate and shape educational policy at the local, state, and federal levels of government.

As public intellectuals, teachers need to provide the conditions for students to learn that the relationship between knowledge and power can be emancipatory, that their histories and experiences matter, and that what they say and do can count as part of a wider struggle to change the world around them. More specifically, teachers need to argue for forms of pedagogy that close the gap between the school and the real world. The curriculum needs to be organized around knowledge that relates to the communities, cultures, and traditions that give students a sense of history, identity, and place. This suggests pedagogical approaches that do more than make learning context specific, it also points to the need to expand the range of cultural texts that inform what counts as knowledge. As public intellectuals, teachers need to understand and use those electronically mediated knowledge forms that constitute the terrain of popular culture. This is the

world of media texts—videos, films, music, and other mechanisms of popular culture constituted outside of the technology of print and the book. Put another way, the content of the curriculum needs to affirm and critically enrich the meaning, language, and knowledge that students actually use to negotiate and inform their lives.

While it is central for teachers to expand the relevance of the curriculum to include the richness and diversity of the students they actually teach, they also need to correspondingly decenter the curriculum. That is, students should be actively involved with issues of governance, "including setting learning goals, selecting courses, and having their own, autonomous organizations, including a free press" (Aronowitz, in press). Not only does the distribution of power among teachers, students, and administrators provide the conditions for students to become agents in their learning process, it also provides the basis for collective learning, civic action, and ethical responsibility. Moreover, such agency emerges as a lived experience rather than as the mastery of an academic subject.

In addition, as public intellectuals, teachers need to make the issue of cultural difference a defining principal of curriculum development and research. In an age of shifting demographics, large scale immigration, and multiracial communities, teachers must make a firm commitment to cultural difference as central to the relationship of schooling and citizenship (Giroux, 1992). In the first instance, this means dismantling and deconstructing the legacy of nativism and racial chauvinism that has defined the rhetoric of school reform for the last decade. The Reagan and Bush era witnessed a full-fledged attack on the rights of minorities, civil rights legislation, affirmative action, and the legitimation of curriculum reforms pandering to Eurocentric interests. Teachers can affirm their commitment to democratic public life and cultural democracy by struggling in and outside of their classrooms in solidarity with others to reverse these policies in order to make schools more attentive to the cultural resources that students bring to the public schools. At one level, this means working to develop legislation that protects the civil rights of all groups. Equally important is the need for teachers to take the lead in encouraging programs that open school curricula to the narratives of cultural difference, without falling into the trap of merely romanticizing the experience of "Otherness." At stake here is the development of an educational policy that asserts public education as part of a broader ethical and political discourse, one that both challenges and transforms those curricula reforms of the last decade that are profoundly racist in context and content. In part, this suggests changing the terms of the debate regarding the relationship between schooling and national identity, moving away from an assimilationist ethic and the profoundly Eurocentric fantasies of a common culture to one which links national identity to diverse traditions and histories.

In short, as public intellectuals, teachers need to address the imperatives of citizenship. In part, this means addressing how schools can create the conditions for students to be social agents willing to struggle for expanding the critical public cultures that make a democracy viable. Consequently, any notion of pedagogy must be seen as a form of cultural politics, that is, a politic that highlights the role of education, as it takes place in a variety of public sites, to open up rather than close down the possibilities for keeping justice and hope alive at a time of shrinking possibilities.

NOTES

1. This is particularly true with respect to those mainstream reformers arguing for national standards and testing. In this discourse, students are always on the receiving end of the learning experience. It is as if the histories, experiences, and communities that shape their identities and sense of place are irrelevant to what is taught and how it is taught. See, for example, Hirsch (1987); Finn, Jr. and Ravitch (1987); for an alternative to this position, see Apple

(1993); Giroux (1988a); Giroux (1993). For an examination of schools that view teachers as more than clerks and technicians, see Wood (1993).
2. I have taken up this issue more extensively in Giroux (1988b), and Aronowitz and Giroux (1993).
3. For a trenchant analysis of the political correctness movement, see Aronowitz (1993), especially Chapter 1; see also Frank (1993).
4. I take this issue up in Giroux (1988b).

REFERENCES

Apple, M. (1993). *Official knowledge*. New York: Routledge.
Apple, M., & Christian-Smith, L. K. (Eds.). (1992). *The politics of the textbook*. New York: Routledge.
Aronowitz, S. (1993). *Roll over Beethoven: The return of cultural strife*. Hanover: Wesleyan University Press.
Aronowitz, S. (in press). A different perspective on educational inequality. *The Review of Education/Pedagogy/Cultural Studies*.
Aronowitz, S., & Giroux, H. A. (1993). *Education still under siege*. Westport, CT: Bergin & Garvey.
Baldwin, J. (1988). A talk to teachers. In Simonson & Waler (Eds.), *Multicultural literacy: Opening the American mind* (pp. 3–12). Saint Paul, MN: Graywolf Press.
Finn, C., Jr., & Ravitch, D. (1987). *What our 17-year olds know*. New York: Harper & Row.
Frank, J. (1993). In the waiting room: Canons, communities, "Political Correctness." In M. Edmunson (Ed.), *Wild Orchids: Messages from American universities* (pp. 127–149). New York: Penguin.
Giroux, H. A. (1988a). *Teachers as intellectuals*. Westport, CT: Bergin & Garvey.
Giroux, H. A. (1988b). *Schooling and the struggle for public life*. Minneapolis: University of Minnesota Press.
Giroux, H. A. (1992). *Border crossings*. New York: Routledge.
Giroux, H. A. (1993). *Living dangerously: The politics of multiculturalism*. New York: Peter Lang.
Graff, G. (1992). Teaching the conflicts. In D. J. Gless & B. H. Smith (Eds.), *The politics of liberal education* (pp. 57–73). Durham: Duke University Press.
Hirsch, E. D. (1987). *Cultural literacy*. Boston: Houghton Mifflin.
Oaks, J. (1985). *Keeping track: How schools structure inequality*. New Haven: Yale University Press.
Simon, R. (1922). *Teaching against the grain*. Westport, CT: Bergin & Garvey.
Wood, G. (1933). *Schools that work*. New York: Penguin Books.

Henry A. Giroux holds the Waterbury Chair Professorship in Secondary Education, Pennsylvania State University, University Park.

QUESTIONS FOR REFLECTION

1.   Why does Giroux advocate "inserting the political back into the discourse of teaching"? Do you agree? What arguments might be raised by critics of Giroux's recommendation?

2.   If teachers were to become "public intellectuals," how would this influence their curriculum planning activities? In other words, what would they do differently?

3.   In regard to the educational setting with which you are most familiar, what would it mean if you were to "go for broke" in the manner that Giroux suggests? What forms of resistance might you encounter? Does Giroux exaggerate when he says that teachers and other responsible citizens who "go for broke" should realize "that in the attempt to correct so many generations of bad faith and cruelty, when it is operating not only in the classroom but in society, [they] will meet the most fantastic, the most brutal, and the most determined resistance"?

4.   Do you agree with Giroux that the dominant view of educational leadership has served to limit teacher involvement in the development and planning of curricula? On the basis of your professional experiences, can you cite evidence that teacher involvement in curriculum planning is increasing?

Who Should Plan the Curriculum?

GLEN HASS (1915–1997)

ABSTRACT: *Several groups have important roles to play in curriculum planning. Scholars from the disciplines can provide input on what should be taught and how to implement the curriculum. Parents and other citizens in our pluralistic society can help to formulate goals and values to be included in the curriculum. Students, since they are well positioned to identify advantages and disadvantages of the current curriculum, can participate in seven aspects of curriculum planning, from determining what shall be studied to identifying methods for evaluating success in learning. Lastly, educators can play a key role by creating structures that facilitate the processes of collaborative curriculum planning.*

In these times of complex, often insoluble problems and rapid change, it is urgent that professionals in curriculum planning take a new look at the question, "Who Should Plan the Curriculum?" It is apparent that the curriculum planning and teaching that is needed involves many factors that go beyond the scope of any single discipline or profession. In addition, change is now so rapid in our society and world, that today's curriculum is unsuited for tomorrow's world and is as outmoded as the Model T for the world of twenty years from tomorrow—the world whose leaders are now in the classrooms.

THE CURRICULUM WE NEED

Today's curriculum planners should study conditions and trends in contemporary society and probable conditions and requirements for democratic living . . . at the beginning of the twenty-first century. Education for the future is almost useless unless it prepares learners to meet problems that are new and that neither they nor anyone else has ever encountered before. All professionals in education need an image of tomorrow as curricula are planned. All too often we now see a "good curriculum" as the present one with its problems removed.

In facing toward the future we must find ways to teach innovation, problem solving, a love of learning; students must acquire the tools of analysis, expression, and understanding. We will surely find that learners of all ages must be prepared for work that does not yet exist. We will see that we all will have numerous increasingly complex tasks as buyers, voters, parents, legislators, and cooperative planners.

All interested citizens, parents, learners, and scholars from many of the disciplines should be encouraged to work with teachers, principals, curriculum leaders, state department of education and federal education agency personnel in the planning. This involvement in planning by all interested parties should begin in the local school and school district, but it should also occur regularly on a state, national and international basis. A democratic society cannot permit uniformity and centralization. The undefined, but onrushing future requires many different autonomous, alternative efforts to cope with its challenges and problems.

In the past many curriculum writers have stated that laypersons and scholars should be encouraged to work with professional educators in planning the curriculum. They have also frequently stated that collaborative models for planning are needed. They have, however, often given inadequate attention to the particular role of each type of planner in the planning process. Lacking adequate role definition we have often, as educators, overemphasized our mission to instruct the public, and have been undersensitive to, or intolerant of, suggestion and dissent. Let us try to define the particular role of each group in curriculum planning.

ROLE OF SCHOLARS

What is the role in curriculum planning of scholars from disciplines other than education? There are at least two ways in which they can help. They can often give crucial advice regarding *what* should be taught; and they can often suggest *means of implementing* curriculum decisions.

For instance, in the 1960s, scholars in biology, mathematics, and physics worked with teachers and other curriculum workers in determining what should be taught. These planners found that the textbooks in use contained almost none of the modern concepts, although greater change in knowledge had occurred in the past fifty years than in the preceding 500. They also learned that greater emphasis was needed on unifying concepts so that the total number of basic ideas to be learned might be reduced. Now the collaboration of scholars is needed to identify the concepts which are most relevant to alternative futures so that they may become the focus of the curriculum.

Sociologists can give particular assistance in determining the means by which goals of education may be achieved and in identifying the essential values and behavior patterns which must be learned as society changes. Of equal importance is the fact that sociologists, as future planners, can aid the educator in understanding some of the characteristics of the society in which his or her students will live in the future. Together they can devise a better educational program to prepare for it.

Anthropologists can shed light on the reasons for the direction of the development of various aspects of the culture. They can help the school to plan to counterbalance pressures for conformity and to attach greater emphasis to creativity and critical judgment. They can help in planning to develop in each student an understanding of his or her powers and limitations for creating and modifying society. Anthropologists can also help in developing curriculum plans for the future.

Scholars from many disciplines can aid in curriculum planning by identifying the central concepts and rules for discovering the nature of the discipline. In the terms in which they are now represented, many of the disciplines are increasingly unteachable. We need a philosophical synthesis, appropriate to our world, the future, and to the learners, that can be taught—and only the scholars working alongside educators can achieve this synthesis.

ROLE OF PARENTS AND OTHER CITIZENS

In the long run, we can only build the curriculum and use the teaching methods which the active public will accept. We must work with the public and have orderly patterns for its participation. People need to be involved in the process of planning the curriculum in order to change their beliefs, attitudes, and behavior regarding it.

A fundamental question is, whose values are to be represented in the curricula for the learners of a particular community? Curriculum planners must recognize that a monolithic curriculum is not acceptable to parents and other citizens in a pluralistic society. Curriculum leaders and teachers should work with parents and other active citizens in setting the yearly educational goals for a particular classroom, school, or district. Within the larger framework of the school system, local communities, teachers, and principals should define *together* what each school community sees as the most important focus for the coming year. Public education transmits values and beliefs as well as knowledge. Since values and beliefs are very much family and community matters, parents and other citizens must be involved in curriculum planning.

From 1960 to the present, the prevailing practice in many school districts has been to curtail opportunities for citizen participation, and, increasingly, to try to confine curriculum decision-making to the professional educators. In the late 1960s this led to the press for community control through decentralization of large, urban school districts—a prime example of our failure to involve citizens in curriculum planning. Such in-

volvement would have helped teachers and other curriculum planners to be sensitive to the realities of life in the school community.

Many parents are concerned today about whether their children seem to be learning the "basics" needed for survival in our society. Some parents are concerned as to whether the content and operation of the school and its curriculum give students pride in their own race and ethnic background. All parents often wonder whether teachers genuinely accept and share their concern about the learning of their children. Without cooperative planning each group often sees the other as insensitive, as having unreasonable expectations, and as making unrealistic demands.

It is a matter of crucial importance that many school systems invent and use structural devices to bring about a sharing of thinking about the curriculum by the lay citizens of the community and professional staff members.

Staff members must learn to work with citizens; citizens must take part but not take over. This should begin at the level of the parents planning with the teacher about their concerns for their children and should move from there to the citizens advisory council and the systemwide curriculum committee. The profession, in each community, and the teacher, in each classroom, is responsible for establishing these channels.

ROLE OF STUDENTS

The student is the major untapped resource in curriculum planning. Students are in the best position to explain many of the advantages and deficiencies of the present curriculum. Their ideas and reactions are of very great importance. Research has shown many times that learning is significantly improved when students share in planning and evaluating the curriculum.

In the process of instruction, learners should share in setting goals and objectives. In a particular learning experience the initial objectives should be those that the student sees, at that time, as interesting and meaningful. While the objectives the teacher uses to guide his or her planning and those sought by learners need not be identical, there should be much overlapping. The teacher's and learner's goals for a learning experience certainly must be understood by both, and they must be compatible or they are not likely to be achieved.

Too little use is made of teacher-student planning. The understanding and skills of planning are among the most important outcomes of education. Perhaps more teachers would plan with their students if they realized that student-teacher planning has at least seven aspects, and that they might begin to plan with students about any one of them:

1. What is to be studied?
2. Why are we having this learning activity?
3. How shall we go about it?
4. Where might we do what needs to be done?
5. When shall we do it?
6. Who will do each part of the job?
7. How can we evaluate our success in learning?

While student participation in the choice of topics may be possible only in certain subjects, there is no reason why extensive use of the other aspects of teacher-student planning should not be used in all subjects.

ROLE OF EDUCATORS

The role of professional educators is one that will grow and develop as they work with the scholars, parents, other citizens, and students.

It is the job of the teacher, principal, and curriculum consultant to provide structure for planning with others, to inform, to offer recommendations, to bring together contributions from many sources, and to work out a recommended plan of action. In the analysis of the curriculum that is planned, professional educators must be certain that it takes account of the nature of the learner, of the society of which he or she is a part, and of the future. This part of the educa-

tor's role is not new, but it has increasing importance as he plans with others who are not so likely to give adequate attention to the various bases for curriculum decisions.

The professional curriculum planner should be alert to the necessity for relating schools to the surrounding political, economic, and social forces so that the means and goals of the curriculum harmonize with the lives of learners in particular circumstances.

Frequently, educators need to take a stand for what they believe, sharing what they know and feel. The public relies on the vision and courage of educators to present recommendations for curriculum improvement. Such recommendations should be related to a sense of purpose, the ability to think and analyze, and a proper respect for the requirements of human response. The educator, in recommending, must carefully avoid the appearance that the curriculum is solely the professional's business. Experience over time in working together helps to solve this problem.

A most important part of the teacher's role is to communicate to students his or her own valuing of learning. Teachers often motivate learners by their own motivations. Learners learn to like to learn from teachers who exhibit the intellectual accomplishment of regularly acquiring and acting on new knowledge.

Finally, professional educators must evaluate and interrelate the contributions from other planners and evolve a curriculum plan which they implement in their own classrooms or which they submit for the approval of the curriculum council or committee.

MOVING AHEAD

If it is recognized that all public policy in education is the product of professional-lay interaction, then one of the main roadblocks to progress can be removed. Increasing the communication between scholars in various disciplines and professional educators would be a valuable step forward. A next step is to make greater use of that largely untapped resource—student contributions to curriculum planning. In each community, professional educators should move to establish the structural devices needed so that scholars, citizens, students, and professional educators may share in planning the curriculum needed. Because of the importance of education, each should be enabled to make his or her particular contribution to curriculum planning.

Who should plan the curriculum? Everyone interested in the future; everyone concerned for the quality of education being experienced by the leaders of the future who are now in our classrooms.

Glen Hass was Professor of Education, Emeritus, University of Florida, Gainesville, and twice National President of the John Dewey Society.

QUESTIONS FOR REFLECTION

1. Do you agree that "The student is the major untapped resource in curriculum planning"? Why or why not?
2. In regard to the level and curricular area with which you are most interested, what "structures" could you create to increase the involvement of the following groups in planning the curriculum: students, parents, and community members, and other educators?
3. What guidelines should educators follow in facilitating collaborative curriculum planning?

A Principal Looks Back: Standards Matter

KIM MARSHALL

ABSTRACT: After 15 years as the principal of Boston's Mather School, the nation's oldest public elementary school, Marshall takes a critical look at his accomplishments and his failings. With approximately 600 inner-city students—many of whom did not speak English at home—Marshall faced the challenges of countless urban principals. Given that, he credits the improvements Mather School saw in the 1990s to rigorous state standards and the high-stakes Massachusetts Comprehensive Assessment System (MCAS) test.

After fifteen years as principal of an inner-city elementary school, I am a battle-hardened veteran with his ideals still intact. I welcome this opportunity to look at how the introduction of standards affected the day-to-day struggle to bring a first-rate education to all students.

I became principal of Boston's Mather School after three experiences that neatly framed some of the challenges of school leadership. Fresh out of college in 1969, I taught sixth graders in a Boston middle school and operated pretty much as a lone wolf, writing my own curriculum and at one point actually cutting the wires of my classroom public address speaker to silence the incessant schoolwide announcements. In my nine years in the classroom, I know that students learned a lot, but I was never held accountable to any external standards.

In 1980, intrigued by the "effective schools" research (including the work of Ron Edmonds and the British study, *Fifteen Thousand Hours*), I spent a year at the Harvard Graduate School of Education and sat at the feet of Edmonds himself. I steeped myself in his research on what seemed to make some urban schools work (strong instructional leadership, high expectations, a focus on basics, effective use of test data, and a safe and humane climate) and said "Amen" to his searing comment on failing urban schools: "We can, whenever and wherever we choose, successfully teach all children whose schooling is of interest to us. We already know more than we need in order to do this. Whether we do it must finally depend on how we feel about the fact that we haven't so far." I was eager to become a school leader and put these ideas to work.

But while I was in graduate school, the voters of Massachusetts passed a tax-limiting referendum that sent Boston into a budget tailspin and closed twenty-seven schools. This nixed any chance I had of being made a principal in the near future, and I prepared to return to my classroom.

Instead, I was hired as chief architect of a new citywide curriculum by Boston's Superintendent of Schools, Robert Spillane, a forceful advocate of higher student achievement and more accountable schools. This was right around the time *A Nation at Risk* came out, and I found myself in the thick of Boston's response to the "rising tide of mediocrity." Later, under Spillane's successor, Laval Wilson, I directed an ambitious systemwide strategic planning process. My colleagues and I did some useful work, but throughout my years in the central office I felt that our efforts were often like pushing a string. Without like minded principals pulling our initiatives into the schools, we often didn't make much of a difference.

When I finally became a principal in 1987, my experiences as a teacher, graduate student, and bureaucrat had shown me three aspects of the urban school challenge: (a) talented but often cussedly independent teachers working in isolation from their colleagues and external standards; (b) provocative research theories about the key factors associated with effective urban schools; and (c) the limited power of the central office to

push change into schools that had a great deal of autonomy and very little accountability. Now that I was in the principal's office, I thought I was ideally situated to make a difference for teachers and kids. Was I right?

First, the good news. Over the last fifteen years, Mather students have made significant gains. Our student attendance went from 89 percent to 95 percent and our staff attendance went from 92 percent to 98 percent. Our test scores went from rock bottom in citywide standings to about two-thirds of the way up the pack. A recent in-depth review gave us a solid B+ based on an intensive inspection of the school and standardized test scores. And in 1999, the Mather was recognized for having the biggest gains in the MCAS (the rigorous Massachusetts statewide tests) of any large elementary school in the state. I am proud of these gains and of dramatic improvements in staff skills and training, student climate, philanthropic support, and the physical plant.

But now some more sobering news. The gains we made came in agonizingly slow increments, and were accompanied by many false starts, detours, and regressions. Graphs of our students' test scores did not show the clean, linear progress I had expected. Far too many of our students score in the bottom category on standardized tests, too few are Proficient and Advanced, and our student suspension rate is too high. Serious work remains to be done.

When judging schools, everyone is an expert. If the Mather's student achievement was extraordinary, people would attribute it to certain "obvious" factors: the principal's leadership, his 78-hour workweek, recruiting great teachers, raising money and bringing in lots of resources, using the research on effective schools, and so on. But our student achievement is not extraordinary. This means that despite a lot of hard work, some key ingredients were missing.

I have a theory. I think that the absence of meaningful external standards before 1998 prevented our strenuous and thoughtful efforts from having much traction. I would like to test this theory by examining ten notorious barriers to high student achievement, our struggle with each of them before the introduction of external standards, and what changed when Massachusetts finally mandated high-stakes tests.

1. Teacher isolation. In my first months as principal, I was struck by how cut off Mather teachers were from each other and from a sense of schoolwide purpose. I understood teachers' urge to close their classroom doors and do their own thing; I had done the same thing when I was a teacher. But my reading of the effective schools research and my experience in the central office convinced me that if Mather teachers worked in isolation, there would be pockets of excellence but schoolwide performance would continue to be abysmal.

So I struggled to get the faculty working as a team. I circulated a daily newsletter (dubbed the Mather Memo) and tried to focus staff meetings on curriculum and effective teaching strategies. I encouraged staff to share their successes, publicly praised good teaching, and successfully advocated for a record-breaking number of citywide Gold Apple awards for Mather teachers. I recruited a corporate partner whose generosity made it possible, among other things, to have occasional staff luncheons and an annual Christmas party.

But morale never seemed to get out of the sub-basement. Staff meetings gravitated to student discipline problems, and as a young principal who was seen as being too "nice" to students, I was often on the defensive. We spent very little time talking about teaching and learning, and did not develop a sense of schoolwide teamwork. The result? Teachers continued to work as private artisans, sometimes masterfully, sometimes with painful mediocrity—and the overall results continued to be very disappointing.

2. Lack of teamwork. Having failed to unite the staff as one big happy family, I decided that grade-level teams were a more manageable arena in which to work on improving collegiality. I began to schedule the school so that teachers at the same grade level had the same free periods.

Teams began to meet at least once a week and held occasional after-school or weekend retreats (for which they were paid). A few years later, a scheduling consultant taught me how to create once-a-week 90-minute team meetings by scheduling Art, Computer, Library, Music, and Phys Ed classes back-to-back with lunch. This gave teams even more time to meet.

After much debate, we also introduced "looping," with the entire fourth-grade team moving up to fifth grade with the same students (fifth-grade teachers looped back to fourth). Teachers found that spending two years with the same class strengthened relationships with students and parents and within their grade-level teams, and a few years later the kindergarten and first-grade teams decided to begin looping.

But despite the amount of time that teams spent together, there was a strong tendency for the agendas to be dominated by field trips, war stories about troubled students, and other management issues, with all too little attention to sharing curriculum ideas. I urged teams to use their meetings to take a hard look at student results and use the data to plan ways to improve outcomes, and I tried to bring in training and effective coaches to work with the teams, but I had limited success shifting the agendas of these meetings. In retrospect, I probably would have been more successful if I had attended team meetings and played more of a leadership role, but I was almost always downstairs managing the cafeteria at this point in the day and reasoned that teachers needed to be empowered to run their own meetings.

3. Curriculum anarchy. During my early years as principal, I was struck by the fact that most teachers resisted using a common set of grade-level standards. In the central office, I had been involved in creating Boston's citywide curriculum goals, and I was stunned by the degree to which they were simply ignored. While teachers enjoyed their "academic freedom," it caused constant problems. While teachers in one grade emphasized multiculturalism, teachers in the next grade judged students on their knowledge of traditional history facts. While one team focused on grammar and spelling, another cared deeply about style and voice. While one encouraged students to use calculators, the next wanted students to be proficient at long multiplication and division. These ragged "hand-offs" were a frequent source of unhappiness. But teachers almost never shared their feelings with the offending colleagues in the grade just below theirs. That would have risked scary confrontations on deep pedagogical disagreements, which teachers were sure would undermine staff morale. But the absence of honest discussion—culminating in an agreed-upon grade-by-grade curriculum—doomed the Mather to a deeper morale problem stemming from suppressed anger—and lousy test scores.

I saw curriculum anarchy as a major leadership challenge, and tried again and again to get teachers to buy into a coherent K–5 sequence. At one staff retreat, I asked teachers at each grade level to talk to those at the grade just below and just above theirs and agree to better curriculum hand-offs. People listened politely to each other, but made very few changes in what they were teaching. Undaunted, I brought in newly written Massachusetts curriculum frameworks and national curriculum documents, but they did not match the tests our students were required to take and could therefore be ignored with impunity. When the Boston central office produced a cumbersome new curriculum in 1996, I "translated" it into teacher-friendly packets for each grade level—but these had little impact on the private curriculums in many classrooms.

As a result, far too many of our students moved to the next grade with uneven preparation, and our fifth graders, although better prepared than most Boston elementary graduates, entered middle school with big gaps in their knowledge and skills. It was not a pretty picture, and I was intensely frustrated that I could not find a way to change it.

4. Weak alignment. As I wrestled with the curriculum issue, I saw that tests were a vital part of getting teachers on the same page. But virtually all of the standardized tests that students took were poorly aligned with the classroom curriculum (whatever that was) and were not well respected by most teachers. Boston's attempt to write citywide curriculum tests in the 1980s was not well received, and the tests quickly fell into disuse. The tests that teachers gave every Friday and at the end of each curriculum unit were of uneven quality and covered a wide variety of topics with an even wider range of expectations and criteria for excellence. The only tests that got a modicum of respect were the Metropolitan Achievement Tests, which were given in reading and math at every grade level except kindergarten, with school-by-school results published in Boston newspapers.

Sensing that teachers cared about the Metropolitan, I thought that might be a lever for getting teachers on the same curriculum page and making predictable hand-offs of skills and knowledge to the next grade. I did a careful analysis of the Metropolitan and, without quoting specific test items, told teachers at each grade level what the test covered in reading and math. Did teachers use my pages and pages of goals? They did not. And hard as it was for me to admit it, they had a point. Teachers did not think they could improve their students' scores by teaching toward the items I had extracted from the tests—or toward Boston's curriculum, for that matter. The Metropolitans, being norm-referenced tests, were designed to spread students out on a bell-shaped curve and were not aligned to a specific set of curriculum goals or "sensitive" to good teaching (you could work hard and teach well and not have your efforts show up in improved scores). What's more, I was pushing the ethical envelope by briefing teachers on the standards that were covered by a supposedly secret test. If Mather scores had skyrocketed, there might have been a major scandal.

But I had stumbled onto an important insight. The key to turning around teachers' well-founded cynicism about the tests they were required to give and the curriculum they were supposed to teach was to make sure that tests really measured a thoughtful K–12 curriculum. We needed to find both missing elements—a clear grade-by-grade curriculum and aligned tests—at the same time. I could not persuade teachers to buy into one without the other, and without both I could not coax teachers out of the isolation of their classrooms.

5. Low expectations. Another barrier in my early years as principal was teachers' pessimism about producing significant student achievement gains. Hamstrung by the lack of aligned curriculum and tests, gun-shy about addressing their colleagues' idiosyncratic classroom goals, and discouraged by the visible results of poverty (85% of our students qualified for free and reduced-price meals and the community around the school was plagued by unemployment and violence), most teachers regarded themselves as hard-working martyrs in a hopeless cause.

Going for broke in my second month as principal, I brought in Jeff Howard, the charismatic African American social psychologist, and his "Efficacy" message hit home. Jeff spoke of combating our students' lack of achievement motivation by getting them to see that you are not just born smart—you can get smart by applying effective effort. He grabbed the faculty's attention with the notion that we could dramatically improve our results by directly confronting the downward spiral of negative beliefs about intelligence and effort. Over lunch, most of the staff buzzed with excitement.

But after lunch Jeff had to go to another school, and the consultant he left in charge was swamped by defensive and increasingly angry reactions. Was he suggesting that teachers were racist? Was he saying that teachers were making the problem worse? And what did he suggest they do on *Monday*? By late afternoon, it was clear that my gamble to unite the staff around this approach had failed.

Licking my wounds, I took a more incremental approach over the next few years, using private conversations, team meetings, the Mather Memo, and research articles to drive home the message that much higher student achievement was doable at the Mather School. I sent small groups of teachers to Efficacy training, and eventually brought in one of Jeff Howard's colleagues to train the whole staff. It was an uphill battle, but gradually Efficacy beliefs were accepted as part of the school's mission and it became taboo to express negative expectations about students' potential.

But we still did not see dramatic increases in our Metropolitan test scores. Belief was not enough. We needed something more to boost achievement in every classroom.

6. Negativism. The area in which I was least effective in my early years was dealing with some strong personalities who declared war on my goals as principal. It's been observed that inner-city schools attract and nurture strong personalities and can develop a negative culture. When a leader starts to mess around with the unspoken expectations and mores of such a culture, he is playing with fire. When I appeared on the scene preaching that "All Children Can Learn," these teachers reacted with disbelief and active resistance. A parody of the Mather Memo ridiculed my idealism: "For Sale: Rose-Colored Glasses! Buy Now! Cheap! Get that glowing feeling while all falls apart around you."

I was often aghast at the vehemence with which these teachers attacked me. Monthly confrontations with the Faculty Senate invariably got my stomach churning, and I took to quoting W. B. Yeats: "The best lack all conviction, and the worst are full of passionate intensity." I jokingly dubbed my antagonists the Gang of Six, but I could not hide my dismay when it was reported to me that on the day of the first Efficacy seminar, one of these teachers was overheard to say in the bathroom, "If I had a gun, I'd shoot Jeff Howard dead." I was continually off balance, and every mistake I made became a major crisis ("People are outraged! Morale has never been worse!"). On several occasions, I failed to set limits on outrageous and insubordinate behavior and assert my prerogatives as principal.

Over a period of years, the most negative people realized that I wasn't going anywhere and transferred out. They had understudies, and there were struggles almost every year in which I battled with them (not always very skillfully) for the hearts and minds of the silent majority, but the school gradually developed a more positive culture. However, it was only when we were confronted with a compelling external mandate that the positive folks found their voice and the remaining negative staff members fell silent.

7. A harried principal. As every busy principal knows, the hardest part of the job is making time for instructional leadership while dealing with the myriad administrative and disciplinary challenges of running a school. The limitless number of tasks that need to be done can also serve as a very plausible excuse for not dealing with the more intractable work of improving teaching and learning. After my initial setbacks with the staff, I plunged into a major campaign to raise money for a gala 350th anniversary celebration and was successful in sprucing up the aging and neglected building and garnering a great deal of publicity for the school. Although these improvements were important, I had no illusions that they were the heart of the matter.

As I got better at handling the constant stream of "over-the-transom" demands on my time, I prided myself at being able to juggle several balls at once and often quoted an intern's observation that I had two hundred separate interactions in a single day—and that did not include greeting students in the halls. I became an "intensity junkie," addicted to being frantically busy and constantly in demand. I had fallen victim to H.S.P.S.—Hyperactive Superficial Principal Syndrome—and was spending far too little time on teaching and learning.

This realization led me to devise a plan for dropping in on five teachers a day for brief, unannounced supervisory visits. These visits and my follow-up conversations with teachers gave me a much better handle what was going on in classrooms, improved my rapport with the staff, and

formed the basis for much more insightful performance evaluations.

But like a recovering addict, I continued to struggle with H.S.P.S. on a daily basis. I gradually accepted that I could not (as I had naively hoped) be the school's staff developer. I began to bring in "coaches" in literacy, math, and science to work with teachers in their classrooms and team meetings. I stopped sending teachers off to isolated workshops and invested in training within the building. These changes greatly improved the quality of staff development for teachers—but test scores were still not improving as much as we hoped.

8. Not focusing on results. I became increasingly convinced that the most important reason for our disappointing scores was that we were spending too little time actually looking at what students were learning. The teachers' contract allowed me to supervise classroom teaching and inspect teachers' lesson plans, but woe betide a principal who tries to evaluate a teacher based on student learning outcomes. Resistance to evaluating teachers on results is well-founded at one level: unsophisticated administrators might use unsuitable measures like norm-referenced tests or unfairly evaluate teachers for failing to reach grade-level standards with students who were poorly taught the year before or had significant learning deficits.

But not looking at the results of teaching during the school year is part of a broader American tendency to "teach, test, and hope for the best." The headlong rush through the curriculum (whatever that might be) is rarely interrupted by a thoughtful look at how students are doing and what needs to be fixed right now or changed next year. For a principal to ask for copies of unit tests and a breakdown of student scores is profoundly counter-cultural. These private artifacts are none of the principal's business. Teacher teams don't use them much either. They rarely pause at the end of a teaching unit to look at which teaching "moves" and materials produce the best gains, which are less successful, and which students need more help. With one notable exception, I failed to get teachers to slow down, relax about the accountability bugaboo, and talk about best practices in the light of the work students actually produced.

9. Mystery grading criteria. Looking at student work, especially writing and other open-ended products, is virtually impossible without objective grading tools. In many schools, the criteria for getting an A are a secret locked up in each teacher's brain, with top grades going to students who are good mind readers. The absence of clear, public, usable guides for scoring student work prevents students from getting helpful feedback and robs teacher teams of the data they need to improve their performance.

In 1996, the Mather made a successful foray into the world of standards-based thinking. Spurred on by a summer workshop with Grant Wiggins, the author of two books on assessment, including *Assessing Student Performance,* we wrote rubrics (scoring guides) for student writing that described in a one-pager for each grade the specific criteria for getting a score of 4, 3, 2, and 1 in Mechanics/Usage, Content/Organization, and Style/Voice. It was striking how much higher our standards were once we had written these rubrics; now we knew what proficiency looked like! We could also guarantee that the same piece of student writing would get the same scores no matter who graded it. Encouraged by our success, we began to give students a "cold prompt" writing assignment (a topic they had never seen before, no help from the teacher) in September, November, March, and June. Teachers scored the papers together and then discussed the results.

This process was a breakthrough. We had found a way to score student writing objectively; we were sharing the criteria with students and parents in advance (no surprises, no excuses); we were giving "dipstick" assessments at several points each year; teachers at each grade were working as a team to score students' work; and teachers were analyzing students' work, giving students feedback, and fine-tuning their teach-

ing. We began to see significant improvements in our students' writing.

But after a few years of regular scoring meetings and charting of students' progress, our efforts began to flag. Finding enough time was always an issue, especially since the scoring/data analysis meetings were hard to fit into our 90-minute team meetings and many teachers had after-school family commitments. It takes very strong leadership—or another equally powerful force—to sustain this kind of work.

10. No schoolwide plan. Over the years, we eyeballed many different programs to turn around student achievement—Effective Schools, Efficacy, Success for All, Core Knowledge, Accelerated Schools, Comer, Schools Without Failure, Multiple Intelligences, Whole Language, Multicultural, and others—but none got the buy-in needed for successful implementation. As a result, we kept trying to "grow our own"—an exhausting and frustrating process. In the late 1990s, one "whole school" reform program was mandated as part of a Boston grant program. We appreciated the help (and the money!) but felt there were crucial pieces missing and drove the program administrators crazy by constantly second-guessing their model and adding components of our own. Perhaps we were asking for too much. Perhaps we should have committed to a less-than-perfect program and given it a chance to work. But we were on a constant quest for a better mousetrap.

As we continued our search, two more narrowly focused programs had a big impact. The first was Reading Recovery, a highly effective, low-tech, data-driven program for struggling first graders. What caught the attention of the whole staff was that most of the students who appeared to be doomed to school failure got back on track after twelve weeks of hard work with the highly trained Reading Recovery teachers.

After a few years of successful implementation, there was enough support to get all primary-grade teachers to buy into the Literacy Collaborative program, which was created by Irene Fountas and Gay Sue Pinnell to align the way reading and writing are taught in regular class-rooms with Reading Recovery. All of our K–3 teachers bought into the program and were trained by one of their colleagues through in-class coaching and a 40-hour after-school course in which teachers looked at student work and data (using a new scale of reading proficiency) and talked constantly about best practices in a low-stakes, collegial atmosphere. The program produced significant gains in our student achievement in the lower grades, and during the 2001–2002 school year we introduced the upper-grade version of Literacy Collaborative.

But these very effective literacy programs were not part of a coherent schoolwide change plan. And this, along with all the other factors discussed above, prevented us from getting the kinds of achievement gains we knew our students could produce. . . .

Children who enter school with middle-class home advantages tend to do well, even if they attend ineffective schools. But disadvantaged children desperately need effective schools to teach them key life skills and launch them into success. Unless there is strong leadership pushing back, the ten factors will make things much worse for these children. If teachers work in isolation, if there isn't effective teamwork, if the curriculum is undefined and weakly aligned with tests, if there are low expectations, if a negative culture prevails, if the principal is constantly distracted by non-academic matters, if the school does not measure and analyze student outcomes, and if the staff lacks a coherent overall improvement plan, then students' entering inequalities will be amplified and poor children will fall further and further behind, widening the achievement gap into a chasm.

This presents a tremendous professional—and moral—challenge to principals, because they are ideally situated to influence each of these factors. If the principal is an effective instructional leader, the forces will be pushed back (at least for the time being) and the gap will narrow. For vulnerable, school-dependent children, this is a godsend.

How did I measure up to this challenge? For more than a decade, I had limited success pushing back the powerful gap-widening forces. Mather students only began to make real progress when strong external standards were introduced, and that did not happen until Massachusetts introduced high-stakes tests (the MCAS) in 1998.

When we heard that 800-pound gorilla knocking on our door, the turnaround happened with amazing speed. As our fourth graders took the first round of MCAS tests, one of our most effective teachers (who taught fourth grade) burst into tears at a staff meeting and proclaimed, "No more Lone Ranger!" She pleaded with her colleagues in kindergarten, first grade, second grade, and third grade to prepare students with the necessary building blocks so that she would never again have to watch her students being humiliated by a test for which they were so poorly prepared.

Some of our colleagues joined the handwringing across Massachusetts about making students the victims of a forced march to high standards. But in a subsequent meeting, the staff sat down and actually took portions of the MCAS and came to these conclusions: (a) although the test is hard, it really does measure the kinds of skills and knowledge students need to be successful in the twenty-first century; (b) the MCAS is a curriculum-referenced test whose items are released every year, making it possible to align the curriculum and study for the test (we are lucky to live in Massachusetts; some states use norm-referenced tests and keep their tests secret); (c) our students have a long way to go; but (d) most of our kids *can* reach the proficient level if the whole school teaches effectively over time.

The only problem was that the Massachusetts frameworks and tests were pegged to grades four, eight, and ten, leaving some uncertainty about curriculum goals for the other grades. But the grade-four tests and accompanying "bridge" documents gave us much more information than we had before. We set up committees that worked with consultants to "tease back" the standards, and we then worked as a staff (with parent input) to create booklets with clear grade-by-grade proficiency targets accompanied by rubrics and exemplars of good student work. We also set a schoolwide achievement target four years into the future (an idea suggested by Jeff Howard), and then spelled out SMART goals (Specific, Measurable, Attainable, Relevant, and Time-bound) for each grade level to act as stepping-stones toward the long-range target. Each year since, we have updated the SMART goals with higher and higher expectations.

I believe that the rigorous, high-stakes MCAS tests had a dramatic impact on all of the areas with which we had struggled for so long. The grade-by-grade MCAS-aligned targets put an end to curriculum anarchy and kicked off the process of locating or writing during-the-year assessments aligned with those goals. This in turn focused the curriculum and produced data that teams could sink their teeth into, giving much more substance to their meetings. The rubrics we had developed just a year before were key tools in objectively measuring student writing and displaying data in ways that encouraged effective team discussions on improving results. As teachers gave up some "academic freedom," their isolation from each other was greatly reduced and grade-level teams had a common purpose. Our staff confronted the issue of teacher expectations when we took portions of the MCAS ourselves, and there was much less negative energy as we united in a relentless push for proficiency—a term we had never used before. My work as an administrator was much more focused on student learning results, which helped in the continuing struggle with H.S.P.S. And, finally, the perennial search for the perfect school improvement program came full circle to a very straightforward mission: preparing students with the specific proficiencies needed to be successful at the next grade level and graduate from fifth grade with the skills and knowledge to get on the honor roll in any middle school. We began to focus all our energy on continuously improving each of the components of a "power cycle": clear unit goals, pretests, effective teaching, formative assess-

ments, data analysis, feedback to students and parents, and a safety net for students who fall through the cracks.

The elements for greatly improved achievement are falling into place, and there's help from the central office: Boston's citywide curriculum goals are being aligned with the MCAS and reframed in a compact format for each grade level, and additional coaching and professional time are being given to all schools. I believe that the Mather's student achievement will take off as the staff hones all the elements and captures big enough chunks of focused staff meeting time to process student work and data effectively. The most important work is hard to do within the school day, even in 90-minute meetings. Special afterschool retreats have to be in teachers' calendars well in advance, money has to be available to pay stipends, and teachers need some initial coaching on making these data analysis meetings really effective. With strong leadership and continuing staff buy-in, these ingredients ought to make it possible for virtually all students to reach at least the proficient level.

In closing, I want to return to the Ron Edmonds statement cited earlier. Edmonds often said that the existence of even *one* effective urban school (and he found a number of them) proved that we knew how to turn around failing schools—which meant that there was no excuse for any urban school to be ineffective. With these words, Edmonds laid a colossal guilt trip on urban educators who were not getting good results. His stinging rebuke may have jolted some educators out of fatalistic attitudes and gotten them thinking about ways to improve their schools. But was Edmonds right that we knew in 1978 how to turn around failing schools? Was he fair to thoughtful, hard-working school leaders? Was he a little glib about what it would take to close the gap?

From my experience as a principal, I can testify that Edmonds and his generation of researchers did not provide a detailed road map to help a failing school find its way out of the woods. Without that, success depended too much on extraordinary talent, great personal charisma, an impossibly heroic work ethic, a strong staff already in place, and luck—which allowed cynics to dismiss isolated urban successes as idiosyncratic and say they proved nothing about broader school change.

But Edmonds' much more basic contribution was in getting three key messages into the heads of people who cared about urban schools: 1) demographics are not destiny, and inner-city children can achieve at high levels; 2) some specific school characteristics are linked to beating the demographic odds; and 3) we therefore need to stop making excuses and get to work.

Turning around failing schools is extraordinarily difficult. My 15-year struggle to make one school effective has brought me face to face with my own personal and professional limitations and made me a student of school effectiveness and the key factors that get people and institutions to work more successfully. I have learned that the starting point has to be an almost religious belief that it can be done, and Edmonds served as high priest in that regard. A second necessity is an outline of what an effective school looks like, and the correlates of effective urban schools (which have held up remarkably well over the years) have given me a vision of the pieces that need to be in place for all children to learn at high levels. A third key piece is real expertise on turning around failing schools. Craft knowledge has increased by leaps and bounds. If I could go back to 1987 and start over again as principal with current knowledge about school improvement, progress would be made much more rapidly.

But student achievement would still not have reached its full potential without a fourth tool: strong external standards linked to high-stakes curriculum tests. I believe that the arrival of standards and tests in the late 1990s provided the traction needed for a principal to push back the powerful gap-widening forces that operate within all schools.

Building on the accumulated lessons of researchers and practitioners, today's principals are in a much better position to be successful. If they believe passionately that their students can achieve proficiency, if they have a clear vision of what makes a school effective, if they learn the lessons of school change, and if they take advantage of external assessments, principals should be able to lead a school staff to bring a first-rate education to every child. Ron Edmonds would have smiled about that. So should all of us.

Kim Marshall resigned from Boston's Mather School in 2002. He was principal there for 15 years.

QUESTIONS FOR REFLECTION

1. What does Marshall list as the ten notorious barriers to high school achievement? Looking back on your high school experience, would you say his list is accurate? What would you add or remove from the list? Why?
2. Marshall credits one single thing as the greatest contribution to improved performance at Mather School. What is it? How did this come to have such a tremendous impact on student performance?
3. What does Marshall wish he had done differently at Mather School in his tenure there? What can you learn from his experiences to help you when dealing with issues of student achievement?

The Muddle Machine: Confessions of a Textbook Editor

TAMIM ANSARY

ABSTRACT: Why are so many textbooks bland and unimaginative? A former editor describes the daunting combination of bureaucratic hurdles, political correctness, and self-appointed censors that stand in the way of a good educational read.

Some years ago, I signed on as an editor at a major publisher of elementary and high school textbooks, filled with the idealistic belief that I'd be working with equally idealistic authors to create books that would excite teachers and fill young minds with Big Ideas.

Not so.

I got a hint of things to come when I overheard my boss lamenting, "The books are done and we still don't have an author! I *must* sign someone today!"

Every time a friend with kids in school tells me textbooks are too generic, I think back to that moment. "Who writes these things?" people ask me. I have to tell them, without a hint of irony, "No one." It's symptomatic of the whole muddled mess that is the $4.3 billion textbook business.

Textbooks are a core part of the curriculum, as crucial to the teacher as a blueprint is to a carpenter, so one might assume they are conceived, researched, written, and published as unique contributions to advancing knowledge. In fact, most of these books fall far short of their important role in the educational scheme of things. They are processed into existence using the pulp of what already exists, rising like swamp things from the compost of the past. The mulch is turned and tended by many layers of editors who scrub it of anything possibly objectionable before it is fed into a government-run "adoption" system that provides mediocre material to students of all ages.

WELCOME TO THE MACHINE

The first product I helped create was a basal language arts program. The word *basal* refers to a comprehensive package that includes students' textbooks for a sequence of grades, plus associated teachers' manuals and endless workbooks, tests, answer keys, transparencies, and other "ancillaries." My company had dominated this market for years, but the brass felt that our flagship program was dated. They wanted something new, built from scratch.

Sounds like a mandate for innovation, right? It wasn't. We got all the language arts textbooks in use and went through them carefully, jotting down every topic, subtopic, skill, and subskill we could find at each grade level. We compiled these into a master list, eliminated the redundancies, and came up with the core content of our new textbook. Or, as I like to call it, the "chum."

But wait. If every publisher was going through this same process (and they were), how was ours to stand out? Time to stir in a philosophy.

By *philosophy*, I mean a pedagogical idea. These conceptual enthusiasms surge through the education universe in waves. Textbook editors try to see the next one coming and shape their program to embody it.

The new ideas are born at universities and wash down to publishers through research papers and conferences. Textbook editors swarm to events like the five-day International Reading Association conference to pick up the buzz. They all

Publisher (A) decides to create a new high school textbook from scratch. Idea lightbulb heats compost heap of similar textbooks (B), causing them to break down into sludge, which is simmered into master list of topics (C). Redundancies are boiled off (D) and philosophy (E) is mixed in. Elixir of topics drains into brain of editor, who starts worrying (F) about conservatives in Texas and liberal zealots in California. Editor transforms topics into outline (G), which flows to writers (H), causing them to begin scribbling. Editor begins worrying about finding name author (I). Text from writers is forced into mold of key curriculum guidelines (J). State frameworks for most states (K) are ignored. Tail (L) of key adoption state of Texas wags dog, which responds by taking textbook-size bites (M) from bales of compressed text. Name author (N) is signed to book. Book is reviewed (O). Too much evolution? Conservatives shoot it down. Not multiracial enough? Liberals shoot it down. Editor patches up holes and end-runs objections (P). Books finally make it to students (Q).

run around wondering, What's the coming thing? Is it critical thinking? Metacognition? Constructivism? Project-based learning?

At those same conferences, senior editors look for up-and-coming academics and influential educational consultants to sign as "authors" of the textbooks that the worker bees are already putting together back at the shop.

CONTENT LITE

Once a philosophy has been fixed on and added, we shape the pulp to fit key curriculum guidelines. Every state has a prescribed compendium of what kids should learn—tedious lists of buffeted objectives consisting mostly of sentences like this:

> The student shall be provided content necessary to formulate, discuss, critique, and review hypotheses, theories, laws, and principles and their strengths and weaknesses.

If you should meet a textbook editor and he or she seems eccentric (odd hair, facial tics, et cetera), it's because this is a person who has spent hundreds of hours scrutinizing countless pages filled with such action items, trying to determine if the textbook can arguably be said to support each objective.

Of course, no one looks at all the state frameworks. Arizona's guidelines? Frankly, my dear, we don't give a damn. Rhode Island's? Pardon me while I die laughing. Some states are definitely more important than others. More on this later.

Eventually, at each grade level, the editors distill their notes into detailed outlines, a task roughly comparable to what sixth-century jurists in Byzantium must have faced when they carved Justinian's Code out of the jungle of Roman law. Finally, they divide the outline into theoretically manageable parts and assign these to writers to flesh into sentences.

What comes back isn't even close to being the book. The first project I worked on was at this stage when I arrived. My assignment was to reduce a stack of pages 17 inches high, supplied by 40 writers, to a 3-inch stack that would sound as if it had all come from one source. The original text was just ore. A few of the original words survived, I suppose, but no whole sentences.

To avoid the unwelcome appearance of originality at this stage, editors send their writers *voluminous* guidelines. I am one of these writers, and this summer I wrote a 10-page story for a reading program. The guideline for the assignment, delivered to me in a three-ring binder, was 300 pages long.

BON APPÉTIT

With so much at stake, how did we get into this turgid mess? In the '80s and '90s, a feeding frenzy broke out among publishing houses as they all fought to swallow their competitors. Harcourt Brace Jovanovich bought Holt, Rinehart and Winston. Houghton Mifflin bought D.C. Heath and Co. McGraw-Hill bought Macmillan. Silver Burdett bought Ginn—or was it Ginn that bought Silver? It doesn't matter, because soon enough both were devoured by Prentice Hall, which in turn was gobbled up by Simon & Schuster.

Then, in the late '90s, even bigger corporations began circling. Almost all the familiar textbook brands of yore vanished or ended up in the bellies of just four big sharks: Pearson, a British company; Vivendi Universal, a French firm, Reed Elsevier, a British-Dutch concern; and McGraw-Hill, the lone American-owned textbook conglomerate.

This concentration of money and power caused dramatic changes. In 1974, there were 22 major basal reading programs; now there are 5 or 6. As the number of basals (in all subject areas) shrank, so did editorial staffs. Many downsized editors floated off and started "development houses," private firms that contract with educational publishers to deliver chunks of programs. They hire freelance managers to manage freelance editors to manage teams of freelance writers to produce text that skeleton crews of development-house executives send on to publishing-house executives, who then pass it on to various committees for massaging.

A few years ago, I got an assignment from a development house to write a lesson on a particular reading skill. The freelance editor sent me the corresponding lessons from our client's three major competitors. "Here's what the other companies are doing," she told me. "Cover everything they do, only better." I had to laugh. I had written (for other development houses) all three of the lessons I was competing with.

THE CRUELEST MONTH

In textbook publishing, April is the cruelest month. That's when certain states announce which textbooks they're adopting. When it comes to setting the agenda for textbook publishing, only the 22 states that have a formal adoption process count. The other 28 are irrelevant—even though they include populous giants like New York, Pennsylvania, and Ohio—because they allow all publishers to come in and market programs directly to local school districts.

Adoption states, by contrast, buy new textbooks on a regular cycle, usually every six years, and they allow only certain programs to be sold in their state. They draw up the list at the beginning of each cycle, and woe to publishers that fail to make that list, because for the next 72 months they will have zero sales in that state.

Among the adoption states, Texas, California, and Florida have unrivaled clout. Yes, size does matter. Together, these three have roughly 13 million students in K–12 public schools. The next 18 adoption states put together have about 12.7 million. Though the Big Three have different total numbers of students, they each spend about the same amount of money on textbooks. For the current school year, they budgeted more than $900 million for instructional materials,

more than a quarter of all the money that will be spent on textbooks in the nation.

Obviously, publishers create products specifically for the adoptions in those three key states. They then sell the same product to everybody else, because basals are very expensive to produce—a K–8 reading program can cost as much as $60 million. Publishers hope to recoup the costs of a big program from the sudden gush of money in a big adoption state, then turn a profit on the subsequent trickle from the "open territories." Those that fail to make the list in Texas, California, or Florida are stuck recouping costs for the next six years. Strapped for money to spend on projects for the next adoption period, they're likely to fail again. As the cycle grows vicious, they turn into lunch meat.

DON'T MESS WITH TEXAS

The big three adoption states are not equal, however. In that elite trio, Texas rules. California has more students (more than 6 million versus just over 4 million in Texas), but Texas spends just as much money (approximately $42 billion) on its public schools. More important, Texas allocates a dedicated chunk of funds specifically for textbooks. That money can't be used for anything else, and all of it *must* be spent in the adoption year. Furthermore, Texas has particular power when it comes to high school textbooks, since California adopts statewide only for textbooks from kindergarten though 8th grade, while the Lone Star State's adoption process applies to textbooks from kindergarten through 12th grade.

If you're creating a new textbook, therefore, you start by scrutinizing *Texas Essential Knowledge and Skills* (TEKS). This document is drawn up by a group of curriculum experts, teachers, and political insiders appointed by the 15 members of the Texas Board of Education, currently 5 Democrats and 10 Republicans, about half of whom have a background in education. TEKS describes what Texas wants and what the entire nation will therefore get.

Texas is truly the tail that wags the dog. There is, however, a tail that wags this mighty tail. Every adoption state allows private citizens to review textbooks and raise objections. Publishers must respond to these objections at open hearings.

In the late '60s a Texas couple, Mel and Norma Gabler, figured out how to use their state's adoption hearings to put pressure on textbook publishers. The Gablers had no academic credentials or teaching background, but they knew what they wanted taught—phonics, sexual abstinence, free enterprise, creationism, and the primacy of Judeo-Christian values—and considered themselves in a battle against a "politically correct degradation of academics." Expert organizers, the Gablers possessed a flair for constructing arguments out of the language of official curriculum guidelines. The Longview, Texas-based nonprofit corporation they founded 43 years ago, Educational Research Analysts, continues to review textbooks and lobby against liberal content in textbooks.

The Gablers no longer appear in person at adoption hearings, but through workshops, books, and how-to manuals, they trained a whole generation of conservative Christian activists to carry on their work.

Citizens also pressure textbook companies at California adoption hearings. These objections come mostly from such liberal organizations as Norman Lear's People for the American Way, or from individual citizens who look at proposed textbooks when they are on display before adoption in 30 centers around the state. Concern in California is normally of the politically correct sort—objections, for example, to such perceived gaffes as using the word *Indian* instead of *Native American*. To make the list in California, books must be scrupulously stereotype free: No textbook can show African Americans playing sports, Asians using computers, or women taking care of children. Anyone who stays in textbook publishing long enough develops radar for what will and won't get past the blanding process of both the conservative and liberal watchdogs.

Responding to citizens' objections in adoption hearings is a delicate art. Publishers learn never to confront the assumptions behind an objection. That just causes deeper criticism. For example, a health textbook I worked on had a picture of a girl on a windy beach. One concerned citizen believed he could detect the outlines of the girl's underwear through her dress. Our response: She's at the beach, so that's her bathing suit. It worked.

A social studies textbook was attacked because a full-page photograph showed a large family gathered around a dinner table. The objection? They looked like Arabs. Did we rise up indignantly at this un-American display of bias? We did not. Instead, we said that the family was Armenian. It worked.

Of course, publishers prefer to face no objections at all. That's why going through a major adoption, especially a Texas adoption, is like earning a professional certificate in textbook editing. Survivors just *know* things.

What do they know?

Mainly, they know how to censor themselves. Once, I remember an editorial group was discussing literary selections to include in a reading anthology. We were about to agree on one selection when someone mentioned that the author of this piece had drawn a protest at a Texas adoption because he had allegedly belonged to an organization called One World Council, rumored to be a "Communist front."

At that moment, someone pointed out another story that fit our criteria. Without further conversation, we chose that one and moved on. Only in retrospect did I realize we had censored the first story based on rumors of allegations. Our unspoken thinking seemed to be, If even the most unlikely taint existed, the Gablers would find it, so why take a chance?

Self-censorship like this goes unreported because we the censors hardly notice ourselves doing it. In that room, none of us said no to any story. We just converged around a different story. The dangerous author, incidentally, was celebrated best-selling science fiction writer Isaac Asimov.

TURN THE PAGE

There's no quick, simple fix for the blanding of American textbooks, but several steps are key to reform.

- Revamp our funding mechanisms to let teachers assemble their own curricula from numerous individual sources instead of forcing them to rely on single comprehensive packages from national textbook factories. We can't have a different curriculum in every classroom, of course, but surely there's a way to achieve coherence without stultification.

- Reduce basals to reference books—slim core texts that set forth as clearly as a dictionary the essential skills and information to be learned at each grade level in each subject. In content areas like history and science, the core texts would be like mini-encyclopedias, fact-checked by experts in the field and then reviewed by master teachers for scope and sequence.

    Dull? No, because these cores would not be the actual instructional material students would use. They would be analogous to operating systems in the world of software. If there are only a few of these and they're pretty similar, it's OK. Local districts and classroom teachers would receive funds enabling them to assemble their own constellations of lessons and supporting materials around the core texts, purchased not from a few behemoths but from hundreds of smaller publishing houses such as those that currently supply the supplementary-textbook industry.

- Just as software developers create applications for particular operating systems, textbook developers should develop materials that plug into the core texts. Small companies and even individuals who see a niche could produce a module to fill it. None would need $60 million to break even. Imagine, for example, a world history core. One publisher might produce a series of historical novellas by a writer and a historian working together to go with various places and periods in history. Another might create a map of the world, software that animates at the click of a mouse to show political boundaries swelling, shrinking, and shifting over hundreds of years. Another might produce a board game that dramatizes the connections between trade and cultural diffusion. Hundreds of publishers could compete to produce lessons that fulfill some aspect of the core text, the point of reference.

The intellect, dedication, and inventiveness of textbook editors, abundant throughout the industry but often stifled and underappreciated, would be unleashed with—I predict—extraordinary results for teachers and students.

Bundling selections from this forest of material to create curriculum packages might itself emerge as a job description in educational publishing.

The possibilities are endless. And shouldn't endless possibility be the point?

Tamim Ansary, a columnist for Encarta.com and author of *West of Kabul and East of New York,* has written 38 nonfiction books for children. He was an editor at Harcourt Brace Jovanovich for nine years and has written for Houghton Mifflin, McDougall Littell, Prentice Hall, and many other textbook publishers.

QUESTIONS FOR REFLECTION

1. What should be the content of textbooks in today's classrooms? Should there be a common textbook curriculum, or should there be local control over what teachers use to teach with?

2. What does Ansary point to as the biggest problem in today's textbook market? What are some possible solutions? Can the problem be fixed or is it too late?

3. Certain states, namely Texas and California, dominate control of the textbooks many other states adopt for their own curriculum. What are the consequences of this kind of centralized control?

4. What do the Gablers teach us about influence and control within the curriculum? Should so few people ever have this kind of power within the curriculum? Who should be responsible for addressing small interest groups like the Gablers and their nonprofit corporation?

Teachers' Voices—
Putting Theory Into Practice

How To Integrate Character Education Into the Curriculum

JANE GILNESS

ABSTRACT: *Having become convinced that all teachers need to be actively involved in raising their students' moral awareness, Jane Gilness shares the formula she devised that has enabled her to weave character education seamlessly into her content lessons. Learning that character education cannot be isolated as a separate discipline, she states that her content lessons will continue to be laced with community, manners, and ethical decision-making.*

To educate a person in mind and not in morals is to educate a menace to society.

—Theodore Roosevelt

As a teacher of language arts, I never fail to be astonished by the rhetorical impact of a well-worded quote. I collect and savor those that strike me. I indulge in philosophical wallowing. A pithy quote speaks volumes. When I first read the quote by Roosevelt, I was overwhelmed with the sense of my responsibility as a teacher. I had always felt fairly confident in my ability to impart content, but this was an added obligation I could not ignore. I grappled with the following question: How can I use my position as an instructor to imbue my students with a strong sense of moral awareness and still commit to the job of teaching content at the same time?

Character education has become a primary concern of mine, and I have searched the Web, pored over many a curious volume, and come to the conclusion that character education cannot be isolated, codified, and packaged into tidy little instructional units in a how-to manual. Assessments of character can't be conjured up with checklists, rubrics, and clearly defined results. That would be too easy.

As I pursued my research, I kept running into complex philosophical constructs that finally led me to circle back on a few homely truths. From these I put together what I have come to call the "character cocktail," a full-bodied and harmonious blend of community, manners, and ethical decision making.

COMMUNITY

"The best and the deepest moral training is that which one gets by having to enter into proper relations with others," wrote John Dewey. "Present educational systems, so far as they destroy or neglect this unity, render it difficult or impossible to get any regular, moral training." Another truth. The first truth I discovered in the classroom is that a teacher cannot begin to think about fostering character without first creating a positive classroom climate replete with a strong sense of community and proper relations among members. Could I integrate this concept into my instructional strategies? It would surely be difficult, but it seemed well worth the effort. I decided to rely on one of my finer qualities: unabashed deviousness. If kids think you're too obvious, they'll think you're preachy.

One method I found of integrating the concept of community into my Honors English 10 classroom was through the use of eulogies. I told the students that we were studying prefixes and roots. As an example, I asked them what a eulogy was. They all knew and were quick to tell me that everyone knows eulogies are given at funerals. Nice words and kind thoughts about dead people are delivered to the mourners. I then instructed them to look up the prefix (*eu*) and the root (*logy*). I asked them to define them, and they came to the conclusion that "eulogy" simply means to "speak well."

Once they had thought about the word, I asked them why we wait until our loved ones can no longer hear us before we say something nice about them. Because I was new to the district, I told the students that, while I didn't know them, they knew one another very well. I asked them to give eulogies for one another so I could get a sense of who they were. They loved the idea. I allowed them to set the criteria for delivering a eulogy, but I was quick to point out that students who were uncomfortable with being in the limelight would not be required to participate. Being genuinely ghoulish creatures, they insisted on playing the role of the dearly departed, selecting background music, and so on. I was surprised by how much thought and planning some of them put into sharing their thoughts about their classmates. We had a few happy tears and much laughter. The result? A stronger sense of community and camaraderie. (They thought it was a vocabulary lesson and ice-breaking activity).

I've also found that giving students ownership of the curriculum promotes a positive classroom climate and gives them a sense of being a vital part of a community. When students write something that I feel has instructional value, for example, I request their permission to make an overhead of it for use as a teaching tool. I am always quick to acknowledge when student ideas or strategies are better than mine, and I thank them for, in effect, helping me do a better job. They are genuinely flattered. In fact, they become so empowered that I continue to squeeze high-quality work out of them because they know that there's always a chance that they will be immortalized in an overhead. The idea that they are respected by an instructor as valuable classroom assets certainly promotes a sense of social responsibility.

Last—but certainly not least—among my efforts to build community is my use of classroom rituals. Such rituals can give students a real sense of belonging. I always keep a stash of penny candy on hand. If I call someone by a wrong name, I give him or her candy as a form of apology for my rudeness. It gives the the opportunity to show students, not just talk to them about, the value of making others feel important and respected. I also give students candy if they catch me making an error in grammar or usage. Usually I make these errors on purpose, but the students don't always know that, and they do pay close attention. And if they're attentive, they're learning. Granted, their motive may be to pounce on my mistakes, to show me up, and to mooch some candy. But inadvertently they are learning because they have to hang on my every word. Simply having such rituals promotes a sense of community, but it is also possible to integrate them into instructional strategies.

MANNERS

John Fletcher Moulton refers to "the domain of obedience to the unenforceable. That obedience is the obedience of a man to that which he cannot be forced to obey. He is the enforcer of the law upon himself." During many hours of research on citizenship, civility, and democratic thinking, I kept underlining similar ideas. Thus I discovered what I consider to be the second ingredient in my character cocktail: "the domain of obedience to the unenforceable." Simply put, it means "doing the right thing" even when no one is looking or imposing a law that forces you to do it. It's the stuff of daily life—basic humanity and decency. In a word, its manners.

I make the distinction between etiquette and manners here. For example, knowing which fork to use is a matter of etiquette, which does not have any inherent moral value. On the other hand, the essence of good manners does have a distinctly moral base. It has to do with the most fundamental premises—making sure one never intentionally makes someone else uncomfortable and avoiding saying or doing anything that diminishes another person's sense of dignity or self-worth.

It is absolutely essential for educators to subtly thread such a conception of manners into the tapestry of our daily classroom life. In order to do this, I decided to ratchet up my efforts to be a good example and role model. Because you get what you give, I treat students with the same re-

spect I would another adult. If I make a mistake, I admit it, I apologize, and I move on. The students mimic what they observe. I act like a hostess who tries to make her guests as comfortable as possible, and eventually they respond graciously. I keep reminding them that, while my classroom is a dictatorship, it's a benevolent one. Again, I show them how manners work by trying to be mannerly myself.

Once the students have a clear feel for the kind of classroom courtesies that I extend to and expect from them, I simply teach them manners and the fundamentals of etiquette. Or rather, I have them teach one another. I found a wonderful book on manners for teens by Alex Packer. It's titled *How Rude!* Packer's book is delightful and immensely appealing to teens. I integrate a manners unit into my interpersonal skills curriculum by having students do group presentations. Each group selects a section of Packer's book to work into a presentation that includes visual aids, graphics, audience interaction, role playing, and skits. We cover topics that range from introductions to telephone and cell phone manners.

The students thoroughly enjoy the unit, especially when they are allowed to demonstrate the dos and don'ts of civilized conduct. Indeed, they are particularly adept at demonstrating *uncivilized* conduct (their area of expertise). When we are finished, I have them write group analysis papers. No time is wasted, and the teaching and learning of manners is fully integrated into the curriculum.

ETHICAL DECISION MAKING

"The good of a nation," A. K. Benjamin states, "demands the consideration of serious ethical questions. If education ignores the value and moral aspect of the human psyche, where will society find citizens able to make moral decisions?" Benjamin's words inspired me to find a way to stir the final ingredient into the character cocktail: ethical decision making. Of course, my motive here isn't entirely noble. Who will some day pick up the torch and make decisions that will affect us as we slide into senescence? Do we want our future leaders to have acquired their decision-making skills in an ethical vacuum? I think not. I recognized a clear need to help my students acquire a set of universal values that will enable them to make ethical decisions.

My job as a language arts instructor lends itself particularly well to this task, but it requires a formidable amount of work. All good literature explores universal themes that involve such ethical dilemmas as truth versus loyalty, the individual versus community, short-term versus long-term, and justice versus mercy. Such conflicts are complex, and it would be much easier to simply assign readings and conduct follow-up assessments that include trivial reading checks and objective questions. However, unless we help students develop critical thinking skills and see connections to other contexts, they will merely be skimming the surface of a story. So I ditched my tests in favor of reading literature aloud to my students and following up with Socratic dialogues and fishbowl debates. I have my students write in reflection journals. After all, how could I, in good conscience, teach *A Separate Peace* without asking them to record their feelings about jealousy, friendship, loyalty, and betrayal? I would certainly not be doing justice to *Antigone* without connecting the theme of anarchy versus social order to its modern applications. How could I not discuss the concept of the Golden Mean as it relates to the tragic flaw of a Greek hero? All of these ideas are presented, discussed, and written about in journals. When my students write reflections that show some depth and substance, I write back to them in their journals.

The more I write in their journals, the more thought students put into their writing in an effort to evoke a personal response from me. Yes, it's work for me, but it's well worth it.

I also make use of some warm-up activities that stimulate critical thinking and allow students to practice decision-making skills. I use dilemma cards from a Milton Bradley game called A Question of Scruples (available in both adult and kid editions). Each card contains an ethical dilemma. Instead of allowing my students to answer the questions with a mere yes, no, or it depends, I have them walk through the reasoning behind their decisions. In a whole-class activity, we discuss unknown factors that might affect our decisions. We also focus on how decisions will affect other people. They enjoy the game, and it forces them to think about making decisions on the basis of universally held values.

For my Honors English 10 class, I stumbled on some examples of real-life dilemmas in *How Good People Make Tough Choices,* by Rushworth Kidder. I use the situations described in this book in conjunction with thematic exercises that relate to similar conflicts found in fiction. These dilemmas provide excellent closing activities for literature units.

My quest to integrate character education into my teaching is far from over. I have learned that we can't isolate character education as a separate discipline. My content lessons will continue to be laced with community, manners, and ethical decision making, the ingredients of my "character cocktail." Bottoms up!

Jane Gilness is an adjunct instructor at Mesabi Range Community and Technical College, Virginia, Minnesota.

QUESTIONS FOR REFLECTION

1. Does the moral awareness of students need to be raised in today's society? By whose standards should students' "moral compass" be set? In other words, how will we know when we have successfully brought morality and character education into the curriculum?
2. What is Gilness' formula for weaving character education into her content lessons and do you think this kind of formula is possible for all teachers to use?
3. How does Gilness couple critical thinking with ethical reasoning? Do the two concepts go hand-in-hand? Is ethical reasoning possible without critical thinking?

LEARNING ACTIVITIES

Critical Thinking

1. Review the four questions in the Tyler rationale for curriculum development. What additional questions would need to be asked when developing a curriculum? Give reasons for your choices.
2. Testing is obviously an important part of the effort to raise standards. To what extent do you think the current emphasis on standardized tests encourages teachers to "teach to the test"?
3. If teachers "teach to the test," is this an effective or ineffective way to promote student learning?

Application Activities

1. Reflect on your experiences taking standardized tests. What factors increased your anxiety about taking such tests? What factors reduced that anxiety? Based on your own experiences, how might you help your students reduce their anxiety about taking tests?
2. Is it fair to hold teachers accountable for student learning? Should teachers of students whose home backgrounds are less supportive of education be held as accountable as teachers of students whose backgrounds are highly supportive?
3. Ask your instructor to arrange for a curriculum coordinator from the local school district to visit your class. In addition to finding out about this coordinator's work, ask him or her to describe how the effort to raise standards and No Child Left Behind legislation have influenced curriculum development in the district.
4. Using the " 'Generic' Lesson Plan for a Unit of Study" presented in this chapter, prepare a lesson plan at the grade level and in the subject area for which you teach (or are preparing to teach). Include at least one authentic classroom assessment of students' learning in your plan.

Field Experiences

1. Spend a half-day at a school at the level at which you plan to teach. Take note of your impressions regarding the extent to which the curricula you observe are student-centered or subject-centered. Share your observations with others in your curriculum class.
2. Interview a few students outside of the classroom during a school day. Ask them to comment on the degree of "fit" between their teachers' curriculum goals and the curriculum goals they have for themselves. Share your findings with others in your class.

Internet Activities

1. Go online to your state's department of education homepage and find the link to the state's standards. Then compare your state's standards with the standards from another state. How are the two sets of standards similar? Different? Is one set of standards clearer than the other?
2. Visit the homepage of a professional association in the subject area for which you are preparing to teach. Locate the curriculum standards developed by the association and compare them with the curriculum standards developed by your state. How are the two sets of standards similar? Different? Is one set of standards clearer than the other?

C H A P T E R **6**

Curriculum and Instruction

FOCUS QUESTIONS

1. What are the interrelationships between curriculum and instruction?
2. What are the characteristics of learning tasks that students find meaningful and authentic?
3. What are the elements of "authentic pedagogy"?
4. What are some models of teaching that are based on behavioral psychology, human development, cognitive processes, and social interactions?
5. How can classroom assessments enhance student learning?
6. What are some "alternative assessments" teachers can use to assess student learning?

This chapter focuses on the interrelationships between curriculum and instruction. The articles in this chapter illustrate, in varying ways, that *what* teachers teach (the content of the curriculum) is as important as *how* they teach (the instructional methods used).

Within the curriculum field, some theorists consider curriculum and instruction as separate, yet related, dimensions of education (see Beauchamp's *Curriculum Theory* [1981], for example). Others see the distinction between the two as an artificial construct (see Dewey's *Democracy and Education* [1916], for example). Regardless of how one views the relationship between curriculum and instruction, both are vital elements of the educative process. As the following comments by a teacher suggest, teaching requires expertise at developing the curriculum—*and* expertise at using instructional methods to reach curriculum goals:

Before becoming a teacher, I imagined that I would teach my students, they would take a test, and I would evaluate my teaching based on their test scores. Actually, that cycle happens very little. It is a part of teaching, but relating to kids, being able to encourage them, being able to laugh with them matters more and more as I develop my teaching style. Encouragement, respect, and trust—those things really make a difference. I am really interested in my subject, mathematics, but I am learning that what matters most to students and to me is becoming excited about learning. When I feel that excitement from the kids . . . that's what makes teaching great.

Curriculum and instruction are not separate, mutually exclusive elements of teaching; they are connected, as the figure below suggests. They are both part of teaching; each influences the other. When a teacher decides to include certain content in the curriculum, that decision means that some methods of instruction will be better suited than others to teach that content to students. On the other hand, a particular instructional method (cooperative learning, for example) is more effective at presenting certain types of content than others. Effective teachers know that they must develop knowledge and skills in both areas—from planning the *what* of the curriculum to planning the *how* of instruction.

Curriculum   ⟵————————⟶   **Instruction**
(What)   (How)

INSTRUCTIONAL METHODS

Appropriate instructional methods, as well as a meaningful curriculum, are key elements of an effective learning environment. What the teacher does and what students do have powerful influences on learning and on the quality of classroom life.

After developing a curriculum, a teacher must answer the question "What instructional methods will enable me to achieve my curricular goals?" Teachers also must realize that instructional activities should meet *students'* goals. The activities must be meaningful and authentic for students. As Dewey points out in "Progressive Organization of Subject Matter" in this chapter, knowledge should be viewed as progressing out of the learner's experiences rather than as something outside of those experiences. Developing appropriate learning activities, therefore, requires thoughtfulness, insight into the motivations of students, and good judgment.

Authentic learning tasks enable students to see the connections between the curriculum and the world beyond the classroom—both now and in the future. To understand how authentic learning tasks can motivate students to learn, the reader may wish to reflect upon his or her own school experiences. Do you recall memorizing facts only because they would appear on a test? Did you ever wonder why a teacher asked you to complete a learning task? Did you ever feel that a teacher asked you to do "busywork"? What kinds of learning tasks motivated you the most?

Herbert A. Thelen (1981, p. 86) contends that authenticity represents "the first criterion all educational activity must meet." According to Thelen, an activity is authentic for a person if he or she "feels emotionally 'involved' and mentally stimulated . . . is aware of choices and enjoys the challenge of making decisions," and feels he or she "has something to bring to the activity and that its outcome will be important" (Thelen, 1981, p. 86).

A comprehensive nationwide study of successfully restructured schools reported that "authentic pedagogy" helps students to (1) "construct knowledge" through the use of higher-order thinking, (2) acquire "deep knowledge" (relatively complex understandings of subject matter), (3) engage in "substantive conversations" with teachers and peers, and (4) make connections between substantive knowledge and the world beyond the classroom (Newmann & Wehlage, 1995; Newmann et al., 1996). In addition, as Figure 6.1 shows, high authentic pedagogy classes boost achievement for students at all grade levels.

FIGURE 6.1

Level of Authentic Student Performance for Students Who Experienced Low, Average, and High Authentic Pedagogy in Restructuring Elementary, Middle, and High Schools

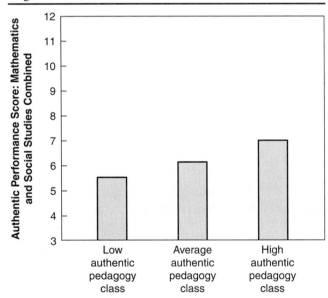

Note: The analysis included 2,100 students in 125 classrooms in 23 schools. Most students had either a mathematics or social studies score, and the two subjects were scored on the same 12-point scale. There were no major differences in the effect of authentic pedagogy on achievement between the two subjects.

Source: Fred M. Newmann and Gary G. Wehlage, *Successful School Restructuring: A Report to the Public and Educators by the Center on Organization and Restructuring of Schools.* University of Wisconsin-Madison: Center on Organization and Restructuring of Schools, 1995, pp. 21, 55.

A REPERTOIRE OF MODELS OF TEACHING

As stated above, the curriculum goals to be attained significantly influence the instructional methods (or "models" of teaching) a teacher uses. In addition, variables such as the teacher's style, learners' characteristics, the culture of the school and surrounding community, and the resources available influence the selection of instructional methods. Together, these variables contribute to the repertoire of models of teaching a teacher develops to reach curriculum goals.

A model of teaching provides the teacher with a "blueprint" of sorts for attaining curriculum goals. In addition, "models of teaching are really models of *learning*. As we help students acquire information, ideas, skills, values, ways of thinking, and means of expressing themselves, we are also teaching them how to learn" (Joyce, Weil, and Calhoun, 2004, p. 7). Table 6.1 presents brief descriptions of five widely used models of teaching: mastery learning, cooperative learning, theory into practice, behavior modification, and nondirective teaching.

To attain a variety of curricular goals and objectives, accomplished teachers have developed a broad repertoire of models of teaching. They have, as David T. Gordon points out in "The Limits of Ideology: Curriculum and the Culture Wars" in this chapter, "techniques in their teaching repertoire that reflect how children learn and make sense of things." In actual practice, each model in the repertoire is eclectic—in other words, a combination of two or more models of teaching. The following sections describe models of teaching that are based on behavioral psychology, human development, cognitive processes, and social interactions.

Models Based on Behavioral Psychology

Many teachers use models of teaching that have emerged from our greater understanding of how people acquire or change their behaviors. Direct instruction, for example, is a systematic instructional method that focuses on the transmission of knowledge and skills from the teacher (and the curriculum) to the student. Direct instruction is organized on the basis of observable learning behaviors and the actual products of learning. Generally, direct instruction is most appropriate for step-by-step knowledge acquisition and basic skills development but not appropriate for teaching less structured, higher-order skills such as writing, the analysis of social issues, and problem solving.

Extensive research was conducted in the 1970s and 1980s on the effectiveness of direct instruction (Gagné, 1974, 1977; Good & Grouws, 1979; Rosenshine, 1988; Rosenshine & Stevens, 1986). The following eight steps are a synthesis of research on direct instruction and may be used with students ranging in age from elementary to senior high school.

1. Orient students to the lesson by telling them what they will learn.
2. Review previously learned skills and concepts related to the new material.
3. Present new material, using examples and demonstrations.
4. Assess students' understanding by asking questions; correct misunderstandings.

TABLE 6.1
Five Models of Teaching

	Goals and Rationale	*Methods*
Mastery Learning	Virtually all students can learn material if given enough time and taught in the appropriate manner. Students learn best when they participate in a structured, systematic program of learning that enables them to progress in small sequenced steps.	• Set objectives and standards for mastery. • Teach content directly to students. • Provide corrective feedback to students on their learning. • Provide additional time and help in correcting errors. • Follow cycle of teaching, testing, reteaching, and retesting.
Cooperative Learning	Students can be motivated to learn by working cooperatively in small groups if rewards are made available to the group as a whole and to individual members of the group.	• Small groups (4–6 students) work together on learning activities. • Assignments require that students help one another while working on a group project. • In competitive arrangements, groups may compete against one another. • Group members contribute to group goals according to their talents, interests, and abilities.
Theory into Practice	Teachers make decisions in three primary areas: content to be taught, how students will learn, and the behaviors the teacher will use in the classroom. The effectiveness of teaching is related to the quality of decisions the teacher makes in these areas.	The teacher follows seven steps in the classroom: 1. Orients students to material to be learned. 2. Tells students what they will learn and why it is important. 3. Presents new material that consists of knowledge, skills, or processes students are to learn. 4. Models what students are expected to do. 5. Checks for student understanding. 6. Gives students opportunity for practice under the teacher's guidance. 7. Makes assignments that give students opportunity to practice what they have learned on their own.
Behavior Modification	Teachers can "shape" student learning by using various forms of reinforcement. Human behavior is learned, and behaviors that are positively reinforced (rewarded) tend to increase while those that are not reinforced tend to decrease.	• Teacher begins by presenting stimulus in the form of new material. • The behavior of students is observed by the teacher. • Appropriate behaviors are reinforced by the teacher as quickly as possible.
Nondirective Teaching	Learning can be facilitated if teachers focus on personal development of students and create opportunities for students to increase their self-understanding and self-concepts. The key to effective teaching is the teachers' ability to understand students and to involve them in a teaching-learning partnership.	• Teacher acts as a facilitator of learning. • Teacher creates learning environments that support personal growth and development. • Teacher acts in the role of a counselor who helps students to understand themselves, clarify their goals, and accept responsibility for their behavior.

5. Allow students to practice new skills or apply new information.
6. Provide feedback and corrections as students practice.
7. Include newly learned material in homework.
8. Review material periodically.

A direct instruction method called *mastery learning* is based on two assumptions about learning: (1) virtually all students can learn material if given enough time and taught appropriately and (2) students learn best when they participate in a structured, systematic program of learning that enables them to progress in small, sequenced steps (Bloom, 1981; Carroll, 1963). The following five steps present the mastery learning cycle:

1. Set objectives and standards for mastery.
2. Teach content directly to students.
3. Provide corrective feedback to students on their learning.
4. Provide additional time and help in correcting errors.
5. Follow a cycle of teaching, testing, reteaching, and retesting.

In mastery learning, students take diagnostic tests and then are guided to do corrective exercises or activities to improve their learning. These may take the form of programmed instruction, workbooks, computer drill and practice, or educational games. After the corrective lessons, students are given another test and are more likely to achieve mastery.

Models Based on Human Development

As pointed out in Chapter 3, human development is a significant basis of the curriculum. Similarly, effective instructional methods are developmentally appropriate, meet students' diverse learning needs, and recognize the importance of learning that occurs in social contexts. For example, one way that students reach higher levels of development is to observe and then imitate their parents, teachers, and peers, who act as models. As Woolfolk (2001, p. 327) points out:

> Modeling has long been used, of course, to teach dance, sports, and crafts, as well as skills in subjects such as home economics, chemistry, and shop. Modeling can also be applied deliberately in the classroom to teach mental skills and to broaden horizons—to teach new ways of thinking. Teachers serve as models for a vast range of behaviors, from pronouncing vocabulary words, to reacting to the seizure of an epileptic student, to being enthusiastic about learning.

Effective teachers also use modeling by "thinking out loud" and following three basic steps of "mental modeling" (Duffy & Roehler, 1989):

1. Showing students the reasoning involved
2. Making students conscious of the reasoning involved
3. Focusing students on applying the reasoning

In this way, teachers can help students become aware of their learning processes and enhance their ability to learn.

Since the mid-1980s, several educational researchers have examined how learners *construct* understanding of new material. As pointed out in Chapter 4, constructivist views of learning focus on how learners make sense of new information—how they construct meaning based on what they already know. Teachers with this constructivist view of learning focus on students' thinking about the material being learned and, through carefully orchestrated cues, prompts, and questions, help students arrive at a deeper understanding of the material. The common elements of constructivist teaching include the following:

- The teacher elicits students' prior knowledge of the material and uses this as the starting point for instruction.
- The teacher not only presents material to students, but he or she also responds to students' efforts to learn the material. While teaching, the teacher must *learn about students' learning*.
- Students not only absorb information, but they also actively use that information to construct meaning.
- The teacher creates a social milieu within the classroom, a community of learners that allows students to reflect and talk with one another as they construct meaning and solve problems.

Constructivist teachers provide students with support, or "scaffolding," as they learn new material. By observing the child and listening carefully to what he or she says, the teacher provides scaffolding in the form of clues, encouragement, suggestions, or other assistance to guide students' learning efforts. The teacher varies the amount of support given on the basis of the student's understanding. If the student understands little, the teacher gives more support. On the other hand, the teacher gives progressively less support as the student's understanding becomes more evident. Overall, the teacher provides just enough scaffolding to enable the student to "discover" the material on his or her own.

Models Based on Cognitive Processes

Some models of teaching are derived from the mental processes involved in learning—thinking, remembering, problem solving, and creativity. Information processing, for example, is a branch of cognitive science concerned with how people use their long- and short-term memory to access information and solve problems. The computer is often used as an analogy for information-processing views of learning:

> Like the computer, the human mind takes in information, performs operations on it to change its form and content, stores the information, retrieves it when needed, and generates responses to it. Thus, processing involves gathering and representing information, or encoding; holding information, or storage; and getting at the information when needed, or retrieval. The whole system is guided by control processes that determine how and when information will flow through the system (Woolfolk, 2001, p. 243).

Although several systematic approaches to instruction are based on information processing—teaching students how to memorize, think inductively or deductively, acquire concepts, or use the scientific method, for example—they all focus on how people acquire and use information. Inquiry learning (often called *discovery learning*) is one example of a widely used model of teaching that develops students' abilities to acquire and use information. Students are given opportunities to inquire into subjects so that they "discover" knowledge for themselves. In "Structures in Learning" in this chapter, Jerome Bruner points out that discovery learning also enables students to see that knowledge has a structure, an internal connectedness and meaningfulness.

When teachers ask students to go beyond information in a text to make inferences, draw conclusions, or form generalizations; and when teachers do not answer students' questions, preferring instead to have students develop their own answers, they are using methods based on inquiry and discovery learning. These methods are best suited for teaching concepts, relationships, and theoretical abstractions, and for having students formulate and test hypotheses.

Inquiry learning and discovery learning approaches frequently use a *research-share-perform* cycle. During the *research* phase, students generate their own questions and hypotheses about a topic. They reflect on their prior experiences and knowledge and formulate a main question for inquiry. Research is carried out in small groups that focus on specific parts of the larger research question. During the *share* phase, knowledge is developed during a dialogue between students and teacher and among students themselves. The usefulness of the knowledge is evaluated by the group which, ideally, functions as a *learning community*. During the *perform* phase, students integrate and synthesize their shared knowledge by making presentations to the public.

The following example shows how inquiry and discovery learning in a first-grade classroom fostered a high level of student involvement and thinking.

> The children are gathered around a table on which a candle and jar have been placed. The teacher, Jackie Wiseman, lights the candle and, after it has burned brightly for a minute or two, covers it carefully with the jar. The candle grows dim, flickers, and goes out. Then she produces another candle and a larger jar, and the exercise is repeated. The candle goes out, but more slowly. Jackie produces two more candles and jars of different sizes, and the children light the candles, place the jars over them, and the flames slowly go out. "Now we're going to develop some ideas about what has just happened," she says. "I want you to ask me questions about those candles and jars and what you just observed" (Joyce, Weil, & Calhoun, 2004, p. 3).

Another form of inquiry learning is known as contextual teaching and learning (CTL). CTL is an approach to teaching based on the theory that students learn best in a concrete manner. They learn best when they are involved in hands-on activities and have opportunities for personal discovery within the context of relationships that are familiar to them. In a CTL environment, students construct, apply, and demonstrate knowledge in relevant contexts. They learn material that is meaningful, relevant, and vital to their futures. Students construct, apply, and demonstrate knowledge in relevant contexts.

Actually, contextual teaching and learning is not new. CTL is derived from the ideas of John Dewey. In *Democracy and Education* (1916), Dewey observed that "the great waste in school comes from . . . the isolation of the school—its isolation from life." During the 1970s, contextual teaching and learning was referred to as *experiential learning* or *applied learning*.

In contextual teaching and learning classrooms, "it is the major task of the teacher to broaden students' perceptions so that meaning becomes visible and the purpose of learning immediately understandable. This is not an add-on or something nice to do. It is fundamental if students are to be able to connect knowing with doing" (Parnell, 2000).

Models Based on Social Interactions

As every teacher knows, student peer groups can be a deterrent to academic performance; however, they can also motivate students to excel. Because school learning occurs in a social setting, models of teaching based on social interactions—cooperative learning, for example—can provide teachers with options for increasing students' learning.

A powerful model of teaching based on social interactions is group investigation, in which the teacher's role is to create an environment that allows students to determine what they will study and how. Students are presented with a situation to which they "react and discover basic conflicts among their attitudes, ideas, and modes of perception. On the basis of this information, they identify the problem to be investigated, analyze the roles required to solve it, organize themselves to take these roles, act, report, and evaluate these results" (Thelen, 1960, p. 82).

The teacher's role in group investigation is multifaceted; he or she is an organizer, guide, resource person, counselor, and evaluator. The method is very effective in increasing student achievement (Sharan & Sharan, 1989/90), positive attitudes toward learning, and the cohesiveness of the classroom group. The model also allows students to inquire into problems that interest them and enables each student to make a meaningful, authentic contribution to the group's effort based on his or her experiences, interests, knowledge, and skills.

Another model of teaching based on social interactions is project-based learning (PBL). In PBL classrooms, students work in teams to explore real-world problems and create presentations to share what they have learned. Compared with learning solely from textbooks, this approach has many benefits for students, including deeper knowledge of subject matter, increased self-direction and motivation, and improved research and problem-solving skills. However, the benefits of project-based learning are not always assured, as Kathleen Vail cautions in "Making Schools Value Student Intellect" in this chapter: "Project-based learning always has the potential to be based on fun rather than content."

A three-year 1997 study of two British secondary schools—one that used open-ended projects and one that used more traditional, direct instruction—found striking differences between the two schools in understanding and standardized achievement data in mathematics. Students at the project-based school did better than those at the more traditional school both on math problems requiring analytical or conceptual thought and on those requiring memory of a rule or formula. Three times as many students at the project-based school received the top grade achievable on the national examination in math (George Lucas Educational Foundation, 2001).

Project-based learning, which transforms teaching from *teachers telling* to *students doing,* includes five key elements:

1. Engaging learning experiences that involve students in complex, real world projects through which they develop and apply skills and knowledge.
2. Recognizing that significant learning taps students' inherent drive to learn, their capability to do important work, and need to be taken seriously.
3. Learning for which general curricular outcomes can be identified up front, while specific outcomes of the students' learning are neither predetermined nor fully predictable.
4. Learning that requires students to draw from many information sources and disciplines in order to solve problems.
5. Experiences through which students learn to manage and allocate resources such as time and materials (Oaks, Grantman, & Pedras, 2001, p. 443).

ASSESSMENT OF LEARNING

A key element of any model of teaching is how student learning is assessed. For most people, the term *assessment* brings to mind a four-step process: (1) the teacher prepares a test (or selects a preexisting test) to cover material that has been taught, (2) students take the test, (3) the teacher corrects the test, and (4) the teacher assigns grades based on how well students performed on the test. Classroom assessment, however, "is more than accurate recall," as Jay McTighe, Elliott Sief, and Grant Wiggins point out in "You *Can* Teach for Meaning" in this chapter. Assessment provides information teachers use (1) to determine how well students are learning the material being taught; (2) to identify the type of feedback that will enhance student learning; (3) to develop strategies for improving their effectiveness as teachers; and (4) to determine if students have reached certain levels of performance.

There is no single "right way" to assess student learning. Clearly, it is important to provide students with multiple opportunities to demonstrate what they know and are able to do. If students know that they have different ways to demonstrate their success, they develop more positive views of themselves as learners. They find learning to be an enjoyable experience.

Students who previously might have disliked a subject because they associated assessments of learning in that area with failure, can develop positive views about a subject if they know they have different ways to demonstrate their learning. They know that they have multiple opportunities to be successful. As a specialist in assessment puts it, "We [now] understand how to use classroom assessment to keep students confident that the achievement target is within reach. . . . We must build classroom environments in which students use assessments to understand what success looks like and how to do better next time. . . . If teachers assess accurately and use the results effectively, then students prosper" (Stiggins, 2004, pp. 24–26).

Increasingly, teachers are using alternative assessments—that is, "forms of assessment that require the active construction of meaning rather than the passive regurgitation of isolated facts" (McMillan, 2001, p. 14). If assessments are limited to "regurgitation of isolated facts" they can foster what Nelson Maylone terms "TestThink" (see "TestThink" in this chapter). The following sections examine several forms of alternative assessments: authentic assessments, portfolio assessments, peer assessments, self assessments, performance-based assessments, alternate assessments, and project-based learning.

Authentic Assessment

Authentic assessment (sometimes called *alternative assessment*) requires students to use higher-level thinking skills to perform, create, or solve a real-life problem, not just choose one of several designated responses as on a multiple-choice test item. A teacher might use authentic assessment to evaluate the quality of individual and small-group projects, videotaped demonstrations of skills, or participation in community-based activities. In science, for example, students might design and conduct an experiment to solve a problem and then explain in writing how they solved the problem.

Authentic assessments require students to solve problems or to work on tasks that approximate as much as possible those they will encounter beyond the classroom. For example, authentic assessment might allow students to select projects on which they will be evaluated, such as writing a brochure, making a map, creating a recipe, writing and directing a play, critiquing a performance, inventing something useful, producing a video, creating a model, writing a children's book, and so on. In addition, authentic assessment encourages students to develop their own responses to problem situations by allowing them to decide what information is relevant and how that information should be organized and used.

When teachers use authentic assessment to determine what students have learned—and the depth to which they have learned it—student achievement and attitudes toward learning improve. For example, a study of eleven pairs of K–12 science and math teachers found that when teachers assess student learning in real-life problem-solving situations, learning and attitudes toward school improve (Appalachia Educational Laboratory, 1993).

Portfolio Assessment

Professionals in the fine arts, architecture, photography, and advertising routinely compile portfolios to document their best work. They show their portfolios to prospective clients or employers. Periodically, the professional will update the portfolio contents to reflect his or her latest, and best, accomplishments.

Similarly, portfolio assessment in education is based on a collection of student work that "tell[s] a story of a learner's growth in proficiency, long-term achievement, and significant accomplishments in a given academic area" (Tombari & Borich, 1999,

p. 164). In short, a portfolio provides examples of important work undertaken by a student, and it represents that student's best work. For example, a high school physics student might include in a portfolio (1) a written report of a physics lab experiment illustrating how vector principles and Newton's laws explain the motion of objects in two dimensions, (2) photographs of that experiment in progress, (3) a certificate of merit received at a local science fair, and (4) an annotated list of Internet sites related to vector principles and Newton's laws.

For students, an important part of portfolio assessment is clarifying the criteria used to select work to be included in the portfolio, and then selecting, organizing, and presenting that work for the teacher to assess. The following purposes have been suggested for student portfolios:

- Growth monitoring, in which portfolio content is used to document student progress toward goals or improvement in proficiency.
- Skill certification, in which the portfolio is used to establish which instructional goals the student has adequately accomplished.
- Evidence of best work, in which the portfolio contains a student's exemplary work and presents the highest level of proficiency the student has achieved with each goal.
- External assessment, in which the portfolio is used to establish student proficiency by agencies outside the classroom, such as the school, school district, or a state agency.
- Communication with parents, in which a portfolio is taken home or maintained at home to convey how the child is performing at school (Oosterhof, 2003, p. 186).

Three general guidelines should be followed to maximize the learning that results from students' involvement in portfolio development:

1. Students should individualize their portfolios—that is, portfolios should focus on the attainment of instructional goals that are important and meaningful for the students.
2. Portfolios should focus on students' accomplishments, their best work—not on their mistakes or limitations.
3. Portfolios should be collaboratively evaluated by teacher and students.

Peer Assessment

Peer assessment occurs when students assess one another's work. Typically, peer assessment is done informally during a class session. At times, a student may be more open to accepting critical feedback from a peer than from the teacher. Also, a peer may use a manner of speaking typical of his/her age level (word choice, for example), and it may be easier for another student to understand the feedback. Lastly, as the following teacher indicates, peer assessment frees the teacher to observe the peer assessment process and to provide input when necessary:

We regularly do peer marking—I find this very helpful indeed. A lot of misconceptions come to the fore, and we then discuss these as we are going over the homework. I then go over the peer marking and talk to pupils individually as I go round the room (Black et al., 2004, p. 14).

Self Assessment

Self assessment occurs when students assess their own work and their thought processes while completing that work. It has been suggested that "[self assessment] is the most underused form of classroom assessment but has the most flexibility and power as a combined assessment and learning tool" (Tileston, 2004, p. 99). When students assess their own work they become more aware of the factors that promote, or hinder, their learning. Students may, for example, ask assessment questions such as the following: What have I learned as a result of this activity? What problems did I encounter during my learning? How will I overcome these problems in the future?

Performance-Based Assessment

Put simply, performance-based assessment is based on observation and judgment (Stiggins, 2001). In some cases, the teacher observes and then evaluates an actual performance or application of a skill; in others, the teacher evaluates a product created by the student. For example, a teacher might observe a student perform a task or review a student-produced product and then judge its quality. Or, a teacher might observe a student's science experiment and judge the quality of the thinking involved, or read a student's research report in history and judge the quality of argumentation and writing. In sum, performance-based assessment is used to determine what students can *do* as well as what they *know*.

Alternate Assessments

Alternate assessments are designed to measure the performance of students who are unable to participate in traditional large-scale assessments used by school districts and state departments of education. This approach to assessment emerged as a result of the reference to "alternate assessment" in the 1997 reauthorization of the Individuals with Disabilities Education Act (IDEA), which called for states to have alternate assessments in place by the year 2000. An alternate assessment is an alternative way of gathering data about what a student, regardless of the severity of his or her disability, knows and can do. Alternate strategies for collecting data might consist of observing the student during the school day, asking the student to perform a task and noting the level of performance, or interviewing parents or guardians about the student's activities outside of school. For students with disabilities, alternate assessments can be administered to students who have a unique array of educational goals and experiences, and who differ greatly in their ability to respond to stimuli, solve problems, and provide responses.

Most states are in the process of developing alternate assessments for students with severe disabilities. The National Center on Educational Outcomes at the University of Minnesota suggests six principles for developing inclusive assessment and accountability systems:

Principle 1. All students with disabilities are included in the assessment system.

Principle 2. Decisions about how students with disabilities participate in the assessment system are the result of clearly articulated participation, accommodation, and alternate assessment decision-making processes.

Principle 3. All students with disabilities are included when student scores are publicly reported, in the same frequency and format as all other students, whether they participate with or without accommodations, or in an alternate assessment.

Principle 4. The assessment performance of students with disabilities has the same impact on the final accountability index as the performance of other students, regardless of how the students participate in the assessment system (i.e., with or without accommodation, or in an alternate assessment).

Principle 5. There is improvement of both the assessment system and the accountability system over time, through the processes of formal monitoring, ongoing evaluation, and systematic training in the context of emerging research and best practice.

Principle 6. Every policy and practice reflects the belief that *all students* must be included in state and district assessment and accountability systems (Guenemoen, Thompson, Thurlow, & Lehr, 2001).

The U.S. Department of Education decided in 2003 that the achievement of students with severe learning problems could be compared to the achievement of students without learning problems. The new ruling would enable more schools to demonstrate that they had made adequate yearly progress (AYP), a key requirement of the No Child Left Behind Act.

Prior to the Department of Education ruling, students who took alternate assessments could not be considered "proficient." In addition, many schools failed to make adequate yearly progress because their students with disabilities scored low on "regular" assessments or did not take the assessments. Thus, schools were "penalized" when they reported their yearly achievement scores for all students. Furthermore, schools that received federal aid for the poor but failed to make adequate yearly progress could face increasing sanctions from the government.

According to the new ruling, states could develop their own criteria to identify students with "significant cognitive disabilities." The federal government required that standards for students with disabilities be tied to state academic standards, however. Identified students would be tested against standards appropriate for their intellectual development, and their scores counted as part of their school's overall academic performance.

BASIC PRINCIPLES OF CURRICULUM AND INSTRUCTION

In *Basic Principles of Curriculum and Instruction* (1949), Ralph Tyler stressed the importance of analyzing educational purposes, learning experiences, organization of those experiences, and evaluation of outcomes. Tyler's paradigm for the interrelationships between curriculum and instruction is viewed by many as "the perennial paradigm of curriculum studies that dominates the field to this day" (Schubert, 1986, p. 82).

Clearly, the "educational purposes" discussed in Tyler's seminal book are realized by a curriculum if it results in the following three outcomes for learners: (1) they acquire an understanding of the subject at hand; (2) they can apply what they have learned to new situations; and (3) they have a desire to continue learning. However, identification of these outcomes does not tell us exactly *how* to attain them. Tyler's book notwithstanding, we are still confronted with the question: What *are* the basic principles of curriculum and instruction? What do effective teachers do when they are teaching? How do they communicate with students? How do they manage classroom activities? What models of teaching do they use? As Carol Lupton points out in this chapter's *Teachers' Voices* section ("Ideals vs. Reality in the Classroom"), "today's educators are encouraged to provide a variety of teaching experiences—linguistic, logical-mathematical, musical, spatial, bodily kinesthetic, interpersonal, and intrapersonal—to increase opportunities for success for all students. Easy to say, hard to do."

As the previous chapters of this book suggest, answers to questions such as the preceding are not easy to formulate. The interrelationships between curriculum and instruction are reciprocal and complex. Ultimately, our quest to identify *the* principles of curriculum and instruction yields results similar to the "Principles of Effective Teaching" presented in an International Academy of Education publication titled, simply, *Teaching*. We close this chapter by presenting these 12 principles, re-titled "Basic Principles of Curriculum and Instruction," in Table 6.2. The principles, based on extensive research on teaching and learning, illustrate the complex interrelationships between curriculum and instruction. While the principles may appear deceptively simple, they require a high degree of skill and understanding to put into practice in actual classrooms.

CRITERION QUESTIONS—CURRICULUM AND INSTRUCTION

The articles in this chapter examine the interrelationships between curriculum and instruction. The criterion questions for this chapter are as follows:

1. Are appropriate instructional methods (or models of teaching) used to attain the purposes and goals of the curriculum?
2. Are the instructional activities meaningful and authentic for students?
3. Are multiple, diverse forms of assessment used to determine what students know and are able to do?
4. Do assessments of student learning require the active construction of meaning, not just recall of information?

TABLE 6.2
Basic Principles of Curriculum and Instruction

1. **Supportive Classroom Environment:** Students learn best within cohesive and caring learning communities.
2. **Opportunity to Learn:** Students learn more when most of the available time is allocated to curriculum-related activities and the classroom management system emphasizes maintaining their engagement in those activities.
3. **Curriculum Alignment:** All components of the curriculum are aligned to create a cohesive program for accomplishing instructional purposes and goals.
4. **Establishing Learning Opportunities:** Teachers can prepare students for learning by providing an initial structure to clarify intended outcomes and cue desired learning strategies.
5. **Coherent Content:** To facilitate meaningful learning and retention, content is explained clearly and developed with emphasis on its structure and connections.
6. **Thoughtful Discourse:** Questions are planned to engage students in sustained discourse structured around powerful ideas.
7. **Practice and Application Activities:** Students need sufficient opportunities to practice and apply what they are learning and to receive improvement-oriented feedback.
8. **Scaffolding Students' Task Engagement:** The teacher provides whatever assistance students need to enable them to engage in learning activities productively.
9. **Strategic Teaching:** The teacher models and instructs students in learning and self-regulation activities.
10. **Cooperative Learning:** Students often benefit from working in pairs or small groups to construct understandings or help one another master skills.
11. **Goal-Oriented Assessment:** The teacher uses a variety of formal and informal assessment methods to monitor progress toward learning goals.
12. **Achievement Expectations:** The teacher establishes and follows through on appropriate expectations for learning outcomes.

Source: Brophy, J. *Teaching—Educational Practice Series-1.* Brussels, Belgium: International Academy of Education, 1999, pp. 366–367.

REFERENCES

Appalachia Educational Laboratory. *Alternative assessment in math and science: Moving toward school a moving target.* Charleston, WV: Author, 1993.

Beauchamp, G. A. *Curriculum theory.* Itasca, IL: F. E. Peacock, 1981.

Black, P., Harrison, C., Lee, C., Marshall, B., and Wiliam, D. Working inside the black box: Assessment for learning in the classroom. *Phi Delta Kappan* (September, 2004): 9–21.

Bloom, B. S. *All our children learning: A primer for parents, teachers, and other educators.* New York: McGraw-Hill, 1981.

Carroll, J. A model of school learning. *Teachers College Record, 64* (1963): 723–733.

Dewey, J. *Democracy and education.* New York: Macmillan, 1916.

Duffy, G., and Roehler, L. The tension between information-giving and mediation: Perspectives on instructional explanation and teacher change. In J. Brophy (Ed.), *Advances in research on teaching,* vol. 1. Greenwich, CT: JAI Press, 1989.

Gagné, R. M. *Essentials of learning for instruction.* Hinsdale, IL: Dryden, 1974.

Gagné, R. M. *The conditions of learning,* 3rd ed. New York: Holt, Rinehart and Winston, 1977.

George Lucas Educational Foundation. *Project-based learning research.* Retrieved November 2001 from http://www.glef.org./index.html.

Good, T. E., and Grouws, D. The Missouri mathematics effectiveness project: An experimental study in fourth-grade classrooms. *Journal of Educational Psychology, 71* (1979): 355–362.

Guenemoen, R. F., Thompson, S. J., Thurlow, M. L., and Lehr, C. A. *A self-study guide to implementation of inclusive assessment and accountability systems: A best practice approach.* Minneapolis, MN: University of Minnesota, National Center on Educational Outcomes, 2001.

Joyce, B., Weil, M., and Calhoun, E. *Models of teaching,* 7th ed. Boston: Allyn and Bacon, 2004.

McMillan, J. H. *Classroom assessment: Principles and practice for effective instruction,* 2nd ed. Boston: Allyn and Bacon, 2001.

Newmann, F. M., and Wehlage, G. G. *Successful school restructuring: A report to the public and educators by the Center on Organization and Restructuring of Schools.* Madison, WI: University of Wisconsin, Center on Organization and Restructuring of Schools, 1995.

Newmann, F. M., et al., eds. *Authentic achievement: Restructuring schools for intellectual quality.* San Francisco: Jossey-Bass, 1996.

Oaks, M. M., Grantman, R., and Pedras, M. (2001). Technological literacy: A twenty-first century imperative. In F. W. Parkay and G. Hass (Eds.), *Curriculum planning: A contemporary approach,* 7th ed., pp. 439–445. Boston: Allyn and Bacon, 2001.

Oosterhof, A. *Developing and using classroom assessments.* Upper Saddle River, NJ: Merrill Prentice Hall, 2003.

Parnell, D. *Contextual teaching works.* Waco, TX: Center for Occupational Research and Development, 2000.

Rosenshine, B. Explicit teaching. In D. Berliner and B. Rosenshine (Eds.), *Talks to teachers.* New York: Random House, 1998.

Rosenshine, B., and Stevens, R. Teaching functions. In M. C. Wittrock (Ed.), *Handbook of research on teaching,* 3rd ed. New York: Macmillan, 1986.

Schubert, W. H. *Curriculum: Perspective, paradigm, and possibility.* New York: Macmillan, 1986.

Sharan, Y., and Sharan, S. Group investigation expands cooperative learning. *Educational Leadership* (December/January 1989/90): 17–21.

Stiggins, R. New assessment beliefs for a new school mission. *Phi Delta Kappan* (September 2004): 22–27.

Thelen, H. A. *Education and the human quest.* New York: Harper and Row, 1960.

Thelen, H. A. *The classroom society: The construction of educational experience.* New York: John Wiley, 1981.

Tileston, D. W. *What every teacher should know about student assessment.* Thousand Oaks, CA: Corwin Press, 2004.

Tombari, M. L., and Borich, G. D. *Authentic assessment in the classroom: Applications and practice.* Upper Saddle River, NJ: Merrill, 1999.

Tyler, R. *Basic principles of curriculum and instruction.* Chicago: University of Chicago Press, 1949.

Vygotsky, L. S. *Mind in society: The development of higher mental process.* Cambridge, MA: Harvard University Press, 1978.

Vygotsky, L. S. *Thought and language.* Cambridge, MA: MIT Press, 1986.

Woolfolk, A. E. *Educational psychology,* 8th ed. Boston: Allyn and Bacon, 2001.

Progressive Organization of Subject Matter

JOHN DEWEY

ABSTRACT: *In the following, Dewey explains a key principle of progressive education—the continuity of educative experience. Instead of presenting subject matter that is* beyond *the life experiences of learners, the curriculum should begin with material that falls* within *those experiences. Once this connection has been established, the subject can be developed progressively into a fuller, richer, and more organized form; and this new knowledge becomes an "instrumentality" for further learning.*

One consideration stands out clearly when education is conceived in terms of experience. Anything which can be called a study, whether arithmetic, history, geography, or one of the natural sciences, must be derived from materials which at the outset fall within the scope of ordinary life-experience. In this respect the newer education contrasts sharply with procedures which start with facts and truths that are outside the range of the experience of those taught, and which, therefore, have the problem of discovering ways and means of bringing them within experience. Undoubtedly one chief cause for the great success of newer methods in early elementary education has been its observance of the contrary principle.

But finding the material for learning within experience is only the first step. The next step is the progressive development of what is already experienced into a fuller and richer and also more organized form, a form that gradually approximates that in which subject-matter is presented to the skilled, mature person. That this change is possible without departing from the organic connection of education with experience is shown by the fact that this change takes place outside of the school and apart from formal education. The infant, for example, begins with an environment of objects that is very restricted in space and time. That environment steadily expands by the momentum inherent in experience itself without aid from scholastic instruction. As the infant learns to reach, creep, walk, and talk, the intrinsic subject-matter of its experience widens and deepens. It comes into connection with new objects and events which call out new powers, while the exercise of these powers refines and enlarges the content of its experience. Life-space and life-durations are expanded. The environment, the world of experience, constantly grows larger and, so to speak, thicker. The educator who receives the child at the end of this period has to find ways for doing consciously and deliberately what "nature" accomplishes in the earlier years.

It is hardly necessary to insist upon the first of the two conditions which have been specified. It is a cardinal precept of the newer school of education that the beginning of instruction shall be made with the experience learners already have; that this experience and the capacities that have been developed during its course provide the starting point for all further learning. I am not so sure that the other condition, that of orderly development toward expansion and organization of subject-matter through growth of experience, receives as much attention. Yet the principle of continuity of educative experience requires that equal thought and attention be given to solution of this aspect of the educational problem. Undoubtedly this phase of the problem is more difficult than the other. Those who deal with the preschool child, with the kindergarten child, and with the boy and girl of the early primary years do not have much difficulty in determining the range of past experience or in finding activities that connect in vital ways with it. With older children both factors of the problem offer increased difficulties to the educator. It is harder to find out the background of the experience of individuals and harder to find out just how the subject-matters already contained in that experience shall be directed so as to lead out to larger and better organized fields.

It is a mistake to suppose that the principle of the leading on of experience to something different is adequately satisfied simply by giving pupils some new experiences any more than it is by seeing to it that they have greater skill and ease in dealing with things with which they are already familiar. It is also essential that the new objects and events be related intellectually to those of earlier experiences, and this means that there be some advance made in conscious articulation of facts and ideas. It thus becomes the office of the educator to select those things within the range of existing experience that have the promise and potentiality of presenting new problems which by stimulating new ways of observation and judgment will expand the area of further experience. He must constantly regard what is already won not as a fixed possession but as an agency and instrumentality for opening new fields which make new demands upon existing powers of observation and of intelligent use of memory. Connectedness in growth must be his constant watchword.

The educator more than the member of any other profession is concerned to have a long look ahead. The physician may feel his job done when he has restored a patient to health. He has undoubtedly the obligation of advising him how to live so as to avoid similar troubles in the future. But, after all, the conduct of his life is his own affair, not the physician's; and what is more important for the present point is that as far as the physician does occupy himself with instruction and advice as to the future of his patient he takes upon himself the function of an educator. The lawyer is occupied with winning a suit for his client or getting the latter out of some complication into which he has got himself. If it goes beyond the case presented to him he too becomes an educator. The educator by the very nature of his work is obliged to see his present work in terms of what it accomplishes, or fails to accomplish, for a future whose objects are linked with those of the present.

Here, again, the problem for the progressive educator is more difficult than for the teacher in the traditional school. The latter had indeed to look ahead. But unless his personality and enthusiasm took him beyond the limits that hedged in the traditional school, he could content himself with thinking of the next examination period or the promotion to the next class. He could envisage the future in terms of factors that lay within the requirements of the school system as that conventionally existed. There is incumbent upon the teacher who links education and actual experience together a more serious and a harder business. He must be aware of the potentialities for leading students into new fields which belong to experiences already had, and must use this knowledge as his criterion for selection and arrangement of the conditions that influence their present experience.

Because the studies of the traditional school consisted of subject-matter that was selected and arranged on the basis of the judgment of adults as to what would be useful for the young sometime in the future, the material to be learned was settled upon outside the present life-experience of the learner. In consequence, it had to do with the past; it was such as had proved useful to men in past ages. By reaction to an opposite extreme, as unfortunate as it was probably natural under the circumstances, the sound idea that education should derive its materials from present experience and should enable the learner to cope with the problems of the present and future has often been converted into the idea that progressive schools can to a very large extent ignore the past. If the present could be cut off from the past, this conclusion would be sound. But the achievements of the past provide the only means at command for understanding the present. Just as the individual has to draw in memory upon his own past to understand the conditions in which he individually finds himself, so the issues and problems of present *social* life are in such intimate and direct connection with the past that students cannot be prepared to understand either these problems or the best way of dealing with them without delving into their roots in the past. In other words, the sound principle that the objectives of learning are in the future and its immediate materials are in present experience can be carried into effect only in the degree that present experience is stretched, as it were, backward. It can expand into the future only as it is also enlarged to take in the past.

John Dewey was, at various times during his career, Professor of Philosophy, Columbia University; head of the Department of Philosophy and director of the School of Education at the University of Chicago; and Professor of Philosophy at the University of Michigan.

QUESTIONS FOR REFLECTION

1. How does a curriculum that is organized according to Dewey's ideas incorporate the past, present, and future?
2. What criticisms might be made regarding Dewey's position that "the beginning of instruction [should] be made with the experience learners already have"? How would Dewey respond to these criticisms?
3. What techniques can curriculum planners and teachers use to determine the learners' "range of past experiences"?

Structures in Learning

JEROME S. BRUNER

ABSTRACT:　Each discipline of knowledge has a structure, and students should be provided with learning experiences that enable them to "discover" that structure. The aim of learning, therefore, is to acquire the processes of inquiry that characterize the discipline, rather than to merely learn "about" the discipline.

Every subject has a structure, a rightness, a beauty. It is this structure that provides the underlying simplicity of things, and it is by learning its nature that we come to appreciate the intrinsic meaning of a subject.

Let me illustrate by reference to geography. Children in the fifth grade of a suburban school were about to study the geography of the Central states as part of a social studies unit. Previous units on the Southeastern states, taught by rote, had proved a bore. Could geography be taught as a rational discipline? Determined to find out, the teachers devised a unit in which students would have to figure out not only where things are located, but why they are there. This involves a sense of the structure of geography.

The children were given a map of the Central states in which only rivers, large bodies of water, agricultural products, and natural resources were shown. They were not allowed to consult their books. Their task was to find Chicago, "the largest city in the North Central states."

The argument got under way immediately. One child came up with the idea that Chicago must be on the junction of the three large lakes. No matter that at this point he did not know the names of the lakes—Huron, Superior, and Michigan—his theory was well reasoned. A big city produced a lot of products, and the easiest and most logical way to ship these products is by water.

But a second child rose immediately to the opposition. A big city needed lots of food, and he placed Chicago where there are corn and hogs—right in the middle of Iowa.

A third child saw the issue more broadly—recognizing virtues in both previous arguments. He pointed out that large quantities of food can be grown in river valleys. Whether he had learned this from a previous social studies unit or from raising carrot seeds, we shall never know. If you had a river, he reasoned, you had not only food but transportation. He pointed to a spot on the map not far from St. Louis. "There is where Chicago *ought* to be." Would that graduate students would always do so well!

Not all the answers were so closely reasoned, though even the wild ones had about them a sense of the necessity involved in a city's location.

One argued, for example, that all American cities have skyscrapers, which require steel, so he placed Chicago in the middle of the Mesabi Range. At least he was thinking on his own, with a sense of the constraints imposed on the location of cities.

After forty-five minutes, the children were told they could pull down the "real" wall map (the one with names) and see where Chicago really is. After the map was down, each of the contending parties pointed out how close they had come to being right. Chicago had not been located. But the location of cities was no longer a matter of unthinking chance for this group of children.

What had the children learned? A way of thinking about geography, a way of dealing with its raw data. They had learned that there is some relationship between the requirements of living and man's habitat. If that is all they got out of their geography lesson, that is plenty. Did they remember which is Lake Huron? Lake Superior? Lake Michigan? Do you?

Teachers have asked me about "the new curricula" as though they were some special magic potion. They are nothing of the sort. The new

curricula, like our little exercise in geography, are based on the fact that knowledge has an internal connectedness, a meaningfulness, and that for facts to be appreciated and understood and remembered, they must be fitted into that internal meaningful context.

The set of prime numbers is not some arbitrary nonsense. What can be said about quantities that cannot be arranged into multiple columns and rows? Discussing that will get you on to the structure of primes and factorability.

It often takes the deepest minds to discern the simplest structure in knowledge. For this reason if for no other, the great scholar and the great scientist and the greatly compassionate person are needed in the building of new curricula.

There is one other point. Our geographical example made much of discovery. What difference does discovery make in the learning of the young? First, let it be clear what the act of discovery entails. It is only rarely on the frontier of knowledge that new facts are "discovered" in the sense of being encountered, as Newton suggested, as "islands of truth in an uncharted sea of ignorance." Discovery, whether by a schoolboy going it on his own or by a scientist, is most often a matter of rearranging or transforming evidence in such a way that one is not enabled to go beyond the evidence to new insights. Discovery involves the finding of the right structure, the meaningfulness.

Consider now what benefits the child might derive from the experience of learning through his own discoveries. These benefits can be discussed in terms of increased intellectual potency, intrinsic rewards, useful learning techniques, and better memory processes.

For the child to develop *intellectual potency,* he must be encouraged to search out and find regularities and relationships in his environment. To do this, he needs to be armed with the expectancy that there is something for him to find and, once aroused by this expectancy, he must devise his own ways of searching and finding.

Emphasis on discovery in learning has the effect upon the learner of leading him to be a constructionist—to organize what he encounters in such a manner that he not only discovers regularity and relatedness, but also avoids the kind of information drift that fails to keep account of how the information will be used.

In speaking of *intrinsic motives* for learning (as opposed to extrinsic motives), it must be recognized that much of the problem in leading a child to effective cognitive activity is to free him from the immediate control of environmental punishments and rewards.

For example, studies show that children who seem to be early over-achievers in school are likely to be seekers after the "right way to do it" and that their capacity for transforming their learning into useful thought structures tends to be less than that of children merely achieving at levels predicted by intelligence tests.

The hypothesis drawn from these studies is that if a child is able to approach learning as a task of discovering something rather than "learning about it" he will tend to find a more personally meaningful reward in his own competency and self-achievement in the subject than he will find in the approval of others.

There are many ways of coming to the *techniques of inquiry,* or the heuristics of discovery. One of them is by careful study of the formalization of these techniques in logic, statistics, mathematics, and the like. If a child is going to pursue inquiry as an eventual way of life, particularly in the sciences, formal study is essential. Yet, whoever has taught kindergarten and the early primary grades (periods of intense inquiry) knows that an understanding of the formal aspect of inquiry is not sufficient or always possible.

Children appear to have a series of attitudes and activities they associate with inquiry. Rather than a formal approach to the relevance of variables in their search, they depend on their sense of what things among an ensemble of things "smell right" as being of the proper order of magnitude or scope of severity.

It is evident then that if children are to learn the working techniques of discovery, they must be afforded the opportunities of problem solving. The more they practice problem solving, the more likely they are to generalize what they learn into a style of inquiry that serves for any kind of task they may encounter. It is doubtful that anyone ever improves in the art and technique of inquiry by any other means than engaging in inquiry, or problem solving.

The first premise in a theory concerning the *improvement of memory processes* is that the principal problem of human memory is not storage, but retrieval. The premise may be inferred from the fact that recognition (i.e., recall with the aid of maximum prompts) is extraordinarily good in human beings—particularly in comparison to spontaneous recall when information must be recalled without external aids or prompts. The key to retrieval is organization.

There are myriad findings to indicate that any organization of information that reduces the collective complexity of material by embedding it into a mental structure the child has constructed will make that material more accessible for retrieval. In sum, the child's very attitudes and activities that characterize "figuring out" or "discovering" things for himself also seem to have the effect of making material easier to remember.

If man's intellectual excellence is the most important among his perfections (as Maimonides, the great Hispanic-Judaic philosopher once said), then it is also the case that the most uniquely personal of all that man knows is that which he discovers for himself. What difference does it make when we encourage discovery in the young? It creates, as Maimonides would put it, a special and unique relation between knowledge possessed and the possessor.

After a career as Professor of Psychology and Director, Center for Cognitive Studies, Harvard University, *Jerome Bruner* was Watts Chair of Experimental Psychology, Oxford University, England, 1972–1979.

QUESTIONS FOR REFLECTION

1. What does Bruner mean when he states that "It often takes the deepest minds to discern the simplest structure in knowledge"? Can you give an example?
2. What is "intellectual potency," and how can it be developed within students?
3. What is "information drift," and what curricular experiences help students avoid it?
4. In recommending the development of "new" curricula, why does Bruner call for the involvement of the "greatly compassionate person" as well as "the great scholar and the great scientist"?

Nurturing the Life of the Mind

KATHLEEN VAIL

ABSTRACT: *Although anti-intellectualism is part of the history and culture of the United States, it does not have to define the nation's schools. Schools must rid themselves of anti-intellectualism and make sure that true intellect has the chance to flourish by taking a critical look at their curriculum, what their teachers are reading, and the way in which they treat academically gifted students. In fact, a reintroduction of the liberal arts—literature, history, poetry, philosophy, and art—might be the best way to rid schools of anti-intellectualism.*

You don't need to look far for evidence that we Americans don't place a very high value on intellect. Our heroes are athletes, entertainers, and entrepreneurs, not scholars. But our schools, with their high academic standards, high-stakes tests, and performance bonuses for improved achievement scores—surely our schools are bastions of intellectualism?

Not necessarily.

Your parents and community, even your teachers and administrators, perhaps even you, might unwittingly be holding back your schools from cultivating intellect in your students and exposing them to the joys of the life of the mind.

Why? Because as a nation, we just don't trust brainy people. The stereotype of the muddle-headed professor—the one who can recite passages of Dante's *Inferno* in the original Italian but doesn't realize his pants are on backwards—is alive and well. We'd rather our children were sociable than scholarly. The results of a 1995 Public Agenda survey clearly point out our distrust of scholars and academics. Seven out of 10 Americans agreed that "people who are highly educated often turn out to be book smart but lack the common sense and understanding of regular folk." Seven out of 10 respondents said they would be very or somewhat concerned if their child earned excellent grades but had only a few close friends and seldom participated in social activities. In focus groups, a New Jersey parent said, "If you focus on the brain, it becomes too tedious." A Cincinnati woman avowed, "If everyone were a genius, it would be a dull world."

Schools are places where we send our children to get a practical education—not to pursue knowledge for knowledge's sake. Symptoms of pervasive anti-intellectualism in our schools aren't difficult to find:

*   A former school board member in Armonk, N.Y., pulled her son and daughter out of the

public schools and placed them in a private school. She'd become increasingly frustrated trying to get more challenging classes for her son. Some staff members resisted creating a gifted program because the other students "would feel bad about not being selected," she said.

- A Columbiana, Ala., school board member asked administrators to investigate middle school English teacher Pam Cooper, who was teaching Shakespeare and Chaucer to eighth-graders. The board member worried that students shouldn't be reading books they'd later encounter in high school literature classes, books that seemed to be beyond their ability level.
- School boards around the country are questioning the merit of homework. The Piscataway, NJ., school board, for example, recently limited the amount of homework teachers could assign, discouraged weekend and holiday assignments, and prohibited teachers from grading work done at home. Parents complained that homework was interfering with their children's extracurricular activities.

"Schools have always been in a society where practical is more important than intellectual," says education historian and writer Diane Ravitch. "Schools could be a counterbalance." Ravitch's latest book, *Left Back: A Century of Failed School Reforms,* traces what she considers the roots of anti-intellectualism in our schools. Schools, she concludes, are anything but a counterbalance to American's distaste for intellectual pursuits.

But they could and should be. When we encourage our children to reject the life of the mind, we leave them vulnerable to exploitation and control. Without the ability to think critically, to defend their ideas and understand the ideas of others, they cannot fully participate in our democracy. If we continue along this path, says writer Earl Shorris, our nation will suffer. "We will become a second-rate country," he says. "We will have a less civil society."

AN AMERICAN TRADITION

"Intellect is resented as a form of power or privilege," wrote historian and professor Richard Hofstadter in *Anti-Intellectualism in American Life,* a Pulitzer-Prize winning book tracing the roots of anti-intellectualism in U.S. politics, religion, and education. Published in 1963, it is considered a watershed book on the subject and rings as true today as it did 30 years ago.

Animosity toward intellectuals is in our country's DNA. From the beginning of our nation's history, according to Hofstadter, our democratic and populist urges have driven us to reject anything that smacks of elitism. Practicality, common sense, and native intelligence have been considered more noble qualities than anything you could learn from a book. Ralph Waldo Emerson and other Transcendentalist philosophers of the 19th century thought schooling and rigorous book learning put unnatural restraints on children. Emerson wrote in his journal: "We are shut up in schools and college recitation rooms for ten or fifteen years and come out at last with a bellyful of words and do not know a thing."

Mark Twain's *Huckleberry Finn* exemplified American anti-intellectualism. The novel's hero avoids being civilized—going to school and learning to read—so he can preserve his innate goodness.

Intellect, according to Hofstadter, is different from native intelligence, a quality we grudgingly admire. Intellect is the critical, creative, and contemplative side of the mind. Intelligence seeks to grasp, manipulate, re-order, and adjust, while intellect examines, ponders, wonders, theorizes, criticizes, and imagines.

School remains a place where intellect is mistrusted. As Hofstadter put it, our country's educational system is in the grips of people who "joyfully and militantly proclaim their hostility to intellect and their eagerness to identify with children who show the least intellectual promise."

Anti-intellectualism is part of our history and our culture, but it doesn't have to define our schools. Many ideas exist on how to make school a place where the life of the mind is valued as much as high test scores or athletic prowess or social status. Some of those ideas contradict each other, and some of the people who espouse them have distinct political agendas or leanings. But true intellect is nonpartisan. The best way to make sure it can flower in your schools is to start by taking a critical look at your curriculum, your teachers, and your school culture.

WHAT ARE YOU TEACHING?

The idea that children must be entertained and feel good while they learn has been embraced by many well-meaning educators. In many classrooms, as a result, students are watching movies, working on multimedia presentations, surfing the Internet, putting on plays, and dissecting popular song lyrics. The idea is to motivate students, but the emphasis on enjoyment as a facile substitute for engagement creates a culture in which students are not likely to challenge themselves or stretch their abilities. After all, if students are not shown the intrinsic rewards that come from working hard to understand a concept, they won't do it on their own. The probable result? A life spent shying away from books, poetry, art, music, public policy discussions—anything that takes an effort to understand or appreciate and has no immediate or obvious payoff.

Project-based learning always has the potential to be based on fun rather than content, says former teacher and administrator Elaine McEwan, who wrote *Angry Parents, Failing Schools: What's Wrong with Public Schools and What You Can Do About It*. She uses the example of a class of academically struggling elementary school students in Arizona that spent 37 hours—more than a school week—building a papier-mache dinosaur. The local newspaper even ran a photo of the students and their handiwork. "Those kids couldn't read well, and they spent all that time messing with chicken wire and wheat paste," says McEwan.

The trend toward teaching skills rather than content has become especially popular with the advent of the Internet. Because information is changing so quickly, the argument goes, it makes more sense to teach students how to find information than to impart it to them. But if students are deprived of content and context, their forays into the Internet might not go beyond looking up the Backstreet Boys web site.

One of the most prominent proponents of imparting knowledge to children along with the skills to probe more deeply is E. D. Hirsch, the founder of the Core Knowledge curriculum approach and author of *Cultural Literacy: What Every American Needs to Know*. The University of Virginia English professor once gave a reading comprehension test to a community college class in Richmond, Va. The students were tested on a passage comparing Robert E. Lee to Ulysses S. Grant. Hirsch was astounded to discover that most of the students, living in an area rich with Civil War history, had no idea who either man was. This experience gave Hirsch the idea for compiling his dictionary of cultural literacy—a basic body of knowledge that educated people should have at their command to be successful in school and in life.

The idea of a core body of knowledge appeals to educators such as McEwan, who worry that many teachers value process over content. Project-based learning is popular with parents, she says, because they want their children to have fun.

The quality of content concerns Santa Monica, Calif., English teacher Carol Jago, who directs the California Reading and Literature Project at the University of California Los Angeles. Jago resists assigning popular novels in her English classes, believing that students at all grade levels should read the classics.

"In the interests of being more inclusive, we've backed away from making demands on students," says Jago. "We should expand and challenge them." Teachers should help students enter into intelligent discourse about what is enduring about a particular piece of literature, she says, but it's hard for teachers to provide the necessary connections for their students and help them develop critical thinking skills. In some classrooms, Jago says, the teachers have a pact with their students: "I won't work too hard; you won't work too hard."

Jago worries that the well-publicized trend toward school boards limiting homework could have repercussions in districts all over the country. If English teachers can't assign homework, she asks, how will they teach novels to their students? The fastest way to create two classes of students is to do away with homework, she says. The Advanced Placement kids will do the reading anyway. The kids who need the extra help the most will fall by the wayside.

Diane Ravitch points to the no-homework trend as a symptom of anti-intellectualism in the schools. "Homework is more time for students to read and write," she says. Cutting back on homework to give students more time to socialize hardly encourages them to take their schoolwork more seriously.

WHAT ARE YOUR TEACHERS READING?

"All too often . . . in the history of the United States, the school teacher has been in no position to serve as a model to the intellectual life," Hofstadter wrote. "Too often he has not only no claims to an intellectual life of his own, but not even an adequate workmanlike competence in the skills he is supposed to impart."

Harsh words, perhaps, but Hofstadter's idea makes sense: If teachers—on the front line of education—don't have an active intellectual life, they're not likely to communicate a love of learning and critical thinking to their students.

In his 1995 book, *Out of Our Minds: Anti-Intellectualism and Talent Development in American Schools*, Craig Howley cites several studies about the education and habits of public school teachers. According to one study, prospective teachers take fewer liberal arts courses than their counterparts in other arts and science majors—and fewer upper-division courses in any subject except pedagogy. It appears, Howley writes, that prospective teachers do not often make a special effort during their college years to pursue advanced study in fields other than pedagogy.

Frequent reading of literature in academic fields is the mark of the scholar, Howley says, so it's logical to look at teachers' reading habits. Readers tend to be more reflective and more critical than nonreaders, argues Howley, who found that studies of teachers' reading showed two patterns: One is that teachers don't read very much—on average, just 3.2 books a year. (In fact, 11 percent of those surveyed said they had not read a single book during the current year.) The second pattern is that when teachers do read, they prefer popular books rather than scholarly or professional literature. Of those who were reading about education, most were reading books intended for the general public.

It's true that U.S. teachers have traditionally been poorly paid and not well respected, which means that the best and the brightest are often not attracted to teaching. But until teachers can be role models and exhibit their own love of learning and academics, the children won't get it.

"Create a culture among the adults, a community of adults who are learners, who are excited about ideas in the other disciplines," says Deborah Meier, educator and author of *The Power of Their Ideas*. "The school must represent the culture it wants to encourage. If we want kids to feel that an intellectual life belongs to them, it must belong to the teacher, too."

HOW DO YOU TREAT YOUR SMART KIDS?

"Far from conceiving the mediocre, reluctant, or incapable student as an obstacle or special problem in a school system devoted to educating the interested, the capable, and the gifted," wrote

Hofstadter, "American education entered upon a crusade to exalt the academically uninterested or ungifted child into a kind of cult-hero."

If schools were strongholds of intellect, then the most academically able students would be the stars. But take a look at any web site aimed at parents of gifted children, and you'll see they say gifted students have almost as much trouble in school as students who don't do well. Children with advanced intellectual ability often are not given the tools they need to succeed. Ridiculed by classmates, resented by teachers, unchallenged by the standard curriculum, they're often ostracized, unhappy, or just plain bored.

Carolyn Kottmeyer, a Pennsylvania mother of two gifted daughters, recounts how a resentful fifth-grade math teacher taunted the older daughter, who received individual instruction from another math teacher. More than once, the regular math teacher walked past the library where the girl was studying. Once she stopped and asked her, "What's a Box-and-Whiskers Plot?" When the girl didn't know, the teacher turned to the class of students standing in the hallway and said, "And you think you're such a genius in math."

Such stories are shockingly common. One parent on Kottmeyer's web site says a teacher told her it was good for her sixth-grade son to be bored because "it prepares him for real life." These parents have tales of teachers who say excessive reading will hurt their child's eyesight; administrators who don't want to allow a boy to skip a grade because others will be getting their driver's licenses before him; principals who don't want to advance students because other parents will ask for the same privilege. Parents tell of teachers and principals who recommend Ritalin for children who are acting up in class because they are bored, or who deny gifted kids entrance to advanced classes because they say the students have behavior problems brought on by boredom.

Smart kids question teachers and are often nonconformists. They are taunted by their peers for being too smart or knowing too much. Some children, in desperation to fit in, hide their academic gifts. "Parents see kids who are excited about going to school, then slowly getting turned off," says Peter Rosenstein, executive director of the National Association for Gifted Children, in Washington, D.C. "Parents find out that nothing the teacher taught that day was new to the child."

Lynne Bernstein, the New York school board member who took her children out of the public school, says her son had a teacher who told him to stop raising his hand and let other children answer some questions. "You get ridiculed, you stop talking," says Bernstein.

The academic reputation of the affluent Armonk school district was the reason Bernstein and her family moved to the community. Instead, she found that a culture of noncompetition was preventing the teachers and staff from pushing kids to do more. "My kids are bright students, and they weren't being challenged," she says.

After winning election to the school board three years ago, Bernstein started a committee to look at what the district was offering gifted students. There was a great deal of resistance even to studying the issue, she says—let alone establishing a program for more advanced students.

But small changes are coming to the district now, including offering additional honors classes at the high school level. Parents are growing nervous because their children aren't being accepted into top colleges, says Bernstein. These parents are pressuring the district to change.

"Learning comes with hard work. It's a struggle," says Bernstein. "We aren't pushing these kids enough, on the bottom, top, and middle."

When the smartest students aren't rewarded and sometimes even feel punished for being academically gifted, other students in a school are hardly likely to see any rewards in doing well, either.

"Schools must create a culture where learning is valued and people get excited about information," says former teacher McEwan. "You don't have to be embarrassed to use big words. We have to make learning cool."

BUT IS IT PRACTICAL?

The purpose of public schools has never been to create thinking, analyzing, intellectual citizens, charges John Taylor Gatto, a 30-year New York City public school teacher and New York State Teacher of the Year in 1991. And that's why they're not doing it now. Today's schools are products of 19th-century industrialists, whose purpose was to prepare people to be good employees—docile, productive, and addicted consumers. And if that's what the public wants, says Gatto, using the Socratic method to teach children to critique great works and question the way things are is a hazard to society.

"Intellect requires a critical mind, not a retentive mind," says Gatto. "Schools can't tolerate questioning."

Gatto is an outspoken critic of the public schools and an advocate of home schooling. He argues that our schools are modeled after factories where repetition and conformity are stressed over thought and expression. "The bell schedule is insane," says Gatto. "It's a rat-training device to make nothing mean very much." When you are interrupted over and over again, what you are doing loses importance, he says. "It creates apathy."

In fact, Gatto and others contend, most of what we consider to be education is actually training. The children at poorer schools receive vocational training. The children in middle-class and affluent schools receive training to become what Hawley calls "intelligent careerists." In this role, he says, they are capable of responding efficiently and pragmatically to work-related problems but unable, or at least disinclined, to examine the broad social, economic, and political context in which the problems are set.

The emphasis on training over education clearly stems from Americans' love of practicality. It's easy to convince parents that their children need certain courses so they can get high-paying jobs when they graduate. But when we believe that the only reason to get an education is to make money, says Howley, "we create a society that thinks about jobs and profit making as universals."

Worse, he says, the idea that education is solely a means to earn money has made us into narcissists whose only goal in life is to make more money—not to be responsible to each other or our community.

A CASE FOR THE HUMANITIES

Propose a rigorous course of study in the humanities and liberal arts, and you'll hear protests: It's traditional. It's elitist. It's full of dead white European males. It's not inclusive. It's not relevant. It's not practical. And besides, it's too hard for our students.

Perhaps the best way to rid schools of antiintellectualism is to reintroduce liberal arts: literature, history, poetry, philosophy, art. Through these subjects, students can learn mankind's best ideas, and they can begin constructing their own life of the mind.

When New York writer Earl Shorris started research for a book on the poor in the United States, he ended up establishing a program that brings the humanities to the inner-city poor. Students are chosen on the basis of their income, their ability to read, and their desire. Some are homeless, some never finished high school, some are in prison, some struggle with drug addiction, but they are taught by professors from elite universities.

"You've been cheated," Shorris tells his students. "Rich people learn the humanities; you didn't. The humanities are a foundation for getting along in the world, for thinking, for learning to reflect on the world instead of just reacting to whatever force is turned against you. . . . Will the humanities make you rich? Yes, absolutely. But not in terms of money. In terms of life."

Shorris sees evidence that the humanities can improve the quality of our lives. In his book, *Riches for the Poor,* he recounts a conversation with one of his students. The man called Shorris to tell him about a problem with a colleague who was making him so angry that he wanted to hit her. He restrained himself, and saved his job, he said, by asking himself, "What would Socrates do?"

After five years, with the support of private foundations and government grants, Shorris' Clemente Course in the Humanities is being taught at about two dozen sites in the United States, Canada, and Mexico. And he is working on a program that would bring the course to public school teachers who would, in turn, pass their knowledge on to their students.

Teaching the humanities is ultimately more practical than training students to perform specific jobs, says Shorris: "If you give human beings the best that human beings have produced, they are changed."

Kathleen Vail is an associate editor of the *American School Board Journal*.

QUESTIONS FOR REFLECTION

1. Do you agree with Vail that there is a spirit of anti-intellectualism in America's schools? Who does she blame for what she sees as an anti-intellectualism and what has caused this trend?
2. What are Vail's solutions to rid the schools of anti-intellectualism and does she offer a practical and realistic plan for educators? What barriers within the school might teachers and school leaders face when attempting to implement her ideas?
3. Is anti-intellectualism too culturally embedded in the American psyche for schools to make a difference regarding intellectual pursuits or can schools accomplish the task of reintroducing intellectualism into the culture by way of the curriculum?

The Limits of Ideology: Curriculum and the Culture Wars

DAVID T. GORDON

ABSTRACT: Gordon examines the culture wars that broke out in the wake of A Nation at Risk—*between conservatives and liberals—over what was required to best teach literacy in America's schools. He observes that ideological orthodoxy for setting educational agendas is very limited and inevitably leads to conflict and poorly served students in the classroom. Gordon stresses the need for a balanced, or integrated, approach to curricular reforms—one that makes the most of what different strategies offer in order to reach the widest range of children. Finally, policymakers and education researchers need to do a better job of clarifying the goals, means and justifications for reforms. Once those objectives have been clarified, teachers need to be given comprehensive training, support, and incentive if reforms are to be taken to scale.*

Just months before she died in 1999, Jeanne Chall, a leading literacy scholar of the twentieth century, participated in a forum at the Harvard Graduate School of Education called "Beyond the Reading Wars." In the 1960s, Chall had written *Learning to Read: The Great Debate* to address the rancorous debate over whether beginning readers should learn letters and sounds before delving into books or immerse themselves in texts, picking up the sights, sounds, and meaning of words along the way. *Learning to Read* had displayed a mountain of research about the need for beginning readers to have both phonics instruction and access to interesting reading material. What more was there to say? Yet here was Chall more than thirty years later discussing a whole new round of reading debates.

In a comical exchange with the moderator, Chall was asked if a certain high-profile report issued earlier that year would settle the matter. "Well," she replied, "the basic knowledge was known for the longest time. Even the Greeks knew what kind of combination [of instruction] you needed in teaching reading. Thirty years ago I said the research showed that you do need phonics. And then you *do* need to read, you see."

"So why do we keep fighting about whole language and phonics?"

"I know many of my friends say it's a political thing," Chall replied. "The ones who like the alphabet are right-wingers, Republicans. Can you imagine? At any rate, somebody discovered along the way that you really didn't need to know all the letters. You could remember the words. That is more fun. You don't have to drill."

"And those fun people are the Democrats? The ones who don't do any work?" the moderator asked.

"Yes, the liberals," said Chall.[1]

The banter was humorous—and meant to be. But it also revealed some frustration over the tenor and substance of the disputes about reading instruction during the 1980s and 1990s. Chall, it has been said, was one to "follow the evidence fearlessly wherever it might lead."[2] Yet the curriculum debates that came after *A Nation at Risk* were often fueled not by a sober and fearless analysis of what the evidence said is best, but by ideological and political partisanship. More often than not, it led to the kind of absurd characterizations Chall was poking fun at, the oversimplifications that turned reading- and math-teaching strategies into salvos within the culture wars.

Somewhere along the line phonics and arithmetic became "conservative"—the pedagogical equivalents of Reaganomics, mink coats, and Anita Bryant—while whole language and reform math became "liberal," lumped in with the progressive income tax and *Mother Jones*.

Given the sense of urgency to improve education following *A Nation at Risk*, school reform was bound to take on the look of blood sport in certain cases, particularly regarding reading and math instruction. Bitter squabbles have broken out over science and social studies instruction, high-stakes testing, and school choice. But the reading and math wars have been generally nastier and more emotional than even those conflicts. It's not hard to understand why. Reading and math are the bedrock of children's learning, the primary subjects of elementary education. Later success in school and college depends on success in those subjects during the preK–3 years.

The broad bipartisan support for the No Child Left Behind Act (NCLB) of 2001 may prove to be something of a truce, if not a peace treaty, in the curriculum wars. Conservatives and liberals, traditionalists and progressives agreed that an emphasis on "scientific," or research-based, instruction and standards was needed so that K–12 decisionmaking would be influenced less by ideology and more by practical and proven solutions to classroom dilemmas.

If the wars really are ended, what can be learned from them? One thing they teach us is the limits of ideological orthodoxy for setting educational agendas. When ideologues impose lopsided solutions, conflict is inevitable—and children are poorly served. A related lesson is about the importance of a balanced, or integrated, approach to curricular reforms—one that makes the most of what different strategies offer in order to reach the widest range of children. Not only does that usually make the most sense, but research shows that teachers seldom incorporate new materials and reform strategies whole hog. Without some evidence that proposed changes are indeed an improvement, and without a specific plan for putting those changes into practice, teachers will take it on themselves to interpret and integrate them into the practices they already know. Which suggests a third lesson: that policymakers and education researchers need to do a better job of clarifying the goals, means, and justifications for reforms. Finally, once those objectives have been clarified, teachers need to be given comprehensive training, support, and incentive if reforms are to be taken to scale.

THE PROBLEM OF IDEOLOGY

Educational ideologies are a useful starting point for discussion, for *describing* the ideal positions of different sides in a debate, but they are not very helpful for *prescribing* solutions. The post–*Nation at Risk* years have shown that reality trumps ideology time and again. California's reading and math reforms are good examples.

The state's 1987 English/Language Arts framework tried to overhaul reading instruction by installing a curriculum meant to convey "the magic of language" and "touch students' lives and stimulate their minds and hearts." It called for a radical change in instructional practice. Out was phonics: proponents of the new method argued that such skill-building exercises—"drill-and-kill"—bored students and stymied their natural excitement about reading. In came whole language, which would immerse students in texts and do away with direct instruction in letter-sound relationships, spelling, and so forth. Students would learn to read as they learned to speak—by jumping right in and doing it—and focus on the meaning of words, not their sounds or particular parts. Fundamental skills would be picked up along the way, in context. This dispute is an old story in American education—from the "alphabetic method" of Noah Webster's speller and McGuffey's readers to attacks by Horace Mann and John Dewey on phonics-based instruction to *Why Johnny Can't Read*, the 1955 bestseller that induced a public outcry for a return to direct phonics instruction.

That's where Jeanne Chall comes in. In 1961, the Carnegie Corporation of New York asked Chall, then at the City University of New York, to determine what the evidence said. She analyzed dozens of studies published from 1910 to 1967, reviewed the most widely used reading textbooks and their teachers manuals, talked with authors and editors of beginning reading programs, and visited hundreds of classrooms in the United States and the United Kingdom. She published her results in 1967 in *Learning to Read*.

The verdict? A combination of phonics for beginners and good literature for all was best. "To read, one needs to be able to use *both* the alphabetic principle and the meaning of words," she wrote. "What distinguished the more effective beginning reading instruction was its early emphasis on learning the code. Instruction that focused, at the beginning, on meaning tended to produce less favorable results." Early phonics instruction in which children learn letter-sound relationships by sounding out words as they read was especially beneficial to children of low socioeconomic status who did not come from language-rich or literacy-rich homes.[3]

In the 1970s and 1980s, when education research was exploring new territory in beginning reading through the lenses of psychology and neurology, evidence continued to mount showing the efficacy of early phonics instruction combined with exposure to high-quality reading material. Later editions of *Learning to Read*, published in 1983 and 1996, reported even stronger support of the advantages of "code emphasis over meaning emphasis" for beginning readers.[4]

But whole language, the latest incarnation of the whole-word method, was winning the ideological battle. It got the approval of teachers unions, schools of education, and others sympathetic to its progressive underpinnings. Its idealized view of children as self-motivated, joyful learners who, with the right encouragement, could construct meaning out of texts without having to know a bunch of rules had a highly romantic appeal.[5]

Whatever its merits, whole language was done a disservice by those adherents who presented it in increasingly strident ways, turning the reading debate into a conflict between good and evil rather than what it should have been: a difference of opinion between people of good will. In California, the discussion took on an almost "theological" character, as journalist Nicholas Lemann puts it, shaped by the crusading, absolutist fervor of its participants.[6]

California's education leaders bought into an ideology rather than a proven, research-based instructional plan. Consulting with whole-language advocates, they were presented with a "choice": (a) provide beginning readers with a humane, nurturing whole-language environment in which their natural interest and love for rich reading material would flourish, or (b) offer them mind-numbing phonics-based instruction. Bill Honig, California's superintendent of public instruction at the time, would later claim, "We thought we were pushing literature. We were neutral on phonics. Then the whole-language movement hijacked what we were doing."[7] The new framework didn't mention whole language directly, but it was full of the theory's romantic language, as its references to the "magic" of language and efforts to "stimulate hearts and minds" suggest.

A similar theological good-versus-evil hue colored the state's math reforms, which included the introduction of new frameworks in 1985 and 1992. Familiar themes emerged, pitting a child-centered ideology emphasizing "real-life" problem-solving against the boring, factory-floor experience of arithmetic drills and pencil-and-paper computation. With reform math, students would use calculators and manipulatives—objects such as beans, sticks, or blocks—to understand numeric relationships. They would read about math problems and discuss them in an effort to understand not just computational value but how such knowledge applies in life. They would work in small groups, tackling together the sorts of problems one encounters in everyday life. Basic skills would—like phonics in the reading reforms—get picked up by students along the way in an informal or indirect manner. This same departure from a basic-skills emphasis characterized the 1989 standards issued by the National Coun-

cil of Teachers of Mathematics (NCTM). To reformers, traditional instruction was "mindless mimicry mathematics."[8]

Of course, ideological excess was not limited to reformers. By the early 1990s, grassroots opposition to both the math and reading frameworks in California had swelled into a statewide movement. Helped by the relatively new technologies of the World Wide Web and email, parents and mathematicians founded Mathematically Correct, an advocacy group that became a powerful opponent of what was now being called "fuzzy math" after the reform's endorsement of estimation rather than computation. Meanwhile, the media began seeking and fording extreme examples of the new methods in action. In one memorable anecdote, *Time* magazine reporter Margot Hornblower visited a fifth-grade class in Sun Valley, California, where the teacher began class by asking, "What if everybody here had to shake hands with everyone else? How many handshakes would that take?" The kids split into small groups and puzzled over the activity for some time—the reporter said for an hour, the teacher later said twenty minutes. Regardless, none of the children could arrive at an answer, and the class tried it again the next day.[9]

Such stories were often exaggerated by opponents of the reforms as representative of the depth and scope of reforms. This was unfair. But they had a potent political effect. In 1997, California revised its framework again to blend traditional instruction with reform methods, putting a greater emphasis on arithmetic, computation, and paper-and-pencil algorithms such as long division. In 2000, the NCTM did the same. But the NCTM also made a point of spelling out more clearly how the standards should be applied, especially in the elementary and middle grades. In some ways, the NCTM saw the math wars as a great misunderstanding and suggested that the revised standards were a clarification, not a correction, of the 1989 framework.[10]

A similar uprising took place over reading. Years after overseeing the 1987 reform, California's former superintendent of public instruction

Bill Honig would say, "The best antidote to a zealous philosophy is reality."[11] The coup de grace for whole language in his state came with the publication of the 1994 National Assessment of Educational Progress (NAEP) reading scores. In just eight years, California had fallen from first among states to dead last, tied with Louisiana. Fifty-nine percent of fourth graders could not read at the fourth-grade level, compared to a national average of 44 percent reading below grade level. African American and Hispanic children fared worst, with 71 percent and 81 percent, respectively, lacking necessary reading skills, compared with 44 percent of white students.

Whole-language proponents cited a number of factors to explain the change, such as larger class size, a new surge of immigration, the high percentage of students from families of low socioeconomic status, and poor training of teachers in whole-language teaching. They pointed out that other states using whole language, such as New Hampshire, had improved test scores significantly.[12] But those arguments fell on deaf ears, especially the arguments about immigration and poverty, given that 49 percent of those who read below basic levels had college graduates for parents. Nowhere else in the nation did the children of college-educated parents score lower than in California.[13]

Something was clearly wrong with California reading instruction, and conservatives had a field day promoting an image of a huge state bureaucracy imposing illiteracy on its children with its politically correct theory. Even before the NAEP scores came out, Republicans had held up whole language from coast to coast in 1994, when they won their first congressional majority in half a century, as a symbol of failed "liberal" ideas. They were not above their own ideological excesses: fundamentalist Christians suggested that whole language's goal of helping students make meaning out of texts was an effort to undermine a literal, or fundamentalist, reading of anything, but especially the Bible.[14]

After the NAEP embarrassment, California amended its reading framework in 1996, calling for a "balanced, comprehensive approach" to reading instruction in its schools that would provide direct instruction in phonics, vocabulary, and spelling while acknowledging whole-language advocates' concern that, of course, "the best instruction provides a strong relationship between what children learn in phonics and what they read."[15] It was a point Jeanne Chall had made in *Learning to Read* twenty-nine years earlier.

THE NEED FOR BALANCE

Chall had warned against taking phonics to an extreme. Early phonics instruction was a necessary tool that should be replaced with reading good stories as quickly as possible. But she had also criticized education professionals for ignoring half a century of research evidence because of their ideological bias against skills-based phonics instruction—the belief that phonics was incompatible with progressive education.[16]

Even as research continued in the 1990s to demonstrate the need for a balanced reading approach, whole-language theorists attacked advocates of balance in baldly political terms. A founding theorist of whole language bizarrely accused Jeanne Chall of doing the bidding of "right-wing" groups bent on destroying public education because she had unmasked the potential harm of a radical application of his theory.[17]

At this time, the federal government did what the Carnegie Corporation had tried to do in supporting Chall's work in the 1960s: get beyond the ideological squabbles to determine what reading research actually said. The National Research Council (NRC), the research arm of the National Academy of Sciences, took up the task. Three shifts in thinking during the 1980s made the project compelling, according to Catherine Snow, the Harvard literacy expert who directed the study. First, a large body of new research increased our understanding of the importance of preschool experiences in the development of literacy—that during those years, children are not just getting ready for reading instruction but actively developing literacy skills. Second, research conducted in the previous two decades about the nature of the reading process had resolved many of the issues phonics and whole-language advocates were fighting about, demolishing some theoretical underpinnings of what Snow calls "radical whole-language practice"—research that had yet to filter down to the trenches. Third, given this consensus on instructional matters, prevention of reading problems rather than reading instruction per se became more of a concern.

In 1998, the NRC issued its verdict: both sides in the reading wars were right—and both were wrong. "The reading wars are over," the panel declared. The findings, published in a book titled *Preventing Reading Difficulties in Young Children,* emphasized the need for reading instruction that balanced and integrated what phonics and whole-language proponents were advocating. Good readers accomplish three things, said the report: "They understand the alphabetic system of English to identify printed works; they have and use background knowledge and strategies to obtain meaning from print; and they read fluently." In other words, they understand and appreciate both the sounds and the meanings of words. The report placed special emphasis on the impact of the preschool years. What kinds of experiences do children need *before* they get to school and formal reading instruction begins?[18]

In a later edition of the book, the authors expressed concern about the use of the term *balance,* a metaphor that, they said, could imply "a little of this and a little of that" or suggest evenly dividing classroom time between phonics and comprehension activities. Instead, they clarified their findings as a call for *integrating* these strategies so that "the opportunities to learn these two aspects of skilled reading should be going on at the same time, in the context of the same activities, and that the choice of instructional activities should be part of an overall, coherent approach to supporting literacy development, not a haphazard selection from unrelated, though varied, activities."[19]

Mathematicians opposed to radical reforms made similar arguments in favor of balanced math instruction that teaches basic skills but also links them to real-life contexts. They argued that having a rich understanding of the abstract concepts and basic facts of mathematics is essential to being able to adapt that knowledge to a variety of plausible and authentic circumstances. Since there is inevitably an abstract or theoretical aspect to any principle, separating the conceptual from the actual is counterproductive and confusing.

TEACHERS TAKE MATTERS INTO THEIR OWN HANDS

While researchers and policymakers have come to the realization that balanced instruction works best, school practitioners seem to have known that all along. Their natural gravitation toward balanced instruction is typical of how school reform works, according to historians David Tyack and William Tobin: "Reformers believe their innovations will transform schools, but it is important to recognize that schools change reforms. Over and over again teachers have selectively implemented and altered reforms."[20]

For example, in one 1995 study, researchers found that children in classes identified as "whole language" made greater gains in reading comprehension than those in classes tagged "basic skills." They also became independent readers more quickly. But when the researchers took a closer look, they found that those whole-language classrooms actually provided abundant instruction in basic skills.[21]

Meanwhile, in their decade-long study of California math reform, researchers David K. Cohen and Heather C. Hill found that teachers by and large reported using a mix of methods, taking parts of the curriculum that made sense and ignoring those that didn't:

> What reformers and opponents packaged tidily, teachers disaggregated and reassembled. Their logic was different from and more complex than

both the logic put forward by reformers in the frameworks, who saw what we call "conventional" and "reform" ideas about teaching and student learning as opposed to each other, and to the critics of reform, whose view of these matters was at least as black and white as that of the reformers. Though many teachers expressed strong allegiance to the principal reform ideas, most did not discard the corresponding conventional ideas.[22]

A 1999 report by the *Harvard Education Letter* found a similar pattern among teachers in Massachusetts, where teachers and curriculum coordinators using materials based on the 1989 NCTM reform math standards began supplementing materials that focused heavily on problem-solving with paper-and-pencil, skills-building worksheets. For example, the math curriculum coordinator for public schools in Braintree, William Kendall, told education journalist Andreae Downs, "It's often good to blend curricula. Kids need practice. It's not enough just to get the big idea and move on, you need practice before you get it right."[23]

Why do practitioners take matters into their own hands? Cohen and Hill ventured a few guesses. First, school practitioners often get conflicting messages from policymakers at various levels about whether, for example, to teach basic skills or discard them. State directives may be contradicted by district-level directives or by leaders in schools—principals, teacher leaders, or the strong lobbying of local parents' groups that are at odds with state policy. So many different messages may make teachers feel that the best thing to do is keep on keeping on until the problem is sorted out.

Another explanation cited by Cohen and Hill is that "teachers learn things from experience that reformers, critics, and policymakers can never know because they lack the experience and rarely inquire of teachers." When math reforms didn't work in California, policymakers accused teachers of not committing to the framework or of implementing the reforms ineffectively by mixing innovative practices and content with traditional ones. But teachers often told researchers that

their professional experience might require them to adjust on the fly to help certain students or classes build essential skills. Like lawyers, doctors, architects, or other professionals, teachers knew that what is drawn up on the board rarely translates easily into practice.

In their analysis of the California math reforms, Cohen and Hill found a great gap between what was prescribed as policy and what took place in practice.[24] This complicated the effort to try to evaluate reforms and assign blame or credit for failure or success—a point California whole-language advocates also made when trying to explain the state's miserable showing in reading in 1994. The interpretation and implementation of standards can vary in each district, school, and classroom. New standards-based curriculum materials often have errors, and the commitment of time and resources to preparing teachers to use such new materials also varies widely.

Because reform efforts often produce glass-half-full and glass-half-empty results, the conclusions we draw from those results must be carefully weighed so that, to paraphrase Bill Honig, reality maintains the upper hand over ideology. For example, researchers at Northwestern University and the University of Chicago compared international math scores to determine how fifth-grade students who had been enrolled in the K–4 reform program Everyday Mathematics matched up with their U.S. and foreign counterparts. The researchers found that the Taiwanese and Japanese fifth graders performed better than all of the American students. Students in Everyday Mathematics outperformed U.S. students from traditional math classes, scored higher than the Taiwanese in some cases, and, on average, scored only slightly lower than Japanese students. Is this good news or bad news? Do we see progress being made through the reform program and should we build on these apparent gains? Or do we just see continued failure—Americans languishing behind the world *again*—and scrap the program?

The value of education research to practice and policymaking naturally depends on the quality or the trustworthiness of the research itself. In 2000, the *Christian Science Monitor* reported that two math reform programs—Core-Plus and the Connected Math Project—got favorable reviews from the U.S. Department of Education based on research conducted by people affiliated with the curricula's developers. Core-Plus was evaluated by an education researcher from the University of Iowa who was a co-director of the program—and in line to receive royalties from sales of its textbooks. "Nobody, including research ethicists, argues that [the Core-Plus study is] invalid," wrote reporter Mark Clayton. Many observers noted that the study would probably provide useful data and analysis about the program. But without a truly independent review, the DOE's recommendation is suspect—and gives ample fodder to skeptics of reforms.[25]

Concerns about skewed research have also been raised by whole-language proponents about recent reports on reading instruction. They note, for example, that the study *Teaching Children to Read,* commissioned by the National Institute of Child Health and Human Development and published in 2000, clearly favored an increased emphasis on phonics instruction. The report, which laid the groundwork for the "Reading First" initiative passed into law as part of the No Child Left Behind Act, focused on quantitative research—that is, studies connecting teaching strategies to test scores. By ignoring qualitative research studies—such as case studies, small-group studies, and in-school observation—the report gave an incomplete picture of the role of classroom instruction in improved reading scores, critics said. In 2002, a new panel went back to the drawing board, looking at qualitative research as well.[26]

New York Times education columnist Richard Rothstein suggests that the current emphasis in federal legislation on "scientifically based research"—the language used in the Reading Excellence Act of 1998 and repeated numerous times in No Child Left Behind—may undermine the balanced approach by tilting policy in favor of phonics because "scientific study is easier for

phonics than whole language." He writes: "Researchers can teach about phonemes, then test if children they know get 'car' by removing a sound from 'cart.' It is harder to design experiments to see if storytelling spurs a desire to read." Rothstein also points out that "[s]cientific studies of separate parts of a reading program exist, but there is no well-established science that precisely balances phonemic awareness, phonics, vocabulary lessons and storytelling. The balance differs for each child. Teachers fluent in both skill- and literature based techniques are needed."[27]

HELPING TEACHERS SUPPORT REFORMS

The past twenty years of reform have also shown that getting teachers to change their practice has been more difficult than expected. The teaching profession is by nature a conservative one. For example, Cohen and Hill report that the math-reform ideas that got the most teacher approval were those that did little to challenge conventional practice and required only modest effort to implement—a little more time here, a change in activities there. Anything that appeared to subvert or challenge what they considered to be essential math teaching and learning got only reluctant attention, if any. "All of this suggests one final explanation," write Cohen and Hill. "[L]earning is often slow and painful, and even when rapid, it attaches to inherited ideas, intellectual structures, and familiar practices."[28]

A comparative study of math teaching in the United States and China demonstrates the importance of teacher knowledge. In an effort to learn why Americans did more poorly, researcher Liping Ma, senior scholar at the Carnegie Foundation for the Advancement of Teaching, found that a high percentage of U.S. teachers had a weak grasp of basic math concepts, particularly at the elementary school level. Teachers lacked a fundamental understanding of standard algorithms, as well as alternative means of problem-solving and why the standard ones have been determined most efficient. A teacher "should know these various solutions of the problem, know how and why students came up with them, know the relationship between the nonstandard ways and the standard way, and know the single conception underlying all the different ways," she writes in her influential book, *Knowing and Teaching Elementary Mathematics.* Ma suggests that to improve mathematics instruction in the United States, more attention must be paid to fundamental math knowledge in preservice teacher training, teacher preparation time, and professional development.[29]

But knowing how to teach math involves more than simply knowing mathematics, and attention to content knowledge alone won't improve teaching and learning. According to the research of Stanford University's Linda Darling-Hammond, students learn best from teachers who have university-level courses in math education as well as a fundamentally sound math knowledge. "Sometimes very bright people who are not taught to teach are very poor teachers because they don't know what it is to struggle to learn, and haven't thought much about how people learn. Content is important, but it isn't enough," she told the *Harvard Education Letter.* Teachers' ability to adapt curricula to the needs of each student is crucial to improved instruction in any curriculum, she says.[30] Critics of education programs who say that teacher training should focus primarily on content, not pedagogy, fail to appreciate the special skills required for good teaching. Katherine K. Merseth, director of teacher education at Harvard and a former math teacher, says fundamental content knowledge is of course essential. But teachers also need techniques in their teaching repertoire that reflect how children learn and make sense of things:

Can you explain to me why one-half divided by two-thirds is three-fourths? Don't tell me how to do it, because that's what many people will do. Give me an example. Tell me a story that represents that equation. We all know you invert and multiply. But why? Or as a kid once said, "If *x*

equals five, why did you call it *x*? Why didn't you just call it five?" You need to be able to draw on the content knowledge itself. But simply having the content background will not make you an effective teacher. To be an effective teacher, you must understand your audience.[31]

In their study, Cohen and Hill found that efforts were successful "only when teachers had significant opportunities to learn how to improve mathematics teaching. When teachers had extended opportunities to study and learn the new mathematics curriculum that their students would use, they were more likely to report practices similar to the aims of the state policy. These opportunities, which often lasted for three days or more, were not typical of professional education in U.S. schools." Having the opportunity to examine student work with colleagues and discuss it in the context of what reforms were trying to achieve was crucial to making classroom improvements.[32]

That same lesson is true of reading. Both preservice and inservice training of teachers is essential to improving reading instruction. John Goodlad, a founder of the Center for Educational Renewal at the University of Washington, Seattle, has argued that the paltry preparation of most primary-grade teachers—the average teacher takes one university-level course in reading instruction—makes intervention to help poor readers almost impossible: "Diagnosis and remediation of the nonreaders lie largely outside the repertoire of teachers whose brief pedagogical preparation provided little more than an overview."[33] Meanwhile, the NRC found that "[p]rofessional development of teachers, teachers aides, and professional or volunteer tutors [was] integral to each program—there is an important relationship between the skill of the teacher and the response of the children to early intervention. Effective intervention programs pay close attention to the preparation and supervision of the teachers or tutors."[34]

At the twentieth anniversary of *A Nation at Risk,* that is a recurring theme, not only in discussions about curriculum reform but also about reform in general. Improving the work of teachers must be central; that is, proposed solutions should be practice based and not simply responses to ideological braying in the public arena. Although it often takes partisan firebrands to get the attention of policymakers, the ideas and prescriptions of ideologues are usually too simplistic and unbending to be helpful in shaping effective reform practices. They make good conversation starters but poor plans for action. The curriculum battles of the post–*Nation at Risk* period have long since demonstrated their limits.

Only a sober assessment of what works on the classroom level—which requires a complex, intensive, and ongoing discussion of the work schools and teachers do, both generally and in very specific, on-the-scene ways—can bring about the kinds of improvements and reforms the writers of *A Nation at Risk* hoped to inspire with their rhetorical alarms. In its 1998 report calling for an end to the reading wars, the NRC committee noted, "The knowledge base is now large enough that the controversies that have dominated discussions of reading development and reading instruction have given way to a widely honored *pax lectura,* the conditions of which include a shared focus on the needs and rights of all children to learn to read."[35] One can only hope that such a peace will pervade future discussions about how best to educate children, giving sobriety and reason the upper hand over the ideological excesses that Jeanne Chall laid bare in 1999. To do so, we, like Chall, must be willing to go fearlessly wherever the evidence leads.

NOTES

1. The Askwith Education Forum "Beyond the Reading Wars" was held at the Harvard Graduate School of Education on 8 April 1999.
2. The quotation is attributed to E. D. Hirsch, Jr., in "A Tribute to Jeanne Chall," *American Educator 25,* no. 1 (Spring 2001), 16.
3. See "Introduction to the Third Edition" in Jeanne S. Chall, *Learning to Read: The Great Debate,* 3rd ed. (New York: Harcourt Brace, 1996).
4. Ibid.
5. See E. D. Hirsch's critique of the Romantic underpinnings of progressivism in *The Schools We Need and Why We Don't Have Them* (New York: Doubleday, 1996).
6. See an interview with Lemann in "The President's Big Test," *Frontline,* 28 March 2002. Online at www.pbs.org/wgbh/pages/frontline/shows/schools/nochild/lemann.html
7. Honig is quoted in Nicholas Lemann, "The Reading Wars," *Atlantic Monthly* 280, no. 5 (November 1997), 128–134.
8. National Research Council, *Everybody Counts* (Washington, DC: Author, 1989).
9. Romesh Ratnesar et al., "This Is Math? Suddenly, Math Becomes Fun and Games," *Time,* 25 August 1997, pp. 66–67.
10. See Andreae Downs, "Will New Standards Quiet the Math Wars?" *Harvard Education Letter* 16, no. 6 (November/December 2000), 4–6.
11. Quoted in Barbara Matson, "Whole Language or Phonics? Teachers and Researchers Find the Middle Ground Most Fertile," *Harvard Education Letter* 12, no. 2 (March/April 1996), 3.
12. Diane Ravitch provides an overview of the debate in "It Is Time to Stop the War" in Tom Loveless, ed., *The Great Curriculum Debate* (Washington, DC: Brookings Institution Press, 2001).
13. See G. Reid Lyon's statement to the U.S. Senate's Committee on Labor and Human Resources on reading and literacy initiatives, 28 April 1998. Lyon is chief of the Child Development and Behavior for the National Institute of Child Health and Human Development.
14. See Ellen H. Brinkley, "What's Religion Got to Do with Attacks on Whole Language?" in Kenneth S. Goodman, ed., *In Defense of Good Teaching* (Portland, ME: Stenhouse, 1998).
15. California Department of Education, "Teaching Reading: A Balanced, Comprehensive Approach to Teaching Reading in Prekindergarten through Grade Three," Program Advisory (Sacramento: Author, 1996).
16. Chall, *Learning to Read,* pp. 288–300.
17. Matson, "Whole Language or Phonics?"
18. See Catherine E. Snow, "Preventing Reading Difficulties in Young Children: Precursors and Fallout" in Tom Loveless, ed., *The Great Curriculum Debate,* pp. 229–246.

19. Preface to the third edition of Catherine E. Snow, M. Susan Burns, and Peg Griffin, *Preventing Reading Difficulties in Young Children* (Washington, DC: National Academy Press, 2000). Online at http://www.nap.edu/readingroom/books/prdyc/

20. See David Tyack and William Tobin, "The 'Grammar' of Schooling: Why Has It Been So Hard to Change?" *American Educational Research Journal* 31, no. 3 (Fall 1994), 478.

21. Matson, "Whole Language or Phonics?"

22. David K. Cohen and Heather C. Hill, *Learning Policy. When State Education Reform Works* (New Haven, CT: Yale University Press, 2001), pp. 70–71.

23. Downs, "Will New Standards Quiet the Math Wars?"

24. Cohen and Hill, *Learning Policy,* p. 71.

25. Mark Clayton, "Flaws in the Evaluation Process," *Christian Science Monitor,* 23 May 2000.

26. National Reading Panel, *Teaching Children to Read;* Kathleen Kennedy Manzo, "New Panels to Form to Study Reading Research," *Education Week,* 30 January 2002, p. 5; Kathleen Kennedy Manzo, "Reading Panel Urges Phonies for All in K–6," *Education Week,* 19 April 2000, pp. 1, 14;

also of interest is Thomas Newkirk, "Reading and the Limits of Science," *Education Week,* 24 April 2002, p. 39.

27. Richard Rothstein, "Reading Factions Should Make Amends," *New York Times,* 5 September 2001, p. B7.

28. Cohen and Hill, *Learning Policy,* pp. 71–72.

29. See Liping Ma, *Knowing and Teaching Elementary Mathematics* (Mahwah, NJ: Lawrence Erlbaum, 1999), pp. 144–153.

30. Downs, "Will New Standards Quiet the Math Wars?"

31. "Arming New Teachers with Survival Skills," *Harvard Education Letter* 18, no. 5 (September/October 2002), 8.

32. Cohen and Hill, *Learning Policy,* p. 3.

33. John I. Goodlad, "Producing Teachers Who Understand, Care, and Believe," *Education Week,* 5 February 1997, p. 36.

34. Catherine E. Snow, M. Susan Burns, and Peg Griffin, *Preventing Reading Difficulties in Young Children* (Washington, DC: National Academy Press, 1998), p. 273. Online at http://www.nap.edu/readingroom/books/prdyc/

35. Ibid., p. vi.

David T. Gordon is editor of the *Harvard Education Letter* and a former associate editor at *Newsweek*.

QUESTIONS FOR REFLECTION

1. Gordon writes that ideological orthodoxy for setting educational agendas is very limited and inevitably leads to conflict and poorly served students in the classroom. What does he mean by the term "ideological orthodoxy" and how does it lead to conflict and poorly served children? What evidence does he cite to support his claims?

2. Do you think politics belongs in the K–12 curriculum? Should political ideologies determine the content, even the methodology, used to teach students? If so, whose political ideas should be represented? How would you go about ensuring equal representation? Is equal representation even possible or desirable?

3. How should we end what has been labeled "the reading wars"? Is the country too culturally divided for a truce, or is some kind of compromise possible? How would we know if we have ideologically "balanced" the curriculum? What would a balanced curriculum look like?

TestThink

NELSON MAYLONE

ABSTRACT: For all the debate in America over the state of its public schools, those on the political Left and Right agree that the achievement gaps are real. According to Maylone, the skills that standardized tests truly measure may be useful in only one context: taking tests. In this article, Maylone also examines the notion of student testing behaviors, which he calls TestThink, *and questions what students really learn from all these tests.*

For all the fractious debate in America over the state of our public schools, those on the political Left and Right agree that the "achievement gaps" are real. But what do most people mean when they say *achievement gaps*? Gaps in standardized test scores, of course. The gaps consist of the differences between test scores of students of color and those of white students and between scores of poor children and those of their wealthier peers.

Referring to those test score gaps as achievement gaps naturally implies acceptance of the tests as valid measures of student knowledge and skills. But the perceived academic achievement gaps might actually reflect differences in students' abilities (or willingness) to behave in idiosyncratic ways while taking standardized tests—ways which are unconnected to content knowledge or to "general aptitude." I call such student testing behaviors TestThink. In the context of the current "No Child Left Untested" environment, I think it's appropriate to reexamine this notion.

Let's assume that TestThink is real. Is it possible to articulate how a student with well-developed TestThink skills behaves while taking a standardized or other traditional objective test? From my own experience, including years of interviewing students and educators, I believe we can do so.

Perhaps more than anything else, Test-Thinkers are fast. Not only can they spot correct multiple-choice answers, they can do it *quickly.* TestThinkers know they don't generally have time to ponder or to thoughtfully analyze or to thoroughly consider ways in which alternative answer choices might reasonably be considered correct. Furthermore, TestThinkers understand that collaboration with others is out of the question and that the use of external resources and experts is forbidden. After all, standardized tests aren't assessing students' resourcefulness.

TestThinkers are in full command of helpful test-taking techniques that exist independent of knowledge and mastery of skills. They recognize the process of elimination as a good method for increasing their chances of guessing correct multiple-choice answers when they are otherwise clueless (thus generating false-positive test scores). TestThinkers are on the lookout for implausible answers and syntactic clues. They spend time—but not too much!—thinking about which answers the makers of the test might want them to choose.

That's a tough challenge, even for skilled Test-Thinkers. And they clearly meet their match in dubiously worded test questions, where dumb luck rules. What is all but a theme of standardized tests is that the test writers knew what *they* meant but didn't notice that there was at least one other logical way to interpret the question or task.

NOT FUNNY

This is a common phenomenon in everyday conversation. We're always asking others to clarify their statements or their questions. Think of the anxious kindergartner being dropped off for her first day of school. She asks her mother, "When will I be through?" The mother answers, "At lunch-time." "No," the child responds, "I mean, how old will I be when I don't have to go to school any more?"

TestThinkers always simply focus on *what the test-makers want,* even though, without a stretch, more than one of the choices which are offered for a given test question might make sense.

One good way to ensure that the issue of item ambiguity would get a proper public airing would be to have all education policy makers—legislators, in particular—take the tests they're foisting on children. My experience, though, is that elected state and federal officials are loath to undertake such an enterprise. I believe they have an intuitive understanding, developed during their own school days, that the tests aren't fair and their scores might be embarrassingly low.

In the area of mathematics, which is where I spent most of my K–12 teaching career, Test-Thinkers use crystalline, no-nonsense, analytic, strictly linear thinking. They know that a sharp-edged, coldly logical, "adult" model of problem solving is preferred by test writers and scorers (ignoring for a moment the fact that test-makers always *want* some students to do poorly). An attitude of "crack the conundrum" is effective.

FORGET IT

TestThinkers know that peripheral factors that might truly determine the correct answer in real life are to be disregarded. Students whose comments reveal practical thinking are clearly *not* TestThinkers. There's no time for musing. Test-Thinkers speedily distill math problems down to their computational essentials. They know that they must ignore otherwise-important contextual realities.

If asked to round $443 to the nearest hundred, TestThinkers know not to ask if that amount is someone's Internal Revenue Service tax bill, in which case rounding down is ill advised. In fact, they know that they shouldn't be asking any questions at all.

If a test item begins by noting, "Thomas, an eighth-grader, ran the second mile of a three-mile cross-country race in four minutes and 50 seconds," TestThinkers know to discount the fact that a middle-schooler couldn't run a solo mile

that quickly, let alone the second mile of a three-mile run. TestThinkers don't look for real-world constraints; they just *solve the problem*.

If Tania read five books in March, 10 in April, and 15 in May, TestThinkers know that she will surely read 20 in June. No matter that school will be out and that the pizza-party rewards for reading books will have ended. TestThinkers know that trends are always constant.

If a test item asks how many square feet of carpeting one should buy to cover the floor of a room that measures 10 ft. by 11 ft., TestThinkers know to simply multiply to get an answer of 110 sq.-ft., even though carpet rolls are typically 12 ft. wide, meaning that buying only 110 sq.-ft. would leave you with either lots of bare wood floor or unnecessary seams.

For TestThinkers, there is great clarity regarding the high stakes associated with standardized tests, even at early ages. Knowing that scores affect college admission, scholarships, and labels of success or failure, TestThinkers with money (or those with moneyed parents) take advantage of test-preparation courses that can make them even better TestThinkers.

Students blessed with a flair for TestThink have at least a vague awareness that policy makers and—even more important—their parents generally view standardized test scores as reliable indicators of . . . *something*. Intelligence? Accumulated knowledge? Aptitude? Inherent reasoning ability? It depends on whom one asks.

TestThinkers may even discern parents' and legislators' attitudes: "I survived standardized tests, and, by God, it built character. It'll do the same for today's kids!" To quote President Bush on the apparent increase in student test anxiety today, "Too bad."

Society in general and employers in particular are telling educators that we should prepare students to be resourceful and innovative team members. TestThinkers know, however, that they must think "*inside* the box" in order to do well on standardized tests and that problems must be solved alone—collaboration would obviously be cheating.

Let us ignore for the moment the clear test-taking advantages that TestThinkers possess. Are the skills associated with TestThinking useless? I don't think so. Speedy, Mr. Spock-style logical thinking can be an important skill. Computer programmers must think analytically, and airline pilots need to make good decisions instantly (although in both cases informed intuition may be just as important).

Working quickly can sometimes be good, but speed *can* also equal impulsiveness, thoughtlessness, and haste. This raises a nasty question: Are students who do well on standardized tests (i.e., good TestThinkers) less likely to be collaborative, creative adults? Even nastier, might the current pressures on educators and children to produce high standardized test scores be inadvertently promoting *undesirable* social characteristics?

NASTIER STILL

If so, that runs counter to the statements of those who produce and administer the big tests. In my state, these advocates of the tests claim that "competitive scholastic experience" provides students with excellent preparation for the real world that awaits them after high school graduation.

In Michigan, a school's designation of success or failure under new accreditation rules will be based primarily on students' scores on the state test. In other words, schools with high percentages of TestThinkers will do very well. (Give Tom Watkins, state superintendent of public instruction, credit for capping the tests' impact on accreditation at only 67%.)

If that's true, I'm not sure that it's fair. All sorts of questions come to mind. First, if TestThink is real, how many children are skilled at TestThink? Which ones? Is being a TestThinker normal? Is doing well on tests the only thing TestThink is good for? What percentage of children at each stage of development are capable of good TestThinking?

Then, too, TestThinkers may be especially adept at choosing correct responses on selected-response items as opposed to producing them on constructed response items. How is *choosing* the correct answer from a list cognitively different from *producing* an answer from scratch and then having to defend that response?

NO BUZZ

To illustrate the importance of the issue, try to answer this question: Who was the first American to travel into space? Maybe you answered it correctly, maybe you didn't. If you didn't, the odds are that you'll get it right anyway when it's posed in a multiple-choice format: Who was the first American to travel into space? A. Neil Armstrong; B. Buzz Aldrin; C. Alan Shepard; D. Christa McAuliffe.

Let's see. I have no idea who it was, but . . . it can't be Armstrong or Aldrin. I think they were the first guys to land on the moon. And wasn't Christa McAuliffe the teacher on the *Challenger*? Must be Shepard.

Still more questions are lurking in the shadowy world of TestThinking. Are alternative, non-TestThink approaches to demonstrations of knowledge and problem solving legitimate? If so, are standardized tests biased against *non*-TestThinkers who have otherwise mastered the curriculum? Does high socioeconomic status tend to promote good TestThinking?

And more provocatively, we might ask if some subgroups in America intuitively recognize Test-Think as inconsistent with their definitions of healthy ways of thinking. Are the shrillest cynics correct when they claim that standardized testing is more about sorting and maintaining the status quo than it is about legitimate assessment? Are standardized tests closely aligned with white, middle-, and upper-class culture?

I honestly don't know the answers to these questions, but I believe that, now more than ever, it's important for educators, parents, and policy makers to wrestle with them. Maybe Test-Think is a cynical construct. Maybe it's perfectly appropriate to ask kids to don their specialized testing hats at times and to expect them to draw on a narrow (and teachable) set of skills for obtaining high scores.

Still, if we are going to attach immensely high stakes to standardized test scores, shouldn't we be sure that the real subject matter isn't the tests themselves?

Nelson Maylone is assistant professor of Educational Psychology, College of Education, Eastern Michigan University, Ypsilanti, MI.

QUESTIONS FOR REFLECTION

1. What is "TestThink" and is there any value for students to be good at it? Besides school, what are situations in life when being able to take a test well matters? Make a list and compare it with others.
2. What do you think should be the role of tests in the current curriculum? Are there subjects which more easily lend themselves to testing as a measure of competence? In which subjects do tests provide little, if any, value? In which subjects are they quite valuable?
3. Make a list of the advantages and disadvantages of using tests to measure learning. Do the advantages outweigh the disadvantages? Explain.
4. If you where able to abolish all tests, but had to find some other mechanism to measure student learning, what would you use? How would you use it to measure learning? Like tests, what would be the limitations? What would be the advantages? Finally, how would you know if your measurement worked at measuring what students have learned?

You *Can* Teach for Meaning

JAY MCTIGHE
ELLIOTT SEIF
GRANT WIGGINS

ABSTRACT: Is teaching for meaning impractical in the real world of content standards and high-stakes testing? Teachers seem to think so as they devote greater amounts of time to practicing for the test and covering large amounts of facts and figures that hold out a promise of proficiency. The authors debunk two prevailing misconceptions: that covering tested items and test format is the only way to safeguard or raise test scores; and, that breadth of coverage is preferable to a deeper and more focused approach to content.

Teaching is more than covering content, learning is more than merely taking in, and assessment is more than accurate recall. Meaning must be made, and understanding must be earned. Students are more likely to make meaning and gain understanding when they link new information to prior knowledge, relate facts to "big ideas," explore essential questions, and apply their learning in new contexts.

Consider the following classroom scenarios (Tharp, Estrada, & Yamauchi, 2000). A 6th grade teacher asks students to collect data from home on the height and weight of various family members. Students discuss the following questions in groups: How could we represent these data? What is the most effective way? Students decide on specific approaches and share them with the class. A spirited discussion takes place on the best approach.

A 4th grade teacher asks students to explore the Eskimo culture through research and discussion. Using the textbook and multiple resources, the class tackles the following question: What makes Eskimo life similar to and different from your life? Students define and describe ideas about Eskimo life, using a graphic organizer to make connections between concepts and facts. In small groups, they develop a project on an aspect of Eskimo life, conduct research, organize data, and draw conclusions that compare Eskimo life with their own lives. The teacher has shared a rubric identifying the key features of successful project work. She regularly collects samples of student work to provide feedback and offer suggestions for improvement.

These two examples illustrate a curricular and instructional approach that we call *teaching for meaning and understanding*. This approach embodies five key principles:

- Understanding big ideas in content is central to the work of students.
- Students can only find and make meaning when they are asked to inquire, think at high levels, and solve problems.
- Students should be expected to apply knowledge and skills in meaningful tasks within authentic contexts.
- Teachers should regularly use thought-provoking, engaging, and interactive instructional strategies.

- Students need opportunities to revise their assignments using clear examples of successful work, known criteria, and timely feedback.

Teachers who regularly use this approach center their planning on three recurring questions that should be at the heart of any serious education reform: What are the big ideas and core processes that students should come to understand? What will teachers look for as evidence that students truly understand the big ideas and can apply their knowledge and skills in meaningful and effective ways? What teaching strategies will help students make meaning of curriculum content while avoiding the problems of aimless coverage and activity-oriented instruction?

Such an approach to teaching and learning is more apt to engage the learner and yield meaningful, lasting learning than traditional fact-based and procedure-based lecture, recitation, or textbook instruction. Yet when well-intentioned teachers and administrators are asked to put these ideas into practice, it is not uncommon to hear a chorus of *Yes, but's*. The message? Teaching for meaning is fine in the abstract, but such ideas are impractical in the real world of content standards and high-stakes testing. The current focus on state and local content standards, related testing programs, No Child Left Behind, and accountability have strengthened the view that we must use more traditional teaching approaches to produce high levels of achievement.

Ironically, a key lever in the standards-based reform strategy—the use of high-stakes external tests—has unwittingly provided teachers with a rationalization for avoiding or minimizing the need to teach for meaning and in-depth understanding. Teachers are more likely to spend time practicing for the test, covering many facts and procedures and using traditional lecture and recitation methods in the hope that more students will become proficient.

Two key *Yes, but's* interfere with the promise of teaching for meaning: Yes, but . . . we have to teach to the state or national test. Yes, but . . .

we have too much content to cover. Both are misconceptions.

MISCONCEPTION NUMBER 1: WE HAVE TO TEACH TO THE TEST.

Many educators believe that instructing and assessing for understanding are incompatible with state mandates and standardized tests. Although they rarely offer research to support this claim, these educators imply that teachers are stuck teaching to the test against their will. They would teach for meaning, if they could. The implicit assumption is that teachers can only safeguard or raise test scores by covering tested items and practicing the test format. By implication, there is no time for the kind of in-depth and engaging instruction that helps students make meaning and deepens their understanding of big ideas.

We contend that teachers can best raise test scores over the long haul by teaching the key ideas and processes contained in content standards in rich and engaging ways; by collecting evidence of student understanding of that content through robust local assessments rather than one-shot standardized testing; and by using engaging and effective instructional strategies that help students explore core concepts through inquiry and problem solving.

What evidence supports these contentions? A summary of the last 30 years of research on learning and cognition shows that learning for meaning leads to greater retention and use of information and ideas (Bransford, Brown, & Cocking, 2000). One avenue of this research explored the differences between novices and experts in various fields. Psychologists learned that experts have more than just a lot of facts in their heads: They actually *think* differently than novices do. According to the researchers, "expertise requires something else: a well-organized knowledge of concepts, principles, and procedures of inquiry" (p. 239). This finding suggests that students, to become knowledgeable and competent in a field of study, should develop not only a solid foundation of factual knowledge but

also a conceptual framework that facilitates meaningful learning.

Data from the Trends in International Mathematics and Science Study (TIMSS) also challenge the premise that teaching to the test is the best way to achieve higher scores. TIMSS tested the mathematics and science achievement of students in 42 countries at three grade levels (4, 8, and 12). Although the outcomes of TIMSS are well known—U.S. students do not perform as well as students in most other industrialized countries (Martin, Mullis, Gregory, Hoyle, & Shen, 2000)—the results of its less publicized teaching studies offer additional insights. In an exhaustive analysis of mathematics instruction in Japan, Germany, and the United States, Stigler and Hiebert (1999) present striking evidence of the benefits of teaching for meaning and understanding. In Japan, a high-achieving country, mathematics teachers state that their primary aim is to develop conceptual understanding in their students. Compared with teachers in the United States, they cover less ground in terms of discrete topics, skills, or pages in a textbook, but they emphasize problem-based learning in which students derive and explain rules and theorems, thus leading to deeper understanding. A recent TIMSS analysis of data from seven countries indicates that all high-achieving countries use a percentage of their mathematics problems to help students explore concepts and make connections, whereas U.S. teachers tend to emphasize algorithmic plug-in of procedures instead of genuine reasoning and problem solving (Hiebert et al., 2003; Stigler & Hiebert, 2004).

Compatible findings emerged in an ambitious study of 24 restructured schools—eight elementary, eight middle, and eight high schools—in 16 states (Newmann & Associates, 1996). The research showed that students improved their performance in mathematics and social studies and that inequalities among high- and low-performing students diminished when the curriculum included sustained examination of a few important topics rather than superficial coverage of many topics; when teachers framed instruction around challenging and relevant questions;

and when students were required to provide oral and written explanations for their responses.

Two additional studies of factors influencing student achievement were conducted in Chicago Public Schools. Smith, Lee, and Newmann (2001) examined test scores from more than 100,000 students in grades 2–8 and surveys from more than 5,000 teachers in 384 Chicago elementary schools. The study compared teachers who used interactive teaching methods with those who used noninteractive teaching methods. The researchers then looked at subsequent achievement in reading and mathematics.

The researchers described interactive instruction methods as follows:

> Teachers . . . create situations in which students . . . ask questions, develop strategies for solving problems, and communicate with one another. Students are often expected to explain their answers and discuss how they arrived at their conclusions. These teachers usually assess students' mastery of knowledge through discussions, projects, or tests that demand explanation and extended writing. Students work on applications or interpretations of the material to develop new or deeper understandings of a given topic. Such assignments may take several days to complete. Students in interactive classrooms are often encouraged to choose the questions or topics they wish to study within an instructional unit designed by the teacher. Different students may be working on different tasks during the same class period. (p. 12)

The study found clear and consistent correlations between interactive teaching methods and higher levels of learning and achievement.

In a related study (Newmann, Bryk, & Nagaoka, 2001), researchers in Chicago systematically collected and analyzed classroom writing and mathematics assignments given in grades 3, 6, and 8 by randomly selected schools and control schools for a three-year period. Researchers rated assignments according to the degree to which the work required authentic intellectual activity, which the researchers defined as "construction of knowledge, through the use of disciplined inquiry, to produce discourse, products, or performances that have value beyond school"

(pp. 14–15). The study concluded that students who received assignments requiring more challenging intellectual work also achieved greater-than-average gains on the Iowa Tests of Basic Skills in reading and mathematics and demonstrated higher performance in reading, mathematics, and writing on the Illinois Goals Assessment Program.

MISCONCEPTION NUMBER 2: WE HAVE TOO MUCH CONTENT TO COVER.

Teachers from kindergarten to graduate school wrestle with the realities of the information age and the knowledge explosion: There is simply too much information to cover. In theory, the standards movement promised a solution to the problem of information overload by identifying curricular priorities. Content standards were intended to specify what is most important for students to know and be able to do, thus providing a much-needed focus and set of priorities for curriculum, instruction, and assessment. In practice, however, content standards committees at the national, state, and district levels often worked in isolation to produce overly ambitious lists of "essentials" for their disciplines. Rather than streamlining the curriculum, the plethora of standards added to the coverage problem, especially at the elementary level, where teachers must teach standards and benchmarks in multiple subjects (Marzano & Kendall, 1998). The matter is further complicated by teachers' propensity to focus on overloaded textbooks as the primary resource for addressing their obligations to the content standards. U.S. textbook publishers try to cover the waterfront to appease state textbook adoption committees, national subject-area organizations, and various special-interest groups. Project 2061's study of mathematics and science textbooks (Kesidou & Roseman, 2002; Kulm, 1999) found few commercial texts that were not "a mile wide and an inch deep."

Teachers confronted with thick textbooks and long lists of content standards may understandably come to the erroneous conclusion that they must cover huge amounts of content. They feel that "if it is in my book, it has to be taught." The perceived need to "cover" is typically based on two implicit assumptions that we think are unfounded. The first assumption is that if a teacher covers specific material—that is, talks about it and assigns some work—students will adequately learn it for tests. The second is that teachers should typically address standards one at a time in lesson planning.

We know of no research that supports the idea that a coverage mode of instruction increases achievement on external tests. In fact, current research suggests that "uncoverage"—focusing on fewer topics and core understandings—is more likely to increase student achievement. The TIMSS research that demonstrated lower achievement scores for U.S. students found that U.S. mathematics and science curriculums were unfocused and included too many topics (Schmidt, McKnight, & Raizen, 1997). In contrast, high-achieving countries offered fewer topics at each level, coupled with more coherent and focused content. This concentrated focus enabled teachers and students to gradually build more complex understandings in mathematics, to delve deeply into subject matter, and to attain higher levels of achievement (Schmidt, 2004; Schmidt, Houang, & Cogan, 2002).

Recent studies on mathematics reform curriculums described by Senk and Thompson (2003) also support using an "uncoverage" approach to improve student achievement. All the mathematics reform curriculums that Senk and Thompson studied were designed to help students understand fundamental mathematical concepts and ideas. Longitudinal data from middle schools show that students using understanding-based mathematics curriculums demonstrated superior performance in both nonroutine problem solving and mathematical skills. Other studies on high school mathematics reform programs showed that students in these programs developed additional skills and understandings while not falling behind on traditional content.

The second misconception—that content standards and benchmarks should be addressed one at a time through targeted lessons—is often reinforced by state and national standardized tests that typically sample the standards and benchmarks one at a time through decontextualized items. Thus, the presentation of both tests and standards documents often misleadingly suggests that teachers should teach to standards one bit at a time. From this point of view, teachers certainly do not have enough time to address all standards.

We suggest clustering discrete standards under an umbrella of big ideas. This approach renders teaching more efficient while applying a principle of effective learning derived from research. Bransford and colleagues suggest that

> Experts' knowledge is not simply a list of facts and formulas that are relevant to the domain; instead, their knowledge is organized around core concepts or "big ideas" that guide their thinking about the domain. (2000, p. 24)

Similarly, the use of complex performance assessments enables students to apply facts, concepts, and skills contained in multiple standards in a more meaningful way while enabling educators to assess for true understanding, not just for recall or recognition.

IMPLICATIONS

Teaching for meaning and understanding leads to more lasting and significant student learning. Although we have made a strong case against two widely held objections to this approach, we realize that educators must test, debate, and explore these claims in their respective settings.

We therefore encourage you to conduct ongoing action research at the school and district levels that compares the kind of curriculum, assessment, and instruction described here with teaching that focuses on covering content or practicing for standardized accountability tests. Are students more engaged when you frame content in provocative essential questions? Do students show increased understanding when they have some choice in the manner in which they demonstrate their knowledge? Is performance on traditional assessments compromised when learners have the opportunity to apply their knowledge in authentic situations? Do inquiry-based and problem-based instruction energize teachers?

Let the results speak for themselves. We hope that by "uncovering" some of these unfounded claims, we will encourage educators and district leaders to take a more proactive stance and focus on what they *can* do to improve learning in today's standards based world.

REFERENCES

Bransford, J., Brown, A., & Cocking, R. (Eds.). (2000). *How people learn: Brain, mind, experience, and school.* Washington, DC: National Research Council.

Hiebert, J., Gallimore, R., Garnier, H., Givvin, K. B., Hollingsworth, H., Jacobs, J., et al. (2003). *Teaching mathematics in seven countries: Results from the TIMSS 1999 video study* (NCES 2003–013). Washington, DC: U.S. Department of Education.

Kesidou, S., & Roseman, J. E. (2002). How well do middle school science programs measure up? *Journal of Research in Science Teaching, 39*(6), 522–549.

Kulm, G. (1999). Evaluating mathematics textbooks. *Basic Education, 43*(9), 6–8.

Martin, M., Mullis, I., Gregory, K., Hoyle, C., & Shen, C. (2000). *Effective schools in science and mathematics: IEA's Third International Mathematics and Science Study.* Boston: International Study Center, Lynch School of Education, Boston College.

Marzano, R. J., & Kendell, J. S. (1998). *Awash in a sea of standards.* Aurora, CO: Mid-continent Research for Education and Learning.

Newmann, F., & Associates. (1996). *Authentic achievement: Restructuring schools for intellectual quality.* San Francisco: Jossey-Bass.

Newmann, F., Bryk, A., & Nagaoka, J. (2001). *Authentic intellectual work and standardized tests: Conflict or coexistence?* Chicago: Consortium on Chicago School Research.

Schmidt, W. (2004). A vision for mathematics. *Educational Leadership, 61*(5), 6–11.

Schmidt, W., Houang, R., & Cogan, L. (2002). A coherent curriculum: The case for mathematics. *American Educator, 26*(2), 10–26, 47–48.

Schmidt, W., McKnight, C., & Raizen, S. (1997). *A splintered vision: An investigation of U.S. science and mathematics education.* Norwell, MA: Kluwer Academic Publishers.

Senk, S., & Thompson, D. (2003). *Standards-based school mathematics curricula: What are they? What do students learn?* Mahwah, NJ: Erlbaum.

Smith, J., Lee, V., & Newmann, F. (2001). *Instruction and achievement in Chicago elementary schools.* Chicago: Consortium on Chicago School Research.

Stigler, J., & Hiebert, J. (1999). *The teaching gap.* New York: Free Press.

Stigler, J., & Hiebert, J. (2004). Improving mathematics teaching. *Educational Leadership, 61*(5), 12–16.

Tharp, R., Estrada, S., & Yamauchi, L. (2000). *Teaching transformed: Achieving excellence, fairness, inclusion, and harmony.* Boulder, CO: Westview Press.

Jay McTighe and *Grant Wiggins* are coauthors of *Understanding by Design* (Association for Supervision and Curriculum Development [ASCD], 1998) and *The Understanding by Design Handbook* (ASCD, 1999). *Elliott Seif* is a member of the ASCD Understanding by Design cadre.

QUESTIONS FOR REFLECTION

1. The authors debunk two common myths regarding testing in this article. What are they? Do you think that the authors' conclusions are accurate?

2. What does it mean to "teach for meaning" and do you know anyone who *wouldn't* want to teach for meaning? Given that, what do the authors mean by the phrase?

3. How does the notion of action research factor into the major themes covered by the authors? What is action research and how would you go about using it in your own classroom to measure whether or not you have successfully taught the subject material?

TEACHERS' VOICES—
Putting Theory Into Practice

Ideals vs. Reality in the Classroom

CAROL LUPTON

ABSTRACT: *Lupton describes how the ideals of her pre-service teacher preparation program were given a "reality check" when she found herself working in a* real *school with* real *kids. Ultimately, she asks how teachers can engage children when there are so many competing distractions for their attention. She concludes that taking pleasure in the little accomplishments her students make tells her she is reaching them.*

Years ago, as a student at Mary Washington College, I was assigned to write my philosophy of teaching as an exit paper in a class called Foundations of Teaching. I not only wrote it, I believed it. I would be a phenomenal teacher, a leader of students engaged in a lifelong journey in our quest for knowledge. I would guide my students as they searched for deeper meanings. I would encourage them to appreciate insights that increased self-awareness. I would applaud them when they recognized universal truths about mankind. My students would accomplish all of this simply by learning to read and write. I would do the rest. I would be the inspiration, I would be the motivation, I would be Everything for Everybody. I would be *it*.

I smile now when I reminisce about my idealistic theorizing. What was I thinking?! My imaginary classroom was obviously occupied by humanoids from an unknown planet. I had left out the most important factor of all—Today's Kids.

I entered this profession armed with a philosophy that I thought was "profound." Unfortunately, my college didn't provide a course called introduction to Middle School Mentality 101: "Hold on to your hats and prepare for one wild ride." I used to work at a middle school that had a 53 percent minority population, an irony when you think about it. Our majority was called "the

minority." Thirty-four percent of our 1200 students received free or reduced lunch. That's a polite way of saying one-third of our students lived below poverty level. Our mobility rate was 30.4 percent. They came, they went. Sometimes they left because of heartbreaking circumstances. Those were the times when they cried, and so did I. In addition to this recitation of statistics, let me share some of the reality stories from my students' lives—weapons charges, drug violations, Social Services interventions, run-ins with the police, teen pregnancy. You name it, we had it.

Once I became a full-time teacher, I had to reexamine my philosophy. It was a little "unrealistic"—not to mention it focused strictly on me, me, me. Remember? "All my students had to do was learn to read and write. I would do the rest." Now educational research indicates that there are multiple basic learning styles. As a result, today's educators are encouraged to provide students with a variety of teaching experiences—linguistic, logical-mathematical, musical, spatial, bodily kinesthetic, interpersonal, and intrapersonal. This plan increases opportunities for success for all students. Easy to say, hard to do. Teachers must be armed with an arsenal of Attention-Grabbing-Lesson-Plans if they intend to survive. Today's students are not easily impressed. I know *mine* aren't. For example, try pulling out workbooks to do reinforcement exercises. You'll hear students protest loudly, "Busy work!" They expect stimulation. New gimmicks are required to maintain their interest, every day.

The educator's litany of expectations goes something like this, "Be creative, provide variety, cover the curriculum, maintain discipline, and don't forget, students must master reading and writing in the process." Therein lies the rub. How do we engage their interest long enough for them to attain the skills we teach? I grapple with this question every day.

We live in a symbol-based society. People must be able to read and write to attain their full potential in today's job market. When I tell my students this, they respond, "Says who? You?" But look at the facts, I tell them: From first grade through the remainder of school, classes are taught using textbooks. The "I-hate-to-read" student is an unsuccessful student. Will this unsuccessful student all of a sudden become a successful adult? I don't think so. My students love to point out the exceptions, but I believe they accept the logic in my argument.

I truly believe students must participate actively as players, not spectators, in the educational process in order to succeed. However, before I get too carried away with theory, it's time for a reality check. Wouldn't it be grand if a lofty philosophy could accomplish so much? Unfortunately, I work in the real world. Come with me and take a peek into my classroom on a typical day: Do you see the student who twists and turns like a pretzel and absolutely cannot sit still? How about the ones who come late and leave early? Then there are the few who never open their books. . . . if they bring a book at all, or a pencil, or paper. Listen to those pleas for one-on-one attention that are too numerous to count. My classes as a whole are never entirely quiet. I always know if I am holding their attention. The minute interest starts to wane, they let me know (with brutal blows to my ego at times). Demanding too rigid an environment frustrates them. However, certain ground rules must be maintained. For example, I draw the line at comments such as: "This story sucks" "The main character must be LD"

"This is boring" "You're boring" "I'm bored" or any variety on the "too bored for words" theme.

Remember, in today's world we teachers are in constant competition with the world of entertainment. Our students have access to TVs, computers, compact disc players and the list goes on and on. They have zero tolerance for boredom. All they need to do is press a button and change the channel. It's not that easy for students to change *me*. However, I do believe that teaching requires the personality of an entertainer to even attempt to compete. The teacher must be the producer, writer and star of the production each and every day.

Recently, I felt brave enough to ask my students for their evaluation of my teaching techniques this school year. We started with something relatively safe, I thought. I asked them for their definition of reading. The answers included "awesome." Listen to this one: "Books make a path for me. When I'm feeling down and alone, I pick up my book and read. Then my real world disappears and my book takes me on journeys and wild adventures. My book is my world, it's my friend." Wow, right? Remarkable is more like it. A student who spent last summer in a juvenile detention center wrote that response. Here's another one: "I like when words leap out and play basketball with my mind." I was so impressed! Maybe I am doing something right. Maybe I don't have to give up on my cerebral philosophy after all. Of course, not all the responses were complimentary. I got the flip side too. For example, one of my students wrote, "Reading is like putting me in jail and not giving me food." Oh well, I consoled myself—he did use a simile. And then, my nemesis this year, the dreaded "boring" word: "I only read for an assignment or if I am bored and there is absolutely positively with no shadow of a doubt *nothing* to do." But, I remind myself, this comment came from a student who would have written one word (boring) at the beginning of the year. He is now up to 24 words to tell me the same thing. I see growth in this response. Have you ever noticed that teachers are eternal optimists? We have to be.

Otherwise, we couldn't keep coming back day after day.

Actually, I haven't given up my idealistic philosophy about teaching. I am a leader of students engaged in a lifelong journey in our quest for knowledge. There are days when I trudge rather than cavort, as I would have liked. There are days when I lose sight of the path and I have to rely on my students to lead the way. I am battle weary I admit, but I still have the energy to keep repeating the message, "Learn to read; learn to write. Education is the key to success." My philosophy may be tattered, but it's still intact. It's just undergoing the revision process at this time.

Carol Lupton is a seventh-grade language arts teacher at E. H. Marsteller Middle School in Manassas, VA.

QUESTIONS FOR REFLECTION

1. What were the author's unrealistic expectations of teaching when she was in her pre-service program? Do you think this kind of idealism is common amongst soon-to-be teachers?
2. What was the most sobering part of Lupton's "reality check" when she finally got out into the "real world" of teaching? What was Lupton dealing with on a day-to-day basis that her philosophy of teaching statement did not address?
3. Do you think many beginning teachers go through a kind of "reality check" when they begin teaching on their own? How do you think they respond to the experience? How might you expect yourself to respond?

LEARNING ACTIVITIES

Critical Thinking

1. Reflect on your K–12 school experiences. To what extent did you practice self-assessment of your own learning? What effect(s) did this have on your motivation to succeed?
2. How much emphasis do you think teachers should place on using alternative assessments in the classroom?
3. What are the advantages of peer assessment? Disadvantages? To what extent do you plan to use peer assessment in your classroom?

Application Activities

1. In the area and at the level with which you are most familiar, examine a set of curriculum materials (a textbook, curriculum guide, etc.) to determine how student learning is assessed. Based on the information presented in this chapter,

what suggestions do you have for how the assessment of student learning might be improved?

2.   Design a workshop for teachers at the level and in the subject area with which you are most familiar. The aim of the workshop should be to expand teachers' repertoire of knowledge and skills related to assessing student learning.

Field Experiences

1.   Interview one or more teachers to find out how they assess students' learning. To what extent do they use the alternative forms of assessment discussed in this chapter?

2.   Interview a group of students in the subject area and at the grade level you teach (or plan to teach) to find out how they assess their own learning. What are the effects of self-assessment on their motivation to succeed?

Internet Activities

1.   Survey the Internet to begin locating and creating bookmarks or favorites for web sites and teacher discussion groups that focus on different approaches to assessing student learning.

2.   Visit the home pages of three or more of the following research publications on the Internet. These journals frequently have articles that focus on the effectiveness of different teaching methods. Read an article that focuses on a teaching method of interest to you. What does the article say about the effectiveness of that method? What are the implications for the methods you use (or will use) as a teacher?

American Educational Research Journal   *Cognition and Instruction*
Contemporary Educational Psychology   *Educational Psychologist*
Educational Psychology Review   *Educational Researcher*
Journal of Educational Psychology   *Review of Research in Education*
Journal of Teaching and Teacher Education *Review of Educational Research*

CHAPTER **7**

Early Childhood and Elementary Curricula

FOCUS QUESTIONS

1. Why should curriculum planners be familiar with educational programs at levels other than the one at which they work?
2. How can preschool and elementary-level education contribute to the long-range growth and development of students?
3. In light of the three curriculum bases, and other relevant curriculum criteria, what are several goals for childhood educational programs?

In keeping with the definition of *curriculum* presented in Chapter 1, the chapters in Part III of this book focus on *programs of education* that occur not only in schools, but in community agencies, businesses, or other settings where education is provided. The chapters are organized, however, according to the institutional, grade-level structure of education in the United States. For the purposes of this chapter, *education for children* refers to early childhood programs for children between the ages of three and five, and elementary-level programs for children between the ages of six and eleven or twelve. Chapter 8, "Middle-Level Curricula," discusses junior high and middle-level education programs; Chapter 9, "High School Curricula," discusses secondary-level programs; and Chapter 10, "Post-Secondary Curricula," discusses post-secondary programs.

To help you understand some of the "real world" challenges associated with curriculum planning at each level, the chapters in Part III of this book, like those in Parts

I and II, include a *Teachers' Voices* section that presents first-person, classroom-based accounts of teachers' experiences with curriculum planning. In addition, each chapter includes a Case Study in Curriculum Implementation designed to illustrate some of the complexities of providing leadership for curriculum implementation at the institutional or system-wide level.

Curriculum planners and teachers should be acquainted with educational programs at all levels, regardless of the level at which they work. For instance, you should know about goals and trends in childhood education even if your primary interest is at another level. Familiarity with your students' prior educational experiences, or those they will have in the future, will better equip you to meet their needs in the present. Knowledge of educational programs at other levels will also enable you to address important curriculum criteria such as continuity in learning, balance in the curriculum, and provision for individual differences.

ELEMENTARY-LEVEL PROGRAMS

Graded elementary schools as we know them today were established in the nineteenth century when educators had little knowledge of the nature and extent of individual differences or of the stages of human development. Prior to the nineteenth century, elementary-level education was primarily for boys from the middle and upper classes; however, boys from the lower classes and girls were often taught basic literacy skills so they could read the Bible and recite religious catechisms.

Elementary schools were developed in conformity with the then prevalent ideas of child development and education. For the most part, it was believed that individual differences in education were undesirable and that the government had an obligation to educate citizens in the new republic. Horace Mann (1796–1859), Massachusetts senator and the first secretary of a state board of education, championed the *common school movement* which led to the free-public, locally controlled elementary schools of today. Mann was a passionate advocate of a system of universal free schools for all children—as he wrote in one of his *Annual Reports on Education*:

> It [a system of free common schools] knows no distinction of rich and poor, of bond and free, or between those, who, in the imperfect light of this world, are seeking, through different avenues, to reach the gate of heaven. Without money and without price, it throws open its doors, and spreads the table of its bounty, for all the children of the State. (Mann, 1968, p. 754)

Today's elementary school typically consists of self-contained classrooms in which one teacher teaches all or nearly all subjects to a group of about twenty-five children. The curriculum is often integrated, with one activity and subject area flowing into another. Teacher and students usually spend most of the day in the same classroom, with students often going to other rooms for instruction in art, music, and physical education. Individual students may also attend special classes for remedial or enriched instruction, speech therapy, choir, and band.

Some elementary schools are organized around team teaching arrangements, in which two teachers are responsible for two groups of students. One teacher might present lessons in mathematics, science, and health, while another teaches reading, language arts, and history. A variation on this arrangement is for teacher responsibilities to be made according to students' ability levels. For example, one teacher might teach reading to lower-ability students and all remaining subjects to middle- and higher-ability students; while the other teaches reading to middle- and higher-ability students and all remaining subjects to lower-ability students.

The Importance of Elementary-Level Programs

"The early years are transcendentally the most important, and if this nation wishes ultimately to achieve excellence, we will give greater priority and attention to the early years and start affirming elementary teachers instead of college professors as the centerpiece of learning." This statement by the late Ernest L. Boyer, President of the Carnegie Foundation for the Advancement of Teaching, reminds us that the experiences children have in elementary school provide the foundation upon which their education through adulthood is built. Clearly, the elementary school has an intense influence on children; the year the child spends in the first grade is one-sixth of his or her entire life to that point. Therefore, the lack of adequate provision for individual differences in the elementary-level curriculum can result in intense feelings of failure and rejection for some children. Failure to acquire sufficient knowledge and skills at the elementary level can exact a high price at other levels where the resulting deficiencies are very difficult to overcome.

Social changes are placing enormous new pressures on the elementary school. All of the social forces discussed in Chapter 2 are having a major impact on education for children. The title of Christopher Brown's article in this chapter reflects this pressure: "Can Kids Still Play in School? Defining and Defending Early Childhood Education in the Context of Never-ending Reform." In addition, a major challenge for elementary schools in the twenty-first century is to establish meaningful contact with children from diverse backgrounds. The scope of this challenge is captured well in the following excerpt from Ernest Boyer's last book, *The Basic School: A Community for Learning*:

> Last fall, more than three million kindergarten children enrolled in over fifty thousand public and private schools from Bangor, Maine, to the islands of Hawaii. Most of these young students arrived at school anxious, but also eager. Some were cheerful, others troubled. Some skipped and ran, others could not walk. This new generation of students came from countless neighborhoods, from a great diversity of cultures, speaking more languages than most of us could name. And the challenge we now face is to ensure that every child will become a confident, resourceful learner. (Boyer, 1995, p. 3)

Provision for individual differences, and flexibility and continuity in learning, are thus curriculum criteria of major significance.

EARLY CHILDHOOD PROGRAMS

During the last few decades, early childhood programs have received increasing attention and support, and the thrust toward education at this level will continue to be a significant educational trend in the future. United States Census Bureau data, for example, revealed that 65 percent of all five-year-olds attended kindergarten in 1965; by 1980, this figure had risen to almost 96 percent; and in 2004, virtually all five-year-olds attended (National Center for Education Statistics, 2004). The preprimary enrollment rates for three- and four-year-olds have also continued to rise steadily. In 1991, 31 percent of three-year-olds and 52 percent of four-year-olds were enrolled in preprimary educational programs, including Head Start, nursery school, and prekindergarten; by 1996, these percentages had risen to 37 percent and 90 percent, respectively (National Center for Education Statistics, 1999a). In 1982, about 3.2 million children attended kindergarten; by 2007, it is estimated that almost 4 million children will attend (National Center for Education Statistics, 2004).

Educational programs for preschool-age children are provided by public and private schools, churches, and for-profit and not-for-profit day care centers; in addition, a growing number of preschool educational programs are being offered to employees in business and industry. Early childhood education may be a half-day nursery school program organized around play and socialization, or it may be a full-day academic program that focuses on teaching reading and math readiness skills to children. The content and organization of early childhood education programs is examined in Lilian G. Katz and Sylvia C. Chard's "The Reggio Emilia Approach" in this chapter. They explain how teachers can add a new dimension to early childhood education by carefully observing and recording, or "documenting," children's learning and progress in a wide variety of media.

Unfortunately, there is no institutionalized system of early childhood education that guarantees preschool experiences for all children, and resources to support preschool education programs have been inconsistent. Chapter 1 programs such as Head Start, Follow Through, and Success for All have continually been in jeopardy of being phased out and have never served all eligible students. It has been estimated that Head Start and similar programs serve fewer than half of the nation's three- and four-year-olds living in poverty (Elam, Rose, & Gallup, 1992). While some research studies concluded that the benefits of Head Start tend to disappear as children move through elementary school, others concluded that the program was effective and provided a $3 return for every dollar invested (Elam, Rose, & Gallup, 1993, p. 143).

Throughout the country, the number of prekindergarten and full-day kindergarten programs is increasing, mainly as a result of studies confirming the value of early childhood education, especially for "disadvantaged" children (Karweit, 1993, 1987; McKey et al., 1985; Nieman & Gastright, 1981). A few states—Pennsylvania, Alabama, and Virginia—have modified their certification policies to include a birth through third-grade certificate, and some states are seeking to create formal public school programs for four-year-olds.

The growth of early childhood education is also due to theories of human development and learning that emphasize the need for early stimulation and encouragement of curiosity in infants and young children if their intellectual potential is to be developed. Since research indicates that much of a child's intellectual development has taken place by the age of six (Woolfolk, 2005; Slavin, 2003), instruction at the preschool level helps to increase a child's interest in learning at a critical period in his or her development. Two of the most successful early childhood education programs are the federally funded Head Start program and Follow Through.

Head Start

Since 1965, Head Start has served almost 16 million three- to five-year-old children from low-income families. Head Start services, many of which are delivered by parents and volunteers, focus on education, socioemotional development, physical and mental health, and nutrition. In 2003, $6.6 billion was allocated to Head Start, and almost 909,600 children were enrolled in 47,000 Head Start Classrooms (Administration for Children and Families, 2004).

The educational component of Head Start provides children with curricular experiences designed to foster their intellectual, social, and emotional growth. In addition, Head Start curricula reflect the community being served, its ethnic and cultural characteristics. Research on the effectiveness of Head Start indicates that participating children show immediate gains in cognitive test scores, socioemotional test scores, and health status (McKey et al., 1985; Love, Meckstroth, & Sprachman, 1997). Over time, however, cognitive and socioemotional gains dissolve, and former Head Start students tend not to score above nonparticipants. Nevertheless, some studies have shown that former Head Start students are more likely to be promoted to the next grade level and less likely to be assigned to special education classes than their peers (McKey et al., 1985).

A unique feature of Head Start is the staff development and training provided by the program. Head Start operates the Child Development Associate (CDA) program that gives professional and nonprofessional employees an opportunity to pursue academic degrees or certification in early childhood education. Almost 80,000 persons held a CDA credential in 1998 (Administration for Children and Families, 1998).

Follow Through

The purpose of Follow Through is to sustain and augment, in kindergarten and the primary grades, the gains children from low-income families make in Head Start and similar preschool programs. Follow Through meets the educational, physical, and psychological needs of children, including supplementary or specialized instruction in regular classrooms. The program's impact was greatest in the 1970s when hundreds of thousands of children were served and the annual budget was more than $55 million; by 1998, funding had fallen to less than $10 million per year. The Follow Through program is a good example of how the curriculum criterion of individual differences can be used to develop appropriate learning experiences for students. By developing a variety of innovative educational programs for children and then evaluating those approaches over time, Follow Through has produced knowledge about programs that best facilitate the growth and development of children (Wang & Ramp, 1987; Wang & Walberg, 1988).

In the past, parents and guardians may have felt that they were to bring their children to the elementary school door and then leave. But evidence from programs such as Head Start and Follow Through indicate that parents can play an important role in the early development of their children. As a result, parents should have a more active role in developing and delivering education programs for young children. One novel way to induct parents and their children into the life of the school was suggested by John I. Goodlad (1984) in *A Place Called School,* one of the more influential educational reform reports to be released in the early 1980s. Goodlad proposed that children enter school during the month of their fourth birthday. The proposed practice would make possible a warm welcome for each child since school could begin with a birthday party. The child would then participate in subsequent birthday parties for children who followed. Needless to say, the challenge of socializing twenty or more beginning students each fall would be greatly minimized, and schooling could take on a highly individualized character. Teachers could become acquainted with just a few new children and their families each month at the time of admission, and the children would enter a stable classroom environment.

GOALS FOR CHILDHOOD EDUCATION

What should be the goals of educational programs for children? Many goals might be suggested—some derived, of course, from the three curriculum bases: social forces, theories of human development, and the nature of learning and learning styles. A list of goals would surely include many of the following:

1. Helping learners develop a sense of trust, autonomy, and initiative
2. Introducing structure and organization without curbing self-expression and creativity (In "Playing Is My Job" in this chapter, Elizabeth Jones reminds us that children's play is an important form of self-expression and creativity as well as "a crucial precursor to the convergent, right-answer thinking required in school.")
3. Developing social skills through large group, small group, and individualized activities (In "Why Is Kindergarten an Endangered Species?" in this chapter, Lina H. Plevyak and Kathy Morris suggest that today's kindergarten programs should place more emphasis on developing children's social skills.)
4. Providing adequate and appropriate physical and health education
5. Teaching the fundamental skills of communication and computation
6. Establishing a desire to learn and an appreciation for education by providing experiences that enhance interest and curiosity
7. Developing interests in many subject areas through exposure to diverse fields of knowledge
8. Developing feelings of self-worth and security by providing opportunities for each child to build on his or her successes

9. Providing many opportunities for children to experience the satisfaction of achievement (In this chapter's *Case Study in Curriculum Implementation* section ["Learning to Read in Kindergarten: Has Curriculum Development Bypassed the Controversies?"], Bruce Joyce, Marilyn Hrycauk, and Emily Calhoun describe a formal reading curriculum developed by district staff members and teachers in the Northern Lights School Division of Alberta that enables students to experience "joy" and "delight" while learning to read)
10. Developing appreciation for the worth and differences of others
11. Developing the processes of conceptualizing, problem solving, self-direction, and creating (In this chapter's *Teachers' Voices* section ["Building a Community in Our Classrooms: The Story of Bat Town, U.S.A."], Andrea McGann Keech describes how her third- and fourth-grade students conceptualized and then created a model community of their own.)
12. Developing a concern for the environment, the local and global communities, the future, and the welfare of others
13. Helping learners to examine and develop moral values.

What additions or changes would you propose for this list of goals? Review William H. Schubert's "Perspectives on Four Curriculum Traditions" in Chapter 1; what goals would an intellectual traditionalist suggest for childhood education programs? Similarly, what goals would a social behaviorist, experientialist, and critical reconstructionist suggest?

REFERENCES

Administration for Children and Families. *Fact Sheet.* Washington, DC: The Administration for Children and Families, 1998.

Boyer, Ernest L. *The Basic School: A Community for Learning.* Princeton, NJ: The Carnegie Foundation for the Advancement of Teaching, 1995.

Elam, Stanley M., Rose, Lowell C., and Gallup, Alex M. "The 25th Annual Phi Delta Kappa Gallup Poll of the Public's Attitudes Toward the Public Schools." *Phi Delta Kappan* (1993, September).

———. "The 24th Annual Phi Delta Kappa Gallup Poll of the Public's Attitudes Toward the Public Schools." *Phi Delta Kappan* (1992, September).

Goodlad, John I. *A Place Called School.* New York: Highstown, 1984.

Karweit, Nancy. "Effective Preschool and Kindergarten Programs for Students at Risk." In Bernard Spodek, ed., *Handbook of Research on the Education of Young Children.* New York: Macmillan, 1993, pp. 385–411.

———. "Full Day or Half Day Kindergarten: Does It Matter?" (Report No. 11). Baltimore, MD: The Johns Hopkins University, Center for Research on Elementary and Middle Schools, 1987.

Love, John M., Mechstroth, Alicia, and Sprachman, Susan. *Measuring the Quality of Program Environments in Head Start and Other Early Childhood Programs: A Review and Recommendations for Future Research: Working Paper Series.* Washington, DC: National Center for Education Statistics, 1997.

Mann, Horace. *Annual Reports on Education.* In Mary Mann, ed., *The Life and Works of Horace Mann,* vol. 3. Boston: Horace B. Fuller, 1968.

McKey, Ruth Hubbell, et al. *The Impact of Head Start on Children, Families, and Communities. Final Report of the Head Start Evaluation, Synthesis and Utilization Project, Executive Summary.* ERIC Documents No. ED 263 984, 1985.

National Center for Education Statistics. *The Condition of Education 2004.* Washington, DC: National Center for Education Statistics, 2004a.

———. *Projection of Education Statistics to 2013.* Washington, DC: National Center for Education Statistics, 2004b.

Nieman, R., and Gastright, Joseph F. "The Long-term Effects of Title I Preschool and All-day Kindergarten," *Phi Delta Kappan 63* (1981, November): 184–185.

Slavin, Robert E. *Educational Psychology: Theory and Practice,* 7th Ed. Boston: Allyn and Bacon, 2003.

Wang, Margaret C., and Ramp, Eugene A. *The National Follow Through Program: Design, Implementation, and Effects.* Philadelphia, PA, 1987.

Wang, Margaret C., and Walberg, Herbert J. *The National Follow Through Program: Lessons from Two Decades of Research Practice in School Improvement.* ERIC Document No. ED 336 191, 1988.

Woolfolk, Anita E. *Educational Psychology,* 9th ed. Boston: Allyn and Bacon, 2005.

The Reggio Emilia Approach

LILIAN G. KATZ
SYLVIA C. CHARD

ABSTRACT: Schools in the Italian city of Reggio Emilia have made documentation of children's classroom experiences a central feature of early childhood education. The Reggio Emilia Approach involves displaying students' work throughout the school and carefully documenting their progress through such means as teachers' comments; observations; photographs; and transcriptions of children's discussions, comments, and explanations. The approach enhances students' learning, takes their ideas and work seriously, allows for continuous planning and evaluation, encourages parent participation, extends teachers' understanding of how children learn, and makes learning visible.

The municipal preprimary schools in the northern Italian city of Reggio Emilia have been attracting worldwide attention for more than a decade (see "Lessons from Reggio Emilia," *Principal*, May 1994). While interest in what is now called the Reggio Emilia Approach is focused on many of its impressive features (Gandini 1993; Katz and Cesarone 1994), perhaps its unique contribution to early childhood education is the documentation of children's experience as a standard classroom practice.

Documentation, in the forms of observation of children and extensive record-keeping, has long been encouraged and practiced in many early childhood programs. However, documentation in Reggio Emilia focuses more intensively on children's experience, memories, thoughts, and ideas during the course of their work. It emphasizes the importance of displaying children's work with great care and attention, both to content and aesthetic qualities.

In Reggio Emilia schools, documentation typically includes samples of a child's work at several different stages of completion; photographs showing work in progress; comments written by the teacher or other adults working with the children; transcriptions of children's discussions, comments, and explanations of intentions about the activity; and comments made by parents. Observations, transcriptions of tape recordings, and photographs of children discussing their work also may be included. Examples of children's work and written reflections on the processes in which they engaged are displayed in classrooms or hallways. The documents reveal how the children planned, carried out, and completed the displayed work.

We believe this type of documentation of children's work and ideas contributes to the quality of an early childhood program in at least six ways.

1. ENHANCED LEARNING

Documentation can contribute to the range and depth of children's learning from their projects and other work. As Malaguzzi (1993) points out, it is through documentation that children "become even more curious, interested, and confident as they contemplate the meaning of what they have achieved." The process of preparing and displaying documentaries of children's efforts and experiences provides a kind of debriefing or revisiting, during which new understandings can be clarified and strengthened.

Observation of children in Reggio Emilia preprimary classes indicate that they also learn from and are stimulated by each other's displayed work. A display documenting the work of a child or group often encourages other children to become involved in a new topic or to adopt a new representational technique. For example, Susan and Leroy conducted a survey on which grocery stores their classmates' families patronized. When

Susan wanted to make a graph of her data, she asked Jeff about a graph he had displayed to demonstrate his earlier survey about the kinds of cereal their classmates ate for breakfast.

2. TAKING CHILDREN'S IDEAS AND WORK SERIOUSLY

Careful and attractive documentary displays can convey to children that their ideas, intentions, and efforts are taken seriously, and that the displays are not intended simply for decoration. For example, an important element in the project approach is preparing documents for display so that classmates working on different aspects of a topic can learn from each other's findings. Taking children's work seriously in this way encourages in them the disposition to approach their work responsibly, with energy and commitment, and to take satisfaction in the processes and results.

3. CONTINUOUS PLANNING AND EVALUATION

One of the most salient features of project work is continuous planning based on progressive evaluations. As children undertake complex tasks—individually or in small groups—over a period of several days or weeks, teachers examine the work each day and discuss with the children their ideas and new options for the following days. Planning decisions can be based on whatever the children have found interesting, puzzling, or challenging.

In one early childhood center where teachers meet to review children's work weekly—and often daily—they plan activities for the following week collaboratively, based in part on their review. Activities are never planned too far in advance, so that new strands of work can emerge and be documented. After the children have left for the day, teachers can reflect on and discuss the work in progress, and consider possible new directions the work might take. They also become more aware of each child's participation and development, which helps teachers maximize chil-

dren's opportunities to represent their ideas in interesting and satisfying ways.

When teachers and children plan together, with openness to each other's ideas, the resulting activity is likely to be undertaken with greater interest and skill than if the child had planned alone. The documentation provides a kind of ongoing planning and evaluation by the adults working with the children.

4. PARENT PARTICIPATION

Documentation makes it possible for parents to become intimately aware of their children's experience in the school. As Malaguzzi (1993) points out, documentation "introduces parents to a quality of knowing that tangibly changes their expectations. They . . . take a new and more inquisitive approach toward the whole school experience. . . ."

Parents' comments on children's work contribute to the value of documentation. As they learn about the work in which their children are engaged, parents may be able to contribute ideas for field experiences, especially when they can offer help in gaining access to a field site or relevant expert. One parent brought in a turkey from her uncle's farm after she learned that the teacher was trying to help children visualize what a live turkey looks like.

The opportunity to examine a project's documentation can also help parents think of ways they might contribute time and energy to their child's classroom, such as listening to children's intentions, helping them find the materials they need, making suggestions, helping children write their ideas, offering assistance in finding and reading books, and measuring or counting things in the context of a project.

5. TEACHER RESEARCH AND AWARENESS

Documentation is an important kind of teacher research, sharpening and focusing teachers' attention on children's plans and learning, and on their own role in children's experiences. As teachers examine children's work and prepare to document it, their understanding of children's development and their insight into children's learning is deepened in ways not likely to occur from simply inspecting test results.

Documentation provides a basis for modifying and adjusting teaching strategies, and a source of ideas for new strategies, while deepening teachers' awareness of each child's progress. On the basis of rich data made available through documentation, teachers are able to make informed decisions about appropriate ways to support each child's development and learning.

The final product of a child's work rarely allows one to appreciate the false starts and persistent efforts entailed. By examining the documented steps that children take during their investigations, teachers and parents can appreciate the uniqueness of each child's construction of experience, and the ways that group efforts contribute to learning.

6. MAKING LEARNING VISIBLE

Of particular relevance to American educators, documentation provides information about children's learning and progress that cannot be demonstrated by the formal standardized tests and checklists we commonly employ. While U.S. teachers often gain important information and insight from their firsthand observations of children, documentation of the children's work in a wide variety of media provides compelling public evidence of the intellectual powers of young children that is not available in any other way.

REFERENCES

Gandini, L. "Educational and Caring Spaces." In *The Hundred Languages of Children: The Reggio Emilia Approach to Early Childhood Education* by Edwards, C.; Gandini, L.; and Forman, G. Norwood, N.J.: Ablex, 1993.

Katz, L. G. *Talks with Teachers of Young Children: A Collection.* Norwood, N.J.: Ablex, 1995. ED 380 232.

Katz, L. G.; Chard, S. C. *Engaging Children's Minds: The Project Approach.* Norwood, N.J.: Ablex, 1989.

Katz, L. G.; Cesarone, B. (eds.). *Reflections on the Reggio Emilia Approach.* Urbana, Ill.: ERIC Clearinghouse on Elementary and Early Childhood Education, 1994. ED 375 986.

Malaguzzi, L. "History, Ideas, and Basic Philosophy." In *The Hundred Languages of Children: The Reggio Emilia Approach to Early Childhood Education* (op. cit.).

Lilian G. Katz is professor of early childhood education at the University of Illinois at Urbana-Champaign and director of the ERIC Clearinghouse on Elementary and Early Childhood Education; *Sylvia C. Chard* is associate professor of early childhood education at the University of Alberta, Canada.

QUESTIONS FOR REFLECTION

1. In the subject area and at the level of greatest interest to you, would careful documentation of students' work à la the Reggio Emilia Approach enhance their learning? How might you implement such an approach?
2. The Reggio Emilia Approach has attracted worldwide attention. What do you think accounts for the effectiveness of the program?
3. In addition to creating documentary displays of students' work, how can teachers indicate that they "take students' ideas and work seriously"?

Playing Is My Job

ELIZABETH JONES

ABSTRACT: The trend to use direct teaching, worksheets, and drill in many kindergartens and some pre-schools may undermine children's competence and self-esteem. According to Erik Erikson and Jean Piaget's developmental theories, becoming a "master player" is a critical learning task for young children. Through play, children begin to shape their identities, acquire language and social skills, and explore the world around them. A "play curriculum" is therefore a developmentally appropriate learning environment for three- to five-year-olds.

During the past few decades, increased awareness of the importance of the preschool years has led to greater public interest and investment in early childhood education. In many programs, however, the developmental theory base for appropriate practice in the education of young children (Bredekamp 1987; Elkind 1986; Kamii 1985) has been neglected in favor of the behaviorist theory that characterizes common practice in elementary education.

A "push-down" of direct teaching, worksheets, and drill is found in many kindergartens and even in preschools. Such programs, designed to give children a head start in school, fail to take into account the active-learning mode in which young children are most competent. Thus, for some children, early schooling may undermine rather than contribute to their competence and self-esteem.

The developmental stage theories of Erik Erikson (1950) and Jean Piaget (Labinowicz 1980), which are basic to early childhood education, emphasize the different tasks to be accomplished at each stage. Infancy and toddlerhood offer the opportunity to learn first to trust and then to separate from one's primary caregiver, and to gain sensory-motor knowledge through active exploration of one's own physical self and the physical world.

Three- to five-year-olds who have mastered these tasks move on to the exercise of initiative, making choices and learning to sustain their play, relationships, and oral language—their modes for developing knowledge about the world. Children in the primary grades are moving into the next stage, in which they practice tasks to meet others' standards, and develop greater understanding of the logical relationship among the concrete objects in their world.

While the stages overlap, mastery of tasks at each stage is the most important preparation for the next stage, rather than practicing the next stage's tasks.

MASTERING PLAY

To become a master player is the height of achievement for children ages three to five. Master players are skilled at representing their experiences symbolically in self-initiated improvisational drama. Sometimes alone, sometimes in collaboration with others, they play out their fantasies and feelings about the events of their daily lives. Through their pretend play, young children consolidate their understanding of the world, their language, and their social skills. The skillful teacher of young children is one who makes such play possible and helps children to keep getting better at it.

Children at play are constructing their individual identities as well as their knowledge of the world. The child is saying, in effect, "This is who I am. This is what I want to do. This is what I need to do it with. I need to keep playing until I'm done."

Play, for young children, is active; the child does what he or she is thinking about, using body language as well as words. Younger children (ages 2 to 5) need props because they are the actors;

older children (ages 4 to 8) increasingly create dramas in miniature by manipulating puppets, blocks, cars, and small animal and people figures.

Children's play is open-ended and builds skills in divergent thinking, a crucial precursor to the convergent, right-answer thinking required in school. The child who has learned, through play, that he or she is a person-who-knows is then ready to adapt to the knowledge of others who know, including teachers.

Becoming a master player is an intermediate stage in the development of representation, a complex sequence that culminates in the child becoming a writer and reader. All human beings, beginning in early childhood, not only have experiences, they *represent* them for purposes of personal reflection and interpersonal communication. Like the life cycle stages, these stages overlap, with the later stages becoming more abstract (see Table 1).

Children invent writing in a process very similar to their invention of talking if they receive comparable response from adults (Ferreiro and Teberosky 1982; Harste *et al.* 1984; Bissex 1980). Talking begins with babbling; writing begins with scribbling. Just as early talkers move from spontaneous babble to conscious imitation of sounds made by mature talkers, so early writers move from spontaneous scribbling to conscious imitation of the print in their environment. The errors made in each case are not random; they reflect the child's systems of knowledge at that point in his or her development.

APPROPRIATE LEARNING ENVIRONMENTS

A developmentally appropriate classroom for three- to five-year-olds has a play curriculum. Children choose their activities during extended time periods, act physically on available materials, and talk to each other. The environment is rich in props for dramatic play, tools for imagemaking, and print. Teachers spend only brief periods talking to the whole group; while children are playing, teachers circulate, respond, mediate, enrich, observe, and plan (Jones and Reynolds 1992).

TABLE 1
The Development of Representation

Body language is the first mode of representation used by infants. As the child reaches for an object, the adult interprets the gesture as communication and responds accordingly.

Talk, which follows not long after, develops in the same way, as the adult interprets random babbling as communicative language, causing the child to babble with increased selectivity.

Play likewise begins as exploration of the physical world. The toddler puts things in and dumps them out, picks up, stacks, and knocks things over. A cup may elicit the beginning of make-believe as the child pretends to drink from it or give a drink to a stuffed toy. But as the child continues to master play, a real cup is unnecessary; a block or imaginary cup is sufficient to sustain play.

Image-making marks a stage in which children first explore and then make representations using markers, crayons, paint, clay, blocks or wood scraps. Scribbles are given names and move toward increasingly recognizable approximations of what they are meant to represent.

Writing evolves when children as young as three identify some of their scribbles as words while playing at drawing signs, making lists, or writing letters.

Reading begins not with decoding, but with the sequence, learned by watching adult readers, of picking up a book, turning it right side up, opening it, turning the pages one by one, and saying remembered words if the book is a familiar one.

Children are ready for the challenges of the primary grades not when they have memorized colors, shapes, and numbers, but when they have mastered play and the dynamics of being a member of a group. A developmentally appropriate classroom for six- to eight-year-olds continues to build on all the skills of representation that children have been practicing since infancy.

Integrated curriculum in the primary grades (Katz and Chard 1989) encourages children to reflect on their meaningful experiences through many different modes of representation. For example, children in a coastal town, who have many reasons to be interested in fish, will gain both in basic skills and general information if they visit a fish market, talk with a visiting fisherman, feed goldfish, build a fishing boat with large blocks, play at working on the boat, read fish stories, sing chanties, and draw, paint, and write their own related experiences.

School should be a place that provides children tools and time to reflect on personal experiences, to understand them, and to communicate about them (Ashton-Warner 1963; Johnson 1987). Children are highly motivated to talk, play, draw, and write about the important people, places, and events in their lives outside school (Graves 1983; Dyson 1989).

From a developmental perspective, children learn to write by writing and to read by reading. "Readiness" activities which break down global tasks into incremental practice are likely to be both irrelevant and confusing to children. Development, both physical and intellectual, proceeds from whole to part, not from part to whole. A babbling infant acquires the inflections of the family's language before breaking them down into words; a three-year-old plays competently at the drama of reading a book long before becoming interested in the words.

Children should come to school with a repertoire of play skills that represent their understanding of the world as they have so far

encountered it. A developmentally appropriate school acknowledges and expands that repertoire while extending children's skills in creating representations of their experience.

REFERENCES

Ashton-Warner, Sylvia. *Teacher.* New York: Simon and Schuster, 1986.

Bissex, Glenda. *GYNS at Work: A Child Learns to Read and Write.* Cambridge, Mass.: Harvard University Press, 1980.

Bredekamp, Sue. *Developmentally Appropriate Practice in Early Childhood Programs Serving Children from Birth through Age 8.* Washington, D.C.: National Association for the Education of Young Children, 1987.

Dyson, Anne Haas. *Multiple Worlds of Child Writers.* New York: Teachers College, 1989.

Elkind, David. "Formal Education and Early Childhood Education: An Essential Difference." *Phi Delta Kappan* 67:9 (May 1986): 631–636.

Erikson, Erik. *Childhood and Society.* New York: Norton, 1950.

Ferreiro, Emilia; and Teberosky, Ana. *Literacy before Schooling.* Exeter, N.H.: Heinemann, 1982.

Graves, Donald. *Writing: Teachers and Children at Work.* Exeter, N.H.: Heinemann, 1983.

Harste, Jerome; Woodward, Virginia; and Burke, Carolyn. *Language Stories and Literature Lessons.* Exeter, N.H.: Heinemann, 1984.

Johnson, Katie. *Doing Words.* Boston: Houghton Mifflin, 1987.

Jones, Elizabeth; and Reynolds, Gretchen. *The Play's the Thing: The Teacher's Role in Children's Play.* New York: Teachers College, 1992.

Kamii, Constance. "Leading Primary Education toward Excellence: Beyond Worksheets and Drill." *Young Children* 40:6 (September 1985): 3–9.

Katz, Lilian G.; and Chard, Sylvia C. *Engaging Children's Minds: The Project Approach.* Norwood, N.J.: Ablex, 1989.

Labinowicz, Ed. *The Piaget Primer.* Menlo Park, CA: Addison-Wesley, 1980.

Elizabeth Jones is a member of the early childhood education faculty at Pacific Oaks College and Children's School, Pasadena, California.

QUESTIONS FOR REFLECTION

1. How should teachers of three- to five-year-olds respond to parents who do not believe that "Children are ready for the challenges of the primary grades not when they have memorized colors, shapes, and numbers, but when they have mastered play and the dynamics of being a member of a group"?
2. In what ways might the concept of *play* be used to enhance curricula at the K–12 and postsecondary levels?
3. Explain the following statement: "Development, both physical and intellectual, proceeds from whole to part, not from part to whole." Does this perspective apply to development after the early childhood years?

Can Kids Still Play in School? Defining and Defending Early Childhood Education in the Context of Never-Ending Reform

CHRISTOPHER BROWN

ABSTRACT: The landscape of early childhood education is changing, but this pressure for reform is not new. Early childhood is a field that has faced many external pressures for change, and in most cases, the field has produced empirically based responses to defend its practices. Yet the current political climate is ignoring much of this work. Instead, policymakers are implementing a "logic of reform" that they believe will improve the education system and increase student performance. How stakeholders in early childhood education respond to these reforms will shape the educational experience for young children for years to come.

Our memories as young students play a powerful role in why we decide to become teachers (e.g., Goldstein & Lake, 2000; Gomez, Walker, & Page, 2000). In many ways, these experiences led us to this point in our careers.

When I discuss teaching in the early childhood years (the years of a child's life from birth through third grade) with the teacher candidates in my early childhood classes, my students immediately bring their own experiences in kindergarten to our discussions. They remember playing with a sand table, working in the dramatic play area, or finding a comfortable spot to read and explore books.

Yet, no matter how many times that I have these conversations with them about their experiences, someone always asks, "Can kids still play and have fun in kindergarten?"

Immediately, they face me with looks of concern—as if my answer will determine whether they might pursue a career in early childhood education. Typically, I respond by stating, "It depends."

It depends on their pedagogical beliefs. It depends on the needs of their students. It depends on the mandated curriculum. It depends on the demands of their principal. It depends on the expectations of their students' families. It depends on so many things.

However, this list of "it depends" has narrowed in the last few years. Where my students plan to teach—the state, the school district, and even the school—may have already made these choices for them. Federal, state, and local policies have begun to determine what is appropriate for students to learn (typically called content standards) and to be able to do (typically called performance standards). Moreover, various stakeholders are now telling teachers how to teach the content standards so that students will achieve the set performance standards.

The landscape of early childhood education is changing, but this pressure for reform is not new. Early childhood is a field that has faced many external pressures for change and, in most cases, the field has produced empirically based responses to defend its practices. Yet, the current political climate is ignoring much of this work. Instead, policymakers are implementing a "logic of reform" that they believe will improve the education system and increase student performance.

CLARIFYING THE FIELD OF EARLY CHILDHOOD EDUCATION

Early childhood education encapsulates a broad range of programs and services for young children from birth to the third grade. Early childhood teachers work in publicly funded and private childcare programs that serve children from birth to age five; publicly funded and private preschool programs that serve children ages 3–5; and publicly funded and private elementary programs that serve children from ages 3 through the third grade. This range of services makes it difficult to explain how particular reforms in early childhood education affect the varied classrooms my students might enter.

Historically, local government and agencies determined what programs were available for young children before they entered elementary school. For example, only three states offered funding for pre-kindergarten (pre-K) programs prior to the 1960s (Mitchell, 2001).

However, in 1965, this changed. At the federal level, the Johnson Administration's "War on Poverty" created two programs that made a seri-

ous commitment to the education of young children: Head Start and the Elementary and Secondary Education Act (ESEA), currently titled the *No Child Left Behind Act* of 2001.[1] The intent of Head Start is to assist families in readying their children for school by providing a range of health, education, and family services (United States Department of Health and Human Services, 1990). Particular titles under ESEA, primarily Title 1, provide schools with funding for additional teachers, teacher training, and literacy programs designed to improve student performance in the early elementary grades. Two things are important to know about these programs. First, the central goal of these programs is to improve student performance. Second, these programs target particular populations of students—students whose families are in the lower socio-economic strata or have limited experience with the English language and students with special needs. States have and continue to assist the federal government's programs through the Departments of Education and Health and Human Services by providing additional funds and services to improve the academic readiness and performance of these populations of children.

While Head Start and other government programs increased the role of early childhood education in the lives of young children, these services only affect a limited set of children and families. This creates a fractured field of programs that do not adhere to one central focus. However, once children enter elementary school,[2] the curriculum and programs offered become more uniform, even for the private programs.

Upon entering elementary school, state or school district content and performance expectations shape children's learning experiences. However, the federal government, through the *No Child Left Behind Act* (NCLB), requires any state receiving funds through this act to put content and performance standards in reading and math in place for all students from the third to eighth grade.[3] Although this requirement for content and performance standards does not include the early grades, many states have them in place (e.g., Virginia, Texas, and Florida). Thus, any early childhood program, including elementary school programs, that receives federal, state, or district funding has to respond to demands put on them by their funding agency.

In contrast, privately funded early childhood programs must only meet licensure requirements. For non-elementary school programs, they must meet program standards, such as teacher-to-student ratios, health and safety regulations, teacher training, etc. Private elementary schools must teach particular areas of content, but do not have to adhere to their state's content and performance standards.

INCREASED FUNDING RESULTS IN INCREASED ACCOUNTABILITY

The concerns my students have over the direction that the recent demands of standards-based accountability reform is taking early childhood education are not new. As soon as the federal government made a serious investment into the lives of young children, controversy arose. Political conversations revolved around issues such as the role of government in "raising" children, which children should be served, which programs should receive funding, and how much funding should the government provide (Berry, 1993; Beatty, 1995). Furthermore, this influx of money created an increased concern over accountability.

Out of these concerns, two primary questions surfaced: (1) were programs such as Head Start effective in preparing students for school; and (2) once in elementary school, were these programs improving student performance? An example of this scrutiny is the Westinghouse Learning House's (1969) evaluation of Head Start. This report suggested that the IQ gains of students who participated in Head Start over their peers who received no intervention services quickly faded, which raised concerns about the effectiveness of these government-funded programs (Vinovskis, 1999; Cuban, 1998). Under-

standing what effects early intervention programs do have on children became a central policy issue. Developing an effective response to this controversy took time. Researchers found that while increases in IQ might not be sustainable, students who participated in specific early childhood programs (e.g., Perry Preschool Project) were more successful academically and socially as they continued through school (e.g., Schweinhart & Weikart, 1980; Ramey, Dorval, & Baker-Ward, 1983).

This scrutiny over program effectiveness in improving student performance and readiness continued through the 1970s and 1980s. During this time, policymakers and school officials placed a premium on students demonstrating a basic competence in academic skills (Linn, 2000). Local government agencies used minimum competency exams to determine whether a student possessed specific basic skills so that he or she could advance to the next grade level or graduate from high school. Such exams caused educators to determine whether students were ready for school by what skills the children possessed. Typically, if students scored poorly on these tests, they had to repeat their grade or participate in an intervention program. While this sounds like a logical policy response, education research has consistently shown that there is no academic benefit for retaining students (Holmes & Matthews, 1984; Labaree, 1984; Shepard & Smith, 1986; Holmes, 1989; Meisels, 1992; Reynolds, 1992; Rumberger, 1995; Reynolds & Temple, 1997; McCoy & Reynolds, 1999; Zill, 1999; Alexander, Entwisle, & Kabbani, 2000; Graue & DiPerna, 2000). In fact, researchers such as Rumberger (1995) found that at the individual level retention is the single most powerful predictor of students dropping out—retained students were four times more likely to drop out of school.

Academic performance and accountability gained further importance with the publication of *A Nation at Risk* (National Commission in Excellence, 1984). This document questioned the ability of America's public schools in readying its students for the workforce. Rather than focus solely on federally funded programs, the report implicated the country's entire system of schooling. This statement of systemic failure shifted the focus of education policy from what schools are to provide their students (termed inputs) to what students were to know, including which classes they must take, when they leave (termed outcomes). This document promoted rigorous academic work rather than minimum competency (Smith & O'Day, 1990; Dougherty & Hall, 1996). The systemic link between economic performance and academic performance by the NCEE increased the demands placed on young children (Hatch & Freeman, 1988a; 1988b; Shepard & Smith, 1988; Shepard, 1994). School districts increased their use of readiness tests to determine whether students were prepared to enter kindergarten or first grade (Shepard & Smith, 1986; Meisels, 1987; Meisels, 1989; Shepard, 1994), and districts escalated their curricular expectations for the early grades (Hatch & Freeman, 1988a; 1988b).

This drive to improve performance led to a narrowing of the early childhood curriculum (Bredekamp, 1997; Hatch & Freeman, 1988a; 1988b; Shepard & Smith, 1988). Policymakers, administrators, and other stakeholders pushed practitioners in early childhood programs and early elementary classrooms to focus their efforts on developing a child's cognitive ability while ignoring the child's physical, social, and emotional needs. The National Association for the Education of Young Children (NAEYC) responded to this pressure for performance through more teacher-directed academic instruction by publishing its guidelines for what it considers developmentally appropriate practices for young children (Bredekamp, 1987).

Bredekamp (1987) and Bredekamp and Copple (1997) based NAEYC's guidelines for developmentally appropriate practice on empirical research that examines how children learn and develop. These documents promote child-centered curricula that emphasize learning opportunities rooted in the children's interest that fosters growth in all of their developmental domains.

Politically, these developmentally appropriate guidelines provided the field with a response to concerns over the use of inappropriate assessments and curriculum with young children. Furthermore, researchers now had a set of standards to compare appropriate and inappropriate environments (Freeman, 1988a, 1988b; Fleege, Charlesworth, Burts, & Hart, 1992; Burts, Hart, Charlesworth, Fleege, Mosley, & Thomasson, 1992; Hart, Burts, Durland, Charlesworth, DeWolf, & Fleege, 1998). For example, Hart et al. (1998) found that students in developmentally inappropriate environments exhibited twice the level of overall stress behaviors than those students in appropriate environments.

Policymakers' concerns over readiness remained an important political issue throughout the 1990s. For example, the first of eight goals from President Clinton's *Goals 2000* legislation stated that all children must enter school ready to learn by the year 2000. However, policymakers and practitioners proceeded with more caution. Work by agencies such as NAEYC (e.g., Bredekamp, 1987; Bredekamp & Rosegrant, 1992; Bredekamp & Rosegrant, 1995), the American Educational Research Association, the American Psychological Association, the National Council on Measurement in Education (1999), and the National Education Panel Goal 1 Early Childhood Assessments Resource Group (Shepard, Kagan, & Wurtz, 1998) informed policymakers and practitioners about the appropriate types of curriculum and assessment measures to use with young children. While inappropriate practices such as retention were not eliminated (Shepard, Taylor, & Kagan, 1996; Hauser, Pager, & Simmons, 2000), this emerging collection of empirical studies provided stakeholders with a clear picture of what are appropriate expectations for young children.

Soon after the passage of Clinton's *Goals 2000* legislation, the federal government reauthorized ESEA, titled the *Improving American School Act* (IASA) of 1994. This policy, as well as a few other incidents (e.g., the publication of the National Council of Teachers of Mathematics' *Curricu-*

lum and Evaluation Standards for School Mathematics in 1989), began the standard-based accountability movement. This legislation emphasized the development of content and performance standards in reading and math for K–12 that received Title 1 funds. States, such as Texas, Maryland, and Virginia, were also putting in place their own standards-based accountability systems. Some of these states, including Texas and Virginia had high-stakes consequences (grade-retention or denying a high school diploma) attached to the performance standards.

An obvious question is what does this have to do with the early childhood years? Research (e.g., Allington & McGill-Franzen, 1992; Roderick, Nagaoka, Bacon, & Eaton, 2000) is beginning to show that what takes place in the older grades affects the educational experiences of students in the early grades. For example, Roderick et al. (2000) found that the improvement in third grade test scores for students in the Chicago public schools might be due to the statistically significant increase in the retention of students in kindergarten through grade two.

Thus, this history of reform in early childhood education exemplifies how my students' concern over the increased demand for readiness and performance is a recurring theme for the field. In fact, many of the issues that field struggled with over the past four decades are reappearing in the current standards-based accountability reforms.

THE CURRENT LANDSCAPE OF EARLY CHILDHOOD EDUCATION

Currently, a divide exists between those early childhood programs that receive public funds and those that do not (Kagan & Scott-Little, 2004). Those programs that do receive any type of public assistance are in the process of adapting their practices to the principles of standards-based accountability (SBA). Typically, my students' practicum experiences are in three- and four-year-old pre-K and kindergarten programs in the public schools. Thus, they gain first-hand experience about how these reforms affect particular early childhood classrooms.

Three primary forms of policy are the cause for these changes. First, elementary schools, which include pre-K and kindergarten students, must implement their state and district content and performance standards. These standards now directly tie themselves to the federal government's implementation of the *No Child Left Behind Act* (2002), the second policy.

NCLB calls for improved student performance in reading, math, and eventually science. By the end of the 2013–2014 school year, 95% of all students in systems of education that receive money from this policy must be performing at the proficiency level on their state's performance standards. Failure to achieve this demand for improved annual yearly performance will result in a series of sanctions for the school, the district, and the state while invoking a series of choice options for the students. Thus, as this demand for annual yearly progress advances towards the 95% requirement, schools, districts, and state departments of education will pay further attention to what types of learning experiences students are having before they enter the third grade (Kauerz & McMaken, 2004)—do they possess the skills the assessments demand that they have? Additionally, NCLB provides additional grants for scientifically based reading instruction through a program titled *Reading First*. These competitive and criteria-based grants provide additional monies to states if they implement those scientifically based reading instruction programs that follow the guidelines put forth in the National Reading Panel's report, *Teaching Children to Read* (2002). Although the validity of this report has been challenged (e.g., Yatvin, 2002), it emphasizes that students in the early grades receive teacher-directed instruction in phonemic awareness, phonics, fluency, vocabulary, and comprehension.

Finally, President George W. Bush's *Good Start, Grow Smart* (GSGS) initiative is the single policy program that specifically targets early childhood programs that exist outside elementary school. The goal of this proposal is to ensure that every child begins "school with an equal chance at achievement so that no child is left behind" (Office of the White House, 2002). Bush's initiative has three components:

- Strengthening Head Start, which includes the development of an accountability system for Head Start and implementing a national training program for Head Start teachers in early literacy teaching techniques
- Partnering with states to improve early childhood education, which includes having states develop early learning standards, that incorporate guidelines on pre-reading and language skills that align with their K–12 standards
- Providing information to teachers, caregivers and parents to assist them in developing partnerships in early education.

Similar to NCLB, the GSGS initiative provides additional grants for improving reading through a program titled, *Early Reading First*. The goal of this funding source is to develop programs based on scientific evidence that prepares young children to enter kindergarten with the necessary language, cognitive, and early reading skills to prevent reading difficulties and ensure school success.

Because of this initiative, 36 states currently have some form of early learning standards (Jacobson, 2004).[4] Furthermore, Head Start has implemented the Head Start Outcomes Framework, which encompasses 100 indicators of what children in Head Start should know and be able to do when they leave the program and enter kindergarten. Furthermore, the program also implemented the Head Start National Reporting System, which uses an assessment tool to measure students' literacy and math skills (see Raver and Zigler (2004) and Meisels and Atkins-Burnett (2004) for a critique of these reforms). Finally, Head Start and publicly funded pre-K programs are competing for and receiving Early Reading First grants to implement reading programs that emphasize oral language, phonological awareness, alphabet recognition, and print awareness.

These initiatives redefine the goal of early childhood education programs that receive federal dollars to be preparing students for academic performance in the early elementary years. Students achieve this success by meeting defined learning standards that incorporate literacy skills and align with a state's K–12 content and performance standards.

The early childhood community supports standards (e.g., National Association for the Education of Young Children & National Association of Early Childhood Specialist in State Departments of Education, 2002) and many stakeholders in the field make the point that standards emphasize content rather than pedagogy (e.g., Griffith & Ruan, 2003; Neuharth-Pritchett, de Atiles, & Park, 2003). However, these federal initiatives do move teacher practice towards a particular pedagogy that implements specific curricula in a standardized format. Under the mantra of scientifically based best practices, NCLB and the *Good Start, Grow Smart* initiatives emphasize instruction in literacy-based skills that align with a state's reading content and performance standards. Moreover, academic readiness becomes the preparation of young children to fit specific curricular expectations, particularly in reading. This raises many questions about the future goals and direction of early childhood education. How stakeholders answer these questions affects how my students will do their jobs in programs that receive public monies, including elementary school.

THE FUTURE

As I stated in the beginning of this article, a primary concern for my students is that if they choose to teach in an early childhood education classroom they will have to teach a mandated curriculum or implement instructional practices that do not meet the needs of their students—a struggle the field has been grappling with for decades. My students' concern is not whether young children are capable of learning academic skills

(Bowman, Donovan, & Burns, 2000; Shonkoff & Phillips, 2000). Rather, they are worried that their administrators will expect them to do things that they know are inappropriate for their students. They want to know if they will be able to implement curricula that is child-centered and child-directed (e.g., Katz & Chard, 1989; Edwards, Gandini, & Forman, 1993; Helm & Katz, 2001). These concerns are very real and get at the heart of the struggle over reform in early childhood education.

Empirically, the research base of early childhood supports my students' desire to provide learning experiences that challenge all of their children's developmental domains. For example, Shonkoff and Phillips (2000) and Bowman et al. (2000) argue that early childhood programs must also develop young children's emotional, regulatory, and social development skills so that they become curious, confident, and persistent students in the classroom. Simply emphasizing particular content or curricula is not enough to ensure the success of young children.

However, politically, the current system of reform is developing a divided field of experiences for children based on whether they attend a public or private early childhood program. Bowman et al. (2000), Shonkoff and Phillips (2000), and Kagan and Scott-Little (2004) argue that this fractured system of early childhood programs and policies needs to be reconceptualized into a uniform set of programs for children that support the development of the whole child from birth through entry into elementary school. The current push towards SBA reform ignores this, which is why my students are so concerned. Moreover, to achieve such a goal would necessitate an increase in funding for existing programs and further expansion in government services for young children, something that contradicts the current state of education reform (e.g., *The Trust for Early Education*, 2004).

A primary question for early childhood reform is, how can it implement policies that emphasize the development of the whole child across the various early childhood programs?

One option is for state departments of education to tie certification to adoption of early learning standards and to ensure that elementary school programs implement these standards. Because of the limited public investment in early childhood education programs outside of elementary school, monitoring implementation would have to occur through some form of accountability that measures student performance as they enter the elementary grades. If states or the federal government implements such a system, it faces the distinct possibility of turning into a readiness test, which school district might use as a "gate-keeping" device for young children (e.g., Florida's current kindergarten screener program).

Policymakers must proceed with caution (Bodrova, Paynter, & Leong, 2001; Kagan & Scott-Little, 2004). If early childhood education follows the roadmap of SBA reform in K–12 schooling, which many states are in formulating their early learning standards, performance standards that emphasize cognitive skills will decide what learning experiences are of most worth (Kagan & Scott-Little, 2004). Nonetheless, if performance standards continue to be the driving force of reform, one must still question whether students are learning more or are they simply taught the test (e.g., Koretz, Linn, Dunbar, & Shepard, 1991).

Thus, as I tell all my students, if they decide to enter the field of early childhood education, they must be prepared for change. More importantly, they must recognize their role in the discourse of "it depends." As teachers, they must be ready to defend their practices by possessing a thorough understanding of the field of early childhood education and the empirical research that defines appropriate practices. Additionally, they need to be advocates for their students in the school and the community in general. Finally, they need to recognize their role in the politics of education. By following the lead of previous early childhood researchers and advocates, they must work to inform their families, their communities, and their legislators about how particular practices and policies affect the education of their students.

REFERENCES

Alexander, K. L., Entwisle, D. R., & Kabbani, N. (2000). Grade retention, social promotion, and 'third way' alternatives. *The CEIC Review, 9,* 18–19. Retrieved March 23, 2004, from http://www.edrs.com/Webstore/Download2.cfm?ID=470459

Allington, R. L., & McGill-Franzen, A. (1992). Unintended effects of educational reform in New York. *Educational Policy, 6,* 397–414.

American Educational Research Association, American Psychological Association, & National Council on Measurement in Education (1999). *Standards for educational and psychological testing.* Washington, D.C.: American Educational Research Association.

Beatty, B. (1995). *Preschool education in America: The culture of young children from the colonial era to the present.* New Haven, CT: Yale University Press.

Berry, M. F. (1993). *The politics of parenthood: Child care, women's rights and the myth of the good mother.* New York: Viking/Penguin.

Bodrova, E., Paynter, D. E., & Leong, D. J. (2001). Standards in the early childhood classroom: Measuring the progress of preschoolers and kindergartners toward achievement standards is a challenge that requires close attention to specific benchmarks. *Principal, 80,* 10–15.

Bowman, B. T., Donovan, M. S., & Burns, M. S. (2000). *Eager to learn: Educating our preschoolers.* Washington, D.C.: National Academy Press.

Bredekamp, S. (Ed.) (1987). *Developmentally appropriate practice in early childhood programs serving children birth through age 8.* Washington, D.C.: National Association for the Education of Young Children.

Bredekamp, S., & Copple, C. (Eds.) (1997). *Developmentally appropriate practice in early childhood programs.* (Rev. ed.) Washington, D.C.: National Association for the Education of Young Children.

Bredekamp, S., & Rosegrant, T. (Eds.) (1992). *Reaching potentials: Appropriate curriculum and assessment for young children.* (Vol. 1.) Washington, D.C.: National Association for the Education of Young Children.

Bredekamp, S., & Rosegrant, T. (Eds.) (1995). *Reaching potentials: Transforming early childhood curriculum and assessment* (Vol. 2.). Washington, D.C.: National Association for the Education of Young Children.

Burts, D. C., Hart, C. H., Charlesworth, R., Fleege, P. O., Mosley, J., & Thomasson, R. H. (1992). Observed activities and stress behaviors of children in developmentally appropriate and inappropriate kindergarten classrooms. *Early Childhood Research Quarterly, 7,* 297–318.

Cohen, A. J. (1996). A brief history of federal financing for childcare in the United States. *Financing Child Care, 6,* 26–40.

Cuban, L. (1998). How schools change reforms: Redefining reform success and failure. *Teachers College Record, 99,* 453–477.

Dougherty, K. J., & Hall, P. M. (1996). Implications of the Goals 2000 legislation. Issue sheet complied by J. Z. Spade & A. R. Sadovnik. In K. M. Borman, P. W. Cookson, Jr., A. R. Sadovnik, & J. Z. Spade (Eds.) *Implementing Educational Reform: Sociological Perspectives on Education Policy* (pp. 459–467). Norwood, NJ: Ablex Publishers.

Edwards, C., Gandini, L., & Forman, G. (Eds.) (1995). *The hundred languages of children: The Reggio Emilia approach to early childhood education.* Norwood, NJ: Ablex Publishing Corporation.

Fleege, P. O., Charlesworth, R., Burts, D. C., & Hart, C. H. (1992). Stress begins in kindergarten: A look at behavior during standardized testing. *Journal of Research in Childhood Education, 7,* 20–25.

Goldstein, L. S., & Lake, V. E. (2000). "Love, love, and more love for children"; exploring preservice teachers' understanding of caring. *Teaching and Teacher Education, 16,* 861–872.

Gomez, M. L., Walker, A. B., & Page, M. L. (2000). Personal experience as a guide to teaching. *Teaching and Teacher Education, 16,* 731–747.

Graue, M. E., & DiPerna, J. C. (2000). The gift of time: Who gets redshirted and retained and what are the outcomes? *American Educational Research Journal, 37,* 509–534.

Griffith P. L., & Ruan, J. (2003). The missing piece in the standards debate: Teacher knowledge and decision making. *Dimensions of Early Childhood, 31,* 34–42.

Hatch, J. A., & Freeman, E. B. (1988a). Who's pushing whom? Stress and kindergarten. *Phi Delta Kappan, 70,* 145–147.

Hatch, J. A., & Freeman, E. B. (1988b). Kindergarten philosophies and practices: Perspectives of teachers, principals, and supervisors. *Early Childhood Research Quarterly, 3,* 151–166.

Hart, C. H., Burts, D. C., Durland, M. A., Charlesworth, R., DeWolf, M., & Fleege, P. O. (1998). Stress behaviors and activity type participation of preschoolers in more and less developmentally appropriate classrooms: SES and sex differences. *Journal of Research in Childhood Education, 12,* 176–196.

Hauser, R. M., Pager, D. I., & Simmons, S. J. (2000). Race, ethnicity, social background, and grade retention. Retrieved on October 25, 2004 from http://www.ssc.wisc.edu/~hauser/retain_03.pdf

Helm, J. H., & Katz, L. (2001). *Young investigators: The project approach in the early years.* New York: Teachers College Press.

Holmes, C. T. (1989). Grade level retention effects: A meta-analysis of research studies. In L. S. Shepard & M. L. Smith (Eds.) *Flunking grades: Research and policies on Retention* (pp. 16–33). New York: Falmer Press.

Holmes, C. T., & Matthews, K. M. (1984). The effects of nonpromotion of elementary and junior high school pupils: A meta-analysis. *Review of Educational Research, 54,* 225–236.

Jacobsen, L. (2004). Pre-K standards said to slight social, emotional skills. *Education Week, 23,* 13.

Kagan, S. L., & Scott-Little, C. (2004). Early learning standards: Changing the parlance and practice of early childhood education. *Phi Delta Kappan, 85,* 388–396.

Katz, L. G., & Chard, S. C. (1989). *Engaging children's minds: The project approach.* Norwood, NJ: Ablex Publishing Corporation.

Koretz, D., Linn, R. L., Dunbar, S. B., & Shepard, L. A. (1991, April). *The effects of high-stakes testing on achievement: Preliminary findings about generalizations across tests.* Paper presented at the annual meeting of the American Educational Research Association, Chicago, IL.

Labaree, D. F. (1984). Setting the standard: Alternative policies for student promotion. *Harvard Educational Review, 54,* 67–87.

Linn, R. L. (2000). Assessments and accountability. *Educational Researcher, 29,* 4–16.

McCoy, A. R., & Reynolds, A. J. (1999). Grade retention and school performance: An extended investigation. *Journal of School Psychology, 37,* 273–298.

Meisels, S. J. (1987). Uses and abuses of developmental screening and school readiness testing. *Young Children, 42,* 4–6, 68–73.

Meisels, S. J. (1989). High stakes testing in kindergarten. *Educational Leadership, 46,* 16–22.

Meisels, S. J. (1992). Doing harm by doing good: Iatrogenic effects of early childhood enrollment and promotion policies. *Early Childhood Research Quarterly, 7,* 155–174.

Meisels, S. J., & Atkins-Burnett, S. (2004). The Head Start National Reporting System: A critique. *Young Children, 59,* 64–66.

Mitchell, A. (2001). Prekindergarten programs in the states: Trends and issues. Retrieved October 15, 2004 from http://www.nccic.org/pubs/prekinderprogtrends.pdf

National Association for the Education of Young Children, & National Association of Early Childhood Specialist in State Departments of Education (2002). *Early learning standards: Creating conditions for success.* Retrieved March 20, 2004 from http://naecs.crc.uiuc.edu/position/creating_conditions.pdf

National Commission on Excellence in Education (1984). *A Nation at Risk: The Full Account.* Cambridge, MA: USA Research.

National Council of Teachers of Mathematics (1989). *Curriculum and evaluation standards for school mathematics.* Reston, VA: National Council of Teachers of Mathematics.

Neuharth-Pritchett, S., Reguero de Atiles, J., & Park, B. (2003). Using integrated curriculum to connect standards and developmentally appropriate practice. *Dimensions of Early Childhood, 31,* 13–17.

Office of the White House (2002). *Good start, grow smart: The Bush Administration's early childhood initiative.* Retrieved June 21, 2003 from http://www.whitehouse.gov/infocus/earlychildhood/sect1.html

Ramey, C. T., Dorval, B., & Baker-Ward (1983). Group day care and socially disadvantaged families: Effects on the child and family. *Advances in Early Education and Day Care, 3,* 69–106.

Raver, C. C., & Zigler, E. F. (2004). Another step back? Assessing readiness in Head Start. *Young Children, 59,* 58–63.

Reynolds, A. J. (1992). Grade retention and school adjustment: An explanatory analysis. *Educational Evaluation and Policy Analysis, 14,* 101–121.

Reynolds, A., & Temple, J. (1997, September 17). Grade retention doesn't work. *Education Week.* Retrieved March 25, 2004, from http://www.edweek.org

Roderick, M., Nagaoka, J., Bacon, J., & Easton, J. Q. (2000). *Update: Ending social promotion. Passing, retention, and achievement trends among promoted and retained students, 1995–1999.* Consortium on Chicago School Research: Chicago, IL.

Rumberger, R. W. (1995). Dropping out of middle school: A multi-level analysis of students and school. *American Educational Research Journal, 32,* 582–625.

Schweinhart, L. J., & Weikart, D. P. (1980). Young children grow up: The effects of the Perry Preschool Program on youths through age 15. *Monographs of the High/Scope educational research foundation, 7.* Ypsilanti, MI: High Scope Education Research Foundation.

Shepard, L. A. (1994). The Challenge of Assessing Young Children Appropriately. *Phi Delta Kappan, 76,* 206–212.

Shepard, L., & Smith, M. L. (1986). Synthesis of research on school readiness and kindergarten retention. *Educational Leadership, 44,* 78–86.

Shepard, L., & Smith, M. L. (1988). Escalating academic demand in kindergarten: Counterproductive policies. *Elementary School Journal, 89,* 135–145.

Shepard, L. A., Kagan, S. L., & Wurtz, E. (Eds.) (1998). *Principles and recommendations for early childhood assessments.* Washington, D.C.: National Education Goals Panel.

Shepard, L. A., Taylor, G. A., & Kagan, S. L. (1996). *Trends in early childhood assessment policies and practices.* Los Angeles: Center for Research on Evaluation, Standards, and Student Testing. ED450926.

Shonkoff, J. P., & Phillips, D. A. (2000). *From neurons to neighborhoods: The science of early childhood development.* Washington, D.C.: National Academy Press.

Smith, M. S., & O'Day, J. A. (1990). Educational equity: 1966 and now. In D. A. Verstegen & J. G. Ward (Eds.), *Sphere of justice in education: the 1990 American Finance Association handbook* (pp. 53–100). New York: Harper Business.

The Trust for Early Education (2004). Quality prekindergarten for all: State legislative report. Retrieved October 10, 2004 from http://www.trustforearlyed.org/docs/Legislative%20Report-9-9.pdf

United States Department of Health and Human Services (1990). *Head Start: A child development program.* Washington, D.C.: Administration of Children, Youth, and Families.

Vinovskis, M. A. (1999). *The road to Charlottesville: The 1989 education summit.* Washington, D.C.: National Educational Goals Panel.

Westinghouse Learning Corporation (1969). *The impact of Head Start: An evaluation of the effects of Head Start on children's cognition and affective development.* Washington, D.C.: Clearinghouse for Federal Scientific and Technical Information. ED036321.

Yatvin, J. (2002). Babes in the woods: The wanderings of the National Reading Panel. *Phi Delta Kappan, 83,* 364–369.

Zill, N. (1999). Promoting educational equity and excellence in kindergarten. In R. C. Pianta and M. J. Cox (Eds.), *The transition to kindergarten* (pp. 67–105). Baltimore: Paul H. Brookes Publishing Co.

NOTES

1. The federal government provided funding for early childhood programs prior to 1965, e.g. policymakers used funding from the Lanham Act (1940) to assist communities in providing childcare for women who worked in war related services (Beatty, 1995; Cohen, 1996). Nonetheless, such funding was limited, and when the need for care subsided, the federal government ended funding.

2. In some cases, school districts and state governments do offer three- or four-year-old prekindergarten programs, but again, these programs usually target particular populations of students.

3. In 2007, NCLB requires states to measure students' progress in science at least once in each of three grade spans (3–5, 6–9, 10–12).

4. The majority of these standards emphasize what children should be able to know and do before they enter kindergarten, but states such as Wisconsin have early learning standards that emphasize what a child should do by the time he or she leaves kindergarten.

Christopher Brown is an assistant professor of Curriculum and Instruction at the University of Texas at Austin. His research interests include the intersection of education policy, curriculum, and instruction, standards-based accountability and assessment, early childhood education, and elementary education.

QUESTIONS FOR REFLECTION

1. What does it mean for a student to be ready for school? Should all students be able to meet your "standard"? What should happen to a student who does not meet your standard?
2. What should be the role of the government (federal, state, and local) in funding early childhood education programs? Which level of government is most responsible for providing access to such programs? Explain.
3. Should education policies be the same for early childhood programs as elementary and secondary school programs? Explain.
4. How can policymakers, educators, and parents work together to create policies that meet the needs of young children?

Why Is Kindergarten an Endangered Species?

LINDA H. PLEVYAK
KATHY MORRIS

ABSTRACT: The pressure to perform on standardized tests in the upper primary grades is having an impact on the curriculum in both kindergarten and preschool programs. The push for including more academics in the kindergarten classroom requires children to already have specific skills prior to entering kindergarten. Standardized testing and the desire to incorporate academics earlier are challenging developmentally appropriate practice in both kindergarten and preschool.

All I ever needed to know I learned in kindergarten, or so the saying goes. But kindergartens today, with their focus on academic skills instead of social skills are very different from the kindergartens of a couple of generations ago. Too many children are learning in kindergarten that they are not smart enough or are lacking, somehow. They can't sit still long enough, they can't go outside and play, they have homework to do, or they didn't get recess because their teacher couldn't spare the "educational time." One concern parents, teachers, and school administrators are grappling with is what children need to know *before* entering kindergarten.

THE TRICKLE-DOWN EFFECT

When standardized testing began to be used to measure absolute academic standards that all children had to meet before moving on to the next grade, a "backward domino effect" occurred. According to research conducted by the University of Colorado, first and second grade teachers began to feel the pressure to cover higher level content and to retain students who were likely to score poorly on the third grade standardized test (Shepard, 2000). A philosophy of buying a year (retaining or starting late) to ensure future success was born. Eventually kindergarten teachers began to feel the pressure to turn out kindergartner children with sight word recognition, phonics and math skills that used to be covered in first grade (Gubernick, 2000).

Parents began to feel the academic pressure as well. When observing kindergarten programs, speaking with other parents, or from personal experience, many parents realized that their child was "not ready" for this kind of academic program. Instead of questioning the program, they either bought another year for their child, and/or enrolled their child in an "academic" preschool that would get them ready for kindergarten. Too often, however, they sent their mature pre-kindergartner to kindergarten the next year and found that their child was older, taller, heavier, more socially mature—and bored!

May (1994) found that by third grade there is very little evidence to suggest that the extra year had any benefit on cognitive skills and abilities. More importantly, those children who are older than the majority of their peers are more likely to engage in dangerous sexual behaviors and use alcohol and cigarettes (Byrd & Weitzman, 1997). These studies may be startling for parents and teachers who just want the best for children. An important question that needs to be answered is what signs should parents and educators consider to be evidence of kindergarten readiness?

KINDERGARTEN READINESS SKILLS

There are many different readiness tests and evaluations that school districts currently use to determine kindergarten readiness. A study presented at the Annual Meeting of the American Educational Research Association in 1996 found that parents, childcare givers and kindergarten teachers all ranked the same three categories as being the most indicative of kindergarten readiness (Harradine & Clifford, 1996). The three categories include: (1) being healthy, well-fed, and well rested; (2) being able to express their needs, wants, and thoughts; and (3) being enthusiastic and curious about new activities.

Another study that looked at teacher and parent expectations for kindergarten readiness found that there were statistical differences between both groups' expectations (Welch & White, 1999). Parents were more likely than teachers to rate academic skills, i.e., counting, writing, and alphabet recognition as necessary pre-kindergarten skills. The teachers' responses mirrored Harradine and Clifford's (1996) study that ranked physical health, effective communication systems, curiosity and enthusiasm as better indicators of readiness. It may be that in the five years since this study was done more kindergarten teachers mirror the parents ranking of pre-academic skills as more necessary. An assumption for this possible change may be that kindergarten teachers feel the pressure to include academic skills in the curriculum even though their beliefs may say otherwise.

PRESCHOOL BENEFITS CHILDREN

Preschool experience offers children many benefits. One documented benefit is that children who attend preschool score higher on kindergarten screening tests. For early childhood educators this is only a minimum benefit and not a primary goal of preschool. Perry conducted a study in 1999 that looked at two groups of children age four to six. Forty children attended a quality preschool and forty children did not attend any preschool program. The study found that preschool experience had a positive effect in regards to being ready for kindergarten. The experimental group scored higher on the Slosson Kindergarten Readiness Test than those children who did not attend preschool.

This finding was consistent with a statement from a Public Policy Report which also showed that programs such as Head Start, and other center-based programs were statistically linked to higher literacy and math skills than for those children who received no preschool (Zill, Collins, West, & Hausken, 1995). It is important to note that quality preschool programming, as it was defined in these studies, is based upon a constructivist philosophy. Children in these studies had many opportunities to play with a wide range of materials, engage in new activities frequently, and were immersed in language, literacy, and math skills daily.

These types of preschools are not mini-versions of kindergarten with an emphasis on the alphabet, number and writing skills. While there are some programs that are based on skill development and report improvement on tests and reading readiness as positive outcomes, studies consistently report that by grade three, these gains have leveled out among students (Shepard, 1996). A distinction needs to be made between a child's cognitive and school performance gains. Sawhill (1999) shows that attending preschool has greater positive outcomes on raising overall school performance rather than just the initial cognitive gains, which again, level off by third grade. School performance continues to remain higher for those students who attended preschool as well.

WHERE DO WE GO FROM HERE?

The pressures facing kindergarten teachers in schools today are enormous. Administrative pressure for academic achievements and emphasis on academic time at the expense of art, gym, music and recess time is a reality facing all kindergarten teachers. There are increasing numbers of students who are coming to school lacking adequate health practices, language skills, and positive emotional skills and are ill equipped to deal with the rigorous demands and pace of our kindergartens today. Kindergarten teachers need to promote their philosophy of how children learn, and document their students' development in creative ways. Studies have shown that teachers'

perceptions of how students learn affect what materials they select, the placement of those materials, and the use of classroom space that are found in a kindergarten room.

Teachers' perceptions of literacy achievement affect how children move around the room and interact with materials and each other. It is imperative that kindergarten teachers be reflective of themselves and their practices in order to face the challenge of heavy academic and skill development proponents. Administrators of elementary schools also need to be educated on the development and learning styles of young children. Children at kindergarten age do not learn in the same manner as other school-age children. Elementary school administrators typically do not have course work or a background in early childhood education. The early childhood programs and schools that are successful in terms of standardized testing scores and other external measurements should be used as models to evaluate programs. Finally, schools should be competing with themselves to continuously improve the academic and social/ emotional lives of its students.

Schools are faced with populations of children who have real emotional and family needs. While schools like to say that they exist to educate children, the reality that must be faced is that children are, in a real sense, only as healthy as their families. Schools must be more of a community-based outreach for families and should not be forced to take on increased academic skills at the kindergarten level to make up for lacking test scores in the higher grades.

On a personal note, Kathy Morris, one of the authors, is a preschool teacher who has struggled, along with many parents, with the question of when to send children on to kindergarten. Last year, Kathy had three students she recommended not move on to kindergarten, despite being age ready, because they demonstrated difficulty with regulating their emotions, struggled with peer relationships and had a difficult time using their language skills to express themselves. She attributes her conclusions to the research that placed a great deal of emphasis on these three skills for success in kindergarten and upper grades. Kathy believes in standing firm in the wake of the academic pressure to run a more "academic" preschool, and will encourage kindergarten teachers to find ways to bring play into their programs.

Early childhood educators must find their own way to be heard in their schools. There are numerous resources and a good deal of research that supports play-based preschools and kindergartens as the best practice for young children.

REFERENCES

Byrd, R., & Weitzman, M. (1994). Predictors of early grade retention among children in the United States. *Pediatrics, 93*(3), 481–87.

Gubernick, L. (2000). Holding back the years. *Offspring* (April/May), 57–60.

Harradine, C., & Clifford, R. (1996). *When are children ready for kindergarten? Views of families, kindergarten teachers, and child care providers*. Raleigh, NC: North Carolina State Department of Human Resources. ERIC Document Reproduction Service No. ED 399 044.

May, D. (1994). School readiness: An obstacle to intervention and inclusion. *Journal of Early Intervention, 18*(3), 290–301.

Perry, D. (1999). *A study to determine the effects of pre-kindergarten on kindergarten readiness and achievement in mathematics*. ERIC Document Reproduction Service No. ED 430 701.

Sawhill, I. (1999). Kids need an early start. *Blueprint* (Fall), 137–140.

Shepard, L. (1996). Effects of introducing classroom performance assessments on student learning. *Educational Measurement: Issues and Practice, 15*(3), 7–18.

Welch, M., & White, B. (1999). *Teacher and parent expectations for kindergarten readiness*. ERIC Document Reproduction Service No. ED 437 225.

Zill, N., Collins, M., West, J., & Hausken, E. (1995). Approaching kindergarten: A look at preschoolers in the United States. *Young Children, 51*(1), 35–38.

Linda H. Plevyak is assistant professor of early childhood education, University of Cincinnati. *Kathy Morris* is a preschool teacher, Brantner Elementary School.

QUESTIONS FOR REFLECTION

1. Why do the authors say that kindergarten is becoming an endangered species? What has changed in the curriculum to make such a transformation?

2. What do you think is the appropriate balance of academic skills and social skills for kindergartners? Why? What is it that kids of this age really need to learn?

3. What kinds of external pressures do kindergarten teachers face when developing a developmentally appropriate curriculum? Is there too much unnecessary pressure on today's kindergartners and their teachers? What might the consequences be of this kind of pressure and where is it coming from?

CASE STUDY IN CURRICULUM IMPLEMENTATION

Learning to Read in Kindergarten: Has Curriculum Development Bypassed the Controversies?

BRUCE JOYCE

MARILYN HRYCAUK

EMILY CALHOUN

with the NORTHERN LIGHTS KINDERGARTEN TEACHERS

ABSTRACT: The prevailing assumption has been that a formal reading curriculum is inappropriate for kindergartners. However, district staff members and teachers in the Northern Lights School Division of Alberta were convinced that a "nurturing" approach to teaching reading would not endanger the children and might in fact prevent some of them from encountering academic difficulties in the primary grades and beyond.

We'll begin with a simple proposition: Let's teach our kindergarten students to read. We already know how to do it, so why don't we?

Within schools and school districts, decisions about curriculum and instruction in literacy have to be made on the basis of present knowledge and judgment. Such decisions can't wait until all controversies have been resolved and all the evidence is in with regard to available options. In the case of kindergarten, decisions about curriculum are complicated by debates about whether there should be a formal curriculum in reading or whether the components of the kindergarten program should be designed to develop the dimensions of emergent literacy only. But research on how to teach beginning readers grows apace, and we believe that we should take advantage of it.

In the Northern Lights School Division in Alberta, Canada—a district of 20 schools and about 6,500 students—we decided to design a formal reading curriculum for kindergarten, prepare the teachers to implement it, and conduct an action research study of student learning. Our decision stemmed from the judgment that research on be-

ginning reading had reached the point where an effective, engaging, and multidimensional curriculum could be designed and implemented without placing our students at risk in the process. And if such a curriculum proved successful, it seemed likely that the much-publicized "learning gap" would be reduced.

Over the past five years in Northern Lights, we ("we" includes the superintendent, Ed Wittchen; the trustees; and representative teachers and administrators) had concentrated on the development of "safety nets" for low-achieving students at the second-grade level and in grades 4 through 12.[1] We based the two curriculum designs on strands of research on beginning literacy for young children and for older struggling readers and writers.[2] Currently, in both safety net curricula, about three-fourths of the students are progressing well and narrowing the distance between themselves and the district's average students. The others are holding their own.

The need for the safety net programs and our observation of the frustration and hopelessness experienced by students who needed help caused us to consider the K–3 literacy curricula and to explore whether we could strengthen them and so reduce the need for the later safety nets. We take seriously the statement by Connie Juel, who, in reacting to the National Research Council report *Preventing Reading Difficulties in Young Children*, wrote that "children who struggle in vain with reading in the first grade soon decide that they neither like nor want to read."[3] Our teachers who work in the safety net programs confirm that their job is half instruction and half therapy.

For some decades, because of the concerns about not generating demands beyond the capabilities of the students or introducing students to reading in unpleasant ways, there has been a dearth of studies on formal reading programs for kindergarten. A few studies did suggest that formal reading programs in kindergarten could have positive effects that lasted throughout schooling.

For kindergarten interventions as such, though, we had to go back to Delores Durkin's work of 30 years ago. In building a kindergarten curriculum, we were not able to draw on a body of recent research on, say, alternative kindergarten reading programs or dimensions of learning to read at age 5. We drew on the literature relevant to learning to read in grades 1 through 3 and above. Building greater literacy is a matter of considerable importance, and not damaging our students is of even greater importance. But it may be that the concerns about hurting students are based on images of brutal and primitive curricula rather than on humane and sophisticated approaches. Certainly those concerns are not based on reports of failed attempts.[4]

We made the decision that there would be no danger to the students if we proceeded deliberately and, particularly, if the teachers tracked the responses of the children carefully and were prepared to back off or change their approach if a student appeared to be stressed. Not to challenge students cognitively might be an even larger mistake than challenging them. In addition, we wanted the early experience to be not only effective but joyful—learning to read should be a delightful experience.

Our view of a nurturing curriculum appears to differ widely from the image that many people have of a reading curriculum for young children, and we believe it is that image that causes them to shy away from formal literacy instruction for kindergartners. We did not imagine students with workbooks, alphabet flash cards, or letter-by-letter phonics drills. Instead, we imagined an environment in which students would progress from their developed listening/speaking vocabularies to the reading of words, sentences, and longer text that they had created, where they would examine simple books in a relaxed atmosphere, where they would begin to write with scribbling and simple illustrations, where they would be read to regularly, and where comprehension strategies would be modeled for them through the reading and study of charming fiction and nonfiction books. If the work of childhood is play, we imagined the students playfully working their way into literacy.

PATHWAYS TO LITERACY: DESIGNING THE CURRICULUM

Our idea for a nurturing curriculum came from developments in the field of curriculum having to do with several of the emergent literacy processes. Most of the literature in this area presents ideas about and studies of students in grades 1 through 6. We saw this literature as defining dimensions for early literacy that could be incorporated into components of a kindergarten curriculum. Essentially, we categorized dozens of studies around the several dimensions:

- The development of sight vocabulary from the students listening/speaking vocabulary and the study of words encountered through wide reading.[5] Words are recognized in terms of their spelling, and, once a hundred or so are learned, the phonetic and structural categories are available to the students.
- The need for wide reading at the developed level. At the beginning, students can engage

at the picture level and, gradually, can deal with books at the caption level as they learn how meaning is conveyed by the authors.[6]

- The regular study of word patterns, including spelling. The students need to learn to classify words, seeking the phonetic and structural characteristics of words and seeing the language as comprehensible. For example, as the students study the beginnings and endings of words ("onsets" and "rimes"), they build concepts, such as "Words that begin with xxxx sounds often begin with xxxx letters," and they apply those concepts when they encounter unfamiliar words: "If it begins with xxxx letter(s), then it might sound like xxxx usually does."[7]

- The need for regular (several times daily) writing and the study of writing.[8] Writing involves expressing ideas through the learned words and patterns—the essential connection between reading and writing. The attempt to write consolidates what is being learned through reading.

- The study of comprehension strategies. Although most of the research on comprehension has been done with older students, the search for meaning begins early, and the modeling of comprehension strategies is important from the beginning.[9]

- The study, by both teacher and students, of weekly and monthly progress, including the levels of books the students can read, sight words learned, phonetic and structural analysis skills, information learned, and fluency in writing.[10] For example, students can build their own files of words and can see what they are learning. Or students can record their classifications of words, can see that they have developed categories of words (e.g., these begin with . . .), and can add to them. Knowing what you know enables you to assess progress and to celebrate growth.

For our early literacy curriculum, we found that the Picture Word Inductive Model—derived from the tradition of "language experience" with the addition of concept formation and attainment models of teaching—was very important. The core of the language experience approach is the use of the students' developed listening/speaking vocabulary.[11] The students study topics and discuss them and dictate to the teacher. The dictated material becomes the source of their first sight words, and their first efforts to master the alphabetic principle come from their study of the structures of those words.

The Picture Word Inductive Model, as the name suggests, begins with photographs of scenes whose content is within the ability of the students to describe. For example, the photographs might show aspects of the local community. The students take turns identifying objects and actions in the picture. The teacher spells the words, drawing lines from the words to the elements in the picture to which they refer and so creates a picture dictionary. The students are given copies of the words, and they identify them using the picture dictionary. They proceed to classify the words, noting their similarities and differences. The teacher then selects some of the categories for extended study. Both phonetic features and structural characteristics are studied. The teacher models the creation of titles and sentences, and the students create some of their own by dictating them and learning to read the dictations. In the same fashion, the teacher creates paragraphs, and the students gradually learn to assemble titles and sentences into paragraphs about the content of the picture. The picture word cycles (inquiries into the pictures) generally take from three to five weeks.

A major assumption underpinning this view of the curriculum is that students need to become inquirers into language, seeking to build their sight vocabularies and studying the characteristics of those words as they build generalizations about phonetic and structural characteristics.

The curriculum was designed to facilitate growth through each of its strands—building vocabulary, classifying, creating sentences and paragraphs, and reading—in an integrated fashion so that each strand will support the others. As indicated above, as sight words are learned, phonetic and structural concepts will be developed through the analysis of those words. Similarly, the construction of sentences and paragraphs will be related to the sight vocabularies that are being developed. As the children read, they will identify known words and attack new ones through the phonetic, structural, and comprehension skills they are developing.

PROVIDING STAFF DEVELOPMENT TO SUPPORT IMPLEMENTATION

Once we decided that such a curriculum was feasible, designing staff development was the next step. We needed a program that was oriented to help the teachers both implement the curriculum and become a positive learning community that would study student learning and take pleasure in colleagueship and inquiry. Eight teachers in three schools in the Grand Centre/Cold Lake area were involved in the initial effort. The school faculties had agreed formally to participate, and all eight kindergarten teachers had agreed as well. Two had taught reading in the primary grades in the past, but none had attempted a formal literacy curriculum in the kindergarten. Two were first-year teachers. The superintendent, cabinet, and board of trustees were supportive, and meetings explaining the curriculum were held with parents in the spring and early fall.

The staff development included demonstrations, the study of early literacy, the analysis of practice, and the study of student learning, following the format developed by Bruce Joyce and Beverly Showers.[12] Peer coaching was embedded in the workplaces of the teachers.

THE ACTION RESEARCH INQUIRY

For the action research component of the initiative, the eight teachers and the district staff members were asked to focus on two questions: Did the multidimensional curriculum work? Did the students learn to read and to what degree, including the extent of their comfort with the process and their feelings about reading?

Informal observation was important, but the teachers were also provided with tools for the formal study of the students' learning of the alphabet, acquisition of vocabulary, general language development (including phonemic awareness), books studied or read, and development of the competence to manage unfamiliar books, including extended text, using the procedure developed by Thomas Gunning.[13] A team made up of district staff members and consultants administered the Gunning procedure in June in order to ensure standardization of the tricky process of measuring the reading competence of very young children.

To what extent is the variance in achievement explained by gender, by developed language competence as students entered kindergarten, and by class group—variables that occur repeatedly in the literature and are reported as factors in many studies? In the first year, all 141 kindergarten-age students in the three schools were enrolled and were included in the study. In all three schools, students came from a considerable variety of socioeconomic levels, and some 15 students came from First Nations reservations. Teacher judgment indicated that just one of the children entered kindergarten reading at any level. Just one student could recognize all the letters of the alphabet (tested outside the context of words).

Throughout the year the data were collected, summarized, and interpreted with respect to the response of the students. Here we concentrate on the most salient aspects of the students' learning. All eight kindergarten classes followed similar patterns. Differences between the classes were small by comparison to the general effects. For us, this was very important. Had it been that only half of the teachers had been able to implement the curriculum successfully, we would have had to do some heavy thinking.

Recognition of Letters of the Alphabet.

In early October, the mean number of letters recognized (out of 52 upper- and lower-case letters) was 31. In January, the mean was 46. In March, it reached 52. That is, all the students could recognize all the letters out of context. Letter recognition was associated with the acquisition of sight vocabulary, but one was not necessarily a function of the other. The learning of sight vocabulary appeared to pull letter recognition as much as the learning of the letters facilitated the acquisition of sight vocabulary.

Acquisition of Sight Vocabulary.

Our inquiry focused both on how many words were being learned and on the students' ability to learn new words. The learning of words was studied in terms of the Picture Word cycles, which ranged from about four to six weeks in length. Both the number of words learned in the cycles and the increased efficiency developed by the students were of interest here. The data below are taken from one of the classes.

Cycle 1.   Twenty-two words were "shaken out" of the picture. At the end of the first week, the average number of words identified in an out-of-context assessment was five. By the end of the fourth week, the average was 16, and one student knew all 22.

Cycle 2.   Twenty-two words were shaken out. At the end of the first week, the average number that the students could identify out of context was 12, and by the end of the third week, the average number identified was 20.

Cycle 3.   Twenty-eight words were shaken out. At the end of the first week, the mean number of words recognized out of context was 20, and at the end of the second week, the mean was 26, with just three students recognizing 24 and none recognizing fewer than 24.

All the students appeared to increase in efficiency so that, by the end of January, they were able to add to their sight vocabularies, within the first week or two, just about all the words shaken out of the picture. For all sections, the mean percentage of words recognized after two weeks of the first cycle was 30%. By the third cycle, the mean for two weeks had risen to 90%.

Retention of Words.

In May, random samples of six students in each class were tested with respect to out-of-context recognition of the words that had been shaken out through the year—for example, about 120 words in the class cited above. Mean retention was 110. In addition, words added through the generation of titles, sentences, and paragraphs were learned, many of them in the high-frequency "useful little words" category. In the class used as an example, those additional words added up to over 100.

Had the students had difficulty developing a sight vocabulary or retaining it, we would have had a serious warning signal. But such a signal did not develop, and, more important, the increase in capability was a positive signal. By midwinter, the students were mastering words within two weeks that had taken them four or five weeks in the first cycle.

Classification of Words.

Once the words were shaken out, they were entered into the computer, and sets of words were given to each student. (The students could examine them and, if they did not recognize one, could use the picture dictionary to identify it.) Classifying the words was an important activity. The students were asked to sort their word cards according to the characteristics of the words. The teachers modeled classifications of various types throughout the year. In the first cycles, most students built categories on the presence of one or more letters. Later, more complex categories emerged. The teachers selected categories for instructional emphasis and led the students to develop new words and unlock unfamiliar words by using the categories. For example, having dealt with work, works, worked, worker, and working, the students could hunt for other words from which derivatives could be made. Or, knowing work and encountering working in their reading, they could try to unlock it as they learned how the -ing suffix operates.

The teachers studied the categories that students were developing, keeping an eye on the phonetic and structural principles that were emerging. The results are too complex to summarize briefly, but, on the whole, about 30 phonetic and about 20 structural concepts were explored intensively.

Transition to Reading Books.

Throughout the year, a profusion of books was available to the students. Books were carried home for "reading to and with," and little books generated from the Picture Word activities went home to be read to parents. As the students began to learn to read independently, books at their levels accompanied them home. Our records show that 80% of the students encountered 50 or more books in this fashion, in addition to any books from home or libraries.

The assessment of independent reading levels was built around the Gunning framework, in which the students attempt to read unfamiliar books at the following levels:

- Picture Level: single words on a page are illustrated.
- Caption Level: phrases or sentences, most but not all illustrated.
- Easy Sight Level: longer and more complex, mostly high-frequency words.
- Beginning Reading: four levels, progressively longer passages, and less repetition and predictability.
- Grade 2A: requires good-sized sight vocabulary and well-developed word-attack skills.

When an assessment is administered, students read aloud books at each level, beginning with the simplest, and their deviations from print are noted. They are asked comprehension questions after the book has been read. Reaching fluency with total comprehension places a student at a particular level.

In the December assessment, all the students were able to deal with books at the Picture Level, and about one-fourth could manage Caption Level books comfortably. By February, about one-fourth had progressed to the Easy Sight Level, and a handful could manage books at a higher level.

Once again, had the students not been able to approach any level of text competently, we would have had a warning that our curriculum was failing. However, the children were progressing beyond the reading of the sentences and paragraphs developed in each Picture Word cycle and were beginning to be able to manage simple books "almost independently."

In June, the independent test team administered the assessment using a specially assembled set of books from United Kingdom publishers to reduce the likelihood that the books would be familiar to the students. The aggregated results for the eight classes were indeed encouraging.

All eight classes apparently succeeded in bringing all the students to some level of print literacy. About 40% of the students appeared to be able to read extended text, and another 30% manifested emergent ability to read extended text. Indeed, 20% reached the Grade 2A level, which includes long and complex passages and requires the exercise of complex skills both to decode and to infer word meanings. All the students could manage at least the simplest level of books.

We felt it was very important that there were no students who had experienced abject failure. Even the student who enters first grade reading independently at the picture level is armed with skills in alphabet recognition, possesses a substantial storehouse of sight words, and owns an array of phonetic and structural concepts. However, a half dozen students will need to be watched closely because, even if they were able to handle books at the caption level, they labored at the task, manifesting difficulty either in recognizing relationships between text and graphics or in using their phonetic or structural generalizations to attack unfamiliar words.

We studied the data to determine whether gender or socioeconomic status influenced levels of success, and they did not. The distributions of levels for boys and girls were almost identical, as were the distributions for students having or not having subsidized lunches.

Typically, in our district, about 20 kindergarten students would have been referred as having special needs in those eight schools. At the end of this year, just two students were referred, both for speech problems.

Comfort and Satisfaction.

During the year, parents voiced their opinions regularly, and in May we prepared simple questionnaires for both the parents and the children. We asked the parents a series of questions about the progress of their children and whether they and the children believed they were developing satisfactorily. The children were asked only whether they were learning to read and how they felt about their progress. We were trying to determine whether there was any discomfort that we were not detecting. But in response to our survey, no student or parent manifested discomfort or dissatisfaction related to the curriculum. However, some parents were anxious at the beginning and remained worried at the end of the year. Some were concerned that we had not taken a "letter by letter" synthetic phonics approach and worried that future problems might develop as a consequence. But even these parents appeared to believe that their children were progressing well "so far."

A YEAR LATER: LEAVING FIRST GRADE

Throughout first grade, we followed the students, and, at the end of the year, we gave them the Gray Oral Reading Test,[14] administered by a team of external testers. The mean Grade Level Equivalent (GLE) was 3.5 (the average for students at the end of grade 1 is 2.0). Five percent of the students were below 2.0, which is quite a distance from the 50% typical in our district in previous years.

In June 2003, 47 students, a randomly selected half of the 94 students still enrolled in the district, were administered the Gray Oral as they exited grade 2. Their average GLE was 5.0 (the national average of exiting grade-4 students). The distributions of male and female scores were almost identical. Five students (10%) scored below the average of exiting second-grade students. Typically, 30% of the students in this district or nationally in the U.S. and Canada do so.

In subsequent years, we will continue to monitor the progress of the students from each year, and we will follow the lowest-achieving students most intensively.

INTERPRETATION

The problem that faced us was whether research on beginning literacy had reached the point that we could design multidimensional curricula to introduce young children to reading with comfort and satisfaction. In our efforts to learn how much an initiative in kindergarten curriculum might improve literacy learning, reduce the likelihood of failure by students thought to be at risk, and also benefit students not thought to be at risk, our first experience must be described as positive. We will follow the students through the grades, and we will continue to scrutinize the curriculum.

The teachers were all new to a formal kindergarten reading curriculum. In the first year, they were scrambling to master a considerable number of unfamiliar instructional models, particularly the Picture Word Inductive Model, and they spent considerable energy tracking the progress of the students and trying to figure out whether they were proceeding optimally and whether the tasks were well matched to them. With greater experience, they will no doubt provide many ideas for improvement.

The issues of "developmental readiness" become moot if the knowledge base permits us to design effective and humane kindergarten curricula in reading. The progress of the students in these eight classes equals the progress of students in average first-grade classrooms and surpasses it in one very important way: no children failed, whereas one-third of the students in average first grades usually do. The half-dozen students who gained the least nonetheless arrived at first grade with substantial knowledge and skill.

In the next few years, we'll learn how these students do in the upper elementary grades, where similar efforts to change the curriculum are under way. Thus far, our results have been encouraging, but there are 400 students to follow now. We certainly want to continue the outstanding achievement we have seen so far, but we also hope to close the door on poor achievement and eliminate the need for the safety net programs. We'll see. Right now, our hypothesis is that a strong, multidimensional, formal reading program for kindergarten students can change the picture of achievement in the primary grades. Moreover, 5-year-old children, given a strong and humane curriculum, can learn to read at least as well as first-graders usually do, but without the high failure rates of so many first-grade classrooms.

We hope that our Northern Lights teachers, and all others in every venue, will set high standards and also treat their students affirmatively. We are bothered when states, provinces, and districts set goals at such a low level that they expect that 2% or 3% of the students will creep up to the next level of achievement in any given year. Ninety-five percent is a better goal. Nearly all of our little second-grade graduates can now read with the best of upper-elementary-grade students. So could nearly all of the students in all school systems.

NOTES

1. See Marilyn Hrycauk, "A Safety Net for Second-Grade Students," *Journal of Staff Development,* vol. 23, 2002, pp. 55–58; and Bruce Joyce, Marilyn Hrycauk, and Emily Calhoun, "A Second Chance for Struggling Readers," *Educational Leadership,* March 2001, pp. 42–47.

2. Emily Calhoun, *Literacy for the Primary Grades* (Saint Simons Island, Ga.: Phoenix Alliance, 1998).

3. See Connie Juel, "Learning to Read and Write," *Journal of Educational Psychology,* vol. 80, 1988, pp. 437–47.

4. In a long-term study of students who had experienced formal reading instruction in kindergarten, Ralph Hanson and Donna Farrell followed them through their high school years and found that the effects could be detected even as they graduated. See Ralph Hanson and Donna Farrell, "The Long-Term Effects on High School Seniors of Learning to Read in Kindergarten," *Reading Research Quarterly,* vol. 30, 1995, pp. 908–33. Delores Durkin's work on the positive effects of learning to read early is well known but has not changed the minds of the large number of experts on early childhood education who are more worried about damage than about benefits. See Delores Durkin, *Children Who Read Early* (New York: Teachers College Press, 1966).

5. See, for example, William Nagy, Patricia Herman, and Richard Anderson, "Learning Words from Context," *Reading Research Quarterly,* vol. 19, 1985, pp. 304–30.

6. A crisp general review can be found in Nell Duke and P. David Pearson, "Effective Practices for Developing Reading Comprehension," in Alan Farstrup and Jay Samuels, eds., *What Research Has to Say About Reading Instruction,* 3rd ed. (Newark, Del.: International Reading Association, 2002), pp. 205–42.

7. Students need to learn to inquire into word patterns and build word-identification skills around concepts about word structures. A fine summary is provided by Linnea Ehri, "Phases of Acquisition in Learning to Read Words and Instructional Implications," paper presented at the annual meeting of the American Educational Research Association, Montreal, 1999.

8. The connection of early writing to beginning reading is growing clearer. See Carol Englart et al., "Making Strategies and Self-Talk Visible," *American Educational Research Journal,* vol. 28, 1991, pp. 337–72.

9. Several lines of research are gradually discovering a great deal about comprehension strategies and

how to develop them. See Ruth Garner, *Metacognition and Reading Comprehension* (Norwood, N.J.: Ablex, 1987); and Michael Pressley et al., *Cognitive Strategy Instruction That Really Improves Student Performance* (Cambridge, Mass.: Brookline, 1995).

10. The Picture Word Inductive Model provides a set of ways to track student progress. Some variables (such as vocabulary development) are tracked weekly or more often. Others are tracked a little less frequently. See Emily Calhoun, *Teaching Beginning Reading and Writing with the Picture Word Inductive Model* (Alexandria, Va.: Association for Supervision and Curriculum Develop-

ment, 1999); and Bruce Joyce and Beverly Showers, *Student Achievement Through Staff Development* (Alexandria, Va.: Association for Supervision and Curriculum Development, 2002).

11. Russell Stauffer, *The Language-Experience Approach to the Teaching of Reading* (New York: Harper & Row, 1970).

12. Joyce and Showers, op. cit.

13. Thomas Gunning, *Best Books for Beginning Readers* (Boston: Allyn and Bacon, 1998).

14. J. Lee Wiederholt and Brian Bryant, *Gray Oral Reading Tests* (Austin, Tex.: Pro-Ed, 2001).

Bruce Joyce is director of Booksend Laboratories, St. Simons Island, Georgia. *Marilyn Hrycauk* is director of instruction in the Northern Lights School Division #69, Alberta. *Emily Calhoun* is director of the Phoenix Alliance, St. Simons Island, Georgia. The Northern Lights Kindergarten Teachers are Bev Gariepy, Christine Reynolds, Melanie Malayney, Carol Kruger, Jennifer Lawton-Codziuk, Elaine Blades, Christine Cairns, Andrea Fama, and Gloria Lane.

QUESTIONS FOR REFLECTION

1. What did the authors learn by their experiment to present the kindergarteners in the Northern Lights School District with a "nurturing" curriculum? How can what they learn inform practice within other districts?

2. What were the "safety nets" the authors referred to as having been used for certain students in the district? How does the research used by the authors address the use of these safety nets?

3. What conclusions can you draw from this article regarding the use of action-based research in schools? What does research have to teach us about the day-to-day activities of our students, teachers, and administrators?

Teachers' Voices—
Putting Theory Into Practice

Building a Community in Our Classroom:
The Story of Bat Town, U.S.A.

Andrea McGann Keech

ABSTRACT: As the passing of time and the changing of the landscape became familiar concepts to them, children in one combined third and fourth grade class at Roosevelt Elementary School in Iowa City, IA used their growing knowledge of their town's past as the starting point for creating a model community of their own. Keech profiles the class and their project community, "Bat Town, U.S.A."

"I've got a problem" said one of my students with a thoughtful frown, "and I'd like to call a city council meeting about it. I'm not getting enough help from my business partner, and I need some advice."

"Fine," I told him, acting in my official capacity as city manager. "We can do that this afternoon right after recess."

"Then I'll need to reschedule my Resource Room time," a girl sitting near us chimed in. "I'll check with my teacher and get back to you."

"Okay," the boy replied with a nod. "This problem needs our attention now!"

I couldn't help smiling at this very serious conversation in my third and fourth grade combination class. With just a few changes in wording, the interchange could have been taking place between the actual members of our town's city council members. Instead, it was occurring in a classroom of students who were participating in a social studies simulation exercise known as *Classroom City*.[1] We had certainly come a great distance from that first day several weeks ago when we held our ribbon cutting ceremony and officially opened the simulated city fondly known as Bat Town, U.S.A.

In our combination classes, the curriculum rotates between topics every other year. This year in

social studies our focus was on communities. We had already studied communities in Japan and China. As participants in the national Kid's Voting USA project, we had followed developments in the local election. Finally, we were ready to take a long look at changes in the community of our own school, Roosevelt Elementary in Iowa City, Iowa, and to begin work on creating a thriving model classroom community of our own in room 116.

Today, Roosevelt Elementary is a school with international connections. Our proximity to the University of Iowa and programs there which attract scholars and their children from around the world makes our school fortunate enough to have an extremely rich diversity of learners. In our classroom alone there were recent arrivals from China, Japan, Sudan, Indonesia and Korea. Children representing many ethnicities come together here and learn together about their world and about themselves. Finding common ground to study the meaning of "community" presents my group with a challenge.

We focused our study of the community on the school itself, using the social studies standards themes of **PEOPLE, PLACES AND ENVIRONMENTS,** and **TIME, CONTINUITY AND CHANGE.**[2] To mark our school's sixtieth birthday a few years ago, a wonderful book called *Reflections of Theodore Roosevelt Elementary School* had been created by Dr. Nora Steinbrech, principal of the school for more than eighteen years. It tells the stories, sometimes moving, sometimes gently humorous, of students, teachers, principals, parents and friends who walked these halls before us.

We read this book together and reflected on our own stories, experiences that we'd like to pass along to future generations about our days at Roosevelt. These were recorded in memory books to keep and to share. Ideas came easily. We included a visit from Echo, the bat, and a trip to a real bat colony in an old schoolhouse; our Chinese New Year feast when we sampled all of those new and delicious foods, and the staging of our very own original drama, *The Terrible Tragedy of the Titanic*.

Next, we made an effort to begin really observing those little details of our school's architecture and design around us, the things we'd always hurried by and taken for granted without a second thought before now. Our appreciation for the passing of time heightened. "Look," someone would say as we walked past the old original facade of the building, "that's the 1931 entrance. Isn't it beautiful? Look at the carved stone!" On our way to P.E. one day, another student pointed out the place where large Palladian windows once brought in the western sunlight. "Why did they brick them in?" several children wanted to know. Well, think about the problems that could result by having enormous glass windows in a building now used as a gymnasium. "Why can't we sled down 'Suicide Hill' in the Ravine anymore?" That question had a fairly obvious answer!

We noticed the additions to our school over the years, variations in building materials, hidden "secret" passages, the signs small and large of changes which had taken place over the decades. Along with the *Reflections* book of "old" Roosevelt, we read several other excellent stories which provided us with a real sense of the passing of time and what that means in the life of a child and a community.

Who Came Down that Road? by George Ella Lyon is a book of few words and many beautiful images.[3] We used it to heighten our awareness of Time, Continuity and Change. As a young boy and his mother walk down a well-traveled path, they imagine all of those long-ago footsteps falling upon the very same path. Mastodon and woolly mammoth, buffalo and elk, Native Americans, settlers, soldiers in blue and gray, and finally a mother and her child. "Who will come next," they wonder—and we wondered, too. We composed our own original pages filled with writing and illustrations to add to the book. Each of us provided a new page, suggestions for the "next" entry, about who or what might follow the young boy and his mother down the path. Some students suggested the boy's own child might one day pass that way. An understanding of our past can provide us with a better preparation for the future.

Another book with lovely illustrations and a haunting tale of time's passing is Dyan Sheldon's *Under the Moon*.[4] Finding an arrowhead in her backyard, a young girl tries to picture a world without automobiles, airplanes, and cities. What did this place look like with open fields and clear streams? Who lived here? Who made this arrowhead she holds today? She begins to imagine what life might have been like when the "land was as open as the sky." Cultures have maintained their traditions and customs over time. We wanted to learn more about the culture that had produced the arrowhead.

Inspired by this book, I brought in a number of arrowheads turned up by the blade of my grandfather's mule-pulled plow on his farm in the 1920s for the children to examine firsthand. We then took a class trip to the natural history museum at Iowa Hall on the University of Iowa campus, where knowledgeable tour guides helped us to understand the history and uses of a wonderful variety of Native American cultural artifacts, such as arrowheads, axes, spearheads, pottery, beadwork, and clothing. We viewed and discussed several life-sized historical dioramas depicting the Meskwaki people who have lived here on the banks of our Iowa River for thousands of years. Our trip to the museum helped us to understand continuity and change in the culture of the Meskwaki, early residents of our community.

In *The House on Maple Street* by Bonnie Pryor, we read another story of an arrowhead and a small porcelain cup, how they were lost by children long ago and how they came to be found many years later by two sisters digging in their garden.[5] We wrote about treasures we might leave behind in our Roosevelt Ravine for others to find one day. What would our special things tell future "diggers" about us? Would those archeologists really appreciate the significance of beloved Beanie Babies? Taking a walk around the neighborhood, we even found an old house like the house on Maple Street. We talked about the many changes the people in the house must have seen from those windows.

We also used a series of seven amazing posters called "The Changing American Cityscape."[6] The fictional town of New Providence as depicted in the posters is actually a composite of many buildings from real cities throughout the United States at various time periods. As we looked at the first poster showing 1875, we saw horses and buggies, muddy streets, and a town just getting started. Over the weeks we added the subsequent posters in the series to the wall. "That's how our town might have looked when Roosevelt Elementary School was built," I told the children as we hung the poster from the 1930s. "There's even an airship!" a sharp-eyed boy who was then engrossed in a study of the Hindenburg pointed out. The posters range from 1885 to the 1990s. The incredible detail in this beautiful series sparks lively discussion and comparisons among the various attributes of the many decades.

We used the posters as models, and working in cooperative learning groups students did research and made our own posters of our changing Roosevelt "schoolscape" through the decades. They showed teachers' and students' clothing and hair styles, games played on the playground, popular music selections, and an outline of the school building's dimensions during a particular period of time. It became a common sight to see small clusters of students around the sets of posters throughout the day, happily discussing history and its changes—what teacher of social studies can ask for more than that?

Finally, we read Alice McLerran's story of the little community known a *Roxaboxen* set in the 1930s "on a hill on the southeast corner of Second Avenue and Eighth Street, in Yuma, Arizona."[7] The children in the story, one the author's mother, built their own town with rocks and boxes, bits of jewel-colored glass and sticks. There was a mayor and a town hall, a bakery, and *two* ice cream parlors, because in Roxaboxen "you can eat all the ice cream you want." It's just the sort of town any child would love. Everyone always had "plenty of money" because there were "plenty of shops." The story in the book took place during the Great Depression, just when our own Roosevelt School was being built. The availability of money and the ice cream were only real in the imaginations of the citizens of Roxaboxen.

Through our readings, discussions, and reflections, we learned many things about communities and the reasons which bring people together. The passing of time and the changing of the landscape became familiar concepts to us. Traditions, conventions, and common goals all played a part in our studies. Now we were ready at last to create our very own model of a community, right in the classroom. This simulation would be a more structured way of making our small community run smoothly and successfully.

To help us organize our own town, we used many elements from a unit available through Interaction Publishers called *Classroom City*. We didn't follow the sequence of the lessons precisely, nor did we feel bound to do every aspect of the simulation. My students would have had some difficulty computing "financial interest on accounts" or figuring up their "income tax." Even adults, after all, can experience difficulty with those! We used the basic organizational guidelines and general format provided by the *Classroom City* lesson plans.

Persuasive speeches were written and delivered as children ran for public office. The election of officials followed. City council meetings were held to get things organized. Everyone submitted a flag design to represent our city and one with a prominent flying fox bat, designed by a talented girl who would eventually open The Artistic Bat Store, was chosen by popular vote. Students brainstormed together about what kinds of businesses they might like to have in Bat Town, U.S.A. and what products or services they could offer for sale to other residents and visitors. This simulation expanded our study to incorporate the social studies standards themes of **POWER, AUTHORITY AND GOVERNANCE** as well as **PRODUCTION, DISTRIBUTION AND CONSUMPTION.** A detailed listing of everyone's job duties, citizen roles and responsibilities, goals, and activities are provided in the *Classroom City* teacher's guide. Our own special touches like the classroom museum, the cookie shop, and the play station were suggested by the students themselves as our simulation progressed.

A ribbon-cutting ceremony opened the town, which the children had decided to call Bat Town, U.S.A. In science we studied bats as a part of our Physics of Sound unit, and their fascination with the world's only flying mammal continued unabated throughout the year, contributing to their interest in naming the model city for these important animals.

As teacher, I held the title of city manager to keep things smoothly on track. **CIVIC IDEAS AND PRACTICES** are an integral aspect of our model city. Thanks to a helpful and informative booklet called "The Children's Guide to Local Government" published by the Iowa City city manager's office, we were able to compare the organization of our model community, Bat Town, U.S.A., with that of our own Iowa City. A mayor and vice mayor were elected by the students. The mayor greets all visitors to the city, is the ribbon cutter at the town's opening, and conducts city council meetings. The vice mayor is second in command. S/he votes on the city council and can remove from office any public officials who fail to perform their duties.

Our city council members were elected as well. Only members of the council and the vice mayor could start a motion or vote on a motion during meetings, but anyone could approach a member with a concern and have it brought before the council. Our class meetings were lively affairs filled with spirited debates and a free exchange of ideas. The council members reviewed all citations issued by health, fire and police departments and assigned fines. They also reviewed and voted on all student applications to open a business. Potential business owners wrote a description of the purpose of their store or service, and the application needed to win the approval of three-fourths of the council before "construction" could proceed.

In addition to the elected officials, there were a myriad of positions to fill, such as police officers to enforce "speeding" violations in the hallways and "noise" ordinances; bankers to distribute income paid weekly; an editor of our illustrious newspaper, appropriately called the *Night Times;* and a fire marshal to monitor litter in desks, keep our "streets" clear of clutter, and hold fire drills as necessary. There were lots and lots of storekeepers, those entrepreneurial types who quickly learned how to make their money grow.

Busy afternoons were spent learning and practicing Robert's Rules of Order, holding city council meetings to approve or disapprove of permits for businesses, making a map of the town for visitors, designing a town logo and flag to fly, writing columns for the *Night Times* ("Dear Batty" proved a popular favorite), and preparing our town for the coming "tourist season" when younger guests would come to visit Bat Town and patronize our stores with "bat dollars" distributed by our bankers.

All students had jobs and were paid a weekly wage, according to principles suggested in the *Classroom City* teacher's guide. Money could also be earned by taking on a duty like editing or contributing features to the newspaper, assessing and collecting fines for violations of city codes, operating a popular business where students could spend their wages, or holding elected office. Fate cards that were drawn weekly either awarded money ("You specialize in decorating book covers for your friends and make $12") or deducted it ("A lost book costs you $9 to replace"). Students came up with many creative ideas for earning those sought-after "bat dollars."

We used cardboard boxes and construction paper to make store-fronts. Among the many options Bat Town shoppers could choose from were homemade cookies or Girl Scout cookies with free ice water, books for rent, origami paper cranes, samurai hats folded from newspaper, pen and ink drawings from a girl with artistic gifts in abundance, stuffed toy rentals, small erasers, stickers, handmade book markers, and a play station offering games of skill. Once the town was up and running, the excitement was tremendous. My students used some of the "bat dollars" they had earned as wages in the earlier weeks of the simulation to spend in the various shops run by their friends. There were two shifts on successive days so that everyone had turns both to sell and shop. They bought items from the businesses run by fellow students, munched cookies from the cookie shop, and visited the play station to try their luck at games like "Ghost Toss" and the tricky "Balancing Bears." They insisted on trying out everything themselves before the "tourists" arrived! Who could blame them?

As the younger children came to visit, they were welcomed by the mayor, vice-mayor, and members of the council. They were given maps of the town and the latest edition of *Night Times,* hot off the presses. Our guests were learning to count money, so each was given twenty "bat dollars" to spend and twenty minutes to spend them. One kindergartner remarked to his teacher as he departed Bat Town, "I can't believe they were only third and fourth graders!"

Seeing those happy young tourists and my even happier Bat Town citizens, so proud of their hard work and efforts, I thought to myself that this experience was truly a Roosevelt memory worth making, something the children will remember long after they've left these hallways for wider roads which beckon them to futures yet unknown. The efforts of all, and the small community we built together in room 116, will live in our memories, just as sweet old Roxaboxen lingered in the memories of those long ago children of the 1930s even "as the seasons changed and the years went by."

NOTES

1. Rod Stark, *Classroom City: A Simulation for Young Persons of Economics and Government in a Small American City, Grades 4–9* (El Cajon, CA: Interaction Publishers, 1995).
2. National Council for the Social Studies, *Expectations of Excellence: Curriculum Standards for Social Studies* (Washington, DC: Author, 1994). Time, Continuity, and Change is the second of the ten standards themes, and People, Places, and Environments is the third.
3. George Ella Lyon, *Who Came Down that Road?* (New York: Orchard Paperbacks, 1996).
4. Dyan Sheldon, *Under the Moon* (New York: Dial Books for Young Readers, 1994).
5. Bonnie Pryor, *The House on Maple Street* (New York: Mulberry Books, 1987).
6. Renata Von Tscharner, Ronald Lee Fleming and the Townscape Institute, "The Changing American Cityscape Poster Set," seven posters, portfolio, 32-page teaching guide (Palo Alto, CA: Dale Seymour Publications, 1996).
7. Alice McLerran, *Roxaboxen* (New York: Puffin Books, 1992).

Andrea McGann Keech teaches at Roosevelt Elementary School, Iowa City, Iowa.

QUESTIONS FOR REFLECTION

1. How does Keech use the concept of "community" to impact the community within her own classroom?
2. What kinds of media and artifacts did Keech use in her classroom to raise awareness of the community around the students at Roosevelt Elementary? What kinds of media or artifacts are around you that you could use to teach about the community in which you are located?
3. What kind of town was Bat Town, U.S.A.? How close was it to a *real* town and what kinds of lessons can the students in Keech's class take from their experience in Bat Town and apply to their real community?

LEARNING ACTIVITIES

Critical Thinking

1. In what ways does the Reggio Emilia Approach reflect John Dewey's educational philosophy? (See the following articles by Dewey: "Traditional vs. Progressive Education," Chapter 1; "The Sources of a Science of Education," Chapter 5; and "Progressive Organization of Subject Matter," Chapter 6.)
2. What are the characteristics of learning experiences in the elementary curriculum that help children master the challenges that come with each stage of their development as human beings?
3. What are some of the challenges that children face today that were unknown or little known to their parents or grandparents? To what extent can (or should) these challenges be addressed in childhood education?
4. Reflect on your experiences as an elementary student. What curricular experiences enhanced your growth and development? Impeded your growth and development? What implications do your reflections have for your curriculum planning activities, regardless of the level of education which interests you most?

Application Activities

1. Invite a group of elementary-level teachers to your class and ask them to describe the steps they take in planning curricula for their students. What do they see as the most important curriculum criteria to use in planning?
2. Obtain a statement of philosophy (or mission statement) from a nearby elementary school. Analyze the statement in regard to the thirteen goals for childhood education presented in this chapter. How many of the goals are reflected in the statement?

3. Conduct a comparative survey, at ten-year intervals, of an education journal that addresses childhood education. Have there been any significant changes over the years in regard to curriculum-related issues and trends discussed in the journal? Among the journals to consider are *Child Development, Child Study Journal, Childhood Education, Children Today, Early Childhood Research Quarterly, Elementary School Journal, Exceptional Children, Gifted Child Quarterly, Gifted Child Today, International Journal of Early Childhood, Journal of Early Intervention, Journal of Research in Childhood Education, New Directions for Child Development, Teaching Exceptional Children,* and *Young Children.*

Field Experiences

1. Interview a school psychologist, mental health worker, child protective services (CPS) worker, or similar individual to find out about the sources, signs, and treatment of psychosocial problems that can interfere with children's learning. Ask him or her to suggest ways that teachers can help students overcome these problems.
2. Visit a nearby elementary school and obtain permission to interview a few students about their curricular experiences. Take field notes based on these interviews. The following questions might serve as a guide for beginning your interviews: Do the students like school? What about it do they like and dislike? What are their favorite subjects? What about those subjects do they like? Then, analyze your field notes; what themes or concerns emerge that would be useful to curriculum planners at this level?
3. Visit an agency in your community that offers services to children and their families. Ask a staff member to explain the services that are offered. Report your findings to the rest of your class.

Internet Activities

1. Go to the home page for the National Clearinghouse for Bilingual Education (NCBE) and gather information and resources on effective elementary-level programs for limited English proficiency (LEP) students. Also visit NCBE's page titled "School Reform and Student Diversity: Case Studies of Exemplary Practices for LEP Students"; from this location, "visit" several exemplary elementary schools and gather additional information and resources.
2. Go to the George Lucas Educational Foundation and gather curriculum resources and ideas relevant to your subject area and level of interest. For example, you may wish to examine the *Learn & Live* kit which contains a documentary film, hosted by Robin Williams, and a resource book that showcases innovative K–12 schools.

3. Go to one or more of the following professional organization web sites dedicated to the education of young children and gather information, fact sheets, research results, resources, and publications of interest.

   Association for Childhood Education International (ACEI)
   Early Childhood Care and Development (ECCD)
   National Association for the Education of Young Children (NAEYC)
   Professional Association for Childhood Education (PACE)

CHAPTER 8

Middle-Level Curricula

FOCUS QUESTIONS

1. What important developmental tasks confront students at the middle level?
2. How do middle-level students differ in their physical, social, psychological, and cognitive maturation?
3. What factors can threaten the healthy development of middle-level students?
4. What are some appropriate curricular goals for middle-level students?
5. How do educational programs organized around middle school concepts address the unique needs of students at the middle level?

Middle-level students are *transescents*—that is, they are passing from childhood to early adolescence. In our society, transesence and early adolescence is a period from about age ten to age fifteen. Young people at this age must cope with a wide range of life stresses because they mature physically more quickly than they mature cognitively or socially. For example, the average age of menarche has dropped from sixteen years of age 150 years ago to twelve and one-half today; similarly, boys reach reproductive maturity at an earlier age. As a result, young people often do not have the social and emotional maturity to handle the freedoms and stressors that characterize our modern society. "Many life-threatening behaviors, such as drug and alcohol abuse and early sexual experiences, begin in early adolescence," Peggy A. Grant points out in "Middle School Students and Service Learning: Developing Empowered, Informed Citizens," in this chapter. The vulnerability of today's adolescents is portrayed graphically in this chapter's "Great Transitions: Preparing Adolescents for a Changing World" excerpted from a report by the Carnegie Council which built on an earlier Council report, *Turning Points: Preparing American Youth for the 21st Century* (1989): "Altogether, nearly half of American adolescents are at high or moderate risk of seriously damaging their life chances. The damage may be near-term and vivid, or it may be delayed, like a time bomb set in youth."

MAJOR TRANSITIONS AND CRITICAL TURNING POINTS

Individual differences among students are greater during transesence and early adolescence than at other stages of life. There is a four-year range within each sex group from the time that the first significant fraction of the group attains puberty to the time that the last member of that sex reaches it. Generally, by the time they are twenty, both boys and girls have reached full physical growth and biological maturity. But social, psychological, and cognitive maturation are usually not in step with physical maturation. Many pressures in modern society tend to force the social, psychological, and cognitive changes of this period on the young person ahead of the biological.

As with any age group, it is important to consider the three bases of curriculum—social forces, human development, and learning and learning styles—when planning curricula for transescents and early adolescents. Toward this end, it may be helpful to review the perspectives on human development covered in Chapter 3, particularly David A. Hamburg's "Toward a Strategy for Healthy Adolescent Development" and James P. Comer's "Organize Schools around Child Development." These articles identify cultural, psychological, cognitive, and social factors that influence students' learning during this period.

Transescence and early adolescence are characterized by rapid physical growth, which is frequently uneven, with some parts of the body growing faster than others. As these physical developments occur, self-concepts must often be adjusted. Both boys and girls may go through periods where they are clumsy and awkward, only to become graceful and athletic as they become older. Since rapid growth requires a great deal of physical energy, children need plenty of food and sleep to maintain good health during this period. On many occasions, though, they may have excess energy that needs to be discharged through vigorous physical activity.

The physical changes that take place during this period are not the only changes that are occurring. In regard to Erik Erikson's eight-stage model for the human life cycle, identity versus identity confusion is the salient psychosocial crisis for early adolescents. During this time, early adolescents use new, more complex thinking abilities and begin to shape a sense of personal identity. Identity confusion can result, however, when the early adolescent is confronted with the variety of roles available to him or her.

Erikson's theory suggests that when early adolescents identify with a peer group, with their school, or with a cause beyond themselves, their sense of *fidelity*—the "virtue" of this stage—can be the "cornerstone of identity." During this stage, early adolescents are loyal and committed—in fortunate instances, they are motivated by growth-enhancing goals, aspirations, and dreams; in unfortunate instances, by people, causes, and life styles that alarm parents, teachers, and other adults in their lives. An example of how curricular experiences can help early adolescents "sort out [their] place in the world" and identify with a worthwhile cause is found in this chapter's *Teachers' Voices* article.

The transescent child who has looked to his or her family for care, affection, and guidance must begin to find independence in order to fulfill the developmental tasks of this period and to prepare for adulthood. They must learn to make decisions on their own and to accept the consequences of those decisions. Parents and teachers can facilitate the growth of early adolescents by praising their accomplishments and not over-dwelling on shortcomings, encouraging independence with appropriate limitations, and giving affection without expecting too much in return. In "Benchmarks of Student-Friendly Middle Schools" in this chapter, M. Lee Manning outlines seven characteristics of school environments that provide young adolescents with "caring and nurturing educational experiences." Similarly, Peter C. Scales and Judy Taccogna describe forty "developmental assets" that promote the growth and development of middle- and high-school level students. *External assets* "are the relationships and opportunities that surround young people with the support and situations that guide them to behave in healthy ways and make wise choices. *Internal assets* are those commitments, values, competencies, and self-perceptions that, when nurtured, provide the 'internal compass' that guides a young person's behavior and choices so that he or she becomes self-regulating."

Great Transitions, an excerpt of which appears in this chapter, reminds us that, indeed, education can be a "turning point" in the lives of early adolescents: "early adolescence is the phase when young people begin to adopt behavior patterns in education . . . that can have lifelong consequences. At the same time, it is an age when, much like younger children, individuals still need special nurturing and adult guidance. For these reasons, early adolescence offers a unique window of opportunity to shape enduring patterns of healthy behavior" (Carnegie Council on Adolescent Development, 1995, p. 1). The same point, perhaps more compelling because it is in the language of her peers, is made elsewhere in *Turning Points* by sixteen-year-old Sarah:

> I think that being a kid is the most important stage of your life. It's a time when you start to develop a personality. It's when you start to learn about who you are, and what you want to do with yourself. And it's a time when you develop trust. It's a time when you learn how to be a person in society. Unfortunately a lot of kids don't have that. If you don't grow up learning how to be a productive person, then you're going to have a problem once you grow up. (Carnegie Council on Adolescent Development, 1995, p. 2)

CURRICULAR GOALS FOR MIDDLE-LEVEL STUDENTS

Turning Points asserts that there is a "volatile mismatch . . . between the organization and curriculum of middle grade schools and the intellectual and emotional needs of young adolescents" (Carnegie Council on Adolescent Development, 1989, p. 2). The "mismatch" noted in *Turning Points* is reflected in the number of today's parents who are "revolting" against the increasing amounts of homework assigned their children (see David Skinner's "The Homework Wars" in this chapter). Pressure to achieve academically, these parents maintain, increases the likelihood that children's emotional and social needs will be overlooked. Similarly, in this chapter's *Case Study in Curriculum Implementation* section, Donald E. Larsen and Tariq T. Akmal suggest that academic achievement in schools can be overemphasized. In "International Curriculum Planning in an Age of Accountability: Explorer Middle School's Approach," they present a case study of a school, while it has yet to meet the academic requirements of No Child Left Behind, is a "rich, vibrant school" that is improving students' lives. Lastly, in this chapter's *Teachers' Voices* section, Nancy King Mildrum describes a TLC

(Ten Lessons in Creativity) model for elementary and middle school classrooms (see "Creativity Workshops in the Regular Classroom"). "When children have experiences with expansive attitudes related to creativity, they begin to feel more confident about who they are and what they have to contribute," Mildrum observes.

What, then, should be the goals of educational programs for middle-level students? Many goals might be suggested; some derived from social forces, some from theories of human development, and some from theories of learning and learning styles. The list would surely include helping learners to:

1. Build self-esteem and a strong sense of identity, competence, and responsibility
2. Understand and adjust to the physical changes they are experiencing
3. Deal with wider social experiences and new social arrangements
4. Explore different areas of knowledge and skill to help determine potential interests
5. Make the transition between childhood education and education for middle adolescents, and prepare for the eventual transition to senior high school
6. Deal with value questions that arise because of their developing cognitive abilities, their growing need for independence, and rapid changes in society
7. Cope with social pressures from some of their peers to engage in risk-taking behaviors
8. Develop concern for the environment, the local and global communities, and the welfare of others

DEVELOPMENT OF THE MIDDLE SCHOOL

A major issue for transescents and early adolescents is whether their education is best provided in a junior high school, a middle school, or some other form of school organization. During the 1950s and 1960s, dissatisfaction with junior high schools became evident as many people pointed out that junior high schools were "scaled-down" versions of high schools, complete with departmentalization, extensive athletic programs, and age-inappropriate social activities. Junior high schools, it was felt, were not providing students with a satisfactory transition into the high school, nor were they meeting the unique needs of early adolescents.

During the early 1960s, an organizational framework for a "school in the middle" was introduced. The new middle school arrangement called for moving the ninth grade into the high school, placing grades 5–8 in the middle school, and developing curricula to meet the needs of ten- to fourteen-year-olds. By 1970, almost 2,500 middle schools had been created, and by 1990 this number had increased to almost 15,000 (George, 1993).

At first, middle schools were quite different from junior high schools—often, middle schools had more interdisciplinary, exploratory curricula; team teaching; teacher/advisor programs; flexible scheduling; smaller athletic programs; and less ability grouping. Today, the distinctions between junior high schools and middle schools have become somewhat blurred, and many innovative practices initially developed to meet the needs of students in middle schools have been incorporated in junior high schools as well.

Evidence to support the effectiveness of middle school concepts—whether they were part of middle-level or junior-high programs—accumulated as the middle school movement expanded during the 1970s and 1980s. The August 1985 issue of *Middle School Journal* presented the results of a major study of "schools in the middle" (grades 5–9), which found that most of the "effective schools" in the study were organized in 6-7-8 or 5-6-7-8 grade patterns. Moreover, principals of these schools were knowledgeable about middle-level programs and research, and they evidenced familiarity with block scheduling, interdisciplinary teaming, cocurricula programs, learning styles, teacher/advisor programs, and developmental age grouping.

Currently, the well-documented effectiveness of educational programs organized around middle school concepts is having a positive influence on schooling at other levels. For example, in this chapter's *Case Study in Curriculum Implementation* article, "Intentional Curriculum Planning in an Age of Accountability: Explorer Middle School's Approach," Donald E. Larsen and Tariq T. Akmal identify three critical elements of school effectiveness at all grade levels: "school-wide leadership whose moral purpose is manifested in a vision for intentional improvement, a web of caring and personal relationships, and ongoing planning guided by relevant data."

REFERENCES

Carnegie Council on Adolescent Development. *Great Transitions: Preparing Adolescents for a New Century,* abridged version. New York: Carnegie Council on Adolescent Development, Carnegie Corporation of New York, 1995.

Carnegie Council on Adolescent Development. *Turning Points: Preparing American Youth for the 21st Century.* Carnegie Council on Adolescent Development, Carnegie Corporation of New York, 1989.

George, Paul. "The Middle School Movement: A State-of-the-Art Report and a Glimpse Into the Future." In Hass, Glen, and Parkay, Forrest W., eds., *Curriculum Planning: A New Approach,* 6th Ed. Boston: Allyn and Bacon, 1993, pp. 446–455.

Great Transitions: Preparing Adolescents for a Changing World

CARNEGIE COUNCIL ON ADOLESCENT DEVELOPMENT

ABSTRACT: This excerpt from the Carnegie Council on Adolescent Development's report, Great Transitions: Preparing Adolescents for a New Century, *stresses the importance of education for early adolescents in a complex, changing world. Eight principles for developing new middle-level education programs based on research and the experiences of educators, policy makers, and advocates for children and youth are described. A program to improve curricula, instruction, and assessment at middle schools in fifteen states resulted in achievement gains for students, increased self-esteem, and reduced feelings of alienation, fearfulness, and depression.*

If it were possible to reach any consensus about high-priority solutions to our society's problems, a good education throughout the first two decades of life would be a prime candidate. Every modern nation must develop the talents of its entire population if it is to be economically vigorous and socially cohesive. A well-educated young adult is rarely found in our nation's prisons. In the past two decades, however, the achievement levels of American adolescents have virtually stagnated. The performance of our students is too low to support adequate living standards in a high-technology, information-based, transnational economy.

A persistent misconception among many educators is that young adolescents generally are incapable of critical or higher-order reasoning. Many school systems do a disservice to middle grade students by not offering challenging instruction. Education to capture the young person's emergent sense of self and the world, and to foster inquiring, analytical habits of mind, is not only feasible but constitutes essential preparation for life.

FACILITATING THE TRANSITION TO THE MIDDLE GRADES

In the move from elementary school, where a student has spent most of the day in one classroom with the same teacher and classmates, to the larger, more impersonal environment of middle school or junior high school farther from home, an adolescent's capacities to cope are often severely tested. Such an abrupt transition coincides with the profound physical, cognitive, and emotional changes of puberty, a juxtaposition that for some students can result in a loss of self-esteem and declining academic achievement.

Middle grade education was largely ignored in the education reforms of the 1980s. With the publication in 1989 of the Carnegie Council's report, *Turning Points: Preparing Youth for the 21st Century,* however, the nascent movement to reorganize middle schools to make them more developmentally appropriate for young adolescents was powerfully reinforced.

Middle grade education, said the report, should be more intellectually challenging, in line with young adolescents' new appreciation for the complexity of knowledge and ideas, and supportive of their desire for individual attention. Schools should have curricula that provide the information, skills, and motivation for adolescents to learn about themselves and their widening world. They should promote a mutual aid ethic among teachers and students, manifest in team teaching and cooperative learning. They should integrate students of varying ability levels in a single classroom, and they should provide opportunities for academically supervised community service.

EIGHT PRINCIPLES FOR TRANSFORMING THE EDUCATION OF YOUNG ADOLESCENTS

At the heart of *Turning Points* is a set of eight principles for transforming the education of young adolescents. These rest on a foundation of knowledge from current research and from the experience of leading educators, policymakers, and advocates for children and youth.

Create Communities for Learning

Large schools should be brought to human scale through the creation of smaller units, or schools-within-schools, where stable relationships between teachers and students and among students can be cultivated and smaller class sizes can ensure that each student is well known and respected.

Teach a Core of Common Knowledge

In many middle grade schools, the curriculum is so fragmented by subject matter that students have few opportunities to make connections among ideas in the different academic disciplines. A primary task for middle grade educators, especially as part of teaching teams, is to identify the most important principles and concepts within each discipline and concentrate their efforts on integrating the main ideas to create a meaningful interdisciplinary curriculum. The current emphasis on memorization of a large quantity of information must yield to an emphasis on depth and quality of understanding of the major concepts in each subject area as well as the connections between them.

Provide an Opportunity for All Students to Succeed

Numerous studies of cooperative learning approaches, in which students of varying ability learn together, have demonstrated their efficacy for everyone. Cooperative learning helps high achievers to deepen their understanding of the material by explaining it to lower achievers, who in turn benefit by receiving extra help as needed from their peers. Students master course material faster, retain the knowledge longer, and develop critical reasoning powers more rapidly than they would working alone. Cooperative refining also enables young people to get to know classmates from backgrounds different from their own, which sets the stage for them to learn the requirements for living together in a pluralistic society.

Prepare Teachers for the Middle Grades

At the present time, there are only a few graduate education programs that prepare middle grade teachers, as opposed to elementary or secondary school teachers. Yet the early adolescent transition is a distinct phase requiring special understanding of the conjunction of changes that a young person is undergoing and that have a bearing on learning. To orient teachers effectively for the middle grades, professional education programs must incorporate courses in adolescent development, team teaching, and the design and assessment of demanding interdisciplinary curricula. They must also offer special training to work with students and families of different economic, ethnic, and religious backgrounds.

Improve Academic Performance through Better Health and Fitness

Middle grade schools often do not have the support of health and social service agencies to address young adolescents' physical and mental health needs. Developmentally appropriate adolescent health facilities, in or near schools, are urgently needed for middle and high school students, especially in areas where there is a high proportion of uninsured families. Such school-related health centers should be linked to health education programs and a science curriculum that helps students understand the biological changes they are experiencing and the impact of various health-damaging as well as health-promoting practices.

Reengage Families in the Education of Adolescents

As discussed in the previous chapter, schools must involve parents of young adolescents in all aspects of their education. As it is, they are often considered as part of the problem of educating adolescents rather than as a potentially important educational resource.

Strengthen Teachers and Principals

States and school districts should give teachers and principals the authority to transform middle grade schools. They and other members of the school staff know more about how to do their jobs than those far removed from the classroom. Teachers, especially, need control over the way they meet curricular goals. The creation of governance committees composed of teachers, administrators, health professionals, support staff, parents, and representatives from community organizations is one way to make schools more effective.

Connect Schools with Communities

In the 1980s, social service professionals and community organization leaders began moving their youth services into the schools, where the young people are. The result is a major innovation called "full-service schools." Led by individual states, full-service schools offer a variety of social and health services to young people and their families, paid for and rendered by outside agencies. As an example of a school-community partnership, these interventions are showing that

they not only can help to reduce high-risk behavior in adolescents, but they enhance the environment for learning.

THE MIDDLE GRADE SCHOOL STATE POLICY INITIATIVE

Turning Points' comprehensive framework became the basis of a Carnegie Corporation effort to stimulate widespread middle grade reform beginning in 1990. Called the Middle Grade School State Policy Initiative (MGSSPI), it is a program of grants to fifteen states (usually the state department of education) whose schools are adopting promising practices in line with *Turning Points'* principles. Included are schools using approaches that are effective with young adolescents from disadvantaged communities, who make up a growing proportion of the nation's public school enrollments.

To improve curricula, instruction, and assessment under MGSSPI, the states have developed week-long summer institutes on interdisciplinary instruction, portfolio-based assessment, on-site professional development seminars facilitated by university faculty, formal networks to exchange information and resources between schools, systems for deploying expert consultants, and many other forms of assistance. At the local level, MGSSPI has stimulated improvements in curricula, instruction, and assessment in more than one hundred middle schools, some of which have worked to integrate education and health services for young adolescents and anchored health education firmly in the middle grade curriculum.

A group of Illinois middle grade schools, first as part of a federally supported effort called Project Initiative Middle Level, and now as part of the MGSSPI, has been implementing *Turning Points'* recommendations. Results thus far from an evaluation of the Illinois project show that, in forty-two schools participating at least one year, students are showing significant improvements in their reading, mathematics, and language achievement. They have higher self-esteem and are less likely to feel alienated, fearful, or depressed in school than they otherwise would, as a result of the implementation of reforms.

These promising findings demonstrate that, although most schools do not now meet the needs of young adolescents, the potential is there and can be readily tapped. With the support of schools redesigned expressly to prepare youth for the future, all adolescents will have a better chance at educational and personal success.

The *Carnegie Council on Adolescent Development* was established in 1985 by the Carnegie Corporation of New York to generate public and private interest in measures that prevent problems during adolescence and promote healthy adolescent development. *Great Transitions* was the Council's concluding report.

QUESTIONS FOR REFLECTION

1. Review the eight principles for transforming the education of young adolescents. What can curriculum planners, teachers, parents, and community leaders do to implement these principles? To what extent do you believe these principles will characterize educational programs for early adolescents during the first decade of the twenty-first century?

2. The Carnegie report states that "In the past two decades . . . the achievement levels of American adolescents have virtually stagnated. The performance of our students is too low to support adequate living standards in a high-technology, information-based, transnational economy." How might the following authors whom you read in the preceding chapters react to this point of view: Nel Noddings, Michael W. Apple, Ashley Montagu, and Henry A. Giroux?

3. Imagine that you are a member of a middle-level teaching team that is following the Carnegie Council's recommendation "to identify the most important principles and concepts within each discipline." How would you proceed?

Middle School Students and Service Learning: Developing Empowered, Informed Citizens

PEGGY A. GRANT

ABSTRACT: Service learning provides students with opportunities to serve their communities while engaging in reflection on the meaning of those experiences. Several examples illustrate how service learning helps middle school students—who are at a critical point in their personal, moral, social, and cognitive development—create a sense of who they are and what they can contribute to the world around them. Successful service learning activities require organization, careful planning, and commitment.

Students are growing vegetables for a homeless shelter in a school garden using recycled water. They have created a computer database on the nutritional content and growth cycles of different plants, solicited donations of materials, and even written a grant to the National Gardening Association for equipment (Hayes, 1997, p. 12).

Seventh graders are reading to preschool children. They have selected and critiqued appropriate children's books and developed oral reading skills. "We liked the look on [the children's] faces when we read them stories and gave them cookies and stuff," they explain (Simon, Parks, & Beckerman, 1996, p. 175).

These teenagers were participating in service learning projects, an educational idea whose purpose is to reconnect young people to their communities while providing real-life contexts for academic learning. This article will discuss the following aspects of service learning: (1) its definition and purpose, (2) how it meets the goals for school reform and content area standards, (3) the ways in which it fits the particular needs of middle school students, and (4) guidelines for incorporating service learning into the middle school classroom.

WHAT IS SERVICE LEARNING?

The twenty-first century is one fraught with dangers and with opportunities, especially for teachers and the young people they serve. Although many teenagers seem to be experiencing, as the former Executive Director of the National Association of Secondary School Principals claims, ". . . disinterest in classwork, a tragic 'drift' and lack of motivation" (Eberly, 1989, p. 53), many are idealists, eager to make a positive difference in their world. Service learning, while not a panacea for what ails us in these postmodern times, does offer exciting possibilities for rejuvenation among teachers and pupils alike.

Teachers who practice service learning create activities in which their students apply the knowledge and skills of their academic classes to improve the communities in which they live, both locally and globally. These activities fall generally into one of the following categories: (1) cross-age tutoring or teaching, such as reading to kindergarten children or helping new immigrants learn English, (2) creation of a product within the classroom to be donated to an outside agency, institution, or other classroom, such as translating government pamphlets about recycling for non-English speaking citizens or performing skits about peer pressure for elementary age students, (3) taking on an issue and attacking it from several fronts, such as working for flood relief or supporting drunk driving legislation, or (4) going into the community to perform service, such as working in a soup kitchen or creating an inner-city flower garden. These areas overlap to a great degree, as authentic learning experiences do, but all of them serve to use skills from the classroom, whether it is the learning of a foreign language to knowledge about reading strategies, to help others that need the service.

THE ROLE OF SERVICE LEARNING IN SCHOOL REFORM

Several of the reform movements of the eighties included involving students in service within their communities in their recommendations. Ernest Boyer, John Goodlad, and the Carnegie Foundation all suggested community service as an important part of the traditional school program. More recently, goal number 3 of the National Education Goals: Building a Nation of Learners, includes the following objectives:

- All students will be involved in activities that promote and demonstrate good citizenship, good health, community service, and personal responsibility.
- The percentage of all students who demonstrate the ability to reason, solve problems, apply knowledge, and write and communicate effectively will increase substantially (National Education Goals Panel, 1998).

Service learning is also compatible with the standards currently being written and implemented in the content areas, such as science, mathematics, social studies, and the language arts. The standards in science demand a "classroom that is inquiry-oriented, activity-based, and engaging. The role of the teacher changes from that of disseminator of information to one of a mentor-scholar as children present ideas, challenge ideas, and reconceptualize these ideas" (Shymansky, Jorgensen, & Marberry, 1997). The K–12 standards for the teaching of mathematics also require a pedagogy radically different from that currently practiced in many of today's schools, one that is compatible with the goals and practice of service learning. "These goals imply

that students should be exposed to numerous and varied interrelated experiences that encourage them to value the mathematical enterprise" (National Council of Teachers of Mathematics, 1989). Real-life connections between science and mathematics, such as those made by students who created a garden to raise vegetables for the homeless using recycled water, embody what is described in the standards for conceptual learning (Hayes, 1997).

The most natural content link for service learning is the social studies. According to Hatcher (1997), "[S]ervice learning is distinguished from other types of experiential education by its commitment to and its potential to clarify values related to social responsibility and civic literacy." Benjamin Barber (1992), a leading proponent of community service, writes, "Civic empowerment and the exercise of liberty are simply too important to be treated as extracurricular electives" (p. 25).

The content of the social studies is also being conceived in a new light, beyond just learning important names and dates in order to be familiar with our nation's history and culture. According to the National Council for the Social Studies, teaching and learning are powerful when they are active, when they "emphasize authentic activities that call for real-life applications using the skills and content of the field" (NCSS, 1994).

An excellent example of how service learning can provide authentic application of classroom subjects and foster civic action is the unit "Trails to Colorado: Past and Present" designed by teachers in the SSEC service learning project. In this unit, students studied "the impact of human settlement and economic development on the environment." They held community information sessions about "environmental problems related to economic development" and educated the local businesses about environmentally responsible endeavors (Schukar, 1997, p. 181).

A complex, student-driven activity such as this one gives young people an opportunity to combine the knowledge from their math and science classes with what they were learning in social studies about world problems to create something original and useful. Working together, they practiced problem-solving and developed interpersonal skills, all the while using the communication skills from their language arts classes. What they produced became an ongoing, self-sustaining project that improved the quality of life in their neighborhood.

With the inclusion of students with disabilities into regular classrooms, instructors must also think about how educational programs such as service learning will affect these students who have special needs and must be dealt with on an individual basis. Fortunately, there is also support within the special education community for service activities. Special educators recommend an "integrated, activity-based learning model" in which the "learning must take place in a community context" where students work cooperatively with others (Edgar & Polloway, 1994). Contact with community agencies gives students with special needs exposure to a variety of vocational opportunities, and working collaboratively with their peers can provide them with modeling of the social and academic skills they will need for success both in and out of school.

A reporter was interviewing a group of eighth graders who were building bat houses in a local park. To his question, "Why bat houses?" a student replied, "We have reclaimed this park for the people of our community who want to enjoy the surroundings." Unfortunately, the environment was also enjoyable to unpleasant insects, especially mosquitoes. Another student explained, "In class we learned that bats consume thousands of insects each day." Thus, middle school students used their science knowledge, their communication and interpersonal skills to solve a problem in their local neighborhood. This environmental lesson, learned in a social context, in the real world of mud and grass and bugs could be the beginning of an environmental awareness that will grow as these children mature into informed adult citizens.

Clearly there is broad support for service learning as an instructional activity. Activity-based, experiential learning is in alignment with the standards of the subject area organization and is appropriate for those students with special needs. It also addresses those skills important in business and personal relationships, working with others, taking on different points of view, in addition to strategic planning and evaluation.

WHY SERVICE LEARNING WORKS IN THE MIDDLE SCHOOL

Service learning is an instructional strategy that is especially appropriate for middle school students who are at a crucial point in their personal, moral, social, and cognitive development. Exposure to diverse work environments, numerous adult role models, and real-life problem solving can provide students in the middle-school years with more options for their future. Many of the most important skills required in service learning projects, although necessary for academic, emotional, and social growth, are not addressed specifically in the academic curriculum. Schine (1997) describes these areas of emphasis:

> Among these [skills] are the need to acquire and test new skills, develop a range of relationships with both peers and adults, be permitted to make real decisions within appropriate and clearly understood limits, have the opportunity to speak and be heard, and discover that young people can make a difference. (p. 171)

When preteenagers enter the middle school years they begin to acquire the ability to think abstractly, to engage in "reflection, introspection, comparisons with others and a sensitivity to the opinions of other people" (Irwin, 1996). They begin a search for identity, especially in relationship to career choices, sexuality, and a view of life (Marcia, 1987). Young people moving from concrete thinking to more formal reasoning are at an ideal place to begin looking at themselves and the world around them in a new light.

Self-esteem is an important issue for middle school students, especially for young women.

Kohn (1994) observes that, "When members of a class meet to make decisions and solve problems, they get the self-esteem building message that their voices count, they experience a sense of belonging to a community, and they hone their ability to reason and analyze" (p. 279). This assertion is supported by the experiences of middle school students working with young children. The teacher reports that "helpers become more mature, responsible and self-assured as a result of their service" and "can see the importance of education since they have been educating others" (NCSL, 1991, p. 29).

Since many life-threatening behaviors, such as "drug and alcohol abuse and early sexual experiences, begin during early adolescence, it seems logical that success in developmental tasks and positive interactions with adults may reduce the need that some adolescents feel to engage in those behaviors" (Irwin, 1996, p. 222). Even anti-social behaviors such as aggression and fighting can be affected by community service activities. A middle school student with a well-deserved reputation as a fighter and troublemaker, while doing service in a pre-school, found himself confronted with two small children about to come to blows on the playground. His developing self-awareness, combined with his service role as an authority figure, prompted him to reconsider his own behavior (NCSL, 1991).

For students at-risk of dropping out of school, the middle school can be the last place where they will receive formal education. Serna and Smith (1995) list several skills that can help these students be more successful in school and reduce the chances that they will leave without a diploma. These skills, all of which are integral to service learning projects, include the following: (1) asking for help and advice from trusted adults, (2) collaborating with others to achieve goals, (3) planning, (4) implementing, and (5) evaluating strategies, as well as (6) risk-taking, and (7) dealing with stress.

As students interact with others during service learning activities, they become engaged and develop a sense of what they can contribute to the world around them. These interactions contribute to motivation for school, for learning, and for participating in community life. Teachers who participated in a service learning program directed by the Social Science Education Consortium reported that one of the most positive aspects of the projects in which their students participated was the enthusiasm of the "trouble-makers" who "did especially well in the service learning portion of the unit" (Schukar, 1997, p. 182).

At this point in the development of young people, community service can provide the concrete experiences through which they can examine values and beliefs from new perspectives, and develop habits of mind that will help them become thoughtful, compassionate, well-informed, and active members of their communities.

GUIDELINES FOR SUCCESSFUL SERVICE LEARNING ACTIVITIES

Because of the many individuals, agencies, even equipment involved, service learning requires an exceptional amount of organization, planning, and commitment. Ruggenberg (1993) suggests the following guidelines for planning successful service learning activities.

- Allow the students to do work of a significant nature;
- Connect the students directly with the people who benefit from their work;
- Present challenges that require students to test and expand their abilities;
- Require students to use decision-making skills, putting them in a position to "do" and not merely to observe;
- Reflect on and discuss the consequences of their work with staff and supervisors (p. 16).

Alan Haskvitz, a longtime practitioner of service learning in his own classroom, recommends using students' interests and behaviors to guide them into worthwhile service projects. "Go after what they're doing," he advises. "If you see a kid wad up a piece of paper and throw it in the corner, there's your recycling. Ask: 'Why did you do that?' 'How much are we really throwing away here?' 'What can we do about this?' " (Hayes, 1997, p. 12).

The ideal format for service learning is to encourage students to initiate them. They can create their own service projects by examining their communities and looking for needs and then thinking of ways to meet them. Schine (1997) describes one such activity. Following the shooting of a Dominican drug dealer by a police officer in their community, a group of sixth graders examined the relationships among the community members and the police. Deciding that one reason for the hostility stemmed from language differences, the students decided to participate in the cross-cultural training offered by the police department. They invented games to help officers learn Spanish, volunteered as language tutors at the police station, and produced skits to illustrate issues important to young people in the community.

Service learning, like all experiential learning, requires more of the teacher than traditional in-class instruction, even instruction based on active learning. One only has to visualize fifty or so thirteen-year-olds wandering an inner-city neighborhood unclear about what they are doing, unmotivated to accomplish it, and unsure about their reasons for participating, to appreciate the seriousness of careful planning for effective service learning activities. The meaning that students derive from the service learning activity has its roots in what happens in the classroom before, during, and after the project itself.

Classroom activities must give students an opportunity to expand their knowledge and skill base in ways that will help them better understand the reasons for the service learning project. Egan (1997) explains this essential link between concrete experience and abstract understanding. ". . . [T]he practical activity is certainly useful, but it can best support meaningful learning in a context of powerful abstractions, it is within the

abstract context that the concrete content makes sense" (p. 52). A well-planned service experience can be an anchor to which the instructor can attach the material of the required curriculum.

Haskvitz explains, "Almost any factual knowledge that students acquire can be related to a service project either by research or an activity" (Hayes, 1997, p. 10). Haskvitz always requires research for service learning projects. "You can't just send students out to clean up a beach," he explains. "That's just free labor. If there's going to be a beach cleanup, my students must research how the beaches got dirty in the first place. . . . If students don't do research, beach cleanups will just go on forever" (p. 10).

The most significant component in student learning is the emphasis that is placed on reflecting on the experience. Conrad and Hedin (1981) explain, "Perhaps students can make personal meaning of their experiences on their own, but if this meaning is to affect their broader social attitudes and intellectual skills, systematic and directed reflection must be added" (p. 36).

The teacher's role in this process is significant because he or she structures the reflection experiences to focus on those aspects that are important for students: (1) to learn the factual, content material, (2) to think about values in terms of their own beliefs and what they have observed in the service experience, (3) to identify the communication and problem-solving skills they used, and (4) to place their own concrete experiences in broad, universal contexts. Because service learning experiences, if they work the way they should, are highly engaging and active, stopping to make personal and intellectual meaning of what is happening will probably not happen unless a teacher provides the opportunity.

CONCLUSION

Students at Mansfield Middle School in Tucson, Arizona, used their social studies knowledge to create a hunger awareness campaign within their own school. After a unit on world hunger, they produced a videotape about the local food bank, then traveled from homeroom to homeroom showing the video and soliciting food for the school food drive. As a result of their actions, Mansfield collected more food than any other middle school in their district (Schukar, 1997). This experience, one that they surely will not forget, allowed them to use knowledge about geography, demographics, and current events in a practical, authentic way. They also exercised their reading, writing, and speaking skills, while working with others in collaboration to accomplish real goals. Most important of all, they learned that they could *do* something about the events going on around them. Imagine the twenty-first century populated with people who learned this lesson early in life.

RESOURCES

Many organizations provide information about how teachers can connect community service with the curriculum: 1) The Citizenship Education Clearing House (CECH) located at the University of Missouri-St. Louis and 2) Learn and Serve America (http://www.whitehouse.gov/WH/EOP/cns/html/cns-index.html).

In addition, the following web sites have information related to service learning: 1) Prophets—www.kn.pacbell.com/wired/prophets/index.html; 2) the National Service Learning Clearinghouse—www.nicsl.coled.umn.edu/; and 3) Youth in - Action Network—www.mightymedia.com/yia/mainmenu.cfm?StateTag=0).

Finally, several books offer ideas and resources for using service learning. *A Kid's Guide to Social Action* by Barbara Lewis has practical, specific advice for organizing service experiences and teaching students the skill they need to be successful. Also useful are *Combining Service and Learning: A Resource Book for Community and Public Service Vol. 1* edited by Jane C. Kendall; *Serving to Learn, Learning to Serve: Civics and Service from A to Z* by Cynthia Parsons; *The Kid's Guide to Ser-* *vice Projects* by Barbara A. Lewis and Pamela Espeland; *Social Issues and Service at the Middle Level* edited by Samuel Totten and Jon E. Pedersen; *A Student's Guide to Volunteering* by Theresa Foy Digeronimo; and *Enriching the Curriculum through Service Learning* edited by Carol Kinsley and Kate McPherson.

REFERENCES

Barber, B. (1992). *The aristocracy of everyone.* New York: Ballantine.

Conrad, D. & Hedin, D. (1981). *Experiential education evaluation project, executive summary of the final report.* St. Paul, MN: Minnesota University.

Eberly, D. J. (1989). National service and the high school. *NASSP Journal, 73* (516). 53–60.

Edgar, E. & Polloway, E. A. (1994). Education for adolescents with disabilities: Curriculum and placement issues. *The Journal of Special Education, 27.* 438–452.

Egan, K. (1997). *The educated mind.* Chicago: University of Chicago Press.

Hatcher, J. A. (1997). Reflection: Bridging the gap between service and learning. *College Teaching, 45.* Retrieved July 24, 1998 from the World Wide Web: http://www.elibrary.com.

Hayes, B. (1997). From the classroom to the community: An interview with Alan Haskvitz. *Social Studies Review, 36* (2). 10–12.

Irwin, J. L. (1996). Developmental tasks of early adolescence: How adult awareness can reduce at-risk behavior. *The Clearing House, 60.* 222–225.

Kohn, A. (1994). The truth about self-esteem. *Phi Delta Kappan, 76.* 272–283.

Marcia, J. (1987). The identity status approach to the study of ego identity development. In T. Honess & K. Yardley (Eds.). *Self and identity: Perspectives across the life span.* London: Routledge & Kagan Paul.

National Center for Service Learning in Early Adolescence. (1991). *Connections: Service learning in the middle grades.* New York: City University of New York.

National Council for the Social Studies. (1994). Expect excellence: Curriculum standards for social studies. Retrieved October 10, 1998, from the World Wide Web: http://www.ncss.org/standards.

National Council of Teachers of Mathematics. Curriculum and Evaluation Standards for School Mathematics. Reston, VA: National Council of Teachers of Mathematics, 1989. Retrieved October 10, 1998, from the World Wide Web: http://www.enc.org/reform.

National Education Goals Panel. National education goals: Building a nation of learners. Retrieved October 10, 1998, from the World Wide Web: http://www.negp.gov, last modified May 28, 1998.

Ruggenberg, J. (1993). Community service learning: A vital component of secondary school education. *Moral Education Forum, 18* (3). 11–19.

Schine, J. (1997). School-based service: Reconnecting schools, communities, and youth at the margin. *Theory into Practice, 36* (3). 170–176.

Schukar, R. (1997). Enhancing the Middle School Curriculum through Service Learning. *Theory into Practice, 36.* 176 183.

Serna, L. A. & Smith, J. L. (1995). Learning with purpose: Self-determination skills for students who are at risk for school and community failure. *Intervention in School and Clinic, 30.* 142–153.

Shymansky, J. A.; Jorgensen, M. A.; & Marberry, C. A. (1997). Science and mathematics are spoken and written here: Promoting science and mathematics literacy in the classroom. In Reform in Math and Science Education: Issues for the Classroom. Columbus, OH: Eisenhower National Clearinghouse. Retrieved October 10, 1998, from the World Wide Web: http://www.enc.org/reform/.

Simon, K.; Parks, B. S.; & Beckerman, M. (1996). Effects of participatory learning programs in middle and high school civic education. *The Social Studies, 87* (3). 171–176.

Peggy A. Grant is Assistant Professor, School of Education, Purdue University Calumet, Hammond, Indiana.

QUESTIONS FOR REFLECTION

1. To what extent could service learning activities be incorporated into the curriculum across all levels of education (i.e., K–12 schools and higher education)? What "adjustments" would have to be made at the various levels?
2. How might you incorporate service learning into the curriculum with which you are most familiar?
3. How should teachers assess students' learning as a result of their participation in service learning activities?

Benchmarks of Student-Friendly Middle Schools

M. LEE MANNING

ABSTRACT: Several benchmarks usually indicate the extent to which middle schools implement student-friendly perspectives. While individual student-friendly schools differ, M. Lee Manning introduces the seven characteristics or benchmarks that most clearly differentiate student-friendly environments. He also discusses how student-friendly teachers emphasize academic achievement and appropriate behavior while providing educational experiences that reflect a genuine consideration of individual learners.

The need for student-friendly middle schools that provide young adolescents with caring and nurturing educational experiences is clear. Tom Erb (1997) called for "student-friendly classrooms" (p. 2) in which middle school educators acknowledge and validate student needs in a humane way. Plus, several reports (Carnegie Council on Adolescent Development, 1990; National Middle School Association, 1995) call for middle schools to be caring and concerned institutions that serve as advocates for young adolescents. Yet, when interviewed by M. Lee Manning (1997), John Lounsbury commented that adults often compound the problems facing young adolescents, thus making middle schools unfriendly. Adults often talk about young adolescents in negative and belittling ways such as calling them "hormones with feet" (p. 262) and "the range of the strange" (p. 262). Such comments indicate some educators do not consider young adolescents from student-friendly perspectives.

Several benchmarks usually indicate the extent to which middle schools implement student-friendly perspectives. While individual student-friendly schools differ, the seven characteristics or benchmarks include: a recognition of learner diversity, educators trained in middle school education, exploratory programs that encourage learner interest, developmentally responsive guidance and counseling programs, equal access to educational experiences, a positive school environment, and the involvement of parents and families in the education of young adolescents.

BENCHMARKS OF STUDENT-FRIENDLY MIDDLE SCHOOLS

Several benchmarks of student-friendly schools can be identified. It is important to state that student-friendly middle schools do not downplay academic achievement and appropriate behavior. Quite the contrary, student-friendly teachers emphasize academic achievement and appropriate behavior; however, they provide educational experiences that reflect a genuine consideration of individual learners.

Benchmark 1—Student-friendly middle schools provide educational experiences that address young adolescents' tremendous diversity.

Middle school educators provide developmentally responsive educational experiences (National Middle School Association, 1995) based upon young adolescents' physical, psychosocial, and cognitive development; gender and cultural differences; and learning styles and multiple intelligences.

Rather than providing educational experiences that assume too much homogeneity among young adolescents, educators learn to know individual young adolescents and provide experiences that meet individual needs. For example, all young adolescents' cognitive development has not reached Piaget's formal operations stages (Toepfer, 1988); some students' psychosocial development might be to a point where they are socially outgoing—others might still be shy and

honors class

withdrawn. Gender and cultural differences should also be addressed, that is, some girls and some cultural groups might prefer collaborative learning efforts rather than competitive activities (Manning & Baruth, 2000).

While addressing such a wide array of diverse characteristics may appear to be an unwieldy task, learner's individuality can be identified through diagnostic assessments, suggestions from previous teachers, and learning inventories. Student-friendly instruction can be accomplished through individualization, cooperative learning, small group instruction, and peer tutoring.

Benchmark 2—Student-Friendly Middle Schools Provide Teachers Who Are Trained in Middle School Concepts and Early Adolescence Development.

Unfortunately, some middle school teachers received teacher education training in either elementary or secondary education. While they might be committed and excellent teachers, they might lack knowledge of middle school concepts and the early adolescence developmental period. Also, an even worse situation exists when middle school teachers actually want to teach in the elementary or secondary school and are "biding their time in the middle school" until an elementary or secondary position becomes available.

Young adolescents benefit when educators receive appropriate professional training (Dickinson & McEwin, 1997) whether it be during initial teacher preparation or on-going professional development. Appropriate professional training contributes to teachers better understanding middle school concepts that contribute to student-friendly educational experiences (i.e., advisory programs, exploratory programs, and positive school climates). Also, in student-friendly middle schools, educators genuinely want to teach young adolescents and want to provide educational experiences that reflect the needs and challenges of individual young adolescents.

Benchmark 3—Student-Friendly Middle Schools Provide Exploratory Programs.

Exploratory programs, long considered an essential middle school concept, provide young adolescents with six week, eight week or semester-long learning experiences (both curricular and special interest) for 40–50 minutes, depending on the school schedule. Learners have opportunities to discover their talents, unique abilities, and values (Arnold, 1991). Developmentally responsive exploratory programs address young adolescents' shorter attention spans, rapidly changing interests, and fluctuating motivational levels (Manning, 1993).

Exploratory programs also build interest, that is, young adolescents learn about possible career opportunities. Typical examples of exploratory courses include business, keyboarding, choir, homemaking and independent living, print making, drama, foreign languages, arts and crafts, independent study opportunities, dance, music, or nearly any areas that young adolescents want to explore (Arnold, 1991).

For exploratory programs to truly focus on learner needs, students should have a fairly wide choice of topics to explore. Exploratories should be carefully planned and taught by teachers with genuine interest and expertise, those who can teach the exploratory with enthusiasm. Teachers take responsibility for developing programs in their areas of interest and focus learning experiences, to the degree possible, on individual learners. Educators should expect active participation of all learners; yet also realize, because of young adolescents' tremendous diversity, some learners might develop an intense interest in the exploratory, while others might have only a casual interest.

Benchmark 4—Student-Friendly Middle Schools Provide Developmentally Responsive, Comprehensive Guidance and Counseling Programs.

Contemporary young adolescents challenge middle school educators and counselors with concerns such as home situations, school problems, at risk conditions and behaviors, and peer pressure. To address young adolescents' problems, educators implement a team approach to guidance whereby both teachers and counselors collaboratively provide advisement and counseling services. Student-friendly middle schools take several major approaches such as individual, small- and large-group counseling, as well as advisor-advisee programs (Cole, 1992).

The advisor-advisee program can be defined as planned efforts in which each student has the opportunity to participate in a small interactive group with peers and staff to discuss school, personal, and societal concerns (James, 1986). The advisory program, perhaps 25 minutes a day (Cole, 1992), helps each student develop a meaningful relationship with at least one significant adult in the middle school. Student-friendly advisories promote young adolescents' social and emotional growth while providing personal and academic guidance. Topics for advisor-advisee sessions include peer pressure, substance abuse, friendships, health-related issues, career exploration, development, school rules, understanding parents, contemporary issues, and leisure time activities.

Benchmark 5—Student-Friendly Middle Schools Ensure Equal Access to All Educational Experiences.

Certainly equal access is a worthwhile goal for student-friendly middle schools. The gap between exclusivity and equal access has narrowed somewhat during the past few decades, predominantly in the areas required by legal mandates. Unfortunately, however, some schools continue to deny opportunities to students by grouping students homogeneously or requiring students to "try out" for a limited number of opportunities.

However, there are also middle schools which actively develop inclusive activities. For example, in one middle school, teachers announced the opportunity to participate in a play. All students participated—some had speaking roles while others sang as a group. Everyone wanting to be in the play had some respectable opportunity to participate. No one was "cut" and no one was encouraged to quit and try again next time. In fact, the students showed so much interest that the teachers decided to have five one-act plays rather than one longer play, so all students could participate.

Benchmark 6—Student-Friendly Middle Schools Ensure a Positive and Safe Learning Environment.

Student-friendly middle schools ensure a school environment that provides young adolescents with opportunities to learn and interact in a humane, respectful, and psychologically safe learning environment—one that emphasizes cooperation and peaceful existence.

The student-friendly school environment demonstrates a sense of collaboration among students and educators, promotes harmony and interpersonal relations among students, and reflects positive verbal interactions. Teachers and students listen to others with empathy and support others in a nonthreatening manner. In essence, they promote a nurturing school environment, one described by Green (1998) as a sense of community where all individuals are valued and where people feel respected and nurtured, with everyone accepting responsibility for student success.

Educators in student-friendly middle schools want an environment that lessens conflicts between educators and students, reduces discipline referrals, and reduces confrontations, teasing, bullying, and harassment among students. By eliminating the "students versus educators" mentality, young adolescents perceive the harmonious relationships in the school and see less need to engage in hostile and confrontational behaviors. To ensure a student-friendly environment, educators will need to implement schedules, discipline procedures, teaching methods, school organization, and guidance programs that place priority on the learner.

Benchmark 7—Student-Friendly Middle Schools Involve Parents, Families, and Community Members.

The number of parents moderately or highly involved in their children's education drops to about 50% when children reach middle school (Seline, 1997). Therefore, educators often feel challenged to recapture parents' and families' interest and to reengage them in the education of young adolescents. Middle school educators in student-friendly schools recognize the importance of involving parents in young adolescents' education and attempt to do so through parent involvement or conferences.

Students of interested and involved parents usually demonstrate higher levels of motivation and commitment to education; educators and parents get to know one another and assist each other in the education of the child; parents get more involved in school activities and homework; and parents learn the various purposes of middle school education.

CONCLUDING COMMENTS

In student-friendly middle school classrooms, expectations for academic achievement and appropriate behavior should always be clear to young adolescents. These expectations should be conveyed in middle schools that recognize learner diversity, provide appropriately trained educators, ensure learners have exploratory programs, provide responsive guidance and counseling programs, ensure equal access, instill a positive school environment, and involve parents and families. Only when middle schools achieve these benchmarks will young adolescents have truly student-friendly educational experiences.

REFERENCES

The revolution in middle school organization. *Momentum, 22*(2), 20–25.

Carnegie Council on Adolescent Development. (1990). *Turning points: Preparing American youth for the 21st century.* Washington: Author.

Cole, C. (1992). Nurturing a teacher advisory program. Columbus, OH: National Middle School Association.

Dickinson, T. S., & McEwin, C. K. (1997). Perspectives and profiles: The professional preparation of middle school teachers. *Childhood Education, 73*(5), 272–277.

Erb, T. O. (1997). Student-friendly classrooms in a not very child-friendly world. *Middle School Journal*, (4), 2.

Green, R. L. (1998). Nurturing characteristics in schools related to discipline, attendance, and eighth grade proficiency test scores. *American Secondary Education, 26*(4), 7–14.

James, M. (1986). *Adviser-advisee programs: Why, what, and how.* Columbus, OH: National Middle School Association.

Manning, M. L. (1993). *Developmentally appropriate middle level schools.* Olney, MD: Association for Childhood Education International.

Manning, M. L. (1997). An interview with John H. Lounsbury. *Childhood Education, 73*(5), 262–266.

Manning, M. L., & Baruth, L. G. (2000). *Multicultural education of children and adolescents* (3rd. ed). Boston: Allyn and Bacon.

National Middle School Association. (1995). *This we believe: Developmentally responsive middle schools.* Columbus, OH: Author.

Seline, A. M. (1997). Parents as partners: Schools seek to build better relationships with families, *High Strides: The Bimonthly Report on Urban Middle Grades, 9*(5), 1, 2–5.

Toepfer, C. F. (1988). What to know about young adolescents. *Social Education, 52,* 110–112.

M. Lee Manning is a professor in the Department of Educational Curriculum and Instruction, Darden College of Education, Old Dominion University, Norfolk, VA.

QUESTIONS FOR REFLECTION

1.   What are the seven characteristics that differentiate student-friendly environments? Are these characteristics realistic for most schools to accomplish? What conditions would make it more difficult for some schools to meet these benchmarks?
2.   What is the effect of a student-friendly middle school for student learning? What is the connection between the environment students occupy and their capacity for learning?
3.   Manning writes that student-friendly teachers emphasize academic achievement and appropriate behavior while providing educational experiences that reflect a genuine consideration of individual learners. How is this accomplished? Is there a threat that a focus on a "student-friendly" environment and curriculum could dilute academic rigor?

The Homework Wars

DAVID SKINNER

ABSTRACT: *In the current hyperproductive, overachieving setting, a curious educational debate has broken out. The parents of the younger K–12 students are revolting against the reportedly increasing amounts of home-work assigned their children. A major lightning rod for this debate has been* The End of Homework, *a book by Etta Kralovec and John Buell, whose argument found an appreciative audience in* Time, Newsweek, The New York Times, People *magazine, and elsewhere. Understanding the book's argument—its strengths and weaknesses—is not necessary to understanding the debate over homework, but it is helpful to understanding the overall tenor of this controversy.*

The American child, a gloomy chorus of news-papers, magazines and books tells us, is over-worked. All spontaneity is being squeezed out of him by the vise-like pressures of homework, extracurricular activities, and family. "Jumping from Spanish to karate, tap dancing to tennis—with hours of homework waiting at home—the overscheduled child is as busy as a new law firm associate," reports the *New York Times*. The arti-cle goes on to describe a small counter-trend in which some parents are putting a stop to the frenzy and letting their children, for once in their little harried lives, simply hang out or, as one of the insurgent parents explains, enjoy an informal game of pickup.

What's this? A game of catch is news? And this is said to be sociologically significant? Something

must be amiss in the state of childhood today. The common diagnosis is that too much work, too much ambition, and an absence of self-directedness are harming American children. In an influential 2001 article in the *Atlantic Monthly*, David Brooks, author of *Bobos in Par-adise*, christened the over-achieving American child the "Organization Kid." Reporting on the character of the generation born in the early 1980s, in which he focused on those attending some of America's most prestigious colleges, Brooks found a youth demographic of career-oriented yes-men, with nary a rebel in the bunch. Called team players and rule-followers, they are best captured by a 1997 Gallup survey Brooks cites in which 96 percent of teenagers said they got along with their parents.

In this hyperproductive, overachieving setting, a curious educational debate has broken out. The parents of the younger K–12 worker-bees are revolting against the reportedly increasing amounts of homework assigned their children. A major lightning rod for this debate has been *The End of Homework,* a book by Etta Kralovec and John Buell, whose argument found an appreciative audience in *Time, Newsweek,* the *New York Times, People* magazine, and elsewhere. For a novel polemic against a long-established educational practice, such a widespread hearing suggests that the issue has struck a chord with many American families. Understanding the book's argument—its strengths and weaknesses—is not necessary to understanding the debate over homework, but it is helpful to understanding the overall tenor of this controversy.

THE END OF HOMEWORK

What makes *The End of Homework* stand out is that it was written by academics. Etta Kralovec holds a doctorate in education from the Teachers College at Columbia University and, for over 12 years, she directed teacher education at the College of the Atlantic. John Buell, too, has spent time on the faculty at the College of the Atlantic. Now a newspaper columnist, the onetime associate editor of *The Progressive* has authored two books on political economy. In an afterword, the authors say *The End of Homework* grew out of a series of interviews with high school dropouts, many of whom cited homework as a reason they discontinued their education. This snapshot of homework's dire effect, unfortunately, requires much qualification.

Kralovec and Buell show little restraint when describing the problems brought on by the reported increase in homework. Attacking the proposition that homework inculcates good adult habits, the authors cite the historical trend in psychology away from viewing children as miniature adults, but then quickly lose perspective. "In suggesting that children need to learn to deal with adult levels of pressure, we risk doing them untold damage. By this logic, the schoolyard shootings of recent years may be likened to 'disgruntled employee' rampages." Nor do Kralovec and Buell inspire confidence by quoting a report attributing a spate of suicides in Hong Kong to "distress over homework." The report they cite is from the *Harare Herald* in Zimbabwe, not exactly a widely recognized authority on life in Hong Kong.

The End of Homework's alarmist tone is best captured, however, in its uncritical acceptance of a 1999 report from the American Association of Orthopedic Surgeons (AAOS) "that thousands of kids have back, neck, and shoulder pain caused by their heavy backpacks." The book's cover photo even shows two little kids straining like packmules under the weight of their bookbags. It so happens that orthopedic professionals themselves, at the AAOS no less, dispute the report. To pick a recent example, a study presented at the 2003 meeting of the AAOS, based on interviews with 346 school-age orthopedic patients, found only one patient who attributed his back pain to carrying a bookbag.

Kralovec and Buell's case against homework is further diminished by the book's clear political agenda. Indeed, the telltale signs of an overriding left-wing social critique are sadly abundant. Twice inside of 100 pages, the same unilluminating quotation is trotted out from "the great radical sociologist C. Wright Mills," whose influence on this book, however, pales next to that of Harvard economist Juliet B. Schor. Schor is most famous for her controversial 1992 bestseller *The Overworked American: The Unexpected Decline of Leisure,* which argued that American adults were losing their disposable time to the steady encroachments of longer work schedules. But the book's primary findings were contradicted by existing research and just about every mainstream expert asked to offer an opinion on the subject.

Nevertheless, Schor's laborite call for a new consensus on the proper number of hours and days that should be devoted to employment (approximately half of current levels) finds an echo in *The End of Homework*'s call to American families to throw off their homework shackles and reclaim the evenings for family time. Indeed, one notices in this book more than a little overwrought socialist rhetoric. For example, after bemoaning the failure of standards-based reforms to improve achievement scores, the authors comment that the continued emphasis on homework "fits the ideological requirement of those who maintain the status quo in our economy and politics" and that homework "serves the needs of powerful groups within our society."

The book's other patron saint is Jonathan Kozol, the influential left-wing author of *Savage Inequalities* who has done more than anyone to swamp mainstream education debate with radical social criticism. In the style of Kozol, whom they cite a dozen or so times, Kralovec and Buell binge on the theme of equality when they should be carefully picking over social science data, insisting that homework "pits students who can against students who can't." And when they're not raising the specter of class warfare, Kralovec and Buell are lecturing readers on their unwillingness to recognize its insidious influence: "We suspect that many Americans may be unwilling to acknowledge the existence of an entrenched class system in the United States that serves to constrain or enhance our children's life chances." Economic inequalities, the authors inveigh, fly in the face of "our most cherished values, such as democracy and freedom." Typical of their tempestuous approach to this discrete pedagogical question, Kralovec and Buell devote their final chapter to "Homework in the Global Economy."

Hidden amid the authors' polemic, however, is a persuasive and warranted case against an educational practice of limited value. Homework, in some cases, deserves to be attacked, which makes it all the more a pity that Kralovec and Buell couldn't confine themselves to their primary subject. Their opinion that "homework is almost always counterproductive for elementary schoolchildren" is not the product of some left-wing fever swamp and deserves further consideration.

HOW MUCH

Kralovec and Buell's more serious case against homework begins with a standard social-science discussion of the difference between correlation and causality. But as often happens in critical examinations, the fact that there are obvious limits to human understanding is used to argue for a radical skepticism when it comes to the methods and aims of research. One author's qualifiers and caveats become, in the hands of his opponents, arguments for the proposition that it is impossible to know anything about what condition brought about which effect. So what if students who did a lot of homework performed well on achievement exams? Maybe it was the case that they did a lot of homework because they were high-achieving students?

Down that road, many a worthy illusion comes undone, but few usable lessons can be drawn. Down the opposite road, however fraught it may be with epistemological limitations, we can nevertheless develop a vague picture of solid educational practice.

University of Missouri professor of psychological sciences Harris Cooper, whose research on homework is widely cited by critics on both sides of the debate, including Kralovec and Buell, offers conditional support for the practice. "Is homework better than no homework at all?" he asks in a 1980s literature review. On the basis of 17 research reports examining over 3,300 students, Cooper found that 70 percent of comparisons yielded a positive answer. In terms of class grades and standardized test scores, he found that "the average student doing homework in these studies had a higher achievement score than 55 percent of students not doing homework." Break down such average findings, however, and this modest advantage gained through homework is lost through other variables.

Perhaps the most commanding factor in deciding the homework question is age or grade level. "Older students benefited the most from doing homework," writes Cooper. "The average effect of homework was twice as large for high school as for junior high school students and twice as large again for junior high school students as for elementary school students." This raises interesting questions about homework's distribution among age groups.

Much of the homework controversy is fueled by stories of very young children burdened with lengthy assignments and complicated projects that require extensive parental involvement. Searching for evidence that such work is important to their child's education and development, the parent of a fifth grader will find only cold comfort in the research examined by Cooper. "Teachers of Grades 4, 5, and 6 might expect the average student doing homework to outscore about 52 percent of equivalent no-homework students." A 2 percentile-point advantage gained by a practice that could be interrupting dinner, stealing family time, and pitting child against parent hardly seems enough to justify the intrusion.

For high school students, however, homework can do a lot of good. "If grade level is taken into account," Cooper finds, "homework's effect on the achievement of elementary school students could be described as 'very small,' but on high school students its effect would be 'large.' " If the average fourth- through sixth-grade student who does homework can expect only a 2 percentile-point advantage over one who does none, junior high school students doing homework can expect a 10 percentile-point advantage and high school students a 19 percentile-point advantage. What's more, this effect translates into high achievement not only in class grades—which more readily reflect a positive homework effect—but also on standardized tests, which are quite significant to a student's educational future.

WHAT KIND

There are other wrinkles worth attending to. For one, Cooper himself still favors homework, but possibly not the kind that is causing the most heartache and the most headaches. "Not surprisingly, homework produced larger effects if students did more assignments per week. Surprisingly, the effect of homework was negatively related to the duration of the homework treatment—treatments spanning longer periods produced less of a homework effect." Which is to say, homework comprised of short regular assignments is probably the most effective.

One underlying lesson here should cause many enemies of homework to groan. Kralovec and Buell, for example, marshall the classic complaint, usually made by children, that homework is boring, repetitive, and basically has nothing to do with the developing child's true self. Interesting homework—the fun stuff that allows a child to express himself, that supposedly promotes "creativity" and "critical thinking" and "planning skills"—does not come off well in Cooper's study. Examining broad national and state-wide studies of the relationship between time spent on homework and its effects, Cooper found that the correlations between time spent and positive effects increased "for subjects for which homework assignments are more likely to involve rote learning, practice, or rehearsal. Alternately, subjects such as science and social studies, which often involve longer-term projects, integration of multiple skills, and creative use of non-school resources show the smallest average correlations." Note the collision of opposing pedagogical trends: improving standards by increasing homework and the movement away from rote learning. Indeed, there may be nothing more unhelpful to a student than a teacher of high standards who doesn't want to bore his students.

Interestingly, no one involved in the fight over homework has argued that parents might consider encouraging their children to put in less effort on homework that is overly time-consuming and pedagogically unproductive. Which seems a pity. Why shouldn't a parent tell his overworked fifth-grader to spend less time on that big assignment on American subcultural narratives? Or occasionally have him not do his homework at all? A little civil disobedience might be a useful way of sending a message to a teacher whose assignments are overly ambitious. And if the child gets a lower grade as a result, then it's a small price to pay. It's not as if his entire educational future is on the line.

The homework critics never suggest such a course of action, needless to say, but not because it might undermine teachers' authority, a result they otherwise happily pursue. Odd as it sounds, the fight against homework is largely about achievement, specifically about setting the price of officially recognized excellence at an acceptable rate. Reading Kralovec and Buell and the many newspaper and magazine articles depicting the rebellion against homework, one comes away with an impression in keeping with David Brooks's "Organization Kid," but with an egalitarian twist. The whole movement reflects an organization culture that wants high grades to be possible for all kids, regardless of their varying levels of ability or willingness to work, regardless of what other commitments these children have made, regardless of the importance of family.

TIME AND HOMEWORK

A significant underlying question remains to be addressed. The evidence that there is a widespread homework problem—that too many students are carrying too heavy a homework load—is largely anecdotal. There are some empirical indications of a modest increase in homework over the last 20 years or so, but other indications suggest the problem is being overstated. While some parents and families may have rather serious homework problems, these would generally appear to be private problems, hardly in need of national or even local solutions.

At least there is a consensus on standard reference points. One constant in this debate are the data gathered from the University of Michigan's 1997 Child Development supplement to the Panel Study of Income Dynamics and 1981 Study of Time Use in Social and Economic Accounts, a collection of time-use studies of children. Often appearing in the press cheek-by-jowl with quotes

from overstretched parents, most reporting on the study suggests its findings support the conclusion that American children lack for leisure time amid demands imposed on them by parents and school. But the study's authors, who arguably know more than anyone about how American children are actually spending their time day-in and day-out, do not see the story this way. In fact, in a *New York Times* article, the study's primary researcher, Sandra L. Hofferth, dismissed the whole notion that the American child is overworked and overoccupied. "I don't believe in the 'hurried child' for a minute. . . . There is a lot of time that can be used for other things."

On the question of homework, Hofferth and co-author John F. Sandberg reject the claim that homework has seen a significant general increase. The average amount of time spent studying for 3- to 12-year-olds has increased from 1981 to 1997, but the vast majority of those increases (studying and reading are measured separately) are concentrated among 3- to 5-year-olds (reading) and 6- to 8-year-olds (studying). "The main reason for the increase in studying among 6- to 8-year-olds was an increase in the proportion who did some studying at all, from one-third to more than one-half. The fact that significant increases in reading occurred among 3- to 5-year-olds probably reflects parents' increasing concern with preparing children for school."

Which is to say, homework appears to be increasing most where there was no homework before, and among age groups for whom it will do the least good. Far from a situation of the straw breaking the camel's back, we see many unburdened camels taking on their first tiny handfuls of straw, and a number of others carrying little if any more than they did in the past. This is where the story of the debate over homework takes a major turn. While arguably some American children have been turned into walking delivery systems for wicked educators bent on upsetting the home life of innocent American families, this is clearly not true across the board. In fact, one might say that a good number of American children and teenagers are already deciding how much time they want to spend on homework, and the amount of work they've opted for is not exactly back-breaking.

The Brookings Institution recently weighed in on the homework debate on this very point, arguing that "almost everything in this story [of overworked students] is wrong." Like Hofferth and Sandburg, Tom Loveless, the Brookings author, points out that most of the increase noted in the University of Michigan study is concentrated among the youngest subjects who are reading earlier and being introduced to homework at a younger age. The most telling finding in the Brookings report, however, is that "the typical student, even in high school, does not spend more than an hour per day on homework." Needless to say, this picture is quite different from the homework situation described by Kralovec and Buell, to say nothing of the dire drama described over and over in newspaper and magazine stories.

The 1997 University of Michigan time-use studies do report average increases for time spent on homework against a 1981 benchmark, but analysis by the Brookings Institution shows these increases are nearly negligible. The amount of time 3- to 5-year-olds spent studying increased from 25 minutes per week in 1981 to 36 minutes per week in 1997. This translates to an increase of two minutes a night if studying takes place five nights a week. The next group, 6- to 8-year-olds, as mentioned, saw the biggest increase, from 52 minutes a week to 2 hours and 8 minutes a week, which translates to an average increase of 15 minutes a night, bringing average homework time to a grand total of 25 minutes or so a night. The oldest group, 9- to 12-year-olds, saw only an increase of 19 minutes on average per week, an increase of less than four minutes a night. Other data culled by Brookings from the University of Michigan study show that over one-third of 9- to 12-year-olds reported doing no homework. Indeed, half of all 3- to 12-year-olds said that they were doing no homework whatsoever, despite data showing a small average increase in homework for this group.

Other research supports these findings. The National Assessment of Education Progress (NAEP) reports that a significant number of 9- and 13-year-olds are assigned no homework at all. Between 1984 and 1999, at least 26 percent and as much as 36 percent of 9-year-olds reported receiving no homework assignments the day before filling out the questionnaire. Among 13-year-olds, the numbers show a relatively large and increasing number of students assigned no homework: 17 percent in 1988, increasing to 24 percent in 1999. As for older students, the 1999 National Center for Education Statistics (NCES) reports that 12 percent of high school seniors said they were doing no homework during a typical week. Of the remaining 88 percent, most said they spent less than 5 hours a week doing homework. This, remember, is in high school, where teachers assign more work, students are expected to do more work, and homework is agreed to have the most benefits. And yet, the above NCES number tells us that most high school students who do homework spend less than an hour a day, five days a week, doing it. According to the NAEP, only about a third of 17-year-olds have more than one hour of homework a night.

What about examining the homework habits of students who go on to college, thus controlling for the downward pull of low performers in high school? In the national survey of college freshmen performed by the University of California at Los Angeles, a surprising number report having worked no more than one hour a night as high school seniors. In 1987, only 47 percent of college freshmen surveyed said they had done more than five hours of homework a week. By 2002, that number had fallen to 34 percent—meaning only about one-third of American college freshman said they'd spent more than one hour a night on homework as high school seniors. As the Brookings report comments, such a homework load makes American high schoolers look underworked compared with their peers in other developed nations.

PLEASED WITH OURSELVES

The evidence suggests that while a significant portion of students are not carrying an insupportable burden of homework, a small percentage of students work long hours indeed—and some of them not for any good reason. We are giving the wrong kind of homework and in increasing quantities to the wrong age groups. As the Brookings report notes, 5 percent of fourth graders have more than 2 hours of homework nightly. Whether such a figure is surprising or not may merely be a question of expectations, but it hardly seems reasonable to expect 9-year-olds to be capable of finishing such quantities of after-school work. Still, that a small percentage of students are unnecessarily overworked does not justify the national press coverage and research interest this story has generated.

Why the homework controversy has received the attention it has may result from our national preference for stories that make our children seem one and all to be high achievers. Also, it's no secret that many professional and upper-class parents will undertake extraordinary measures to help their children get ahead in school in order to get ahead in the real world: These children are sent to elite schools that liberally assign homework, even as they are signed up for any number of organized activities in the name of self-improvement. And, of course, this segment of the population does more than its share to direct and set the tone for press coverage of news issues of interest to families. That surely helps explain spectacular headlines like "The Homework Ate My Family" (*Time*), "Homework Doesn't Help" (*Newsweek*), and "Overbooked: Four Hours of Homework for a Third Grader" (*People*).

So, while the overworked American child exists, he is not typical. Strangely enough, he seems to be more of an American ideal—drawn from our Lake Woebegone tendency of imagining that we're so good and hard-working, we might be too good and too hard-working. Thus do we ask ourselves why Johnny is doing so much homework, when in fact he is not.

David Skinner is an assistant managing editor at *The Weekly Standard*. Before working at *The Standard* in November 1998, he was managing editor of the *Public Interest*. He has written for the *Washington Times, Salon, Philanthropy,* the *Public Interest,* and the *Wall Street Journal.*

QUESTIONS FOR REFLECTION

1. What should be the role of homework in today's curriculum? Should there be an end to homework or should homework continue much the same as it does today? If changes to homework were to be instituted, what should change and who would monitor the change?

2. Given how many distractions there are outside of school—television, video games, sports, etc.—is there a compelling argument that homework keeps students from becoming too reliant on entertainment rather than intellectual growth?

3. Do you agree with Skinner's assertion that the "overworked American child" is not typical and that most children today have more free time than people think they do? Skinner suggests that a relatively small percentage of overworked students contributed to an unnecessarily large amount of national press coverage and research interest. Why do you think this is? Is the media to blame for creating a crisis where one doesn't truly exist?

Building Developmental Assets to Promote Success in School and in Life

PETER C. SCALES
JUDY TACCOGNA

ABSTRACT: Both a sense of belonging and a belief in their own competency seem to be missing from the school experiences of disengaged, underachieving students. Building students' developmental assets is a promising practice for reconnecting students and supporting achievement. Looking at schools through an "assets lens" can promote concrete changes in school organization, curriculum and instruction, cocurricular programs, support services, and community partnerships that make the whole environment more conducive to great teaching and learning.

Students live in a school environment that is increasingly dominated by accountability measures such as standardized tests. Consequently, many schools focused on teaching tightly prescribed content knowledge and related skills in order for students to meet state benchmark standards in a variety of subject areas. In Chicago, for example, 500 education standards are aligned with 18 state goals, and more than 1,500 curriculum frameworks that dictate what content is to be taught are in turn aligned with the benchmark standards (Newmann, Lopez, and Bryk 1998). Yet standardized curriculum prescriptions often work against authentic and effective instruction (Newmann, Secada, and Wehlage 1995), and against engaging students who are most in need of more solid connections to their schools.

A PROMISING PRACTICE FOR RECONNECTING YOUTH AND SUPPORTING ACHIEVEMENT

One promising approach to increasing the likelihood of student success in both school and life is to build "developmental assets"—those relationships, opportunities, values, and skills that, when present in the lives of youth, make young people less likely to become involved in risk behaviors and more likely to be successful in school, rela-

tionships, and life in general (Benson et al. 1999). Building developmental assets is essentially about building positive, sustained relationships, not only among students and teachers but also among parents and students, parents and teachers, students and students, and among teachers and other school staff themselves (Scales 1999). What is crucial, however, is that the use of relationships as a lens through which to view school policies and practices can effect concrete changes in curriculum and instruction, school organization, cocurricular programs, community partnerships, and support services that make the entire school environment more conducive to engagement and achievement, and to great teaching and learning (Starkman, Scales, and Roberts 1999).

One of the main strengths of asset building is that it is less a scripted program and more a way of living, a way of looking at and relating differently to students as people, a way of creating a classroom and school environment that is supportive of children and adolescents. That strength means that it does not take a significant amount of time to learn new strategies and incorporate them into a discrete portion of time during the day. Rather it means rethinking what one already does in the classroom and reframing these activities in an "asset-building lens"—for example, greeting students by name, responding to student questions and concerns, providing students with differentiated assignments, and communicating with parents.

DEVELOPMENTAL ASSETS

Developmental assets are the positive relationships, opportunities, competencies, values, and self-perceptions that youth need to succeed (see Table 1). Researchers at Search Institute, a nonprofit research organization located in Minneapolis, Minn., believe that these assets make a difference in the success and health of young people. Many studies, including research being conducted at Search Institute, indicate that building students' developmental assets is related to a variety of antecedents to achievement as well as to measures of actual performance and achievement. For example, students who report experiencing 31–40 of the developmental assets are several times more likely than students reporting an average level of 11–20 assets to get mostly As in school (38 percent versus 19 percent, according to Benson et al. 1999). Studies also have found significant relationships among variables defined similarly to the 40 developmental assets and key achievement outcomes (such as level of effort, academic goal orientations, competency beliefs, beliefs about the value of education,

TABLE 1

Forty Developmental Assets for Middle and High School Youth (ages 12 to 18)

Class and Type	*Name and Definition*
External	
Support	1. **Family support:** Family life provides high levels of love and support.
	2. **Positive family communication:** Young person and her or his parent(s) communicate positively, and young person is willing to seek parent(s) advice and counsel.
	3. **Other adult relationships:** Young person receives support from three or more nonparent adults.
	4. **Caring neighborhood:** Young person experiences caring neighbors.
	5. **Caring school climate:** School provides a caring, encouraging environment.
	6. **Parent involvement in schooling:** Parent(s) are actively involved in helping young person succeed in school.
Empowerment	7. **Community values youth:** Young person perceives that adults in the community value youth.
	8. **Youth as resources:** Young person is given useful roles in the community.
	9. **Service to others:** Young person serves in the community one hour or more per week.
	10. **Safety:** Young person feels safe at home, school, and in the neighborhood.
Boundaries and Expectations	11. **Family boundaries:** Family has clear rules and consequences, and monitors the young person's whereabouts.
	12. **School boundaries:** School provides clear rules and consequences.
	13. **Neighborhood boundaries:** Neighbors take responsibility for monitoring young person's behavior.
	14. **Adult role models:** Parent(s) and other adults model positive, responsible behavior.
	15. **Positive peer influence:** Young person's best friends model responsible behavior.
	16. **High expectations:** Both parent(s) and teachers encourage the young person to do well.

TABLE 1
Continued

Class and Type	*Name and Definition*
External *(cont.)*	
Constructive Use of Time	**17. Creative activities:** Young person spends three or more hours of time per week in lessons or practice in music, theater, or other arts.
	18. Youth programs: Young person spends three or more hours per week in sports, clubs, or organizations at school and/or in community organizations.
	19. Religious community: Young person spends one hour or more per week in activities in a religious institution.
	20. Time at home: Young person is out with friends "with nothing special to do" two nights or fewer per week.
Internal	
Commitment to Learning	**21. Achievement motivation:** Young person is motivated to do well in school.
	22. School engagement: Young person is actively engaged in learning.
	23. Homework: Young person reports doing at least one hour of homework every school day.
	24. Bonding to school: Young person cares about her or his school.
	25. Reading for pleasure: Young person reads for pleasure three or more hours per week.
Positive Values	**26. Caring:** Young person places high value on helping other people.
	27. Equality and social justice: Young person places high value on promoting equality and reducing hunger and poverty.
	28. Integrity: Young person acts on convictions and stands up for her or his beliefs.
	29. Honesty: Young person "tells the truth even when it is not easy."
	30. Responsibility: Young person accepts and takes personal responsibility.
	31. Restraint: Young person believes it is important not to be sexually active or to use alcohol or other drugs.
Social Competencies	**32. Planning and decision-making:** Young person knows how to plan ahead and make choices.
	33. Interpersonal competence: Young person has empathy, sensitivity, and friendship skills.
	34. Cultural competence: Young person has knowledge of and comfort with people of different cultural/racial/ethnic backgrounds.
	35. Resistance skills: Young person can resist negative peer pressure and dangerous situations.
	36. Peaceful conflict resolution: Young person seeks to resolve conflict nonviolently.
Positive Identity	**37. Personal power:** Young person feels he or she has control over "things that happen to me."
	38. Self-esteem: Young person reports having high self-esteem.
	39. Sense of purpose: Young person reports that "my life has a purpose."
	40. Positive view of personal future: Young person is optimistic about her or his personal future.

Note: This table may be reproduced for educational, noncommercial uses only. Copyright © 1997 by Search Institute, 700 S. Third St., Suite 210, Minneapolis, Minn. 55415; 800-888-7828; www.search-institute.org.

grades, graduation rates, and test scores), as well as among the developmental assets and those outcomes that support learning (such as lessened alcohol and other drug use, greater problem-solving skills, greater social skills, and less depression). In addition to being associated with higher levels of school achievement, the assets have also been linked to lower drug use; less sexual intercourse in the teen years; fewer conduct problems; lessened use of marijuana; and increased helping of others, leadership, and ability to overcome adversity, among other desirable outcomes (Benson et al. 1999; Leffert et al. 1998; Scales et al. 2000; Scales and Leffert 1999).

The assets (see table 1) fall into two main classes: external and internal. *External assets* (grouped into the categories of support, empowerment, boundaries and expectations, and constructive use of time) are the relationships and opportunities that surround young people with the support and situations that guide them to behave in healthy ways and make wise choices. *Internal assets* (commitment to learning, positive values, social competencies, and positive identity) are those commitments, values, competencies, and self-perceptions that, when nurtured, provide the "internal compass" that guides a young person's behavior and choices so that he or she becomes self-regulating.

Unfortunately, research at Search Institute indicates that the typical sixth to twelfth grader experiences less than half the assets overall, and too few experience those assets that are most directly related to school success. Over the past decade, Search Institute has surveyed more than one million youth in more than 1,000 cities and towns nationwide to measure their asset levels. The basic findings have remained distressingly consistent from year to year, community to community. From the perspective of teachers and administrators at the secondary level, the situation is even more troubling: the average level of developmental assets that students report drops from sixth grade through twelfth grade, with a particularly large drop across the middle-level school years (Benson et al. 1999). Following is just one statis-

tical highlight from Search Institute research for each of the asset categories, suggesting the depth of the challenge facing educators, parents, and students.

From the external classes, in the support category, only 25 percent of students say they experience a caring school climate. In the empowerment category, only 50 percent of students say they feel safe in their schools and neighborhoods. In the boundaries and expectations category, less than 50 percent of students think their teachers and parents have high expectations for their performance. In the constructive use of time category, fewer than six in ten students spend at least three hours per week in organized clubs, sports, or other activities sponsored by schools or community organizations, even though involvement in structured activities beyond school hours is associated with lower involvement in risk behaviors, encourages the development of other positive attributes, and assists young people in developing positive social supports and skills.

For the internal classes, in the commitment to learning category, nearly 40 percent of students do not feel engaged with school or motivated to achieve. In the positive values category, nearly 40 percent of students do not take personal responsibility for their actions. In the social competencies category, more than 70 percent of students do not consider themselves good planners and decision makers. In the positive identity category, less than 50 percent of students feel they have control over the things that happen in their life.

ASSET BUILDING IN THE SCHOOLS

Schools and districts seeking to infuse their school community with the developmental assets approach should spread efforts across these five main areas of schooling: curriculum and instruction, school organization (the building and the school day), cocurricular programs (i.e., before- and after-school programs), community partnerships (i.e., with families, neighbors, and other community members, volunteers, and business people), and support services (i.e., counseling services, health care providers, and support staff).

Before looking at each of these areas in more depth, it is useful to make explicit six basic principles of asset building.

- Everyone can be an asset builder. Administrators, teachers, custodians, bus drivers, counselors, food service staff, and countless individuals contribute to the roles played by parents and other adults in the community.
- All young people need assets. These developmental assets are crucial for all students, not just at-risk students, gifted students, or students with special needs.
- Relationships are the key. Strong, nurturing relationships support youth, engage them in learning, and focus them on positive thinking and behaviors. How often do teachers receive letters from students who write with stories about how their connections with individual teachers have made a tremendous difference their lives?
- Asset building is an ongoing process. Educators add to what parents and many others have already contributed to students' development, and they help students benefit from future relationships and opportunities.
- Consistency of messages is important. When all the people in all the settings in an adolescent's life say the same things about values and expectations, and they provide similar support and challenges, his or her world is more psychologically secure and sensible, increasing the adolescent's sense of motivation.
- Redundancy is crucial. Asset building is not a one-shot program but a commitment to provide for all students repeated exposure to caring relationships and challenging opportunities that will allow them to develop their talents, interests, and values in ways that help them reach personal goals and contribute to society.

With those six principles of asset building as background, school administrators should consider how they, in partnership with other commu-

nity resources, can best build all 40 developmental assets. However, in reading the following examples, readers might keep in mind primarily the 13 assets that research (see Scales and Leffert 1999) suggests are most important to academic success: school engagement, achievement motivation, positive peer influence, youth programs, bonding to school, school boundaries, homework, interpersonal competence, other adult relationships, high expectations, parent involvement in schooling, caring school climate, and reading for pleasure (Starkman, Scales, and Roberts 1999).

Examples of how the main areas of school functioning are tied to the school-related developmental assets include the following:

Curriculum and Instruction

Cross-curricular integration, team teaching, and exploratory programs of high interest to students help keep young people engaged, help teachers coordinate and monitor homework, and provide opportunities for youth to build adult relationships beyond those with their parents. Heterogeneous grouping (versus academic tracking) and the use of authentic assessment contribute to achievement motivation. Service learning experiences not only help students meet standards in many states but also provide students with opportunities to feel valuable and to make contributions to their community. Cooperative learning strategies reinforce the skill building needed to develop the positive peer influence and interpersonal competence assets. A comprehensive health education curriculum builds both the values and social competencies asset categories. Teachers provide clear school boundaries when they state explicitly what students must know and be able to do to receive a particular grade. Many curricula already incorporate skill-building in communication, decision making and planning; thinking about those as asset-building instructional strategies makes teaching to the assets more deliberate and intentional than it otherwise might be. One of the key skills necessary for success is the ability to read; providing training in teaching and supporting reading skills for both meaning and pleasure to teachers in all content areas at middle and high schools would not only build the reading for pleasure asset, but more important, contribute to greater reading success through continual, targeted reinforcement.

Organization

Several organizational structures currently advocated in schools support more and deeper relationships between adults and students, increase motivation, and ensure consistency in boundaries and expectations. Examples include organizing schools so that there are smaller communities within large middle or high schools (houses and teams), establishing advisor/advisee systems, using flexible scheduling, and keeping students in the same teams and with the same adults over several years (known as looping). Providing ways that students can have input into the operations of the school, including decision making and development of rules and sanctions, enhances the empowerment assets and helps develop interpersonal competencies. Asking parents to participate on committees, in learning situations, or in making decisions about what is purchased for the library increases the parent involvement asset. Opening the school doors to before- and after-school programs for young people supports all of the assets in the constructive use of time category, and can provide opportunities for peer and adult tutoring as well, enhancing the positive peer influence and relationship with adult assets.

Cocurricular Programs

Before- and after-school programs provide a wide variety of opportunities through which youth can develop assets, from involvement in the creative arts, sports, and clubs, to additional academic enrichment from tutors. Many of those opportuni-

ties also help to develop social-emotional intelligence and leadership skills and provide opportunities for service learning. To reinforce asset building most successfully, active recruitment of all students in those programs is an important element, so that participation is as inclusive as possible. Cocurricular programs are also an ideal place for parents to become involved in school-related, youth-friendly activities conducted in safe environments.

Community Partnerships

Corporate

Links with businesses and other community organizations create additional opportunities for youth to build assets and enhance educational programs by providing "real world" environments in which students can learn content-related knowledge and skills at the same time. Partners such as the YMCA, Boys and Girls Clubs, and parks and recreation organizations are key providers of before- and after-school programs and all typically advocate for similar positive youth outcomes. Framing the accomplishment of those outcomes in the common language of developmental assets also brings consistency and redundancy to the messages a community and school system wants to send.

Support Services

Schools typically offer counseling and health services, but there are many other support services as well that bring caring, encouragement, and resources to students. Examples of providing potentially asset-building services within school systems include establishing on-site family resource centers; creating articulation programs to ease the transitions of students from elementary to middle and from middle to high schools; making peer mediation programs a key element in the operation of the discipline system; and providing counselors to students in ratios that allow them time to talk explicitly about issues of immediate developmental importance to them, as well as about short- and long-term planning.

CHALLENGES FOR IMPLEMENTATION

Several challenges exist in introducing and incorporating such asset-building strategies into school communities. First, it may be a challenge to communicate the relevance of asset building quickly and convincingly to school audiences who sometimes feel they have little time or energy to invest in looking at or thinking about anything that does not relate to content or instructional strategy development. Yet building assets in students is something that educators throughout America are already doing, though perhaps unsystematically.

Second, it can be a challenge to help staff learn the strategies involved in asset building and identify ways in which they can intentionally build assets through (a) relationships with students, (b) the instructional program, (c) schoolwide discipline codes, (d) mission statements, and (e) policy directions. Woven through the five areas of schooling (curriculum and instruction, school organization, cocurricular programs, community partnerships, and support services) are three approaches to incorporating asset building: building relationships, creating supportive environments, and aligning programs and practices with asset-building principles. For example, one of the basic principles of asset building is that "relationships are the key." Hence, searching for ways to build relationships with young people within each of those five areas of schooling would be productive. Teachers might provide instructional activities (e.g., cooperative learning opportunities) that foster relationships between the teacher and students and among classmates at the same time that content and skills are being taught.

Teachers and principals can help create supportive environments for students by reconsidering school organization (lengthening periods, creating houses or teams), incorporating cocur-

ricular programs (enabling clubs or theater groups to meet after school), and implementing support services (i.e., advocating for improved counselor to student ratios). Many programs and practices already in place in schools are aligned very well with asset-building principles.

A third challenge is finding the time to learn about developmental assets and to be more intentional about building them in all students. Setting aside time involves acknowledgment that change of any kind takes some amount of thinking and assimilation of new information before a change in behavior occurs. Most school personnel advised of the concept of asset building can almost immediately identify practices they routinely use that are asset building. Nevertheless, becoming more intentional about using those practices with all students (rather than only with the preferred or at-risk students, or those labeled special education or gifted and talented) and thinking about ways to extend the approaches to building developmental assets requires deliberate planning and a focus on changing one's behavior.

The time investment is cost-effective: The amount of time needed to expand one's ability to build assets through practices already in use is presumably far less and is more easily infused into one's thinking and current practice than the time needed to receive inservice training; learn a new practice, program, or curriculum; and begin teaching that. Asset building lends itself to being embedded into programs and practices that are already part of the school culture or classroom environment and into educators' ways of relating to students.

REFERENCES

Benson, P. L., P. C. Scales, N. Leffert, and E. C. Roehlkepartain. 1999. *A fragile foundation: The state of developmental assets among American youth.* Minneapolis, Minn.: Search Institute.

Carnegie Council on Adolescent Development. 1992. *A matter of time: Risk and opportunity in the nonschool hours.* New York: Carnegie Council on Adolescent Development.

Leffert, N., P. L. Benson, P. C. Scales, A. Sharma, D. Drake, and D. A. Blyth. 1998. Developmental assets: Measurement and prediction of risk behaviors among adolescents. *Applied Developmental Science* 2: 209–30.

Newmann, F. M., G. Lopez, and A. S. Bryk. 1998. *The quality of intellectual life in Chicago schools: A baseline report.* Chicago: Consortium on Chicago School Research.

Newmann, F. M., W. G. Secada, and G. G. Wehlage. 1995. *A guide to authentic instruction and assessment: Vision, standards, and scoring.* Madison, Wisc.: Center on Organization and Restructuring of Schools.

Scales, P. C. 1999. Care and challenge: The sources of student success. *Middle Ground* 3(2): 19–21.

Scales, P. C., P. L. Benson, N. Leffert, and D. A. Blyth. 2000. Contribution of developmental assets to the prediction of thriving among adolescents. *Applied Developmental Science* 4: 27–46.

Scales, P. C., and N. Leffert. 1999. *Developmental assets: A synthesis of the scientific research on adolescent development.* Minneapolis, Minn.: Search Institute.

Starkman, N., P. C. Scales, and C. Roberts. 1999. *Great places to learn: How asset-building schools help students succeed.* Minneapolis, Minn.: Search Institute.

Peter C. Scales is senior fellow, and *Judy Taccogna,* a former district director of curriculum and instruction, school principal, counselor, and teacher, is director/education sector; both are with Search Institute, Minneapolis, Minnesota.

QUESTIONS FOR REFLECTION

1. What are "developmental assets" and do you believe they have the power that Scales and Taccogna think they do? How might you help students build developmental asset lists in your school? What might be barriers to building a list such as this for students?

2. How do the authors recommend that a school use its "asset lens" to promote concrete changes in school organization, curriculum, co-curricular programs, support services, and community partnerships? What obstacles might prevent a school from carrying out such a task? What can be done to improve the chances that a school would be successful making these kinds of changes?

3. How does asset building lend itself to being embedded into programs and practices that are already part of the school culture or classroom environment and into educators' ways of relating to students? What specific characteristics can you identify that make this possible?

Case Study in Curriculum Implementation

Intentional Curriculum Planning in an Age of Accountability: Explorer Middle School's Approach

Donald E. Larsen
Tariq T. Akmal

ABSTRACT: The following case study documents the school improvement efforts at Explorer Middle School, a school where more than 90 percent of students qualify for free or reduced-priced lunches. Although the school has yet to achieve "adequate yearly progress" as mandated by No Child Left Behind, the authors explain how, through a "model of intentional curricular and instructional planning . . . Explorer's administration, teachers, staff, students, and parents are moving [the school] forward."

"It was the best of times, it was the worst of times, it was the age of wisdom, it was the age of foolishness, it was the epoch of belief, it was the epoch of incredulity, . . . it was the spring of hope, it was the winter of despair, we had everything before us, we had nothing before us, we were all going direct to Heaven, we were all going direct the other way" (Dickens, 1859, p. 1). So begins Charles Dickens' classic novel, *A Tale of Two Cities*. Although the novel's scenes and characters are rooted in the late eighteenth century, many educators might readily apply this dichotomous description to the state of American public education in the first decade of the twenty-first century.

No Child Left Behind (NCLB) sets ambitious expectations for *all* teachers and students. Even before the reauthorization of the Elementary and Secondary Education Act in 2001, most states adopted reform measures that focused on fixed standards for student achievement (Orfield & Kornhaber, 2001; Stecher & Chun, 2001). The competence of teachers and the success of students are now being gauged by "adequate yearly progress" (AYP), a composite total of students' test scores on various state-mandated exams. Schools that do not meet the AYP standard are

readily and publicly identified as having fallen short of the mark; improvement plans followed by other, more dire, sanctions are specified when a school shows a pattern of failing to meet AYP. The U.S. Secretary of Education insists that improved student achievement and a higher standard of education will result from the mandates handed down by the U.S. Department of Education.

For those who equate standards with requiring that each student reach a specified score on a state-mandated assessment, No Child Left Behind may represent a call to accountability, an antidote to "wishy-washy" educational practices— the best of times. However, many teachers believe that state tests implemented in response to the call for higher standards in education, in fact, limit their teaching effectiveness (Barksdale-Ladd & Thomas, 2000; Sack, 1999) and even cause a *de-skilling* effect (McNeil, 2000). Furthermore, test scores may be unrealistically equated with school effectiveness and teacher quality (Reeves, 2004; Smith, Heinecke, & Noble, 1999)—the worst of times.

Teachers, particularly those who guide students in developing skills that will be assessed by the state assessment in the spring, labor under the microscope of media scrutiny and public

The Curriculum in Action

comparison of schools and school districts. The dissection that occurs ritually each fall in the local press suggests that standardized test scores can be analyzed by the numbers and schools neatly quantified, in much the same way that an article in *Consumer Reports* might advise the potential buyer which manufacturer produces the best can opener, and which the worst. Successful schools are seen as those that post improved test scores from the previous year. The assessment report issued each year by the Office of the Superintendent of Public Instruction in State A presents the data without acknowledging that when 82 percent of the seventh graders in Affluence Valley pass the math section of the assessment, and 16 percent of their peers in Poverty Gulch meet that standard, the scores do not compare apples with apples. The report fails to mention that the seventh grade teacher in Poverty Gulch may have coaxed 16 percent of her students to proficiency despite challenges and ethical considerations more daunting than anything the Affluence Valley teacher could imagine or acknowledge.

Some may aver that high-stakes mandates such as NCLB will result in little more than external commitment (Fullan, 2001) on the part of those charged with implementing a new requirement. However, our research (Akmal & Larsen, 2004a; Akmal & Larsen, 2004b) suggests that, even in schools whose demographics would seem to justify low expectations, teachers and administrators may intentionally embrace effective teaching practices tailored to the needs of the student populations they serve.

EXPLORER MIDDLE SCHOOL: A SCHOOL INTENT ON IMPROVEMENT

Over the past five years, we have made Explorer Middle School a focus of our research. By every conventional measure, the circumstances at Explorer might give rise to despair. Of the 720 or so sixth-, seventh-, and eighth-grade students at Explorer, more than 90 percent qualify for free or reduced-priced lunch benefits. For nearly half of the students at Explorer, English is not the language of the home. Some of the students will not begin the next school year until late September, after the last crop in the valley has been harvested; a few students will not return from Christmas vacation in Mexico until February. From 1999–2001, Explorer averaged more than a 50 percent turnover of students during the course of the school year. In 2002, the flow had slowed to 31 percent, a rate that still justifies concern for the stability of the student population. On the seventh grade benchmark state test, few of the students show proficiency in mathematics; reading scores are slightly better. Explorer is now in year three of a state-mandated "School Improvement Plan," a consequence of failing to achieve "adequate yearly progress" as defined by state standards and No Child Left Behind.

A wooden fence across Arroyo Street from the school office bears spray-painted evidence that Explorer Middle School lies in a neighborhood that rival gangs claim as home turf. A police department cruiser rests at the curb in front of the school. The local police department and the school district have collaborated to make a "school resource officer" (SRO) a daily presence on the Explorer campus to reduce external influences on some members of the student body. Estimates of the number of students who are gang members or "junior" gang members indicate that more than half of the students, some as young as 11 years of age, are affiliated with local gangs.

Given these facts, one would not be surprised to find a building in disrepair, hardened and discouraged staff members, parents eager to take advantage of the first opportunity to transfer their children to another school within the district, and administrators who have reached the point of disheartened, apathetic management. What we have found at Explorer belies any such pessimistic assumptions.

Held to the standard of adequate yearly progress as defined by NCLB, Explorer *is* a failing school. For the teacher in the classroom, the prospect of pushing 100 percent of the student population to proficiency by 2014 might daunt the most sanguine idealist. However, staff members at Explorer have adopted a purposeful plan. They distinguish between (a) the state's expectation that pedagogy and curriculum materials will align with what will be assessed in the spring and (b) the need to do much more with their population than raise test scores. This intentionality reflects a commitment to an internalized set of values (Fullan, 2001). The carefully cultivated relationships and data-guided decision making we have observed suggest that teachers and administrators are collaborating in an explicit " 'making-a-difference' sense of purpose" (Fullan, 2001, p. 20), manifested in strategies aimed at improving the achievement *and* the lives of their students. To break the cycle of poverty and low student achievement, these educators are taking a holistic approach that connects students, teachers, and schools in ways that, heretofore, had not been achieved.

Two years ago, at the request of the Explorer staff, the state assigned a school improvement facilitator to guide steps that might help the school emerge from the cloud of failure. Vern Madison, a veteran K–12 educator who works with 16 other failing schools, answered the call.

The initial steps in Explorer Middle School's journey began with what Madison describes as a "readiness-to-benefit" audit. A high-functioning school, Madison says, has three important components in place: (1) staff development targeted to student learning needs, (2) a curriculum that aligns with assessments, and (3) the universal belief that "all kids can learn." Assured that the Explorer staff members held a core belief that ability to learn is not delimited by wealth, family stability, ethnicity, or primary language, Madison has helped in drafting strategies and targets aimed at improving student achievement. Explorer's teachers and administrators have written an improvement plan that focuses on intentionality. "No Child Left Behind has forced us to become more intentional," he says. "The ultimate goal is to be more intentional tomorrow than we were today."

INTERPRETING AND USING DATA TO GUIDE PLANNING

A major part of this intentionality relies on using available data to shape plans and decisions for the school. Assessment scores from the previous spring arrive in the district office in mid-July. In August, the members of the Instructional Leadership Team (ILT) meet to examine the data and develop a narrative around that information. A comparison of Explorer seventh graders' scores with those earned by students in other schools in the district or, more likely, other parts of the state, verifies Explorer's steep uphill journey to meet improvement goals. However, Madison insists that assessment information points toward opportunities as much as toward challenges.

A central function of Explorer's ILT is to make decisions based on the learning attributes and needs of students. As the ILT members examine the assessment numbers, they disaggregate the data in order to focus also on specific populations within the school. Madison says, "It becomes not just [a matter of] presenting data but also asking, 'What do the data mean for the classroom?' "

The administrators and the teachers also critically examine the data for evidence of high achievement. One seventh grade teacher observed, "When one teacher sees that another seems to be having real success with 'Four Square Writing,' the rest of us should be asking, 'What's she doing that works?' " Because the Explorer instructional plan is built around blocks of core subjects, each core team can also examine individual student achievement from subject to subject and class to class.

Jolene Zimmerman, Explorer's principal, notes that, at a comprehensive level, her role is, "to see the bigger data picture. I try to point out [positive and negative] trends that we're experiencing, but more importantly, that we ask why those trends exist." Following this self-analytical process, the ILT submits an updated school improvement plan to the district office by October.

Research suggests that standards-based initiatives tend to reduce teaching to a "one-size-fits-all" formula that prescribes how lessons will align with state-mandated assessments (Barksdale-Ladd & Thomas, 2000; Dutro, Collins, & Collins, 2002; Kohn, 2000). In a study by Barksdale-Ladd and Thomas (2000) that included interviews with 59 teachers, one teacher lamented, "All of the most powerful teaching tools I used to use every day are no good to me now because they don't help children get ready for the test, and it makes me a robot instead of a teacher" (p. 392).

At Explorer, the school improvement process has had its detractors. A district policy adopted in 2003 requires middle schools to reserve 90 minutes daily for reading. This reading initiative has displaced lessons that some teachers prized. "We have teachers who are 'mourning' the loss of autonomy," Madison says. "And they really *are* mourning the loss of autonomy." However, while a few may lament that they have lost their favorite history unit or whale unit, even the most skeptical have been gratified as the increased focus on reading has paid dividends in the classroom. "My goodness," teachers say, "My kids are reading!"

When one subject—reading, for example—is singled out to be the focus of campus-wide efforts, other subjects may suffer a proportionate de-emphasis. Madison and several teachers observed that pressure on the content areas increased as the school plan zeroed in on reading and writing. However, Madison says, the goal of school improvement is to raise student performance to a point where the intensive intervention is no longer necessary. "As [student] skills get higher," Madison says, "our hope is that teachers can bring more of the content back into the classroom."

Though cautiously optimistic about this time-consuming investment in reading improvement that in one year alone—2003–2004—paid a 100 percent dividend, teachers at Explorer worry about all the other variables in their students' lives that may adversely affect that achievement. Empathy with the day-to-day realities of their students' lives may not occur automatically to teachers who commute to Explorer each morning from comfortable homes. As one teacher reflected, it can be difficult for a teacher who was raised in—and now lives in—a middle-class setting to comprehend why one student didn't bring her textbook to class and why another offers no explanation for not completing the homework assignment.

> It's difficult for us to relate to all the different *stuff*—how many of our students are actually *being* the adults in their homes and running their homes and things like that. . . . How many of our students go home and don't know if there's going to be anyone there.

One of Explorer's assistant principals added, "When you have kids who are afraid to go home at night because the gangs are after them, they're not exactly worried about reading and writing!" Still, the goal remains to help students improve their lives while also gaining the academic skills they need to leave poverty behind.

Developing and implementing the improvement plan at Explorer has been a creative process. To ensure that all teachers might benefit from team-based planning time, as well as common teaching time, the staff requested a waiver from the union's contractual agreement. The 90-minute reading block is one departure from the contractual agreement. Classes at Explorer are delayed by 90 minutes once a week so teachers can collaborate and plan together. Both principal Zimmerman and Madison note that these teacher-initiated waivers from a contract that governs all certified staff in the district are manifestations of intentionality and moral purpose. In addition, every member of the staff has a staff development calendar for the entire school year, a document developed by the Instructional Leadership Team.

RELATIONSHIPS AS KEYS TO EFFECTIVE PLANNING

"If moral purpose is job one, relationships are job two, as you can't get anywhere without them"

(Fullan, 2001, p. 51). At Explorer, intentionality is accompanied by a second, equally important part of school-wide improvement: a focus on building and maintaining relationships, beginning with the unified efforts of the staff, faculty, and administration of the school and concluding with the inclusion of students and parents in the improvement process. For teachers at Explorer Middle School, creating a vision for their learning community and charting the steps needed to attain purposeful objectives for student learning have been facilitated by development of strong bonds within the staff.

The strong friendships and high levels of respect among teachers and administrators foster deeper conversations that are more grounded in student assessment data. "Sometimes we have to look at each other, eyeball-to-eyeball across the table until we come to agreement," says Principal Zimmerman, "But at the end of the day, we're still friends and colleagues." These tight bonds also permit teachers an opportunity to lay their frustrations and concerns on the table, knowing that their colleagues are not going to criticize, but instead offer empathy and solutions.

One teacher notes, "I think what this faculty does most effectively is take care of each other. It's just amazing how many personal situations have come up with our faculty and how we have always been so supportive of each other." At the heart of this behavior is the philosophy that if the faculty and staff care about and support one another, they will be in a better position to care and provide support for their students.

Relationships at Explorer are not happenstance; they, too, are intentional and part of the overall strategy of the ILT. The School Improvement Plan contains specific reference to building teams through collaborative planning times, ensuring that teachers have enough time and professional development to be proficient in their use of data and decision-making. At an informal level, all staff birthdays, individual and team achievements, and familial occurrences are celebrated or, in time of crisis, supported. During the summer vacation the staff meets—voluntarily—simply to gather and enjoy one another's company. On weekends, many of the staff socialize or do outdoor recreation, pursue home or community projects, or shop together. Invariably, school comes up. "We sometimes solve some of our toughest problems when we aren't in school," says one member of a teaching team that spends almost every other weekend together. Is the planned curriculum affected by these relationships? "Absolutely!" says Principal Zimmerman. "We no longer see any hidden agendas at meetings. Everybody knows what I want and they feel comfortable voicing their disagreement or support for an idea. So when we talk about something, it's an honest, no-holds-barred talk."

LEADERSHIP BY DESIGN

Intentionality, moral purpose, and relationships are essential components of a culture in which internal motivation drives the organization (Fullan, 2001). But what are the characteristics of the leader of such an organization? Fullan suggests that effective leaders instill a "can-do" ethos in those around them. "They are always hopeful—conveying a sense of optimism and an attitude of never giving up in the pursuit of highly valued goals" (Fullan, 2001, p. 7).

The ideal school administrator might be described as not just a generic manager, but an instructional leader. In practice, however, few administrators live up to this lofty expectation.

> Most principals spend relatively little time in classrooms and even less time analyzing instruction with teachers. They may arrange time for teachers' meetings and professional development, but they rarely provide intellectual leadership for growth in teaching skill (Fink & Resnick, 2001, p. 598).

At Explorer Middle School, Jolene Zimmerman may well serve as the prototypical principal whose energy, optimism, and vision set the tone for an entire learning community.

Their prior experience with a secretive, divisive, and penny-pinching administrator left the

Explorer staff distrustful of administrators and each other. "There was a lot of hurt on this faculty," Zimmerman acknowledges, "a lot of people who had not been well treated and who were not willing to trust me just because I said they should or wanted them to." Zimmerman's open style of leadership that invited and accepted input from teachers, staff, students, and parents promised to align mission with practice.

What has allowed Zimmerman to connect with a staff that had developed the "duck and cover" mentality of a shell-shocked foot soldier? For one thing, Zimmerman cultivates an open communication style. "I like to put everything on the table so that everyone can see it," Zimmerman says. Her secretary agrees:

> One thing's for sure: you always know where you stand with Jolene. If she's unhappy with something you've done, you'll know it. If she's happy about it, you'll know it. But one of the things that we all know around here is that if we don't like something, we'll have the chance to say so.

Whether inspired by Zimmerman's open communication, her follow-through on promises, or her unquenchable energy and optimism, the Explorer staff has rallied to her side. Eighteen of the staff members had requested transfers to other schools before Zimmerman received the call to Explorer. They all stayed. Zimmerman empowered the ILT to dictate the school budget. Transparency became the norm in faculty meetings and core team meetings.

The process and pace of change at Explorer since the state identified it for school improvement has elevated and accelerated the expectations of the staff. Simultaneous with this acceleration has come the potential for staff members to throw up their hands in exasperation. Jeffrey Abood, a teacher who has been on the Explorer staff for 10 years, says that the unrelenting focus on intentional instructional practices might tempt a teacher to look for a school that places fewer demands on its staff. "Quite frankly, it would be easier [to leave]," he says,

There are probably people [at Explorer] who would like to be doing something else, but we're in this together. Ms. Zimmerman has built in that sense of interdependence. I don't know . . . it's just that sense of "roll up your sleeves and get it done."

Zimmerman says the process of breaking the inertia and moving Explorer toward improvement involved more than setting goals on which everyone could agree. She was learning to be a principal while the staff members were learning to work together. "It was sort of like building the airplane while flying it."

A can-do culture has replaced the self-protective climate that Zimmerman first encountered at Explorer. Even when teachers complain, they want to do the right thing. They want to help. Brian Morales, a special education teacher, notes that he and his colleagues have learned to trust the vision that Zimmerman has brought to the school. "People get frustrated," he observed.

> Jolene knows it's the same thing like with [our students], so you have to say, "Let's give it a shot and see how it goes." It just kind of gets everybody to level out a little bit, calm down a little bit. And then people go, "Aaaah, all right, it'll be okay." I think that people, whether they are kids or adults, just want reassurance that things are going to be okay.

Today, instead of focusing on pennies spent or developing and supporting factions, the Explorer staff focuses on kids. A "whatever-it-takes" attitude prevails. The slightest upturn in student achievement or test scores is cause for celebration. All communication with parents is published in English and in Spanish. A framed and matted copy of Explorer's state assessment scores is the first thing one sees upon entering the main office. The school custodian helps coach wrestling. One of the cooks uses her computer to keep track of and celebrate students' birthdays. During vacation breaks, as part of the school's interventional academic program, the school gym and selected classes remain open. Student volunteerism is at an all-time high, and student pride in the spotless campus is evident. "I've seen it [Explorer] go from a shell to a rich, vibrant school," says Madison.

To many educators, Explorer's recipe for school improvement might represent the pinnacle—or perhaps the precipice—of innovation. However, as Abood remarks,

> If you sit down and really think about some of the changes that we've made, they're common sense. They're common sense. I think what has been most difficult for us has been change. Change. It's just something that we needed to do.

Zimmerman acknowledges that keeping a focus both on the moral purpose behind change and on the relationships required to motivate and sustain change takes a delicate balance, but she also believes Explorer is on the right track. "But if our students' reading doesn't substantially improve next year," she says, grinning, "they [the teachers] will be ready to string me up!"

WHAT LIES IN STORE FOR EXPLORER?

Explorer Middle School's effort to improve their students' learning and lives is firmly grounded on intentionality. School-wide leadership whose moral purpose is manifested in a vision for intentional improvement, a web of caring and personal relationships, and ongoing planning guided by relevant data are the hallmarks of this school.

Explorer has developed as a kind of "nested learning community" (Fink & Resnick, 2001), a metaphor drawn from the nesting dolls sold as souvenirs in places such as Russia.

> The [nesting dolls] image seems to work because the dolls are each independent, free-standing "people," but they share a common form. And you can't decide which is the most "important" doll, the tiny one in the middle that establishes the shape for them all or the big one on the outside that encloses them all (Fink & Resnick, 2001, p. 600).

The professionals at Explorer distinguish between the state's expectation that pedagogy and curriculum materials will align with what will be assessed in the spring and the need to do much more with their population than raise test scores. In the spring of 2004, after three years under the shadow of a school improvement plan, the seventh graders' scores on the state assessment doubled. Yet no one in this learning community is ready to erect a banner that declares "Mission Accomplished." As the faculty and staff continue to focus their efforts on helping students develop basic skills for learning (reading, writing, and mathematics), test scores will continue to climb. "Even if we don't see the scores we want," Madison insists, "Explorer is still a good place for kids to be."

According to the rubric set by NCLB, Explorer is a failing middle school, but a glance beyond the numbers shows this to be anything but true. Through a model of intentional curricular and instructional planning, Explorer's administration, teachers, staff, students, and parents are moving Explorer forward, from the worst of circumstances to the best of times.

REFERENCES

Akmal, T. T., & Larsen, D. E. (2004a). Keeping History from Repeating Itself: Involving Parents about Retention Decisions to Support Student Achievement. *Research in Middle Level Education Online, 27*(2).

Akmal, T. T., & Larsen, D. E. (2004b, April). *Aligning state reform with middle school needs: Contextualizing accountability pressure for school renewal.* Paper presented at the annual meeting of the American Educational Research Association Conference, San Diego, CA.

Barksdale-Ladd, M. A., & Thomas, K. F. (2000). What's at stake in high-stakes testing: Teachers and parents speak out. *Journal of Teacher Education, 51,* 384–397.

Dickens, C. (1859). *A tale of two cities.* New York: Walter J. Black, Inc.

Dutro, E., Collins, K. M., & Collins, J. (2002, April). *Teachers' responses to the standards movement:*

Perspectives from literacy practitioners in three states. Paper presented at the annual meeting of the American Educational Research Association, New Orleans, LA.

Fink, E., & Resnick, L. B. (2001, April). Developing principals as instructional leaders. *Phi Delta Kappan, 82*(8), 598–606.

Fullan, M. (2001). *Leading in a culture of change.* San Francisco: Jossey-Bass.

Kohn, A. (2000). Burnt at the high stakes. *Journal of Teacher Education, 51,* 315–327.

McNeil, L. M. (2000). *Contradictions of school reform: Educational costs of standardized testing.* New York: Routledge.

Orfield, G., & Kornhaber, M. L. (Eds.). (2001). *Raising standards or raising barriers? Inequality and high-stakes testing in public education.* New York: The Century Foundation Press.

Reeves, D. B. (2004). *Accountability for learning: How teachers and school leaders can take charge.* Alexandria, VA: Association for Supervision and Curriculum Development.

Sacks, P. (1999). *Standardized minds: The high price of America's testing culture and what we can do to change it.* Cambridge, MA: Perseus Publishing.

Stecher, B., & Chun, T. (2001). *School and classroom practices during two years of education reform in Washington state* (National Center for Research on Evaluation, Standards, and Student Testing/ RAND). Los Angeles: University of California.

Donald E. Larsen is Assistant Professor, Educational Administration and Leadership, University of the Pacific, Stockton, CA; and *Tariq T. Akmal* is Associate Professor, Teaching and Learning, Washington State University.

QUESTIONS FOR REFLECTION

1. What are the implications for a school that has more than 90% of its students qualifying for free or reduced lunch? How might this school be different with regards to community, outside support, and achievement than one in which no students qualify for free or reduced lunch?

2. What key features of Explorer Middle School's yearly progress have school leaders and teachers been addressing and how have they been able to move the school forward? What do you think will be necessary to bring the school to a place where it can meet NCLB's requirement for improved annual progress?

3. Does Explorer Middle School sound like a school you would like to teach in? Why or why not? What characteristics about the school influence your answer?

Teachers' Voices—
Putting Theory Into Practice

Creativity Workshops in the Regular Classroom

Nancy King Mildrum

ABSTRACT: Although gifted students are sometimes best served in homogeneous settings specifically tailored to their intellectual and emotional needs, creativity lessons can be transferred to heterogeneous settings without compromising instructional quality for the gifted population. Nancy King Mildrum discusses how her conviction that creativity workshops are effective in regular classrooms has strengthened over the years because the original findings are consistently repeated in each new situation. It is a joy to watch creative potential unfold in all types of children, she writes.

"Although the creativity lessons were completed several weeks ago, my class still feel the effects. Can you teach/encourage/learn creativity? Yes. Everyone benefits all ages and all abilities."

—First Grade Teacher

For the last eight years I have experimented with teaching creativity in elementary and middle school classrooms. In each situation, I adapted a creativity curriculum model designed for use in the regular classroom. The model is called TLC, Ten Lessons In Creativity, coauthored with Robin Hands as part of a masters thesis in gifted education at Johnson State College in Vermont.

The techniques developed for this model were based on:

- development of creative abilities (Davis, 1986; Shallcross, 1981; Torrance, 1977)
- development of positive attitudes related to creativity (Davis, 1986; Shallcross, 1981)
- experimented with perceptual shifts (Davis, 1986; Perkins, 1981)
- practice with imagery (Eberle, 1971; Lowery, 1982)
- developing an understanding of meta-creativity (Brunch, 1988; Pesut, 1990)

- opportunities for product development (Renzulli & Ries, 1985; Treffinger, 1986)
- reinforcing a belief in one's own calling (Shallcross, 1981; Torrance, 1989).

The purpose of the research was to determine the effects of the TLC model on attitudes and abilities related to the creativity of students in the regular classroom. We field tested the model in a self-contained sixth grade classroom and used both qualitative and quantitative pre- and post-treatment measures. Although creativity is usually part of the curriculum in gifted education, we believed that all children could benefit from this instruction, and felt that the field testing of TLC should occur in the regular classroom setting.

The results revealed that the children who participated in the lessons demonstrated:

- increased knowledge of creative abilities and attitudes as evidenced by use of vocabulary

- increased meta-creative awareness
- increased creative abilities
- increased development of attitudes related to creativity (Hands, 1991 & Mildrum 1991).

Although gifted students are sometimes best served in homogeneous settings specifically tailored to their intellectual and emotional needs, creativity lessons can be transferred to heterogeneous settings without compromising instructional quality for the gifted population. My conviction that creativity workshops are effective in regular classrooms has strengthened over the years because the original findings are consistently repeated in each new situation. It is a joy to watch creative potential unfold in all types of children.

MODEL CONSIDERATIONS

The lessons based on Ten Lessons in Creativity engage students in reflection, production and presentation. Woven throughout is an emphasis on developing a personal understanding of one's own creative process and the creative processes of others. There is consistent teacher reinforcement of a working vocabulary of the creative abilities: fluency, flexibility, originality, and elaboration; and of creative attitudes such as persistence, risk taking, independence, and curiosity.

Usually the classes meet once a week for one hour over six to ten weeks. The classroom teacher and I collaborate on the planning and implementation. Everyday household objects, art supplies, biographies of creative people and some trade books are used for materials. At the beginning of each lesson the class is told what creative abilities or attitudes they will work with, and the objectives are clearly stated.

In the first lesson, the children compose a class definition of creativity. After a brainstorming session, one fourth grade settled on, "Creativity is cool, it is everything around you. It is thinking, it is learning new things, it is solving problems." Then we make a class mural; using creativity as a

metaphor, we finish the sentence, "Creativity is . . ." The students use markers to create a section on mural paper which includes the finished sentence and an illustration. When the mural is completed, each child explains his or her work, and the group responds with questions and comments. Immediately in the first lesson, creative talent jumps off the paper and recognition is given to the unique ideas that appeal to others in the group.

After establishing the general topic in the first class, following lessons deal directly with specific creative abilities and attitudes. In the flexibility lesson, for example, the children are asked to apply the synectic method of combining two ideas to create a novel idea. As an introduction, flexibility is defined as the ability to look at things differently, or trying a new approach—stretching into something new. Inventions are then discussed that are combinations, such as clock-radios and snow-boards. In the activity, students pair up and select two things out of a collection of miscellaneous items which might include: a flashlight, forks, bottle caps, paper towel rolls, plastic toys, a top, string . . . They are asked to put their two things together to invent something novel that has a function different from either of the individual items. When each pair is ready, they explain their creation. The audience is very interested to see what their peers have come up with, and they always respond enthusiastically to the "stand out" ideas. This simple activity gets them thinking about flexibility as a creative ability.

Although it is a paradox to teach creativity using a rigidly defined structure, many of the techniques are simply sound teaching methods: introduction, practice, reinforcement, review and evaluation. The students are prompted to notice exceptional interpretations to learn from each other, and to piggy back on interesting ideas. The classes develop an atmosphere of cooperation, experimentation and appreciation for outstanding work. As the lessons progress the children realize that, like any skill, creativity improves with practice.

CREATIVITY INSTRUCTION: AN AMBASSADOR FOR GIFTED EDUCATION

> "I was challenged by the teaching approach in the creativity lessons. It is more convenient for me to fall back on books and workbooks. Hopefully this will bring me to use more of a mixture in my approach to teaching."
>
> —Seventh Grade Teacher

In gifted education, original thinking, the world of possibilities, and an appreciation of the unusual are often highlighted. In regular education, teachers are primarily focused on getting through a curriculum and student achievement of academic skills. There is an emphasis on convergent rather than divergent thinking and most often, the creative potential of students is not a consideration.

Working on creativity lessons collaboratively with an enrichment teacher gives classroom teachers first hand experience with child centered philosophies in gifted education such as recognizing and supporting talent and working from areas of strength. During the creativity lessons, classroom teachers see the effects of teaching strategies based on these principles. In the classes, the students are energetic and motivated because they sense that their ideas are important. Teachers become much more comfortable with supporting individual creative expression as they experience the positive learning environment that develops when each child's unique abilities are honored.

I believe that many classroom teachers are skeptical about the child centered nature of gifted education. They are not accustomed to working with students as the center of the process, and are entrenched in a teacher down mentality. In gifted education one is almost forced to be child centered because we work with children who need challenges beyond the basics. We have to listen carefully to our students; they are dead serious about their interests, and are emphatic about their own learning preferences. In partnership with our students, we build on strengths and interests to create meaningful experiences that synthesize and integrate information. Many classroom teachers are afraid to take that leap of faith which gives students more control over their own learning.

As cooperating teachers have observed me in the stance of total respect for each child's ideas during the creativity lessons, they begin to understand that honoring and respecting each child's contribution isn't a threat to education, it's a catalyst for learning. Maybe the teacher doesn't always have to be right, maybe there can be more than one way to approach a problem, maybe the children know more than the teacher!

An extraordinary alchemy occurs when the practical wisdom of a classroom teacher mixes with skills in nurturing the creative potential of students. Sometime after completing a series of lessons with a first grade teacher she wrote to me saying, "The creativity spills over into everything they do, they have more self-confidence and are much more productive."

CREATIVITY WORKSHOPS AFFIRM THE HIGHLY CREATIVE CHILD

> "The kids were really supportive of each other, they were positive in complimenting each other on what they did for their projects, and gave supportive suggestions."
>
> —Seventh Grade Teacher

Highly creative children often experience negative social cues in a heterogeneous classroom because of their off beat approach and unusual perspective is sometimes misunderstood or not appreciated. Most of the time, their unique ideas have no outlet in a classroom environment geared toward acquisition of basic skills.

When a class is focused on lessons that have creative development as the goal, children with creative ability are given an audience and an opportunity to use their talent! Each lesson has time built in for explanation of work and peer response. The children are generous with positive feedback, knowing instinctively when something is exceptional! Often the praise takes the form of curiosity and questions.

"Where did you get that idea?"

"Why did you decide to make it with those materials?"

"How did you do that?"

Excitement and interest explode when a student's work captures the group's imagination.

During the elaboration lesson, students are asked to come up with a novel use for a paper plate. We provide them with a wide array of art materials for elaboration such as: glue, felt squares, pipe cleaners, sequins, yarn, feathers, buttons, wood scraps and tissue paper. They then create something unique using a paper plate as the base. Typically ordinary responses include: masks, flowers, containers or mobiles, but one of a kind ideas also emerge. One seventh grade boy worked diligently on a computer designed to store the tales of his Native American grandfather. "Each button represents different subjects, like animal stories, tales of the hunt or tales of ancestors," he proudly told his classmates. "The idea is to keep the stories in a safe place so that they will never be lost, and can always be found," he said as he pointed out details for headphones and disk storage.

The other students and his teachers were impressed and asked many questions about his work. This particular child was often disruptive in school and the object of negative attention from teachers and students. Yet during this class, he displayed a sense of pride, he was productive and articulate, and his classmates and teachers demonstrated a new level of respect for him. The experience of being appreciated and respected by age peers strengthens the self-esteem of highly creative children, who often feel alienated by their talent.

CREATIVITY AND SELF-ESTEEM

"I want to say, that I am doing something on self-esteem with my students and the creativity lessons definitely increased their self-esteem."
—Sixth Grade Teacher

As students participate in creativity workshops they modify their work without fear of failure, learning to trust their own ideas, and developing the ability to reflect on the process. Each child feels successful in the non-competitive environment where flexibility and cooperation are encouraged.

Abraham Maslow made a distinction between special talent creativeness which refers to achievements resulting from rigorous training, talent and commitment, and self-actualizing creativeness, which springs from personality and the tendency to approach all aspects of life in a creative manner. He viewed great talent to be irrelevant to the concern of pursuing life in a creative manner and realizing a healthy existence which he termed, "essentially human" (Maslow, 1968). When children have experience with expansive attitudes related to creativity, they begin to feel more confident about who they are and what they have to contribute. When they sense it is safe to be themselves within the structure of a school setting, they demonstrate increased self-confidence.

Shallcross suggests that highly creative individuals respect themselves as a source as much as they respect external sources (Shallcross, 1981). As students gain experience with creativity lessons, I have seen attitudes of self-respect influencing their behavior. They work with serious determination, they cooperate with each other to refine ideas, and they take pride in presenting and responding to each other's work.

CREATIVITY INSTRUCTION: NOT JUST FOR GIFTED AND TALENTED

"I saw some creative abilities that I had not tapped into at all, especially in writing. One girl's spelling and mechanics are terrible, but her ideas are fantastic, that kind of appeared on the first mural that we did."
—Seventh Grade Teacher

Creative abilities exist in varying degrees in all students (Shallcross, 1981). Unfortunately, as children become socialized in school, they are conditioned to find the correct answer. In their quest to be right, their abilities to experiment with ideas and to trust their instincts are neglected. If they do not learn to distinguish their unique voice, it can be irretrievably lost.

When children define creativity, have opportunities to be creative, and learn the language to articulate their own creativity, they celebrate their individuality. There is no fear of failure because all ideas have value. At the same time, they experience the struggle of working through frustration to arrive at a product that reflects their intention. They become aware of outstanding creative contributions by classmates, and internalize what they have noticed. As students explain their work at the end of each class, an atmosphere of mutual respect develops and competition gives way to a sense of community. There is always enough creativity for everyone and every child's work is validated as he or she gets feedback from the group.

During the course of the creativity lessons, classroom teachers begin to see individual students through a new lens. For example, children who resist structure often demonstrate fluency, flexibility or original thinking. In many cases, classroom teachers were surprised by the children who emerged as highly creative, because some of them were not successful in school. It follows that when a classroom teacher has knowledge of a student's creative abilities he or she will capitalize on this area of strength to support academics.

My course work in gifted education has helped me acquire the skills necessary to teach creativity with intention. No doubt, gifted education is an essential hot house for originating programs in creativity. However, it is important to bring this information into mainstream education because some students who do not qualify for gifted programs are highly creative, and all children have some degree of creativity that can be developed further. Every child benefits from learning about creativity and their own creative process, and the lessons learned in creativity workshops relate to all areas of a child's development. I've had many unforgettable experiences teasing out and supporting creative potential in students and teachers in heterogeneous settings, piecing together crazy quilts of creative expression, made more beautiful by the diversity they represent.

REFERENCES

Bruch, C. (1988). Meta-creativity: Awareness of thoughts and feelings during creative experiences. *Journal of Creative Behavior, 22,* 2, 112–122.

Davis, G. (1989). *Creativity is forever.* Dubuque, Iowa: Kendall Hunt Publishing Co.

Eberle, B. (1987). *Scamper.* Buffalo, New York: DOK Publishing.

Hands, R. (1991). *Implementing ten lessons in creativity in the regular classroom: Effects on abilities associated with creativity.* Johnson, Vt.: Johnson State College.

Lowery, J. (1982). Developing creativity in gifted children. *Gifted Child Quarterly, 26,* 3, 133–138.

Maslow, A. H. (1968). *Creativity in self-actualizing people, toward a psychology of being.* New York, New York: Van Nostrand Reinhold Company.

Mildrum, N. K. (1991). *Implementing ten lessons in creativity in the regular classroom: Effects on abilities associated with creativity.* Johnson, Vt.: Johnson State College.

Perkins, D. (1981). *The mind's best work.* Cambridge, Mass.: Harvard University Press.

Pesut, D. J. (1990). Creative thinking as a self-regulatory meta-cognitive process—a model for education training and further research. *Journal of Creative Behavior, 24,* 4, 105–109.

Renzulli, S. J., & Reis, S. (1985). *The schoolwide enrichment model.* Mansfield Center, Conn.: Creative Learning Press.

Shallcross, D. (1981). *Teaching creative behavior: How to teach creativity to children of all ages.* Englewood Cliffs, NJ.: Prentice Hall.

Torrance, E. P. (1977). *Creativity in the classroom.* Washington, D.C.: National Education Association.

Torrance, E. P. (1998). On the shoulders of giants. *The Educational Forum, 53,* 2, 117–124.

Treffinger, D. J. (1986). Research on creativity. *Gifted Child Quarterly, 30,* 1, 15–19.

Nancy K. Mildrum is the Enrichment Coordinator at the Georgia Elementary and Middle School in Georgia, Vermont.

QUESTIONS FOR REFLECTION

1. What lessons did Mildrum learn from working with gifted children that she is now able to bring to the regular classroom? What made the transformation from one population of students to another work?
2. Is there, or should there be, such a thing as an "exclusive curriculum," one that is only appropriate for a given population (such as gifted students), or should the curriculum be fluid and adaptable to many populations? What might be the benefits of an exclusive curriculum? What might be the drawbacks?
3. What is creativity instruction? Likewise, what is teaching creativity with intention? How might you take what Mildrum presents here into your own classroom? What are key features of her observations that are generalizable to many different kinds of students, classrooms, and schools?

LEARNING ACTIVITIES

Critical Thinking

1. Which developmental changes discussed in Chapter 3 should guide curriculum planners in designing educational programs for transescents and early adolescents?
2. What are the essential elements of effective curricula for transescents and early adolescents?
3. William M. Alexander, generally acknowledged as the "father" of the middle school, once said, "Every student should be well known as a person by at least one adult in the school who accepts responsibility for the student's guidance." What does it mean to be "known as a person"? Why is such a relationship with an adult of critical importance to middle-level students? What steps can teachers and administrators take to ensure that each student has such a relationship?

Application Activities

1. Pioneering work in developing curricula for transescents was done by Carleton W. Washburne at the Skokie Junior High School in Winnetka and is described in Chapter 7 of *Winnetka: The History and Significance of an Educational Experiment* by Washburne and Sidney P. Marland (Prentice-Hall, 1963). Would the activities described in that chapter be appropriate and challenging for today's transescents? Which of the four perspectives on curriculum that William H. Schubert discusses in Chapter 1 do those activities represent?
2. When you were an early adolescent, what school experiences helped you to grow and learn? What experiences hindered you? What implications do these experiences have for your current and future curriculum planning activities?

3. Drawing from the material in this chapter, develop a short questionnaire or set of interview questions that curriculum planners could use to learn more about early adolescents.

4. Invite a group of junior high/middle school teachers to your class and ask them to describe the steps they take in planning curricula for their students. What do they see as the most important curriculum criteria to use in planning?

Field Experiences

1. Talk with a group of early adolescents about the social forces of concern to them in their school, their community, their nation, and the world. Compare your findings with those of your fellow students.

2. Visit a junior high or middle school and ask to see the school's statement of philosophy (or mission statement) and/or set of schoolwide goals. To what extent do these materials reflect the points of view expressed in this chapter?

3. Visit an agency in your community that offers services to transescents and early adolescents and their families. Ask a staff member to describe the services that are offered. Report your findings to the rest of your class.

Internet Activities

1. Go to one or more of the following locations and gather information, research results, publications, and resources on effective educational programs for transescents and early adolescents.

   Center for Adolescent Studies
   National Middle School Association
   Online Educational Resources
   Center of Education for the Young Adolescent
   Middle Level Leadership Center
   The Middle School Information Center

2. Go to Kidlink, an organization dedicated to using the Internet to link children and youth through the age of fifteen from around the world. From this location, visit areas accessible to adults to determine the educational interests, needs, and concerns of transescents and early adolescents.

3. Go to Kidlink, an educator-oriented site where you will find instructional activities that integrate various areas of the curriculum. Compile a list of activities appropriate for transescents and early adolescents. From here you can "visit" school sites where students and teachers use Kidlink in the classroom.

CHAPTER 9

High School Curricula

FOCUS QUESTIONS

1. What are the major developmental concerns of high school–level students?
2. What are some of the "internal problems" that confront today's high schools?
3. What were the reasons behind the development of the comprehensive high school in America?
4. What recommendations have been made for restructuring high schools?
5. What are some appropriate curricular goals for high school–level students?

DEVELOPMENTAL CHALLENGES OF HIGH SCHOOL–LEVEL STUDENTS

High school–level students are beginning to seek some assurance of eventual economic independence from parents and other adults. They sense their new intellectual powers and their need to develop additional cognitive skills. Their dominant motivation most often is to achieve social status within the adolescent community and to meet the expectations of their peers. Often, they feel the tension between two orientations—engaging in behavior approved by adults versus engaging in behavior approved by peers. In this chapter's *Case Study in Curriculum Implementation* section, Hugh Campbell, a high school principal, outlines how teachers at his school developed a curriculum to help students adjust to the transition between the middle school and high school (see "Going the Extra Mile to Smooth the Transition to High School"). According to Erik Erikson, students at this level seek a "sense of identity" and the development of values they can call their own. According to Bennett M. Berger, a well-known sociologist and author of *An Essay on Culture: Symbolic Structure and Social Structure* (1995), adolescence is one of the ways that culture violates nature by insisting that, for an increasing number of years, young persons postpone their claims to the privileges and responsibilities of common citizenship. At this point, you may wish to review the perspectives on human development that have been advanced by Lawrence Kohlberg, Carol Gilligan, and others by turning to Chapter 3.

The world of today's high school–level students is dramatically different from the one their parents experienced. Technological changes, a multiplicity of social options and values, the pervasiveness of crime and violence, the media's intrusion and influence, and the blurring of the lines separating adults and children have a tremendous impact on today's youth. Adults may have difficulty comprehending the realities that characterize the lives of many youth today—for example, results from the South Carolina Youth Risk Behavior Survey revealed that 47 percent of adolescent males and 13 percent of adolescent females carried weapons, and large numbers reported fighting; the strongest predictors of weapon carrying and fighting were alcohol and drug use and sexual intercourse (Valois and McKewon, 1998). In this chapter's *Teachers' Voices* article, "A Tale of Two Curriculums," Mira Reisberg describes an approach to curriculum development that helps students understand and transcend the harsh realities of their lives by creating "heartfelt connections among student's lives, communities, creative intelligences, bodies, and spirits."

THE QUEST FOR SELF-IDENTITY

As young people move through their high school years, they usually come to attach less importance to the reactions of their peers and more to their quest for a strong self-identity. They tend to move from relying on others to self-reliance; their own sense of what matters, rather than the reactions of peers, guides their actions. Eliot Wigginton, the originator of the Foxfire approach to the high school curriculum, says in *Sometimes a Shining Moment: The Foxfire Experience* that the needs of high school students are best met by allowing them "to do things of importance—to do real work of real consequence in the real world" (1985, p. 236). To the extent that they have these experiences they are less likely to see the school curriculum as meaningless and to turn to self-destructive activities such as drug abuse, dropping out, school absenteeism, suicide, teenage pregnancy, vandalism, criminal activity, and cultism. In "A Tale of Two Curriculums" in this chapter, Mira Reisberg explains how she uses place-based pedagogy similar to Wigginton's Foxfire approach to prepare pre-service teachers to enter the high-stakes testing environment of today's schools.

Often, though, high school–level students gain their independence and sense of identity only after going through a period of conflict with parents, teachers, and other adults. In far too many instances, they express their defiance and rebellion by turning to the self-destructive activities mentioned above. The challenge for those who plan high school curricula, then, is to provide them with appropriate ways to express their emerging sense of independence or, as Carolyn Mamchur (1990) suggests, opportunities to use their "power" to decide what and how they learn. To help middle adolescents traverse this challenging period of their lives and prepare for their eventual transition into adulthood, M. Lee Manning and Richard Saddlemire (see "Implementing Middle School Concepts into High Schools") suggest that high schools adopt four middle-level practices: advisor–advisee programs, exploratory programs, interdisciplinary teams, and school climate enhancement efforts.

CHALLENGES TO THE AMERICAN HIGH SCHOOL

In addition to being buffeted by frequent waves of criticism and calls for reform from external sources, high schools in the United States have been coping with a myriad of internal problems during the last few decades. Many high schools are plagued by hostility, violence, despair, alienation, and drug abuse. Their expansive campuses, large enrollments, and bureaucratic organizational structures make matters worse; and students often express underlying negativity toward teachers, administrators, and staff. Some students find their school experiences unenjoyable, if not painful. Minority group students may feel that they receive differential treatment. Typically, students ask for more openness and mutual respect. Neither students themselves nor teachers see students as influential in setting school policies. Many students believe they are not learning as much as they should. The high school typically does not use the rich resources of the community.

In addition, confirmation that high school curricula are not as rigorous as they ought to be comes from the students themselves. One survey of college students for their views on what should be included in the high school curriculum indicated that students wanted more reading, literature and vocabulary, speaking and writing skills, research papers, and computer courses (Sandel, 1991). Instead, what students often experience in America's high schools—even "good" high schools—is a curriculum of "edutainment," according to Kay S. Hymowitz (see "Tales of Suburban High" in this chapter). Similarly, Susan Black maintains that many high school students are "disengaged" because they experience only a narrow, skills-based curriculum while at school.

DEVELOPMENT OF THE "COMPREHENSIVE" HIGH SCHOOL

To meet the needs of middle adolescents and to catch up with the Soviet Union in the production of engineers and scientists, former Harvard University President James B. Conant and others called for the development of the "comprehensive" high school during the 1950s and 1960s. The comprehensive high school would "provide learning opportunities for all . . . adolescents within a range from barely educable to the gifted and talented. Its purpose [would be] to enable each pupil (a) to develop to his [sic] greatest potential for his [sic] own success and happiness and (b) to make a maximum contribution to the American society of which he [sic] is a part" (Gilchrist, 1962, p. 32).

Conant recommended that "every pupil who can do so effectively and rewardingly should take a minimum of eighteen academic subjects" (1962, p. 29). This course of study, which Conant estimated 15 to 20 percent of students could complete "with profit," would include four years of mathematics, four years of one foreign language, three years of science, four years of English, and three years of social studies.

Expectations for the comprehensive high school were high. As the superintendent of University City Public Schools in Missouri wrote in 1962: "America desperately needs the developed abilities of all its youth. Citizens and educators have, in the comprehensive high school, an exciting and valuable tool to fulfill America's needs for the future" (Gilchrist, 1962, p. 33).

The comprehensive high school, however, has proven inadequate for the program of education many middle adolescents need. Some observers believe that attempts to develop comprehensive high school curricula that address the needs of all middle adolescents have resulted in curricula that lack coherence. High schools tend to try to teach "too much" to students. As a result, high school curricula focus more on *covering content* than on *developing understanding.*

THE GREAT DEBATE ON HIGH SCHOOL REFORM

The 1980s saw a plethora of reform-oriented reports and books on American education, most of which focused on the high school and called for raising standards, promoting excellence, and rebuilding public confidence in the schools. The 1983 report by the National Commission on Excellence in Education, *A Nation at Risk: The Imperative for Educational Reform,* launched a great national debate on how to improve high schools in the United States. With alarm, the report claimed that the nation had "been committing an act of unthinking, unilateral educational disarmament" and cited the high rate of illiteracy among seventeen-year-olds and minority youth, a drop in SAT scores, and the need for college and business to offer remedial reading, writing, and computation. In response to the perceived ineffectiveness of America's schools, *A Nation at Risk* recommended raising standards (not clearly defined), requiring "Five New Basics" (four years of English, three years of mathematics, three years of science, three years of social studies, and one-half year of computer science) for graduation, assessing students' learning more frequently, and lengthening the school day and the school year.

Another widely discussed report was Ernest Boyer's (1983) *High School: A Report on Secondary Education in America* sponsored by the Carnegie Foundation for the Advancement of Teaching. *High School* recommends first and foremost a "core of common learnings" and service-oriented activities for all, more flexibility in scheduling, a program of electives to develop individual interests, the mastery of language, and a single track for academic and vocational students.

Broad, sweeping reform of America's high schools was also called for in *Horace's Compromise: The Dilemma of the American High School* by Theodore Sizer (1984). Through his analysis of the professional dilemmas encountered by Horace Smith, a hypothetical high school English teacher, Sizer built a case for "revamping the structure" of the high school. He asserted that higher-order thinking skills should form the core of the high school curriculum and they should be learned through students' confrontations with engaging, challenging problems. Sizer also believed that high schools should have fewer and clearer goals, and should require mastery of subject matter for graduation. Interdisciplinary nongraded curricula were essential, he believed, and instruction should be adapted to students' diverse learning styles. To put his ideas into practice, Sizer began the Coalition of Essential Schools at Brown University. From a modest beginning with five schools in 1984, the Coalition grew to more than one thousand schools and twenty-four regional support centers by the end of the century.

In *Horace's School: Redesigning the American High School* (1992), Sizer further described the Coalition's approach to restructuring high schools. A basic premise of the Coalition is that top-down, standardized solutions to school problems don't work and that teachers must play a key role in changing schools. Since no two Coalition schools are alike, each is encouraged to develop an approach to restructuring that meets the needs of faculty, students, and community. However, the restructuring efforts of Coalition schools are guided by ten common principles, two of which specifically address the content of the educational program:

1. The school should focus on helping young people develop the habit of using their minds well. Schools should not attempt to be comprehensive if such a claim is made at the expense of the school's central intellectual purpose. Schools should be learner centered, addressing students' social and emotional development, as well as their academic progress.

2. The school's academic goal should be simple: that each student master a limited number of essential skills and areas of knowledge. The aphorism "Less Is More" should dominate. Curricular decisions should be guided by student interest, developmentally appropriate practice, and the aim of thorough student mastery and achievement. Students of all ages should have many opportunities to discover and construct meaning from their own experiences (Coalition of Essential Schools, 1998).

In *Horace's Hope: What Works for the American High School* (1996), Sizer describes thirteen lessons he learned from a decade of efforts to reform America's high schools. In this chapter's "New Hope for High Schools: Lessons from Reform-Minded Educators," excerpted from *Horace's Hope*, Sizer describes four of those lessons.

GOALS FOR THE EDUCATION OF HIGH SCHOOL STUDENTS

What goals should be included in educational programs for high school–level students? As we have emphasized throughout this book, curriculum goals should be derived, in large measure, from the three curriculum bases—social forces, theories of human development, and the nature of learning and learning styles. With this perspective in mind, the goals would surely include the following:

1. Encouraging the development and practice of critical thinking, what the Coalition of Essential Schools has described as "the habit of using [one's] mind well"
2. Helping learners begin the process of career development, whether through vocational guidance, vocational education, or additional academic development
3. Providing learners with experiences that enhance their citizenship skills, sense of responsibility, and understanding of and concern for the world about them
4. Helping students to become self-directed, lifelong learners
5. Assisting learners to become self-actualized and secure in their identities
6. Assisting learners in making the transition to the world of work, to participation in their communities, and to the world of the future

Currently, virtually every state has responded to the recurring calls to reform high schools in America. Teachers are playing a greater role in restructuring and curriculum change. For example, many schools participate in collaborative school reform networks, and through these networks, teachers receive training and resources for facilitating change in their schools. As the articles in this chapter confirm, more and more educational programs for high school students are being developed in light of the following recommendation from the Coalition of Essential Schools: ". . . decisions about the details of the course of study, the use of students' and teachers' time and the choice of teaching materials and specific pedagogies must be unreservedly placed in the hands of the principal and staff" (Coalition of Essential Schools, 1998).

REFERENCES

Berger, Bennett M. *An Essay on Culture: Symbolic Structure and Social Structure.* Berkeley: University of California Press, 1995.

Boyer, Ernest. *High School: A Report on Secondary Education in America.* New York: Harper and Row, 1983.

Coalition of Essential Schools. "Ten Common Principles." Oakland, CA: Coalition of Essential Schools, 1998.

Conant, James B. "The Comprehensive High School." *NEA Journal* LI, No. 5 (May 1962): 29–30.

Gilchrist, Robert S. "What Is a Comprehensive High School?" *NEA Journal* LI, No. 8 (November 1962): 32–33.

Mamchur, Carolyn. "But . . . the Curriculum." *Phi Delta Kappan* 71, no. 5 (April 1990): 634–637.

Sandel, Lenore. "What High School Students Need to Know in Preparation for Success in College." *The High School Journal* 74, no. 3 (February/March 1991): 160–163.

Sizer, Theodore R. *Horace's Hope: What Works for the American High School.* Boston: Houghton Mifflin, 1996.

———. *Horace's School: Redesigning the American High School.* Boston: Houghton Mifflin, 1992.

———. *Horace's Compromise: The Dilemma of the American High School.* Boston: Houghton Mifflin, 1984.

Valois, Robert F., and McKewon, Robert E. "Frequency and Correlates of Fighting and Carrying Weapons Among Public School Adolescents." *American Journal of Health Behavior* 22, no. 1 (January–February 1998): 8–17.

Wigginton, Eliot. *Sometimes a Shining Moment: The Foxfire Experience.* Garden City, NY: Anchor Press, Doubleday, 1985.

Tales of Suburban High

KAY S. HYMOWITZ

ABSTRACT: *Kay Hymowitz observes that even in America's "good" (suburban) schools, classroom travesties are the order of the day. She explores and comments on several factors that are responsible for the decline of public education, even in the more affluent areas of the United States. A critical examination of "edutainment" as curriculum is at the center of her analysis.*

When Americans think about public education, they tend to see a stark divide. On the one hand, there are the failed school systems of our big cities, blackboard jungles where drugs abound, gangs rule the hallways, and dropouts outnumber the barely literate graduates. On the other hand, there are the shining, achievement-oriented public schools of the suburbs, the institutions that have led so many middle-class parents to flee New York City for Westchester or Chicago for Highland Park. In these greener pastures, public education seems to be working fine: students do not have to pass through metal detectors each morning, most of them go on to college, and their parents (according to opinion surveys) are basically content.

The problem with this picture, as we have learned in recent decades, is that, despite their obvious advantages, all is far from well in suburban schools. In 1983, the National Commission on Excellence in Education cautioned that, across the country, SAT scores were flat, and students were falling behind their peers in other nations. College professors began to gripe about incoming students who, even with sterling records in high school, had never heard of the Renaissance, or thought Winston Churchill was a Civil War general.

Compounding these pedagogic worries have been concerns about the often poisonous social and moral environment of the high schools in more prosperous communities. After two teenagers turned Columbine High School in Colorado into a killing field in 1999, just about every suburban district in the country began fretting about potential violence. Many launched curriculums to combat sexual harassment, to root out homophobia, to discourage cattiness among girls, and, of course, to stop bullying among boys, the supposed root cause of the massacre at Columbine. More recently, cheating has become an issue, especially with the temptations posed by the Internet. In one much-publicized scandal, a biology teacher at a high school in suburban Kansas City discovered that 28 of her students had downloaded whole sections of their term papers. But when the teacher tried to fail the offenders, the superintendent and parents refused to back her up, apparently seeing nothing remarkable in the transgression. As one student told the chastened teacher, "We won."

That matters are as bad as these instances suggest is amply confirmed by two new books that take us inside the classrooms of today's suburban high school: Elinor Burkett's *Another Planet: A Year in the Life of a Suburban High School* and Denise Clark Pope's *Doing School: How We Are Creating a Generation of Stressed-Out, Materialistic, and Miseducated Students*. Burkett, an astute journalist with many previous books to her name, introduces us to Prior Lake High School outside Minneapolis, an overwhelmingly white, middle-class school that sends its better graduates to state universities. The pseudonymous Faircrest High School described by Pope, a lecturer at Stanford's School of Education, is located in a "wealthy California suburb," and is a more diverse institution. Though a third of its students are lower-income Hispanics, Filipinos, or blacks, it also boasts more National Merit scholars than Prior Lake, and more Ivy League aspirants.

For all their differences, both institutions are considered "good" schools. They feature plenty of Advanced Placement (AP) courses, college-hungry kids, and attentive teachers, and their facilities are so fine that one parent in Burkett's account, observing plans for a new school complete with archery and golf ranges, quipped that it looked more like a sports-entertainment complex. The question is: what exactly are these "good" schools good *at*?

An instructive place to start is with the teachers. In dress, demeanor, and interests, many of the pedagogues at Prior Lake High School can hardly be distinguished from the hormonal crew they are supposed to be educating. There is the math teacher who brags to his students that he has read only two books in his life, one about high school football and the other about Elvis Presley. There is the English teacher, with bleached hair and a "Tommy" shirt (because "kids love brand names"), who performs card tricks for his students and regales them with stories about his lost career as a basketball player. And there is the memorable Sandra Sterge, an English teacher—I think—who makes constant sexual innuendos in class, calling attractive male students "hotties" and joking about spending the weekend with them at the Day's Inn.

I say I *think* Sandra Sterge is an English teacher, but it is hard to tell. She sees her role as making sure students "are happy and feel like they belong," which seems to boil down to keeping them entertained. We do not see this former beauty queen instructing students in grammar, essay-writing, or literature—the subjects traditionally associated with her profession. Instead Burkett shows her to us teaching public speaking with a "lip-sync unit," an exercise in which students rap songs with lyrics such as "I like big butts and I cannot lie" and "I'm long and I'm strong and I'm down to get the friction on."

Nor is Sterge alone at Prior Lake in using popular culture as a tool for . . . well, it is unclear for what. During study hall, students watch the melodramatic psychobabble of *The Maury Show*. The English department insists that students study *The Scarlet Letter*—the movie, not the book. Other teachers show educational fare like the cross-dressing Dustin Hoffman in *Tootsie*.

Keeping students properly diverted is also a key part of the program at Faircrest High in California. Especially striking is Pope's depiction of American-history classes. In one of them, the teacher assigns only two projects for the entire semester, so that the students can, in her words, focus "in-depth" and become "experts." As a practical matter, this means that aside from watching a few videos about World War II, they spend most of their time listening to each other's "brief, disconnected reports on . . . topics as varied as the history of the automobile or the life of Lucille Ball." Another history teacher begins a unit on the 1960's by dressing in a tie-dyed shirt and lighting incense.

As for Faircrest's elite AP course in American history, its chief distinction seems to be higher production values. Eve Lin (as Pope calls one of the school's star students) worked for 250 hours on her part of an "intensive" group research project. Pope describes the culmination of this effort, a presentation in which the members of the group, wearing NASA name tags and T-shirts, escort their classmates into a darkened room decorated with twinkling stars. Through several scene and costume changes, they take the class on makeshift rockets, show film clips about space travel, and, using cardboard cones and Styrofoam cups, demonstrate how the Apollo 13 crew managed to fix their damaged spacecraft—all of this while the music from *Star Wars* blasts in the background. The teacher pronounces the show "magnificent" and gives the group an A+.

Not all the teachers at Prior Lake and Faircrest confuse education with entertainment. Some are serious and demanding, and they attract the most motivated students. But almost all of these exceptional teachers seem to be tired soldiers from a different era, readying themselves for retirement. One math teacher at Prior Lake, a veteran of 27 years, drives her calculus students so hard that they get perfect scores on the AP test at twice the national rate. While most students at the school do a total of two or three hours of homework a week, hers do more than that for her class alone.

But with no school-wide policies on matters like tardiness, plagiarism, and grading, even the most conscientious teachers find themselves without support and sorely tempted to compromise their standards. Sick of excuses for unfinished homework, they hand out worksheets to be completed in class and hold special study groups before each test, resigned to the fact that their students will cram the past month's assignments into a single all-nighter. The hard-driving calculus teacher at Prior Lake compares her school to East Berlin before the wall fell, a place where "nobody did much work because rewards bore little relationship to merit."

What may be the saddest part of these accounts is that the students at Prior Lake and Faircrest are not the least bit engaged by the "edutainment" that increasingly dominates their curriculum. To the contrary, they are often contemptuous of their chummy, "with-it" teachers. Eve Lin walks away from the NASA demonstration knowing that her A+ does not add up to much. "All that work for a one-hour performance. . . . I think people really underestimate what students can do." Others are disgusted by the condescension they constantly experience in the classroom. "She thinks she redefines cool," says one student of Sandra Sterge, the lip-sync queen. "I'm embarrassed for her. Can't she behave like an adult?"

Still, unlike their inner-city peers, the vast majority of these middle-class kids accept their tiresome four years as fate, a necessary prelude to college, which is itself a necessary prelude to a good paycheck. They do not play hooky, threaten teachers, or get into knife fights. Rather, they size up the situation and treat high school like a game, knowing what it takes to win. As one girl tells Burkett, "You can get all A's without learning anything."

This is what Pope means by "doing school," and it takes many forms. Students sign up for courses that include a lot of group projects and

then befriend smarter, more conscientious classmates who will perform most of the work. They try to be "interactive," as they sometimes put it, asking a question every few minutes to impress the teacher even as they sit at their desks doing homework for the next class. They whine that a test was too hard, even—or especially—if they know it was not. They try to win over teachers by asking how their training for the marathon is going or whether they enjoyed a weekend date. "I have no interest in the personal lives of the teachers," one girl says of the young man who teaches her government course, "but it's a game, and Mr. Carr is losing."

Whenever possible, they also pick teachers who are reputed to be easy graders or who assign journals or "creative writing" instead of research papers or tests. One of the five "ideal students" whom Pope follows in her book chooses to write her English report on Cesar Chavez—not for reasons of political commitment but because she has saved an A paper about him that she wrote in middle school. They use Cliffs Notes and log onto sparknotes.com to get summaries of the books they are supposed to read, and if such resources do not provide enough help, they cheat.

In all of this, moreover, the students are actively aided and abetted by their parents. In an interview with the *Atlantic Monthly,* Burkett said that nothing shocked her more about Prior Lake than the attitude of the parents, who see themselves not as the allies of the teachers and administrators but as their children's agents. If a teacher is too academically demanding, they lobby to get their child transferred to another class. If junior's grades flag, they demand extra-credit work to let him bring them up. And they gripe: "Why isn't my child getting a higher grade?" "My son never got a B before." As Burkett writes of Prior Lake, "I didn't meet one teacher there demoralized by the low pay. But I met dozens of teachers demoralized by abusive parents who were not willing to let them do their jobs by holding kids to higher standards or by making them work."

Their authority undermined at every turn— not least by their own behavior—teachers find that order in their classrooms is pretty much dependent on adolescent whim. After being called to task for runaway talking, one girl at Prior Lake protests, "It's not my fault, I have ADHD [Attention Deficit Hyperactivity Disorder]." A special-ed student whose disability gives him the right to copies of a teacher's lecture notes feels free to sleep during class. At Faircrest, when several students pull down their pants and moon their classmates, a teacher can do nothing more than tell them to "cut it out."

One of Pope's subjects, a talented but under-challenged student named Michelle, finds herself paired for a project with a class slacker who failed the last test and had not done the reading since the fall, when she lost her textbook. Just as Michelle begins their joint presentation, her partner saunters out of the classroom to go to the bathroom. Michelle presents the material as her classmates take notes. "Slow down!" they yell. "Shit, you weren't supposed to write a book!" The teacher pleads, "Be nice" and "No swearing," but no one listens.

In her inability to make sense of these chaotic scenes, Denise Clark Pope unwittingly illustrates how little our self-styled education experts have to tell us about the problems of suburban schools. She views Faircrest through the prism of ed-school cliché. Such schools, she argues, are too focused on achievement and competition, and give short shrift to cooperative learning—even as her examples demonstrate that the latter approach simply leaves the better students to carry the weaker ones. She also suggests, contradictorily, that they do not provide enough opportunities for individualized learning—even as Faircrest students choose paper or research topics that let them get away with as little original work as possible.

Pope is right to object to the cynicism of the game the schools ask their students to play, but she offers no vision of what an educated person should look like. Her chief concern is that young people become "passionately committed" to learning; *what* they learn seems to be a matter of indifference. As she sees it, a Faircrest student who adores her Mexican dance class and another who is deeply involved in his community-service project are models of educational excellence.

Elinor Burkett, who comes to her subject with fewer preconceptions and more curiosity, provides a fresher picture of the suburban high school. But she is no more able than Pope to explain what she has so astutely observed. Indeed, as their two accounts make clear, *none* of the usual suspects takes us very far in assigning blame for the stubborn mediocrity of schools like Prior Lake and Faircrest.

Multiculturalism certainly does not play much of a role; Burkett notes that most of the assigned books are by white males. Nor are the educators at those schools sophisticated enough to have been corrupted by postmodernism—most have not heard of Faulkner, much less Foucault. Burkett makes a strong case for the woeful influence of the religion of self-esteem, but this too seems insufficient. Indulgent as they may be at times, teachers and parents alike do set real goals for the students. At both schools, caffeine-driven, sleep-deprived teenagers have date books crammed with lab-report assignments, church activities, tennis practice, theater and band rehearsals, student-council meetings, and part-time jobs. Finally, the schools impose a measure of order and discipline. Administrators search students' cars, test them for drugs, send them home for wearing T-shirts with provocative messages, and even take them to task for hanging out with the wrong people.

Why, then, do so many middle-class Americans now act as if education is nothing more than a "game"? The ultimate culprits no doubt lie deep in our national character, and most of all in our relentless pragmatism, which here expresses itself in the inability of a single adult in this educational universe to offer a broader view. Along with any serious commitment to subjects like English and history, the idea of education as a way to sharpen mental discipline, to cultivate higher cultural interests, or to teach civic principles has simply disappeared. The course offerings at Prior Lake include journalism, theater, stress management, and "death education" (which includes field trips to a cemetery and an undertaker), and educators now refer to activities like student council and football as "co-curricular" rather than "extra-curricular."

When everyone accepts that education is simply a means to acquire a McMansion and an SUV, the distinction between reading a classic novel and producing an entertaining video dissolves, especially if both efforts are rewarded with a coveted A. When students see teachers standing in front of them lighting incense or nodding approvingly during student presentations about *I Love Lucy,* it is perfectly understandable if they conclude that these adults have nothing serious to offer them, and are undeserving of their respect.

In a discussion of Thomas Jefferson during an honors class at Prior Lake, students demand, "How is this relevant to my life?" When the subject is the Electoral College, they complain, "Why do we have to learn this?" To some extent, this is just typical adolescent provocation. But the truth is, their teacher, an amiable but vapid young man whose literary taste has never evolved beyond John Grisham, does not have the slightest idea how to answer them—how to explain, that is, the importance of something like citizenship, which does not impinge directly on their immediate wants and needs.

But teenagers are not simply looking to be amused and flattered. At the end of her book, Burkett is surprised to run into one class goof-off who, after graduation, had enlisted in the Marines. He finished basic training with a perfect score on his final exam. "In boot camp," he tells her, "they kick your butt if you don't try your hardest."

Most graduates of our suburban high schools must wait until after graduation—if then—to experience satisfaction of this sort. The education they receive during the decisive years of adolescence not only fails to spark their intellectual and moral imaginations, it hardly even tries. Instead it aims to produce students like Eric, a top academic achiever at Prior Lake, highly regarded by his teachers. "My belief is that every part of life is a game," he tells Burkett. "The question is: what can I get away with before it's a problem."

Kay S. Hymowitz is a contributing editor of City Journal *and the author of* Ready or Not: What Happens When We Treat Children as Small Adults.

QUESTIONS FOR REFLECTION

1.   What is "edutainment" in Hymowitz's observation? Did you feel any of your own education strayed too far into entertainment and too far away from academics? What are examples you can remember for this entertainment component of the curriculum?

2.   Does Hymowitz's observation of "good" schools matter in this article? Would it influence the reader's interpretation if the author had looked at poor performing schools instead?

3.   What solutions does Hymowitz offer to correct many of the bad habits she sees in the curriculum? Do you agree with her recommendations? What other solutions are possible?

Engaging the Disengaged

SUSAN BLACK

ABSTRACT: In this article, Susan Black explores why some kids in the classroom are immersed in learning, while others are unmotivated and indifferent about it. She offers observations and advice to help teachers engage students in the learning process.

The 10th-graders are supposed to be writing essays in their English class. But student researchers from the University of California, Irvine, observing this Orange County classroom, report that most of the kids are indifferent to the assignment, preferring to while away their time napping, daydreaming, talking, or putting on makeup.

Researchers have no trouble spotting disengaged students—the kids who lack motivation to study and learn and spend their time watching the clock and waiting to escape from what one 10th-grader called "my private prison." In fact, disengaged students are highly visible, and their numbers are disconcerting, as I discovered during a recent tour of a city high school in upstate New York.

As we made the rounds, an assistant principal and I noticed disengaged students throughout the school. Kids nonchalantly sauntered into their rooms with no concern for the tardy bell, slouched into their desks, and tuned out the lesson, preferring to stare out the window, listen to music on personal CD players, snooze, or catch up on news with their friends.

To be sure, learning sparkled in some classrooms. But why, I wondered, are some kids immersed in learning, while others are unmotivated and indifferent? And what can schools do about this problem?

TEACHERS WHO ENGAGE STUDENTS

Schools can do plenty to keep students engaged in learning, says Charlotte Danielson, of the Ed-

ucational Testing Service. Students who are deeply engaged in learning are not simply spending "time on task," she says, but are intellectually involved with curriculum topics and mentally involved in what she calls "minds-on learning."

Making that happen, not surprisingly, starts with the teacher. The best teachers, according to Danielson, keep students highly engaged throughout an entire lesson and encourage students to contribute their ideas and insights as a way of enhancing their own and other students' learning.

Danielson says the mark of a distinguished classroom is a "distinguished teacher" who has mastered a number of skills in four broad domains: planning and preparation; classroom environment; instruction; and professional responsibilities. Teachers who are adept at engaging students in learning, a skill she defines as the heart of instruction, demonstrate mastery of a number of performance standards. They:

- Represent curriculum content appropriately
- Expect students to help define topics and determine how they can be studied
- Link content to students' prior knowledge and experiences
- Ensure that students are mentally engaged in all activities and assignments
- Allow students to initiate and adapt learning activities and projects
- Form instructional groups that work to achieve learning goals
- Choose suitable instructional materials for lessons and encourage students to select resources that will help them learn

- Teach highly coherent, well-planned, and well-paced lessons that include time for student reflection.

HIGH SCHOOL SLUMP

Student disengagement occurs at all levels—in fact, some first-graders I've observed have as much apathy toward learning as many 10th-graders. But, according to Cori Brewster and Jennifer Fager, researchers at the Northwest Regional Educational Laboratory, disengagement is more frequent and more pronounced in the upper grades.

Outside influences take a particular toll on susceptible high school students, Brewster and Fager say. Such factors as unsupportive families and downtrodden neighborhoods can diminish kids' motivation and engagement in learning. In the early grades, kids from such environments can be hard to reach and difficult to motivate. By middle school, their interest in schoolwork steeply declines. And by high school, these researchers say, seriously disengaged students completely lose touch with learning. Many drift out of their classrooms and drop out for good.

Linda Lumsden, a researcher with the University of Oregon's ERIC Clearinghouse on Educational Management, says younger children generally maintain their self-confidence and believe they can succeed despite repeated failures. But older students easily lose self-confidence, attributing their failures to low ability and believing that no matter how much effort they put forth they won't succeed.

Schools can counteract negative influences and other factors that contribute to student disengagement. But first, say Brewster and Fager, it's important to know what *not* to do.

For one thing, teachers should avoid using extrinsic motivators such as pizza parties or free time. Teachers might believe that token rewards motivate students, but research shows that, in the long run, they actually diminish students' desire to learn and lower their achievement. Brewster and Fager advise teachers to develop students' intrinsic

motivation by making classrooms inviting, designing challenging and compelling lessons, and giving students choices. (For more information see "The Praise Problem," August 2000 *ASBJ*.)

They also advise schools to forego ranking and comparing students according to achievement scores. Competition ends up with winners and losers, and kids who lose soon give up on themselves, detach from school, and disengage from classroom learning. Students are more likely to be engaged when teachers pay close individual attention to their interests and the ways they learn. Students stay engaged when teachers create lessons centered on "big ideas" and design assignments at the correct level of difficulty—not too easy and not impossibly difficult—so students are challenged but still able to succeed.

Focusing on intrinsic motivation pays off in the long run, Brewster and Fager say. They cite a number of research studies showing that, compared with students who are motivated by rewards, students whose motivation comes from within are more likely to:

- Earn higher grades and test scores
- Adjust better to school
- Apply more effort
- Feel more confident about their ability to learn
- Use more decision-making strategies
- Persist and complete difficult assignments
- Retain information and concepts longer
- Avoid the need for remedial courses and review
- Work on more challenging tasks
- Value lifelong learning.

Teachers who are most successful in drawing students into deep and thoughtful learning develop activities that keep students' psychological and intellectual needs in mind. Brewster and Fager cite research showing that student engagement is higher when teachers give students a strong sense of competence, grant them autonomy and opportunities to work with others, and allow them to be original and creative. Teachers who keep students engaged also give them time for self-assessment and reflection about what they've learned and how.

A PLAN FOR ENGAGEMENT

District 186 in Springfield, Ill., is one district that takes engaged learning seriously. Teachers are expected to follow the school's checklist for assessing engaged learning by answering questions such as these:

- Are students able to select resources and strategies thoughtfully and apply them to unfamiliar tasks?
- Are students excited about their learning and eager to spend extra time and effort?
- Are tasks complex and designed for students to stretch conceptually and take greater responsibility for learning?
- Do students have frequent opportunities to get to know and work with all students?
- Are groups formed for specific purposes, and are they re-formed as needs require?
- Do students have time to explore "uncharted territory"?

Springfield's expectations correspond with Vito Perrone's principles for engaging students in learning. Perrone, former director of teacher education at Harvard's Graduate School of Education, says students' intellectual engagement depends on studying topics that relate to their own lives.

Students report feeling most engaged in learning, he says, when they help define the content to be studied; have time to wonder and pursue areas of most interest; are prompted to view topics in new ways; are encouraged to raise questions; have teachers who are passionate, inventive, and respectful; become "resident experts"; create original products that demonstrate their learning; and sense that their study is open-ended rather than predetermined and predictable.

Perrone says that teachers should start by defining their goals and sharing them with their students. Then, he says, teachers need to find primary sources—such as government documents, original photographs, and genuine objects and artifacts—that can help students gain entry into new topics. As part of their planning, Perrone urges teachers to "leave room for student choices, for inquiry for interpretation, for role-playing."

Perrone's hope is that teachers avoid teaching what he calls narrow, skills-based, understanding-poor lessons. He believes all students—including those assigned to remedial or low-track classes—should have opportunities to reach understanding, not just knowledge, by "making connections among and between things, about deep and not surface knowledge, and about greater complexity, not simplicity."

Imagine the world of difference teachers in your district can make in kids' learning—and in their lives—by taking these ideas to heart and engaging your most disengaged students.

REFERENCES

Brewster, Cori, and Jennifer Fager. *Increasing Student Engagement and Motivation: From Time-on-Task to Homework*. Portland, Ore.: Northwest Regional Educational Laboratory, October 2000; www.nwrel.org/request/oct00/textonly.html.

Danielson, Charlotte. *Enhancing Professional Practice: A Framework for Teaching*. Alexandria, Va.: Association for Supervision and Curriculum Development, 1996.

Lumsden, Linda. *Student Motivation: Cultivating a Love of Learning*. Portland, Ore.: ERIC Clearinghouse on Educational Management, 1999.

Lumsden, Linda. "Student Motivation to Learn." ERIC Digest Number 92, 1994. ED370200; www.ed.gov/databases/ERIC_Digests/ed370200.html.

Perrone, Vito. "How to Engage Students in Learning." *Educational Leadership*. February 1994; www.ascd.org/readingroom/edlead/9402/perrone.html.

"Student Disengagement in High School: A Precious Waste of Talent and What Can Be Done About It." Report from the Spring 1996 Class of Education 150:

Changing the High School Experience. University of California, Irvine; www.gse.uci.edu/doehome/deptinfo/faculty/becker/HS-Disengagement/Intro Chaptl.html.

Source: Jones, Beau, and others. *Designing Learning and Technology for Educational Reform*. Oak Brook, Ill.: North Central Regional Educational Laboratory, 1994.

Susan Black is a contributing editor to the *American School Board Journal* and is an education research consultant in Hammondsport, New York.

QUESTIONS FOR REFLECTION

1. What does Black see as the main difference between kids who are immersed in learning and those who are unmotivated and indifferent about it? Are unmotivated kids "reachable" at some point, or have they become so distant from learning that many of them will never become engaged?
2. How does Black recommend teachers engage the unengaged? Is this a realistic expectation? How much responsibility do students have to engage with their own learning?
3. How can schools that wish to better engage students learn from District 186 in Springfield, Illinois? Is the school's checklist for assessing engagement easy to follow for all schools or is it specific to those in certain conditions? Should this checklist be the basis for how all schools approach learning?

Implementing Middle School Concepts into High Schools

M. LEE MANNING
RICHARD SADDLEMIRE

ABSTRACT: Four middle school concepts shown to increase students' achievement; promote positive, humane behaviors; and improve attitudes toward school hold promise for the high school level: advisor–advisee programs, exploratory programs, interdisciplinary teams, and efforts to promote a positive school climate. Discussions of each concept include implementation tasks, characteristics of effective high school efforts, and recommended readings.

During the last ten years, research and scholarly writing on effective middle school concepts and practices have resulted in clear directions for middle level educators. A wealth of information on effective middle school practices has come from several sources: *Turning Points: Preparing American Youth for the 21st Century* (Carnegie Council on Adolescent Development 1989), the National Middle School Association's position paper *This We Believe* (National Middle School Association 1992), middle school textbooks (Allen, Splittgerber, and Manning 1993; Irvin 1992; Manning 1993), recommendations of professional associations (National Association of Secondary School Principals 1993), and reports from several state departments of education (California State Department of Education 1987; Maryland Department of Education 1989).

Responding to this information, middle schools increasingly have implemented concepts that have the potential to increase students' academic achievement, promote positive and humane behaviors, and improve attitudes toward school. In this article, we propose that there are four middle school concepts that hold promise for being effective in high schools. For each concept, we list implementation tasks, the characteristics of effective high school efforts, and recommended readings.

Before choosing to implement one or more of the concepts, high school educators should ask themselves the following question: Considering the characteristics of our high school, which concepts hold the most promise for (1) improving academic achievement, (2) improving student behavior, (3) fostering positive interpersonal relationships between students and between educators and students, and (4) enhancing the school's ability to address adolescents' cognitive and psychosocial needs?

CONCEPT 1: ADVISOR-ADVISEE PROGRAMS

The advisor-advisee program, sometimes called a teacher advisory, ensures that each student has at least one adult who knows him or her well and also that each student belongs to a small interactive group. Advisory groups promote students' social, emotional, and moral growth, while providing personal and academic guidance. To reduce the student-teacher ratio, all professional staff members serve as advisors. Advisories should be held daily and can be twenty-five to forty minutes long, depending on the school schedule (Allen, Splittgerber, and Manning 1993). Advisories can focus on students' concerns and suggestions or can be based on "advisory plans" prepared by professional writers.

Most high schools have guidance counselors and guidance programs that operate in accor-

dance with district policy and/or accrediting associations. It should be noted that adding advisor-advisee programs to the high school guidance program neither negates nor undercuts the work of counseling professionals.

Implementation Tasks

To implement an advisor-advisee program, members of the school staff will need to

- write a rationale for implementing the program based on an examination of actual student behaviors and school conditions;
- list ways that the program and the guidance and counseling services can work collaboratively toward agreed-upon goals;
- design an advisory guide that shows daily or monthly topics; and
- write a letter to parents describing the newly implemented advisor-advisee program.

Characteristics of Successful Programs

Successful advisor-advisee programs share several characteristics: (1) all students feel known by at least one caring adult; (2) students participate in advisor-advisee sessions on concerns and issues that they consider personally relevant (e.g., developmental matters, school rules and policies, higher education opportunities, and dealing with parents and other adults); (3) students and educators get to know one another on a personal teenager-adult basis; and (4) educators have sufficient professional development to know how to select appropriate topics and plan effective advisor-advisee sessions.

Recommended Reading

High school educators will find two publications especially useful in the area of advisor-advisee programs: *Advisor-Advisee Programs: Why, What, and How* (James 1986) and Neila Connors's

"Teacher Advisory: The Fourth R" in *Transforming Middle Level Education: Perspectives and Possibilities* (Irvin 1992). Also, an article in the May 1994 issue of the *Middle School Journal* addresses teacher attitudes and advisor-advisee programs.

CONCEPT 2: EXPLORATORY PROGRAMS

An exploratory program gives students the opportunity to explore areas of interest and concern. Recognizing adolescents' developing interests and capacities to learn, such a program introduces a variety of topics, skills, and content fields, without requiring mastery. The program may consist of short courses or elective units, each of which should give students a sense of control over the kind of learning they are pursuing. Various numbers and types of exploratory programs may be established, depending on school schedules, student interest, and teacher expertise. An exploratory usually lasts a month or six or nine weeks; a semester-long exploratory may be too long, considering adolescents' changing interests (Manning, 1993).

Exploratory programs provide an interesting "retreat" from the prescribed curriculum and the rigid routine of the school. Also, for students who have few opportunities to explore areas of interest outside the prescribed curriculum, exploratory courses can spark new interests, lead them to take previously unconsidered academic courses, or even motivate them to investigate new career fields.

Implementation Tasks

To undertake an exploratory program, administrators and teachers will need to perform the following tasks:

- write a rationale for having exploratory programs on the high school level;

- identify what the teachers' roles will be in the program;
- identify appropriate time frames (minutes per day, days per week, six or nine weeks, and so forth) for the exploratory program;
- select topics for the program;
- write a syllabus that outlines an exploratory program; and
- write a letter to parents that describes the program, its rationale, and possible topics.

Characteristics of Successful Programs

Several characteristics of effective exploratory programs can be identified: (1) The high school considers students' interests when choosing exploratory topics. (Possible topics include dramatic, home, and industrial arts; technology; developmental and health concerns; foreign languages; extensions of specific academic areas; theatrical performances; independent study opportunities; historical, cultural, and studio art; various elements of visual art, drawing, and pottery; and consumer education.) (2) The exploratory program has a time frame shorter than a semester (e.g., six or nine weeks), so that students can explore a number of topics rather than only one or two during the school year. (3) The program does not assign grades to students' work, so students do not feel pressured to achieve in areas that they are only exploring.

Recommended Reading

An extensive discussion of exploratory programs, *Teaching and Learning in the Middle Level School* (Allen, Splittgerber, and Manning 1993) suggests time frames, topics, and procedures. Also, *Exploration: The Total Curriculum* (Compton and Hawn 1993) provides readers with a comprehensive treatment of this key middle school concept.

CONCEPT 3: INTERDISCIPLINARY TEAMS

Interdisciplinary teaming has proved to be a workable concept that is highly valued and enjoyed by both middle school teachers and students. It can be equally successful in the high school, especially when teachers see its advantages and are allowed to maintain allegiances to their subject area departments.

Interdisciplinary teams are made up of three or more teachers representing different subject areas. The team shares the same students, schedules, and classroom areas and thereby has increased autonomy and responsibility for significant decision making. It is important to note that while teachers from various subject areas plan together, they do not teach together in the same classroom.

Most high schools are organized by subject area departments. Teachers are experts in their respective subject areas; however, they are often unfamiliar with the skills and abilities of other subject area teachers. As a result, little curricular integration occurs, and students are left with knowledge of individual courses but without a clear perspective of the many relationships between subject areas.

Suggestions that teachers break away from their subject area teams and reorganize into interdisciplinary teams may be met with opposition. Teachers' concerns might be assuaged by allowing them to continue with their respective departmental organizations (thus having both subject area departments and interdisciplinary teams) either permanently or during the transition periods. Such a decision could be made by administrators and teachers.

Implementation Tasks

Tasks that need to be undertaken in order to put interdisciplinary teams into effect include the following:

- write a rationale for adopting the interdisciplinary approach;
- list several characteristics of effective interdisciplinary teams;
- list the roles and responsibilities of team leaders;
- list several means of evaluating interdisciplinary projects; and
- identify any conflicts that might arise and possible ways of handling them.

Characteristics of Successful Programs

The characteristics of effective interdisciplinary teams are (1) teams that are balanced among content, instruction, and skills; (2) teams that emphasize the fruits of positive teamwork, such as caring, respect, success, and a sense of interdependence; (3) teachers sharing time, materials, and resources; (4) the participation of team members in conflict resolution training; and (5) for team leaders, training in effective leadership skills.

Recommended Reading

Helpful publications on interdisciplinary teaming include *The Team Process: A Handbook for Teachers* (Merenbloom 1991), *Interdisciplinary Teaching in the Middle Grades: Why and How* (Vars 1993), and the March 1994 issue of the *Middle School Journal,* which includes articles that focus on integrating subject areas and selecting interdisciplinary themes.

CONCEPT 4: EFFORTS TO PROMOTE A POSITIVE SCHOOL CLIMATE

The middle school philosophy holds that the overall climate of the school is itself a "teacher." *This We Believe* compares a good middle school to a good family—all people in the building are respected and all have particular roles and responsibilities (National Middle School Association 1992). A true middle school provides evidence of warmth, caring, and respect; those conditions should be apparent in all aspects of the school and should be firmly rooted in a sense of harmony and togetherness (California State Department of Education 1987).

Undoubtedly, high school students will benefit from a positive school climate. Such a climate promotes better interpersonal relationships, more humane environments, improved student behavior, and more helpful behavior-management methods. Some high schools subscribe to aggressive (and, in fact, sometimes abrasive and offensive) discipline policies. Educators often place rules and punishments upon students, sometimes in a harsh manner. Although educators have a responsibility to maintain safe and orderly environments, programs designed simply to suppress aggressive or negative behaviors often fail. Teachers and administrators who, on the other hand, implement humane behavior-management programs and model positive behaviors will influence students to treat educators and other students in the same positive manner.

Implementation Tasks

To promote a positive school climate, adults in the school community will need to do the following:

- identify school "hot spots"—either times of the day or locations of the school where aggressive behaviors might begin;
- extend "invitations" for positive school environments (such as listening to students; speaking courteously; using students' interests as a basis for conversations; and refraining from making hurtful remarks) (Kostelnik, Stein, and Whiren 1988);
- identify ways that students can become involved in the governance of the school; and
- name specific alternative (and positive and humane) practices that promote positive behavior and reflect middle school concepts.

Characteristics of Successful Programs

Several characteristics are shared by schools with positive climates. (1) Educators understand the importance of positive interpersonal relationships and their effect on daily school routines. (2) A positive verbal environment sets a tone for students to emulate. (3) Educators plan behavior management systems that enforce school rules and policies yet allow students to retain self-respect. (4) Educators encourage behavior that demonstrates respect for all cultures and both sexes.

Recommended Reading

Irvin's (1992) *Transforming Middle Level Education: Perspectives and Possibilities* includes an article (Johnston 1992) that addresses school climate and collaborative behavior. Also, Thomas and Bass (1993) examine the relationship between school climate and the implementation of middle school practices. Last, the *Middle School Journal* and *The Clearing House* periodically include articles on promoting positive school behaviors.

TIME FRAME

High school educators should be commended for their visions of more positive and humane high schools. They will find, however, that the implementation of middle school concepts into the high school requires both dedicated effort and considerable time. For example, staff development sessions that give educators only an introduction to middle school concepts likely will result in "business as usual." A sustained yet patient effort will prevent educators from feeling overwhelmed by change, will provide time for a genuine change of attitudes and improvement of skills, and will allow educators to feel that they are a part of the change process rather than that change is being imposed on them. Determining a time frame will require a consideration of the individual school, its current practices and policies, the extent to which the middle schools that feed into the high school adhere to the concepts, and the enthusiasm of administrators and faculty. An excellent resource for educators wanting to implement middle school concepts is *Planning for Success: Successful Implementation of Middle School Organization* (Williamson and Johnston 1991).

SUMMARY

Implementing middle school concepts into the high school years can have a positive impact on both adolescents and their educators. Adolescent learners will benefit from advisor-advisee and exploratory programs. They and their teachers will benefit from interdisciplinary teams and from a positive and humane school climate. The challenge lies in determining which middle school concepts to adopt and in reaching agreement on a realistic time frame for implementation. Although implementing the concepts into a high school requires considerable time and effort, educators should not feel overwhelmed in their efforts, especially because students might already have a working knowledge of essential middle school concepts. Similarly, many valuable journal articles and books provide clear directions for implementing those concepts.

REFERENCES

Allen, H. A., F. L. Splittgerber, and M. L. Manning. 1993. *Teaching and learning in the middle level school.* Columbus, Ohio: Merrill.

California State Department of Education. 1987. *Caught in the middle.* Sacramento, Calif.: California Department of Education.

Carnegie Council on Adolescent Development. 1989. *Turning points: Preparing American youth for the 21st century.* Washington, D.C.: Carnegie Council on Adolescent Development.

Compton, M. F., and H. C. Hawn. 1993. *Exploration: The total curriculum.* Columbus, Ohio: National Middle School Association.

Connors, N. A. 1992. Teacher advisory: The fourth r. In *Transforming middle level education: Perspectives and possibilities,* edited by J. L. Irvin, 162–92. Boston: Allyn and Bacon.

Irvin, J. L. 1992. *Transforming middle level education: Perspectives and possibilities.* Boston: Allyn and Bacon.

James, M. 1986. *Advisor-advisee programs: Why, what, and how.* Columbus, Ohio: National Middle School Association.

Johnston, J. H. 1992. Climate and culture as mediators of school values and collaborative behavior. In *Transforming middle level education: Perspectives and possibilities,* edited by J. L. Irvin, 77–92. Boston: Allyn and Bacon.

Kostelnik, M. J., L. C. Stein, and A. P. Whiten. 1988. Children's self-esteem: The verbal environment. *Childhood Education* 65:29–32.

Manning. M. L. 1993. *Developmentally appropriate middle level schools.* Wheaton, Md.: Association for Childhood Education International.

Maryland Department of Education. 1989. *What matters in the middle grades.* Baltimore, Md.: Maryland Department of Education.

Merenbloom, E. 1991. *The team process: A handbook for teachers.* Columbus, Ohio: National Middle School Association.

National Association of Secondary School Principals. 1993. *Achieving excellence through the middle level curriculum.* Reston, Va.: National Association of Secondary School Principals.

National Middle School Association. 1992. *This we believe.* Columbus, Ohio: National Middle School Association.

Thomas, D. D., and G. R. Bass. 1993. An analysis of the relationship between school climate and the implementation of middle school practices. *Research in Middle Level Education* 16:1–12.

Vats, G. F. 1993. *Interdisciplinary teaching in the middle grades: Why and how.* Columbus, Ohio: National Middle School Association.

Williamson, R., and J. H. Johnston. 1991. *Planning for success: Successful implementation of middle school organization.* Reston, Va.: National Association of Secondary School Principals.

M. Lee Manning is an associate professor in the Department of Educational Curriculum and Instruction, Darden College of Education, Old Dominion University, Norfolk, Virginia; *Richard Saddlemire* is superintendent of the Antilles Consolidated School System, Fort Buchanan, Puerto Rico.

QUESTIONS FOR REFLECTION

1. Select one of the four middle school concepts discussed in this article and critique the recommendations for implementing that concept. What additional implementation strategies would you suggest?
2. Review the articles in Chapter 8 on educational programs for transescents and early adolescents. What additional middle school concepts would you suggest for the high school level?
3. The authors identify four general characteristics shared by schools with positive climates. If you were evaluating the climate of a school, what specific "evidence" would you look for to indicate the presence, or absence, of each characteristic?

New Hope for High Schools: Lessons from Reform-Minded Educators

THEODORE R. SIZER

ABSTRACT: This excerpt from Horace's Hope: What Works for the American High School *examines four factors that account for the "extraordinary gap between common sense and common school practice": the symbolic, rather than substantive, purposes of high schools; the highly complex and interconnected high school "mechanism"; similar high school routines across the country; and decisions about policy and practice made by those who do not have to live with those decisions. The author then discusses four of the thirteen lessons he has learned from working with reform-minded schools—these schools have stable leadership; perceive each child as an individual; continually readjust goals based on children, staff, and community; and have a climate based on respect and genuine communication.*

The leap from traditional school practice to commonsense reform is for most Americans a heroic one. Contrast familiar life outside school with that commonly found inside school. Few parents want to spend, or can even rationally contemplate spending, a full day all alone penned up in one room with 27 12-year-olds, day after day. . . . Nonetheless, most parents assume that a middle-school teacher can cope well every day of the week with five groups of 27 12-year-olds drawn from every sort of community, following a regimen over which that teacher has almost no control.

Most college English department faculty members would mightily object—and do strenuously object—if those of them who teach writing classes are forced to carry more than 60 students at once, in four classes of 15 students each. Nonetheless, most school boards assume that high school English instructors can teach 120 to 180 students, in groups of 20 to 40, to write clearly and well.

Few businesses hire people on the basis of test scores alone, or even principally so. Most businesses hire people on the basis of evidence about their previous work, its substance, and how faithfully and imaginatively they dealt with that substance. Yet most policy makers assume that for serious purposes of judgment, one can pinpoint the present effectiveness and future chances of a child, or even an entire school, on the basis of some congeries of numerical data.

Few successful businesses change the content of each employee's work every hour and regularly and insistently interrupt the workers' efforts with announcements on a public address system. Nonetheless, a seven- or eight-period day and an incessant blare of administrative matters over PA systems characterize most high schools.

Few serious enterprises let all their employees take long vacations at the same time every year. Few such enterprises assume that all work can be reduced to a predictable schedule, which implies that every worker will produce at the same speed. Few serious businesses believe that those who are immediately swifter are always better. Nonetheless, most high schools accept these practices without challenge.

And more. The typical routines of high school . . . often defy elementary logic and the experience of the typical citizen. Yet, curiously, they seem exceedingly difficult to change.

I believe that there are at least four reasons for this extraordinary gap between common sense and common school practice.

First, high schools in America serve more symbolic than substantive purposes. The routines of adolescence carry great weight—taking the expected courses, coping with Mom and Dad over a report card festooned with challenging letter or numerical grades, meeting girls or boys, dating (made possible by the rituals of the high school hallways), attending homecoming, the prom, and above all graduation, that choreographed rite of passage expected of every American around the age of 18. One messes with these very familiar icons of practice at one's peril. . . .

Second, the high school mechanism is highly complex and interconnected. The curriculum, for example, is divided into familiar subjects. To teach a particular subject in a public school, one has to be formally certified in that academic area by the state. One gains certification by attending a college where specified courses leading to that credential are given. The college is divided into departments that correspond with the certification needs of those at the high school. College faculty get their tenure by providing the expected courses and writing their books in the expected areas. The collective bargaining agreements reflect these subject categories. State and federal assessments and regulations depend on them. . . . Seemingly everything important within and outside a high school affects everything else. To change anything means changing everything. The prospect is daunting, usually paralyzing.

Third, and not surprisingly, school routines tend to be remarkably similar in high schools across the country, even those in the private sector, where one might expect significantly different approaches. There are few examples, especially state-endorsed examples, of a school organized in ways and on assumptions that diverge sharply from the conventional. Thus we have a chicken-and-egg problem; there is no critical mass of different schools across the country to bear witness to a better kind of schooling, and this makes the argument in their favor a difficult one, based on promises rather than evidence.

Finally, the people who make many crucial decisions about educational policy and practice— those at the top—do not have to live with those decisions. After giving the order to charge, they do not have to lead the troops—that is, to serve directly in the schools. Accordingly, there is little incentive for many of them to study the realities. . . . They can require and recommend and finance with little immediate accountability. If kids do not improve, someone else is always there to blame. . . .

Change comes hard, even when the need for the change is blatantly obvious. The system carries on, even when the carrying on is irrational. In Essential schools as well as in schools in kindred projects, there is usually a battle over even the most obviously needed reforms. Realistically, we must expect that a majority of the schools attempting significant change will flounder, smothered by the forces of mindless tradition, fear, and obstruction, which, because of the complexity of high school work, are so easy to rally. As a result, we have learned to be very straight with the schools and with the authorities directing them about the rigors and costs of serious change. . . .

Human-scale places are critical. "I cannot teach well a student whom I do not know." How many students at once can one high school teacher know well? At the start, the Coalition, somewhat arbitrarily, asserted that no teacher should have responsibility for more than 80 students. Even though the leap to this number from the more usual 100 to 180 students is heroic, the record of demonstrably successful Essential schools shows that this number is still too large.

However, we have learned that there is much more to the whole matter of scale. It is not only that each teacher must have a sensible load of students. It is that the school itself has to be of human scale—a place where everyone can know everyone else. Of course, smallness is just the beginning, but it is a necessary precondition.

More than one teacher must know each child (and her family) well, and there must be time for those teachers, and, as necessary, her parents, to discuss that child. It is fine for me to know Jessica, a ninth-grader; but my knowledge of her is necessarily limited to her participation in my classes and our personal relationship. She may well be known quite differently by another teacher, who is a different person and who teaches her a different subject. Together that teacher and I and her parents can construct a fuller, fairer portrait of Jessica than any of us can alone.

Such sharing of knowledge about kids requires trusting colleagueship among teachers. If we are hired merely on the basis of our certification areas ("secondary school U.S. and European history teacher") and seniority in the school system ("First hired, last fired"), we join a school as independent operators, are given our classrooms, and consult and collaborate only when the spirit moves us. But when we are chosen to work in a school on the basis of a commitment to the philosophy of that school and because our arrival will strengthen the corps of staff members already there, the relationship of each of us to the others is always crucial, particularly so if the school is taking on tough reforms.

How many colleagues can work effectively together? No more, our hunch is, than can attend a crowded potluck supper. So much of importance in schools depends on trust, and trust arises from familiarity and from time spent together getting divisive issues out on the table and addressing them. A team of 25 to 30 teachers, a number large enough for variety and small enough for trust, might be ideal. This implies, given average secondary school pupil-teacher ratios, a school of 325 to 420 pupils, itself a human-scale number. Adolescent anonymity is unlikely in such a place.

How, some protest, does one create such small units when school buildings are very large? The answer is to divide the students into small, fully autonomous units, each in effect its own school within a large "educational apartment building."

What does it take to work together effectively? A mix of inspired leadership, candor, and restraint. Schools are difficult places, filled with issues over which reasonable people will disagree. A process to work the inevitable kinks out is necessary, as is the time for that process to proceed.

A kid has just been caught with a pinch of marijuana; he is a first-time offender. Should we suspend him? "We need to set an example." Or do we just slap his wrist hard? "He's really scared—he needs support now."

Those English prize essays; which is best and why? Who gets the prize? Should there be a prize? What signals, good and bad, do prizes send?

An unmarried teacher is pregnant. As she comes to term, should she continue to teach? "She models the very behavior that we must not condone." "She's a stellar teacher; the kids love her." "Her private life is her own business." "Each case deserves to be decided on its merits." . . .

The very existence of such confrontations, of course, makes teaching an endlessly stimulating occupation. These are real issues that affect real people every day, and they are issues as influential in people's lives as they are controversial. They can be dealt with well only in schools small enough to allow for trusting relationships among the staff and with the students.

Human scale is only the beginning. The culture of the place is also critical. Essential schools with high morale reflect the dignity deserved by teachers as well as students. The little things symbolize it well. Teachers are given not only the time to struggle with the substance and standards of the students' daily work but also the civilities of access to telephones and trust in their use. A copying machine is available for all, not just the administrative staff. There are no time clocks or check-ins. Teachers are expected to consult with one another, and easy relationships among colleagues—formal or informal, as the individuals like—are the norm. These matters are the important minutiae of school keeping, the little things that send institutional signals.

Work in an Essential school (as in most others) is hard. The pressure is bearable if the work is respected, not only in word but in the way the adult community functions. Essential schools that have worked out their relationships clearly serve their students better than those in which the adults go their own ways civilly or are full of tension and disrespect. . . .

The evidence in favor of human-scale environments and a teacher–student ratio of one to 80 or fewer comes largely from negative findings. Some schools, however devoted to redesign, have not been able to reduce teacher loads dramatically. They thereby remain wracked with faculty dissension, which paralyzes all reform beyond generalized rhetoric. Big schools remain the prisoners of procedures rather than relationships to get through a day, and many of their students thus remain aloof and difficult to engage. The poor performance of such students reflects this.

The limited but growing number of small Essential schools (or small autonomous units within a larger institution) that have been able to build coherent relationships demonstrably outperform their large and bureaucratically ensnared brethren. . . .

Clusters of schools proceed more effectively than schools alone. The Coalition in its early years was a group of individual schools, each making its own way in its own setting. As the numbers of schools grew, for administrative convenience we organized regional centers to pro-

vide the kind of support usually delivered from the Coalition's central office at Brown University. We have since realized that clustering has important substantive virtues.

The schools play off against one another, comparing work, consulting on new directions, promoting honest talk by faculty members across schools, serving each other as sustained "critical friends." A cluster of schools can help others in their midst get started, both through the small staffs they hire and by lending veteran teachers as consultants.

The schools protect one another politically. In one extraordinary instance, a new district superintendent threatened to fire a principal because she had raised substantial moneys on her own for her school's library, which made it far richer than comparable libraries in nearby schools. The superintendent found this inequitable; no school should have a much bigger library than others. The principal had to cease this fund-raising, he ordered. Principals at the other schools in the cluster and the cluster's staff had contacts with the local newspaper, and the story quickly reached page one. The superintendent backed off. Entrepreneurial energy was applauded, and the poverty of school library budgets was exposed.

In some places, such as New York City, clusters in fact operate in some respects as formal school districts. They collectively prepare standards and expectations for exhibitions, and they make the work of their students public. They monitor and support one another. When it is efficient, they make collective purchases. They have negotiated with the state for collective waivers of regulations. They are professional and governmental units in all but name. They profoundly redefine what is meant by the top and the bottom.

The relationship between the top and the bottom of the educational hierarchy must be fundamentally rethought. Our experience with the governance of schools has led to four principal conclusions. First, stability of leadership within the system is crucial. Schools endlessly affected by changes—new superintendents, each with a new plan; new governors, also with "new initiatives"; new legislative leadership—are pulled in frustratingly different directions. We have seen school principals and teachers figuring out practically, and often cynically, how to fend off the worst of any new order, knowing that this year's innovation may well not be operative next year. . . .

Second, the way the policy community and the bureaucracy view schooling is crucial. If the metaphor of the bloodless assembly line persists, little change happens. Dealing with children in the aggregate ("all the eighth-graders in this state," "all children from families below the poverty line") and perceiving each child as an individual ("just like each of my own very different children") lead policy in very different directions. The latter, obviously—as it reflects reality—is preferable.

Policy makers, of course, have to view the large scene, but they do not have to reduce the scene to crude generalities. Accepting both the diversities implicit in schooling—the differences among children, neighborhoods, and professionals—and the need to attend carefully to the wishes, commitments, and proper rights of parents make system policy and practice complex, and thus a nuisance. We have found that when the subtleties are honored and when there has been bipartisan commitment to a reform direction, the results are promising.

In 1988, the Coalition of Essential Schools formally allied with the Education Commission of the States (an association of state governments for collective study of educational policy and practice) in a project dubbed Re:Learning to pursue what we called a strategy of reform "from the schoolhouse to the statehouse." The assumption here was that the governmental "top" and the school-level "bottom" would work as close allies, with the demands and particular needs of the bottom—the individual schools—profoundly shaping the top's specific policies.

Over the past years some 15 states have been involved, directly or indirectly, in this project, which has led to efforts to bring together the teaching and policy communities for greater understanding of each other's roles (gatherings rarely held in previous times), state assignment of staff to support Essential schools and kindred reforming schools, state funds to support the reform, and waivers of regulations to give the schools room to redesign their work. In several states this activity has led to reform legislation—specific support to risk-taking schools. Most important, Re:Learning has given legitimacy to the work of those schools trying to break with unwise practices. The informed blessing of the top has provided substantial support for the bottom, as the rapid growth of Essential schools after 1988 evidences.

Third, leaders at both the top and the bottom have to understand that managing a school is rather like sailing a boat. There is a chart, there is a planned course, and there are plotted shoals and sandbars, but those on board have to adjust all the time to changing winds and attitudes, even redrawing the course to the destination from time to time. There are goals for a school and a framework of expectations for how those goals may be reached, but the means, and even the framework itself, are subject to constant adjustment on the basis of what is going on with the children, the staff, and the community. The hand of government has to be a light one, and a trusting one. Directing the sailboat from an office ashore is as imprudent as directing the activities of an individual school from a school system's central headquarters.

Finally, respect and sustained, genuine communication between top and bottom are essential. Where there are differences, they should be addressed. Too often they are swept under a rug while the state or district tries to ram its views home and the locals sit on their hands, griping.

Of course, the conventional wisdom implies that higher government has the right to overrule lower government. The fact that these "levels" of government arise more from the realities of scale (towns are smaller than states) and from political arrangements than from citizens' rights obscures the fact that the compulsory nature of public education puts an enormous responsibility for restraint on governmental leaders. Some give that responsibility too little respect, with predictable resentment and opposition at the bottom.

The shape and obligations of all the pieces of the public school system as we know it are under fresh scrutiny. State and city leaders' willingness to contemplate radical changes in that system is strikingly more prevalent today than when the Coalition's work started. The system is under criticism unprecedented in this century. We hope that the new forms it takes adhere carefully to the convictions represented by Re:Learning's slogan, "*from* the schoolhouse *to* the statehouse."

Theodore R. Sizer is university Professor Emeritus, Brown University, and Chairman of the Coalition of Essential Schools, Oakland, California.

QUESTIONS FOR REFLECTION

1. After his brief discussion of the symbolic purposes of high school, Sizer says "One messes with these very familiar icons of practice at one's peril. . . ." What does he mean by this statement?
2. After discussing the complexity and interconnectedness of the "high school mechanism," Sizer concludes that the prospect of change is "daunting, usually paralyzing." Do you agree? Can you cite evidence to suggest that Sizer's view is too pessimistic?
3. Reflecting on the educational setting with which you are most familiar (K–12 through higher education; school or nonschool program), to what extent does the climate of this setting reflect concern for the "human scale"? How does this concern (or lack of concern) affect students' learning?

Can Depth Replace Coverage in the High School Curriculum?

FRED M. NEWMANN

ABSTRACT: *The emphasis on broad content coverage is a fundamental limitation of the high school curriculum. This "addiction to coverage" allows students to develop only superficial understanding of what they study. As an alternative, the curriculum should emphasize depth. If given time to differentiate, elaborate, qualify, and integrate, students will acquire a rich understanding of content. To overcome the obstacles to depth will require cutting content from the existing curriculum, developing new approaches to assessment, and changing instructional strategies.*

Debates about the high school curriculum tend to focus on two general questions. First, are students studying the proper content? In other words, are they taking the right number of courses in each content area, and do these courses provide an appropriate blend of knowledge, skills, attitudes, and values? Second, what are the best ways to organize and teach a given body of content to certain groups of students? These important questions seem likely to persist, due to a lack of definitive research and to the political nature of education policy making. Meanwhile, a more fundamental problem continues to plague our efforts. Despite an abundance of sophisticated rationales, pedagogical approaches, and curriculum designs, we usually try to teach too much.

In our research on higher-order thinking in high school social studies classes, we asked students whether they ever had the opportunity to really dig into a given topic and study it in depth for at least two weeks. John responded to our question:

> I got totally immersed in a project when the teacher forced us to do a paper on some guy. We couldn't pick him, but we had to read at least four books and write at least 100 note cards—big cards—and develop at least a 10-page paper. I got Montaigne. It ended up real interesting. As Mr. Foster pointed out, it was kind of cool that I got to be a real expert and to know more than probably five million people in America about this guy. I'm not sure what made it so interesting—whether it was Montaigne's own works and life or just the fact that I got to know so much about him.

Asked whether he had such opportunities very often, John replied:

> Most of the time, you don't get this in school. A lot of times it's a total skim; it's very bad. The course in European history is a classic example. We covered 2,000 years. Every week we were assigned to cover a 30-page chapter. The teacher is a stickler for dates and facts. We had 50 dates a week to memorize. The pity of it all is that now I don't remember any of them. I worked so hard, and now basically all I remember is Montaigne. There's like maybe five dates I remember, when I probably learned 300 or 400 dates all year. I can't even remember a lot of the important guys we studied.
>
> I'd like to have worked where you dig in depth, but it's a double-sided sword, because if you're constantly going in-depth about each thing you come across, then you're not going to get very far. It's quantity versus quality. The only reasonable thing is you've got to find a balance. I guess there's

more of a superficial quality to school now—teachers trying to cover as much as they can. They're not going into depth.

ADDICTION TO COVERAGE

We are addicted to coverage. This addiction seems endemic in high schools—where it runs rampant, especially in history—but it affects all levels of the curriculum, from kindergarten through college. We expose students to broad surveys of the disciplines and to endless sets of skills and competencies. The academic agenda includes a wide variety of topics; to cover them all, we give students time to develop only the most superficial understandings. The press for broad coverage causes many teachers to feel inadequate about leaving out so much content and apologetically mindful of the fact that much of what they teach is not fully understood by their students.

For several reasons, the addiction to coverage is destructive. First, it fosters the delusion that human beings are able to master everything worth knowing. We ought to realize that the knowledge explosion of this century has created a virtual galaxy of material worth knowing. Moreover, we ought to recognize that a crucial task of curriculum builders is to choose from this vast quantity of valuable knowledge a relatively infinitesimal portion to teach. The more we attempt to make this infinitesimal sample of knowledge representative or comprehensive, the more we delude ourselves, given the swift pace at which knowledge is accumulating. It is both arrogant and futile to assume that we can keep up with the knowledge explosion.

Furthermore, survey coverage is often a waste of time. Students learn most material in order to use it on one or two brief occasions (a quiz and a test), after which the material is quickly forgotten. When knowledge is used only rarely, it is seldom available for transfer to new situations.

Beyond simply wasting time or failing to impart knowledge of lasting value, superficial coverage has a more insidious consequence: it reinforces habits of mindlessness. Classrooms become places in which material must be learned—even though students find it nonsensical because their teachers have no time to explain. Students are denied opportunities to explore related areas that arouse their curiosity for fear of straying too far from the official list of topics to be covered. Teachers' talents for conveying subtle nuances and complexities are squelched. Not surprisingly, many students stop asking questions soon after they leave the early elementary grades. Instead, they passively allow teachers and textbooks to pour material into their heads, where they will try to store it for future use in educational exercises. However, the press to "cover" offers little opportunity to develop that material in ways that will help students meet more authentic intellectual challenges.

Most of us recognize the negative consequences of an addiction to coverage. We all want our curricula to foster fundamental understandings and complex, higher-order thinking. But despite our best intentions, we cannot break the habit.

THE ALTERNATIVE: DEPTH

The alternative to coverage, though difficult to achieve, is depth: the sustained study of a given topic that leads students beyond superficial exposure to rich, complex understanding. The topic might be "broad" (e.g., liberty, ecological balance) or "narrow" (e.g., John Winthrop's leadership in colonial America, the effect of acid rain on sugar maple trees). To gain rich understanding of a topic, students must master a great deal of information, use that information to answer a variety of questions about the topic, and generate new questions that lead to further inquiry. In demonstrating their knowledge of the topic, they should go beyond simple declarative statements to differentiation, elaboration, qualification, and integration.

Depth has been summarized as "less is more."* But *less* in this context does not mean less knowledge or information, for depth can be achieved only through the mastery of considerable information. Rather, *less* refers to less mastery of information that provides only a superficial acquaintance with a topic. In general, depth is preferable as a principle of curriculum development, because depth is more likely to facilitate lasting retention and transfer of knowledge, more likely to cultivate thoughtfulness than mindlessness, and more likely to enable us to cope in some reasonable fashion with the explosion of knowledge.

It is important to head off two possible misinterpretations of my advocacy of depth over coverage. First, I do not suggest that skills should replace knowledge as the focus of the curriculum. Instead, I maintain that knowledge in depth is more valuable than superficial knowledge and that, in order to achieve knowledge in depth, we must radically reduce the number of isolated bits of information that are transmitted to children.

Second, some readers may worry that emphasis on depth will produce excessive specialization and thus undermine the quest for a common core of knowledge, which is necessary for communication and social cohesion. However, there is no logical contradiction between knowledge in depth and attempts to achieve a common core. A common core can consist either of in-depth knowledge of a few topics or of superficial knowledge of many topics. What to include in the common core and what proportion of the curriculum the common core should occupy are difficult questions, but they should remain separate from the issue of superficial familiarity versus complex understanding. I am arguing here only that we should be devoting a far greater proportion of formal education to the development of complex understanding of fewer topics, whether those

*Theodore R. Sizer, *Horace's Compromise: The Dilemma of the American High School* (Boston: Houghton Mifflin, 1984).

topics are unique to certain classes and schools or common to all of them.

OBSTACLES TO DEPTH

Why is depth so difficult to achieve? What are some of the major obstacles?

First, we must recognize that the point of education *is,* in a sense, to cover material—that is, to expose students to and make them familiar with new information. Conversely, to be unaware of information considered "basic" for productive living within a society is to be uneducated. In our society, becoming educated involves learning the meanings of thousands of words and mastering hundreds of conventions for manipulating information and communicating effectively with others. Clearly, to master ideas and techniques, students must be exposed to information.

Unfortunately, this legitimate need for a certain degree of coverage has fostered the illusion (firmly held by professional educators and by the general public) that it is possible to teach a reasonably comprehensive sample of all the worthwhile knowledge that is currently available. We are remarkably unwilling to accept the consequences of the knowledge explosion. Instead, we cling to a conception of education more appropriate to medieval times, when formal public knowledge was relatively well-defined, finite, and manageable. Although we know that times have changed and that we can't teach everything, we apparently retain our faith in the ideal of comprehensiveness, because we continue to try to cover as much as possible.

The mounting pressure for schools to be accountable and to prove their effectiveness through students' test scores gives added impetus to an emphasis on coverage over depth. It is more convenient to test for superficial coverage, because thousands of multiple-choice test items can be constructed to tap countless bits of knowledge.

We teachers have been socialized to construe knowledge as outlines of the content of introductory textbooks. Seldom in our own undergraduate or graduate education did our professors engage us in deep inquiry, except for such special experiences as participating in an honors program or writing a graduate thesis (rare instances that are reserved for individuals who have already endured many years of ritualistic coverage). Thus many of us would hardly know what to do with students if the pressure for coverage were suddenly lifted.

Even teachers who have a commitment to depth and a vision of how to achieve it in the classroom are frustrated by the lack of suitable textbooks and other instructional materials. Literary works, journal articles, and primary sources are useful with highly motivated and able readers, but such materials are too difficult for many students, and few alternatives are available.

Another obstacle to depth is the orientation that students bring to their schoolwork. They have been rewarded primarily for completing discrete tasks that require the recognition of countless bits of knowledge. Those knowledge bits are organized into many separate subjects, and students' learning schedules are divided into small chunks of time. A variety of topics must be studied each day. Therefore, continuous and sustained study of any one topic seems virtually impossible.

Television further undermines intense and sustained concentration on a single topic. Teachers report that young people of the television generation have no patience for study in depth; they want quick, simple, unambiguous answers. Moreover, college-bound students want some assurance that they have been exposed to the range of information covered by admissions tests.

OVERCOMING THE OBSTACLES

The obstacles are formidable indeed. But teachers, administrators, and state-level policy makers who seek to overcome them may find the following recommendations helpful.

First, schools and school districts must continue to develop a rationale for study in depth. At the same time, they must focus the public's attention on the problems of addiction to coverage. In other words, they must help policy makers, academics, business leaders, and the general public to see that well-intentioned efforts to cover a broad range of material have developed into an obsession that is undermining education.

Second, instead of focusing immediately on which courses to eliminate, schools and school districts would probably find it less divisive to work first on ways of achieving depth within existing courses. Later, criteria such as the following might be used to decide which content to cut from the curriculum:

- Does the topic occupy a critical position in a hierarchy of content, so that students must master it in order to understand the important ideas that follow? Does failure to understand this particular topic put students at risk?
- If the topic is of critical importance, could it be readily learned outside of school through reading, televiewing, or some other form of independent study? Or does mastery of this topic require special guidance by a professional educator?
- Are teachers likely to spend a large amount of time developing this topic and assessing students' understanding of it, or will they simply give students a superficial exposure to the topic and then test for recognition or recall?

These criteria alone cannot resolve all the complicated issues related to the selection of curricular content. But they illustrate the kinds of educational principles (as opposed to teachers' personal preferences or faculty or school district politics) on which curriculum decisions might be based.

Third, in any individual school that tries to foster depth at the expense of coverage, the teachers will need special support as they wrestle with such issues as what content to cut from the curriculum, how to teach for depth, and how to assess new and more complex forms of mastery. Such support ought to include resources that would enable teachers to participate more fully in the development of curriculum materials and new approaches to testing and that would enable them to help one another more frequently in planning, teaching, and evaluating lessons.

At the state level, policy makers affect the coverage of content in at least five areas: assessment, textbook selection, curriculum requirements, school improvement programs, and teacher education. Let us consider the nature of state influence in each area and how the states might encourage a greater emphasis on depth.

Assessment. To the extent that state testing programs rely primarily on short-answer, multiple-choice tests that cover a broad range of subjects, the states contribute to the disease of coverage. There are two basic strategies for improving assessment. First, test developers can reduce the number of isolated bits of information covered by the tests, using instead items that allow students to demonstrate in-depth mastery of a smaller number of topics. Second, test developers can replace multiple-choice, short-answer questions with writing exercises—perhaps even speaking exercises—that require students to synthesize their ideas and to show the development of their thinking on selected topics.

Textbook Selection. States spread the disease of coverage when they adopt textbooks written primarily for survey courses aimed at comprehensive exposure. Publishers must be persuaded to prepare textbooks that take a more selective, in-depth approach; meanwhile, the states should adopt and publicize existing textbooks and other instructional materials that reflect this approach. One of the students I interviewed remarked that he had enjoyed a course in European history. "What made the course so interesting?" I asked. "Was it the teacher?" "No, the teacher was not particularly exciting," he said. "But the textbook was really terrific." He recalled neither the title of the book nor the name of its author. What he remembered was that the book did not inundate readers with dates and facts, headings, review questions, and test questions. "It was like a book you'd find in the library—a real book," he added.

State Curriculum Requirements. State legislators are pressured by every conceivable organization to insert subjects into the curriculum, and a reasonable case can be made for almost every proposed course or unit of instruction. Individually, each requirement seems legitimate; collectively, however, they often resemble a disorganized smorgasbord. Current efforts to reduce the number of electives and to return to a common core of required courses may seem to address the problem. But elective courses often enable students to inquire more deeply into specific topics than do core courses, which often become superficial surveys. We should avoid sanctifying either approach and instead support having students study fewer topics in greater depth.

School Improvement Programs. Moving away from an emphasis on coverage will be difficult. Many teachers regard coverage as a primary educational goal. Others recognize that the pace of instruction makes thoughtful inquiry impossible, but they worry that they will do a disservice to students if they fail to cover all the territory required by state mandates and standardized tests. To resolve this complex professional dilemma, teachers need time to think, to argue, to select, and to develop new instructional materials. States should appropriate funds to help the schools pay for programs of staff development and for the production by staff members of curricula and tests that emphasize in-depth study.

Teacher Education. Colleges and universities perpetuate the addiction to coverage through survey courses and broad distribution requirements. These offerings permit many students to complete their degrees without ever having to engage in a sustained struggle to master the complexity of a field or topic. Thus higher education encourages teachers to conceive of knowledge as that which is contained on the table of contents of an introductory text. The states should counter this tendency by requiring that prospective teachers devote a greater proportion of their training to the in-depth study of an academic area.

Regardless of what we teach or how we teach it, we try to teach too much. The addiction to coverage is a futile attempt to offer students a comprehensive education; it wastes time and it undermines intellectual integrity. Instead of superficial exposure, curricula should emphasize sustained study aimed at developing complex understanding. But powerful obstacles—illusions about the nature of knowledge, pressures for accountability, patterns of socializing teachers and students, the organization of schooling, and the quality of instructional materials—stand in the way of a shift to study in depth. Moving in that direction will require action at the school, district, and state levels to cut content from the curriculum, develop new approaches to assessment, and change instructional materials and pedagogy. Most important, schools, districts, and states will have to carefully reexamine the goals of education.

Fred M. Newmann is Director, National Center on Effective Secondary Schools, School of Education, University of Wisconsin, Madison.

QUESTIONS FOR REFLECTION

1. To what extent does an "addiction to coverage" characterize curricula at the elementary, junior/middle, and postsecondary levels of education? What examples can you cite?
2. In what ways does an emphasis on coverage "reinforce habits of mindlessness"?
3. What steps can curriculum planners take to help policy makers, other educators, business leaders, and the general public understand how the "addiction to coverage" undermines the educative process?

CASE STUDY IN CURRICULUM IMPLEMENTATION

Going the Extra Mile to Smooth the Transition to High School

HUGH CAMPBELL

ABSTRACT: Although many schools have structures in place to ease the transition between middle level and high school, some students need more help. In this article, Campbell describes how Norwich Free Academy in Norwich, Connecticut, extended its freshman program into the tenth grade to help these students achieve greater success.

Many educators are concerned about ninth grade students who enter high school lacking the skills necessary for success. At the Norwich Free Academy (NFA) in Norwich, Conn., our guiding belief is that all students can learn, but several of the young people entering the NFA are one, two, or three years behind their classmates. Maybe they are missing some of the basic elements required to meet the demands of a high school curriculum. Weak study or organizational skills or gaps in their learning may have limited their success in the eighth grade, and they have to play catch-up for four years. Perhaps they are socially immature. Or they may have rarely received the attention they needed to tackle academic challenges independently. Schools often address these issues during the ninth grade, but what happens to these students after they finish their ninth grade year?

NFA is an independent high school of 2,300 students that is the designated high school for the city of Norwich and seven surrounding towns. NFA is a large school, and students travel to and from its five classroom buildings, athletic facility, and library media center each period. Although we are confident that our ninth grade program successfully integrates students into the school community, we recognize that we have students who need extra support and attention during their second year. As both a teacher and an administrator, I saw many tenth graders struggle to complete the transition.

THE NINTH GRADE HOUSE

Ninth grade students are taught in the Cranston Building. Students are scheduled in one of five units with teacher teams from four core subject areas—English, civics, mathematics, and science—which carries over an essential component from middle level philosophy. Curriculum is often integrated to allow the students to make better connections from one subject to another. In a school our size, with students coming from eight sending communities, the teams make NFA seem smaller and more inviting.

This structure encourages a more personalized approach as the students begin their high school experience. But despite the teachers' best efforts to enhance students' skills and encourage solid study habits, not all of the students receive the messages that we are trying to send. When we researched composite GPAs over a 10-year period for each grade level, we found that our freshmen had a composite GPA of 2.35 during the first semester and 2.27 during the second semester. This was at least .4 points below any other grade. This finding reinforced our belief that not all of our ninth graders are prepared to fly independently when they leave our freshmen house. What kind of safety net could we create for our tenth graders?

THE TENTH GRADE SOLUTION

In spring 1998, a group of colleagues, including teachers from both ninth and tenth grade, guidance counselors, and the curriculum director, brainstormed ways to meet our tenth graders needs. We felt strongly that extending the unit concept for those students who needed another year of firm structure and support was a good beginning. We agreed that tenth grade might be our last chance to make any significant changes in how students approach school—before students are distracted by driver's licenses, dating, and jobs. Meanwhile, we could target one of NFA's strategic goals: Provide a private school education to a public school population.

Could a tenth grade unit fit with this strategic goal? We thought so.

First, we reviewed research on this idea. *Lessons from Privilege* provided an excellent starting point (Powell, 1996). Powell notes that "the glory of the private school is taking the third rate student and making him/her second rate." He maintains that personalizing education for each student is the answer and class size is a key component. Other research supports Powell's claims. Diana Oxley (1994) points out:

> Organizing schools by units encourages a coordinated, cross-disciplinary approach to instruction. Within a unit, teachers share a group of students in common rather than a discipline. They take collective responsibility for their students' success, and they work together to unify instruction and allow students the opportunity to exercise skills and knowledge across subjects. (P. 521–526)

Second we took a closer look at our ninth grade house to determine which practices were most effective for students. Ninth grade teams have been in existence at NFA since 1988. It was

important to carefully examine which of the original concepts were still useful; what needed to be priority for change; and most important, what positive components we could replicate in a tenth grade unit. The ninth grade teachers and their house principal provided insights and experiential anecdotes on successes and failures. It was clear that the pros far out weighed the cons, and we gained a better sense of what could be done with a unit of 80 students rather than an entire class of 560 students.

Then we started to paint a picture of what we wanted the tenth grade unit to look like. We asked ourselves questions:

- What are the criteria for student selection?
- Who makes the recommendations?
- Who determines acceptance?
- Where do we set the bar for student achievement?
- How do we get the parents to buy in so there is a consistent message at home and at school?
- What kinds of interventions are we prepared to make for students who fall below expectations?
- How will teachers be selected to teach within the unit?

We decided to give the first three questions priority. We felt that we had to clearly define the types of students who would be included in the program before we could begin to recruit teachers.

We determined that the criteria for identifying students would include:

- Students who struggled freshman year, but should be doing better according to their Connecticut Mastery scores (CMT) from eighth grade and Educational Records Bureau (ERB) performance scores from ninth grade.
- Students who have an apparent weakness in one or more subject areas.
- Students with poor motivation or poor work ethics.
- Students who may have little support at home.

- Students who struggle with maturity issues connected to handling the increased responsibility of being a high school student.
- Students who were prepared to take Geometry, Biology, World History, English II, or certain electives in NFA's sequence of study. (These students took Algebra their freshman year.)

The committee decided that the unit leaders in the ninth grade house, the ninth grade guidance counselors, and the ninth grade principal would make recommendations in late January. All recommendations were forwarded to my office by the end of February. To our amazement, 160 recommendations were submitted, far exceeding our expectations.

We compiled data on each of the recommended students, including their grades, CMT scores, and ERB scores. Our director of guidance, the ninth grade house principal, and I scrutinized the data and added pertinent anecdotal information from student records and guidance counselors' observations. We whittled the list to about 90 names.

After we selected the students, we sent letters to their parents or guardians, explaining the purpose of our pilot tenth grade unit. We emphasized that the unit would provide a safety net of support for another year, and that the unit would emphasize organizational skills and good study habits. Goal setting would be an important component, so students would learn to make good long-term decisions, rather than live for the moment. Classes would have no more than 22 students. The letter also emphasized that we had high expectations for the students in the unit. We pointed out that anytime a student's performance fell below that expectation, the student's parents would be notified by a teacher. We included a postcard for the parent to return to indicate whether they were interested in having their child included in the unit.

The positive response was overwhelming. Of the 90 letters that were sent, only two parents declined. I invited each selected student to my office to discuss the unit and to encourage them to make a commitment to the program and to himor herself. This was very important: It didn't matter so much that the parents wanted their children to be included, but how badly the students wanted it themselves. Conversations lasted anywhere between 10 to 20 minutes. It was exciting to see how many of the students were honest about their struggles in ninth grade and anxious to make a commitment to self-improvement.

The students' biggest concern about being part of the unit was being isolated. They did not want to be stuck in one building, as they were in the ninth grade, or worse, one section of one building for their core classes. I assured them that this would not be the case. Although they would share a team of teachers, these teachers would be spread out all over campus, and they would go from building to building, just like any other tenth grader. Their homerooms and guidance counselors would be assigned, like the other tenth graders and would remain the same until they were graduated.

FACULTY SELECTION

Finally, the faculty had opportunities to ask questions. The biggest concern of a few teachers was that this pilot might become the first step toward teaming the entire tenth grade. We assured them that we didn't intend to do so at present. Not all tenth grade students needed the safety net that we were planning to provide.

The committee was asked to recommend members of the faculty who had experience with the tenth grade curriculum and students. Some recommendations were made, but no one expressed overwhelming interest until I began to contact individual teachers and thoroughly explained the intent of the program. Four excellent faculty members were genuinely excited about working as a team and being part of the pilot program. These teachers were integral to the eventual success of this program.

DESIGNING CURRICULUM

The teachers and I met in spring and summer 1999 to set goals for the students and to modify our standard tenth grade curriculum to allow more integration. The teachers were excited to have this opportunity to experiment and design. We decided that they would teach four-fifths of their teaching load in the unit and teach one class outside the unit and have a common planning period. The biology and geometry teachers attended a workshop during the summer about integrating math and science curricula.

The teachers left for summer break with a complete data sheet for each student in the unit so the teachers could contact the ninth grade teachers if they had questions about a particular student.

Before the students left for the summer, we gave them two books to read. Normally, tenth grade students choose three books from the tenth grade reading list. But we required that the pilot program students read *The Seven Habits of Highly Effective Teens* by Stephen Covey (1998) and *A Separate Peace* by John Knowles (1985). The students were also required to read a book of their choice from the tenth grade reading list. Reading *The Seven Habits* gave the students some thoughtful information about how they could fine-tune their personal lives. It was very easy to read and humorous. *A Separate Peace* was chosen by our English and history teachers for an integrated lesson. These books were common topics for class discussion after the school year began.

Scheduling the unit was a challenge. We decided that scheduling the unit in four consecutive periods would allow time for guest speakers and field trips. After announcing the schedule, we immediately lost four students who preferred to take electives that conflicted with the schedule.

ORIENTATION

Orientation sessions with both the students and the parents were held on the evening of the first day of school. We gave parents a handout titled "Back to School Tips for Parents," and we borrowed ideas from a variety of sources, including *The Complete Idiot's Guide to Parenting a Teenager* (Kelley, 1996), *Teen Tips: A Practical Survival Guide for Parents with Kids Ages 11–19* (McMahon, 1996), and a few ideas of our own. Each teacher introduced briefly discussed his or her expectations and curriculum.

The parents filled out questionnaires on how they perceived their children as students and what their hopes were for their children. Parents or guardians of 52 of the 80 students attended. The next day, we had a similar meeting with the students, and they also filled out questionnaires. The teachers received copies of the parents' and students' responses. The students were very honest in their responses, recognized their weaknesses, and seemed to welcome the opportunity to improve within the framework of the unit.

We felt that we were off to a solid start. The teachers and I met every Friday during the teachers' common prep time to compare notes, plan, and decide whether any interventions were needed. We quickly established lines of communication among the teachers, the students, and the parents or guardians. Most of our students were comfortable asking for extra help when they needed it. When a student's work fell below 80 percent in a subject, the teachers notified the student's family. The teachers divided the students into four groups and one teacher was responsible for communicating our concerns to those students' families. Individual teachers made additional calls if they felt an issue was serious enough to warrant personal contact. E-mail became the most popular means of communication for both teachers and families and allowed teachers to send assignments to students who were absent.

When the first marking period ended, we had our first bit of data to look at. We were excited that 34 percent of the students received all As or Bs in core subject areas. Only five Fs were given. It was amazing improvement for that group of students. The teachers felt that because they expected the students to meet high standards and communicated consistently with parents, the students responded. The parents did not have to wait until the end of the marking period to discover how their children were doing; they were notified regularly.

We also asked the students to fill out a first quarter review sheet. We wanted to know what differences they saw in themselves. Questions included:

- In regard to your studies, what are you doing better now as compared to last year? What do you think the reason is for your improvement?
- What do you still need to work on, and what do you intend to do about it?
- We have spoken to you a lot about how important it is to set goals and to establish relationships with people who can help you achieve those goals. What short- and long-term goals have you set?

Responses varied, but a couple of messages came through loud and clear. Students felt much more organized in their studies and they were beginning to make long-term goals. As students started to feel better about themselves and school, making long-term decisions seemed practical to them.

Prior to midyear exams, we invited parents to the school. We gave parents review sheets similar to the ones the students received. The resulting dialogue was productive, and we shared hints with parents on ways they could assist their children's study and time management.

Semester grades indicated that our efforts had been fruitful. We compared our students' grades from their first semester, ninth grade classes to their grades in their first semester, tenth grade classes. Seventy percent improved their grades in science, 65 percent improved in mathematics, 77 percent improved in English, and 77 percent improved in history. We brought the students together to applaud their efforts and encourage them to continue.

The second semester was more challenging for our teachers. The students, feeling good, naturally wanted to relax a bit. Unfortunately, there are no vacations built into our calendar at midyear. Teachers continued to keep parents apprised of student progress. Second semester results, although not as good as first semester, were still impressive. Comparing second semester grades from ninth and tenth grades: Sixty-one percent of students improved in science, 62 percent in mathematics, 61 percent in English, and 66 percent in history.

The individual success stories were many. Tina is a student of color who is extremely bright, but struggled in her freshman year. She got caught up in socializing with friends and did not pay enough attention to her studies. At the end of her freshman year, she had a GPA of 1.91. She admitted that she did not have good organizational skills and really did not know how to prepare herself for class everyday or how to study for tests.

Tina took full advantage of lessons on organizational skills and started keeping meticulous assignment books and notebooks. After a slow start, she blossomed during the second marking period and did a truly remarkable job during the second semester earning no grade lower than a B in her core subject areas. By the end of the year, she raised her GPA to 2.27.

David often clowned around in class, rarely keeping a focus on the tasks at hand. When motivated, he demonstrated that he could do excellent work, but those instances were few and far between. Because of the behavior issue, David's situation was a bit more complex than Tina's. We had a conference with his parents to obtain further insight into his patterns of behavior. We found that David had a history with attention deficit disorder and had been taken off medication when he started high school. It was quite obvious that his distractibility was getting in the way of his academic success. His parents were willing to take David back to his doctor to reassess his attention deficit issue. He was given a new prescription, and the academic dividends were almost immediate. David raised his freshman

GPA of 1.16 to 1.83 at the end of tenth grade. David earned nothing lower than a B during the second semester.

There were many success stories in our tenth grade unit. Because of our teachers' dedication and the pilot program's small class sizes, teachers were able to personalize lessons for the students, which resulted in significant improvements by those students who were open to making changes in the way they studied. At the beginning of the next school year, many of the students visited their teachers to touch base. The students are anxious to share their summer activities and their new successes in school.

We will continue to monitor the students' performance in school through the eleventh and twelfth grades. We want to determine whether the lessons we taught about how to succeed in school are lasting. We will examine the students' performances on the Connecticut Academic Performance Test (CAPT), which the students took in May 2000, and their performances on the PSAT and SAT exams.

Our superintendent and our board of trustees were impressed enough by our success with this pilot program that they gave me permission to expand the program to two units during the 2000–2001 school year. A second team of teachers was recruited, and all of the teachers from last year were anxious to return. This year, each team of teachers is teaching three classes within their units. Each unit will contain approximately 65 students. The parent support and student commitment has been excellent.

Keeping students connected to school often takes extra effort and some creative thinking on the part of the school community. We feel strongly that our efforts with the tenth grade unit saved some students who might have otherwise fallen through the cracks into the sea of academic indifference.

REFERENCES

Covey, S. 1998. *The seven habits of highly effective teens.* New York: Simon and Schuster.

Kelley, K. 1996. *The complete idiot's guide to parenting a teenager.* New York: Alpha Books.

Knowles, J. 1985. *A separate peace.* New York: Bantam Books.

McMahon, T. 1996. *Teen tips: A practical survival guide for parents with kids ages 11–19.* Pocket Books.

Oxley, D. 1994. Organizing schools into small units: Alternatives to homogeneous grouping. *Phi Delta Kappan* 75(7): 521–526.

Powell, A. 1996. *Lessons from privilege.* Cambridge, Mass.: Harvard University Press.

Hugh Campbell is principal of the Tirrell Building of NFA in Norwich, Connecticut.

QUESTIONS FOR REFLECTION

1. What is the ninth grade house and what features about it are appropriate for tenth graders' success in school?
2. Campbell's article demonstrates how collaborative work between teachers and administration can lead to system changes within a school district. How might other schools accomplish this same kind of collaboration? What are key characteristics of this collaborative effort that made it successful at Norwich Free Academy?
3. What positive outcomes can the teachers and administration point to to demonstrate that their program was a success? Is "proof" necessary to justify this kind of endeavor, or are there times when faith that a system has been improved is enough?

TEACHERS' VOICES—
Putting Theory Into Practice

A Tale of Two Curriculums

MIRA REISBERG

ABSTRACT: *The author, a teacher educator and illustrator of children's books, contrasts the progressive, constructivist curriculum found in most teacher education programs with the conservative, traditional curriculum that pervades today's schools. To prepare pre-service teachers for the curricular realities they will encounter in schools, the author's students experience a curriculum that incorporates a pedagogy of pleasure, place-based pedagogy, critical race theory, and social reconstructionist arts education.*

Here lies a tale of two curriculums. One is a progressive, constructivist curriculum that employs strategies such as cooperative learning, inquiry-based learning, scaffolded instruction, multiple intelligences theory, and authentic assessments. The other is a conservative, traditional curriculum that, for the most part, employs teacher-delivered, top-down rote memorization activities and basic skill building techniques. These activities typically culminate in a series of high-stakes tests that determine both the child's and the school's future (McNeil, 2000). In general, teacher education programs are structured around progressive, constructivist pedagogy, while an increasingly conservative legislative body favors the traditionalist, conservative pedagogy.

Federal mandates such as No Child Left Behind (NCLB) have helped create an educational climate privileging the traditional conservative curriculum. Funding connected with NCLB is tied to "scientifically based" programs that have a traditionalist orientation of skill and drill and rote memorization (Coles, 2002; Garan, 2004). For children who struggle with issues of motivation and comprehension, focusing primarily on skill and drill programs while ignoring issues of cultural congruence and personal connection does not promote a love of learning (Delpit, 1995; Taylor, 2004).

Anyone who has learned to play a musical instrument will remember the boredom and tedium of repetitive practice and basic skills acquisition. Without this practice they would never have been able to play. However, if the learning focused solely on technique, chances are they never connected with the heart and soul and love of music and dropped it as soon as they could. Those fortunate enough to have a teacher who taught them using culturally relevant, meaningful music and who also encouraged them to explore music in many ways frequently developed a lifelong love of music. In other words, a combination of traditional and constructivist pedagogies are needed for an effective education. Cowen (2003) has termed this a "balanced approach" to education.

This paper posits that, although basic skills and rote memorization are necessary for learning, teachers do their students a great disservice if they focus primarily on such pedagogy at the expense of meaningful experiences such as those I try to provide my students. As a teacher of pre-service elementary teachers at a major university, I have noticed the polarization between the two curriculums. However, because my future teachers will be provided with an abundance of conservative skill building materials in the field, my curriculum focuses on teaching critical, constructivist pedagogies that are vitally important. Before detailing the specifics of my curricular approach, I will provide further background information on the differences between the two curriculums.

DIFFERENCES BETWEEN THE TWO CURRICULUMS

A traditional curriculum is based on learning discrete parcels of information (or facts) that are acquired through rote memory. These facts are discipline specific and taught in a prescribed skill and drill manner within a delineated time frame. Students work alone on basal, textbook-centered problems, and their learning is assessed by tests.

A constructivist curriculum, in contrast, tends to be integrated, inter-disciplinary and inquiry-based. Learning is socially constructed, and the context of learning and students' prior knowledge are central to the educational experience. Projects are frequently student generated and group oriented, and they involve more flexibility in the use of time. In addition, authentic literature is used with portfolio and other authentic assessment models (Cambourne, 2002; Moursund, 1999).

Traditional conservatives and progressive constructionists both want children to succeed and do well. However, it appears that they have different ideas of what success means and how to go about achieving it. For many traditional conservatives, success appears to be about learning the basic cognitive and class-appropriate vocational skills that enable one to participate in the American dream. For critical, constructivist educators, the goal is less job oriented than about developing higher-order thinking skills and enabling students to become active participants in their own lives.

However, some critical pedagogues believe that constructivism simply serves to "rearrange the furniture" in an institution whose foundations are rotting. By preparing students to take tests, institutionalized constructivists have been co-opted into propping up a system that continues to colonize and dominate humans, animals, and environments (Bowers, 1997; Gruenewald, 2003a). In other words, constructivism is merely "the other side of the same coin" as traditionalism. Such arguments notwithstanding, the reality is that pre-service teachers are entering a world they cannot immediately change. Consequently, it is important to find ways to integrate pedagogies that help them teach critical thinking skills to challenge the status quo and to construct something better, while also teaching successful test-taking strategies so they can keep their jobs and students can progress to the next grade.

Meanwhile, social reproduction theorists (Kozol, 1991; Tozer, Violas, & Senese, 2002) hold that education is consciously and historically constructed to reproduce class and inequality through the different curriculums taught in economically segregated schools. One class of schooling focuses on the basics needed for low-level employment, while the other focuses on the development of creative critical thinking skills needed for positions of management and leadership. Not coincidentally, those in more privileged schools have parents who are educated to take advantage of political power by making decisions about who gets educational resources that influence test scores and opportunities (Kozol, 1991; Ladson Billings, 1998).

DEWEY OR DON'T WE?

Advocates for traditional, top-down education believe that the system of education that worked for them is best for today's children. As President George W. Bush stated in 1996:

> The building blocks of knowledge were the same yesterday and will be the same tomorrow. . . . We do not need trendy new theories or fancy experiments or feel good curriculums. The basics work. If drill gets the job done then rote is right (Coles, 2002).

However, not everyone can or did learn this way, and such approaches ignore a long history of unequal outcomes as well as the question of the purpose of education. The entire history of progressive, constructivist education tells us that students benefit from an experiential curriculum connected to their lived experiences (Dewey, 1916; Freire, 2003).

In contrast to the traditional curriculum, I propose a curriculum that centers on feeling good—about one's self, one's work, and one's place in the world. This approach strives to create heartfelt connections among student's lives, communities, creative intelligences, bodies, and spirits.

Dewey was one of the first to advocate for pleasure, connection, and integration in the curriculum. In *Interest and Effort in Education* he wrote:

> education rises or falls with our ability to make school life an interesting and absorbing experience to the child. In one sense there is no such thing as compulsory education. We can have compulsory physical attendance at school; but education comes only through willing attention to and participation in school activities. It follows that the teacher must select these activities with reference to the child's interest, powers, and capabilities. In no other way can she guarantee that the child will be present. (Dewey, 1913, p. ix)

Although Dewey wrote these words over ninety years ago, they are still profoundly relevant and compelling for today's educators.

THE PRACTICE OF PLEASURE: TEACHING FOR SOCIAL JUSTICE AND ENVIRONMENTAL STEWARDSHIP

Engaging students is central to a curriculum based on the principle of pleasure. If learners enjoy doing something, they will do it frequently and, consequently, get good at it. If students are motivated by connections—to themselves, their communities, their environment, their classmates, and their history; if they see themselves reflected in the literature they read and as creators of literature; if they see their work as having value not only to their teachers, but also to others outside the school and in the real world—they will enjoy learning more, and participate in it with enthusiasm (Dewey, 1913, 1934; Eisner, 1995; Greene, 1978).

In brief, my course, Integrated Fine Arts, teaches pre-service teachers how to teach the various content areas using a creative integration of art and drama. These methodologies are designed to teach critical, higher-order thinking skills as well as to foster a love of learning. The curriculum consists of three conceptual threads:

1. A pedagogy of pleasure, based on the joy of sensory play while making multiple connections across content areas, personal experiences and culture (Cambourne, 2002; Dewey, 1913, 1934; Eisner, 1982, 1995, 1998; Greene, 1978).
2. A pedagogy that employs place-based education (Gruenewald, 2003b; Haas & Nachtigal, 1998; Sobel, 2004), critical race theory (Delpit, 1995; Ladson Billings, 1998, 2000; Nieto, 2000; Schwartz, 1995), and social reconstructionist arts education practices (Cahan & Kocur, 1996; Klein, 1992, 2000; Milbrandt, 2002).
3. A pedagogy that promotes democratic participation through awareness and action for social justice and environmental stewardship (Dewey, 1916; Furman & Gruenewald, 2004; Greene, 1978).

These conceptual threads are woven through a creative and critical combination of authentic, multicultural children's literature and art. What follows is a brief description of these ideas, including examples of how I encourage students to use them in their own classrooms.

Place-Based Pedagogy

In the Deweyan tradition, connection is one of the central tenets of place-based education through which students connect with their local environments as sites for situated learning experiences that benefit both themselves and their communities. Place-based educators and their students promote environmental stewardship and active participation in their "place of being." As Gruenewald (2003b) writes:

> Place-conscious education, therefore, aims to work against the isolation of schooling's discourses and practices from the living world outside the increasingly placeless institution of schooling. Furthermore, it aims to enlist teachers and students in the firsthand experience of local life and in the political process of understanding and shaping what happens there (p. 620).

Critical Race Theory

Critical race theorists advocate for understanding and shaping issues of culture and race. Among other things, they call for authenticity and critical inclusion in children's literature. Describing how the non-critical use of multicultural literature supports an ineffective liberalism that effectively maintains hegemony in the form of existing class structures and racism, they effectively ask: "Who says what and for whom," and "How culturally congruent is the curriculum with students' own cultures?" Multicultural literature that is authentic can truly be a valuable form of storytelling that creates agency and affirmation for all children (Ladson Billings, 2000; Nieto, 2000; Yenika Agbaw, 1997).

Social Reconstructionist Arts Education

Arts based educators taking a more holistic approach note the spiritual, emotional, and practical importance of the arts in educating the whole child while covering the content areas in fun and meaningful ways. At the same time, social reconstructionist arts educators believe that the practice of art with its sensual, reflective, and collaborative qualities can provide an excellent forum to explore and challenge official reifying discourses. As Milbrandt (2002) writes:

> Rather than accepting intellectual and moral complacency, art educators must possess the courage and the skills necessary to initiate art programs that engage students in critical inquiry, connect learning to authentic and meaningful issues in life, and inspire responsible intellectual and moral action (p. 153).

MY CURRICULUM IN ACTION

Curriculum choices strongly influence students' beliefs about race, gender, class, and environment (Parkay & Hass, 2000). Drawing on the transformational theories mentioned above, I encourage my pre-service teachers to build curriculum around a central book that is place specific, culturally authentic, and visually and linguistically aesthetic. This can jumpstart community-oriented art projects that utilize multiple intelligences (Gardner, 1983), as well as the many other forms of knowledge needed to navigate in life. I encourage inclusion of European American stories as part of the multicultural discourse to show that all students have culture and that multiculturalism does not once again marginalize people of color as separate and "other" and European Americans as cultureless (Newling, 2001).

I use quality, place-specific, multicultural literature as the starting point of a unit to model culturally congruent teaching for my pre-service students to use in their own future teaching. By starting here, they are able to find themselves and others reflected and affirmed. While exploring concepts of embedded racism, they are provided opportunities to learn about and respect the many cultures that make our world. These books also help promote environmental awareness by providing opportunities to compare and contrast place. The books also stimulate connections with students about their own communities and environments to facilitate the creation of situated learning experiences that benefit students and their communities (Gruenewald, 2003b; Haas & Nachtigal, 1998). After conducting a close reading of a book, the class compares and contrasts the embedded themes in the text and illustrations and makes connections to their own race, place and culture. From this awareness, they can then create projects that promote awareness of social and environmental issues.

For example, the book *Where Fireflies Dance* (Corpi, 1997) promoted a range of projects in my class. One was the creation of portraits and intergenerational oral histories with local senior citizens, which were exhibited and celebrated in the public library. These histories showed seniors connected to "lived history" in contrast to "official histories," while using art to address state standards of science, history, communication, reading, and writing.

A second place-based project involved creating large cut-paper murals of our local wildlife and landscape through the seasons. This project modeled how to integrate math and science with art by embedding math concepts in the numbers of animals depicted while learning about our local environment.

A third project integrated dance, drama, and science through the creation of "Science Theater": body-based interpretive dances of the life cycles of endangered and at-risk local animals with instructions on how to save them.

In a fourth example, inspired by the work of contemporary African American artist Fred Wilson, my pre-service teachers learned how to teach about embedded racism in how language is used. After creating paper-maché Halloween insect masks, students created labels for them showing how the kind of language used to exhibit African and minority art is radically different than that used to exhibit European and European Ameri-can art. Their labels used demeaning vocabulary like primitive and ritual and were un-credited except for the geographic area they came from.

These examples are just some of the many projects that provide rich and meaningful ways to integrate all the content areas. They are also frequently fun and pleasure-based. These methodologies are student driven, culturally relevant, and center on collaborative learning. They incorporate time-outs for teaching content areas with more traditional methods, and the framework is there to provide connected, concrete, learning opportunities. These are valuable skills that children need to know along with the basics. What could be more important than learning how to be a multiliterate, caring, and capable member of one's community?

JUSTIFICATION AND ACCOUNTABILITY

Because teachers are frequently called upon to justify and provide accountability for their teaching methodologies, I also provide examples of research my students can cite showing that children can do well on achievement tests by doing culturally congruent, fun, and rewarding projects while also learning test-taking strategies if needed.

Teachers can also cite examples showing how all students, particularly low socioeconomic status students, do well when their learning is connected to their lives and their communities (Dillard & Blue, 2000; Ladson Billings, 2000). My future teachers can make use of arts-based research (Catterall, 1998; Cornett, 2003; Elfland, 2002; Fowler, 1996; NAEP, 1997) that describes the significantly positive outcomes of arts infused curriculums in high-stakes testing arenas as well as in other areas. As Upitis and Smithrim (2002) note, "Students, teachers, parents, artists, and administrators [can see] how the arts motivate children, referring to the emotional, physical, cognitive, and social benefits of learning in and through the arts" (p. 2). Finally, my future teachers can question why these integrated teaching methodologies are considered ineffective when wealthier schools value them so much (Kozol, 1991; Ladson Billings, 1998).

Accountability to parents and community members occurs when children and their work go out into the community, and when the community comes into the classroom. In utilizing place-based pedagogies of engaged local learning that incorporate art and literature, parents and community members can experience the delightfulness of their children's experiences, while their children learn important, real-life, integrated skills *and* how to pass mandated tests. Stakeholders can see that their children are reading, writing, performing, creating, understanding, and working with challenging math and science concepts. By enriching the traditional teacher education curriculum with these ideas, my pre-service students will be more apt to teach in ways that challenge unfairness and inequality while maintaining or exceeding mandated standards. By bridging the two curriculums and engaging and motivating students to find pleasure and meaning in their education, students will succeed academically, and, in all likelihood, they will also become lifelong learners and valuable community members.

REFERENCES

Bowers, C. A. (1997). *The culture of denial: Why the environmental movement needs a strategy for reforming universities and public schools.* Albany: State University of New York Press.

Cahan, S., & Kocur, Z. (1996). *Contemporary art and multicultural education.* New York: Routledge.

Cambourne. (2002). Holistic integrated approaches to reading and language arts instruction: The constructivist framework of an instructional theory. In *What research has to say about reading instruction* (pp. 25–46). Newark, NJ: International Reading Association.

Catterall, J. (1998). Does experience in the arts boost academic achievement? A response to Eisner. *Art Education, 51*(4), 6–11.

Coles, G. (2002). *Learning to read—"scientifically".* Retrieved 10/20/04, 2004, from http://www.rethinkingschools.org/special_reports/bushplan/Read154.shtml

Cornett, C. E. (2003). *Creating meaning through literature and the arts: An integration resource for classroom teachers.* Upper Saddle River, NJ: Pearson Education.

Corpi, L. (1997). *Where fireflies dance.* San Francisco, CA: Children's Book Press.

Cowen, J. E. (2003). *A balanced approach to beginning reading instruction: A synthesis of six major U.S. research studies.* Newark, NJ: International Reading Association.

Delpit, L. (1995). *Other people's children: Cultural conflict in the classroom.* New York, NY: The New Press.

Dewey, J. (1913). *Interest and effort in education.* Boston, MA: Houghton Mifflin.

Dewey, J. (1916). *Democracy and education: An introduction to the philosophy of education.* New York, NY: The Macmillan company.

Dewey, J. (1934). *Art as experience.* New York: G. P. Putnam and Sons.

Dillard, C. B., & Blue, D. A. (2000). Learning styles from a multicultural perspective: The case for culturally engaged education. In M. Gallegos & S. Hollingsworth (Eds.), *What counts as literacy: Challenging the school standards.* New York, NY: Teachers College Press.

Eisner, E. W. (1982). *Cognition and curriculum: A basis for deciding what to teach.* New York, NY: Longman.

Eisner, E. W. (1995). What artistically crafted research can help us understand about schools. *Educational Theory, 45*(1), n.p.

Eisner, E. W. (1998). *The kinds of schools we need: Personal essays.* Portsmouth, NH: Heinemann Educational Books.

Elfland, A. D. (2002). *Art and cognition: Integrating the visual arts in the curriculum.* New York: NY: Teachers College Press and National Art Education Association.

Fowler, C. (1996). *Strong arts, strong schools: The promising potential and shortsighted disregard of the arts in American schooling.* New York: Oxford University Press.

Freire, P. (2003). *Pedagogy of the Oppressed* (30th Anniversary Edition ed.). New York, NY: The Continuum International Publishing Group.

Furman, G., & Gruenewald, D. A. (2004). Expanding the landscape of social justice: A critical ecological analysis. *Educational Administration Quarterly, 40*(1), 49–78.

Garan, E. M. (2004). *In defense of our children: When politics, profit and education collide.* Portsmouth, NH: Heinemann.

Gardner, H. (1983). *Frames of mind: The theory of multiple intelligences.* New York, NY: Basic Books.

Greene, M. (1978). *Landscapes of learning.* New York: Teachers College Press.

Gruenewald, D. A. (2003a). The best of both worlds: A critical pedagogy of place. *Educational Researcher, 32*(4), 3–12.

Gruenewald, D. A. (2003b). Foundations of place: A multidisciplinary framework for place-conscious education. *American Educational Research Journal, 40*(3), 619–654.

Guthrie, J. T. (2002). Preparing students for high-stakes test taking in reading. In A. Farstrup (Ed.), *What research has to say about reading instruction* (pp. 370–391). Newark, Delaware.

Haas, T., & Nachtigal, P. M. (1998). *Place value: an educators' guide to good literature on rural lifeways, environments, and purposes of education.* Charleston, WV: ERIC Clearinghouse on Rural Education and Small Schools.

Klein, S. (1992). Social action and art education: A curriculum for change. *Journal of multicultural and cross-cultural research in art education, 10,* 111–125.

Klein, S. (2000). Spirituality and art education: Looking to place. *Journal of multicultural and cross-cultural research in art education, 18,* 57–66.

Kozol, J. (1991). *Savage inequalities.* New York, NY: Crown Publishers.

Ladson Billings, G. (1998). Just what is critical race theory and what's it doing in a nice fields like education? *Qualitative studies in education, 11*(1), 7–24.

Ladson Billings, G. (2000). Reading between the lines and beyond the pages. In M. Gallegos & S. Hollingsworth (Eds.), *What counts as literacy: Challenging the school standards.* New York, NY: Teachers College Press.

McNeil, L. M. (2000). Creating new inequalities: Contradictions of reform. *Phi Delta Kappan, 81,* 728–734.

Milbrandt, M. K. (2002). Addressing contemporary social issues in art education: A survey of public school art educators in Georgia. *Studies in art education: A journal of issues and research, 44*(1), 141–157.

Moursund, D. G. (1999). *Project-based learning using information technology.* Eugene, OR: International Society for Technology in Education.

NAEP. (1997). *The NAEP 1997 Arts Report Card: Eighth-grade findings from the National Assessment of educational progress.* Washington, D.C.: U.S. Department of Education, office of educational research and improvement.

Newling, M.-L. (2001). Approaches to critical literacy through literature. In L. Ramírez & O. Gallardo, M. (Eds.), *Portraits of teachers in multicultural settings: A critical literacy approach.* Needham Heights, MA: Allyn & Bacon.

Nieto, S. (2000). *Affirming Diversity: The Sociopolitical Context of Multicultural Education. Third Edition.* New York.

Parkay, F. W., & Hass, G. (2000). Learning and learning styles. In F. W. Parkay, & G. Hass (Eds.), *Curriculum planning: A contemporary approach* (pp. 165–171). Needham Heights, MA: Allyn & Bacon.

Schwartz, E. G. (1995). Crossing borders/Shifting Paradigm: Multiculturalism and children's literature. *Harvard Educational Review, 65*(4), 634–649.

Sobel, D. (2004). *Place-based education: Connecting classrooms and communities.* Great Barrington, MA: The Orion Society.

Taylor, H. (2004). Education expert wonders if NCLB is too focused to accommodate children living in poverty. *School administrator's compliance hotline, 7*(2), 4–5.

Tozer, S. E., Violas, P. C., & Senese, G. (2002). *School and society: Historical and contemporary perspectives.* New York, NY: McGraw Hill.

Yenika Agbaw, V. (1997). Taking children's literature seriously: Reading for pleasure and social change. *Language Arts 74*(6), pp. 446–453.

Mira Reisberg, a former K–6 teacher and literacy consultant for K–12 schools, is an illustrator of children's books and a teaching assistant in the Department of Teaching and Learning at Washington State University.

QUESTIONS FOR REFLECTION

1. Reisberg suggests that "mandates such as No Child Left Behind have helped to create an educational climate privileging the traditional, conservative curriculum." Do you agree or disagree with her observation? Explain your position.
2. With respect to the subject area and grade level with which you are most familiar, how might you employ place-based pedagogy strategies such as those described by Reisberg?
3. Reisberg's article includes the following observations by President George W. Bush:

    > The building blocks of knowledge were the same yesterday and will be the same tomorrow. . . . We do not need trendy new theories or fancy experiments or feel good curriculums. The basics work. If drill gets the job done then rote is right.

    To what extent do you agree or disagree with the President's view of education?

LEARNING ACTIVITIES

Critical Thinking

1. Are a common high school curriculum and uniform standards appropriate in a pluralistic society? Can a common curriculum and uniform standards be implemented with diverse groups of students? Can individual differences be accommodated? Should they be?
2. Reflect on this chapter's recommendations for changing the curriculum for high school students in light of curricular goals for this age group, the three bases of the curriculum, and curriculum criteria. Which recommendations from the articles in this chapter would you like to see implemented?
3. Which developmental changes discussed in Chapter 3 should guide curriculum planners in designing educational programs for high school students?
4. What are the essential elements of effective curricula for high school students?
5. What are some of the challenges that today's high school students face that were unknown or little known to their parents or grandparents? To what extent can (or should) these challenges be addressed in educational programs for high schoolers?

Application Activities

1. When you were a high school student, what school experiences helped you to grow and learn? What experiences hindered you? What implications do these experiences have for your current and future curriculum planning activities?

2. Drawing from the material in this chapter, develop a short questionnaire or set of interview questions that curriculum planners could use to learn more about high school students. Compare your questions with those of your classmates.
3. Invite a group of high school teachers to your class and ask them to describe the steps they take in planning curricula for their students. What do they see as the most important curriculum criteria to use in planning?
4. Obtain a statement of philosophy (or mission statement) from a nearby high school. Analyze the statement in regard to this chapter's six recommended goals for educational programs for high school. How many of the goals are reflected in the statement?

Field Experiences

1. Visit a nearby high school and obtain permission to interview a few students about their curricular experiences. Take field notes based on these interviews. The following questions might serve as a guide for beginning your interviews: Do the students like school? What about it do they like and dislike? What are their favorite subjects? What about those subjects do they like? What are their plans for the future? Then, analyze your field notes; what themes or concerns emerge that would be useful for curriculum planners at this level?
2. Visit an agency in your community that offers services to high school students and their families. Ask a staff member to describe the services that are offered. Report your findings to the rest of your class.
3. Talk with a group of high school students about the social forces of concern to them in their school, their community, their nation, and the world. What implications do their concerns have for curriculum planners at this level?

Internet Activities

1. At the Center for Research on the Education of Students Placed at Risk (CRESPAR), gather research results and curriculum-related resources useful to those who plan educational programs for high school students placed at risk.
2. Go to the State Curriculum Frameworks and Contents Standards page maintained by the U.S. Department of Education's Office of Educational Research and Improvement (OERI) and obtain your state's secondary-level curriculum frameworks. Critique these frameworks in light of the recommendations in Chapter 9.
3. Go to OERI's Blue Ribbon Schools Program which recognizes outstanding public and private schools. From that site, "visit" a few exemplary high schools. To what extent do they reflect the recommendations made throughout Chapter 9?

CHAPTER 10

Post-Secondary Curricula

FOCUS QUESTIONS

1. What are the major developmental challenges of students in post-secondary educational programs?
2. What are several types of community college programs?
3. What challenges confront today's colleges and universities?
4. How has adult education evolved to meet the needs of adult learners?
5. What educational opportunities are available to senior learners?

Students who enter post-secondary educational programs immediately after graduation from high school are entering a critical period in the development of self-concept. This period is important for the individual's psycho-social identity, work or work-related success in terms of what is valued by society, and integration into the life of the local, national, and global communities. At this time, the quest for identity shifts from relying on others to self-reliance. The individual critically examines values, begins to form intimate relationships with others, and develops an identity as worker, parent, and citizen. No longer children, recent high school graduates want to use newly acquired knowledge, skills, and strengths to achieve their own purposes whether through employment, marriage, parenthood, post-secondary education or training, a career, or military service.

DEVELOPMENTAL CHALLENGES OF LATE ADOLESCENCE AND ADULTHOOD

Erik Erikson's eight-stage model for the human life cycle identifies three salient psychosocial crises that characterize late adolescence through adulthood. During young

464

adulthood (intimacy versus isolation), the individual must develop intimate relationships or experience feelings of isolation. Then, during middle adulthood (generativity versus stagnation), the individual must develop a way to satisfy and support the next generation or experience stagnation; this care for the next generation can be expressed through parenting or a career in teaching, for example. Finally, during late adulthood (integrity versus despair), the individual must accept oneself as one is and thereby experience a sense of fulfillment; without this self-acceptance, the individual experiences feelings of despair.

Robert J. Havighurst (1900–1991), a University of Chicago professor who made outstanding contributions to life span developmental psychology, found that some individuals, during late adolescence and early adulthood, lead highly individualistic lives and grow into alienation, loneliness, or ruthlessness with little feeling for the values of community life. While Havighurst (1972, p. 5) believed that early adulthood is the period most full of "teachable moments," he found that period of life "emptiest of efforts to teach." One of the challenges to community college and university programs, then, is to capitalize on these "teachable moments."

HIGHER EDUCATION ENROLLMENTS

Higher education enrollments have steadily increased during the last few decades. Enrollments in public and private, two-year and four-year institutions totaled more than 9 million in 1972. By 1996, this figure had risen to more than 14 million; and by 2013, the figure is expected to rise to more than 18 million (National Center for Education Statistics, 2004a). Since the early 1980s, women have played a major role in the increased higher education enrollments. Between 1983 and 1996, the enrollment of women increased from 6.4 million to 8.0 million, and this figure is expected to increase to 10.4 million by 2013 (National Center for Education Statistics, 2004a). The enrollment of students over age thirty-five increased from 2.2 million in 1988 to 3.0 million in 1996; and this figure is expected to remain unchanged by 2013 (National Center for Education Statistics, 2004a).

Total enrollments in public and private two-year colleges were 5.6 million during fall 1996; by 2013, this figure is expected to increase to 7.1 million (National Center for Education Statistics, 2004a). Among the students enrolled at this level in 1996, almost 50 percent were under 25; about 25 percent were in the 25–34 age group, and 25 percent were in the over-35 age group (National Center for Education Statistics, 2004).

TWO-YEAR COLLEGES

Two-year colleges offer education and training programs that are two years in length or less. These programs usually lead to a license, a certificate, an associate of arts (A.A.) degree, an associate of science (A.S.) degree, or an associate of applied science (A.A.S.)

degree. Colleges with programs less than four years in length are usually called *community colleges, technical colleges,* or *junior colleges.*

The community college, a relatively new educational institution developed in the United States, has become a major element of the American system of postsecondary education. Although it evolved from the junior college, the community college is designed to serve many more social purposes. Community colleges provide their communities with adult education programs in a variety of fields. They provide a college-parallel program for those who wish to transfer to four-year colleges or universities after two years. They offer terminal education in many vocational, technical, and commercial subjects for those who desire a two-year course of study. Several states have developed master plans to provide community colleges within commuting distance of all high school graduates.

The community college has grown from one that served a limited number of students to one that provides education for many youth not in four-year colleges and for many adult learners. Community colleges also offer many programs to help meet the needs of their communities and society. Typically, community colleges offer five types of programs:

1. Junior college transfer programs. High school graduates can pursue the equivalent of the first two years of undergraduate work at a four-year college or university. This program of study leads to the associate of arts (A.A.) degree. For many students, a nearby community college may be preferable to a larger, often more impersonal, college or university.

2. Technical and/or vocational programs. Our technological society provides excellent opportunities to young people who wish to prepare for jobs that require completion of a two-year, or less, preparation program. For example, the *Occupational Outlook Handbook,* published annually by the U.S. Department of Labor, Bureau of Labor Statistics, includes many careers that require two years of training or less.

3. Adult education programs. These programs serve an entire community. Classes, usually formed according to interest and demand, might offer instruction in photography, acting, playing a musical instrument, self-defense, meditation, retirement planning, cooking, or horseback riding, to name only a few. Adult education programs are particularly appealing to individuals who are retired or semi-retired.

4. Developmental programs. These programs serve students whose educational backgrounds may prevent them from enrolling in and successfully completing academic or technical courses of study. Most community colleges offer GED programs for students who have not graduated from high school and need a high school diploma to enroll in a postsecondary program.

5. Community service programs. Some community colleges provide their communities with education and training when and where they are needed. Multiservice outreach programs, extension centers, in-plant training, and programs for traditionally underrepresented groups are examples of community service programs.

Since the 1970s, the number of community colleges and their enrollments have increased dramatically, and the functions and importance of the five types of programs have changed considerably. At first, community colleges emphasized transfer programs because of the expanded opportunities they gave high school graduates to attend college. Later, the emphasis shifted to "nontraditional" students—women "reentering" education after their childbearing years, middle-aged adults seeking new educational experiences and career opportunities, the unemployed, new immigrants, and members of groups traditionally underrepresented in postsecondary educational programs.

A major concern for community colleges today is the large number of students who drop out before completing their programs. Because many students seem unable to succeed, attention to individual learning needs and problems is an important part of curriculum planning and teaching at this level.

The community college serves many young people who mature late (often called "late bloomers") and would not be permitted to enter a four-year college or university on the basis of their high school grades. Many students who need remedial work in basic skills can make up these deficiencies in noncredit "guided studies" programs. Completion of such a program enables them to enroll in other areas of study.

FOUR-YEAR COLLEGES AND UNIVERSITIES

Total undergraduate enrollments in public and private four-year colleges and universities for fall 1996 were about 12.3 million; by 2008, this figure is expected to decrease to about 11.7 million (National Center for Education Statistics, 2004a). Among the students enrolled at this level in 1996, about 71 percent were under 25; about 17 percent in the 25–34 age group; and 12 percent in the over-35 age group (National Center for Education Statistics, 1996).

Total graduate enrollments in public and private universities for fall 1996 were about 1.7 million in 1996; by 2008, this figure was expected to be about the same (National Center for Education Statistics, 1998a). Total first-time enrollments in professional schools (medical, law, etc.) for fall 1996 were about 285,000; by 2008, this figure is expected to be about the same (National Center for Education Statistics, 1998a). Among the students enrolled at this level in 1996, about 19 percent were under 25; about 45 percent in the 25–34 age group; and 36 percent in the over-35 age group (National Center for Education Statistics, 1996).

Since the start of the last decade of the twentieth century, the university has been challenged and its benefits questioned in ways that were unheard of previously in that century. Clearly, universities cannot continue to do for the next twenty years, only better, what they have done for the last twenty. The demand for alternatives and alternative programs is as strong at this level as at the other levels of education addressed in this book. Many students have gone to college after high school by default because they didn't know what else to do, and their parents had been conditioned to believe that higher education was something they owed their children. Over 50 percent of high school graduates in the United States now go on to college (in some communities, 70 or 80 percent) expecting to get better jobs as a result of getting a college degree—in spite of the fact that 80 percent of jobs in the country do not require a college degree. The broad general goals of education at this level are the same as those at the other levels we have studied—*citizenship, equal educational opportunity, vocation, self-realization,* and *critical thinking.* However, alternatives should continually be developed to serve the needs of late adolescents and adults in attaining these goals. And, the curriculum should reflect a "balance" between liberal and professional study, between education for life and education for work.

At one time, the word *college* may have meant four uninterrupted years of full-time enrollment at one institution. During the 1970s, however, alternatives for undergraduate education for late adolescents and adults were increased considerably in many parts of the United States by the development of "colleges without walls" and their "external" (or "extended") degrees. Today, thousands of students earn their bachelor's degrees through such programs. The academic community's acceptance of the best of these programs is indicated by the number of recipients of external degrees who are able to gain admission to graduate studies.

Similar to the "great debate" on high school reform discussed in the previous chapter, several national reports addressing the goals and practices in higher education were released in the mid-1980s. For example, the Carnegie Foundation for the Advancement of Teaching's 1985 report, *Higher Education and the American Resurgence,* called for the restoration to higher education of its original purpose of preparing graduates for lives of involved and committed citizenship. The report also called for increased efforts to recruit minority students into higher education and renewed efforts to develop creativity and independence of mind. In response to the increased focus on academic disciplines and the "gradual retreat from values," the report proposed "active learning" and the "ideal of service."

The National Institute of Education's 1984 report, *Involvement in Learning: Realizing the Potential of American Higher Education,* called for more active modes of learning. The report claimed that college curricula had become excessively vocational in orientation and that curriculum content should address not only subject matter but also the development of students' abilities to analyze, to solve complex problems, and to synthesize. Furthermore, students and faculty should integrate knowledge from various disciplines. Similarly, in "Connectedness through Liberal Education" in this chapter, the late Ernest Boyer draws from the 1987 Carnegie Foundation report titled *College: The Undergraduate Experience in America* and identifies five essential priorities for undergraduate education.

There has also been a widespread recognition that higher education curricula should prepare students to live in a society that continues to become increasingly culturally diverse. For example, in "Diversity, Democracy, and Curriculum Reform in Higher Education" in this chapter, Willie J. Heggins, III, examines the role of curriculum reform in higher education and suggests that minority faculty members can play a critical role to ensure that issues of culture, values, and multiculturalism are reflected in the curriculum. Additionally, in "How Americans Think about International Education and Why It Matters" in this chapter, Susan Nall Bales calls for the development of a clear vision of international education to replace the perception that it is a nonessential add-on to the conventional post-secondary curriculum.

ADULT EDUCATION

Adult education is changing dramatically. Before 1945, it was generally believed that adults, once past adolescence, had little learning capacity. When thousands of World War II veterans returned to college campuses, supported by the Servicemen's Readjustment Act (popularly known as the G.I. Bill of Rights), there was great fear that they would be unable to learn and would lower academic standards. Just the reverse happened; they did better academically than their younger classmates—because they were older, more mature, and often highly motivated. Today, we know that adults, regardless of age, can learn almost anything they are motivated to learn. The fact that almost one-third of all undergraduate students now are over twenty-five and that this percentage will continue to increase for the foreseeable future is compelling evidence of adults' ability to learn.

A major educational issue well into the twenty-first century will undoubtedly be to establish an equilibrium between what might be termed *youth-terminal* and *adult-continuing* education. Two traditionally held assumptions about post-secondary education are being questioned: 1) that the need for organized educational opportunities can be met during the first one-fourth of the life span; and 2) that the need for education during the remaining three-fourths of a lifetime can be met adequately by incidental learning through the daily experiences of living and working. Today's students must develop the ability and desire to continue learning throughout their lifetimes, and they must be provided with appropriate, recurring learning opportunities to achieve that goal. In a world characterized by rapid social, technological, economic, and political changes, continuing education will be essential—a person's education now becomes obsolescent with a rapidity never before known. We must remember that one of the primary purposes of schooling is for students to learn how to learn.

A major emphasis in adult education is to continue to expand learning opportunities for people previously underrepresented in higher education: African Americans, Latino and Hispanic Americans, Asian Americans and Pacific Islanders, Native Americans and Alaskan Natives, and the poor. In this chapter's *Teachers' Voices* section ("How Critical Are Our Pedagogies? Privileging the Discourse of Lived Experience in the Community College Classroom"), Leonor Xóchitl Pérez and Anna Marie Christiansen describe how the first author created a mechanism through which students' psychological, social, and cultural characteristics were acknowledged, discussed, and integrated into a course for students aged seventeen to fifty-five at a community college in a low-income Latino community in Los Angeles.

MEETING THE NEEDS OF NONTRADITIONAL STUDENTS

Colleges and universities are beginning to take seriously the challenge posed by the reentry of adult, "nontraditional" students, who, as Naomi Jacobs (1989, p. 329) points out, may be "unsure of their abilities, rusty in their study habits, and encumbered by family and work responsibilities." Colleges and universities are meeting the educational needs of many nontraditional students whose employment, family obligations, and geographic location make on-campus attendance difficult through distance education—"education or training courses delivered to remote (off-campus) locations via audio, video, or computer technologies" (National Center for Education Statistics, 1998b, p. 1). In addition to creating greater access to higher education, especially for students in rural areas, distance education is seen as a way of reducing costs. For example, in the state of Washington, the Washington Higher Education Telecommunication System (WHETS) is a two-way audio-video microwave system that links ten cities and fourteen educational institutions. As a member of WHETS, Washington State University delivers about seventy courses per semester to several sites around the state, including three branch campuses and two community colleges. More than thirty classrooms on campus are capable of sending and receiving over the system.

Examples of other university and state networks for distance education include the Colorado Electronic Community College, EdNet in Oregon, the Iowa Communications Network, the TeleLinking Network in Kentucky, and BadgerNet in Wisconsin. Other systems involve cooperatives and consortia that cross state lines, such as the Western Governors University, a "virtual university" (sponsored by the governors of fifteen states and one U.S. territory); and the Committee on Institutional Cooperation, a network of twelve large universities, including Pennsylvania State University, University of Iowa, Ohio State University, University of Minnesota, University of Wisconsin, and University of Illinois (National Center for Education Statistics, 1998b).

Distance education is becoming an increasingly important element of higher education. In 1994–95, an estimated 25,730 distance education courses with different catalog numbers were offered by colleges and universities. That year only 4 percent of institutions offered no distance education courses, while 25 percent offered 11 to 25 courses, and 26 percent offered more than 25 courses (National Center for Education Statistics, 1998b). Out of about 14.3 million students enrolled in higher education in 1994, almost 800,000 enrolled in distance education courses. Among the target audiences for distance education courses, 49 percent of institutions targeted workers seeking skill updating or retraining; 39 percent targeted professionals seeking recertification; 16 percent targeted individuals with disabilities; 12 percent targeted military personnel; 7 percent targeted Native Americans/Alaskan Natives on tribal lands; and 3 percent targeted non-English-speaking individuals (National Center for Education Statistics, 1998b).

SENIOR LEARNERS

Another group of learners that is increasing rapidly is senior learners. With computer-age advances in health care—from artificial heart implantation, to diagnoses using magnetic resonance imaging, to the possibility of individuals cloning vital organs for later replacement—the life span of Americans is steadily being extended. The population over the age of 65 is increasing twice as fast as the population as a whole. For example, a *U.S. News & World Report* article titled "If You Live to Be 100—It Won't Be Unusual" estimated that the number of Americans 65 or older will nearly double between 1983 and 2033; more than one out of five Americans in 2033 will be 65 or older. Also, in 1998, approximately 61,000 persons were 100 or older; by 2040, this number is expected to increase to 1.4 million. As John Glenn's return to space in 1998

Post-Secondary Curricula   **471**

at the age of 77 dramatically portrayed, older Americans will increasingly be better educated and more physically, intellectually, and politically active than their predecessors. Thus, it seems highly possible that new opportunities for curriculum planners will become available as educational gerontologists, individuals who specialize in developing educational programs for an aging population.

Many colleges and universities are now opening their doors widely to senior citizens; roughly one-fifth of the 3,000 institutions for higher learning offer courses for retirement age students (many offer free or reduced tuition). Courses vary from cultural enrichment, retirement services, and crafts to liberal arts programs and vocational reeducation.

The greatest group participation of older adults in regular college-level courses has been through Elderhostel, which began as a nonprofit organization in 1975 and offered people sixty and over the chance to take courses, staying in residence while paying only for living expenses. The Elderhostel program, originally based on a few college and university campuses in the New England states, now operates in all states and in many countries. In 1998, more than 270,000 individuals participated in Elderhostel educational programs, and 3,000 courses were offered. Increasingly, curriculum planners are realizing that more attention should be given to teaching senior learners and that the fight against ageism should begin in the minds of the elderly. Elderhostel is based on the idea that retirement does not mean withdrawal and that "learning is a lifelong process; sharing new ideas, challenges and experiences is rewarding in every season of life" (Elderhostel, 1998).

HIGHER EDUCATION AND THE FUTURE

What will be the shape of higher education in the future? In "The Decline of the Knowledge Factory" in this chapter, John Tagg maintains that colleges will need to become "learning-driven institutions" if they are to provide society with its best hope for the future—the educated person. In "Applying the Science of Learning to the University and Beyond" in this chapter, Diane F. Halpern and Milton D. Hakel explain how application of the "science of learning" can promote long-term retention and transfer of learning among college students. Also, in this chapter's *Case Study in Curriculum Implementation* ("Do As I Say, Not As I Do: A Personal Odyssey"), Helen C. Botnarescue, with the assistance of David R. Stronch, explains how the learning of undergraduate students can be enhanced through techniques such as brainstorming, working in small groups, and completing assignments that allow for a variety of interpretations.

In addition, linkages with other institutions will be all-important to the survival and significance of the university of the future. Since more and more jobs depend upon contacts with people throughout the world, what is taught in our colleges and universities must reflect the interrelatedness of global and national events. Colleges and universities should provide young people and adults in our society with the skills and knowledge needed to function in a world community.

In addition to continued calls to provide students with a rigorous liberal education and to prepare them to meet the challenges of a rapidly changing society and world, today's universities are experiencing strong pressure to make their curricula more student centered. For example, in "The Student-Centered Research University" in this chapter, Gershon Vincow maintains that student learning is the principal goal of the research university and that the principal rationale for research should be the extent to which it promotes learning among undergraduate and graduate students. As universities continue to become more student centered, many different approaches to curriculum planning and teaching will be utilized, and much faculty time will be devoted to diagnosing students' needs and prescribing individual courses of study.

What goals of education should be established for late adolescents and adults? As mentioned earlier in this chapter, the broad general goals of education at the post-secondary level are the same as those at the other levels we have studied—*citizenship, equal educational opportunity, vocation, self-realization,* and *critical thinking.* In addition, a major goal of post-secondary education should be to provide a wide array of educational opportunities for learners. Curriculum planners must recognize that the life span for everyone includes critical transitional events that require new adjustments to meet life's challenges.

REFERENCES

Boyer, Ernest L. *College: The Undergraduate Experience in America.* New York: Harper & Row, 1987.

Carnegie Foundation for the Advancement of Teaching. *Higher Education and the American Resurgence.* Lawrenceville, NJ: Princeton University Press, 1985.

Elderhostel. "Elderhostel Mission Statement." Boston: Elderhostel, Inc., 1998.

Havighurst, Robert J. *Developmental Tasks and Education,* 3rd ed. New York: Longman, 1972.

Jacobs, Naomi. "Nontraditional Students: The New Ecology of the Classroom." *The Educational Forum* 53, no. 4 (Summer 1989): 326–329.

Kerr, Clark. "Speculations about the Increasingly Indeterminate Future of Higher Education in the United States." *Review of Higher Education* 20, no. 4 (Summer 1997): 345–356.

National Center for Education Statistics. *Projection of Education Statistics to 2008.* Washington, DC: National Center for Education Statistics, 1998a.

———. "Distance Education in Higher Education Institutions: Incidence, Audiences, and Plans to Expand." Washington, DC: National Center for Education Statistics, 1998b.

———. *The Condition of Education 1996.* Washington, DC: National Center for Education Statistics, 1996.

National Institute of Education. *Involvement in Learning: Realizing the Potential of American Higher Education.* Washington, DC: U.S. Government Printing Office, 1984.

Connectedness through Liberal Education

ERNEST L. BOYER (1928–1995)

ABSTRACT: Drawing from the 1987 Carnegie Foundation report, College: The Undergraduate Experience in America, *Boyer identifies five essential priorities for undergraduate education. Students should (1) become proficient in the written and spoken word, (2) be liberally educated, (3) acquire moral and ethical principles, (4) be taught by teachers who emphasize active rather than passive learning, and (5) be helped to establish connections between theories presented in the classroom and the realities of life.*

In the past 3 years, the Carnegie Foundation has been looking at undergraduate education in the United States. In our report, "College," we recommended many changes to strengthen the undergraduate experience. I would like to highlight what I consider to be five essentials of quality undergraduate education.

Let me begin with a personal illustration. In 1972, I was sitting in my office in Albany, New York, on a dreary Monday morning. To avoid the obligations of the day, I turned instinctively to the stack of third-class mail that I kept perched precariously on the corner of my desk to create the illusion of being very busy. On top of the pile was the student newspaper from Stanford University. The headline read that the faculty at Stanford had reintroduced a required course in Western civilization after having abolished all requirements just 3 years before. The students, in a front-page editorial, opposed the brash act of the faculty. They declared that "a required course is an illiberal act," and concluded that editorial with this blockbuster question. "How dare they impose uniform standards on nonuniform people?"

At first I was amused, and then deeply troubled, by that query—and it has nagged me to this day. I wondered how it was that some of the nation's most gifted students could not understand that while we are not uniform, we still have many things in common. Is it conceivable that we are educating our students to see themselves in isolation while failing to help them discover their connections? Is it possible that, through formal education in the United States, we are stressing

our independence but not affirming the interdependent nature of our existence?

This anecdote brings me to the central theme of my remarks. I believe that all worthy goals we pursue in undergraduate education might be captured by the simple word, "connections." Let me give four or five examples to illustrate my point.

First, we are connected through the exquisite use of symbols. Language is our most essential human function. Our capacity to capture feelings and ideas sets us apart from all other forms of life, the porpoise and the bumble bee notwithstanding. And the top priority of those in undergraduate education must be to help all students become proficient in the written and spoken word. I find it quite amazing that children learn very early that words are both magical and powerful. When I was a young boy in Dayton, Ohio, they used to say "Sticks and stones may break my bones, but names would never hurt me." "What nonsense," I'd usually say, with tears running down my cheeks, thinking all the time, "For goodness sakes, hit me with a stick but stop those words that penetrate so deeply and last so long."

Language begins before birth as the unborn infant monitors the mother's voice in utero. We know that the three middle ear bones—the hammer, the anvil, and the stirrup—are the only bones fully formed at birth. So, we start language development before we're born. We learn language from our parents and our grandparents and all those people around us. It is through this process that we are connected to each other. And now that I am a grandfather and see this process of language acquisition and development unencumbered by dirty diapers and burpings late at night, I stand in awe that this magical, God-given, gene-driven capacity of symbols emerges so majestically. Yet we take language development so carelessly for granted. We accept it unthinkingly, just as we do breath itself. Consider the miracle of this very moment: I stand here vibrating my vocal cords, molecules are bombarded in your direction, they touch your tympanic membrane, signals go scurrying up your eighth cranial nerve, and there is a response in your cerebrum which I trust approximates the images in mine. It is this process through which we are personally and socially empowered and connected.

We say in our report that every college freshman should take a basic course in language. We say that writing should be taught in every class, since it's through clear writing that clear thinking can be taught. We conclude that every student should, before he or she graduates from college, be able to write carefully, think critically, listen with discernment, and speak with power and precision.

In the teaching of language, we should also teach the value of silence, listening to each other and to ourselves. We live in a culture where noise too often is the norm. In fact, we feel uncomfortable in the presence of silence. And yet listening is often a crucial condition for those in the healing arts. I wish that in the classroom students would begin to have periods of silence, not just to keep order but to reflect on what they have heard.

There is, in too many professional arrangements, the protection of our labels that conceal us from each other. Some years ago, when we were having dinner at our home, the children were playing a record at a decibel level that was calculated to destroy the tympanic membrane. I asked them to please tell me what I was hearing. They gave me the lyrics of the song "Eleanor Rigby," the story of a woman who wore a mask she kept in a jar. I think that song quite rightly is a parable of many of our institutions. We protect

ourselves as deans, professors, scientists, scholars, and one wonders where's the humanity of it all. We scurry about, caught up in the thick of things, unwilling and often unable to take the time to listen carefully to each other. I'm talking about teaching language, not as the parts of speech, not just as a process that's technically correct, but as the means by which humans are connected to each other.

When I was chancellor of the State University of New York, I was about to speak to a group of faculty from across the state, when 350 students came barging in through the door, as they often did in those days. They were chanting slogans and waving placards and they demanded that I help free a group of students who had been arrested on another campus. For almost an hour we shouted back and forth. Finally, I concluded we weren't listening to each other. The meeting was in a shambles and, even worse, I realized that I was talking not to people but to a faceless mob. So more out of desperation than inspiration, I left the platform, walked into the crowd, and began to talk to a single student. I asked her name; I asked her about her family; I asked her why she was so angry. Soon several others joined us and I described what I could and couldn't do. Well, to make this story short, the session ended, we reached a compromise, and in the process I learned to know some most attractive students.

What I'm suggesting is that our shared use of symbols connects us to each other, and it is through liberal education that students should be asked to consider the quality of the messages they send. Recently, I happened across a fascinating little anecdote about an 18th century Quaker named John Olmen. He tells of a meeting he had with Indians in Pennsylvania. Olmen said he struggled to communicate with them through an interpreter who was having an extremely bad time with his messages. So Olmen shifted to silence and occasionally to prayer. At the end of the exchange, he was intrigued by what one of the Indian chiefs said of his message. "I love to feel where the words come from." In the end, the quality of the message is not in its correctness alone, but in the integrity of the meaning. Those around us know whether we are just sending messages or are listening as well.

I want to make one final point on the issue of connectedness through language. Connectedness is achieved not just through cleverness or even clarity of expression, but through integrity as well. To borrow again from the Quakers, in the 18th and early 19th centuries, Quakers were unwilling to swear "to tell the truth, the whole truth, and nothing but the truth" in a court of law. It wasn't just that they were against swearing, although they were. The problem was that they were unwilling to swear to tell the truth in a court with their hand positioned on a Bible because to do so meant raising the question of whether or not, outside the courtroom, truth might be an option. So they would say, "Your Honor, I speak truth." "No, No, you have to swear you'll speak it now." "But your Honor, I speak truth." Now, I'm not sure I would be willing to hang for a delicate point like that, but the larger principle cannot be denied. I am suggesting that students should be taught that truth is the obligation they assume when they are empowered with the use of symbols. And that in the end, the quality of a college can be measured by the quality of communication on the campus.

This brings me to priority number two. I believe that students not only need empowerment and connectedness through language, they need to be liberally educated so they can put their work in larger context. As I look at the nature of our world, I'm deeply disturbed that many of our students are becoming increasingly parochial at the very moment the human agenda is more global. And I do not believe that they can act as wise professionals in an interdependent world unless they are able to put their work in an international context.

About 3 years ago, 40 percent of the community college students we surveyed could not locate either Iran or El Salvador on the map. During our study of the American high school, we discovered that only two states require students to complete a course in non-Western stud-

ies. And 2 years ago, when we surveyed 5,000 undergraduates, we learned that over 30 per cent of them said that they had nothing in common with people in underdeveloped countries. The simple truth is that our graduates will live in a world that is economically, politically, and environmentally connected and they increasingly will work with a population in the United States that is more and more diverse. Yet somehow we are not providing a general education that offers the larger perspective that is urgently required, one that affirms our connectedness, not just socially but ecologically as well.

When I was US Commissioner of Education, Joan Ganz Cooney, the creator of Sesame Street, came to see me one day with an idea she had for a new program on science for junior high school students. We found funding for the show, which was called "3-2-1 Contact." Cooney and her staff conducted research to prepare for the show. They asked some junior high school students in New York City such questions as where water came from. A disturbing percentage said, "the faucet." They asked where light came from and the students said, "the switch." And they asked where garbage went and students said, "down the chute." Their answers indicate a frightening almost "anti-connectedness" to much of their world.

We are, as Lewis Thomas put it, embedded in the natural world as working parts. It is no longer possible for us to consume and produce without asking about discarding, too. We must become increasingly sensitive to the interdependent nature of our physical world and our responsibility to live according to the laws of nature, both as a global community and in our personal lives as well. This kind of interdependence, in my judgment, is at the heart of professional education. Lewis Thomas once wrote that "if this century does not slip forever through our fingers it will be because education will have directed us away from our splintered dumbness and helped us focus on our common goal."

This brings me then to priority number three, how we live and how we work—the challenge to bring moral and ethical perspective to our profession. Many of us have been worried about such issues as gene splicing research that might introduce mutations on the planet earth. We have also questioned whether human subjects should be used during experimentation. These, in my judgment, are questions in which there are no experts. There are only human beings trying to solve new and complicated problems.

Again, the challenge is to put our professions in social and ethical perspective. If we do not, we run the risk of creating what I call the "Boesky syndrome," people who know how to succeed but who do not make their decisions within the context of moral judgment; people whose confidence is not guided by conscience. In the Carnegie report on college, we suggest something called the enriched major. We suggest that every professional field should be asked to place its own work in historical, social, and ethical perspective. We drew some of our inspiration from Norman Cousins, who observed some years ago that the doctor who knows only disease is at a disadvantage alongside the doctor who knows as much about people as he or she does about pathological organisms.

Cousins goes on to say that the lawyer who argues in court from a narrow legal base is no match for the lawyer who can connect legal precedence to historical experience. So we suggest in our report that the values professionals bring to their work are every bit as crucial as the work itself. And we argue that general and specialized education should be blended during college; just as inevitably, they should be blended during life.

This discussion leads me to say a word about teachers. We can have a good curriculum in professional training and we can have all the priorities spelled out in a syllabus or in a national report. However, in the end, connectedness is established in the classroom by teachers who serve as models and as mentors.

Several years ago during a sleepless night, I counted all the teachers I've had, instead of counting sheep. I remembered 15 or more rather

vividly. There were, I must admit, a few nightmares in the bunch. But I tried to think of all the great teachers, the outstanding individuals in colleges and schools who genuinely changed my life.

First I thought about Miss Rice, my first grade teacher. My mother walked with me my first day of school. On the way, I asked her if I would learn to read that day. I badly wanted to learn to read. My mother said, "No, you won't learn to read today but you will before the year is out." Well, she didn't know Miss Rice. I walked into the room and there she stood half human, half divine. After a meaningful pause, Miss Rice looked at 28 frightened, awestruck children and said, "Good morning class, today we learn to read." Those were the first words I ever heard in school.

I probably learned to memorize that day, not decode, but Miss Rice taught me something much more fundamental. She taught me that language is the centerpiece of learning. And I find it really quite miraculous that 50 years later in our book on high school, there was a chapter on the centrality of language, and again in our book on college there was a chapter on language. If we do a book on graduate education, I'm sure there will be a chapter on language. And I mention that to credit the influence of an unheralded first grade teacher at Fairview Avenue Elementary School, Dayton, Ohio, 1934.

I also recall Mr. Wittlinger, a high school history teacher, who one day said quietly as I passed his desk, "Ernest, you're doing very well in history. If you keep this up you just might be a student." It sounds like a put-down but it was the highest academic accolade I'd received. I went home that night thinking to myself, "I'm not a baseball player, I'm not a cowboy, I'm not a fire chief, I just might be a student." The redefinition of who I might be at a time when I wasn't very sure was immeasurably powerful.

Great teachers live forever. What made them truly great? First, these teachers were knowledgeable and well-informed. They had something to teach; thus, their knowledge base was firm. Of course, we've all had teachers who were very knowledgeable but also were dreary and ineffectual, so there had to be something else. Second, these teachers could communicate at a level the student understood. They knew their students and they made connections between their knowledge and their students' readiness to receive it.

The third and final characteristic that brought all together was the fact that the truly outstanding teachers in my life were open, authentic, and believable human beings. They laughed, they cried, they said "I don't know," and above all, they made connections. Mentoring by great teachers makes the difference. I suggest that as we look for ways to strengthen the undergraduate experience we need new models of teaching in the classroom. We need, among other things, active learning rather than passive relationships. We need teachers who inspire not conformity, but creativity in the classroom.

During our study of high school and college, we were enormously impressed by the passivity of students. John Goodlad, who has done an excellent job of studying schools, reports that in many classrooms, 6 percent of the time is devoted to student speech in the classroom and almost all of that has to do with logistics such as "Will we have this on this test?" and comments about procedural arrangements, not the substance of their work. Now I wish I could tell you that that's not true in colleges, but passivity dominates the classroom in higher education as well. We are teaching lethargy, not engagement.

During our study of undergraduate colleges, we were on the campus of a well-known university. Just before we got there, one of the ranking professors had observed the graduating senior class. He asked how many of them went through 4 years at this institution, got a baccalaureate degree, and said not one word in class. What would you guess? Seventy-five percent of the students said they could go through that university, never say one word in class, just take notes, and slip in and out. They admitted that they would perhaps have to avoid a few teachers, but that by and large they could do it.

We need to create a climate not only in which there are teachers who mentor, but in which stu-

dents are teachers, too. Students, as they continue to learn, must accept an obligation to be increasingly engaged. We also need cooperative learning as a part of this process. I'm impressed that through all of school, students are in competition with each other, yet in the end, our serious problems will be resolved through collaborative efforts in the sciences, the professions, and in the workplace, too.

It is not insignificant that increasingly we are talking about the health care "team." That language demonstrates clearly that we are going to have to share information and pursue collaborative problem solving. The teaching model in all fields should be built around the collaborative approach where students are pursuing problems together, and even being graded on their group effort rather than in competition with each other. In the end we are going to survive on planet Earth through an understanding that our problems are collective and our solutions must be found through collaboration.

This leads me to one final observation. I believe we must establish connections between the theories of the classroom and the realities of life.

John Gardner said on one occasion that the deepest threat to the integrity of any community is an incapacity on the part of its citizens to lend themselves to any worthy, common purpose. Gardner goes on to reflect on the bareness of a life that encompasses nothing beyond the self. I believe we are creating a culture in which the sense of engagement is increasingly diminished.

When we did our study on high school, for example, I became quite convinced that we have not just a school problem but a youth problem in this nation. Many of our young people during their teenage years are not socially engaged. This is worrisome, because it's particularly during this time that young people need to find out who they are and how they will fit into the larger world. Many college campuses are youth ghettos, too, places where students talk only to themselves. Today in our society we're organizing ourselves horizontally; putting children in day-care centers, young people in high schools, and then finally our seniors into retirement villages. Instead of connections, we're having intergenerational fragmentation. There is something unhealthy about a culture in which the different generations are separated from each other.

My parents will be celebrating their 89th birthdays in a retirement village soon. There's something particularly redeeming about that village. They have a day-care center there, so every morning 50 or more 4- and 5-year-olds come trucking up. It may not be your idea of retirement, but there's something authentic about a community in which the young and the older mingle with each. My father has a little boy whom he calls "his little friend." All of the day-care children have adopted grandparents and they spend time together throughout the day. When I call my father, he talks about the child's drawings on the wall and the conversations they've had. A community in which young children are able to see the agonies and the dignities of aging and in which 80-year-olds can spend time with children who are on the threshold of a hopeful life offers a deep, joyous opportunity for connections.

Increasingly, I believe that an authentic part of education is building connections between the theory of the classroom and the reality of life outside. The school is not simply a monastic retreat; it is a base of operation. And it is my opinion that every professional field has to build in this component of connectiveness so that students can see the relationship between theory and it application.

For that reason, in our report called high school and then later in college, we propose a service term, not just in the professions but in other fields as well; a time when students can teach others, serve as tutors or spend time in retirement villages or work with young children in day-care centers. All of this is to demonstrate a validity between who they are and the realities of life. Vachel Lindsay wrote on one occasion that "It is the world's one crime its babes grow dull. . . . Not that they sow, but that they seldom reap, not that they serve, but have no gods to serve. Not that they die, but that they die like sheep." Students should understand that the tragedy of life is not death. The tragedy is to die with commitments undefined, convictions undeclared, and service unfulfilled.

Ernest L. Boyer was president of the Carnegie Foundation for the Advancement of Teaching from 1979 to 1995; prior to that he was U.S. Commissioner of Education under President Carter and chancellor of the State University of New York.

QUESTIONS FOR REFLECTION

1. Do you agree with Boyer that all worthy goals for undergraduate education might be captured by the word *connections*? What other word captures what the goals for undergraduate education ought to be?
2. In terms of importance, how would you rank order the five priorities Boyer has identified? What is the rationale for your ranking?
3. To what extent do you agree with the following observation by Boyer: ". . . passivity dominates the classroom in higher education as well. We are teaching lethargy, not engagement"? What factors limit the amount of *engagement* found in the college curriculum? What steps can curriculum planners and teachers take to change this?

The Student-Centered Research University

GERSHON VINCOW

ABSTRACT: A model for the goals, priorities, and desired outcomes of the student-centered research university is presented. Ten key actions are essential for an institution to make the transformation to a student-centered research university, a central feature of which is the student-centered course, which focuses more on students' learning and less on faculty interests. Common faculty objections include lowering of standards, an abandonment of research, lack of training in pedagogy, and lack of time.

THE NEED FOR CHANGE

Research universities—independent and state-supported alike—have been the object of society's severe criticism in recent years. Some of it is justified; much of it is uninformed and unfounded. I'm tired of this criticism, but I'm also dismayed by our weak and ineffective response. We need a new approach, the student-centered research university.

Yes, I'm tired of "Profscam," of the charge that the research I did in my day, with such dedication and creativity, published in the leading journals, was arcane, irrelevant and unnecessary. How do you feel about your research and its significance? Is it a "scam"?

I'm annoyed that people claim we cost too much. Is $35,000 a year for an assistant professor in the Humanities too much compared to the starting salaries of engineers and lawyers who have less education and less proven creativity? Beyond that comparison, do you think you are overpaid?

I'm tired of the mindless carping about teaching assistants, most of whom are inspired, involved, and helpful to students. I'm dismayed by the lack of understanding that supervised teaching assistants are like medical residents. They are society's way of regenerating an important profession. Why can't we make that clear?

I'm upset by the imagery of the professor as fat-cat consultant, always on the airplane, hardly ever at the university, and certainly not dedicated to students. How many of us in this room does that picture portray?

I must admit, however, that our responses to these attacks have often been weak and typically ineffective. We acknowledge that we need to put some more effort into undergraduate education, but we assert that overall our house is in order. After all, aren't American research universities the envy of the world—sought by students from around the globe? Don't we still receive the lion's share of Nobel awards?

"Irrelevant," reply our critics, "what we want is better results for our children, improved learning outcomes as they join a globally competitive work force. The solution is simple. Just teach more hours per week, and all will be well." We know that this oversimplified solution will not produce the desired results, but we will not win their hearts and minds so long as the playing field of our discussion is society's conventional exaggeration of the research university model.

Our best course of action is to pursue a new model. I propose that we create a student-centered research university. This student-centered model will produce the learning outcomes our students need, will therefore be valued by society, and will again bring us society's strong support.

My goal in this presentation is to describe one view of the student-centered research university and to persuade you of its value. The theme of this symposium, "Toward a Student-Centered Research University," suggests that you may be disposed to develop your own version of such a model, one best suited to the strengths and traditions of an outstanding university.

THE STUDENT-CENTERED MODEL: GOALS, PRIORITIES, AND DESIRED OUTCOMES

To provide an overview I will first sketch a conceptual framework for the student-centered research university. I start by reformulating the mission statement of the research university. In my view, it ought not be the conventional "teaching, research and service," however elegantly we might phrase it, but rather the following:

> The mission of the research university is to promote learning through teaching, research, scholarship, creative accomplishment, and service.

Our goal is to promote learning. Teaching, research, and service are simply the means to achieve this goal, not the ends in themselves. We will judge the value of each program and each activity by how much and how well it contributes to promoting learning. This statement is important because it helps us prioritize our actions, but even more important because it serves as the clear and ultimate performance measure of our success.

How much and how well has our teaching promoted learning by our undergraduate and graduate students? How much and how well has our research contributed to promoting learning among our students as well as among our colleagues in the discipline? How much and how well has our public service contributed to promoting learning among the citizens of our state and society in general?

Another advantage of this revised mission statement is that it leads us naturally to a student-centered model. Whom do we first think of as the learners at a university? Certainly, our undergraduate and graduate students.

So the mission statement to promote learning refocuses our attention away from a university centered mostly on the faculty and what it does—teaching, research and service—toward a university in which faculty and students share center stage, both as learners. We see the student as learner in our educational programs, the faculty member as learner in his or her research program.

Now we proceed to defining the student-centered research university. Simply put, it is a special kind of research university—in which the principal focus is on students, both undergraduate and graduate.

Since our institutional mission is "to promote learning" and our principal focus is on students, our number one priority becomes promoting learning by our students. We take a fresh look at all our activities from this viewpoint, centered on students. What are some immediate consequences?

- We—the faculty—will judge our success as educators not simply by how well we teach, or transmit knowledge and skills, but rather by how well we promote learning by students. This change in emphasis—that is, the faculty thinking about education not simply as "teaching" but as "teaching and learning"— is the single most important transformation to be achieved by the vision of a student-centered research university.
- A second consequence is that successful research and creative performance will have a significant impact on our students. Our principal rationale for research will be how it promotes learning by our students, both undergraduate and graduate students, including doctoral students. Our secondary rationale for research will be how it promotes learning as it advances our discipline. Among faculty, this flip-flop of rationales for research is the most controversial aspect of the new model. But think of its positive impact on society. Our legislatures, our critics can be led anew to appreciate and value research. They will come to understand that research is essential because it promotes learning by our students.

Another aspect of becoming student-centered follows from recognizing that enormous learning and personal growth occur outside the classroom during the college years. We in Academic Affairs must work together in new ways with Student Affairs so that academic learning and personal development become two mutually supporting, reinforcing, enhancing parts of one whole—the collegiate experience of the student. An improved "campus culture" becomes an important goal.

Having outlined what I mean by student-centered, let me make a few remarks about the research university aspect of the new model. Our basic character will remain that of a research university, with greater emphasis put on the role of research in promoting learning. As a research university, we will continue to feature graduate education, especially doctoral education. The student-centered model will apply both to undergraduate and graduate students. In fact, undergraduate and graduate education should be mutually reinforcing in such a research university and their synergy an important component of the student-centered approach.

How can the research university provide added educational value to students? I believe that a faculty engaged in research and creative professional activity can bring to the classroom not only the cutting edge of new knowledge but also a creative spirit that adds a special quality to education. I believe that we can model in our teaching a curiosity about the world and an excitement in learning and discovery, both of which are essential to inspire students with our passion for the life of the mind. Further, we can better motivate students to be engaged in learning since we are seen by them as fellow active learners and not simply as transmitters of knowledge and skills. Outside the formal classroom, we can and should involve undergraduates, insofar as possible, in research or in a research type of experience. Many science and engineering faculty have long led the way in providing such opportunities for undergraduate students in their laboratories.

I'll conclude this general portrait of the student-centered research university by summarizing it in another way. The following ten key actions are required for becoming a student-centered research university:

- We view each aspect of the university from the perspective of its impact on students.
- We affirm student learning as our principal goal, and our principal rationale for research is the extent to which research promotes learning among undergraduate and graduate students.
- We judge our success in education by how well students learn and not simply by how well we transmit knowledge.
- We revise our courses and our majors to become more centered on students' learning.
- We continually improve courses and academic programs through assessment of learning outcomes.
- We emphasize the value added by a research university experience in promoting students' learning.
- We develop a holistic approach to the experience of students and the culture of the institution—scholarly learning and personal development become mutually supporting goals.
- We support students' success leading to graduation so that student-faculty relationships, including improved advising and mentoring, are central to our efforts.
- We modify faculty roles, evaluations, and rewards to increase the emphasis on teaching and advising; and we redirect institutional incentives and reallocate resources to support these actions.

THE STUDENT-CENTERED COURSE: A MAJOR FEATURE OF THE STUDENT-CENTERED RESEARCH UNIVERSITY

To create the student-centered research university we must proceed from the conceptual to the concrete. We must implement each of these ten key actions. For example, we must revise our courses and our majors to become more centered on students' learning. I will illustrate this point by describing in detail a student-centered course, focusing on how it promotes learning.

We conceptualize and develop the student-centered course from the point of view of its impact on students and their learning. We abandon the old refrain—I teach Physics, not students. We modify the traditional faculty-centered focus on the subject matter content we wish to convey and the skills we wish to impart. To begin the student-centered approach to teaching, we try to understand the starting point from which students enter our classroom. We ask such questions as the following.

- What is our students' background knowledge in our subject and their prerequisite preparation in allied disciplines such as mathematics?
- What are their goals in taking the course? How can we relate their goals to ours?

Answering these leads us to the most important questions:

- What are our goals for the course as they relate to student learning outcomes?
- What do we wish students to come away with in their knowledge of subject matter, critical-thinking skills, communication skills, awareness of values issues, and so on?
- And how will we accomplish these goals in our student-centered course?

There are many additional questions to answer as we focus on the teaching and learning process.

- How can we acknowledge and support our students' learning within their diverse learning styles? (Some are concrete thinkers, others abstract; some are verbal, others visual.)
- How can we communicate high expectations of all our students, motivate their involvement in learning, and provide the support they need to produce optimal learning outcomes?
- How can we get them actively involved in their studies?
- How can we approach each student as an individual, personalizing the experience?

- How can we stimulate students' intellectual curiosity and introduce them to the meaning of scholarship and discovery?
- How can we help students achieve the same pleasure and satisfaction we experience in the process of learning?

These are all important questions we need to answer in order to design a student-centered course. But for most of us, who have developed our careers as subject-matter experts in research universities, they are difficult and indeed uncomfortable questions. I do not pretend to be an expert on pedagogy but will simply report a few illustrations of what some master teachers and experts in the literature of effective teaching have suggested.

Many instructors make special efforts to get to know their students personally, even in large courses. Classroom anonymity—often a contributor to students' lack of involvement and absence from class—can be broken down. Faculty gather information from students, such as their year of attendance, major, reasons for taking the course, background in the subject, and so on. This information helps the instructor shape the course; asking for it indicates a personal interest in students and provides "icebreakers" when students visit during office hours. In some cases, the instructor in large classes can learn the name of each student. One colleague, who teaches a large-enrollment "Introduction to Political Science" course, requires that each student visit him once during office hours, just to get acquainted and give their impressions of the course. Such increased student-faculty contact is essential to promoting students' involvement in learning.

Students frequently tell me that they want to know more about us as people. They want to know where we hail from, our educational background, family, hobbies, and so on. That small degree of personalization adds to a constructive relationship and stimulates their engagement in the course.

Among our first communications with students is the course syllabus that we pass out and review during the first class period. Think about it. Aren't our syllabi typically bureaucratic in tone and course-centered rather than student-centered? What should we add to syllabi from the student's point of view? An interesting statement of the goals, objectives and outcomes of the course is essential.

- These are the main ideas and areas of knowledge that you will learn.
- These are the academic skills that you will acquire, and this is how.
- These are the ways we will support your learning.

Reviewing such a syllabus in class communicates our teaching and learning goals and can set an inspirational tone at the outset. Students will sense our love of the subject, our genuine enthusiasm for teaching it, and will understand our expectations for what they will learn. Such an introduction can go a long way toward promoting student interest in the course.

And what should the syllabus say about classroom attendance? At Syracuse we have a new policy: "Attendance in classes is expected in all courses at Syracuse University. Class attendance requirements and policies concerning nonattendance are established by the instructors of each course and are detailed in the course syllabus." This policy conveys our belief that classroom attendance is essential to promoting learning. (My freshman seminar class last semester was amazed at the back-of-the-envelope calculation that each class costs them the same as a good rock concert, about $30; they won't easily forget that comparison.)

As we teach our course we should look at each aspect to consider how it is student-centered, that is, how it promotes learning by students. For example, are we giving enough assignments early in the semester with prompt feedback? This is particularly important in lower division courses, to help first-year students understand college-level expectations and to guide them in developing skills of independent learning.

In all levels of courses we should ask if we are working our students hard enough. "Reading, writing, thinking, and a lot of it," that's how one master teacher describes his approach. The conventional format—lectures, assigned readings, a midterm, a paper, and a final are far from adequate in a student-centered course.

And what about papers? Are they designed to promote learning? Traditionally many faculty have assigned a topic for a paper, read the paper, assigned a grade and made some comments in the margins. This approach focuses on the faculty evaluating the student. It does not optimally promote the learning of analytic and communication skills. Perhaps a shorter paper should be assigned, with a requirement first to submit an outline, then a draft of the paper and then a revised final version, each of these receiving constructive feedback. That process models our professional approach to research and writing and is much more student-centered and learning centered.

Two other examples to improve learning in the area of writing involve student collaboration:

- In the basic writing course at Syracuse students often work together as a writers workshop, reading and critiquing each other's papers.
- A colleague at Rochester tells me that his students' papers are read by two other students in the class, critiqued by them, and then rewritten and resubmitted for a grade. All three students are graded, the two student readers based on the quality of their critiques.

These are examples of active learning, a variety of approaches stressing the active participation of students with other students in learning. Research shows that students involved in academically-focused groups are more engaged in their learning and learn more. There is a whole variety of active learning strategies to complement the more traditional lectures, seminars, and laboratories. These strategies include study groups, project teams, group work in class, informal discussion groups, learning communities, cooperative learning, and collaborative learning.

Active learning is an important feature of the student-centered course.

Despite our best efforts to provide feedback first-year students frequently are not clear about how well they are doing. At Syracuse we have recently introduced mid-semester progress reports. First-year students receive S or U, satisfactory or unsatisfactory, in four categories: attendance, participation, submitted work (assignments, papers, projects), and exams and quizzes. This feedback signals some students that they need to party less and study more or ask for help in a particular course. These reports also signal advisers and deans' offices about students "at risk" who may need special attention.

It is important that the student-centered course reflect our claim that the faculty's involvement in research and graduate education is a great advantage for undergraduates. We should incorporate into our lectures and course material references to our scholarly activities as well as those of faculty and students at our university. These references may be quite natural in graduate courses or advanced upper-division courses. In lower-division courses it may be necessary to digress intentionally to connect the course material with our scholarship or that of others. In this way, we illustrate the value and importance of a spirit of inquiry, discovery, and creativity and make students aware and proud of their research-university environment.

At the end of each course, I encourage a return to the syllabus, and a review of our goals—now as achieved results. What were the highlights of the course? What have students learned? What have they accomplished? Students need assistance in performing such reflective integration of their educational experience. It's very satisfying for both faculty and students to preview and review teaching and learning accomplishments.

And how can we promote learning at the very end of the course—the final exam? In my opinion, the notion of a cumulative final examination that requires students to review and integrate the entire course is an important capstone experience. At Syracuse, we have a new Academic Calendar starting next year. I pressed for six reading days in fall and four reading days in spring—a significant increase. I will call on the faculty to provide students, whenever possible, a cumulative final exam as yet another aspect of promoting their learning experience.

OBJECTIONS TO THE MODEL CHANGE

Having proposed the new model of the student-centered research university, having summarized it with ten key actions, and illustrated it with the student-centered course, I will now respond to some of the concerns about it that have been raised by my colleagues.

Some faculty object to a student-centered approach, fearing that it might lead to a lowering of standards. That is a possibility, but it can be avoided. Although we will try to promote learning by each student, we ought not achieve or claim success by artificially lowering standards so that all students have "successful" learning outcomes. It is essential that we continue to articulate our standards clearly, teach to standards, and in the long run, strengthen these standards. This is a fundamental part of our value system and must be preserved.

Some faculty fear that the new model will destroy the research university. How far will we go along this path, they ask? What will the university look like when we get there? Will we be spending so much of our time on undergraduate teaching and advising that we are forced to abandon research?

Although that is not our intention, the truthful answer is that we can't know in detail what the student-centered research university will look like in the future. This model cannot yet be understood as a "product"—a defined end point but is rather a "process"—a direction of development. We are just beginning to describe its path and to create the "vehicles" that will propel us along it.

How fast will we change? We should not assume that a dramatic transformation will occur in the short term. Just as the current research university model took several decades to develop, this new model will evolve over time, with more than one generation of faculty involved. The pace of change will depend on the faculty's commitment and on society's positive reinforcement of our efforts.

Faculty must be motivated to proceed along this new and challenging path. To speed this culture change at the university we must revise faculty evaluation and reward systems and align institutional incentives to our new criteria for successful performance.

How much will we change? One fundamental limitation to the degree of student-centeredness that we can achieve is our student-to-faculty ratio, currently in the range 10–15 to one. But who knows how the use of advanced information technology may radically transform teaching and learning, the nature of the student-faculty relationship, and therefore the significance of this limiting ratio?

Another faculty objection to pursuing this model is that it emphasizes improvements in pedagogy that go far beyond what we were trained for. We are basically subject matter experts who have a lot of on-the-job teaching experience. Although this is a legitimate concern, I have great confidence in our flexibility and creativity. We are smart, energetic, and dedicated problem solvers who can take major steps toward creating the student-centered research university.

En route, we must also transform the Ph.D. degree so that it better educates not only in research but also in teaching. At Syracuse we have such a "Professoriate of the Future" project underway, involving more than 150 faculty mentors who are training advanced doctoral students in teaching.

One final and major objection is that faculty members are already working 50–60 hours per week and can't take on additional activities. I fully agree. Developing the student-centered research university can't be viewed as an "add on"; it must be a substitution, achieved through eliminating some low-priority activities and reallocating our time commitments. Some more time will have to be spent on improving teaching and advising and less on research.

What are some specific suggestions for improving faculty productivity—here defined not as numbers of students taught or as classroom hours spent teaching per week but rather as effectiveness in supporting students' learning?

- We can improve overall productivity by increasingly measuring it at the department level, with each faculty member contributing optimally, through an individualized mix of teaching, research and service, which may change with time and stage of career.

- Since research remains an essential component of our mission, faculty can improve productivity by focusing on the quality of their research, scholarship, and creative activity. We should prioritize our scholarly efforts more carefully. With somewhat less time available during the academic year, the quality of research accomplished rather than its quantity should become the leading criterion of performance. Some universities have already reflected this idea by limiting the number of articles that faculty can submit for their tenure evaluation.

- Keeping in mind that the end product is student learning, we can also enhance productivity by requiring students to work harder, longer hours, and more effectively in our courses. This will call for better motivation and engagement by students and better support by faculty.

- To promote instructional efficiency in student learning, we can increase our use of advanced undergraduate students as preceptors, particularly in large-enrollment courses. Some universities involve such undergraduates on a volunteer basis; others give course credit, and still others pay small stipends.

- Faculty can increasingly explore the use of information technology to improve the efficiency and effectiveness of student learning.

- Faculty can reduce the total number of undergraduate courses offered—eliminating

many low-enrollment elective courses—so that they can focus more time and effort on improving the quality of teaching and learning in the remaining courses. The result can be a rich but simplified curriculum, coherent and internally reinforcing.
- Finally, faculty can trim the number and sizes of committees at all levels—department, college, and university while exercising caution not to relinquish faculty governance responsibilities and prerogatives.

CONCLUSION

The obvious difficulty of implementing some of these suggestions to improve our productivity in promoting learning exemplifies the general challenge that faces us in moving toward a student-centered research university. Not all research universities are yet ready to meet that challenge, but some have begun to ask themselves critical questions. Answers can lead to most of the 10 key actions required for becoming a student-centered research university. A few examples of such questions, leading to a change in the campus culture, are as follows:

- Are we too alcohol- and sport-centered?
- Should teachers be more involved in extracurricular activities?
- Should teachers be concerned with teaching character, tolerance, and an ethic across the curriculum?

Positive answers to these and related questions invite us to "develop a holistic approach to the experience of students and the culture of the institution—scholarly learning and personal developments become mutually supporting goals."

To strike at the heart of the matter is to focus on promoting learning as the best way of further-

ing the interests of students. We might ask ourselves the following:

- What is good teaching?
- Are we really teachers, or do we "facilitate learning"?
- What are the advantages of being a research university?
- How does student involvement in research promote learning?

Answers to such questions will "affirm student learning as our principal goal," will acknowledge that "we judge our success in education by how well students learn and not simply by how well we transmit knowledge," and will "emphasize the value added of a research-university experience to promoting students' learning."

The topic of creating student-centered courses and programs raises issues of building a curriculum in a culturally pluralistic academic community. We ask ourselves such questions as the following:

- Are courses taught to meet the needs of students and to promote learning, or are they taught to accommodate the interests of faculty?
- Does the university's curriculum promote learning and meet the needs of students today?
- Should the core curriculum include required courses on other cultures or languages?

Answers lead us to the key action to "revise our courses and our majors to become more centered on students learning."

This symposium at the University of Georgia and other similar efforts beginning at research universities across the country manifest a courageous and visionary response to society's messages. Within the academy we can decide to break the logjam of criticism and denial, to take a positive stance, to move toward the new model of the student-centered research university.

Gershon Vincow is Vice Chancellor for Academic Affairs, Syracuse University.

QUESTIONS FOR REFLECTION

1. What additional key actions should research universities take to become more student-centered?
2. Should teachers at the higher education level be concerned with teaching character, tolerance, and ethical behavior across the curriculum?
3. Why is the development of a student-centered research university a *process* rather than a *product*?

Applying the Science of Learning to the University and Beyond

DIANE F. HALPERN
MILTON D. HAKEL

ABSTRACT: Halpern and Hakel discuss the basic principles of teaching so as to promote long-term retention and transfer among college students. These include practice at retrieval, varying the conditions under which learning takes place, and fostering prior knowledge and experience.

There is nothing more annoying than telling a new acquaintance that we are college professors and getting the enthusiastic reply, "It must be great to have all your summers off." Most of the general public—including the parents of the students we teach, students themselves, and many of the people who ultimately pay our salaries—believe that college faculty are primarily teachers who have little to do when classes are not in session.

Of course, most of the general public know that we also "do research" and committee work. But they believe that these other parts of the professor's job are secondary to teaching. Those outside academia further assume that because we are college faculty, we actually have a reasonable understanding of how people learn and that we apply this knowledge in our teaching.

It is easy to imagine where these fantastic notions come from. Have you actually *read* those glossy brochures (known as "View Books" to those in the trade) that our colleges and universities send out to prospective students and to others they want to impress? Invariably, beautiful images of campus life are presented, together with well-crafted language that explains how our students learn lifelong skills that prepare them for lucrative careers and to face the many challenges of adult life.

It would be reasonable for anyone reading these fine words to assume that the faculty who prepare students to meet these lofty goals must have had considerable academic preparation to equip them for this task. But this seemingly plausible assumption is, for the most part, just plain wrong.

The preparation of virtually every college teacher consists of in-depth study in an academic discipline: chemistry professors study advanced chemistry, historians study historical methods and periods, and so on. Very little, if any, of our formal training addresses topics like adult learning, memory, or transfer of learning. And these observations are just as applicable to the cognitive, organizational, and educational psychologists who teach topics like principles of learning and performing, or evidence-based decision-making.

We have found precious little evidence that content experts in the learning sciences actually apply the principles they teach in their own classrooms. Like virtually all college faculty, they teach the way they were taught. But, ironically (and embarrassingly), it would be difficult to design an educational model that is more at odds with the findings of current research about human cognition than the one being used today at most colleges and universities.

Most faculty do in fact spend substantial amounts of time in teaching-related activities—and this is true at even the most research-centered institutions. Most care about their students' learning and want to be effective teachers. Most also believe that they are good teachers and tell those who ask that their teaching skills are above average. But what most college faculty actually know about adult cognition is generally gained through a process of practical trial and error.

Unfortunately, because their intuitive knowledge of good teaching practices is rarely put to a systematic test, what faculty often "know" to be sound educational practice may not be so at all. Nora Newcombe, a developmental psychologist at Temple University, notes wisely that biology has become the scientific basis for medicine, while cognitive psychology and learning research have not become the scientific basis for education. The study of human cognition is an empirical science with a solid theoretical foundation and research-based applications that we can and should be using in college classrooms.

Psychologists, educators, and other professionals already have available to them a substantial body of research that can be drawn upon to inform those responsible for designing and implementing learning programs. Unfortunately, the research literature is usually ignored, while educational leaders and policymakers grasp at the ephemeral "magic" of quick fixes. How can we apply what research on human learning can tell us to both higher education institutions and the many other places where adults learn?

About 30 experts from different areas of the learning sciences recently met to answer this question. They included cognitive, developmental, educational, motivational, social, cultural, and organizational psychologists, physicists and other science instructors, and representatives from such bodies as the National Science Foundation and regional accrediting agencies.

The empirically validated principles that we offer in this article are based on discussions at that meeting, embellished by our own personal biases and memories. They can be applied in any adult learning situation, including distance education with online components, learning from texts, laboratory and classroom instruction, and learning in informal settings.

THE FIRST AND ONLY GOAL: TEACH FOR LONG-TERM RETENTION AND TRANSFER

Why do we have colleges and universities? The main reason—some might argue the only reason—is transfer of learning. The underlying rationale for any kind of formal instruction is the assumption that knowledge, skills, and attitudes learned is this setting will be recalled accurately, and will be used in some other context at some time in the future. We only care about student performance in school because we believe that it predicts what students will remember and do when they are somewhere else at some other time. Yet we often teach and test as though the underlying rationale for education were to improve student performance *in school*. As a consequence, we rarely assess student learning in the context or at the time for which we are teaching.

Sometimes information learned in a school context will transfer to an out-of-school context and sometimes it won't. If we want transfer, we need to teach in ways that actually enhance the probabilities of transfer. *The purpose of formal education is transfer.* We teach students how to write, use mathematics, and think because we believe that they will use these skills when they are not in school. We need to always remember that we are teaching toward some time in the future when we will not be present—and preparing students for unpredictable real-world "tests" that we will not be giving—instead of preparing them for traditional midterm and final exams.

Teaching for retention during a single academic term to prepare students for an assessment that will be given to them in the same context in which the learning occurs is very different from teaching for long-term retention and transfer. Consider, for example, a common concept like statistical correlation that is taught in many different disciplines. After completing a standard course in statistics or analysis, most students can define the tenor, can compute a correlation coefficient, and can probably explain why correlation is not the same as causation.

As a result, they can usually achieve high grades on an examination at the end of the term that asks straightforward questions about this set of knowledge and skills. But what happens when they are at their own kitchen table reading a newspaper article describing a finding that children who attended preschool are better readers in first grade than those who did not attend preschool? Does it occur to them to ask whether the children who attended or did not attend preschool are distributed randomly? Or do they automatically assume that attendance at preschool *causes* children to be better readers in first grade? Most likely the latter.

BASIC PRINCIPLES

If we want to enhance long-term retention and transfer of learning, we need to apply a few basic laboratory-tested principles drawn from what we know about human learning.

1) *The single most important variable in promoting long-term retention and transfer is "practice at retrieval."* This principle means that learners need to generate responses, with minimal cues, repeatedly over time with varied applications so that recall becomes fluent and is more likely to occur across different contexts and content domains. Simply stated, information that is frequently retrieved becomes more retrievable. In the jargon of cognitive psychology, the strength of the "memory trace" for any information that is recalled grows stronger with each retrieval.

Actual practice at retrieval helps later recall of any learned information more than does additional practice without retrieval, or time expended in learning the information in the first place. For example, the "testing effect" is a term used to describe the frequent finding in educational measurement that the act of taking a particular test often facilitates subsequent test performance—but *only* for those items recalled from the first test.

The benefits of retrieving information learned earlier to produce answers in response to new questions are among the most robust findings in the learning literature. Practice at retrieval necessarily occurs over time and within a particular context. Transfer of learning can be aided by altering the context for retrieval. For example, students can practice retrieval by teaching learned concepts and skills to other students, or by responding to frequent questions asked in class or posed online.

The effects of practice at retrieval are necessarily tied to a second robust finding in the learning literature—*spaced* practice is preferable to massed practice. For example, Bjork and his colleagues recommend spacing the intervals between instances of retrieval so that the time between them becomes increasingly longer—but not so long that retrieval accuracy suffers (see deWinstanley and Bjork in Suggested Readings).

Applying this principle, a first examination to test a given concept or element of knowledge might be given to students one day after the initial learning, the second exam a few days after the first, the third a week after the second, and the fourth a month after the third, with the interval for each subsequent exam determined by the level of accuracy of student performance on the preceding one.

2) *Varying the conditions under which learning takes place makes learning harder for learners but results in better learning.* Like practice at retrieval, varied learning conditions pay high dividends for the effort exerted. In the jargon of cognitive psychology, when learning occurs under varied conditions, key ideas have "multiple retrieval cues" and thus are more "available" in memory. For example, educational research suggests that significant learning gains can occur when different types of problems and solutions are mixed in the same lesson, even though the initial learning can take significantly longer. Like practice at retrieval, variability in constructing learning situations requires greater student effort. As a result, engaging in such situations may be less enjoyable for students and lead to lower student ratings of their instructors.

This can be an important consideration on campuses where small differences in student responses on course evaluations are used—we believe inappropriately—to inform salary, promotion, and tenure decisions. We mention this only because changes in institutional practices and incentives, not only changes in faculty knowledge and behavior, will frequently be necessary to put these principles to work on real college campuses.

3) *Learning is generally enhanced when learners are required to take information that is presented in one format and "re-represent" it in an alternative format.* Cognitive research has established the fact that humans process information by means of two distinct channels—one for visuospatial information and one for auditory-verbal information. A given piece of information can be organized and "stored" in memory in either or both of these representational systems. According to dual-coding theory, information that is represented in both formats is more likely

to be recalled than information that is stored in either format alone.

Learning and recall are thus enhanced when learners integrate information from both verbal and visuospatial representations. For example, requiring learners to draw visuospatial "concept maps" makes them a) create an organizational framework in terms of which to arrange the information they are learning, and b) communicate this framework visually through a "network" of ideas—both of which are activities that enhance learning. Complex concepts can be related to one another in numerous ways, and depicting correct relationships among concepts is central to all graphic organizing techniques.

When students engage in concept mapping, they focus on and identify different types of relationships or links among concepts. Many students report that concept mapping is a challenging experience, but that it pays off in long-term learning gains. Similarly, requiring students to write about or explain verbally what they have learned in a mathematical or schematic learning task also takes advantage of dual coding. Faculty need to use both verbal and visuospatial processing activities in *all* of the learning tasks that they construct.

4) *What and how much is learned in any situation depends heavily on prior knowledge and experience.* Psychologists use the term "construction of knowledge" because each learner creates new meaning using what he or she already knows. Thus, the best predictor of what is learned at the completion of any lesson, course, or program of study is what the learner thinks and knows at the start of the experience. Yet few college faculty try to discover anything about the prior knowledge or beliefs of their students, despite the importance of prior conditions in determining what they will learn.

We need to assess learner knowledge and understanding at the *start* of every instructional encounter, probing for often-unstated underlying assumptions and beliefs that may influence the knowledge, skills, and abilities that we want students to acquire. We also need to test continually for changes in knowledge structures as learning progresses—and look especially for post-learning drifts, because student understanding can easily revert back toward pre-instructional levels.

5) *Learning is influenced by both our students' and our own epistemologies.* Academic motivation is related to underlying epistemological beliefs about learning itself and about how learning works. Many college students complain that they "cannot do math," cannot succeed in a literature course, or will automatically have trouble with some other academic discipline. When questioned about this belief, what most are really saying is that they think learning ought to be easy but, in these disciplines, it is hard.

What they don't know is that learning and remembering involve multiple, interdependent processes. Some types of learning occur implicitly, without conscious awareness. Others occur consciously but are relatively easy. Still other types of learning involve considerable effort, and are perhaps even painful and aversive, like learning how to do long division or how to multiply matrices. It is only after an initial investment in the hard work of learning that additional learning in these fields becomes more automatic, and consequently becomes easier.

Determining the best way for students to learn and recall something will thus depend on *what* you want learners to learn and be able to recall, what they *already know,* and their *own beliefs* about the nature of learning. College faculty can help students articulate their implicit beliefs about learning so that these beliefs can be explicitly examined. And based on this knowledge, instructors' construction of the learning task itself can also help students construct new models of how they learn.

6) *Experience alone is a poor teacher.* There are countless examples that illustrate that what people learn from experience can be systematically wrong. For example, physicians often believe that an intervention has worked when a patient improves after a particular treatment regime. But most patients will improve no matter what intervention occurs. If the patient does not improve, then physicians may reason that he or she was "too sick" to have benefited from effective treatment. There are countless examples of this sort of erroneous thinking in both professional practice and everyday life, where current beliefs about the world and how it works are maintained and strengthened, despite the fact that they are wrong.

People, therefore, frequently end up with great confidence in their erroneous beliefs. Confidence is not a reliable indicator of depth or quality of learning. In fact, research in metacognition has shown that most people are poor judges of how well they comprehend a complex topic.

The fact that most people don't know much about the quality of their comprehension is important, because there is a popular belief that all learning and assessment should be "authentic"—that is, nearly identical in content and context to the situation in which the information to be learned will be used. But what is missing from most authentic situations—and from most real-life situations as well—is systematic and corrective feedback about the consequences of various actions.

To return to the example of physicians, many medical schools have now adopted simulated patients as a teaching testing tool—actors trained to present a variety of symptoms for novice practitioners to diagnose—because unplanned clinical encounters with real patients can't provide the necessary variety and feedback.

7) *Lectures work well for learning assessed with recognition tests, but work badly for understanding.* Virtually all introductory college courses involve a lecture portion, in which a lone teacher mostly talks and writes on the board, while students take notes. This is a satisfactory arrangement for learning if the desired outcome is to produce learners who can repeat or recognize the information presented. But it is one of the worst arrangements for promoting in-depth understanding.

There are two related points in this principle. The first is the fact that lecturing is not optimal to foster deep learning. The second is the consequent reliance on recognition-based tests as an index of learning. These two problems are often related because large-lecture learning settings are often associated with multiple-choice tests.

The combination of large lecture classes and multiple-choice tests constitutes a relatively low-cost approach to instruction, so it is easy to understand the widespread use of this pedagogical model for large-enrollment courses on college campuses. But understanding is an *interpretive* process in which students must be active participants.

Learners need "cues" that trigger interpretation and force them to engage the material actively, even if they are sitting silently in a large lecture hall. For example, it is possible to get students to elaborate on information that is presented in lectures by relating it to information that they already know through the use of imagery or probing questions that test for understanding.

A major problem with recognition-based tests like multiple-choice exams where questions tap only lower-level cognitive processes, or with tests that require students only to repeat back course material, is that both faculty and students believe that achieving a high score is evidence of "good learning."

Unfortunately, it is quite possible for students to achieve high scores on tests like these and not be able to recognize a given concept's application in a slightly altered context, or not be able to apply the concept at some time in the future.

The ability to simply recognize a correct answer on an examination is not a good indicator of whether the learner can recognize other instances in which a concept applies when he or she is outside the classroom. Thus the type of assessment used needs to match the learning objectives. High scores on traditionally constructed tests do not necessarily indicate enduring or transferable learning.

8) *The act of remembering itself influences what learners will and will not remember in the future.* Asking learners to recall particular pieces of the information they've been taught often leads to "selective forgetting" of related information that they were *not* asked to recall. And even if they do well on a test taken soon after initial learning, students often perform less well on a later test after a longer retention interval.

Principles of learning are difficult to discuss in isolation because learning activities that occur at different times—at the point of initial learning, during the retention interval, and at the point of recall—are all interdependent. They work together to determine what is remembered at some point in the future, well after the first recall test is administered. According to standard "memory trace" theories of how we remember, the act of remembering strengthens some memory traces and weakens—or at least fails to strengthen—others.

Few instructors are aware of this effect and inadvertently create learning activities that actually *cause* students to forget information that they want them to retain. This may especially be the case when faculty test for relatively unimportant points, in the belief that "testing for the footnotes" will enhance learning. In fact, it will probably lead to better student retention of the footnotes at the cost of the main points.

Another variable that is often ignored in pedagogical design is the length of the retention interval between the point of initial learning and the first test. When students are tested frequently, they receive higher scores than students who are tested infrequently, thus creating the impression that frequent testing is a sound educational practice.

But frequent testing also leads to overconfidence for learners who erroneously believe that their long-term retention of the information will be better than it actually is. This belief may lead them to invest less time and effort in studying the material for future recall. The detrimental effect of testing soon after information is learned is another example where the short-term benefits of an educational practice can mask important long-term detriments.

9) ***Less is more, especially when we think about long-term retention and transfer.*** Some introductory texts in psychology, biology, or economics seem to weigh almost as much as the students who carry them around. Faculty need to consider carefully the balance between how much and how well something is learned. This is especially the case when external bodies like boards and accreditors favor domain coverage, no matter how thin, of more and more content at the cost of deeper understanding.

Instructional designers need to make careful choices about how much content to include. An emphasis on in-depth understanding of basic principles often constitutes a better instructional design than more encyclopedic coverage of a broad range of topics. Again, it is important to stress that classroom instruction is intended to provide learners with information and skills that they will need sometime in the future when the instructor is not present.

The amount of detail that learners will need at this future, unknown time and place is what should be guiding decisions about how deeply a particular element of content should be learned and what level of detail is important. If cursory knowledge of a broad area is indeed desirable, as it sometimes is, then learners and instructors should be collectively conscious of this goal so that they can learn and teach in ways that will achieve broad coverage.

But if deep understanding of basic principles is what is wanted, then the teaching and learning process needs to be structured accordingly. This means that instructors and learners ought to have clearly articulated goal statements at the start of instruction that guide instructional design and learning activities. And they need to carefully match the learning activities they engage in to these goals.

10) ***What learners do determines what and how much is learned, how well it will be remembered, and the conditions under which it will be recalled.*** There is an old saying in psychology,

"The head remembers what it does." Our most important role as teachers is to direct learning activities in ways that maximize long-term retention and transfer. What professors do in their classes matters far less than what they ask *students* to do.

Regardless of class size or format—in lecture halls, in laboratories, in seminar rooms, or on-line—faculty can use these empirically validated principles to enhance learning. Most of us devote considerable time and energy to the hard work of teaching, and we want to do it well. By applying the science of learning in our classrooms, we practice what we preach in helping students learn.

We need to look constantly for concrete evidence when we evaluate claims about what works in education. Consequently, we urge you to develop a healthy skepticism about all educational claims. If a colleague or a teaching newsletter advises, for example, that you should match student learning styles with your own teaching style, or that giving students an outline of the text will promote retention, employ some basic concepts of critical thinking and ask about the *evidence* that supports these claims.

There is a large amount of well-intentioned, feel-good psychobabble about teaching out there that falls apart upon investigation of the validity of its supporting evidence. As college faculty, we can have a lifelong effect on what our students remember, and consequently on what they will think and do. Or we can have a minimal effect. Most of the difference depends on how we design and direct learning activities. It's time we applied what we know about learning generated in our own cognitive laboratories and applied research settings to systematically enhance teaching and learning practice in college.

AUTHORS' NOTE

We thank the American Psychological Society, the Spencer Foundation, and the Marshall-Reynolds Trust for supporting the conference on this topic. We also thank experts who shared their knowledge with us.

Diane F. Halpern is professor of psychology and director of the Berger Institute for Work, Family, and Children at Claremont McKenna College. She is author of numerous books including *Thought and Knowledge: An Introduction to Critical Thinking* 4th ed. (2003, Erlbaum Publishers) and *Sex Differences in Cognitive Abilities* 3rd ed. (2000, Erlbaum Publishers).

Milton D. Hakel is the Ohio Board of Regents Eminent Scholar in Industrial and Organizational Psychology at Bowling Green State University. He published *Beyond Multiple Choice: Evaluating Alternatives to Traditional Testing for Selection* in 1998. He serves on the Board on Testing and Assessment of the National Academy of Sciences.

QUESTIONS FOR REFLECTION

1. What do the authors identify as one of the major misconceptions the general public has about college level teaching?
2. What is the goal for "long-term retention and transfer" the authors discuss? How does one go about achieving this goal? What are its basic principles?
3. Based on your experiences as a student in higher education, what made your good professors good and the poor ones poor? If you were to teach at the higher education level, how would you create a curriculum that would address the main issues raised by the authors?

The Decline of the Knowledge Factory

JOHN TAGG

ABSTRACT: *Knowledge—rather than capital, labor, or raw materials—will be the "organizing and animating principle" of the twenty-first century. Thus, the educated person will be the hope for America's future, and colleges, the "engine" of the knowledge society, should be our best hope for producing such persons. However, if one considers the criteria against which colleges should be judged—what students learn—it is evident that colleges are failing. Evidence indicates that the quality of undergraduate education on many campuses has been declining, and college selectivity, prestige, and resources have little influence on students' learning. Standardization and bureaucratization in "knowledge factories" has resulted in an undergraduate education characterized by mediocrity and incoherence. An "atomized" curriculum results in students' inability to think globally and to transfer methods of analysis from one subject or problem to another. To reverse their current decline, colleges must become "learning-driven institutions."*

The organizing and animating principle in the world of the next century will be neither capital nor labor nor raw materials but knowledge. As management theoretician Peter Drucker observes, "The shift to the knowledge society . . . puts the person in the center. In so doing it raises new challenges, new issues, new and quite un-precedented questions about the knowledge society's representative, the educated person." If knowledge is the key to our future, the educated person will embody the hope for the future.

When we speak of the "educated person" today, we often assume as a framework for the discussion the institution that defines and certifies education: the college. At a time when high schools cannot persuasively claim to produce even literate graduates, we focus our hopes for the educated person on colleges and universities.

The United States leads the world in the proportion of its people who attend college. We see college as the bridge to social mobility; discussions about the prospects of disadvantaged groups or individuals often become disputes about access, or the lack thereof, to college. In many ways college has become the engine of the knowledge society; if it breaks down, we will be stranded in a strange new place.

Unfortunately, this engine of progress is failing. It makes more noise than ever, but it is no longer turning the wheels. Yet this will not be instantly evident to the casual observer. Behemoth University carries on public and private research in a dizzying array of fields, provides graduate and professional schooling and community service, and offers a stage for the political and cultural dramas of a variety of social causes and groups; with so many shells in constant motion, most observers would be hard pressed to find the pea of undergraduate learning. Most of what we read in the newspapers about colleges and universities concerns the inputs to those institutions—entering students, faculty hired, revenue from taxes or tuition—or the research outputs, such as discoveries in the physical or social sciences. We encounter little news about the central product of colleges—the product that justifies most public investment in higher education. Even the well-informed citizen will find little information in the public press on the issue on which colleges should be judged: what the students learn.

DO COLLEGES WORK?

That question has been asked, and with increasing persistence, over the past two decades—and the answers have been discouraging. In 1985 the Association of American Colleges (now the Association of American Colleges and Universities)

assembled a select committee under the leadership of Mark Curtis, then president of the AAC, to address "the loss of integrity in the bachelors degree." Their report, Integrity in the College Curriculum, asserted that "evidence of decline and devaluation is everywhere." An examination of what students study in college revealed that "what is now going on is almost anything, and it goes on in the name of the bachelor's degree." Assessing the qualities of those who teach undergraduates, they concluded that "if the professional preparation of doctors were as minimal as that of college teachers, the United States would have more funeral directors than lawyers."

Eight years later, in 1993, the Wingspread Group on Higher Education, chaired by former Labor Secretary William Brock and including several prominent college presidents, surveyed the same prospect. They noted that the Department of Education's National Adult Literacy Survey (NALS) found that "surprisingly large numbers of two- and four-year graduates are unable, in everyday situations, to use basic skills involving reading, writing, computation, and elementary problem-solving." They concluded that

> a disturbing and dangerous mismatch exists between what American society needs of higher education and what it is receiving. Nowhere is the mismatch more dangerous than in the quality of undergraduate preparation provided on many campuses. The American imperative for the 21st century is that society must hold higher education to much higher expectations or risk national decline.

A growing body of research over the last two decades has helped to fill in the sketchy picture of what colleges do. A relatively few scholars at our major universities have turned their attention to the central questions that define the value of the institutions where they work. And what they have found is disturbing. In 1991, Ernest Pascarella of the University of Illinois, Chicago, and Patrick Terenzini of the Center for the Study of Higher Education at Pennsylvania State University published a massive volume, *How College Affects Students: Findings and Insights from Twenty Years of*

Research. Their assessments are carefully weighted and qualified, and they find, not surprisingly, that college students learn a good deal while in college and change in many ways. College does make a difference. But perhaps their most striking conclusion is that while attending college makes a difference, the particular college one attends makes hardly any predictable difference at all.

One of the foundational assumptions that guides parents, students, alumni, and taxpayers in thinking about colleges is that a greater investment in human and economic resources produces a better product in terms of educational outcome. Conventional thinking holds that those who run these institutions have some coherent conception of *quality,* and that this conception of quality is embodied in the best colleges, which others seek to emulate. Parents pay the breathtaking tuition charged by Ivy League institutions, and legislators invest public money in enormous state universities, because they believe quality is worth paying for—and because they believe that while they may not be able to define just what that quality consists of, those professionals who govern higher education can define it and, given adequate resources, create it.

But Pascarella and Terenzini found that

> there is little consistent evidence to indicate that college selectivity, prestige, or educational resources have any important net impact on students in such areas as learning, cognitive and intellectual development, other psychosocial changes, the development of principled moral reasoning, or shifts in other attitudes and values. Nearly all of the variance in learning and cognitive outcomes is attributable to individual aptitude differences among students attending different colleges. Only a small and perhaps trivial part is uniquely due to the quality of the college attended.

In other words, if colleges know what quality is in undergraduate education, they apparently do not know how to produce it.

In 1993 Alexander Astin, director of the Higher Education Research Institute at UCLA,

published a new study: *What Matters in College: Four Critical Years Revisited.* Astin attempted to assess the effects of college using longitudinal studies of students at many varied institutions and finding correlations between the institutions' characteristics and selected student outcomes. His research, like Pascarella and Terenzini's, leaves us with a disappointing picture, a picture of colleges that attend least to what matters most and often act in ways that seem almost designed to assure they fail at their avowed mission.

Astin's research reveals that what colleges actually do bears little resemblance to what we would be likely to extract from college catalogs or commencement speeches. This probably should not surprise us. Harvard organizational theorist Chris Argyris has demonstrated that the way people say they act in business organizations—their "espoused theory," Argyris calls it—has little relationship with their "theory-in use," which governs how they actually behave. Astin has discovered essentially the same thing in American colleges:

> Institutions espouse high-sounding values, of course, in their mission statements, college catalogues, and public pronouncements by institutional leaders. The problem is that the explicitly stated values—which always include a strong commitment to undergraduate education—are often at variance with the actual values that drive our decisions and policies.

For an outsider—and for not a few insiders—the first barrier to realistically assessing baccalaureate education is simply finding it in the morass of muddled missions that make up the contemporary multiversity. Astin quotes "one of our leading higher education scholars" as dismissing research about undergraduate learning with the remark, "The modern American university is not a residential liberal arts college." Indeed, Astin responds that

> all types of institutions claim to to be engaged in the same enterprise: the liberal education of the undergraduate student. While it is true that certain kinds

of institutions also do other things—research, vocational education, and graduate education, to name just a few—does having multiple functions "give permission" to an institution to offer baccalaureate education programs that are second-rate?

Does engaging in research and graduate education justify shortchanging undergraduate education? Does engaging in vocational education justify offering mediocre transfer education? The answer to that question today is, for all practical purposes, "yes." A multiplicity of functions does justify mediocrity and incoherence in undergraduate education, at least to the not very exacting standards of most of our colleges.

WHAT HAPPENED?

Why are our colleges failing? Because they have substituted standardized processes for educational substance. They have become bureaucratized assembly lines for academic credit and have largely ceased, at the institutional level, to know or care what their students learn.

If we look at higher education as it exists today, what we see is counterintuitive. In a nation with over thirty-five hundred colleges serving more than fourteen million students, we find an amazing homogeneity. Despite the vast number of colleges, they display more sameness than difference. Why?

Today's system of higher education is a product of the postwar world. With the impetus of the GI Bill of Rights, rapid economic growth, and the baby boom, the college population surged after World War II. Between 1950 and 1970 college enrollment more than tripled. The percentage of Americans over twenty-five who completed a bachelor's degree doubled between the end of the war and 1970 and nearly doubled again by 1993. And the most dramatic growth has taken place in public colleges. In 1947 less than half of the nation's college students attended public institutions. By 1993 nearly 80 percent did.

Today's colleges have developed as part of a nationwide system of higher education, and hence they have become nearly interchangeable. In such a system, colleges, especially public colleges, have been able to thrive only by growing. Thus their operations have become standardized and focused on providing more of their product to more students. The mission of colleges in this system is to offer classes. My colleague Robert Barr has labeled the governing set of assumptions, attitudes, and rules that define colleges in this system—the theory-in-use of most colleges—the Instruction Paradigm. In the Instruction Paradigm, the product of colleges is classes; colleges exist for the purpose of offering more instruction to more students in more classes.

In this system, the "atom" of the educational universe is the one-hour block of lecture and the "molecule" is the three-unit course. The parts of the educational experience have transferrable value only in the form of completed credit hours. For almost any student at nearly any college today, the essential meaning of "being a student" is accumulating credit hours.

A credit hour is a measurement of time spent in class. I do not mean to suggest that credit is automatic for students who merely show up. They must, of course, pass the course. But the amount of credit, the weight of the course in the transcript, is based on the length of time the student sits in a room. What the student does in the room, what the teacher does in the room, what they think after they leave the room—these things are irrelevant to academic credit. The qualifications and experience and attitudes of the teacher are irrelevant to academic credit—three units from a creative scholar passionately interested in her subject and her students are equal to three units from a bored grad student who finds teaching a largely avoidable irritation. The attitude and involvement of the student are irrelevant to academic credit—three units earned by a committed and involved student who finds a whole new way of thinking and a lifechanging body of ideas in a course are equal to three units earned by a student who thinks about the course only long enough to fake temporary knowledge with borrowed notes.

Public funding mechanisms in most states reward colleges for offering courses, credit hours. Not for grades, not for course completion, and certainly not for learning. States pay colleges for students sitting in classrooms. You get what you pay for.

THE KNOWLEDGE FACTORY

The Instruction Paradigm college of the postwar period is a knowledge factory: The student passes through an assembly line of courses. As the students pass by, each faculty member affixes a specialized part of knowledge. Then the students move on down the assembly line to the next instructor, who bolts on another fragment of knowledge. The assembly line moves at a steady pace. Each instructor has exactly one semester or quarter to do the same job for every student, who is assumed to be as like every other as the chassis of a given model of car. The workers on this line tend to view their jobs narrowly, as defined by the part of knowledge that it is their business to affix. No one has the job of quality control for the finished product.

In the college as knowledge factory, students learn that the only value recognized by the system, the only fungible good that counts toward success, is the grade on the transcript. It is a fractured system dedicated to the production of parts, of three-unit classes. The reason colleges fail is that the parts don't fit together. They don't add up to a coherent whole. They add up to a transcript but not an education.

Most of the lower division, the first two years of college, is dominated by general education requirements. These requirements at most colleges consist of lists of classes—in a variety of categories such as the humanities, social science, and physical science—from which the student may choose. William Schaefer, emeritus professor of English and former executive vice chancellor at UCLA, describes general education as "a conglomeration of unrelated courses dedicated to the proposition that one's reach should never exceed one's grasp."

The incoherence of the curriculum flows from the internal organizational dynamic of the knowledge factory. Required classes are shaped by the dominant organizational unit of college facilities: academic departments. At nearly all colleges, the fundamental duty and allegiance of the faculty is to their home departments. Most academic departments hire their own faculty. Most faculty members literally owe their jobs not to the college as an institution but to their departments. Most of the crucial decisions about a faculty member's workload and duties are primarily departmental decisions. As Schaefer notes, "Departments have a life of their own—insular, defensive, self-governing, compelled to protect their interests because the faculty positions as well as the courses that justify funding those positions are located therein."

Departments become large by bolting more of their distinctive parts onto more student chassis in the educational assembly line, by offering those bread-and-butter required general education courses that garner large guaranteed enrollments. But these are often just the kinds of innocuous survey courses that faculty prefer not to teach. And the highest rewards in most universities are reserved not for those who teach undergraduates but for those who are recognized for their research contributions to their academic disciplines. Academic departments have achieved the "best" of both worlds by hiring large numbers of graduate students or part-time instructors, at low salaries and often with no benefits, to teach undergraduate courses, while freeing up senior faculty for research activities.

Our great research universities have for many years subsidized their research programs and graduate schools at the expense of undergraduate programs. They have, in effect, pawned their undergraduate colleges to buy faculty the jewel of research time. There is no penalty to pay for this transaction, because undergraduate programs are funded based on seat time; learning doesn't count; the failure of students to learn exacts no cost to the department or the institution.

Academic departments are ostensibly organized in the service of "disciplines"—coherent and discrete bodies of knowledge or methods of study. While many of the academic disciplines that make up the sciences and humanities are of ancient and proud lineage, their configuration in the modern university is largely a product of academic politics. And their trajectory in the development and deployment of general education courses is almost entirely a product of competition between departments for campus resources. On the academic assembly line of the knowledge factory, each part must be different, so the incentive is to emphasize what makes a discipline unlike others and to shape all knowledge into these highly differentiated disciplines.

Even skills of universal relevance to virtually everything we do in life have become the property of one department or another. Thus, writing in the student's native language becomes the concern of the Department of English; speaking the student's native language is relegated to the Department of Communication. Quantitative reasoning belongs to the Department of Mathematics. The atomized curriculum has taken an increasingly conspicuous toll: the inability of students to think globally or to transfer methods of analysis from one subject or problem to another. The evidence mounts that what students learn in one course they do not retain and transfer to their experience in other courses or to their lives and their work. The fragments never fit together. This has led to a growing demand for the teaching of "critical thinking." But even the subject of thought itself becomes in the knowledge factory an object of competitive bidding among academic departments. Adam Sweeting, director of the Writing Program at the Massachusetts School of Law at Andover, warns that "if we are not careful, the teaching of critical thinking skills will become the responsibility of one university department, a prospect that is at odds with the very idea of a university."

But then much about the modern university is at odds with the very idea of a university. The competition between "academic disciplines" for institutional turf generates a bundle of fragments, a mass of shards, and no coherent whole at all. It lacks precisely that quality of *discipline* that provided the rationale for the enterprise from the beginning. It creates a metacurriculum in which students learn that college is a sequence of disconnected parts, valuable only as credits earned. And what comes off the assembly line of the knowledge factory in the end is an "education" that might have been designed by Rube Goldberg, with marketing advice from the Edsel team.

The result is an institution that satisfies nobody. College faculties complain bitterly, often about the administration, but most often about the students. History and philosophy professors complain that students can't write. English professors complain that students know little about history and culture. Science professors complain that students have only a rudimentary grasp of mathematics. And everyone complains that students can't think. Yet grades have never been higher. The mean grade point average of all college graduates in 1994 was 3.0 on a scale of 4. It seems unfair to penalize students with poor grades for deficiencies that really fall outside the scope of the course, deficiencies that could not possibly be addressed in a three-unit, one-semester class. So the professors blame the students or the administration and fight pitched battles in the faculty senate. Yet nothing seems to work, because the deficiencies that plague students are almost by definition problems that cannot be addressed in any three-unit class. But three-unit classes are all there are; they are what the college is made of.

Perhaps least satisfied with the knowledge factory are the students. Those students who come to college from high school today come hoping for something better, but with no framework of educational value to bring to the experience themselves. For many of them, the defining experience of college becomes drunkenness. While some colleges have begun belatedly to recognize the costs of the culture of irresponsibility that has grown up on many campuses, it remains the case that substance abuse is one of the few measurable outcomes of a college education. A commission chaired by former Health, Education, and Welfare Secretary Joseph Califano Jr. reported in 1994 that a third of college students are binge drinkers and that the number of college women who reported that they drink in order to get drunk had tripled since 1973, now matching the rate for men.

William Willimon, dean of the chapel at Duke University, and Thomas Naylor, emeritus professor of economics at Duke, have characterized the chaos and aimlessness that college is for many students in their book *The Abandoned Generation: Rethinking Higher Education*. They offer an especially telling statement of the experience of the knowledge factory from a University of Michigan senior:

> So you get here and they start asking you, "What do you think you want to major in?" "Have you thought about what courses you want to take?" And you get the impression that that's what it's all about—courses, majors. So you take the courses. You get your card punched. You try a little this and a little that. Then comes GRADUATION. And you wake up and you look at this bunch of courses and then it hits you: They don't add up to anything. It's just a bunch of courses. It doesn't mean a thing.

DO COLLEGES HAVE A FUTURE?

The knowledge factory is breaking down as we approach the twenty-first century. The transformation to the knowledge society means that the demand for higher education will increase both in quantity and quality: More students will require more sophisticated knowledge and skills. But this transformation has also brought into existence something new on the higher education landscape: competition.

Competition has emerged for two reasons. First, private employers who need skilled employees have found that the graduates of conventional colleges are poorly prepared to do the work they need to do. Many corporations have either established their own "universities" or sought the support of outside vendors to provide educational services. The second reason competition has burgeoned is that contemporary information technology has made possible immediate access to educational services from anywhere. Education is no longer bound to the campus. Hence many providers can compete to serve students who were formerly too distant. The competition is real. Stan Davis and Jim Botkin—in *The Monster Under the Bed,* their book about the growing imperative for corporate education—offer little hope to the conventional college: "Employee education is not growing 100 percent faster than academe, but 100 times—or 10,000 percent—faster.

In the face of such competition, if conventional colleges hold fast to the Instruction Paradigm and continue to grant degrees on seat time, many of those colleges will wither and die—going down, we can hardly doubt, in a blaze of acrimony as the nation's great minds culminate in faculty senates across the land. If colleges are to thrive, and in some cases if they are even to survive, they must change.

Colleges need to make a paradigm shift, to set aside a whole body of assumptions and implicit rules and adopt a fundamentally different perspective, a new theory-in-use. They must recognize that the Instruction Paradigm mistakes a means for an end, confuses offering classes with producing learning. To put that end in its proper place would be to embrace what Barr calls "the Learning Paradigm." From the perspective of the Learning Paradigm, the central defining functions of the knowledge factory are trivial. What counts is what students learn. That the mission of colleges is to produce learning should be fairly noncontroversial, since it is consistent with what nearly all college faculty and administrators already say in public.

The problem is that most colleges do not assess in any meaningful way what students have learned. They can tell you what classes their students have taken but not what their graduates know or what they can do. The shift to the Learning Paradigm would require that colleges begin to take learning seriously, to assess and measure it, and to take responsibility for producing it.

A large and growing number of faculty and administrators have seen that major changes in the way colleges do business are both desirable and inevitable. The prestigious California Higher Education Policy Center, in a 1996 report, urged that "colleges and Universities . . . begin a transition toward making student learning, not the time spent on courses taken, the principal basis on which degrees and certificates are rewarded."

Excellent models of such colleges exist. Alverno College in Milwaukee has for decades been developing "assessment-as-learning," an approach that seeks to both monitor and guide students' development toward the mastery of a set of core competencies that define a liberal education. The new Western Governors' University will reward students with credit only when they have established through rigorous assessment that they have mastered the required skills. According to Alan Guskin, chancellor of Antioch University, more than two hundred colleges across the country are seriously discussing major restructuring.

Nonetheless, if we contrast the glacial rate at which colleges and universities seem inclined to change with the lightning speed with which the society they serve is transforming itself, we must be disturbed by the contrast. Many believe that undergraduate colleges cannot meet the challenge of the knowledge society. Davis and Botkin, for example, foresee that "corporations will continue to need traditional universities to carry out basic education and research. Nevertheless they will increasingly take on teaching themselves." Drucker predicts: "Thirty years from now the big university campuses will be relics. Universities won't survive. . . . Such totally uncontrollable expenditures, without any visible improvement in either the content or the quality

of education, means that the system is rapidly becoming untenable. Higher education is in deep crisis."

Should we, after all, care? What matter if many of our colleges pass away or diminish into support institutions for market-driven forces that can adapt more flexibly to the needs of a changing world? What would be lost? Perhaps not much. Perhaps a great deal. For colleges hold a place in American society that no other institution is likely to fill. They hold the place of liberal education, of education for liberty, of the kind of experience through which children grow into citizens, through which men and women learn the exercise of the freedom that is tempered by choosing responsibility. I say that colleges "hold the place" of liberal education today because I cannot say that they serve the function. But they remain the institutional focus of the ideal, which survives as an ideal.

While private industry and the Internet may supplant many of the existing functions of colleges in our society, these media do not seem likely venues for a rebirth of liberal education. Part of the vulnerability of our existing undergraduate colleges lies in the fact that they have become institutions whose chief activities could be done better by others. If what we want is a knowledge factory, let us at least apply the insights of American efficiency engineer Frederick Taylor and organize the work in the most efficient way. If we want an academic assembly line, let us at least give the workers real responsibility for a real product and reward those who do good work more than those who do poor work. If what we want is an efficient knowledge factory, it will not look anything like a modern college.

The real claim that existing colleges have on our loyalty and our resources is not based upon what they are now or what they do now; it is based on what they could be and what they could do, on the ideal of which they remain the emblems. A college, a real college, is a human community, not a civil service bureaucracy or an industrial factory. A college that can become a learning community, can become more than the sum of its parts. John

Henry Cardinal Newman wrote over a century ago in *The Idea of a University:* "A University is, according to the usual designation, an Alma Mater, knowing her children one by one, not a foundry, or a mint, or a treadmill."

Changing the governing paradigm, becoming learning-driven institutions, may seem a daunting task for today's knowledge factories. It seems a little like asking the post office to become a church. Yet the reason that the ideal of liberal education survives in our cultural imagination is that it addresses an ongoing need, the need to nurture in the young the development of both heart and mind, the need to set young people on a course that offers not just facility but maturity, not just cleverness but wisdom.

I am not ready to give up on the ideal of liberal education. Our society is a poorer place because we so often fail to achieve that ideal, and it would be a far richer place if we could revive that ideal in a manner fitting for our time. It is not likely to be revived in any place other than our colleges. The question we face is really what we want the "educated person" of the new millennium to be. Is it worth the trouble to prepare people for life in the knowledge society with a foundation experience that genuinely opens to them the rewards of learning and the satisfactions of discovery, that empowers them with the independence and the discretion to seek not just information but understanding? I think it is worth the trouble. It is, at least, worth a try.

John Tagg is associate professor of English at Palomar College, San Marcos, California.

QUESTIONS FOR REFLECTION

1.   Is the "knowledge factory" an appropriate metaphor for colleges? What other metaphor(s) can you suggest?

2.   Reflect on your undergraduate education; to what extent does (did) it "fit" Tagg's portrayal of undergraduate education in America? Do you possess a "transcript" or an "education"? Were the general education requirements you satisfied "a conglomeration of unrelated courses dedicated to the proposition that one's reach should never exceed one's grasp"?

3.   What are the salient differences between an "efficient knowledge factory" and a "learning-driven institution"? In which direction do you think colleges will evolve during the twenty-first century?

Diversity, Democracy, and Curriculum Reform in Higher Education

WILLIE J. HEGGINS, III

ABSTRACT: The central social dilemma in American history has been the effort to meld a vast spectrum of cultures, classes, and communities into a common political project called democracy. *Within the context of higher education, to what extent is there a connection between the values of diversity and democratic principles that are embedded within the curriculum? This essay explores the role of curriculum reform in higher education and its relationship to enhancing diversity. Heggins highlights how minority faculties play a critical role as transformative agents within the academy and provides strategies for embedding issues of culture, values, and multiculturalism in the curriculum.*

HISTORICAL OVERVIEW

At the founding of this nation, proponents and opponents of the new Constitution engaged in a vigorous debate about the effects of societal diversity on the new political experiment. The First Amendment's protections for free speech both asserted and sought to assure the centrality of a vibrant public dialogue in the life of the young nation. From the founding until well into the twentieth century, U.S. historical records abound with racial stigmatizations against non-white groups that have impacted America's core values.

The central social dilemma in American history has been the effort to reconcile a vast spectrum of cultures, classes, and communities—groups classified or identified by gender, sexual orientation, religion, and race—into a common political project called democracy (Marable, 1997). From a historical perspective, that uneven and often interrupted dialogue and debate has taken many forms including the abolitionist movement of the nineteenth century; the suffragist movement; the struggles for an eight-hour day and the right to organize collectively. Other examples include the Second Reconstruction; the massive movement of nonviolence; the renaissance of the feminist movement; and the Stonewall riot and the emergence of a gay and lesbian rights movement.

What is the connection between the values of diversity and democracy? From Franklin and Moss's (1994) perspective, the impact of affluence on people values impacts their interpretation of freedom and empowerment. Democracy as a political project starts from the theoretical premise that all human beings have value, that they are "created equal" and have "inalienable rights," and that participants within the polity should be able to take part in the fundamental decision-making process. Democracy, in its ideal state, creates an environment of tolerance for diversity and a willingness to work with others to achieve common goals.

Using this as a conceptual framework, this essay will explore the role of curriculum reform in higher education and its relationship to enhancing diversity. Emphasis will focus on how minority faculty play a critical role to issues related to curriculum reform and its connection to learning styles that are present within higher education today. From a perspective that faculty serve as transformative agents within the academy, emphasis will also focus on highlighting strategies toward embedding issues of culture, values, and multiculturalism in the curriculum. By highlighting the social nexus in which all learning occurs, the linkage between diversity and a democratic society challenges us to think more deeply about what individuals learn from their experience and how that learning in turn constrains or enriches the quality and vitality of American communities.

HIGHER EDUCATION

In its commitment to diversity, higher education assumes, therefore, both a distinctive responsibility and a precedent-setting challenge. While other institutions in society are also fostering diversity, higher education is uniquely positioned, by its mission, values, and dedication to learning. In essence, this experience is geared toward fostering and nourishing the habits of heart and mind that Americans need to make diversity work in our daily life. Banks (1997) alludes to the notion that trend data on changing American attitudes and values depict a shift away from xenophobia toward a greater acceptance of diversity.

As higher education fosters campus and public learning about the human experiences, pain and aspirations behind the language of "difference" must be continuously explored as it relates to issues of social justice. In essence, the multicultural reform movement was designed to explore dimensions to revise and enhance curriculum and structural changes within the context of education. Many theorists conclude that educational practices, in conjunction with issues related to race and ethnicity, were harmful to students and reinforced traditional stereotypes and discriminatory practices from a Western perspective.

To combat these assumptions, multiculturalism suggests that concepts including race, ethnicity, culture, language, and diversity are salient parts of the educational experience. In essence, these concepts create a positive element within our system from the perspective that it enriches the ways in which we perceive and view the world. Further, as we look toward the idea of celebrating democracy and embracing difference, we can only grow if our systems and curricula are aligned with creating opportunities to view our own cultures and behaviors from the perspective of learning about other racial and ethnic cultures. The question begs, to what extent is higher education transforming itself in the alignment of its systems, policies, and procedures that embrace difference? What will be the potential gain for its constituents?

Many universities often defend their use of racial and ethnic preferences by appealing to an educational goal—attaining the benefits of diversity. These benefits are often described in areas related to increasing awareness, enhancing campus climate, and fostering growth. However, the connection between racial and ethnic preferences and the benefits of diversity broadly understood is quite ambiguous. Gurin (2002) contends that undergraduates just out of high school are especially susceptible to being provoked into "active thinking processes." In essence, what she is describing is the notion that an eighteen-year-old (traditional college age student) fresh from the comfortable bosom of family and neighborhood, arrives on campus with a set of unreflective prejudices and assumptions. Within the collegiate experience, students such as these are confronted with oftentimes unsettling and discordant experiences. Further, their traditional ideas, beliefs, and assumptions can be challenged. Throughout this experience, they may abandon old ideas and develop new ways of thinking.

This example provides a platform for viewing how racial and ethnic diversity can serve growth in the active thinking process within the educational experience. A racially integrated campus environment confronts many students with new and unfamiliar classmates who serve as a source of enhancing multiple and different perspectives. Furthermore, this experience enables students to connect civic learning experiences associated with preparing individuals to be active participants in our democratic society. Recognizing these benefits as described in having a diverse campus environment, the focus must shift toward minority faculty representation and their role in creating and supporting this agenda.

DIVERSITY WITHIN THE FACULTY

As we look toward a transformative time in the history of higher education, institutions must move beyond the rhetoric that inclusiveness is not merely a policy but rather embedded as an integral part of its mission and vision for the future. Universities today should commit to becoming national and world leaders in the racial and ethnic makeup of its faculty, administrators, students, and staff. Over the past several decades, it is apparent that the diversity within the student body has changed dramatically. However, the makeup of the faculty, particularly pertaining to minority faculty has not changed in the same magnitude. This is particularly problematic as it relates to curriculum reform and its relationship to the differences of learning styles that are apparent in our classrooms today. As suggested earlier in this essay, higher education should focus its attention to the importance of creating viable opportunities for enhancing diverse constituents in doctoral education, serving as a mechanism to increase minority faculty representation.

For example, diversification in terms of minority representation in American higher education continues to be problematic, with African Americans (the largest pool) representing less than 6% of the American professoriate (U.S. Department of Education, 2000). More importantly, this data is stabilized with little prospect of substantial increases especially in light of the sharp decline in the number of African Americans earning Ph.D.s in the 1980s (Carter & Wilson, 1989). The number of doctoral degrees awarded nationally between 1977 and 1994 increased by 30% (from 33,232 to 43,185) among all students. Sadly, the increase was only 7.3% among African Americans (from 1,253 to 1,344). According to the U.S. Department of Education (2000), during 1999 there were 45,394 terminal degrees awarded in higher education. Only 2,607 were awarded to Asian Americans, representing 5.7%; 1,847 were awarded to African Americans, representing 4.1%; and 1,098 were awarded to Hispanics, representing 2.4%.

Magner (1996) concludes that more than a third of all faculty members are in the first seven years of their careers. Still, the composition of this new faculty population is predominantly White and tenure rates show men gaining tenure at far higher rates than women. The largest gains

for any single racial or ethnic group are for those of Asian descent. The largest gains for any demographic component of the faculty population were among those not born as U.S. citizens. Further, the new faculties of today tend to be less likely than their older counterparts to hold tenure-track positions or to explore the core arts and science fields of the modern university (Magner, 1996).

These issues suggest that higher education continues to operate on an unequal playing field. Although gains have been made with the support of legislation—including affirmative action—there continues to be a long journey ahead. However, the implications for a more diverse faculty and its connection with curriculum reform for empowerment, action, and change in the teaching and learning process serves as an opportunity for growth. These proponents are critical from the perspective that as a result of academic freedom, faculty are in the position to decide what is being taught (curriculum design), how the class is managed (delineation of materials), and how students are evaluated (assessment). Institutions of higher education, from a systems perspective, should broaden their idea of reconceptualizing scholarship for transforming the academy.

TRANSFORMING THE ACADEMY

National leaders are calling for more attention to be placed on the teaching and learning process with emphasis on the content of discovery, the language of assessment, and the evaluation of teaching from a value added perspective. Boyer (1990) defines scholarship as having four domains: discovery, integration, application, and teaching. In essence, the scholarship of discovery reflects the excitement of new ideas, exhilarations in new insights, and the search of knowledge for the joy of knowing. Integration implies the work is compiled and interpreted for the purposes of generating new insights. Application reflects the idea of engagement, a dynamic process through which theory and practice interact. Teaching provides the dimension to incorporate these ideas into an environment that enables one to apply what he/she knows, discover new knowledge, and contribute to new understandings. However, the question begs are transformative scholars and intellectual leaders valued that bring an alternative perspective to the academy?

Research suggests that scholars who become intellectual leaders have tremendous impact in their communities as well as the academic environment. For example, Thomas F. Pettigrew was an outspoken advocate of school desegregation during the 1960s and 1970s. Pettigrew made major contributions to race relations research by challenging Coleman's "White flight" thesis, which stated that large school districts risked losing White students and parents when desegregation took place under certain conditions (Pettigrew & Green, 1976). John Hope Franklin considered himself an objective historian, although he promoted civil rights. Throughout his illustrious career as an academician, he prepared the brief for the *Brown v. Board of Education* Supreme Court case, participated in the Selma, Alabama, Civil Rights March in 1965, and presented a statement to the judiciary committee opposing the nomination of Robert H. Bork for the Supreme Court. These examples are used to illustrate a point that these academicians integrated their life experience within the classroom environment from a non-majority perspective. Students who had opportunities to work and conduct research with these scholars were transformed through exploring alternative lenses. Further, their insights were challenged and the process of what Boyer considers discovery, integration, and application was infused through the teaching and learning process.

Higher education today should value the contributions and support this new generation of scholars who bring alternative perspectives to the classroom environment. Historically, scholars who worked within marginalized groups that promoted policies and practices which conflicted with those institutionalized within the mainstream academic community have suffered. In essence, their work has been viewed as political, partisan, and subjective. Academicians who bring alternative perspectives within the classroom environment are keenly aware of the risks; however, they promote concepts of curricular reform by trying to bring awareness to distorted representations in mainstream scholarship. As we embrace the most transformative time period in the history of education, the collegiate experience should reflect in its curriculum, the ideas, viewpoints, and perspective of "all" its constituents. The following section provides a theoretical perspective to employing diverse concepts that can be embedded and incorporated within the curriculum.

THEORETICAL PERSPECTIVES ON CURRICULUM

Within the context of educational experience, the curriculum of higher education should reflect a recognition and respect for all stakeholders. From an historical perspective, Berquist (1977) suggested that curricular models in higher education were considered: (a) *heritage based,* with a premise to inculcate students with knowledge of the past; (b) *thematic base,* where emphasis is based on a problem-solving approach; (c) *competency base,* focusing on factors that enhance proficiency in learning; (d) *career base,* where the focal point is a path toward success; (e) *experience base,* encompassing the notion of theory-to-practice; (f) *student base,* tend to reflect students input in the learning process; (g) *values base,* where learning is aligned to the mission of the University; and (h) *future base,* tend to incorporate an holistic approach to the educational process. This recognition of perspectives encompasses a value added dimension that explores and appreciates the contributions of all members within the classroom environment (e.g., race, ethnicity, religion, gender, orientation, disabilities, etc.) Further, these models have served as a framework to what we do within academe, however, in some instances, they may inhibit the way postsecondary institutions and the curriculum serve, reproduce, and challenge the social order of society. Furthermore, previous research of curriculum development traditionally does not focus on how the change process is linked to the cultural makeup of the faculty and the institution. As alluded to before, until higher education focuses on issues pertaining to valuing the interaction of cultures within the environment, only then will we be in a position to align our systems, policies, curricula, and structures that seek to empower its constituents.

PROCESS FOR CHANGE

Impacting change within the curriculum involves a multifaceted approach. In essence, faculty should create learning environments whereby emphasis is placed on enhancing societal enrichment, cohesiveness, and commitment to social justice. Students within this type of structure should be challenged to facilitate constructive societal change that enhances human dignity and democratic ideals. Further, regardless of academic specialization, these principles can be transferred across all disciplines within the educational experience. The context for what is being taught, how the classroom is managed, and how students are evaluated is still within the hands of the faculty member. Faculty should be willing to explore their own presuppositions of creating a learning environment that embraces these concepts. Faculty members should explore what obstacles their fields present to the participation of discrete groups of underrepresented students and make a strong commitment to eliminating those obstacles.

Becker and Watts (1996) contend that "chalk and talk" is the predominant pedagogical strategy oftentimes utilized in certain academic disciplines. Other scholars have noted that the lecture centered approach may not be the most effective method or technique for college students today. As we look to transforming the learning process,

faculty can utilize a plethora of ideas to stimulate learning. Across the curriculum, faculty should develop ways to balance lectures with active learning through classroom design (e.g., U-shape), incorporated cooperative learning concepts (e.g., structured groups, group activities, or case studies), and learning environments that promote interaction. Johnson, Johnson, and Smith (1991) suggest that cooperative learning environments produced higher achievement and enhanced positive relationships between students.

Faculty can also incorporate concepts related to service learning in their curriculum design. Often referred to as experimental learning, service learning is not a new concept but, instead, represents a fabric of integrating the academic curriculum to practical experiences through the interaction of faculty, students, and their respective communities. This strategy embedded within the curriculum enables students and the faculty to become a "community of learners" as well as partners in the examination of learning from multiple perspectives that provide opportunities for personal growth to occur. Kretchmar (2001) contends that service learning has the capacity to transform lives, an experience that touches the heart and the mind, and teaches valuable lessons beyond those that faculty provide within the confines of their classrooms.

It is apparent that institutions of higher education are still confronting issues of inclusiveness. Even as students from diverse ethnic, racial, and economic backgrounds have entered the academy over the last fifty-years, they still remain underrepresented. More importantly excluding Historically Black Colleges and Universities (HBCUs), the faculty make-up in terms of representation, curriculum design, and campus culture still remains predominantly Eurocentric. Recognizing that the social nexus in which all learning occurs, there exists a critical link between diversity and a democratic society that challenges us to think more deeply about what individuals learn from their experience and how that learning in turn constrains or enriches the quality and vitality of American communities.

Faculty of today as well as the future should commit to establishing curriculum that is coherent to valuing and celebrating difference. Within this environment, faculty should encourage concepts such as engaging in critical perspectives allowing students to share and learn through substantive dialogue. More importantly, connecting the concept of "community of learners" to curriculum design in alignment with an institutional commitment to diversifying the faculty should serve as a framework for what is being taught, how the learning environment is managed, and how students are evaluated throughout the educational experience.

REFERENCES

Banks, J. A. (1997). *Educating citizens in a multicultural society.* New York: Teachers College Press.

Becker, W. E., & Watts, M. (1996). Chalk and talk: A national survey on teaching undergraduate economics. *American Economic Review, 86*(2): 448–53.

Berquist, W. (1977). Eight curricular models. In A. Chickering et al. (Eds.), *Developing the college curriculum* (pp. 87–108). Washington, DC: Council for the Advancement of Small Colleges.

Boyer, E. L. (1990). *Scholarship reconsidered.* Princeton, N.J.: Carnegie Foundation for the Advancement of Teaching.

Carter, D. J., & Wilson, R. (1989). *Eight annual states' report, minorities in education.* Washington, DC: American Council on Education.

Franklin, J. H., & Moss, A. A. (1994). *From slavery to freedom.* New York: McGraw-Hill.

Gurin, P. (2002). Diversity and higher education: Theory and impact on educational outcomes. *Harvard Educational Review, 72*(1): 330.

Johnson, D. W., Johnson, R. T., & Smith, K. A. (1991). Cooperative learning: Increased college faculty instructional productivity. In ASHE-ERIC *Higher Education Report* 4, Washington, DC: George Washington University.

Kretchmar, M. D. (2001). Service learning in general psychology class: Description, preliminary evaluation and recommendation. *Teaching of Psychology 28*(1): 5–10.

Magner, D. (1996). "The New Generation." *Chronicle of Higher Education* vol. 42, no. 21, A17–A18.

Marable, M. (1997). *Black liberation conservative America.* Boston: South End Press.

Pettigrew, T. F., & Green, R. L. (1976). School desegregation in large cities: A critique of the Coleman "White flight" Theses. *Harvard Educational Review, 46*(1), 1–53.

U.S. Department of Education. (2000). National Center for Educational Statistics, *Integrated postsecondary education data systems,* NCES 96-133. Washington, DC.

Willie J. Heggins, III, is an assistant professor of Higher Education at Washington State University.

QUESTIONS FOR REFLECTION

1. What are the challenges associated with the connection between the values of diversity and democracy within the curriculum?
2. How can faculty serve as transformative agents when looking to embed issues of culture, values, and multiculturalism in the curriculum?
3. What strategies can faculty employ to prepare students to think more deeply about what individuals learn from their experiences and how that learning restrains or enriches the quality of American communities?

How Americans Think about International Education and Why It Matters

SUSAN NALL BALES

ABSTRACT: *The public has not yet embraced international education. It is time, Susan Nall Bales argues, to articulate a clear vision of international education to replace the perception that it is a nonessential add-on to the conventional curriculum.*

Scholars of social movements offer important advice for those who would attempt to catapult international education onto the nation's policy agenda: "There is no such thing as a social problem, until enough people, with enough power in the society, agree that there is. Social problems are produced by public opinion, not by particular social conditions, undesirable or otherwise."[1]

Taken in this light, the fact that student knowledge of the world is demonstrably inadequate or that fewer than 40,000 American students study Chinese is unlikely to result in a widespread call for education reform. And, despite the fact that policy leaders in government and business have publicly expressed their concern about "educational isolationism," elite opinion in itself is insufficient to propel the changes that are necessary to transform the curriculum. That will depend on the reactions of constituents and of influential individuals who must weigh international education against other priorities.

The challenge for those who would advance internationalizing the American curriculum as an important public goal lies in helping opinion leaders engage citizens in the issue in a way that makes vivid the transformative power of the educational changes proposed. At the same time, educators and opinion leaders must anticipate and avoid unproductive habits of thinking that are likely to derail public understanding. The public has a lot on its mind just now, from jobs and health care to "failing" schools and terrorist threats. Without a clear and well-stated message about the importance and promise of international education, this issue is unlikely to attach itself to other public goals that Americans are eager to address.

The findings reported here come from an admittedly small sample of research projects on international education conducted by the FrameWorks Institute. FrameWorks interviewed 20 average citizens in Colorado and Connecticut to elicit their associations with international education and conducted two focus groups in North Carolina. However, this body of work is amplified dramatically by FrameWorks' multi-year investigation of American attitudes toward international issues in general—funded by the Rockefeller Brothers Fund and others—which consisted of more than a dozen multi-method studies, including two large-scale surveys of public opinion. The following observations are based on work conducted by FrameWorks' partners, the independent research organizations Cultural Logic and Public Knowledge.

THROUGH A GLASS DARKLY

In a review of previous research on U.S. attitudes toward international education, public opinion expert Meg Bostrom concluded, "In several ways, Americans demonstrate strong support for international education, including foreign language requirements, international education courses, study abroad, and international students on U.S. campuses. However, few say these skills are essential, leaving international education easily displaced by other priorities."[2] The research by FrameWorks confirms this assessment.

"Framing," as it is used by FrameWorks researchers, refers to the subtle selection of certain aspects of an issue in order to cue a specific response. As researchers have shown, the way an issue is framed explains who is responsible and suggests potential solutions conveyed by images, stereotypes, messengers, and metaphors. The advantage of "strategic frame analysis" is that it allows researchers to document and deconstruct the frames currently in the public consciousness and to understand their impact on public policy preferences.

Perhaps the most important finding in Frame-Works' research is the lack of a well-defined public vision or definition of international education. The topic simply does not bring up powerful or specific associations for people. While this fact means that advocates need not fight an uphill battle to dislodge erroneous images, it also leaves international education prey to default patterns of thinking that come into play precisely because the public has little sense of the issue. Put another way, when people lack a vivid, available image of an issue, they reach for the next best thing, any association that can help them reason about the issue.[3] In this case, international education is quickly defined by such narrow associations as language study or geography. Alternatively, international education is sometimes defined as "everything but" American history and English. In either case, the definition does little to advance a new story about how Americans might learn to engage with the world.

Even more problematic, these default associations are likely to connect the issue of international education to current public opinion about American education generally, rather than to the need for students to develop a global perspective. This pattern of thinking instantly derails the conversation into a discussion about what the public readily perceives to be the sorry state of the nation's schools. Such a focus in turn undermines support for any sweeping reforms or additions to the curriculum until the existing education system is "fixed." In the context of a system that is perceived to be failing at the basics, international education is viewed as a luxury or a set of skills that can be postponed to undergraduate education or assigned to specialists. This assessment is exacerbated by the public's beliefs 1) that international education is composed primarily of exotic languages and geographic details with which parents are unfamiliar and 2) that American students are deficient in international "basics," such as foreign languages and world history.

The sketchy picture of international education held by most Americans is partly a result of the fact that it is perceived to be "all over the map"—an endless list of thing students might learn with no endpoint—rather than a basic competency. As scholars affiliated with the research organization Cultural Logic have pointed out, people tend to reason within a "humanities model" in which international education becomes a process of choosing one country at a time and developing an acquaintance with that country.[4] This makes it hard for them to imagine a core curriculum and leaves them skeptical of reforms that appear limitless in their demands on the system.

CURRENT FRAMES IN PLAY

Current communications practices among international education advocates have been tested in qualitative research. Two of these approaches that appear with some frequency in the field demonstrate the vastly divergent effects of communications on public understanding.[5]

The school solutions frame.   This frame is exemplified by the Asia Society's call to "put the world into worldclass education," as well as by other reforms that focus on improving the educational vision and process itself. This particular framing is inspiring to people and can help them see the need to update the curriculum to bring it into the 21st century. Moreover, it does this without falling into such traps as the widely held notions that the schools are already broken, that basics have to come before luxuries, and that we must act locally before addressing global needs. To further improve on this way of framing the issue, specific examples of school systems that are undertaking global curricula should help move the public into a "solutions mindset" rather than a "problems mindset." By painting a vivid picture of what happens in these schools and classes and how it was achieved, advocates can begin the necessary task of defining international education in the public mind.

The knowledge gap frame.   By contrast, framing the issue in terms of a knowledge gap defines the learner as deficient. Moreover, it defines international education as being "about" success and qualifications. This frame often appears in the context of questions about whether American students and teachers are able to locate the world's countries, capitals, and major geographic features. The public response is generally something like, "They can't even find Wisconsin on a map."

However, reminding people of student deficiencies is likely to lead to them to construct a script in which the "basics" come first and knowledge of one's own country comes before knowledge of foreign cultures. Indeed, the public can easily explain away the knowledge gap by asserting that Americans have enough challenges in their education system already and shouldn't undertake new problems until more progress has been made on the old ones. The fact that the public perceives international education as an infinite number of specific facts leads many Americans to conclude that we will never be proficient in this area. Thus we tend to refocus on those areas where change seems possible, say, improving reading test scores in grade schools.

TELLING A STORY THE PUBLIC CAN HEAR

It is difficult to inspire people to want better international education when they lack a concrete image of what is being proposed. The paucity of vivid images associated with international educa-

tion requires that advocates take immediate steps to fix the topic in the public's imagination and to avoid allowing understanding to default to foreign language and geography.

The critical next step for reform proponents is to make global education come alive in the public mind. By exposing people to multiple examples of imaginative programs across the disciplines, advocates can begin to overcome the biggest obstacle to change: the shallow and sketchy perceptions of international education that easily default to problematic interpretations.

In making the issue vivid, it is also important to define international education in terms of people's existing educational values—to emphasize critical thinking and respect for other cultures. As FrameWorks research partner Public Knowledge concluded from the focus groups:

> Advocates need to create a conversation that links to the priorities people already have for the public education system, rather than one that tries to create a new priority. The public wants education to provide opportunity; to teach children how to understand, respect, and value others; to develop good citizens; and to prepare children for success in the workplace. Advocates need to communicate that achieving these objectives in an increasingly interdependent world requires updating the public education system to incorporate a global perspective. When approached in this way, international education is not a separate priority. Rather, it is inherent in the definition of a world-class education.[6]

The entire body of communications research conducted by the FrameWorks Institute strongly suggests that global education should be "about" improving the quality of teaching; getting values of mutual understanding, respect, and cooperation across cultures into the curriculum; and inspiring students' curiosity to explore beyond their borders and boundaries. The frames that worked best in the focus groups were those that inspired a positive vision of what we could be, not those that narrowly addressed problems we have experienced. The FrameWorks research concludes that the argument for international education needs to be changed to tell a different story about the world, about Americans' role in it, and about the opportunities for today's students. The vision of global education should be seen as transformative, not merely additive. Only then can proponents of international education count on a positive public reception for specific policy proposals for reform.

NOTES

1. Armand L. Mauss and Julie Camille Wolfe, *This Land of Promises: The Rise and Fall of Social Problems in America* (Philadelphia: Lippincott, 1977), p. 2.
2. Meg Bostrom, "Building Bridges, or Fences?: Perceptions of America's Role in the World Community," Public Knowledge, for FrameWorks Institute, Washington, D.C., June 2003, pp. 39–40.
3. For more about how people process information, see Susan Nall Bales and Franklin D. Gilliam, Jr., "Communications for Social Good," Practice Matters: The Improving Philanthropy Project, The Foundation Center, 2004; accessible online at http://fdncenter.org/for_grantmakers/practice_matters/index.html.
4. Axel Aubrun and Joseph Grady, with Jeffrey Snodgrass. "Global Systems and Global Education," Cultural Logic, for FrameWorks Institute, Washington, D.C., November 2003.
5. For more on alternative frames and their effects, see Susan Nall Bales, "Making the Case for International Education: A FrameWorks Message Memo," FrameWorks Institute, Washington, D.C., January 2004.
6. Meg Bostrom, "Creating World-Class Education: An Analysis of Qualitative Research Exploring Views of International Education," Public Knowledge, for FrameWorks Institute, Washington, D.C., November 2003.

Susan Nall Bales is president of the FrameWorks Institute, a nonprofit organization based in Washington, D.C., which conducts communications research on social issues. She is a visiting scholar at Brandeis University's Heller Graduate School for Social Policy and Management, Waltham, Massachusetts.

QUESTIONS FOR REFLECTION

1. Why are Americans so adverse to international education? What makes the idea of global awareness so difficult for average American students?
2. Why does Bales believe international education is so important in today's curriculum? How are students today different from students of the 1970s or 1980s? What unique international challenges does today's world present the next generation of world leaders?
3. What could be done to change American attitudes regarding international education? Where does change need to begin? Is it specific to certain topics within education (history or social studies, for example) or does it transcend all topics?

CASE STUDY IN CURRICULUM IMPLEMENTATION

Do As I Say, Not As I Do: A Personal Odyssey

HELEN C. BOTNARESCUE
with assistance from DAVID R. STRONCK

ABSTRACT: Botnarescue offers several teaching strategies across the continuum of age groups, from early childhood to graduate education. She says the most successful techniques are brainstorming and jigsaw. She further concludes that changing the mode of teaching university undergraduate and post-graduate students from using a standard approach to applying the concept of developmentally appropriate practices is a process that takes experimenting, monitoring and evaluation, revising, and, most of all, time.

What does the concept of *best practices* mean when it is applied to college/university teaching? Most instructors at the undergraduate and graduate levels teach in the way they themselves were taught: they lecture. According to popular belief, one history professor used the same notes for his lectures for 30 years. Do instructors in departments of elementary and secondary education do likewise? Since most of them, at one time, taught in pre-kindergarten or K–12 schools and had classes in the methods of teaching, do they, too, lecture when hired to teach college students?

When I first started teaching Psychological Foundations of Education at California State College (now University), Hayward, I did what my role models in college did: I prepared lectures, stood at a lectern or table, and delivered them. I did this in spite of the fact that I had been a science major and a science teacher in both high school and junior high settings. During my three years as a preschool teacher-director, I noticed that 4-year-olds enjoyed science in the discovery center more than my junior high students, who hated reading the text and answering the questions at the end of the chapters. Eventually, as Cal State Hayward's teacher preparation programs

changed, classes that had been offered three times a week for an hour or twice a week for an hour and a half, were offered only once a week for three or four hours. This scheduling change posed a problem. There was no way I could lecture for that long without losing my voice and putting many of my students to sleep.

INITIAL CHANGES AND NEW TEACHING TECHNIQUES

What could I do? My initial changes involved bringing in as much audio-visual stimulation as I could—films and videotapes, overhead masters, diagrams on the chalkboard. Since I am a visual and auditory learner myself, these were the tools I thought I should use for my own students. But I was forgetting two facts: college/university students have multiple learning styles, and textbooks' costs were rising. Thinking back on my own learning in college, I asked myself why science had been such an exciting major. Eventually, I realized that I loved science because it was interactive. After listening to lab instructions, I could get actively involved—and that meant using visual, auditory, and tactile modes to learn.

During my seventh year at Cal State Hayward, I was asked to teach courses in the early childhood master's degree program. Later, stimulated by the concept of developmentally appropriate practices (DAP), I tried using interactive techniques in two of my undergraduate classes, an introductory early childhood course and a child development course. Techniques designed to involve students included brainstorming, having them work in small groups, and designing assignments that provided for a variety of interpretations. (One student, for example, titled her paper "The Left-Hander's Term Paper" and wrote it from back to front. Another turned in a sculpture; now *that* was a challenge to grade!)

Initially, however, some students were confused. What did working in small groups and trying to piece together a puzzle have to do with child development or children's learning? Was not this activity a waste of student time? I used the puzzle activity as an example of problem solving and cooperative learning. Others complained when I assigned them to work in small groups on one of the chapters in the textbook and then report back to the class as a whole. Wasn't *I* supposed to be the instructor? Others, however, understood quickly that working with peers employed their visual, aural, and (sometimes) tactile senses; they understood that in listening to one another, they occasionally gained insight into how they themselves learned best. Best of all, in teaching each other, their presentations were sometimes more relevant and couched in terminology more easily understood than what I might have used.

The most successful techniques for me were brainstorming and jigsaw. In the jigsaw technique, students were assigned to two groups, a *home* group and an *expert* group. Each *expert* group studied the content of one chapter from the textbook, usually a chapter they chose. After an hour or so of cooperative study, students returned to their respective home groups and taught each other the material learned in their expert groups.

NEXT STEP: COLLABORATION

Later, I wondered if I could apply the same instructional strategies to my other courses. Again, how could I change? Many of the education students at Hayward complained that they could not afford to buy all of the textbooks required by their various classes. The educational psychology course Teaching and Learning was only one of four required in the first quarter of a newly state-mandated program designed to prepare teachers in only one post-graduate year.

Having attended many committee meetings with colleagues and established working relationships with several, I approached David Stronck, who taught a methods course, Principles of Education, and inquired about using one textbook for both of our classes. David and I had known each other for several years; both of us had been science teachers prior to the completion of our doctorates, although he had remained in the science education field and I had moved into educational psychology. The text I was using included several chapters related to how students learn, and it seemed appropriate for a methods class. At the same time, I asked David about the instructional methods he was teaching. It seemed logical to me to teach the educational psychology course using the same methodology that he would be teaching in the methods course. Would he be amenable to dropping his methods textbook and adopting the educational psychology one? He could use the chapters related to student learning; instructional planning; behavioral, cognitive, and constructivist approaches; information processing; and discovery learning. I would use those related to theories of growth and development, learning theory, classroom management, special students in regular settings, assessment of student learning, and standardized testing.

TRANSITION DIFFICULTIES

This collaboration proved to be easier to work out on paper than in reality. The principal questions were: Could I teach theories of development, using discovery as a technique? Would the scientific method lend itself to an exploration of theories of development? Did social learning theory apply to the subject of classroom management? How might information processing be applied to tests and measurements? It was easier to employ brainstorming, for example, in exploring the various ways in which students learn, or to the concept of multiple intelligences. Jigsaw proved to be a way to use more of the text and omit fewer chapters. Unfortunately, most textbooks are written with semester schedules, not 10-week quarters, in mind. Notice that my concern still focused on *covering* a text, rather than on choosing what principles I considered essential.

The next step was to apply these different techniques to the educational psychology course, and to convince my colleague that he could use the same textbook. After considering several texts, we chose the Biehler and Snowman (1990) text that several of our colleagues and I had been using.

RESULTS

Fortunately, since David and I (with our science backgrounds) planned our syllabi in similar ways, it was perhaps easier to collaborate. We began with a course description (from which we derived course objectives), and listed course requirements based upon the objectives. The objectives were related to those approved by the California State Commission of Teacher Preparation. We listed our office hours and telephone numbers, as well as those of the textbook and publisher. Then, we presented a detailed week-by-week schedule of class meetings and assignments,

along with what requirements were due on which specific dates. Penalties for absences and late requirements were also given, as were grade expectations. We modeled our mutual respect when visiting each other's classes through our questions to each other, our respectful responses, and even through our disagreements, which were often handled with humor.

Some of my early childhood students were expecting a standard educational psychology course, and they grumbled about working in small groups and complained that the puzzles, for example, had no bearing on learning theory. David faced some of the same complaints: What did a chapter on theories of learning have to do with preparing lessons for their own students? There were some students who understood immediately what David and I were attempting, and they would instruct their peers. Ah, was there a lesson in this? Why shouldn't university students exhibit as much variability as children and students in kindergarten through 12th grade?

It would be wrong to suggest that our cooperative teaching experiment progressed smoothly, because it did not. David and I taught independently of each other. We shared one textbook and we gave each other our respective syllabi, but I was not always careful to check with him about any changes he might have made in his schedule, nor did he always ask me what I was doing in my class. We did rely on each other's syllabus and decide which chapters each would assign.

CONCLUSIONS

The second year went more smoothly and the third was better yet. David and I continued to collaborate in teaching these two courses until I retired. What did I learn? Changing my mode of teaching university undergraduate and postgraduate students from using a standard approach to applying the concept of DAP is a process that takes experimenting, monitoring and evaluation, revising, and, most of all, time. I moved from a lecture-question-answer methodology to providing students with choices and with the right to explore and interact with each other. I learned that covering material in a textbook is less important than focusing on a few major concepts and teaching them in differing ways; this process modeled for my students the same methods they were learning in the general methods course. Both they and I learned more effectively through the repeated exposure to the instructional methods that David and I were using.

REFERENCE

Biehler, R. F., & Snowman, J. (1990). *Psychology applied to teaching* (6th ed.). Boston: Houghton Mifflin.

Helen C. Botnarescue is Professor Emeritus, California State University, Hayward. *David R. Stronck* is Professor and Team Leader, Department of Teacher Education, California State University, Hayward.

QUESTIONS FOR REFLECTION

1. What are the important lessons Botnarescue borrowed from her time teaching younger students which she then used in the college classroom? What teaching methods currently being employed at the college level did she think were most ineffective for student learning?
2. What role did collaboration play in Botnarescue's college classroom? What made collaboration successful and, likewise, what made it challenging? How did Botnarescue, and her colleague, overcome the challenges?
3. Overall, what does Botnarescue say she learned from her experience shifting from a standard teaching approach to the concept of DAP? What do you think she would change were she to repeat the process? What might you take from her experiences and apply in your own classroom?

TEACHERS' VOICES—
Putting Theory Into Practice

How Critical Are Our Pedagogies? Privileging the Discourse of Lived Experience in the Community College Classroom

LEONOR XÓCHITL PÉREZ
ANNA MARIE CHRISTIANSEN

ABSTRACT: *The first author describes her experiences teaching a "Success in College" course at a community college in a low-income Latino community in Los Angeles. The development of a learning community, the author realizes, requires more than an appropriate textbook and teaching strategies. The curriculum should include strategies for addressing the psychological, social, and cultural issues minority students bring to the classroom. By providing students with opportunities for collaborative learning and sharing personal opinions, the author acknowledged, discussed, and integrated students' backgrounds into the course objectives.*

The need for socialization within the academic culture is a common theme in research and recommendations for practitioners that teach or work with minority college students (Bower, 1996). Among factors that place minority students in need of this socialization are: (a) minority students' beliefs about valued adult roles and about the part played by education in structuring access to those roles; (b) minority students' preparation, which involves both developing expectations about higher education and participating in experiences that approximate going to college; and (c) minority students' style of attending college, which distinguishes students who follow traditional full-time patterns of college attendance and those who enter college with adult roles and responsibilities (Richardson & Skinner, 1992). Given this need for socialization about academic culture, many community colleges now offer courses that teach "success in college." The content of these courses most often includes three general topics—the college

experience, academic skill development, and life management.

What becomes problematic at the community college level, however, is how minority students must negotiate everyday experience with formal academic learning. Such negotiations complicate the academic socialization process for these students. While the acquisition of knowledge is expected to impact students' abilities to think critically about the world outside of the academic institution, many educators believe that the elemental experiences of everyday living should not impact what happens in the classroom. For students balancing school with their various nonacademic identities and responsibilities, such negotiation of their experiences can lead to what Signithia Fordham (1988) terms academic "racelessness," in which students "unlearn or modify their own culturally sanctioned interactional and behavioral styles and adopt those styles rewarded in the school context if they wish to achieve academic success." Often, the mere act of attending an institution of higher learning suggests either a conscious or semiconscious rejection of their home culture(s) (Fordham, 1988).

As a novice instructor preparing to teach a class in "success in college" at a community college in a low-income Latino community in Los Angeles, I* invested many hours in developing the curriculum. I thought much about the appropriate textbook and about ways to develop learning communities. I anticipated using Supplemental Instruction (SI), which increases academic achievement and promotes the development of learning communities through collaborative learning. In SI, regularly scheduled, out-of-class, peer-facilitated sessions are held in which students have the opportunity to discuss, process, and interact by reading, studying, and preparing for examinations (Martin, Blanc, & Arendale, 1996). These learning communities have been noted to increase coherence in what is being learned, promote intellectual interaction, and help promote academic and social connections with faculty and students (Tinto, Russo, & Kadel-Tara, 1996).

It wasn't long, however, before I learned that a curriculum should include more than the appropriate textbook and strategies to develop a learning community. A curriculum should include the complete environment for learning that instructors provide. Giroux and McLaren (1994) point out that a curriculum embracing students' cultural politics, or the myriad of everyday negotiations they face as raced, gendered, and social subjects, addresses the nexus of social and curricular theory. Such curricular change can, they argue, provide a "commitment to hope and emancipation [as well as] the desire to link educational practice to the public good" (Giroux & McLaren, 1994). Therefore, the depth and complexity of the educational process must be considered, and thus a curriculum should also account for how an instructor will address the psychological, social, and cultural issues that mi-

nority students bring to the classroom, which will in turn affect learning.

The first day of the "success in college" course was important to me personally. Not only was it my first day teaching at the college level, I was also returning as an instructor to the same college where I started my own higher education, inhabiting the role of Gramsci's (1987) organic intellectual who furthers the interests of her community in scholarly activity. I was making a full circle and anxiously awaiting the opportunity to give back to the Chicano community in which I was raised by teaching at the local community college. As I walked to class, I looked around the campus and noticed that not much had changed. Half of the classrooms were still housed in beige World War II surplus bungalows. Concrete and asphalt, more than grass and trees, covered the campus grounds. I also looked in the women's bathroom and saw that graffiti still covered the walls and doors, the towel dispensers were still empty, and water leaked from under one of the stalls.

My first impression of the students who sat in my class led me to consider what others have said about classrooms at the community college. The classroom was at one time a community of students with shared experiences. The classroom at the community college today, however, is composed of individuals who have nothing more in common than if they were all waiting at a bus stop (Ritschel, 1995). Before me sat students who ranged in age from seventeen to fifty-five. Among them were housewives and grandmothers, while others were recent high school graduates or full-time workers who supported an entire family.

During the first week of instruction I learned that the demands in the lives of most of these students interfered with my plans to use out-of-class Supplemental Instruction (SI) to build learning communities. Olivia, a Latina in her late forties with brown curly hair, large brown eyes, and a noticeable Spanish accent, shared something with the class that demonstrated the personal and cul-

---

* Throughout this article, "I" refers to the first author.

tural conditions that would keep her from participating in SI activities. "My husband, he gets angry when I come to the college," she said in a heavy Spanish accent. "At first I came to school behind his back. He went to work and I went to the college." Eventually he found out that she was attending community college and became enraged. In his view, a woman should never surpass the educational or career status of her husband. His attitude reflected the patriarchal ideology of traditional macho culture as well as Fordham's (1988) notion of how, for some students, further learning functions as cultural two-timing. Olivia's husband started threatening to hurt her physically if she continued attending classes. Eventually he made good on his threat and physically abused her. She chose to report her situation to the police and as a result received a restraining order so that she could continue attending classes. The class was silent as they listened to her story. They also seemed to be moved. This is only one of a variety of stories I heard about what keeps many of these students from participating in traditional college activities that would incorporate them into academic culture.

It then became apparent that learning communities in this class, at this community college, could not be developed through interactions with the institution as a whole or with peers in out-of-class SI sessions but would be developed only in interactions between the students and myself in each individual class session. I had to make adjustments to my planned curriculum to meet the needs of this class. I quickly developed activities and exercises that provided in-class opportunities for collaborative learning that facilitated the development of learning communities.

Even after I developed the opportunity for collaborative learning and thus for the development of learning communities, I often found that many students could not make the connection between what they learned in class and their life experiences. This was the case with Angela. She was one of two African American students in this predominately Latino class. I noticed that some-

thing was happening in her life when, during a class session, I heard tapping on the glass window behind the chair in which I sat. It was Angela. By motioning with her index finger she indicated that she wanted me to attract the attention of a fellow student. I obtained the attention of that student. She pulled out a book from her bag and went outside and took it to Angela. When Angela returned to class, I asked her if all was well. She stated that her mother-in-law was hospitalized. She was dying of cirrhosis of the liver, and Angela was spending a great amount of time caring for her mother-in-law's nine children, aged one through twenty-four. Angela is twenty-seven years old. Later that month, she said in a calm and nonchalant manner, "I thought I almost went into labor last night. I have been having contractions and I went to the doctor. My doctor he said I am three centimeters dilated." "And how many do you need to be, six?" I asked. "I need to be at least five, so I have two more to go. I'll be glad when it comes. I'm tired," she said. "You have been working hard too," I responded. She said, "This year just started off bad. Maybe it will get better, God willing." I then asked her what was happening with the nine children, and she said, "A lot, ooh, well, remember I told you that we were helping with the children? Well, now starting last weekend they are coming out here. The children are staying with me." "With you at your house?" I asked. "Yeah. Just every weekend they've been coming down here and I love them so much but I can't take care of them much longer." "All nine of them are coming to your house?" I asked in disbelief. "Well, actually, only eight are, plus my own baby and then I'm having another baby now. It's hard because those kids can eat! And we don't have that much food in the house. So it's just hard and they, they, I have to have a lot of energy and patience in dealing with them. It's just dreadful, but I can't just say 'no' because they don't have anybody else to turn to," she said. I asked her how her personal situation had been affecting her school work. She said she had not been studying like she was supposed to. She had been too busy at home to give school her all. Angela was in class the day that we discussed the theory of challenge and support, which states that every challenge that is adequately supported dissipates in intensity. Thus I asked her if anything that she had learned in class so far had helped her with this situation. She said, "not this situation, not this situation," as she shook her head. For Angela, challenges in her personal life interfered with her ability to fully benefit from the class. However, had Angela not had external pressures, she still might have not benefited any more from the class. She learned through the Meyers-Briggs inventory that she was an introvert. However, she was unable to translate this knowledge into insights on how her introversion could be affecting her help-seeking behavior in dealing with the challenges in her life. Walsh (1996) points out that educators should collaboratively study with students their real-life problems and find "active, creative ways to make these realities the knowledge base from which other learning emanates and evolves."

I soon learned, however, that for students to consider their real-life problems and beliefs to be a valid springboard from which to learn, they must be encouraged to voice them. Alex, a male Latino who is about twenty years old, appeared to be what we call "the loner type." He always wore polyester pants, T-shirts with slogans on them, and a baseball cap. He also carried a Walkman around that he listened to, shutting himself out further from the world that surrounds him. He carried around a binder with a picture of the revolutionary Che Guevara. This student never participated in class discussions. One day, however, as I asked students how they felt about certain issues, he started to speak about the evils of American corporations. The class laughed. I firmly stated, "Do not laugh at him! He has a right to voice his opinion whether it agrees with yours or not." The class was silent. Embedded within liberatory theories of education is the corollary of student voice. To give students voice is to let them reinvent the world according to what they already know, even if their paradigm

questions that of the dominant structures. Through voice, the context of the learning situation is made familiar to the student. I continually encouraged students to share their personal opinions with the class as well as to make connections between these opinions and what was learned in class by keeping an in-class journal.

My experiences in listening to and observing Olivia, Angela, Alex, and many other students in this class taught me that the curriculum I had planned did not provide a mechanism in which the different psychological, social, and cultural factors brought in by the students could be acknowledged, discussed, and integrated into the course objectives. My ability to adapt to the needs of the class and to apply critical pedagogical practices, however, increased the possibility that students would make meaningful connections between what they learned in class and what goes on in their lives. The Freire (1997) model of education posits a problem-solving methodology in which students practice the power to "perceive critically *the way they exist* [author's emphasis] and in which they find themselves." In this way, their reality is not fixed, but in process and capable of being transformed.

Although I found pedagogical practices that worked for this class, pedagogical practices must constantly be reconceptualized to address each new teaching assignment. Through continual interrogation of how we teach, it then becomes, as Freire (1988) points out, "the form that knowing takes as the teacher searches for particular ways of teaching that will challenge and call forth in students their own act of knowing," thus privileging lived experience alongside formal academic endeavor.

REFERENCES

Bower, B. L. (1996). Promoting new student success in community college. In J. N. Hankin (Ed.), *The community college: Opportunity and access for America's first-year students.* Columbia, SC: National Research Center for the Freshman Year Experience and Students in Transition, University of South Carolina. (ERIC Document Reproduction Service No. ED 393 486).

Fordham, Signithia. (1988). Racelessness as a Factor in Black Students' School Success. *Harvard Educational Review,* 58, 54–84.

Freire, Paulo. (1988). Letter to North American Teachers. In Ira Shor (Ed.). *Freire for the Classroom: A Sourcebook for Liberatory Teaching.* Portsmouth, NII: Boyton/Cook Publishers.

Freire, Paulo. (1997). *Pedagogy of the Oppressed.* New Revised Ed. Trans. Myra Bergman Ramos. New York: The Continuum Publishing Company.

Giroux, Henry A., & McLaren, Peter. (1991). Radical Pedagogy as Cultural Politics: Beyond the Discourse of Critique and Anti-Utopianism. In Donald Morton & Mas'ud Zavarzadeh (Eds.). *Theory/ Pedagogy/Politics: Texts for Change.* Urbana, IL: University of Illinois Press, 152–186.

Giroux, Henry A., & McLaren, Peter. (1994). *Between Borders: Pedagogy and the Politics of Cultural Studies.* New York: Routledge.

Gramsci, Antonio. (1987). *The Modern Prince & Other Writings.* Trans. Louis Marks. New York: International Publishers.

Martin, D. C., Blanc, R., & Arendale, D. R. (1996). Supplemental instruction: Supporting the classroom experience. In J. N. Hankin (Ed.), *The community college: Opportunity and access for America's first-year students.* Columbia, SC: National Re-

search Center for the Freshman Year Experience and Students in Transition, University of South Carolina. (ERIC Document Reproduction Service No. ED 393 486).

Richardson, R. C., Jr., & Skinner, E. F. (1992). Helping first-generation minority students achieve degrees (pp. 29–43). In S. L. Zwerling & H. B. London (Eds.), *First generation students: Confronting cultural issues. New Directions for Community Colleges,* No. 80. San Francisco: Josscy-Bass.

Ritschel, R. E. (1995, Feb./March). The classroom as community. *Community College Journal,* 65(4), 16–19.

Tinto, V., Russo, P. E., & Kadcl-Tara, S. (1996). Learning communities and student involvement in the community college: Creating environments of inclusion and success. In J. N. Hankin (Ed.), *The community college: Opportunity and access for America's first-year students.* Columbia, SC: National Research Center for the Freshman Year Experience and Students in Transition, University of South Carolina. (ERIC Document Reproduction Service No. ED 393 486).

Walsh, Catherine E. (1996). Making a Difference: Social Vision, Pedagogy, and Real Life. In Catherine E. Walsh (Ed.), *Education Reform and Social Change: Multicultural Voices, Struggles, and Visions.* Mahwah, NJ: Lawrence Erlbaum Associates, Publishers. 223–240.

Leonor Xóchitl Pérez is a post-doctoral scholar in higher education at the University of California-Los Angeles; *Anna Marie Christiansen* is an assistant professor at Brigham Young University–Hawaii.

QUESTIONS FOR REFLECTION

1. How can the curriculum contribute to minority and nonminority students' "academic socialization" in institutions of higher education?
2. What characterizes a genuine learning community at the higher education level? Is this description different from that of a learning community at other levels of education?
3. How can students' "real-life problems and beliefs" be a catalyst for learning?

LEARNING ACTIVITIES

Critical Thinking

1. The introduction for this chapter states that the general goals for educational programs at the higher education level—citizenship, equal educational opportunity, vocation, self-realization, and critical thinking—are the same as at other levels. Should the relative emphasis on these goals remain the same for learners at the different stages of life covered in this chapter—late teens through all phases of adulthood? What changes in emphasis would you recommend?
2. What is the role of higher education in regard to today's trend toward lifelong learning? How has this role changed during the last two decades?
3. Reflect upon the college curricula you have experienced thus far in your education. Was most emphasis placed on liberal or professional studies? To what extent were the two integrated? How might this integration have been more extensive and effective?
4. Carl Eisdorfer, noted gerontological psychiatrist, once said that older Americans are less like one another than any other segment of the population. What do you think might be the basis for this statement? If true, what implications does it have for programs of lifelong education?

Application Activities

1. In "Nontraditional Students: The New Ecology of the Classroom" (*The Educational Forum,* Summer 1989, pp. 329–336), Naomi Jacobs suggests that ". . . it will become more and more crucial to develop methods of instruction acknowledging and creatively unifying the varieties of experience to be found in such diverse groups, and even harnessing the potential energy in conflict." Identify and describe three methods of instruction that would be effective for such groups of students. In addition, how would you describe the curricular materials that would be most effective for this group?
2. What curriculum criteria do you consider most important for curriculum planning at the community college level? At the university level? At each level, how should these criteria be applied?
3. The introduction to this chapter states that a major emphasis in adult education is to expand learning opportunities for people previously underrepresented in higher education: African Americans, Latino and Hispanic Americans, Asian Americans and Pacific Islanders, Native Americans and Alaskan Natives, and the poor. How can adult and continuing education curricula meet the needs of students from these groups? Does Willie J. Heggins's article, "Diversity, Democracy, and Curriculum Reform in Higher Education," suggest any guidelines for developing these curricula?

Field Experiences

1. Visit a nearby community college and interview a few students about their curricular experiences. Take field notes based on these interviews. The following questions might serve as a guide for beginning your interviews: What are the students' long-range goals? How will their community college experiences enable them to reach those goals? What emphasis do the students place on the following goals: citizenship, equal educational opportunity, vocation, self-realization, and critical thinking?

2. Obtain materials that describe the undergraduate general education requirements at your college or university. To what extent do they reflect the following curricular goals: citizenship, equal educational opportunity, vocation, self-realization, and critical thinking?

3. Interview an instructor in an adult and/or continuing education program to determine the curricular strategies he/she uses to meet students' needs. To what extent do these strategies reflect the points of view presented in this chapter?

Internet Activities

1. Go to the home page of the Association for the Study of Higher Education (ASHE). From there go to the "Abstracts to the Research Papers" presented at the annual national conference. What issues and trends are reflected in the abstracts? How do they relate to the material presented in this chapter?

2. Go to the Office of Adult Learning Services (OALS) maintained by College Board Online. Gather information related to the recruitment, instruction, and assessment of adult students. Compare this information to the material presented in this chapter.

3. At the National Institute on Postsecondary Education, Libraries and Lifelong Learning sponsored by the Office of Educational Research and Improvement (OERI), gather information of interest on the education and training of adults in postsecondary institutions, community-based education programs, and the workplace.

Credits

PART I: *BASES FOR CURRICULUM PLANNING*

Chapter 1

Deborah Meier, So What Does It Take to Build a School for Democracy? From *Phi Delta Kappan* 85, no. 1 (September 2003): 15–21. © 2003 Phi Delta Kappa, Inc. Used by permission of the author and publisher. Lyrics from "God Bless the Child," written by Billie Holiday and Arthur Herzog, Jr., used by permission of Edward B. Marks Music Company.

Nel Noddings, A Morally Defensible Mission for Schools in the 21st Century. From *Phi Delta Kappan* 76, no. 5 (January 1995): 365–368. © 1995 Phi Delta Kappa, Inc. Used by permission of the author and publisher.

William H. Schubert, Perspectives on Four Curriculum Traditions. From *Educational Horizons* 74, no. 4 (Summer 1996): 169–176. Used by permission.

Theodore Brameld, A Cross-Cutting Approach to the Curriculum: The Moving Wheel. Excerpted from *Phi Delta Kappan* 51, no. 7 (March 1970): 346–348. © 1970 Phi Delta Kappan, Inc. Used by permission of the publisher.

Robert M. Hutchins, The Organization and Subject-Matter of General Education. From an address presented at the annual convention of the National Association of Secondary School Principals at Atlantic City, NJ, February 1938. Used by permission of the National Association of Secondary School Principals.

William C. Bagley, The Case for Essentialism in Education. From *Today's Education: Journal of the National Education Association* 30, no. 7 (October 1941): 201–202. Used by permission of the publisher.

William Heard Kilpatrick, The Case for Progressivism in Education. From *Today's Education: Journal of the National Education Association* 30, no. 8 (October 1941): 231–232. Used by permission of the publisher.

John Dewey, Traditional vs. Progressive Education. From John Dewey, *Experience and Education,* pp. 1–10 (New York: The Macmillan Co., 1938), a Kappa Delta Pi Lecture. © Kappa Delta Pi. Used by permission.

Linda Inlay, Values: The Implicit Curriculum. From *Educational Leadership* 60, no. 6 (March 2003): 69–71. © 2003 Educational Leadership. Reprinted by permission. The Association for Supervision and Curriculum Development is a worldwide community of educators advocating sound policies and sharing best practices to achieve the success of each learner. To learn more, visit ASCD at www.ascd.org.

Chapter 2

Frederick M. Hess & Chester E. Finn, Jr., Inflating the Life Rafts of NCLB: Making Public School Choice and Supplemental Services Work for Students in Troubled Schools. From *Phi Delta Kappan* 86, no. 1 (September 2004): 34–43. © 2004 Phi Delta Kappa, Inc. Used by permission of the authors and publisher.

Lisa Guisbond & Monty Neill. Failing Our Children: No Child Left Behind Undermines Quality and Equity in Education. From *The Clearing House* 78, no. 1 (September/October 2004): 12–16. Reprinted with permission of the Helen Dwight Reid Education Foundation. Published by Heldref Publications, 1319 Eighteenth St., NW, Washington, DC 20036-1802. Copyright © 2004.

Tina M. Anctil, The "Three A's" of Creating an Inclusive Curriculum and Classroom. Article written by Tina M. Anctil for *Curriculum Planning: A Contemporary Approach,* Eighth Edition, 2006. Used by permission of the author. Table 2.2, Assessment Accommodations Framework, used by permission of the Research Institute on Secondary Education Reform.

James A. Banks, Multicultural Education and Curriculum Transformation. From the *Journal of Negro Education* 64, no. 4 (Fall 1995): 390–399. © 1995 Howard University Press. Used by permission.

Erica Scharrer, Making a Case for Media Literacy in the Curriculum: Outcomes and Assessment. From the *Journal of Adolescent & Adult Literacy* 46, no. 4 (December 2002/January 2003): 354–358. © 2003 Journal of Adolescent & Adult Literacy. Used by permission of the author and publisher.

Michael W. Apple, Remembering Capital: On the Connections between French Fries and Education. From the *Journal of Curriculum Theorizing* II, no. 1 (1995): 113–128. © 1998 Corporation for Curriculum Research. Used by permission of the author and publisher.

Kevin Maness, Teaching Media-Savvy Students about the Popular Media. From the *English Journal* 93, no. 3 (January 2004): 46–51. © 2004 by The National Council of Teachers of English. Reprinted with permission.

Chapter 3

Ashley Montagu, My Idea of Education. From *Today's Education,* Journal of the National Education Association, 69, no. 1 (February-March 1980) (General Edition): 48–49. Used by permission of the author and publisher.

David A. Hamburg, Toward a Strategy for Healthy Adolescent Development. From the *American Journal of Psychiatry* 154, no. 6 (June 1997): 6–12. Reprinted by permission of the author and publisher. © 1997, the American Psychiatric Association.

Lawrence Kohlberg, The Cognitive-Developmental Approach to Moral Education. From *Phi Delta Kappan* 56, no. 10 (June 1976): 670–677. © 1976 Phi Delta Kappa, Inc. Used by permission of the author and the publisher.

Table 3.1, Definition of Moral Stages, used by permission of the *Journal of Philosophy*.

Carol Gilligan, Woman's Place in Man's Life Cycle. Reprinted by permission of the publisher from *In a Different Voice: Psychological Theory and Women's Development* by Carol Gilligan, Cambridge, Mass.: Harvard University Press, pp. 8–9, 19–23, © 1982, 1993 by Carol Gilligan.

James P. Comer, Organize Schools around Child Development. From *Social Policy* 22, no. 3 (Winter 1992): 28–30. © 1992 Social Policy Corporation. Used by permission.

Christopher Bamford & Eric Utne, Waldorf Schools: Education for the Head, Hands, and Heart. From *Utne Reader* 117 (May/June 2003): 1–14. © Utne Magazine. Used by permission of the authors and publisher.

Molly Ness, A First-Year Teacher Tells It All. From an article that originally appeared in *The Education Digest* 66, no. 2 (October 2000): 8–12. © 2000 Molly Ness. Used by permission of the author.

Chapter 4

Gary D. Kruse, Cognitive Science and Its Implications for Education. From *NASSP Bulletin* 82, no. 598 (May 1998): 73–79. © 1998 National Association of Secondary School Principals. www.principals.org. Reprinted with permission.

John T. Bruer, Let's Put Brain Science on the Back Burner. From *NASSP Bulletin* 82, no. 598 (May 1998): 9–19. © 1998 National Association of Secondary School Principals. www.principals.org. Reprinted with permission.

Howard Gardner, Probing More Deeply into the Theory of Multiple Intelligences. From *NASSP Bulletin* 80, no. 598 (November 1996): 1–7. Used by permission.

Kathie F. Nunley, Giving Credit Where Credit Is Due. *Principal Leadership (High School ed.)* 3, no. 9 (May 2003): 26–29. © 2003 by Kathie F. Nunley. Used by permission of the author.

Cynthia B. Dillard & Dionne A. Blue, Learning Styles from a Multicultural Perspective: The Case for Culturally Engaged Education. Article written by Cynthia B. Dillard and Dionne A. Blue for *Curriculum Planning: A Contemporary Approach*, Seventh Edition, 2000. Used by permission of the authors.

M. Bruce King, Jennifer Schroeder, & David Chawszczewski, Authentic Assessment and Student Performance in Inclusive Secondary Schools. Adapted from *Authentic Assessment and Student Performance in Inclusive Schools, Brief #5*, Research Institute on Secondary Education Reform for Youth with Disabilities (RISER), December, 2001. © 2001 RISER. Used by permission of the authors. See http://www.wcer.wisc.edu/riser/Brief%205.pdf. The brief was supported by a grant from the U.S. Department of Education, Office of Special Education and Rehabilitative Services, Office of Special Education Programs (#H158J970001) and by the Wisconsin Center for Education Research, School of Education, University of Wisconsin–Madison. Any opinions, findings, or conclusions are those of the authors and do not necessarily reflect the views of the supporting agencies.

Elsa C. Bro, Lifelines: An Ethnographic Study of an IEP Student. From the *English Journal* 94, no. 1 (September 2004): 81–87. © 2004 by The National Council of Teachers of English. Reprinted with permission.

PART II: *DEVELOPING AND IMPLEMENTING THE CURRICULUM*

Chapter 5

Table 5.1, Two Dimensions of Curriculum Development: The Target and Time Orientation. From Forrest W. Parkay and Beverly Hardcastle, *Becoming a Teacher: Accepting the Challenge of a Profession*, Sixth Edition. Published by Allyn and Bacon, Boston, MA. Copyright © 2004 by Pearson Education. Reprinted by permission of the publisher.

John Dewey, The Sources of a Science of Education. From John Dewey, *The Source of a Science of Education* (New York: Horace Liveright, 1929), pp. 7–22. © Dewey Center, Southern Illinois University at Carbondale. Used by permission.

Henry A. Giroux, Teachers, Public Life, and Curriculum Reform. From *Peabody Journal of Education* 69, no. 3 (Spring 1994): 35–47. © 1994 Peabody College of Vanderbilt University. Used by permission of the publisher.

Glen Hass, Who Should Plan the Curriculum? Revised, 1979 by Glen Hass. Portions drawn from *Educational Leadership* 19, no. 1 (October 1961): 2–4, 39. Used by permission of the author and publisher.

Kim Marshall, A Principal Looks Back: Standards Matter. From David T. Gordon (ed). *A Nation Reformed: American Education 20 Years after* A Nation at Risk. Harvard Education Press, 2003, pp. 53–68. Used by permission.

Tamim Ansary, The Muddle Machine: Confessions of a Textbook Editor. From *edutopia* 1, no. 2 (November 2004): 30–35. © 2004 edutopia™. Used by permission of the author and publisher.

Jane Gilness, How to Integrate Character Education Into the Curriculum. From *Phi Delta Kappan* 85, no. 3 (November 2003): 243–245. © 2003 Phi Delta Kappa, Inc. Used by permission of the author and publisher.

Chapter 6

Figure 6.1, Level of Authentic Student Performance for Students Who Experienced Low, Average, and High

Authentic Pedagogy in Restructuring Elementary, Middle, and High Schools. From F. M. Newmann and G. G. Wehlage, *Successful School Restructuring: A Report to the Public and Educators by the Center on Organization and Restructuring of Schools,* University of Wisonsin-Madison, 1995, pp. 21, 55. Used by permission.

Table 6.1, Five Models of Teaching. From Forrest W. Parkay and Beverly Hardcastle, *Becoming a Teacher: Accepting the Challenge of a Profession,* Second Edition. Published by Allyn and Bacon, Boston, MA. Copyright © 1992 by Pearson Education. Reprinted by permission of the publisher.

John Dewey, Progressive Organization of Subject Matter. From John Dewey, *Experiences and Education,* pp. 86–93 (New York: The Macmillan Co., 1938), a Kappa Delta Pi Lecture. © Kappa Delta Pi. Used by permission.

Jerome S. Bruner, Structures in Learning. From *Today's Education* 52, no. 3 (March 1963): 26–27. Used by permission of the author and the publisher, the National Education Association.

Kathleen Vail, Nurturing the Life of the Mind. From the *American School Board Journal* 188 (January 2001): 18–23. © 2001 National School Boards Association. Reprinted with permission from *American School Board Journal.* All rights reserved.

David T. Gordon, The Limits of Ideology: Curriculum and the Culture Wars. From David T. Gordon (ed). *A Nation Reformed: American Education 20 Years after* A Nation at Risk. Harvard Education Press, 2003, pp. 99–113. Used by permission.

Nelson Maylone, TestThink. From *Phi Delta Kappan* 85, no. 5 (January 2004): 383–386. © 2004 Phi Delta Kappa, Inc. Used by permission of the author and publisher.

Jay McTighe, Elliott Seif, & Grant Wiggins, You *Can* Teach for Meaning. From *Educational Leadership* 62, no. 1 (September 2004): 26–30. ©2004 Educational Leadership. Reprinted by permission. The Association for Supervision and Curriculum Development is a worldwide community of educators advocating sound policies and sharing best practices to achieve the success of each learner. To learn more, visit ASCD at www.ascd.org.

Carol Lupton, Ideals vs. Reality in the Classroom. From *Virginia Journal of Education* 94, no. 7 (April 2001): 18–19. Used by permission of the author and publisher.

PART III: *THE CURRICULUM IN ACTION*

Chapter 7

Lilian G. Katz & Sylvia C. Chard, The Reggio Emilia Approach. From *Principal* 76, no. 5 (May 1997): 16–17. © 1997 National Association of Elementary School Principals. Used by permission of the authors and publisher.

Elizabeth Jones, Playing Is My Job. From *Principal* 76, no. 5 (May 1997): 18–19. © 1997 National Association of Elementary School Principals. Used by permission of the author and publisher.

Christopher Brown, Can Kids Still Play in School? Defining and Defending Early Childhood Education in the Context of Never-Ending Reform. Article written by Christopher Brown for *Curriculum Planning: A Contemporary Approach,* Eighth Edition, 2006. Used by permission of the author.

Linda H. Plevyak & Kathy Morris, Why Is Kindergarten an Endangered Species? From an article that originally appeared in *The Education Digest* 67, no. 7 (March 2002): 23–26. © 2002 Linda H. Plevyak. Used by permission of the author.

Bruce Joyce, Marilyn Hrycauk, & Emily Calhoun, with the Northern Lights Kindergarten Teachers, Learning to Read in Kindergarten: Has Curriculum Development Bypassed the Controversies? From *Phi Delta Kappan* 85, no. 2 (October 2003): 126–132. © 2003 Phi Delta Kappa, Inc. Used by permission of the author and publisher.

Andrea McGann Keech, Building a Community in Our Classroom: The Story of Bat Town, U.S.A. From *Social Education* 65, no. 4 (May/June 2001): 232–236. © National Council for the Social Studies. Reprinted by permission.

Chapter 8

Carnegie Council on Adolescent Development, Great Transitions: Preparing Adolescents for a Changing World. From Executive Summary of *Great Transitions: Preparing Adolescents for a New Century,* Carnegie Council on Adolescent Development, Carnegie Corporation of New York, © 1995. Used by permission of the publisher.

Peggy A. Grant, Middle School Students and Service Learning: Developing Empowered, Informed Citizens. Article written by Peggy Grant for *Curriculum Planning: A Contemporary Approach,* Seventh Edition, 2000. Used by permission of the author.

M. Lee Manning, Benchmarks of Student-Friendly Middle Schools. From *Contemporary Education* 71, no. 1 (Fall 1999): 5–8. © 1999 Contemporary Education. Used by permission.

David Skinner, The Homework Wars. Excerpted from *The Public Interest* 154 (Winter 2004): 49–60. © The Public Interest. Used by permission of the author and publisher.

Peter C. Scales & Judy Taccogna, Building Developmental Assets to Promote Success in School and in Life. Excerpted from *NASSP Bulletin* 84, no. 619 (November 2000): 69–78. Used by permission of the author and publisher. © 1998 National Association of Secondary

School Principals. www.principals.org. Reprinted with permission. Table 8.1, the list of Forty Developmental Assets™ is reprinted with permission from Search Institute℠. © 1997 by Search Institute. All rights reserved. No other use is permitted without prior permission from Search Institute, 615 First Avenue N.E., Minneapolis, MN 55413; 800-888-7828; www.search-institute.org. Search Institute℠ and Developmental Assets™ are trademarks of Search Institute.

Donald E. Larsen & Tariq T. Akmal, Intentional Curriculum Planning in an Age of Accountability: Explorer Middle School's Approach. Article written by Donald E. Larsen and Tariq T. Akmal for *Curriculum Planning: A Contemporary Approach,* Eighth Edition, 2006. Used by permission of the authors.

Nancy King Mildrum, Creativity Workshops in the Regular Classroom. From *Roeper Review* 22, no. 4 (April 2000): 162–164. © 2000 Roeper Institute. Used by permission of the Roeper Institute, P.O. Box 329, Bloomfield Hills, MI 48303.

Chapter 9

Kay S. Hymowitz, Tales of Suburban High. From *Commentary* 113, no. 6 (June 2002): 38–41. © Commentary. Used by permission of the author and publisher.

Susan Black, Engaging the Disengaged Student: Research Shows Why some are Immersed in Learning while Others are Indifferent. Excerpted from the *American School Board Journal* 190, no. 12 (December 2003): 58–71. © 2003 National School Boards Association. Reprinted with permission from *American School Board Journal.* All rights reserved.

M. Lee Manning & Richard Saddlemire, Implementing Middle School Concepts into High Schools. From *Clearing House* 69, no. 6 (July/August 1996): 339–342. Reprinted with permission of the Helen Dwight Reid Educational Foundation. Published by Heldref Publications, 1319 Eighteenth St., N.W., Washington, DC 20036-1802. Copyright © 1996.

Theodore R. Sizer, New Hope for High Schools: Lessons from Reform-Minded Educators. Excerpt from *Horace's Hope,* by Theodore R. Sizer. © 1996 by Theodore R. Sizer. Reprinted with permission of Houghton Mifflin Company. All rights reserved.

Fred M. Newmann, Can Depth Replace Coverage in the High School Curriculum? From *Phi Delta Kappan* 66, no. 5 (January 1988): 345–348. Used by permission of the author.

Hugh Campbell, Going the Extra Mile to Smooth the Transition to High School. From *Principal Leadership* 1, no. 6 (February 2001): 36–40. © 2001 The National Association of Secondary School Principals. www.principals.org. Reprinted with permission.

Mira Reisberg, A Tale of Two Curriculums. Article written by Mira Reisberg for *Curriculum Planning: A Contemporary Approach,* Eighth Edition, 2006. Used by permission of the author.

Chapter 10

Ernest L. Boyer, Connectedness through Liberal Education. Excerpted from *Journal of Professional Nursing* 5, no. 2 (March-April 1989): 102–107. Based on a keynote presentation at the semiannual meeting of the American Association of Colleges of Nursing, Washington, DC, March 14, 1988. Used by permission of the publisher.

Gershon Vincow, The Student Centered Research University. From *Innovative Higher Education* 21, no. 3 (Spring 1997): 165–178. © 1997 Human Sciences Press, Inc. Used by permission of the author and publisher.

Diane F. Halpern & Milton D. Hakel, Applying the Science of Learning to the University and Beyond. From *Change* 34, no. 4 (July/August 2003): 37–41. Reprinted with the permission of the Helen Dwight Reid Educational Foundation. Published by Heldref Publications, 1319 Eighteenth St., NW, Washington, DC 20036-1802. Copyright © 2003.

John Tagg, The Decline of the Knowledge Factory. From *The World and I* 13, no. 6 (June 1998). Used by permission of *The World and I* online.

Willie J. Heggins, III, Diversity, Democracy, and Curriculum Reform in Higher Education. Article written by Willie J. Heggins for *Curriculum Planning: A Contemporary Approach,* Eighth Edition, 2006. Used by permission of the author.

Susan Nall Bales, How Americans Think About International Education and Why It Matters. From *Phi Delta Kappan* 86, no. 3 (November 2004): 206–209. © 2003 Phi Delta Kappa, Inc. Used by permission of the author and publisher.

Helen C. Botnarescue, with assistance from David R. Stronck, Do As I Say, Not As I Do: A Personal Odyssey. From *Childhood Education* 80, no. 4 (Summer 2004): 209–211. ©2004 Association for Childhood Education International. Used with permission of the authors and publisher.

Leonor Xóchitl Pérez & Anna Marie Christiansen, How Critical Are Our Pedagogies? Privileging the Discourse of Lived Experience in the Community College Classroom. Article written by Leonor Xóchitl Pérez and Anna Marie Christiansen for *Curriculum Planning: A Contemporary Approach,* Seventh Edition, 2000. Used by permission of the authors.

Name Index

Damasio, H., 173
Darling-Hammond, Linda, 306
Davidson, Lyle, 187
Davies, Máire Messenger, 115
Davis, G., 411
Davis, Stan, 500–501
Deakin-Crick, R., 76
deCourten, Ch., 177, 178
Delpit, L., 90, 193, 455, 457
Demming, William, 154–155
Dewey, John, 7, 20, 23, 25–27, 34–35, 41–43, 124, 136–138, 143, 220, 231–235, 265, 270, 271, 277–278, 287–289, 300, 365, 457
DeWolf, M., 340
Dickens, C., 403
Dickinson, T. S., 385
Digeronomo, Theresa Foy, 382
Dillard, Cynthia B., 170, 193–198, 195, 197, 459
DiPerna, J. C., 339
Donovan, M. S., 342–343
Doolittle, J. C., 99
Dorr, A., 99
Dorval, B., 339
Dougherty, K. J., 340
Downs, Andreae, 304
Drake, D., 398
Drucker, Peter, 494, 501
D'Souza, D., 89
DuBois, W. E. B., 93, 94
Dudley-Marling, Curt, 210
Duffy, G., 275
Dunbar, S. B., 343
Durkin, Delores, 352
Durland, M. A., 340
Dutro, E., 406
Dyson, Anne Haas, 336

Easton, J. Q., 341
Eberle, B., 411
Eberly, D. J., 377
Edgar, E., 379
Edmonds, Ron, 248–249, 256–257
Edwards, C., 343
Edwards, Tony, 105
Egan, K., 381
Eisner, E. W., 457
Elam, Stanley M., 326
Elfland, A. D., 459
Elkin, D., 95
Elkind, David, 163, 334
Elkins, Stanley M., 94–95
Elmore, Richard, 75

Emerson, Ralph Waldo, 293
Englert, C. S., 200
Entwisle, D. R., 339
Epstein, Herman, 123, 180
Erb, Tom, 384
Erikson, Erik, 123, 124, 334, 369, 418, 464–465
Erikson, Joan M., 124
Eron, L. D., 99
Espeland, Pamela, 382
Estrada, S., 313

Fager, Jennifer, 430
Ferreiro, Emilia, 335
Finders, Margaret, 113
Fink, E., 407, 409
Finn, Chester E., Jr., 24, 55, 65–73, 236, 243n
Fischer, P., 99
Fisherkeller, JoEllen, 112–116
Flavel, J., 163
Fleege, P. O., 340
Fletcher, G. H., 228
Foehr, U. G., 100
Fordham, Signithia, 517–519
Forman, G., 343
Foucault, Michel, 110
Fountas, Irene, 254–255
Fowler, C., 459
Frank, J., 243n
Franklin, John Hope, 94, 503, 506
Fraser, Nancy, 110
Freeman, David F., 212
Freeman, E. B., 340
Freeman, Yvonne S., 212
Freire, Paulo, 195, 457, 520
Freud, Sigmund, 149
Frost, R., 99
Fruchter, Norm, 105
Fullan, M., 404–407
Fuller, B., 75
Furman, G., 457

Gabler, Mel, 262
Gabler, Norma, 262
Gagné, R. M., 273
Gallimore, R., 314
Gallup, Alex M., 74, 228, 326
Gamoran, A., 85, 199, 203
Gandini, L., 331, 343
Garan, E. M., 455
Gardner, Howard, 19, 170, 174, 183–187, 216, 217, 458
Gardner, John, 477
Garnier, H., 314

Gartner, A., 199
Gastright, Joseph F., 326
Gatto, John Taylor, 297
Gauld, Joseph, 187
Gay, G., 90
Gelman, R., 163
Genovese, Eugene D., 94–95
George, Paul, 371
Gewirtz, Sharon, 105
Gilchrist, Robert S., 420
Gilligan, Carol, 125, 149–152, 419
Gilness, Jane, 228, 264–267
Giroux, Henry A., 221, 236–243, 518
Gittell, Marilyn, 105
Givven, K. B., 314
Glauberman, N., 95
Glenn, John, 470–471
Goldman-Rakic, P. S., 177–180
Goldstein, L. S., 337
Goleman, Daniel, 158
Gomez, M. L., 337
Gonzalez, G., 76
Good, Thomas E., 168–169, 273
Goodall, Jane, 159
Goodlad, John, 44, 306, 328, 378, 477
Goodwin, B., 74
Gordon, David T., 273, 298–308
Gould, Stephen Jay, 95
Graff, Gerald, 241
Gramsci, Antonio, 518
Grant, Peggy A., 368, 377–383
Grantman, R., 279
Graue, M. E., 339
Graves, Donald, 336
Graves, S., 99
Green, Andy, 105
Green, R. L., 386, 506
Greene, M., 194, 457
Greer, Colin, 105
Gregory K., 314
Griffith, P. L., 342
Gronws, D., 273
Gruenewald, D. A., 456–459
Gubernick, L., 348
Guenemoen, R. F., 283
Guisbond, Lisa, 74–80
Gunning, Thomas, 354
Gurin, P., 504
Guskin, Alan, 501

Haas, T., 457, 459
Hakel, Milton D., 471, 487–494

Hall, P. M., 340
Halloran, J. D., 99
Halpern, Diane F., 471, 487–494
Hamburg, David A., 121, 129–135, 369
Hamilton, L., 76
Hammill, Patricia A., 221
Hands, R., 412
Haney, W., 76–77
Hanley-Maxwell, C., 201
Hansen, D., 44
Harlen, W., 76
Harradine, C., 348
Harrison, C., 282
Harste, Jerome, 194, 335
Hart, A., 99
Hart, C. H., 340
Hart, L., 174
Hartshorne, Hugh, 142
Haskins, Kenneth, 105
Haskvitz, Alan, 380–381
Hass, Glen, 6, 229, 244–248, 458
Hatch, J. A., 340
Hatcher, J. A., 378
Hauser, C., 75
Hauser, R. M., 340
Hausken, E., 348–349
Havighurst, Robert J., 465
Hawkins, R. D., 173
Hawn, H. C., 434
Hayes, B., 377, 378, 381
Healy, Jane, 159
Heath, Shirley Brice, 61, 194
Hedin D., 381
Heggins, Willie J., III, 468, 503–508
Heibert, J., 314
Helm, J. H., 343
Herman, J. L., 75
Herrnstein, R. J., 95
Hess, Frederick M., 55, 65–73
Hickey, Joseph, 146
Hiebert, J., 314
Hill, Heather C., 303–304, 306
Hinde, E. R., 76
Hirsch, E. D., Jr., 10, 24, 243n, 294
Hobbs, R., 98, 99
Hoerr, Tom, 186–187
Hofferth, Sandra L., 392–393
Hofstadter, Richard, 293, 295–296
Holiday, Billie, 12
Hollingsworth, H., 314
Holmes, C. T., 339
Honderich, Ted, 104, 106

Subject Index